I0670190

CITIZEN
OF THE
SHADOWS

CITIZEN OF THE SHADOWS

THE LIVES AND LIES OF LOTHAR WITZKE

PAUL FRIEDLAND & ROBERT HORNICK

LEGACIES OF WAR

G. Kurt Piehler, Series Editor

The University of Tennessee Press
Knoxville

The Legacies of War series presents a variety of works—from scholarly monographs to memoirs—that examine the impact of war on society, both in the United States and globally. The wide scope of the series might include war's effects on civilian populations, its lingering consequences for veterans, and the role of individual nations and the international community in confronting genocide and other injustices born of war.

Copyright © 2025 by The University of Tennessee Press / Knoxville.
All Rights Reserved.
FIRST EDITION.

Library of Congress Cataloging-in-Publication Data

Names: Friedland, Paul, 1962- author | Hornick, Robert N. author
Title: Citizen of the shadows : the lives and lies of Lothor Witzke / Paul Friedland and Robert N. Hornick.
Description: First edition. | Knoxville : The University of Tennessee Press, 2025. |
Series: Legacies of war | Includes bibliographical references and index. | Summary: "This is the first biography of Lothar Witzke, a German spy sentenced to death by the United States during WWI but later pardoned by President Calvin Coolidge. Witzke was convicted for the Black Tom munitions depot explosion in 1916 that killed four and crippled the Allies' resupply and arguably intensified the stalemate faced by the opposing armies of WWI. After his pardon Witzke lived in Latin America and China as a German expat, first joining the Abwehr and later the Nazi party. He ran espionage squads in Great Britain during WWII. After WWII Witzke became a nationalist politician and returned to Hamburg as a prominent businessman. He was killed in East Germany in 1962, presumably by a Stasi agent for suspected double agent work on behalf of the British. The authors trace Witzke's morally complicated life and in doing so focus on whether Witzke was guilty of the Black Tom explosion and how a spy functioned in the interwar years and after"—Provided by publisher.
Identifiers: LCCN 2025015707 (print) | LCCN 2025015708 (ebook) |
    ISBN 9798895270325 hardcover | ISBN 9798895270332 paperback |
    ISBN 9798895270356 adobe pdf | ISBN 9798895270349 kindle edition
Subjects: LCSH: Witzke, Lothar, 1895–1962 | Espionage, German—History—20th century | Espionage, German—United States—History—20th century | Black Tom Explosion, Jersey City, N.J., 1916 | World War, 1914–1918—Secret service—Germany | World War, 1939–1945—Secret service—Germany | Spies—Germany—Biography | LCGFT: Biographies
Classification: LCC D639.S8 W584 2025 (print) | LCC D639.S8 (ebook)
LC record available at https://lccn.loc.gov/2025015707
LC ebook record available at https://lccn.loc.gov/2025015708

From Robert: To my son Will and my brother Joe,
                the two most generous and caring men
                I know. I love you both.

From Paul: To my father, Abner, whose drive
                to learn history lives in me.
                Et à Georges Heywang, ce beau
                père d'Alsace qui m'a donné à voir
                l'histoire allemande du 20ème siècle.

CONTENTS

ILLUSTRATIONS

ACKNOWLEDGMENTS

We thank the following.

Christoph and Claudia Moinian, two of Lothar Witzke's grandchildren, who graciously shared memories of their grandfather, grandmother, father, mother and other relatives, as well as private family correspondence and photographs.

Will Hornick, who capably managed our excellent team of German language researchers and translators, including David Hamann, Anika Hesse, and Andrea Koch in Berlin, Benjamin Haas in Freiberg, and Florian Danescke in Koblenz. The German language component of this project was huge and could not have been done without Will's diligence, oversight, and care.

Colleagues of the coauthor at White & Case LLP contributed materially: Donna Clarke, by superb work on the manuscript; Kerri Spennicchia, by indefatigable retrieval of sources of all kinds; Clemency Wang, by diligent work on footnote formatting and accuracy; Vivi Mendez, by Spanish-language research on conditions in Mexico and Venezuela during the 1920s and 1930s; Suzanne Knijnenburg, by Dutch-language research on Witzke's doings in Belgium and Holland during World War II; and Bettina Braun, by making first contact with the Moinian family.

James Kaplan, for encouraging us in this project and for valuable reactions to a series of possible book titles.

Archivists and staff at the US National Archives, with a special nod to Stanley Fanaras, Thomas Macnear, and their colleagues at College Park, MD, who guided us through NARA's massive collection of Mixed Claims Commission and Military Intelligence Division materials relevant to Lothar Witzke, David Hardin at NARA's St. Louis, MO, branch who helped us find Witzke's trial record and related correspondence, and Lindsay Closterman at NARA's Kansas City, MO, branch, who located Witzke's Leavenworth records.

The staff of numerous other libraries and archives with original material relevant to this book who helped us access that material and were invariably courteous to us, including the New York Public Library, the libraries of the University of Arizona and the UA Rogers College of Law, and the Christopher G. Nason Military Intelligence Library at Fort Huachuca, AZ.

Tom MacGregor, attorney and former JAG lawyer, who responded helpfully to our arcane questions about military law and procedure.

John Vargo and Bob Walters, two experts on the Hudson River, who convinced us both that it would have been possible on the night of July 29–30, 1916, for twenty-one-year-old Lothar Witzke to have rowed from the Manhattan shoreline to Black Tom and back and that a rogue wave might have swamped a rowboat carrying Witzke and Jahnke.

Jeffrey Luber, a handwriting expert, who helped us with questions we had about Witzke's controversial address book, including the timing and authenticity of certain entries.

We are also grateful to Siegfried Elsing, Michael Kort, John MacLennan, David Michaelis, and Dick Snyder, each of whom read earlier drafts of this book and gave us valuable comments that have helped make our writing better than it otherwise would have been.

Finally, we owe our title, *Citizen of the Shadows*, to a passage in Alan Furst's novel, *A Hero of France* (New York: Random House, 2017).

FOREWORD

Paul Friedland and Robert Hornick rescue from obscurity the life and times of Lothar Witzke who had the dubious distinction of being the only German agent captured and sentenced to death in the United States during World War I. Tried and sentenced to hang by a US Army court, Witzke's death sentence was commuted to life imprisonment by President Woodrow Wilson. Later, President Calvin Coolidge commuted his sentence to time served and released him from prison. Witzke's life story suggests the remarkable continuity between Wilhelmine Germany, the Weimar Republic, the Third Reich, and the early Federal Republic of Germany (West Germany). Witzke prospered under all four regimes, and the efforts the Weimar government took to prod the American government to release him from Leavenworth Prison are striking. After returning to Germany, Witzke met with success as a businessman with stints working in China and South America. During World War II, the Nazi state found a place for him in the Abwehr, Nazi Germany's military intelligence organization, where he served in occupied Europe, ending the war stationed in Norway. It is also remarkable how easily Witzke was able to rebuild his life after VE Day and his postwar success as a businessman in Hamburg shows the limits of denazification.

His experiences in World Wars I and II aside, Witzke's life story had many episodes in many settings. Readers of this book are likely to be educated and entertained by the deeply researched descriptions offered about the times and places that Witzke experienced. Few among us, I expect, know what it was like to travel in Mexico in 1918, or about conditions in Leavenworth Prison in the 1920s, or about the ecological devastation caused by the oil industry in Mexico and Venezuela in the 1920s, or about life in the German expatriate community in Hankow, China, in the 1930s. Even where there has been much prior scholarship, such as about the Nazi era, this book offers a fresh perspective, told from the point of view of a resourceful officer, and his family, of the occupation in Greece and Norway and of conditions on the home front in Hamburg. The account of family life in postwar Hamburg is particularly haunting for its lack of reflection or regret about the past.

A leitmotif in Witzke's life was women. He had among many other dalliances a girlfriend in Berkeley, California, in 1917, a fiancée in Mexico in 1917, a wife whom he wed in 1927, and a girlfriend in occupied France in 1942; and he seems to have been murdered in bed by an East German agent in a honey trap in 1962.

Writing the history of intelligence and espionage, especially in wartime, is a difficult task. To mount a successful intelligence operation requires secrecy and subterfuge that often leaves a sparse paper trail that makes it difficult for historians to reconstruct the past. The defeated often have good reason to downplay their wartime covert actions, especially if they lead to civilian deaths. In the case of Witzke, this biography carefully dissects his possible role in the two events that took place in July 1916: the Black Tom explosion which destroyed a munitions depot on the New Jersey side of New York harbor and the terrorist bombing of a preparedness parade in San Francisco. Whether Witzke was in truth responsible, as the Americans claimed, for the Black Tom sabotage—the most spectacular act of sabotage in US history—is the primary historical controversy pertaining to Witzke. Friedland and Hornick display their capacities as historians and lawyers in their examination of the evidence for and against Witzke's responsibility and defy the consensus by their convincing conclusion.

Writing the history of espionage in the United States during World War I must also consider the panic that gripped large sections of American society over the perceived threat of foreign agents and disloyal German Americans. David M. Kennedy in *Over Here: The First World War and American Society* (1980) maintained that fear combined with an effort to suppress dissent led the federal government to enact laws that saw the wholesale violation of the civil rights of pacifists, antiwar activists, leaders of the Industrial Workers of the World (IWW), and many loyal German Americans. *Citizen of the Shadows* offers convincing evidence that the fear of external espionage on the part of the German government during World War I remained a significant threat for American national security. German intelligence sent Witzke to the United States to foster dissent by contacting the IWW to encourage labor turmoil and Black troops with the eye of fueling widespread mutinies. Federal authorities arrested Witzke soon after he crossed into the United States and his plans were foiled before he could contact either group.

How to balance legitimate security concerns while still protecting civil liberties is a question that still divides Americans. President Coolidge in commuting Witzke's sentence in the interest of promoting American reconciliation with Germany ultimately had the unintended consequence of eventually making a skilled agent available to serve the Third Reich. Despite his service with Abwehr and the possibility Witzke may have been implicated in war crimes in occupied territories, the British occupation force only briefly detained him after VE Day. During the postwar years, Witzke managed to forge a partnership with British business interests and there is some circumstantial evidence he may have worked for British intelligence. Friedland and Hornick tell us much about Lothar Witzke, but they also make clear there are some mysteries that still need to be resolved, especially about the extent of German covert activities in the United States during World War I.

G. KURT PIEHLER
Florida State University

INTRODUCTION

When the Statue of Liberty was opened to visitors in 1886, one of its marvels was an internal staircase that allowed the hardy to climb to the tip of the torch. Thousands did so, until July 30, 1916. Since that day, no one has done so. The torch steps have been closed off.

What happened on July 30, 1916, was the biggest explosion in the New York area until September 11, 2001. The explosion was not an accident. It was sabotage, though the target was not the statue herself. The saboteurs' purpose was to destroy an arms depot on a nearby slip of land, called Black Tom, on the New Jersey side of the Hudson River. Black Tom was the railway terminus for freight awaiting shipment across the Atlantic Ocean. On July 30, 1916, Black Tom was full of munitions paid for by the Allied Powers opposing the Central Powers in World War I. The United States was at the time a neutral nation. To keep the munitions from its enemies, German spies and saboteurs working undercover triggered an explosion that destroyed the arms depot and shattered windows throughout Manhattan. Its reverberations were felt as far away as Philadelphia. While the statue did not topple, shrapnel from the explosion weakened the torch, closing it forever to visitors.[1]

The collective memory of Black Tom has faded, but for a few generations its impact endured, and not in salutary ways. Memories of German sabotage on the Hudson River influenced the Roosevelt administration's decision during World War II to intern Japanese-Americans after Pearl Harbor. "We don't want any more Black Toms," President Roosevelt in 1942 told assistant secretary of war John McCloy, who implemented the internment order.[2]

The German operative said to be responsible for the sabotage at Black Tom was Lothar Witzke.

◇　◇　◇

Lothar Witzke was once notorious. A 1931 series entitled "German Spies in America" in the popular magazine *Liberty*, described him as "the most dangerous agent sent by Germany to America."[3]

Though his notoriety has not endured, Witzke's life story is an important part of the history of America during World War I, of international law, and more broadly of twentieth-century Germany. Yet until now no one has written a history of the life of this man.

Befitting a secret agent, Witzke's life story is full of shrouded and contested episodes. To tell the story of Witzke's life has required sorting out the truth from the lies. Many of the latter were promoted by Witzke himself. We have relied on previously untapped sources to separate the truth from the lies.

Distinguishing truth from untruth is but one challenge for the Witzke biographer. The available information about Witzke's life remains frustratingly imperfect and incomplete. For example, we learned from his family that a memoir-like record that Witzke kept during the 1920s and 1930s was used for toilet paper during the final days of World War II and therefore did not survive the war. Still, we have been fortunate to obtain access to a considerable amount of original source material, including hundreds of personal letters and postcards to and from Witzke written during 1913–1923 and 1943–1958, an address book that includes travel notes that Witzke kept during the time that he was a spy in America (1916–1917), thousands of pages of evidence submitted by Germany and the US to the Mixed Claims Commission from 1923 to 1939 in the interstate arbitration regarding Germany's alleged responsibility for Black Tom, Witzke's Leavenworth prison file, formerly classified materials in the US, UK, and Germany, long-overlooked German archival material, and multiple interviews with two of Witzke's grandchildren.

Historians have previously written about Black Tom and German espionage and in so doing have referenced Witzke.[4] There is also one recent book about Witzke's life during 1916–1918.[5] But most of these writings, including the book about Witzke during 1916–1918, accept as true many of the lies that we will disprove. None has reassessed the core assumption that he was responsible for Black Tom. None has gathered the evidence set out in this book. We reexamine the evidence using our skills as international lawyers and litigators, including careful review of hearing transcripts and documentary and testimonial evidence. We reach a conclusion that is different from the consensus.

The controversy about Witzke's responsibility for the sabotage at Black Tom is but one aspect of the extraordinary life of this man. His was a life of unceasing adventure, before and well after 1916. His was also a life of moral compromise, a common thread among those Germans who lived and survived the first half of the twentieth century. Remarkably, amid the extreme discontinuities of twentieth-century German history, from the Wilhelmine Empire to the Weimar Republic to the Third Reich to early postwar West

Germany, Witzke not only survived but prospered. More than once, he was lucky. More than once, his cleverness—the compromises he chose or rejected—made a difference.

This biography had an unlikely origin. We were investigating a possible book on presidential pardons, and we came upon a list that said that Lothar Witzke, a German spy, was pardoned in 1923 by President Coolidge. This led us to wonder: What had Witzke done to be jailed? How was he caught? Why was he pardoned?

Researching those questions, we learned that Witzke, working as a spy and saboteur in the US and Mexico during World War I, was caught at the Mexican border thanks to an improbable set of circumstances involving two double agents. He was then convicted of espionage (not sabotage) in 1918 by a military tribunal and sentenced to be hanged, but the execution was not carried out before World War I ended. He was later pardoned and released under pressure from the Weimar Government. Witzke then became the star witness in the sixteen-year interstate arbitration between the US and Germany over responsibility for Black Tom, he lived and worked for more than a decade in Mexico, Venezuela, and China, and he went on from there to serve with the *Abwehr* in World War II, to be imprisoned once again (this time by the British) and then to participate in the economic miracle of West Germany in the 1950s as a member of the Hamburg Parliament and chief executive of a major company. He died in 1962 under mysterious circumstances, probably murdered in bed by an East German Stasi agent in a honeytrap, as payback for suspected espionage on behalf of the British.

The more we learned, the more we were hooked, and this book is the result.

◇　○　◇

This biography is organized in three sections.

After a prologue that sets the scene of German sabotage in America, and especially at Black Tom during World War I, part 1 recounts the dramatic events of Witzke's capture by American counterintelligence operatives at the US/Mexican border in January 1918, and his subsequent trial, imprisonment, and pardon, leading to his deportation back to Germany in 1923.

Part 2 goes back in time, presenting what is known of Witzke's childhood and his life in the German merchant marine and describing his time as an undercover agent in the United States and Mexico before his capture. The narrative then resumes where part 1 left off, upon Witzke's return to Germany in 1923. The chapters that follow tell Witzke's very German story, first during the Weimar era, then as an expatriate living in privileged German enclaves in Latin America and China, then as a witness for Germany in a long-running arbitration brought by the United States arising from German sabotage in the US during World War I, then as a Nazi and commander in the *Abwehr* during World War II, and then as a prosperous businessman in Hamburg after the war.

Part 3 addresses the unresolved, and until now unexamined, issue of whether Witzke was responsible for the acts of sabotage of which he boasted, both on the West Coast and at Black Tom.

The epilogue recounts the mystery surrounding Witzke's death in 1962 on the first day of his retirement.

PROLOGUE:
SABOTAGE ON
THE HUDSON

"Fate had . . . picked him, as a blonde-
haired, blue-eyed youth of 19 to play one
of the strangest roles of the World War."
REGINALD P. MITCHEL, "SPY," THE AMERICAN
FOREIGN SERVICE JOURNAL (NOVEMBER 1934)

Fifteenth Street between 5th and 6th Avenues in Manhattan resembles to this day the block as it was in the early twentieth century. Four-story brownstones line the north side of the street. At each residence, steps lead up to an entrance, and one enters a hallway with high ceilings. Trees surrounded by plantings interrupt the sidewalk. Not all remains the same. In the early twentieth century, the street was cobblestoned, not paved; there were gaslights, not electric lights; the traffic then was less and included horse-drawn carriages. The area had yet to see a decline in fortunes, or the gentrification that would follow.

On the north side of the street, one of the addresses is today, as it was then, 123 West Fifteenth Street. Easy to remember. It would not occur to the twenty-first-century resident that, a century before, the address had been selected because it would be easy for transient guests to remember. Even less would today's passerby imagine that 123 West Fifteenth Street served during World War I as the meeting place for a cell of German secret agents and saboteurs whose deeds included, we can fairly be sure, the most spectacular and destructive explosion in the eastern United States before September 11, 2001.

Mena Edwards was a very pretty American girl. At the outbreak of World War I, she found employment with the Eastman Kodak Company and became known as one of the "Eastman Girls." She posed for photographs and appeared on magazine covers.[1] Her smile opened doors. One such door was at 123 West Fifteenth Street.

Captain Franz von Rintelen was attached at the outbreak of the war to the Admiralty Staff in Germany.[2] He had spent several years in New York working for a bank before the war and remained a member of the New York Yacht Club, whose only other German members were the Kaiser and the Kaiser's brother.[3] Von Rintelen had wealth, family connections, and looks. His father was the former Imperial Minister of Finance. It made sense that he was sent to New York in 1914 to look after Germany's interests. In New York, von Rintelen's social set included Captain Franz von Papen, who was the Military Attaché of the German embassy in Washington, DC, but mostly resided in New York at the German Club, which had a choice address on Central Park South. Von Rintelen and von Papen and their friends were young, monied, and good-looking, and they had free time and the means to enjoy the best of New York City. Why not do so in the company of good-looking women?

Mena Edwards was pleased to be one of those good-looking women invited into the company of these impressive German officers. She dined often with them at New York's finest hotels and restaurants: the Plaza, the Ritz, the Majestic, Delmonico's. She regularly went horseback riding with them in Central Park. In the morning it was with Captain von Papen, in the late afternoon it was with another German official living in Manhattan. "They would phone me," she said, "and I would meet them at the Sixty-Sixth Street entrance to the Park." It may be that the German officers were so charmed by Mena that her presence sufficed for her to be invited to their many outings and soirees. It is more likely that she was the mistress of at least one of them, presumably von Papen.

Captain von Papen would go on to become chancellor of Germany in 1932, and would serve as Adolf Hitler's vice chancellor in 1933–1934. His visibility in German politics of the 1920s and 1930s offers some explanation for Germany's assiduous efforts to deny and disprove the later sabotage claims raised against Germany for its agents' actions in the US during the period of American neutrality. In his memoirs published after World War II, von Papen dismissed with disdain Mena Edwards' allegations, including about riding with him in Central Park, saying *inter alia* that "the horse that I hired from

Table 1. German Operatives in the US, 1914–1917

Name	Description
Ahrendt, Carl.	Baltimore resident, employed by a shipping company, worked with Hilken and Herrmann.
Gordon, Martha (aka Martha Held).	Owner of 123 West Fifteenth Street, German meeting place.
Herrmann, Frederick.	American of German descent. Baltimore resident. In Mexico in 1917. Author of the 1917 Herrmann Message.
Hilken, Paul.	American of German descent and a representative of the North German Lloyd Line in Baltimore. Paymaster for Herrmann and other German operatives.
Hinsch, Friedrich.	Captain of the SS Neckar, a North German Lloyd ship interned as of 1914 in Baltimore harbor. Took credit for Black Tom.
Jahnke, Kurt.	Master spy. Resident in San Francisco in 1916. Occasionally in New York in 1916. In Mexico in 1917.
Kristoff, Michael.	Slovakian native. New Jersey resident. Accused of participating in Black Tom.
von Papen, Franz.	Military Attaché of the German Embassy in Washington, DC, as of 1914. German Chancellor in 1932.
von Rintelen, Franz.	Captain, Admiralty Staff. In New York as of 1914. Head of espionage operations. Captured by the British in 1916 on a trip to Europe, convicted of espionage and imprisoned.
Witzke, Lothar.	Jahnke's right-hand man. Resident in San Francisco as of May 1916. Occasionally in New York in 1916. In Mexico in 1917. Responsible for Black Tom?
Wozniak, Theodor.	Kingsland worker, accused of starting the Kingsland fire in January 1917.

the Central Park Riding Academy loathed other horses and always had to be ridden alone."[4] If von Papen's memoirs are to be believed, Mena Edwards fabricated her story. It is more likely that von Papen lied in his memoirs.[5]

Mena Edwards' German beaux introduced her to a German woman who had taken the name Martha Gordon. Gordon was known both as a former opera singer from Germany and as a prostitute. Her house at 123 West Fifteenth Street made an impression on Mena. "I remember very distinctly the details regarding this house. . . . The Germans who went there from time to time were accustomed to entering by the basement door. It was an old-fashioned house with a brown stone stoop. There was a large room in the front part of the basement floor and a kitchen in the rear, and a long hall that extended from the front of the basement to the rear."[6]

Gordon understood that decorative and amenable female company was required by her German friends at the nearly constant dinner parties she gave. Mena was flattered that Gordon "took a great fancy" to her. Mena did her best to reciprocate for her "stout" hostess. "She asked me to assist her from time to time in selections of clothes and hats. I remember that I recommended a particular kind of corset to her which was adapted to stout people."

The German officers and secret agents were indiscrete in the presence of their American lady friend. "They appeared to have entire confidence in me. I didn't speak German fluently but I could understand it quite well and as a great deal of wine was consumed the men frequently became very talkative." The overconfident foreign agents did not pause to consider that some day this young American woman might be persuaded by US authorities to speak of what she heard at 123 West Fifteenth Street. And this she would do: "The subject of destroying munitions and factories and other supplies which were being used for the Allied governments was a constant topic of conversation in the dinners and conferences which the men held there and which I overheard."[7]

◊　◊　◊

Germany could say that it was all the fault of the British. Because the British controlled the Atlantic and were blockading Germany and its allies, US companies wishing to trade with Europe could trade either with the Allies or not at all. They unsurprisingly chose the former.

The Atlantic trade corridor was a critical source of munitions and food for the Allies. Germany had the capacity to harass shipping routes through submarine warfare, but u-boat attacks risked bringing the United States into the war on the Allied side. This was an intolerable conundrum for Germany, and German war leaders decided that a covert sabotage campaign, designed to limit munitions supplies without incurring (they hoped) the diplomatic risks associated with submarine warfare, should be tried.[8]

Accordingly, on January 24, 1915, the German Foreign Office sent the following telegram, which was drafted by the German General Staff, to the German Embassy in the United States:

It is respectfully requested to have dispatched the following telegram in cipher to the Imperial Embassy at Washington:

> In United States sabotage can reach to all kinds of factories for war deliveries; railroad, dams, bridges must not be touched there. Under no circumstances compromise Embassy, and equally Irish-German propaganda.

Acting General Staff[9]

Though falling short of an order to commit sabotage in the United States while the US was still a neutral in the war, this telegram, which was intercepted by British intelligence, authorized sabotage to interdict the supply of munitions to Germany's wartime enemies, and directed that such activities be pursued in a manner that would not connect them to the German Embassy.[10]

In response to the telegram, von Rintelen organized a campaign of interdiction, primarily by having incendiary devices, in particular time-delayed explodive cigar-sized lead tubes, placed in munitions-laden ships bound for Europe.[11] There soon followed a series of unexplained accidents at sea. Ships carrying American munitions exploded, destroying their cargoes.[12]

Von Rintelen was unaware that British naval intelligence were intercepting and decrypting his telegrams.[13] In August 1915, he was arrested in England during a stopover on his way to Germany, and he remained in prison in England and later in the US for the duration of the war.[14]

Paul Hilken, an American of German descent who represented the North German Lloyd Line in Baltimore, and another German-American agent named Frederick Herrmann were then summoned to a meeting of German intelligence officers in Berlin, and were told to continue von Rintelen's work.[15] Herrmann would later author a message that would be the decisive piece of evidence in the sixteen-year interstate arbitration between the United States and Germany over responsibility for sabotage in neutral America during the war.

During the first six months of 1916, Hilken involved yet another German agent, Friedrich Hinsch, in the effort to stop American munitions from reaching Allied hands. Hinsch, "in his early forties, was a huge burly individual with . . . fair hair, blue eyes, ruddy complexion, round full face."[16] He had been the captain of a North German Lloyd ship (*the SS Neckar*) interned in Baltimore harbor since late 1914.[17] "At the commencement of the war, he had remained in the South Atlantic, dodging British cruisers and attempting to use his ship as a collier and supply base for German warships still at large.

Late in 1914, he had finally been forced to put into Baltimore, where his ship was interned. Hinsch was fearless. He knew how to handle the men on the docks and commanded their respect by his shrewd intelligence, his flow of seafaring language, and the ready use of his fists when necessary."[18]

One of Hinsch's activities in 1916 was to travel across the United States under the alias Francis Graentnor, gathering information about munitions plants. He was accompanied by Michael Kristoff, a Slovakian oil worker, about whom more will be told in this book.

◇   ◇   ◇

German efforts to prevent munitions shipments to the Allies by interfering with shipping proved futile. The cigar bombs stopped only a tiny portion of ammunition bound for the Allies. German agents in the United States needed to do more.

Black Tom terminal was a shipping and warehouse complex of the Lehigh Valley Railroad Company located on a mile-long promontory that juts into New York Harbor from the New Jersey shore. "Within a short time after the commencement of the war, Black Tom became the most important point in America for the transfer of munitions and supplies to Allied vessels."[19] Millions of pounds of explosives moved through the depot every day.[20]

Von Rintelen, investigating the US munitions industry in 1914, had come upon Black Tom and quickly concluded that it was an ideal site for sabotage:

> One of our visits took us to "Black Tom," a rather curious name for a terminal station. . . . I could not help urging upon myself the advisability of giving Black Tom a sound knock on the head—its mere name sounded so good to me: we could run little risk from paying Black Tom a compliment of this kind. Some peaceful summer evening—all arrangements properly made—a powerful speedboat at hand for us to disappear into the vastness of the Hudson River—it was all so remote from observation, from possible harm that might be done to human life![21]

As of 5:30 p.m. every Saturday, Black Tom emptied out. The terminal had easy, unfenced and unlit access on the landward side, and the bargemen whose boats were tied at the pier occasionally passed through from one end to the other. The few overnight guards on the landward side did not scrutinize individuals who entered the grounds. There were no guards on the seaward side.[22]

On Saturday, July 29, 1916, the terminal was full of explosives bound for Russia.[23]

Mena Edwards remembered the days leading up to July 29/30, 1916:

> I recall overhearing discussions about the plans for destroying that property. This had frequently been a matter of conferences that I overheard for many months. It had been discussed a great deal by Capt. Von Papen and Capt. Boy-Ed before they left. . . . In the immediate few weeks before the explosion I overheard conversations which told me exactly what night it was proposed to blow up the Black Tom terminal. They had selected Saturday night and early Sunday morning because they thought there would be fewer people around at that time.

The intention was not to kill, but to destroy munitions; this was sabotage, not terrorism.

At 2:08 a.m. on Sunday, July 30, 1916, there began a series of explosions at Black Tom Island. The explosions reverberated over parts of New York, New Jersey, Connecticut, Pennsylvania, and Maryland. In New York City, windows were shattered from the Bowery to midtown, from City Hall to St. Patrick's Cathedral. In Jersey City, every window in the town hall was destroyed, as well as those at homes, churches, and businesses. In Philadelphia, 100 miles to the south, the earth trembled. Hundreds of millions of dollars worth of munitions (in 2020 USD) were destroyed. Three men and a child were killed.[24]

Mena Edwards was staying that night at a house on the Palisades in New Jersey, "The vibration of the house was terrible. [The proprietor] awakened with a great start and we both ran out in the yard. She thought at first it was a terrible thunderstorm and said—'Let's get our bathing suits. They will get wet.' We ran out on the lawn in our kimonas [sic]. I remember that it was a clear night and we saw the light, and later watched the fire as it developed at Black Tom."

At 123 West Fifteenth Street, they organized a celebration to be held on Tuesday of that week. Mena might have been shocked by the explosions, but not enough to miss the fête. "Mrs. Gordon called me on the telephone on Tuesday morning—I think it was in the morning—and asked me to come down to the house at 123 West Fifteenth Street for dinner. She said there was going to be 'a large party.' I went down there, arriving at about 7 o'clock. . . ."

A celebration it was. "There was a great deal of champagne and wine and I remember particularly that some wonderful old vintage wines were brought out for the occasion. There was a great deal of drinking and hilarity, and a great deal of singing and toasts to the Kaiser and the Fatherland and also a good deal of hand shaking."[25]

◇ ◇ ◇

US authorities did not initially attribute the explosion to sabotage. As the New York Times reported on July 31, 1916, "the fire and subsequent explosions cannot be charged to the account of alien plotters against the neutrality of the United States, although it is admitted that the destruction of so large a quantity of Allied war materials must prove cheering news to Berlin and Vienna."[26]

Suspicion of sabotage soon arose, though, and the investigation came to center on Hinsch's travel companion, Michael Kristoff, who was a laborer at the Eagle Iron Works adjacent to Black Tom. Kristoff's aunt and cousin had reported to the police that Kristoff had left the cousin's home early on the night of the explosion, saying that he was going to the Iron Works to collect back pay. This made little sense to them because payroll departments were ordinarily closed Saturday evening. Kristoff returned to his aunt's house early Sunday morning exclaiming, "What I do? What I do?" Kristoff's family also reported that they had previously seen him with drawings of bridges and factories.[27]

A detective hired by the Lehigh Valley Railroad later said that Kristoff admitted to him that he had helped to explode Black Tom. But a prison doctor found Kristoff to be of such low intelligence as to be incapable of planning or executing the explosion. The Mixed Claims Commission later constituted to hear claims about the sabotage would ultimately reject the evidence of Kristoff's role because of omissions and inconsistencies in Kristoff's statements.[28] Kristoff died in 1928, before the Commission rendered its decision.

The second instance of massive sabotage in the New York area occurred on January 11, 1917, at Kingsland, NJ, at a munitions plant owned by the Canadian Car and Foundry Company. The plant was located seven miles west of the Hudson River in the Jersey Meadows. The damage caused was less than at Black Tom, though it still exceeded millions of dollars and prompted nearby populations to flee their homes. Unlike the Black Tom explosion, which killed four people, there were no deaths at Kingsland. The fire at Kingsland that caused the explosion began at the bench of Theodor Wozniak. Wozniak quickly came under suspicion, and vanished.

Suspected German sabotage during the period of US neutrality was not limited to New York and New Jersey. "From early 1915 until the United States joined the war in April 1917, there were nearly 100 fires or explosions on merchant ships leaving New York Harbor and at chemical and munitions factories" across the country.[29] The effects of these fires and explosions were terrible for those harmed, but were immaterial to the total war effort except in one way: they contributed, albeit in small part, to the US decision to join the war against Germany.[30]

In April 1917, following an address by President Wilson to Congress, the United States declared war on Germany. The President's speech cited several factors that he said compelled US entry on the Allied side, especially Germany's unrestricted submarine warfare. Suspected sabotage by German operatives in the US was among the factors:

> One of the things that have served to convince us that the Prussian autocracy was not and could never be our friend, is that from the very outset of the present war it has filled our unsuspecting communities and even our offices of government with spies and set criminal intrigues everywhere afoot against our national unity and counsel, our peace within and without, our industries and our commerce.
>
> Indeed, it is now evident that its spies were here even before the war began; and it is unhappily not a matter of conjecture, but a fact proved in our courts of justice, that the intrigues which have more than once come perilously near to disturbing the peace and dislocating the industries of the country have been carried on at the instigation, with the support, and even under the personal direction of official agents of the Imperial Government. . . .[31]

In a speech on Flag Day, 1917, President Wilson invoked again Germany's sabotage campaign against America when it had been neutral: "The extraordinary insults and aggressions of the Imperial German Government left us no self-respecting choice but to take up arms. . . . The military masters of Germany . . . filled our unsuspecting communities with vicious spies and conspirators. . . . They sought by violence to destroy our industries and arrest our commerce. . . .[32]

It is notorious that American engagement in World War I gave rise to domestic repression of civil liberties. The Espionage Act was used to stifle benign dissent.[33] There was a surge of anti-immigrant nativism, featuring a new phrase, "100% Americanism."[34] But it is curious how few histories of the US home front account for the impact on American attitudes of German espionage and sabotage, including Black Tom. The most renowned study of the subject makes not a single mention of undercover German activity.[35] Yet there is ample evidence that widespread reports of undercover German sabotage of US industry poisoned US public opinion against Germany.[36]

Immediately upon the US declaration of war, many of the German agents operating in the United States fled to Mexico.[37]

Two of those who fled the United States for Mexico were Kurt Jahnke, the head of German naval intelligence in 1916 for the western US and from February 1917 the head for the whole of the US, and Lothar Witzke, Jahnke's chief operative and the subject of this book. Both men came to be suspected of planning and committing several of the most egregious acts of sabotage against the US during World War I, including Black Tom and Kingsland. Both denied any involvement.

Jahnke, for his part, later admitted only that he had "collected information" for German military and political bureaus while the United States was neutral, including information about the "nature and volume" of US arms and munitions production and "the destination of arms and munitions transports."[38]

Both Jahnke and Witzke said that they had been in New York City (rooming together at West Fifty-Sixth Street) for two months in the latter part of 1916, and insisted that they were not in New York either at the time of Black Tom or in January 1917 when Kingsland was attacked. Witzke said that he knew nothing about, and had never frequented, the house located at 123 West Fifteenth Street. Nor, he said, had he ever met with or talked to Mena Edwards or Martha Gordon. He did admit that he, like Jahnke, had in 1916 collected and distributed information of interest to Germany while living in San Francisco and that, in 1917 in Mexico, he was tasked to observe ship movements and oil exports from Tampico and Veracruz, and that he worked against America from Mexico as a secret agent.[39]

Lothar Witzke—young, dashing, and unafraid—would be captured by the Americans at the border nine months after fleeing to Mexico, tried for espionage (but not sabotage), convicted, and sentenced to be hanged, the only German agent in World War I so sentenced by the US. "I realize," he said, "the futility of convincing anyone [of my innocence]. My only hope lays in the chance that some day someone will investigate."[40] Now, a century later, we undertake that investigation and explore the life and lies of this now forgotten secret agent who worked against America.

THE SPY'S
CAPTURE,
IMPRISONMENT
AND PARDON

1 CAPTURED AT THE BORDER

If anything happens in the United States,
and you are in danger of being caught . . .
do not allow yourself to be arrested.
Remember you are a sworn man and commit
suicide first.
—KURT JAHNKE TO LOTHAR WITZKE, JANUARY 16,
1918, WHILE EXPLAINING TO WITZKE HIS
FORTHCOMING MISSION TO THE US

THE SECRET AGENT

Lothar Witzke was only twenty-two years old when he was captured in 1918 in the border town of Nogales, Arizona, by the man he was sent there to kill. His legacy of death and destruction was already worthy of one twice his age. He had set forest fires in the American northwest, disabled a US transport steamer, blown up a 250,000 pound powder magazine at a naval station near San Francisco, destroyed half a million shells at the Kingsland munitions factory west of New York City, and, most spectacularly, set the explosion at the Black Tom munitions depot in New York harbor, an explosion so powerful (5.5 on the Richter scale) that the ground shook in Philadelphia one hundred miles away, the torch on the Statue of Liberty, 300 feet above sea level, was permanently damaged by flying debris, and more than one million pounds of munitions (dynamite, TNT, nitro-cellulose, and shrapnel shells) were destroyed. These acts of sabotage caused casualties and extensive damage; at Kingsland and Black Tom alone, property losses exceeded $750 million (in 2020 USD).

Whether Witzke was in fact responsible for all this is the subject of later chapters. That he boasted of having done all of it is reported by multiple sources. His story is one of deception and survival.

We take up Witzke's story in Mexico City in January 1918, two weeks before his capture. His early life—his journeys before going to the United States, his life in the US, including espionage and sabotage, his flight to Mexico—will be addressed later.

Witzke had hurriedly left San Francisco for Mexico City in April, 1917, when the United States entered the war against Germany. Mexico at the time was recovering from years of revolution and civil war, and its conflicts were not resolved. During 1913-1914, the revolutionary armies of Venustiano Carranza, Pancho Villa, and Emiliano Zapata had joined to overthrow the counterrevolutionary dictatorship of Victoriano Huerta. There followed a year of fierce fighting for supremacy among the victors, a fight that Carranza won. The Zapata forces retreated south of Mexico City, the Villa forces went north to the border along the Rio Grande, and multiple warlords and gang leaders retreated to their fiefdoms, each to become some version of guerrilla fighter or bandit. In 1915, Carranza declared himself president of Mexico, entered Mexico City at the head of his army, convened a constitutional convention the following year, and in February 1917 presided over the adoption of a new constitution. In April 1917, as Witzke was making his way to Mexico City, Carranza was elected Mexico's first president under the new constitution.

Although Carranza had been recognized by the United States as the lawful president of Mexico before the civil war ended and had received arms from the US, Carranza was a great admirer of Kaiser Wilhelm II. In 1916 the German minister to Mexico, Heinrich von Eckhardt, approached Carranza with an offer of "cooperation" if Carranza would close the Tampico oil fields to the Royal Navy on Mexico's east coast. In January 1917, the German Foreign Office led by Foreign Minister Arthur Zimmermann, emboldened by Carranza's sympathies for the German cause, cabled Germany's ambassador to the US, Count Johann von Bernstorff, instructing him to advise Mexico that Germany would help Mexico recover the territories of Arizona, New Mexico, and Texas if Mexico would enter the war on Germany's side should the US enter the war against Germany. The cable was intercepted and decoded by the British and then leaked to the American press. The cable, an immense diplomatic blunder by the Wilhemine government and a cause of US entry into the war, has become known as the Zimmermann Telegram. It read in relevant part:

> We intend to begin unrestricted submarine warfare on the first of February. We shall endeavor in spite of this to keep the United States neutral. In the event of this not succeeding, we make Mexico a proposal of alliance on the following basis: make war together, generous financial support and an

understanding on our part that Mexico is to reconquer the lost territory in Texas, New Mexico, and Arizona. The settlement in detail is left to you.

You will inform the president [of Mexico] of the above most secretly as soon as the outbreak of war with the United States is certain. . . . Please call the president's attention to the fact that the unrestricted employment of our submarines now offers the prospect of compelling England to make peace within a few months.

Zimmermann[1]

The Zimmermann Telegram and its offer of an alliance with Mexico had its genesis in Germany's realization by late 1916 that its sabotage campaign had not meaningfully disrupted the flow of munitions and supplies from the US to Germany's European enemies and that, despite substantial territorial gains in Europe, Germany had been unable to bring the Allied Powers to accept defeat. Germany hoped that President Wilson's deep commitment to keep the US out of the war would continue and that, even if the US did declare war, unrestricted submarine warfare would yield a victory before the US could fully mobilize. Additionally, the German command thought that, if the US entered the war, a German alliance with Mexico would divert US manpower and resources to the southern border, thereby further disrupting US mobilization in Europe.[2]

President Carranza was informed of the German offer by von Eckhardt on February 5, 1917. Carranza was unpersuaded. He was content to let German U-boats operate in Mexican waters, and he called for all neutral nations to embargo munitions and other war materials destined for the belligerents, which was a boost for the German cause because of British dependence on maritime imports. But Carranza neither believed that Mexico could successfully invade the US and seize territory nor that Germany could deliver Arizona, New Mexico, and Texas. He therefore prudently refused to declare war, preferring to remain formally neutral. He was however willing to turn a blind eye to German agents, such as Witzke, for taking refuge in Mexico and using Mexican territory as a staging area for espionage and sabotage against the United States.

The operational center of the German Secret Service in the Americas after the United States entered the war was Mexico City, where Kurt Jahnke, the head of naval intelligence operations, was headquartered. Jahnke was credited by Berlin with a series of successful operations in the US before the US entered the war, including a disruptive sabotage campaign on the West Coast undertaken with the assistance of Germany's San Francisco consul, Franz

Bopp. Jahnke was said to be a "guiding spirit among the Germans who were blowing up western munitions factories, sending dynamiters against Canadian railways and tunnels, helping to equip and replenish the stores of German raiders off the coast, and inciting anarchistic elements to riot and strike in industrial centers," and was therefore given a fair amount of autonomy as head of operations.[3] He knew well both Mexico's President Carranza and Germany's Ambassador von Eckhardt, and had worked closely with Lothar Witzke since meeting him in San Francisco in 1916.[4]

On the morning of January 15, 1918, Jahnke invited Witzke and fellow agent Dr. Paul Altendorf to join him for breakfast at his house on Calle Colonia No. Four.[5] Jahnke had just returned to Mexico City from a ten-day trip to Veracruz, where he had received two large bags of papers and money that had been transported to him from Germany via U-boat and Spanish steamer.[6] The papers included detailed plans from Berlin for an invasion of the United States from the Mexican border by a force of 45,000 men. The invasion was to be coordinated with a planned spring offensive in Europe. Jahnke assigned his two breakfast companions key roles in the preparations for the invasion. Witzke, known locally as Pablo Waberski or, sometimes, Wabirski, had recently returned to Mexico City from a reconnaissance mission to Mazatlan and Manzanillo on Mexico's west coast, where he had gathered information to facilitate Germany's expected use of the harbors there to shelter German U-boats that would attack Allied shipping in the Pacific. Altendorf, a German-speaking native of Poland, had been practicing medicine in southern Mexico and the Yucatan since 1914 before he came to Mexico City, signed on with the German Secret Service, and gained Jahnke's trust, even staying at Jahnke's house while Jahnke was at Veracruz and serving in Jahnke's absence as acting head of the service.

During their long breakfast briefing, Jahnke instructed Witzke and Altendorf to prepare to leave Mexico City the next day for the US-Mexican border. Witzke's mission would be to cross the border at Nogales and stir up as much trouble as possible on the US side. "Trouble," in this case, meant three things: first, contact representatives of the Industrial Workers of the World[7] and help them to provoke strikes and riots; second, persuade Black troops at nearby Fort Huachuca to mutiny, (in this Witzke was to be aided by a Black agent of Canadian nationality William Gleaves, who would travel with him and Altendorf to the border); and third, assassinate Byron Butcher, a US intelligence special officer at Nogales who was running troublesome counterespionage operations against the Germans in Mexico.

Altendorf was to accompany Witzke as far as Hermosillo and to stay on the Mexican side of the border. His responsibilities were twofold: first, at Hermosillo to introduce Witzke to General Plutarco Elias Calles, the governor of Sonora, and to procure a gun from him for use by Witzke;[8] and second, to relay back coded information that Witzke would deliver through Altendorf to Jahnke about the progress of his mission.

The conspirators dined together that evening. Dinner was a lavish affair, typical of sendoffs for an important mission. The three agents, joined by two of Jahnke's assistants, drank freely and spoke of past exploits. As Altendorf would later report, Witzke boasted that he had destroyed the boilers of the *Minnesota* while working as a sailor, started a major forest fire in Oregon at a saw mill where he was employed, blown up a 250,000 pound cache of black powder at the Mare Island naval base near San Francisco, and, with Jahnke, detonated the lethal Black Tom explosion in New York Harbor. He also taunted Jahnke with the fact that he (Witzke) had been commended for his work by the Kaiser while Jahnke had not.

Breakfast the next morning was more somber. Jahnke gave Witzke money and papers, including a code that Witzke was to use for sending messages back. His parting words to Witzke were: "Pablo, if anything happens in the United States, and you are in danger of being caught, tear up those papers. Do not allow yourself to be arrested. Remember you are a sworn man and commit suicide first."[9]

The journey in early 1918 from Mexico City to the US border at Nogales, Arizona, was arduous and dangerous. The trip included both train and sea travel, and required eight overnight stops. Departure and arrival times were uncertain. Bandits and rebels lurked along the route, attacking travelers and disrupting schedules. Infectious disease at each stopover was widespread.

Witzke's journey north was comic and consequential. On the train from Irapuato to Guadalajara, Witzke—always the ladies' man—was smitten by the young daughter of a Mexican woman sitting across the aisle from him. His flirtation was thwarted by poor Spanish. Nonetheless aroused, he was eager for a night on the town and that evening in Guadalajara he and Altendorf made the rounds of that city's seamy nightlife. Witzke, who liked his liquor as well as women, got very drunk, so much so that he had to be carried by Altendorf back to their hotel. The next morning, they learned that their train to Colima had been cancelled. Bandits or rebels had attacked the train the previous day midway between Colima and Guadalajara, causing it to be abandoned.

Witzke, with Altendorf in tow, used his down time in Guadalajara to visit a German firm with which he had previously been in touch regarding the procurement for the German Secret Service of a 150 hp engine to power a wireless station that the service planned to build near Mexico City, to enable direct communications with Berlin. Witzke was told that the procurement effort had failed and that the engine would have to be acquired, if at all, from a German firm in Buenos Aires, Argentina. Disappointed, Witzke and Altendorf went to the local German club, where they met several German chemists employed at a local munitions factory. Witzke was in the market for gas masks as well as engines. That effort also came to naught, as the chemists said that they were awaiting supply of materials from Spain that were needed to manufacture the masks.

The next day (January 19), the train for Colima was running again and the journey resumed: to Colima and Manzanillo by rail, to Mazatlan by boat, to Guaymas by rail, arriving on the evening of January 27, the Kaiser's birthday, where Witzke and Altendorf joined the German consul in a toast to the Kaiser's health, and then on to Hermosillo the following morning.

At Hermosillo, Altendorf, as instructed, introduced Witzke to General Calles. "He is a German," Altendorf said, "but goes on a Russian passport as 'Pablo Waberski.' [He] will operate on the border against the United States." Calles replied, "Yes, you know how I am pro-German, I am for Germany, and I shall do everything possible to help him." The three men reviewed Witzke's plans to create mayhem on the border pending the anticipated spring invasion. At Altendorf's request, Calles ordered his attaché to obtain a "good pistol" and gun permit for Witzke, for which Witzke paid 150 pesos.

Witzke left Hermosillo for Nogales by train on January 30 and arrived in the Sonoran sector of the city that same evening. Nogales was "the 1918 equivalent of Cold War Berlin. . . . The split city was the flashpoint between US intelligence and Mexican revolutionary foils that were occasionally augmented by Germans. El Paso and other US cities on the Rio Grande were buffered by the river, but the Sonora-Arizona border zigzagged through the streets of downtown Nogales—a mere 11-strand wire fence that had been erected by the Mexican government in 1917."[10]

Witzke checked into the Nogales Hotel Central. On January 31, Witzke went to the US consulate to obtain a visa for entry into the US. He showed the consul a completed "Declaration of An Alien About to Enter the United States" that had been previously issued to him by the American Consulate in Mexico City as well as a selective service registration card dated June 9, 1917, and said that his purpose in entering the US was to complete his selective service registration in order to serve in the US army. The consul endorsed

Witzke's Russian passport for entry, and told Witzke, who was carrying his pistol and holster, that he would have to leave the weapon in Mexico. The consul then telephoned an officer on the US side to escort Witzke to the immigration office on the Arizona side of the border.[11]

The US immigration inspector on the Arizona side was Charles Beatty. Beatty asked Witzke a series of routine questions, the answers to which were recorded in a document called the "primary manifest." Witzke stated that his name was Paul Waberski, that he was born in Winski, Russia, had lived in the US since 1901, and that his final destination was San Francisco.[12] He told Beatty that he would be meeting a friend there to discuss opening a garage and auto repair business together, possibly in Mazatlan. He also said that his intent was to become a US citizen. He then swore that his statements were true, and Beatty admitted him to Nogales, Arizona.[13]

Witzke went twice that day back and forth across the border, meeting several times during the day with William Gleaves, the Black agent who had accompanied him from Mexico City. At one of those meetings, Gleaves introduced Witzke to a Black American deserter who was to help with the plan to provoke a mutiny among Black cavalry troops at Fort Huachuca, Arizona. Witzke told Gleaves that he was headed back to Hermosillo and would meet him again when he returned to Nogales. Witzke had dinner and played pool until about 8:00 p.m., when Witzke excused himself from his pool companion because, he said, he had an engagement. Witzke returned about 9:00 p.m. and spent the rest of the evening socializing until he turned in for the night.[14]

On Friday morning, February 1, at about 10:00, Witzke crossed again into the United States, intending to buy glue, collars, a necktie, and cigarettes, and to do some banking. He was on Morley Street, near the First National Bank, when two men quietly approached him from behind, one on each side, and thrust the muzzles of two revolvers into his ribs. The two men were special agent Byron Butcher, whom Witzke was supposed to assassinate, and Harry Smart, a US customs inspector. "Halt. Hands up," Butcher shouted. Witzke, according to Butcher, turned "deathly pale." "I suppose you think you have caught a German spy," Witzke replied. "We know what we've caught," Butcher answered, and then hustled Witzke into a nearby waiting car and drove him to the US intelligence office at Camp Stephen A. Little, about a mile outside Nogales, for detention and interrogation.[15]

The man said to be Germany's most sinister agent in America had been captured.

THE DOUBLE AGENT

It was no accident that Byron Butcher knew who was coming, and when and where to stage the capture.

Witzke's capture was made possible by one of the most successful penetrations of a foreign espionage ring in US history. Unknown to Jahnke, to Witzke, to their Mexican collaborators, or to their superiors in Berlin, both of Witzke's fellow travelers on his trip to the border were double agents working against Germany.

Paul Altendorf was a US double agent who had been feeding information to US intelligence for months, regularly updating his US counterparts on Witzke's mission and the details of his journey from Mexico City to Nogales. William Gleaves was also a double agent, but for the British. Neither Altendorf nor Gleaves knew of the other's double affiliation. Thus, of the three German agents traveling to the border to instigate "trouble" in advance of an anticipated spring invasion from the south, two were along for the ride to prevent it.

Paul Altendorf is a singular individual in the annals of counterespionage. His early history is obscure and his later life is mostly lost. If he is to be believed (everything that we think we know about him before his service as a secret agent is based on his own, not always consistent, accounts), he was born June 1, 1875, in Krakow, in the Polish-speaking part of of Austria-Hungary. He studied design and foreign languages at the Jacka Gymnasium and medicine at the Jagiellonian University in Krakow where he specialized in dentistry, or perhaps podiatry, then fled the city to avoid service in the Austro-Hungarian army. For twenty years he travelled in Europe, Africa, and South America (perhaps Canada and England as well), selling jewelry, fighting in the Boer War, practicing medicine. He was fluent, or at least proficient, in German, Polish, Italian, English, and Spanish.[16]

As for Gleaves, little is known of him. He was a British national, born in Montreal in 1870. He had been in Mexico since 1893 and was working for British intelligence before Witzke appeared in Mexico.[17]

In 1917, when the United States entered World War I, Altendorf was living and practicing medicine in Merida, state of Yucatan, Mexico. Typical of Poles raised in the Polish part of Austria-Hungary, he harbored anti-Austrian and anti-German feelings, and he spoke publicly, and incautiously, in favor of the Allied cause. This brought him to the attention of the pro-German authorities in Yucatan, who urged him to move out. He tried booking passage on a steamer to the United States, but was refused by the American steamship line because he was deemed an enemy (Austrian) alien. He then packed his bags containing $3,000 worth of personal effects and $5,000 US gold currency and moved to Mexico City. The journey took forty-two eventful days during which he travelled by rail, push car, motorboat, and cattle barge, surviving storms at sea, bombed trains, landslides, and multiple shootouts with bandits, and finally reached Mexico City, intact, with all his personal possessions and all but $558 of his American currency, the cost of his trip. One incident on Altendorf's journey would have consequence. As his train was pulling into Mexico City, a hotel runner boarded the train, soliciting business for a place called the Hotel Juarez. It was 2:00 a.m., and Altendorf decided to put up there.

The Juarez was not one of Baedeker's preferred hotels. It was, rather, among the many unnamed places of lodging that the guidebook warned were "apt to be poor" and whose "sanitary conditions leave much to be desired. . . . Neither soap nor matches are provided in the bedrooms."[18] One US intelligence officer called it "fourth-rate."[19] It was nonetheless a favorite meeting place of the German expatriate community in Mexico City, including German secret agents; and it was managed by a German sympathizer named Otto Paglasch. Altendorf introduced himself to Paglasch and ingratiated himself by giving Paglasch a collection of carved Mayan statuettes. Over the next several days the two talked, had coffee, and dined together. Altendorf was careful to espouse pro-German sentiments, even speaking to Paglasch in a regional German dialect. Paglasch introduced him to members of the German community. On the fourth day after Altendorf's arrival, Paglasch introduced him at dinner to Kurt Jahnke and Lothar Witzke, the latter being then known as Pablo (or sometimes Harry) Waberski. Jahnke was not feeling well and arranged to see Altendorf the next morning for a medical examination. Altendorf conducted the examination, made his diagnosis, and prescribed treatment, reassuring Jahnke that he would get well. Jahnke did get well quickly, was grateful to Altendorf, and asked him to dinner again, apparently to size him up more carefully. Whether during the course of the medical examination, or shortly thereafter—perhaps at their dinner for two—Jahnke said, according to one of Altendorf's later accounts, that he had conceived the Black Tom operation, reconnoitered the site with Witzke, and delegated its implementation to Witzke. "Jahnke told me how he had fallen out of a boat while reconnoitering Black Tom island in New York harbor preparing for the great explosion there on July 29, 1916, which he planned and delegated Wabirski to execute, and believed he had sustained severe internal injuries."[20] Satisfied that Altendorf could be trusted, Jahkne asked him at dinner whether he had ever done secret service work and would he be interested in doing so.

Altendorf, who was more than interested (but for the purpose of double cross rather than German loyalty), feigned reticence. Jahnke asked him to give his answer the following day. But the next day, Altendorf fell seriously ill with typhoid fever. He was hospitalized for three weeks, during which time Paglasch checked on him daily. Jahnke, who had business out of town, left orders that all his medical costs should be covered by a German slush fund. Jahnke reconnected with Altendorf after he was released from the hospital. On August 23, 1917, Altendorf told Jahnke that he would work for Jahnke as a secret German agent. He was outfitted with two military uniforms, one German and the other Mexican, and sent to Hermosillo to coordinate with General Calles in preparation for the next spring's planned invasion of the United States.

Altendorf soon gained the trust of Calles and spent the rest of the year in and around Hermosillo, training German recruits for the invasion and serving as Calles's personal physician. In late September or early October 1917, he began sending unsolicited reports to US intelligence officials about German spy activities in Sonora. Evidently, US intelligence liked what it got. On December 14, 1917, during a quick trip to Nogales, Altendorf was formally sworn in by Byron Butcher as a US secret agent.

Altendorf was recalled by Jahnke to Mexico City, where he arrived in early January 1918. He was sufficiently trusted and liked by the German Secret Service that Ambassador von Eckhardt personally thanked him for his work, and Jahnke, who was heading off to Veracruz to take delivery of money and papers that had been sent to him from Berlin, asked Altendorf to stay in his house and to serve as acting head of the service during the ten days or so that he would be away. This gave Altendorf access to files kept at Jahnke's house that he could pass along to US intelligence.

On January 14 or 15, after Jahnke returned from Veracruz and briefed Witzke and Altendorf about their imminent mission to the border, a "very nervous and excited" Altendorf appeared at the US Embassy and insisted on meeting the military attaché, Major R. M. Campbell.[21] Campbell ran the US's counterespionage operation in Mexico City. His people had told him the first time that Altendorf showed up in the city and began hanging out with Paglasch and Jahnke that Altendorf was a new German agent in town. Campbell put a tail on him, having no idea that he was a double agent. Now, an astonished Campbell listened as Altendorf introduced himself, repeated several times that he was "Butcher's man," and handed Campbell one of

Butcher's visiting cards. Altendorf laid before Campbell a "mass of papers" that, he said, contained "important information" for Butcher and instructed Campbell on how to mail them to Butcher. Most important, he told Campbell that a German agent named Pablo Waberski, traveling on a Russian passport, would be leaving the next day with him for the border and he showed Campbell copies of a code that Witzke and other German agents in the United States used to communicate between the US and Mexico. Campbell agreed to mail the papers to Butcher, which he did, and Altendorf left.[22]

Over the next two weeks, as Witzke, Altendorf, and Gleaves made their way north, Altendorf continued to gather intelligence and to send secret reports to Butcher. At Guadalajara, on the night that Witzke got drunk, Altendorf encouraged the drinking while imbibing relatively little himself. After carrying Witzke back to their hotel and putting him to bed, Altendorf "spent a large part of the night" examining and copying papers that Witzke was carrying with him and writing a report on all of it for Butcher. The next day, after joining Witzke for meetings with the local German firm that was trying to procure an engine to power the Secret Service's planned wireless station near Mexico City, Altendorf added that information to his report.[23] At Mazatlan, Altendorf wrote up a detailed description of Witzke that he wired to Butcher via the US Consul there, together with an alert as to when Witzke would probably be leaving Mazatlan. He also took photographs of Witzke, had the film developed when he got to Hermosillo, and sent the photographs ahead to Butcher to help US intelligence identify Witzke.[24]

On January 30, after Witzke left Hermosillo for Nogales, Sonora, Altendorf did not stay put in Hermosillo as Jahnke had instructed him to do. Instead, he shaved his mustache, darkened his complexion with iodine to facilitate disguise, and caught a freight train to Nogales. Hiding in Byron Butcher's house in Nogales, Arizona, he peeked through window blinds when Witzke was arrested.[25]

Altendorf's career as an agent, or double agent, in Mexico was brief: it lasted five months before Witzke's capture, and two or three months after. He returned to Mexico in March 1918 but was outed shortly afterwards and had to escape back to the United States with a 20,000 pesos bounty on his head offered by General Calles, dead or alive.[26] Despite the brevity of his service, Altendorf claimed several counterintelligence coups besides Witzke's capture. These included: disclosure to US intelligence of the German-Mexican scheme to invade the US, such invasion to be preceded by a campaign of mutiny and labor unrest at the border that Witzke was supposed to instigate; identification of fifty-six German agents other than Witzke, resulting in their arrest or neutralization as threats; location of two previously unknown German wireless stations; provision of intelligence on German submarine movements; and disruption of smugglers who were supplying blacklisted German firms.[27] He resigned from the service on April 1, 1919, and was issued a letter of commendation by the War Department that stated in part:

> It is with great regret that we part with the services of . . . Dr. P.B. Altendorf, who has, for more than eighteen months, been connected with the intelligence service of the northern department, where he has given most excellent service and been instrumental in the conviction of one of the cleverest spies in the German service.
>
> Dr. Altendorf has shown the greatest evidence of dedication to his work, loyalty to the American government, used wonderful resourcefulness in working up his cases. This department loses its most valued employee in the doctor's separation.[28]

DETENTION, SEARCH, AND INITIAL INTERROGATION

Witzke, handcuffed, was driven to the intelligence office at Camp Little, about a mile outside Nogales, where Butcher searched him in the presence of Henry Smart (the customs inspector who had aided in the arrest) and Capt. Joel A. Lipscomb, the station's assistant intelligence officer.[29] Witzke had on him his Russian passport, a Mexican passport, a Declaration of Alien about to Depart for the US, a small notebook, an Able Seaman certificate from San Francisco, an Efficient Life-boat man certificate, a driver's license, a selective service registration card, and a sealed, unstamped letter to a girlfriend in Berkeley, California. He was also wearing a money belt with gold inside and, tied around his legs, handkerchiefs containing about a thousand dollars in American money.[30] His personal effects were still on the other side of the border, in the Hotel Central at Nogales, Sonora. Butcher made a quick trip across the border to the hotel, talked his way into Witzke's room, retrieved Witzke's suitcase, and brought it back to the downtown intelligence office in the Bowman Hotel Building where Butcher and Altendorf went through its contents together. They then brought the suitcase to the Intelligence Office and turned it over to Captain Lipscomb.[31] The suitcase contained clothing, shaving materials, a revolver, holster and holster belt, a gun permit, correspondence and photos, a sheet of paper containing Spanish and German phrases, and, most intriguing of all, a small scrap of paper with the following series of letter combinations on it: [32]

15-I-18.

seofnatupk	asiheihbbn	uersdausnn
lrseggiesn	nkleznsimn	ehneshmppb
asueasriht	hteurmvnsm	eaincouasi
insnrnvegd	esnbtnnrcn	dtdrzbemuk
kolselzdnn	auebfkbpsa	tasecisdgt
ihuktnaeie	tiebaeuera	thnoieaeen
hsdaeaiakn	ethnnneecd	ckdkonesdu
eszadehpea	bbilsesooe	etnouzkdml
neuiiurmrn	zwhneegvcr	eodhicsiac
niusnrdnso	drgsurriec	egrcsuassp
eatgrsheho	etruseelca	umtpaatlee
cicxrnprga	awsutemair	nasnutedea
errreoheim	eahktmuhdt	cokdtgceio
eefighihre	litfiueunl	eelserunma
znai		

Captain Lipscomb inventoried Witzke's papers, made copies of certain ones, then forwarded the originals by registered mail to Major Robert L. Barnes, the department intelligence officer at Fort Sam Houston in San Antonio, Texas. Barnes would forward the Spanish-German sheet and the letter combination sheet to the recently created American Cryptographic Bureau in Washington, popularly known—like its British counterpart—as MI-8.[33]

The papers that Witzke carried identified him as Paul (sometimes "Pablo") Waberski, a twenty-two year-old Russian national, 5 feet 8 inches tall, weighing 165 pounds, with sandy complexion, light brown or blond hair, and blue or gray eyes, who emigrated to America in 1901 through New York City and resided in San Francisco, California, from January 1905 to November 1917, most recently at the Bay City Hotel. His current occupation was listed as automobile mechanic, although he must have had substantial, prior experience as a sailor too because he had with him both an Able Seaman's certificate for service on the high seas and inland waters and a Life-boat Man Efficiency certificate issued in San Francisco in June 1917. He had also registered with the Selective Service in June. As he told Consul Lawton when applying to cross the border into the United States, he was headed to San Francisco to complete his selective service registration, and his intent was to become a US citizen.

A bit of Witzke's personality can be gleaned from other documents that were in his possession. He seems to have been meticulous and well-organized, a keeper of lists. There is a detailed list of expenses that he incurred on the journey from Mexico City to Nogales, and an equally detailed to-do list for his trip across the border on the day of his capture, items to be purchased and things to be done, such as to buy transparent glue, shirt collars, cigarettes, a small pocket book, and chocolate; go to the National Bank; get a shoe shine. "That's all for the first," he wrote at the bottom.[34]

Witzke's interest in women was also evident. There was an unmailed love letter to a woman in Berkeley, California, dated the previous day and a list of names and addresses of women he apparently met or knew in towns that he passed through on his journey.

There are several amusing discrepancies in Witzke's documents. His Mexican passport, obtained at Laredo, Texas, in November 1917, says both that he is single and that he is accompanied by his wife. But there was nothing to arouse suspicion, except the list of Spanish and German phrases and the scrap of paper with the letter combinations. Neither Butcher nor Lipscomb could make sense of either. Witzke was, of course, questioned about them. He refused to answer. But then, several days into his detention, he sent word to Lipscomb that he wanted to talk. He was brought from the guardhouse to Lipscomb's office, where he told Lipscomb that he was afraid that, were he not to explain the two items, they would be presumed to be something sinister. His explanation was that he had an arrangement with certain opposition newspapers in Mexico to provide them with information about the Yaqui Indian campaign in Sonora, including estimates of relative Yaqui and federal force strength. The Spanish and German phrases were a code he was given for sending information back to the newspapers. The scrap with letter combinations was a memorandum in code introducing Witzke to the papers' representatives in Mazatlan.[35] The man was a resourceful liar.

Witzke was interrogated for two weeks at Camp Little. His interrogators hoped he would break down and admit to the acts of espionage and sabotage that Altendorf and Gleaves, in separate briefings, were detailing for Butcher and Lipscomb, based on admissions that they claimed Witzke had made to them. But it was not to be. Witzke stayed silent. There was, however, one poignant exchange that he had with Butcher at the Calabasas train station while waiting for the train that would take him from Nogales to a jail at Fort Sam Houston, Texas. Butcher transcribed the conversation from memory three or four hours later. Perhaps rattled by his predicament and in a reflective mood, Witzke asked Butcher what he thought the US authorities would do with him. "Pablo," Butcher replied, "I tried to tell you the other day that the best thing for you would be to tell the whole thing. . . . As you have already guessed, we know nearly all about you. We are in war now, and also as you know spies are hung. . . . The only possible chance you have is [to] tell them all you know."[36]

The transcript does not say whether Witzke paused before replying. His reply, when it came, was emphatic, unambiguous, even noble: "No, I can't do that. I am very young to die, twenty-two years. But I have done my duty. If I told you I would be a traitor and that I will never be." Butcher pressed again, but Witzke remained steadfast. The conversation ended with the following exchange.

W. I will probably be the first man to die in the United States for my country, won't I?

B. Yes, probably the first, though I hear that one or two more have been caught since you were. You think it over, for the way I see it, your only chance now is to tell all.

W. No, I think I will go through with it. I had planned to live in Mexico after the War, but now I can never do that. Will it [the trial] be published in the papers?

B. I don't know, probably not.

W. You know all the details all right, and I think it was that Dr. Altendorf who told you, as I told him a lot of things in conversation.[37]

This last statement—"You know all the details all right, and I think it was that Dr. Altendorf who told you, as I told him a lot of things in conversation"—was the closest Witzke would come in his multiple interrogations to an admission that what Altendorf had reported to the Americans was true. If it was an admission, it was an oblique one. Witzke's guilt or innocence would continue to be a matter of who to believe, Altendorf or Witzke?

WHAT WAS HIS CRIME?

I haven't done anybody any harm;
all I did in Mexico was under jurisdiction
of Mexico. I didn't do anybody . . .
harm in the United States.
—WITZKE TO AN INTERROGATOR,
FEBRUARY 1918

American authorities had captured a young man thought to be a dangerous German agent. But what offense had he committed that could be proved in a court of law? The question would befuddle the authorities in the several months after Witzke's detention in early February 1918.

The prisoner did not make it easy for the Americans. Despite intense questioning, a confession did not come. Witzke held for days, and then weeks, to the story that he was a Russian immigrant looking for work, and was on his way to San Francisco to register for the draft. The swiftness of his capture did not help the investigators: Witzke had been apprehended before he even had time to attempt any of the wrongful acts that he was supposedly in the US to commit. True, both Altendorf and Gleaves in their debriefings said that Witzke had admitted to them his intent to do harm when he got to Nogales. Altendorf claimed as well that Witzke had boasted of past acts of sabotage. But there was no hard evidence linking him to any offenses. The authorities wanted—needed—more than a he-said/she-said credibility contest. The cipher message that Witzke was carrying might prove damning, and had been sent up the chain of command to Washington for further analysis, but for months nothing came of it. Witzke's explanation of the cipher message—that he had been doing freelance reporting about the Yaqui Indian

uprisings in Sonora and the cipher message was his editor's letter of introduction to friendly contacts in hostile territory—was disbelieved but stood
unrefuted. After being detained for two weeks at Camp Little in Nogales,
Witzke, manacled and under heavy guard, was taken by train to the guard
house at Fort Sam Houston, Texas, to await trial, after having been held en
route for several days at the Bexar County jail in San Antonio.[1]

MORE INTERROGATIONS

US intelligence officers began interrogating Witzke the morning of his capture on February 1, 1918, and continued to do so until his trial in August
1918. We do not know how many interrogations were conducted or how
long they lasted. Witzke would much later testify that Special Agent Butcher
questioned him every day during the two weeks he was detained at Nogales
and that others questioned him regularly thereafter at each place of detention. He would later say:

> From the very first day of my arrest, I gained the conviction that it was
> attempted to obtain from me a confession . . . particularly as to my alleged
> participation in the destruction of the Black Tom and the Kingsland Plant.
> . . . The attempts to obtain a confession were carried on by all possible
> means: by friendly persuasion, by simulating compassion and pity with
> my situation, by promises of money, of favors or of immunity, by physical
> and mental tortures, by bodily torment and privations.[2]

Such testimony was written years after Witzke's capture and was crafted by
German lawyers representing Germany before the Mixed Claims Commission that at the time was trying the Sabotage Cases relating to the Black Tom
and Kingsland explosions. It is improbable that the Black Tom and Kingsland
explosions were a focus of Witzke's post-capture interrogations. They were
not even mentioned in the interrogation records that survive. Insofar as attention was paid to any prior acts of sabotage, the interrogators were more
interested in the Mare Island bombing in San Francisco and other sabotage
in the western part of the United States than in what might have happened
on the East Coast. This was because the western region was within the area
of responsibility of those involved in capturing and charging Witzke.

As to the conditions of his detention, Witzke asserted in the same statement
to the Mixed Claims Commission that he was "bound hand and foot for two
weeks" at Nogales, deprived of food for two days at El Paso when he was on
his way to Fort Sam Houston in San Antonio, and kept in the "so-called death

cell" in the Bexar County jail in San Antonio where the gallows were in front of the door and sometimes at night the guards would taunt him by dropping the platform on which a condemned prisoner had to stand before his execution.

If Witzke was being truthful, his treatment by the Americans was harsh: "Attempts were also made to crush me by beatings, mistreatment and alternate locking up in hot and cold cells. The nerve-wracking cross examinations were continued after I had been transported to Ft. Sam Houston, where on the first day I received excellent treatment and care but was placed in solitary confinement in the dark when I stubbornly refused to give any information."[3]

There is some contemporaneous corroboration of Witzke's assertions about the conditions of his detention. A letter that Witzke wrote in June 1918 and that was apparently meant for Paglasch was intercepted by the authorities at Fort Sam Houston. In the letter, Witzke said that he was detained in a "small, semi-dark pigeon hole . . . with a strong resemblance to a cave" and that his cell was sometimes as hot as a Turkish bath.[4] Claims of being bound hand and foot at Nogales, deprived of food at El Paso, and even beatings are believable but unverified.

As to the substance of what Witzke told his interrogators, we have summarized in chapter 1 what he said during his detention at Nogales. He was also questioned at Fort Sam Houston in the months before his trial, and two of the Fort Sam Houston interrogations are of special interest because of the autobiographical fantasy that Witzke spun for those sessions. One session was conducted by Major R.L. Barnes who was the Southern Department's intelligence officer at the Fort, the other by First Lieutenant E.V. Spence.[5]

Witzke's Statement to Major Barnes

The life story that Witzke, or "Pablo Waberski" as he was known to Barnes, recounted was detailed and inventive. As young as he was, as dire as his circumstances were, he was already a master of lies.[6]

Wizke told Barnes that his memory was damaged by typhoid fever contracted in Mexico a couple of years before; as best he could recall, his biographical details were as follows. He was born on or about May 15, 1895, in Winske, Russia.[7] His family emigrated to New York City when he was five years old. His father died a year or two later. When he was twelve, he was hired out as kitchen help on an English steamer, never saw or heard from his mother again, and spent most of his life at sea, graduating to deck boy and then sailor. He traveled all over the world and learned to write at sea. Between voyages he worked in the coal mines of Belgium, the copper mines of Chile, and the saltpeter mines of Ecuador. He also worked as a porter in a London saloon and was a sugar smuggler in Valparaiso.

His fluency in English is suggested by the tale that he constructed. He said that his family moved to the US when he was five. Were his English less than excellent, his American interrogators would have disbelieved his story on this basis alone. But how had he learned the language so well and so quickly? He was a skilled linguist, and we will see how fast he mastered the language.

Continuing his story, Witzke told Barnes that, sometime in what must have been 1915 or early 1916, after a long voyage that took him from Asia to the west coast of South America, then around the Cape to New York, he joined an English (later American) steamer to Buenos Aires, the South American west coast, San Francisco, Seattle, and back to South America. He left the ship in Guayaquil, did odd jobs for a year or so, and ended up in Mexico in 1916 or early 1917. On June 5, 1917, he crossed the border on his way to San Francisco, stayed for six weeks where at a saloon he made some acquaintances (mostly sailors) whose names he forgot, and returned to Mexico in mid-July. He tried to find work in Mazatlan and Mexico City, and eventually went into business trading gold and silver bullion. He made $1,000, returned to San Francisco in September, met some girls including one named Sarah Gillespy (he knew that the interrogators had found his unsent letter to Ms. Gillespy). He did not find work, spent most of the money he previously made, and "was up nearly every night dancing."

Witzke returned to Mexico later that fall, got a job in Mazatlan for a newspaper that wanted him to report on events in the state of Sinaloa including troop movements against the Yaqui Indians. He used a code he was given to send telegraphic reports from there to his editor in Mexico City. He was paid $150. He also got reinvolved in the bullion metals trade, earned another $1,000, and sold several pearls that he had bought from a sailor; he thus had accumulated approximately $1,200 (this he had to say, as the cash was found on him) when he decided to make another trip to the United States, this time via Nogales, where he was arrested.

Witzke knew that he had to be both vague enough so that his details could not easily be contradicted but specific enough to incorporate what Barnes was bound to know or could easily check from the documents at hand. For the most part he succeeded. His story was both entertaining and, as we will learn, almost entirely untrue. Among other salient untruths, he was born and raised in Prussia, not Russia; his father and mother (plus his siblings) were alive and well, not dead, and he was in regular contact with all of them; and he had spent not a day in New York City until sometime in 1916.

Witzke's Statement to First Lieutenant Spence

Witzke was interrogated at length at Fort Sam Houston again on the afternoon of April 8, 1918, by US Army First Lieutenant Spence.[8] Spence's report does not provide much detail about the substance of what Witzke said, focusing instead on the purpose and methodology of Spence's interviewing technique. He also offers insight into what he calls Witzke's "style of evasion." Spence's purpose, he says, was "to see if [Witzke] would divulge any information. No leading questions were asked of him, except in a very general way, my idea being to make him admit certain facts without the question being asked him direct." Spence did not get far. Witzke admitted that he had never denied being a "crook," but insisted that he had "never done any crooked work in or against the United States."

Spence pressed Witzke about his final interview with Special Agent Butcher on the train platform at Calabasas station, while awaiting the train to take him to San Antonio and Fort Sam Houston. At first, Witzke denied everything that he had reportedly said to Butcher. But, Spence tells us, "under close cross-examination," he eventually admitted that he had said most of what Butcher had reported. He did not, though, admit to having told Butcher that he was unwilling to give more information and would rather die first.

In a self-congratulatory summation, Spence says that he questioned Witzke so closely that Witzke "was much mixed up and harassed by this interview, and plainly showed it."

The next morning Witzke asked Spence to see him again. He told Spence that he would disclose the name of the newspaper for which he had claimed to be working if Spence could assure him it would not get back to Mexico. Spence says that he made no promises but Witzke gave up the name anyway: "El Universal." Witzke also disclosed the name of the seller from whom he had been buying gold bullion: "Ramon Alderellette" or "Alrellette." Spence ends his report on a confident note: "frequent and close questioning of this spy will soon break him down."

Witzke never broke. It was Witzke who was playing Spence rather than the other way around. The two last-minute disclosures that Spence believed that he had wrung from Witzke were but more inventions.

◇　◇　◇

Despite the lack of a confession, there remained other avenues of investigation for the intelligence authorities to pursue: potential leads from double agents Altendorf and Gleaves about Witzke's mission to Nogales and Witzke's boasts to Altendorf about acts of sabotage; clues left by Witzke himself in his seized papers and personal effects, including friends and acquaintances in the San Francisco area named in his notebook; and, of course, the cipher message he had been carrying.

WHAT THE DOUBLE AGENTS SAID

Coincident with the interrogations of Witzke that began in Nogales on the day of his capture, the Americans debriefed the double agents Altendorf and Gleaves about Witzke. Both men had arrived at Nogales, Sonora, shortly before Witzke's capture. Altendorf arrived in disguise, on the night of January 31, 1918, after a two-day journey from Hermosillo by freight train; Gleaves arrived a day or two before that, also by rail. Altendorf, who quartered on the American side with Special Agent Byron Butcher, was debriefed beginning the night of his arrival.[9] Gleaves was debriefed in Nogales, Mexico, on February 2 and 3.[10]

The double agents' narratives differed sharply from the one Witzke told in his post-capture interrogations.

Gleaves and Altendorf each described Witzke's mission to Nogales in consistent terms. According to Gleaves, the Germans who hired him to accompany Witzke (he did not know their names) said that the plan was for "Hell [to] break loose in the United States" sometime in April or May, with the help of IWW representatives with whom Witzke and Gleaves were to liaise in Nogales. Gleaves was assigned special responsibility for two Black representatives who were supposed to attend.[11] Witzke told Gleaves that the objective was to create havoc in the American southwest, using members of the IWW from the border states (Arizona, California, New Mexico, and Texas), Colorado, and Oklahoma to call labor strikes, foment a Black American uprising, and blow up mines, industrial plants, railroads, bridges, and telegraph and telephone lines. Witzke would manage the campaign of destruction from Nogales, Sonora.

According to Altendorf, Witzke told him that he was going to Nogales to kill someone and "blow up things in the United States." Altendorf did not know who that "someone" was, but he inferred from the discussion that it was an American officer in Nogales with good connections in Mexico who was undermining German efforts in Mexico. This was consistent with the cable that Altendorf had sent to Butcher from Mazatlan (via the American Consul) on January 26, in which he said that the two German spies with whom he was traveling (Altendorf thought Gleaves as well as Witzke was a German spy) were plotting to assassinate "some officials" in Nogales.[12] As to the broader mission, Altendorf said, Witzke insisted that he could not give Altendorf more details, only that what he was going to do was "terrible" and that, if he succeeded, it would be in all the papers and he, Witzke, would have "saved Germany."[13]

Altendorf told Butcher about three incidents involving Witzke on their trip north that, if believed, put substance to the broad outlines of Witzke's mission at the border. On January 27, on the train from Guayamas to Hermosillo, Witzke "busied himself through the coaches" and on his return to where he and Altendorf were sitting told Altendorf that he had "gotten rid of over $100 as he had six men going north with him. The work is moving splendidly."[14] In Hermosillo, Witzke insisted on going to an American hotel, the Arcadia, because he was then posing as a Russian-American. He struck up a conversation with Americans at the hotel in which he exhibited a "deep understanding of American military camps, so much so that his knowledge caused comment." Also in Hermosillo, Altendorf introduced Witzke to his former boss General Calles, who seemed to be "informed" already about Witzke's proposed trip to Sonora, and who told Witzke that he could "give him protection on the Mexican side of the border" but not on the American side. Witzke told Calles that he would be sending coded telegrams to Mexico City via Calles's private telegraph, that Altendorf would act as interpreter, and that Calles would be receiving further instructions from Mexico City. Witzke also bought a pistol from Calles, paying him 150 pesos for the pistol and gun permit.

Gleaves likewise described several incidents relating to Witzke that added details to the outline of Witzke's mission. The most important was a meeting that Gleaves said that he and Witzke attended in Nogales, Mexico, on the evening of January 31 after Witzke arrived by train from Hermosillo the previous evening. The meeting, at a small hotel near the market, was with three IWW delegates from Arizona which lasted an hour. The two Black persons for whom Gleaves was supposed to be responsible did not show up and Witzke asked Gleaves to leave the meeting while Witzke instructed the White delegates. Gleaves' orders were to go to Piedro Negras after the meeting in Nogales, to attend a similar meeting there with IWW delegates from Texas, Oklahoma, and Colorado sometime between February 15 and 20. Money for the trip was to be provided by a mystery man named DoctorDeitz.[15]

The twenty-first century reader might find it ludicrous that German agents were seeking to foment Black Americans to revolt together with labor unrest to deter the Americans from contributing to the war effort against Germany in Europe. Misguided and futile, for sure, and arising from an ignorance and underestimation within German leadership about US conditions and capacities.[16] But there is no hint in the contemporaneous reports and investigations of the undercover plot that the Americans were dismissive of the threat of domestic sedition. World War I America was beset by fear of divided loyalty. Former President Theodore Roosevelt railed against "hyphenated Americans";[17] and German undercover agents looked again and again to Irish Americans to assist in subversion of US assistance of Great Britain.[18]

WHAT WITZKE'S SAN FRANCISCO ACQUAINTANCES SAID

The intelligence service, confronted by the contradiction between what they found to be credible allegations against Witzke (by Altendorf and Gleaves) and Witzke's steadfast denials of any wrongdoing, decided to find and interview Witzke's San Francisco acquaintances whose names and addresses were found in Witzke's belongings at the time he was captured. They decided as well to search for evidence that might link Witzke to the West Coast sabotage that he reportedly boasted to Altendorf that he had done, especially Mare Island. A third track—trying to decipher the cipher message that Witzke was carrying—was to be pursued by the cipher bureau MI-8 in Washington.

The Girlfriend

Prominent among the names and addresses of Witzke's San Francisco acquaintances was Sarah Gillespy. It was to Gillespy, at a Berkeley, California address, that Witzke had written an unmailed amorous letter. The letter, signed "Your Harry," was playful and intimate:

> Dear little kiddo!
> I am in the U.S.A. today as you can see on the stamp, but still far away from you, and I think for a long time there will be no chance to see you, because I am going back the border tomorrow morning. Anyhow I send you a couple pictures of mine to look at. . . . I am kind of warrior like looking, but really it is necessary. The Yaqui Indians are on the warpath and killed more than 300 people already, amongst them some americans. They attacked a train lately and killed all the passengers and over hundred soldiers. I never go without a gun or a rifle not even in town because they are able to attack any one of this small mexican cities. Had some mining and automobile business in Sonora and Mazatlan. That's the reason I am

on this side, expect to go back to Mexico City every day. . . . Have you got more knowledge in kissing fellows, as you used to have before I met you. Well I think I was a pretty good teacher but I really had some experience. I wished I had some certain girl in my arms. . . .

I hope I see you pretty soon and still loving me and not that red haired fellow, with thousand kisses and still loving only you

Your Harry

Miss Bee G my best regards and the same to Katherine and husband.

On February 6, US Operative C-308 interviewed Gillespy.[19] She reported that she was employed as a cook at the address on the envelope, had met Witzke at a picnic in a park in Oakland the previous summer (1917), and had gone out with him "a few times." He told her that he was part Russian and part German. She showed the operative a letter (dated the prior November 24) and a postcard (dated the prior December 31) that she had received from him, both sent from Mexico and signed "Harry." The operative said that "neither . . . contained anything of interest."

Gillespy was interviewed again in late July.[20] The second interview produced more detail but still nothing incriminating. When she was shown three photos of Witzke, she verified that they were photos of him and that she knew him as Harry Anderson.[21] They were introduced at the picnic by a woman named Mrs. Beer, who moved east and with whom Sarah lost touch. Contrary to something she had said earlier—that Witzke would spend as much as $150 in San Francisco in two days— now she clarified that on the one or two occasions when he took her to dinner he may have spent five dollars. There was also a time that he was broke and borrowed money from a man—she thought it was the cashier—at the Heidelberg Cafe. Witzke never gave her one hundred dollars or any other money except to pay back a dollar he borrowed from her one day to buy gas. She did not know when he left San Francisco.

The investigator also asked her about the names mentioned at the bottom of Witzke's unmailed January 31 letter. "Miss Bee G" and "Katherine" turned out to be Sarah's sisters; the husband was Katherine's. None of them knew anything about Witzke.

THE GIRLFRIEND'S BROTHER-IN-LAW

In his Declaration of Alien About to Depart for the United States dated December 10, 1917, Witzke listed one of his references a "G. Jarelli" of "16th St.," Oakland, California. Operative C-308 was sent to find and interview Jarelli. While the operative did not find such person listed on Sixteenth Street, he did find a Thomas L. Jarell who was employed by Kahn's Department Store and who resided at an apartment house on Sixteenth Street. Assuming this person to be Witzke's reference, Operative C-308 went to the address and interviewed Jarell's landlady, and then tracked down and interviewed Thomas Jarell. Jarell said he did not know Waberski.[22]

The following July, agents in the Western Department, believing that someone other than Thomas Jarell was Witzke's intended reference, made a second attempt to find "G. Jarelli." They discovered that a "JP Farrell" worked in the Oakland fire department and lived on Sixteenth *Avenue* (not Sixteenth Street) and suspected that it was this man, rather than Thomas Jarell, whom Witzke had referenced. They interviewed coworkers at the fire department, all of whom vouched for JP Farrell's character and said that he had never done anything "that would cast the slightest suspicion" on him. They then interviewed Farrell himself, who turned out to be Sarah Gillespy's brother-in-law. He said that he had never met Witzke, although he knew that Witzke was "calling on" his sister-in-law. He denied having any business connection with Witzke. Apparently, the agents thought that Farrell and Witzke might have been involved together in trying to establish an auto shop and garage. Farrell's wife, whom the agents also questioned, admitted that she had met Witzke, but only in the presence of her sister. She described him as a "harmless boy." The agents reported their findings, and the investigation was not pursued further.[23]

The Business Partner

The most intensely investigated among Witzke's San Francisco acquaintances was Gustav Wild. Wild was mentioned in an entry in Witzke's expense book as "Wild and Sarah . . . 100," apparently referring to a payment made or debt owed by Witzke. But the principal reason for the focus on Wild was that Altendorf, in his Butcher debriefings, had apparently "implicated" Wild as an accomplice of Witzke in the July 9, 1917 bombing of the Mare Island Naval Station near San Francisco.[24] While it seems unlikely that Witzke would have disclosed to Altendorf the name of an accomplice otherwise unknown to him the authorities believed Altendorf, who as of then had substantial credibility with them.[25] It is more likely that Altendorf, upon searching through Witzke's belongings with Butcher after Butcher brought them back across the border from the Mexican side of Nogales, saw the Wild entry in Witzke's notebook or heard Butcher and Lipscomb discuss it, and then decided to claim that

Witzke had told him that Wild was his accomplice in the Mare Island plot. On Sunday evening February 3, 1918, agents descended on the Heidelberg Café in San Francisco where Wild worked as a cashier and apprehended him.[26]

There ensued a six-month saga during which the unfortunate Wild was jailed, repeatedly interrogated, his home searched, his papers seized, and his acquaintances interviewed. What the authorities learned was inoccuous and did not implicate Wild in the Mare Island bombing in any way. Wild was born and educated in Germany, served in the German army, came to the United States, married a German-American woman, and worked as a riding instructor. One day he was thrown from a horse and suffered a badly broken leg that did not heal properly that left him partially crippled, with one leg shorter than the other. He had worked as a cashier at the Heidelberg Cafe for five years, except for a brief period from May to mid-August 1917 when he was employed at the Inyo Development Company plant at Keeler, located in the remote mountains of southeastern California, which enabled him to be outdoors. He was in Keeler "continuously" throughout that time.[27]

The agents were particularly interested in Wild's whereabouts on July 9, 1917, the date of the Mare Island explosions. Wild remembered very well what he was doing in Keeler on that day because it was his birthday; he and "several of the boys" who worked with him at the plant had a "mild" celebration. The superintendent of the plant corroborated that Wild had been in Keeler at the times he said he was.

As to Wild's relationship with Witzke, they first met in late 1916 or early 1917 at the Heidelberg Café where Witzke came regularly to eat.[28] Witzke was unemployed, Wild had some savings, and they decided to go into business together, operating a jitney for hire that Witzke would drive. Wild put up half the purchase price to buy the car (a Ford) and Witzke agreed to pay his half from future earnings. But the enterprise hit a snag before they could startas Witzke could not get a license to operate a jitney because he was not a US citizen. Wild still owned the car, and Witzke still owed him $125 for half the cost. Witzke nevertheless insisted on driving the Ford around for a few more weeks. He used it to pick up women and get drunk with them. Then he left town and Wild never heard from him again.[29]

Witzke did obtain a regular driver's license on October 17, 1917, which gave a house on Scott Street as his address.[30] The house belonged to a Mr. and Mrs. Walbourn. Agents interviewed the Walbourns. Mrs. Walbourn said she had rented a room to Witzke during October 1917. Both Walbourns identified a photograph of Witzke as their roomer. They did not know much about him. Mrs. Walbourn said that he had owned a Ford, was "addicted to drink," "came in at all hours of the night," never had visitors, slept "very late," received many telephone calls but made few himself, would leave the car in front of the house, and never had anyone in the car with him except once. On that occasion a man was with him but sat outside while Witzke went inside. Wild told the agents that he was the one in the car; he had stayed in the car while Witzke went inside to get his overcoat. The agents judged the Walbourns and Wild totally credible.[31] Acquaintances of Wild who were also interviewed said that Wild was a "loyal American, honest and all right."[32]

As for the one-hundred-dollar entry in Witzke's notebook, Wild insisted that he had never received a penny from Witzke, much less one hundred dollars, whatever the notebook said.[33] The agents believed him, and concluded their report by saying that they believed that Wild knew nothing about the Mare Island explosion or about Waberski beyond what he had told them.[34] Wild's ordeal ended on September 27, 1918, when the US attorney and Justice Department formally opined that the evidence against Wild was "not sufficient to request permanent internment."[35]

What can we derive about Lothar Witzke from these several interviews of his acquaintances in California in 1916-1917? That he liked women and they seemed to like him, that he drank too much, that he had money problems, causing him to hustle for business opportunities and jobs that never materialized, and that he got a lot of phone calls but rarely made any himself—adding a whiff of mystery to the mix. Some of these traits (womanizing and boozing) would figure in his entire life. But this was hardly the portrait of a master spy and saboteur.

WITZKE'S SABOTAGE BOASTS

In his debriefings, Altendorf told Butcher that Witzke repeatedly boasted to Altendorf about acts of sabotage that he had previously carried out against the United States. The most chilling boast, reportedly made over a bottle of wine that the two shared during an overnight stopover in Guadalajara on the journey north, concerned the Mare Island Naval Station bombing. According to Altendorf, Witzke said that he had "blown up a black powder magazine of 250,000 pounds near San Francisco (Mare Island), one morning about five o'clock. Waberski bragged that sixteen lives had been lost including six children. He asserted he was working for the American government as a mechanic on the island at the time of the explosion and laid wires to accomplish his designs."

When Altendorf exclaimed that he [Witzke] "had a lot of nerve," Witzke allegedly replied that he was "a sworn member of the German Secret Service and that he must do the work 'life or death.'"

Witzke also laid claim (according to Altendorf) to other acts of sabotage against America. He had, he said, "ruined or disabled" the boilers on the *Minnesota* while working on the ship, and "crippled or disabled a boat in the Gulf of Mexico by taking a red hot coal in a glove he had soaked in water for twenty-four hours and dropping the coal into a hole he prepared leading to the dynamite magazine," and then made his way safely to the other end of the ship before the explosion took place. "I also did the work in New Jersey [i.e., Black Tom] with Yanke [Jahnke] when the munitions barges were blown up and the piers wrecked," he told Altendorf. "We were out in a small boat and the waves nearly swamped us and we came near drowning. The hardships of this piece of work were many but it was all for 'The Fatherland.' The German ambassador and Yanke think very highly of me for my work and I am very proud to have done it. I am a man they know they can depend on. I have many lives on my conscience and I have killed many people and will now kill more."[36]

The intelligence office undertook investigations of two of these sabotage boasts: Mare Island and the *Minnesota*. They were not able to connect Witzke to either of them.

The investigations of Witzke's San Francisco acquaintances and of his possible connection to the Mare Island explosion or the disabling of the *Minnesota's* boilers had led nowhere. Nothing implicated Witzke in any triable offense of sabotage except the alleged boasts themselves, which he denied. There remained only the cipher message that had been sent to the cryptographic experts at MI-8 in Washington shortly after Witzke's capture. Nothing had been heard from those experts for several months. Was that a dead end as well?

WHAT WITZKE'S CIPHER SAID

The Cipher Bureau

That the United States even had a cryptographic capability in 1918 was fortuitous. The story is worth telling.[37]

A modern intelligence service in the United States began to take shape in 1885 with the establishment of a bureau in the Office of the Army's

Adjutant General to collect and file information about the military organizations of certain foreign countries.[38] In 1888, Congress appropriated funds to pay a clerk for the "collection and classification of military information from abroad." The Military Intelligence Division ("MID"), as it came to be called, was set up as a separate division supervised by the Adjutant General, and in 1889 military attachés were dispatched to legations in major capitals of the world. Over the next two decades, MID's responsibilities expanded beyond information collection and filing to include mapping and reconnaissance, military planning and military liaison work, and the number of personnel in the division grew from a single officer and clerk in 1885 to more than twenty head office personnel in 1898, with sixteen attachés, and forty reporting officers supplemented by paid local agents. During the Spanish-American War in 1898, MID provided critical and accurate information about enemy troop levels, fortifications, climate, and terrain in Cuba, Puerto Rico, and the Philippines.

In 1908, despite strong opposition from MID itself, MID was merged with the War College Division ("WCD," by then both MID and WCD were organizationally part of the War Department's General Staff) to facilitate the growing need of WCD for MID's maps, library, and files; the president of the War College was put in charge of the merged operation. The educational function of WCD in the merged operation came quickly to dominate the intelligence function of MID. After the merger, the intelligence function atrophied and, by 1915, with Europe already several months into the First World War, there were but two officers and two clerks assigned to intelligence, none of whom had experience or training in intelligence matters. In short, there was no longer any meaningful intelligence work being done in Washington.[39]

The situation changed in 1917 after the United States entered the war, when then-Major Ralph H. Van Deman was tasked to recreate an independent, properly functioning MID. Van Deman, a man experienced in intelligence, had been assigned to WCD in mid-1915. He quickly sized up the situation and began pummeling the Army's Chief of Staff, General Tasker Bliss, sounding the alarm with memoranda. At first, the chief of staff was decidedly uninterested. As recounted afterwards by Van Deman, the chief, who was "a fine officer and later in the war became a member of the Supreme War Council in Europe," said "he could see no reason for the US Army to have any such thing as a military information service."[40] When told, in the days immediately following US entry in the war, that the US's British and French allies relied heavily on their intelligence services, the chief replied in substance that "we should simply ask them to hand over to us all the information about the enemy that their intelligence services had obtained." "No amount of talking or argument could change the Chief of Staff's opinion and after two or three such interviews, he became exasperated and ordered [me] to cease [my] efforts with respect to the organization of a military intelligence service."[41] He even forbade Van Deman from approaching the Secretary of War, Newton Baker, on the subject. Then a chance event occurred that changed things. As told by Van Deman:

> At this particular time one of the best-known and respected women novelists of the United States appeared in Washington. She had been engaged for some weeks in visiting various training camps of the Army at the request of the Secretary of War and had come to Washington to make a report to him on the matter. Merely by chance, [I] was detailed to escort this lady to certain of the installations in the immediate vicinity of Washington. In conversations she mentioned the fact that she had lately been in touch with an American young man who had been serving with the British Military Intelligence in Europe and was quite audible on the subject of the importance which the Allied military authorities in Europe placed on the work being accomplished by their intelligence services. [I] explained to this lady that there was no military intelligence service in the United States Army and there had not been since 1908.[42]

Van Deman told the novelist that he had tried, unsuccessfully, to persuade the Chief of Staff to set up an intelligence service and been forbidden to approach the secretary of war about it. "She became quite excited and said that she should certainly report this matter to the Secretary of War that very day." She did so, as did the Chief of Police of the District of Columbia (who had breakfast most mornings with the secretary of war at a local club), to whom Van Deman had also recounted his unsuccessful efforts. Shortly thereafter Van Deman was summoned to a private meeting with Secretary of War Baker, the two talked for half an hour, and forty-eight hours later the Secretary directed the president of the WCD to set up an intelligence organization "as rapidly as possible." Van Deman was put in charge of the effort, and MID was reborn, first as an independent section of WCD, then (in 1918) as a separate division of the General Staff independent of WCD as it had been ten years before. By the time of the armistice in November 1918, MID comprised 282 officers, twenty-nine sergeants, and 1,000 civilians who were providing information to the Departments of War, Justice, and State as well as other government entities.[43]

Van Deman's reconstruction of the intelligence service in America did not, at first, include any serious cryptographic capability. This changed when a former railroad telegrapher with a passion for cryptology, then working as a telegrapher at the State Department, introduced himself to Van Deman and made the case that the country badly needed code-breaking expertise in Washington to solve diplomatic messages and break enemy ones. Van Deman was easily persuaded. He got the young telegrapher, whose name was Herbert Yardley, released from the State Department and commissioned as a first lieutenant in the Army Signal Corps, then put him in charge of a new cryptoanalytic section, or cipher bureau, that came to be known (like its British counterpart) as MI-8: military intelligence, section eight.[44] It was to MI-8 that Witzke's mysterious cipher message (i.e., cryptogram) was transmitted.

DECIPHERING WITZKE'S CRYPTOGRAM

Following Witzke's capture, Agents Lipscomb and Butcher quickly determined, to their disappointment, that the code sheets were irrelevant to decryption of Witzke's cryptogram. They needed help. Van Deman had the cryptogram in hand by February 7, 1918.[45] He promptly summoned Yardley (the head of the cipher bureau) to his office, handed him the cryptogram, and told him, according to an account of the meeting by Yardley: "Don't come back until you can bring me the decipherment."[46] Yardley would later claim that he worked on the cipher through the night, solved it, met with Van Deman the next morning (a Sunday), and handed him a translation of the deciphered message. "Van Deman read the translation over and over again. 'It is a translation of the Waberski cipher,' I explained. . . . Van Deman leaned back in his chair. 'A most amazing document,' he said. 'It ought to hang Waberski. . . . Please offer my sincere congratulations to the personnel of MI-8,' he said. 'If for no other reason, the decipherment of this document justifies your bureau.'[47]

Yardley's self-serving account is untrue. Yardley himself was *not* able to solve the cipher. Nor was it solved in the first twenty-four hours after it was delivered to him, or anytime soon thereafter.[48] On March 3, 1918, a month after getting the cipher message, Yardley admitted this in a letter to MID, "Regarding the Waberski cipher that you sent me some time ago; so far we have been unable to decipher this message."[49]

With Yardley stymied, a US Lieutenant General with the British-sounding name Marlborough Churchill, who worked with Van Deman at MI-8 and would replace Van Deman the following June, sent a copy of the cryptogram to John Manly, another of the cryptographers in the bureau.[50] John Manly had been a professor and (since 1898) head of the English Department at the University of Chicago. His interest in codes and ciphers was long-standing—"from sixteen or seventeen years of age"—and he had read in the intervening thirty-five years "everything I could get on the subject."[51] When the United States entered the war, Manly volunteered to join MID and its cipher bureau.

It was Manly, assisted principally by Edith Rickert, who finally solved the cipher on May 18, 1918, more than three months after it was sent to the bureau for decipherment.[52] Manly could read German (something Yardley could not do) and had taught as an exchange professor at the University of Göttingen in 1909. Manly testified at Witzke's trial that he could not remember exactly when he first saw the Waberski cipher message, but the message had been in the office for awhile, and several others had tried without success to decipher it. He "took it up" when he had some time (around the end of April).[53]

The process by which Manly and Rickert solved the cipher was both technical and intuitive, not to be detailed here. Briefly, they had first to determine what kind of cipher they were dealing with: one in which the letters retained their normal values after being disarranged (a so-called "transpositional" cipher) or one, more complicated, in which the disarranged letters were assigned different values from their original ones; second, they had to figure out how the letters were disarranged so that they could rearrange them into the intended message.

They initially made an educated guess about the language of the cipher: most likely German, because German was Witzke's native tongue. It could have also possibly been Spanish or English because Witzke was coming from a Spanish-speaking country and traveling to an English speaking one when he was captured. They did a frequency test on the letters in the message and observed that the frequency (or percentage) of occurrence of each letter was consistent with the frequency with which such a letter occurred in German. This pointed to the likelihood that German was indeed the language of the message and that the cipher was transpositional.

Manly and Rickert then moved to the second step of trying to figure out how the letters in the cipher were disarranged so that they could reassemble them in a coherent message. By way of illustration, they knew that, in German, the letter "c" is usually paired with "h" and less frequently with "k." By counting intervals between each occurrence of the letters "c," "h," and "k," they found a series of intervals in the "c's" that was repeated and duplicated in the "h's." This showed which "c's" belonged together with which "h's"; they then brought them together, i.e., "lifted the whole string of letters containing these letters and put them side by side."[54] Now they could look to see whether "any two letters made inevitable a third" (in view of the usual sequencing of German lettering), gradually expanding likely letter combinations from two to three, then four, beginning to see words form and patterns of association.

And so on, tediously, for three weeks. There was a special incentive to decipher the message by Sunday, May 19, 1918: the chief of staff and members of a congressional committee were planning an inspection visit to the MID offices that day. By Saturday the eighteenth, Manly and Rickert knew they were close, but at the six p.m. closing time they had not yet finished. They grabbed a quick bite to eat and worked late into the evening, finishing the solution in time for delivery to Van Deman on Sunday. "The triumphant feelings of Colonel Van Deman as he awaited the visit of inspection can easily be imagined," Manly would write later. "Not only was he able to point to a well-organized, smoothly-working division, he could cite a fresh achievement of the Code and Cipher Section, which, in the opinion of the Chief of Staff and the other members of the visiting committee, would alone have justified the whole organization."[55]

The deciphered Waberski message read in translation as follows:

15-1-18
To the Imperial Consular Authorities in the Republic of Mexico. Strictly Secret! The bearer of this is a subject of the Empire who travels as a Russian under the name of Pablo Waberski. He is a German secret agent. Please furnish him on request protection and assistance, also advance him on demand up to one thousand pesos Mexican gold, and send his coded telegrams to this embassy as official consular dispatches.
von Eckhardt [56]

Colonel Van Deman, head of the US Intelligence Service, had cabled the intelligence officer at Fort Sam Houston on Friday May 17, asking if Witzke was still in military custody and whether there were any new developments or evidence.[57] The answer came back Monday, May 20: yes, he was still in the guard house at Fort Sam Houston and, no, there were no new developments or evidence: "Most of corroborative evidence must necessarily be secured in Mexico City."[58] An excited Van Deman replied: "Letter sent you today giving new evidence Waberski case. . . . Hold Waberski for military trial until further advised stop."[59] The "new evidence" was the decoded cipher message.

Here at last was proof, independent of Altendorf and Gleaves, that Witzke was a secret German agent. It gave credence to the double agents' testimony that his purpose in coming north and crossing into the United States was to do harm to America. Witzke's conviction now seemed assured.

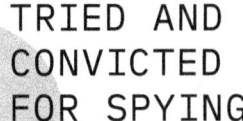

TRIED AND CONVICTED FOR SPYING

SPIES.—Any person who in time of war shall
be found lurking or acting as a spy in or
about any of the fortifications, posts,
quarters, or encampments of any of the
armies of the United States, or elsewhere,
shall be tried by a general court-martial
or by a military commission, and shall,
on conviction thereof, suffer death.
—EIGHTY-SECOND ARTICLE OF WAR

Lothar Witzke could not know that he was doomed once the cipher message was decoded. He continued to try to save himself. But the arena of combat in which he was now caught up was about as foreign as could be to a twenty-three-year-old German agent. Witzke's near-impossible task now was to convince a military tribunal comprised of American officers that he was innocent of spying. The accused had no university education, no legal training, no exposure to any legal system, and would be using a second language. The defense counsel assigned to him was not a lawyer. His foe was a military prosecutor who had gathered eight eyewitnesses, one cryptologist and fourteen documents to prove the case against the captured German.

The Americans who wanted him promptly convicted and hanged had, for their part, two concerns to address, one practical, the other political. Neither involved the merits of the case against Witzke but both were implicated in the question of *who* could try him.

The practical concern was MID's need to protect its methods and sources: MID did not want Altendorf and Gleaves, its two star witnesses and agents, outed in a public trial.[1]

The political concern had to do with preserving MID's authority to engage in domestic surveillance with regard to national security matters such as subversion and sabotage as it had done, for example, in its investigation of Witzke's San Francisco acquaintances: Congress, in the recent Espionage and Sabotage Acts, had given the Justice Department's Bureau of Investigation (the predecessor to the FBI) authority to do the same thing. MID did not want to become subordinate to the bureau in such national security matters or be inhibited by the civil liberties constraints that prevailed in civilian courts.

The surest way for MID to protect its two double agents from public exposure and to hold on to the domestic investigatory authority that it had exercised in Witzke's case was to try Witzke in a closed military court proceeding rather than in a public civilian trial. The problem for MID and the Army was that there was real doubt that a US military tribunal, as distinct from a civilian court, had jurisdiction to try the case against Witzke. The Americans' uncertainty about which court should try Witzke was resolved in the short term in favor of a military tribunal but, in the longer term, it would save Witzke's life. We will tell the latter story in the following chapter. We present in the first section of this chapter a brief explanation of the jurisdictional issue.

MILITARY OR CIVIL TRIAL?

MID had kept its intentions regarding Witzke close to its vest while it determined what to do with him. Witzke's capture and detention were carefully guarded secrets, and it was not until April 1918 that Attorney General Thomas Gregory learned of them. He was furious and ordered the Intelligence Office, Southern Department, to turn Witzke over to the local district attorney in San Antonio.[2] The Espionage Act made spying a crime and provided that spies could be tried in a civilian court. It was Gregory's intention to do just that in the case of Witzke. Although the attorney general would later back down, he demanded—and got—something important to him in return. MID's Van Deman had made enemies while recreating the intelligence department— among them Attorney General Gregory. In exchange for dropping his demand that the military yield custody of Witzke, the attorney general secured Van Deman's demotion within MID. Van Deman was transferred to a lesser post in Europe and replaced in June by General Marlborough Churchill. Attorney General Gregory would exact still more revenge against Van Deman after Witzke's trial was done (see chapter 4.)[3]

The attorney general's retreat notwithstanding, there remained the problem for the Army and MID of establishing a credible legal basis for trying Witzke in a military rather than civilian court. To proceed in a military court, the Army needed to find a plausible violation by Witzke of the Articles of War. The statutory provision upon which the military chose to rely for purposes of asserting military jurisdiction over the civilian Lothar Witzke was Article Eighty-Two of the Articles of War. It provided that "any person who in time of war shall be found lurking or acting as a spy in or about any of the fortifications, posts, quarters, or encampments of any of the armies of the United States, or elsewhere, shall be tried by a general court-martial or by a military commission, and shall, on conviction thereof, suffer death." This article was a separate basis for trying accused spies that was not pre-empted by the Espionage Act. Indeed, the act stated explicitly that nothing therein should be deemed to limit the jurisdiction of courts-martial and military commissions.

There were questions about whether Witzke was a spy within the meaning of Article Eighty-Two. First, did the article apply to non-military persons of foreign nationality such as Witzke? Second, even if it did, had Witzke been "lurking or acting as a spy" either one, in or about a military facility or two, "elsewhere" within the meaning of that catch-all term in Article Eighty-Two? The Army's answer to both questions was "yes." But the Army's evidence to support its conclusion was debatable. In light of the cipher message, would the evidentiary issues matter before a military commission trying Witzke? The answer, we will see, is "no."

Application of the Articles
of War to Non-Military Persons

Article Two of the Articles of War sets forth a list of persons subject to military law, i.e., to the Articles of War. Although the principal subjects of military law are persons in the military, certain civilians are expressly covered as well. In time of war, all so-called "retainers" and persons accompanying or serving with the armies of the United States "in the field," in other words, family members who travel with an army in the field, the army's civilian service providers in the field, and the like. In addition, Article Twelve provided that military courts could try "any other person," who, by the laws of war, was subject to military courts. It had long been custom and practice that military courts could try any civilian for breaches of civil, criminal, or military law in areas where the civil courts were not operating because of war, insurrection, or where martial law had been imposed.

None of these categories fit Witzke: he was not a civilian retainer or service provider to the US Army, there was no martial law in effect where

Witzke was captured, and the civilian courts in the United States were open for business. That said, the term "any person . . . in time of war" was broad, the US was at war with Germany when Witzke was captured, and there were examples, dating to the Revolutionary War and the War of 1812, of civilians being tried by military courts for spying. An argument could, therefore, be made that Article Eighty-Two of the Articles of War did apply to Witzke, assuming that he was engaged in spying for Germany.

LURKING OR ACTING AS A SPY NEAR A MILITARY FACILITY

The "lurking" in or about a military facility language of Article Eighty-Two seemed to be a stretch when applied to Witzke. Though Camp Little was only a mile from the border crossing, Witzke was going shopping, not headed for Camp Little, when he crossed the border on February 1 and was captured only a few yards into the United States. The previous day he had been in Nogales trying to complete and file his selective service questionnaire. Those activities did not fit any common understanding of lurking or acting as a spy near a military facility.

OR ELSEWHERE

The term "or elsewhere," though extremely broad, must have been intended to mean something less than "everywhere not a military facility." Otherwise, it would have been unnecessary to mention military facilities at all; the statute could simply have prohibited spying "anywhere." Still, even if "elsewhere" meant something less than "anywhere," it might encompass places far from the battlefield where activities in support of the war effort were being performed, such as mines and factories producing war materials, both of which were objects of Witzke's mission. Thus, if Witzke's mission could be characterized as spying, then "elsewhere" might fit the offense.

The Army's Case for Jurisdiction

The Army's opinion that it had jurisdiction to try Witzke in a military court was issued by then-Acting Judge Advocate General James Mayes on May 31, 1918.[4] "A spy," Mayes said, citing international law and custom as well as US military law treatises, is someone (military or civilian, citizen or alien) who, acting "in disguise" or "under false pretenses," contrives to obtain material information about his adversary (numbers or resources, the state of his defenses, and the like) and to communicate such to the enemy, all of which

Witzke was accused of doing. Moreover, according to the treatises, spies "may operate in places not in the immediate vicinity of military operations," and if they act as spies in those places then their offense is punishable under Article Eighty-Two. Thus, without parsing the specific words of Article Eighty-Two, Mayes based jurisdiction on that Article. There was, he conceded, a Civil War Supreme Court case that said, or seemed to say, that civilians who were not retainers, service providers, or members of one of several other limited categories of persons that did not include Witzke could not be tried by the military, but those statements were dicta and not binding. Therefore, Witzke could be tried by the military.

THE LEGACY OF THE WITZKE CASE

The decision to try Witzke before an American military tribunal was controversial in its time. The struggle between military and civilian authorities over which had jurisdiction to try Witzke was won by the military. But as we will see, President Wilson, among others, was so troubled by the dubious jurisdiction of the military tribunal that he delayed ordering that Witzke's death sentence be carried out. This delay spared Witzke's life, allowing him to go on to a life of continued adventure. Because the Witzke trial was a ruling by a military commission rather than by a court, it was unreported in publications that track judicial rulings. Few litigants and courts, if any, took heed of the case in situations where it might have been a precedent. The use of military commissions was followed in World War II with respect to non-citizen, civilian spies captured in the United States, without reference to the Witzke case.[5] Since 9/11, courts have considered whether military commissions should be used to try terrorists, including terrorists captured outside the United States. The issues presented differed sharply from the jurisdictional issue that befuddled American authorities in 1918.[6] There is no reason to think that the outcome of these cases, limiting the jurisdiction of military commissions, would have helped Witzke in his very different circumstance, but in any event the limitation came about ninety years too late for him.[7]

THE MILITARY TRIAL

The military trial of accused spy Lothar Witzke took place on August 16-17, 1918, at Fort Sam Houston. The case was officially known as *United States vs. Lathar Witcke, alias Pablo Waberski*.[8] The mispelling of Witzke's name was never corrected on the record.

The military tribunal, or commission, trying the case (a military commission, not a court-martial, because Witzke was not a member of the US armed forces) was comprised of five individuals, including two distinguished army brigadier generals, James A. Ryan and James J. Hornbrook, two cavalry colonels, and a lieutenant colonel from the Quartermaster Corps.[9] Ryan, a West Point graduate and professor of modern languages at the academy, had participated in campaigns against Geronimo and the Arizona Apaches, the Santiago Campaign in Cuba during the Spanish-American War, fighting in the Philippines against Filipino insurrectionists, and the punitive expedition in Mexico with Pershing against Pancho Villa. Hornbrook, who had also participated in the punitive expedition against Villa, had served in France since the US entered the War and returned to the States only three weeks before Witzke's trial.

The prosecutors, Major A. P. Burgwin assisted by Captain T. H. Brown, were from the Judge Advocate General's Reserve Corps and Quartermaster Reserve Corps respectively. Bergwin was a graduate of St. Paul's and Trinity College in Hartford, Connecticut, and had been assistant general counsel of the Pennsylvania Railroad before the war.

The defense counsel assigned to Witzke was career army officer W. J. Glasgow. He, too, had ridden with Pershing against Villa. At the time of the trial, he was a senior instructor at San Antonio for brigade and field officers of the National Guard and a special investigator of border incidents involving American and Mexican troops along the frontier between the Big Bend of the Rio Grande and Nogales, Arizona. He would eventually rise to the rank of brigadier general and would live to be 101. He was not a lawyer.

The trial began at 1:00 p.m with the reading of the charge and specification: that on or about January 31, 1918, in violation of the Eighty-Second Article of War, the accused "acted as a spy" in and about an army encampment near Nogales, Arizona, and there attempted to collect "material information" about "the numbers, resources and operations" of US military forces "with intent to communicate the same to the enemy." Witzke pleaded not guilty.[10]

Prosecution

The prosecution's case was based on witness testimony, especially the testimony of double agents Altendorf and Gleaves, special agent Butcher, and cryptologist Manly as well as documents found on Witzke's person when he was apprehended and in his luggage that was retrieved thereafter from his hotel in Nogales, Mexico.[11] The case against Witzke was as follows:

At meetings in Mexico City in early January 1918, Witzke was ordered to go to the US, among other reasons, to obtain information for Germany about the US military.

Acting on these orders, Witzke left Mexico City for Nogales, Arizona on January 16, 1918, in the company of several others, including Altendorf and Gleaves. The threesome made stops along the way at Irapuato, Guadalajara, Colima, Manzanillo, Mazatlan, Guyamas, and Hermosillo before arriving at Nogales.

At Manzanillo, Mazatlan, and Guaymas, Witzke met with the German consuls.

At Hermosillo, Witzke was introduced by Altendorf to General Calles, the governor of Sonora. Witzke procured from Calles a gun and gun permit and made arrangements with Calles to transmit messages from Nogales to Witzke's German superiors in Mexico City via coded wires, using Calles's good offices as intermediary.

Witzke arrived at Nogales on January 31, 1918. There, he falsely represented himself to be a Russian citizen named Pablo Waberski, presented a Russian passport, and by means of such false representation was admitted to the US, apprehended shortly thereafter by US intelligence agents, and taken to Camp Little about one mile away for questioning.

At Camp Little, Witzke's person was searched, along with his luggage that agents retrieved from his hotel in Mexican Nogales. The search produced various papers and documents that purported to show that Witzke was a Russian citizen.

The search also produced a list of coded phrases and a cipher message that showed that Witzke, though traveling as a Russian citizen, was in reality a German and a sworn member of the German secret intelligence service.

For the prosecution, the most problematic evidentiary hurdle was with regard to Witzke's alleged spy mission, i.e., the supposed order he received to collect "material information" about "the numbers, resources and operations" of US military forces. Even accepting the testimony of Altendorf and Gleaves about meetings that they said they had attended with Witzke and his bosses in Mexico City, those meetings had little to do with collecting military information.

According to Altendorf, the goal of the mission was revolution, to provoke an uprising that would divert the US from sending troops to Europe and force it instead to send them to protect the southern border of the US. In particular, Witzke was supposed to instigate the IWW and others in the

Nogales area "to burn and kill everybody they could," to cause Black soldiers at Fort Huachuca to mutiny, and ultimately to lead an invasion by South Americans and German volunteers then being trained on the Mexican side of the border. Altendorf also testified that Witzke was supposed to kill Butcher.[12]

According to Gleaves, acting under the direction of Witzke, Gleaves was supposed to contact Black soldiers at Fort Huachuca, explain the coming revolution to them, and bring their representatives to meet Witzke in Nogales. There were also to be strikes by workers at nearby mining sites, and Gleaves, using money to be provided by Witzke, was supposed to bribe Black soldiers at Fort Huachuca not to break the strikes.[13]

The only witness who testified about spying as such was special agent Butcher. He described in some detail his conversation with Witzke on February 14, 1918 at Calabasas Station, waiting for the train that would take Witzke to Fort Sam Houston to await trial. According to Butcher, the two men "discussed spy work in general." Butcher pointed out to Witzke that the penalty for spying in wartime was death, and he told Witzke that his only chance to avoid the death penalty was to tell the authorities at Fort Sam Houston "his whole story." Witzke replied, in substance, "No, I can't do that. I am very young to die, twenty-two years old, but I have to do my duty. I will never be a traitor." Witzke was also said to have told Butcher, as they discussed "spy work in general," that he (Butcher) had done "some excellent work" or "very good work" or "words to that effect," and that "at the same time I [Witzke] have been doing mine."[14] These exchanges prompted the commission to ask Butcher, "Did the accused admit to you that he was a spy?" to which Butcher responded, "Indirectly, but not directly."[15]

In addition to the foregoing, there was testimony from Altendorf and Gleaves about the method to be used by Witzke including code phrases to communicate information from Nogales to his superior Kurt Jahnke in Mexico City.[16] Although the type of information to be communicated was not identified, the intent surreptitiously to communicate information to the enemy was further indirect evidence of an intent to spy.

Finally, there was the cipher message, signed by the German Ambassador to Mexico von Eckhardt, identifying Witzke as a German national and secret agent traveling as a Russian national under the false name of Pablo Waberski, entitling Witzke to the protection and assistance (including financial) of German consuls in Mexico.

The prosecution's evidence, in sum, proved that Witzke was a spy, but not that his mission was to gather material information about US military forces. There was also no evidence that Witzke was "lurking" near a military base, as required by the statute (Article Eighty-Two) that was invoked to empower the military commission to try Witzke. Absent that proof, Witzke could fairly have been acquitted. But this was not to be.

Defense

Witzke's defense consisted of three principal parts: first, it was argued that there was no evidence to show that Witzke acted as a spy within the meaning of the charge and specification, i.e, he never collected any material information and never lurked around a military encampment, second, defense counsel attacked the credibility of Altendorf and Gleaves, and third, Witzke testified in his own defense and presented a counternarrative very different from, and more innocent than, that presented by the prosecution.

No act of spying. The defense argued that the prosecution had failed to prove that Witzke had acted as a spy in and about a US Army encampment near Nogales, Arizona, by attempting to collect material information regarding the numbers, resources, and operations of the US military, in contravention of Article Eighty-Two. True, there was a military encampment—Camp Little—about a mile away from the border crossing, but the uncontroverted testimony was that Witzke never went anywhere near the camp before he was apprehended. He had been to the US Immigration Office ten yards from the border to process his admission to the US, he had been to the city hall and back to try to complete his draft questionnaire. And the next day he had stepped about ten paces into the US for the purpose of making some purchases in town when he was arrested. There was no evidence whatsoever to show that he attempted to collect material information about the US military or that he ever lurked in and about a military encampment. "He acted as anybody else would have to act who came into Nogales, at all. He could not help getting near that encampment, which was only a mile away. There was only one place he could have crossed the line. . . . But he was not lurking around that encampment."[17]

The defense was a good one. The prosecution responded by citing the Army's Manual for Courts-Martial, which said that the principal characteristic of being a spy was "a clandestine dissimulation of the object sought, which object is an endeavor to obtain information with the intention of communicating it to the hostile party." It was sufficient proof of this that "the accused was found at a certain place within our lines, acting clandestinely, or under false pretenses."[18] According to the prosecution, the testimony of Altendorf and Gleaves was that Witzke's "express object . . . unmistakably was for the purpose of obtaining valuable information on the American side with reference to

American encampments, American soldiers, and American miners" and then transmitting that information back to the enemy in Mexico City by means of the system arranged with General Calles.[19] But this was wrong: Altendorf and Gleaves had not "unmistakably" testified that Witzke's purpose was to collect information about American encampments, soldiers, and miners; at best, this was an inference to be drawn from their testimony. There was, however, considerable evidence, both testimonial and documentary, that Witzke entered the US under false pretenses: that he was a German national posing as a Russian national, traveling on a Russian passport, and using a false name (Pablo Waberski). To the extent that the government needed to prove only that spying was "acting under false pretenses," the case for spying was strong. But on the face of the charge, the prosecution needed to prove more than that, and the prosecution's response did not account for the failure of evidence of lurking near an encampment to gather information.

Impeaching the credibility of Altendorf and Gleaves. The second prong of Witzke's defense was to try to impeach the credibility of Altendorf and Gleaves. In the case of Altendorf, the main point of attack was testimony that Altendorf gave at trial about alleged disclosures made to him by Witzke and his handler Jahnke. Altendorf had testified that the day after arriving in Mexico City in August, 1917 and putting up at the Juarez Hotel, the proprietor of the hotel, a Mr. Paglasch, introduced himself and told Altendorf that he would like to present him to two gentlemen who would be interested in meeting him, and that they were both working in the German Secret Service. He then introduced Altendorf to Jahnke and Witzke. They had a short conversation, briefly discussed the war, and then Jahnke asked him if he had ever done secret service work. Altendorf replied no. They invited Altendorf to dinner that evening. At dinner, they had a long conversation about the war and the United States. Jahnke said that he was a German agent operating in the US. Witzke said that he was Jahnke's assistant and that the two of them were responsible for the "big explosion that happened in New Jersey," that the two of them "were laying mines off an island in New Jersey, and how a wave came up and almost washed away Jahnke" and that he (Witzke) helped to save him.[20]

The defense immediately raised the issue of credibility on cross-examination:

Q Did it ever occur to you that a German Secret Agent in Mexico City would be very frank in telling a perfect stranger all about these things, the day he met you?

A There was nothing strange about it. . . .

DEFENSE: The German Secret Service, gentlemen, is not as careful as I thought they were.[21]

The defense also pressed the point in argument and in its closing. Responding to a reprimand from the commission about his straying from the subject matter of the prosecutor's direct examination, defense counsel said that he was trying to attack the credibility of the witness: "It seems most remarkable to me that the accredited German agents in Mexico City would so open their hearts within twenty-four hours to a perfect stranger, no matter who he claimed to be, to tell him their most intimate secrets. He was not employed by them, by his own admission, until [a number of] months later; but still, all during this time, they were telling him the most intimate secrets."[22] In his closing statement, defense counsel returned to the credibility point:

> I would like to call attention again particularly to Dr. Altendorf's testimony; if the Commission will just read Dr. Altendorf's testimony as written here they will find that the Imperial German secret service in the City of Mexico, after knowing him twenty-four hours or less, immediately began disclosing all of their secrets, what they had done and what they proposed to do, and began trusting him like a brother. He said that he was not employed by them until some time in December, I believe. Now, here is a man not even in their employ, to whom they tell all these things, and the whole testimony in this case is what Altendorf says this man told him, or what Jahnke told him . . .
>
> If you will read Dr. Altendorf's testimony, I think you will come to the conclusion that about nine-tenths of it is made out of whole cloth . . . .[23]

The argument was a powerful one, or anyway should have been seen as such. The factual implausibility of Altendorf's narrative should have led the commissioners to consider carefully whether the government had met its burden of proof. But they did not, as shown by the brevity of their deliberations.

Much less was said about Gleaves' credibility—a single, conclusory sentence in the closing, "Gleaves' testimony is just about the same thing as the other" [i.e., nine-tenths made out of whole cloth].[24] Perhaps the fact that Gleaves was Black was thought sufficient to undermine his credibility.

The prosecution's reply to the defense's impeachment effort was to insist that Altendorf's testimony was amply corroborated by other evidence presented, especially Butcher's uncontroverted testimony and the cipher message that Witzke admitted was his.[25]

Witzke's narrative. Witzke testified in his own defense. He was the only defense witness. His task was formidable. Not only did he have to present a coherent narrative to counter that of Altendorf and Gleaves, but he had to do so in what was for him a foreign language—English—and to account for harmful elements in their testimony that could not easily be denied. Most daunting, he had to explain away damning documentary evidence that was now before the commission, the cipher message being the most problematic item. In retrospect, he might have served himself better to not testify at all. But it was not in Witzke's nature to shrink from a challenge, especially one on which his life depended. At a minimum, he had to explain away the cipher message. It did not go well.

"The Commission, of course, realizes," defense counsel began, "that it is impossible to compel the attendance of witnesses from Mexico. The accused, then, is forced to depend entirely upon what he can say for himself, and he desires to be sworn as a witness in his own behalf." Witzke was sworn, and told a story that we have already heard in substance because it was a polished version of the narrative that he told Major Barnes during Barnes's interrogation of him on February 18.[26]

First, there was the innocent immigrant and life of the sailor. As Witzke told it, he was Russian, not German. Because his mother was from a German-speaking area in Russia, he learned to speak German from her. The family emigrated from Russia to New York in or about 1901. His father died shortly thereafter, and a friend of his father took Witzke on board a steamer as a kitchen helper. He was about eight or ten, and since then spent most of his time traveling the world as a sailor on a steamer. There followed years of mining in Latin America.

Then he met a man named Ramirez. They went to Mexico City, and Witzke started acting as an intermediary between Ramirez and some Mexican bandits in the nearby mountains, transporting silver and gold bullion from the bandits to Ramirez at night. Witzke lived at the Hotel Juarez, was hired by the hotel's owner Paglasch to register guests arriving during the day, got to know Paglasch pretty well, and gave his money to Paglasch for safekeeping. Witzke had saved about $1,000 at the time. After a falling out with Ramirez, in July 1917 Witzke (in his own words) "beat it" to San Francisco.[27] The accused man's fluency in colloquial English was impressive.

Then came the American episode in his life, one in which Witzke was overwhelmed by circumstance. In San Francisco, he got mixed up with the wrong crowd, they cheated him, he got drunk, lost most of his money, and ended up with only "about one hundred and fifty dollars . . . and a second-hand Ford automobile." In November 1917 he decided to return to Mexico City, got in touch with Ramirez once again, and they restarted their bullion business. One night he learned that Ramirez had been shot, and that ended that.

Then there was his supposed unwillingness to serve as a German agent. Otto Paglasch asked him to do some work for the German government. Witzke refused. Paglasch asked again, and Witzke again said no. A few days later, Paglasch overheard Witzke speaking German to some guests. Paglasch expressed surprise that he could speak German (they had always spoken in English) and once again raised the idea of working for Germany, "Don't you think you'd better go to the United States and do some work for our people?" Once again Witzke said no. Then Paglasch told him there was a man he had met the other day, Ramon Alderate, who wanted to meet Witzke and had a work proposition for him on Mexico's west coast. Witzke went to meet Alderate at a local saloon and he offered Witzke a job reporting on military matters. "There is a big 'Yaki' campaign on in the State of Sonora," he said, and there are three armies fighting against the Indians and we would like to have information about them, would you like to furnish it?" Witzke agreed.

Then there was the innocent explanation for the cipher message. Because this was anti-government work, and perilous, Alderate gave him a code to use, in Spanish, which Witzke translated into German. He also gave Witzke a small, second code, that he said was "an identification card." The card (a cipher message) could be presented to Alderate's people in Mazatlan, and they would help him in whatever way he needed.

Then came the chance encounter with a man named Altendorf. Witzke left for Mazatlan on January 16 on his way to Sonora to undertake his reportorial duties for Alderate. In Irapuato, he "met a man by the name of Altendorf," and the next morning they travelled together. Altendorf told Witzke that he was from Hermosillo and knew lots of people there, so Witzke asked him if he knew any military people. The answer was yes, he had worked for two months as a doctor for General Calles and knew "all the German people, and everybody of military influence." Witzke said: "You might be useful to me, to make me acquainted with those people." They travelled together to Colima by train, Manzanillo by steam engine, and steamer to Mazatlan. They met a negro on the way "who seemed to be quite well acquainted with the doctor."[28]

At Mazatlan, Witzke introduced Altendorf to his new fianceé. He also met with the girl's father, a Mr. Garcia. Witzke's prospective father-in-law said he had friends in the mining business in San Francisco. If Witzke married his daughter and could get to San Francisco, he might be able to go into business with them. Witzke tried to figure out how he could enter the United States.

Finally, the bewildering arrest of an innocent Russian. Witzke left for

Nogales, got there on January 30, met the American consul the next morning, and pleaded with him to let him into the United States on his overdue passport. The consul phoned over to the US and got Butcher to come to help him get across. Witzke crossed back and forth a couple of times on the 31st, trying to sort out his draft questionnaire so that he would not be deemed a deserter, then spent the night on the Mexican side of the border. "The next morning there was a man [who] asked me to get him some paste [glue], said he could not get it in Mexico there, because they didn't make it over there, and then I went over to the United States side and walked about a half a block and got arrested. That is about all I have got to say."

The prosecutor asked Witzke several questions on cross-examination. Witzke then asked if he could make a short, further statement about a matter he had forgotten to mention. There was no objection, and Witzke added to his story that, before he left Mexico City, he gave Otto Paglasch $2,000 in cash to keep for him. The commission asked him why he wanted to add this. He replied that, from the minute he was arrested and questioned by the Department of Justice agent, "I found out somebody got me into this, not only because he had something against me, but he wanted to get me out of there,—I had an enemy or somebody interested in getting me out of the way." He surmised it was Paglasch, after his money.

Not a word of what Witzke testified was true.

VERDICT AND SENTENCE

The Commission took little time to deliberate. After brief closing arguments and a short adjournment, they reconvened to announce their verdict and sentence:

> The Commission . . . finds the accused, LATHAR WITCKE, alias PABLO WABERSKI:
>
> Of the Specification: Guilty
>
> Of the . . . Charge: Guilty
>
> The Commission sentence the accused, LATHAR WITCKE, alias PABLO WABERSKI, to be hanged by the neck until dead, 2/3 of the members concurring therein.[29]

In different circumstances, the government's failure to adduce evidence that Wizke had lurked anywhere, let alone near a military base, with the purpose of gathering information about the base, might have doomed the government's case.[30] Here, though, the cipher message, together with the testimony of Altendorf and Gleaves, proved that Witzke was a German spy, and had entered the country under false pretenses with the purpose of doing harm to US interests. It was wartime; the US and Germany were enemies. The verdict in these circumstances was a foregone conclusion, and there is no indication that Witzke ever considered wrongful the commission's interpretation of Article Eighty-Two. Nevertheless, he would for many years be infuriated that the commission heeded the testimony of Paul Altendorf.

◇ ◇ ◇

The condemned twenty-two year-old Lothar Witzke was returned to solitary confinement in his cell at the Fort Sam Houston guard house and stripped to his underwear. A special guard was stationed by his cell, presumably on suicide watch. At about 8:00 that evening, First Lieutenant Charles Miller, the officer of the day at the main guard house, got a call from the commanding general at Fort Sam Houston, instructing him to "take every precaution in guarding War Prisoner Witche." Miller went immediately to get Corporal Roy Stephens, the corporal of the relief on duty with him, and the two went upstairs to Witzke's cell. Miller ordered Stephens to search it. Witzke was removed, and Stephens and Miller searched the cell, removing everything except the bedstead and mattress. They found nothing.[31]

When Witzke was returned to his cell, the special guard, Private Henry Brackett, told Miller that he had earlier seen the prisoner with a safety razor, that the prisoner had hid it somewhere in his cell, and that Brackett had searched but could not find it. Miller questioned Witzke, who said he had thrown the razor away. Miller then ordered Stephens to conduct another search. Stephens "took a knife and inserted it between the bars and steel sheeting" of the cell, and after "working the knife around in different places the blade fell out onto the floor." Miller ordered him to search on top of the cell, where he eventually found, "on top of the cell under an iron bar," a cigarette paper, rolled up in a ball. There was writing on both sides of the paper in a foreign language that none of the three soldiers could read. Miller turned the razor and cigarette paper over to Captain John Ulrick, a federal prison officer. The handwritten language of the writing on the cigarette paper was German. Translated, it read as follows:

> My right name is Lathar Witzke. Born in Posen and for that reason I only understand Polish but not Russian. I was lieutenant on cruiser Dresden

that was sunk near Valparaiso, Chile. I lay two months in the hospital, which is the reason I escaped internment. The rest of the crew is interned.[32]

The cigarette paper note reads, at first, as the confession of a death row prisoner. Written in his own language, acknowledging for the first time his true place of birth, it seems that the prisoner facing death by hanging has finally decided to tell the truth. But aside from his birthplace, the note is nothing but a pack of false boasts. Witzke did not serve on the *Dresden*, was never a naval officer, and did not escape internment. We show this in chapter 6, where we consider the evidence of Witzke's pre-capture life.

Why, in this darkest hour of his life, did he choose to continue to lie? It may be that he considered that he would get better treatment if the American authorities thought that he was a naval officer. But if so, why write this in German and why hide the message? We offer answers to these questions in chapter 6. But there is a shadow about the man, a history of lies and inexplicable false boasting. For now, in any case, Witzke was on death row.

ON DEATH ROW

There is an unfortunate general impression
that not even in the most flagrant cases
of espionage does your country intend to
impose the death penalty.
—SIR REGINALD HALL (DIRECTOR OF BRITISH
INTELLIGENCE) TO EDWARD BELL (AMERICAN
DIPLOMAT AND LIAISON WITH BRITISH
INTELLIGENCE), 1918

Incarcerated at Fort Sam Houston, the convicted spy was deemed dangerous. His guards had orders not to talk to him. Some authorities pushed to accelerate his execution, but others in the government were uncertain about the jurisdiction of the military tribunal that had convicted and sentenced Witzke to death by hanging. During the ensuing months of internal debate as to the validity of his conviction, a debate that engaged President Wilson himself, the US Government considered whether to commute Witzke's death sentence to life imprisonment. One consequence of the delay was that it gave Witzke time to mount a prison break, an effort that would have led to his definitive escape but for the circumstance that Witzke had been deprived of clothing and needed after breaking out of prison to find something to wear. His stop to look for clothing led to his re-capture; the two other prisoners who escaped with him were never caught. The delay also allowed those interested in Witzke's role, if any, in sabotage at Black Tom and Kingsland to seek evidence from him, a futile quest. This chapter recounts these events.

THE RUSH TO HANG WITZKE

Because of the extra precautions that needed to be taken to guard Witzke, army personnel at Fort Sam Houston were anxious to get on with his execution and be done with it. The fort's commanding general, J. A. Ryan, (the same General Ryan who had presided over Witzke's trial) quickly approved the execution. But the judge advocate general in Washington, DC, needed to sign off as well, and six weeks after the trial he had not yet done so. An exasperated General Ryan wrote to then Acting Judge Advocate General Ansell. "The papers in this case were forwarded over a month ago," he said. "[Waberski] is a dangerous prisoner and one over whom we must exercise extraordinary vigilance. The strain is heavy and I wish you would take up this matter and see if his case cannot be rushed."[1]

British Intelligence, too, was anxious for the army to get on with the execution, albeit for different reasons. Their secret agent Gleaves had testified against Witzke, risking exposure, and the risk was magnified the longer Witzke remained alive. In late September 1918, six weeks before the armistice, the Director of British Intelligence Sir Reginald Hall wrote a blunt letter to Edward Bell at the US embassy in London:

> There is an unfortunate general impression that not even in the most flagrant cases of espionage does your country intend to impose the death penalty. In my opinion and experience, a nominal sentence of twenty or thirty years is small deterrent to espionage. The Germans have themselves sentenced so many Belgians and French to these long terms that a general mutual release of such cases after the war seems inevitable. . . .
>
> In many cases only a death sentence will open a spy's mouth, and increase apprehension of exposure among the other spies with whom he has consorted and lessen the chances of revenge on persons giving evidence.
>
> I can quote as an instance a negro agent of mine in Mexico who gave information which enabled your people to arrest one Waberski at Nogales. His guilt as an enemy agent was proved to the hilt, I believe, by papers on him, and Gleaves was to give evidence of his intentions as regards sabotage, but G. was very reluctant to give evidence if W. was not to be shot. He did, however, and now it seems that the only person to be shot will be Gleaves when W. is ultimately released.[2]

Acting Judge Advocate General Ansell was unmoved by Ryan's plea for haste. On October 22, 1918, he returned the trial record to Ryan unapproved. "In view," he said, "of the gravity of the questions of policy and, possibly, of international concern, which are presented by this case, it is recommended that the record herewith returned be forwarded for the action of the President, under the 51st Article of War."[3] Article Fifty-One authorized the Judge Advocate General to suspend a sentence of death "until the pleasure of the

President be known." Ansell also convened a Board of Review to advise the Secretary of War (and, through him, the President) whether Witzke was lawfully convicted and sentenced to hang and, if so, whether the sentence should be carried out or mitigated.[4]

HANGING DEFERRED

The "questions of policy" to which Ansell referred in his letter to General Ryan were the same as those that had concerned Attorney General Gregory in the months before Witzke's trial, namely, whether it was the Army or a civil court that had jurisdiction to try Witzke? Gregory had refrained from formally opposing the army's jurisdiction over Witzke before the trial, in exchange for Van Deman's demotion and transfer out of the country. Now that the issue was to be put to President Wilson, Gregory decided to weigh in.

The Attorney General's Opinion

On November 25, 1918, two weeks after the armistice, Attorney General Gregory sent a letter to President Wilson, giving his opinion as to why the Army did not have jurisdiction to try Witzke. Gregory's opinion was, in essence, that for the army to have jurisdiction under Article Eighty-Two of the Articles of War, Witzke would have had to be found "lurking in or about" a military facility. He was not. He was arrested the moment he stepped onto US territory. True, Article Eighty-Two also said "or elsewhere." But the latter term was constrained by the Constitution. The Supreme Court said in 1866 during the Civil War that, under the constitution, the military's jurisdiction over civilians is limited to offenses committed inside army lines or the field of military operations or territory under martial law—not the case here. Therefore, the only place Witzke could be tried was in a civil court for breach of the Espionage Act,which made it a crime to commit espionage anywhere in the US.[5]

The Review Board's Opinion

The Review Board issued its own opinion six months later. Contrary to the attorney general, it concluded that the army did have proper jurisdiction over Witzke under Article Eighty-Two.[6] Its analysis was in two parts: first, it sidestepped the "or elsewhere" issue and took the view that the accused was "in or about" an encampment of the US Army when he crossed the border into Nogales, Arizona on January 31 and February 1; and, second, it concluded that the accused acted as a spy there within the meaning of Article Eighty-Two.

As to place, the accused had admitted being in Nogales, Arizona, on February 1, the date of his capture. Other evidence, which the accused did not deny, showed that a US Army facility (Camp Little) was about a mile from the center of Nogales. Therefore, in the board's opinion, the allegation of place, i.e., that Witzke was in or about a US military facility on the relevant date, was "clearly proved." The conclusion is strained and unconvincing.

As to spying, the board was on solid ground. The board said that, by "ordinary usage," three elements had to be proved: first, that the accused obtained or endeavored to obtain information; second, that he intended to communicate the information to the enemy; and third, that his action was clandestine or under false pretense.

Each of these elements, the board concluded, was proved beyond doubt. First, the testimony of Altendorf and Gleaves proved that one of Witzke's purposes in coming to the United States was to obtain information for the enemy, and their testimony was corroborated by phrases in the code book that the accused was carrying that were "consistent" with such purpose. Second, the cipher message that Witzke was carrying proved that he intended to communicate the information he obtained to the enemy. It directed German consular representatives to send his coded messages to the German embassy in Mexico City as official consular dispatches. Third, the evidence proved that the accused acted clandestinely or under false pretenses. He traveled under a false name (Pablo Waberski). He presented a Russian passport at the border crossing and misrepresented himself as a Russian even though he was a German national. He also misrepresented that he was coming to the United States for the purpose of complying with the US Selective Service law and entering into business in San Francisco. Lastly, the cipher message itself, signed by the German Ambassador to Mexico, stated that the accused was a "subject of the (German) Empire" and a "German secret agent."

Reconciling the Two Opinions

The Review Board was well aware that its opinion was contrary to the Attorney General's and that opinions of an attorney general ordinarily should be accorded "very great weight and consideration." The way it reconciled the two opinions was to say that Attorney General Gregory had been given the wrong facts and that, if he had been given the correct facts, he would have reached the same conclusion as the board. For example, the attorney general had been told that the accused was a Russian national (i.e., a friendly national during the Great War) whereas he was a German national and member of the German Secret Service (i.e., an enemy alien). Enemy aliens (unlike friendly nationals) were not constitutionally entitled to a jury trial.

Most important, the attorney general had assumed that the accused crossed the border to commit offenses "in the United States" rather than "in or about" a military facility near Nogales, and that therefore it was the "or elsewhere" language of Article Eighty-Two that applied, language that the Supreme Court in 1866 had said was limited to circumstances that did not apply to Witzke. The "overwhelming" evidence at trial, though, showed that Witzke's real purpose was to incite mutiny among the troops stationed near the guarded border (including at Fort Little), to cause insurrection among the civilian population in the vicinity of Nogales, to prepare for an invasion of the US from Mexico, and to gather important information about the foregoing with intent to transmit it to the enemy. Thus, the relevant part of Article Eighty-Two that applied to Witzke was the "lurking in or about" a military facility language (not the "or elsewhere" language), and the precedents were clear that military courts could constitutionally try accused spies under this narrower language. The board said that whether the evidence at trial established that Witzke violated this provision went to the merits of the charge against Witzke, not the military court's jurisdiction to try him.

As for the Supreme Court case, the Review Board said that it was not on point because the accused in that case was a US citizen entitled to all constitutional protections, whereas Witzke was an enemy alien not entitled to such protections.

The Sentence

The attorney general did not address whether Witzke's death sentence should be mitigated. The Review Board did. It recommended that the sentence be commuted to "confinement at hard labor" for twenty years at Leavenworth Disciplinary Barracks. In the board's view, Witzke was young (only twenty-two years old at the time of the offense), and "likely . . . dominated to a considerable extent by his superiors." Of course, he was not innocent or inexperienced. To the contrary, "he was apparently either hardened or vainglorious." [7] But he was being tried only for spying, not for his past offenses. Had the war not now (May 1919) been over, there would be no reason to show mercy. However, the war was "practically at an end, hostilities have ceased, an armistice has been signed and a treaty of peace among the belligerents is about to be concluded." In these circumstances, the board concluded, mitigation was appropriate.

◇   ◇   ◇

The army heartily endorsed the Review Board's opinion. Former Acting Judge Advocate General Ansell, who had slowed the rush to hang Witzke and initiated the review, was now fully on board. "I have no doubt, he said after reading the opinion, "of our military jurisdiction to try [Witzke] as a spy."[8] The only dissent was with regard to the board's clemency recommendation. "There is no reason why the death penalty should not be enforced," one officer complained. "We are too easy and make ourselves absurd in other people's eyes. Remember Edith Carvell [sic] et al."[9]

PRESIDENT WILSON CONSIDERS WITZKE'S CASE

It was now time to involve President Wilson and find out what his "pleasure" was with regard to the fate of Lothar Wizke, as prescribed by Article Fifty-One of the Articles of War. On June 26, 1919, Secretary of War Baker forwarded Witzke's trial record to the president together with a cover letter summarizing the evidence against Witzke and confirming that the reviewing authority had approved the death sentence but rcommended that it be commuted to twenty years of hard labor at Leavenworth's Disciplinary Barracks. The Secretary concurred in the Review Board's recommendation for clemency but thought twenty years was too light a penalty for spying. He recommended confinement at hard labor "for life." He also recommended that such life sentence be served at the Leavenworth Penitentiary, not the disciplinary barracks.[10] The penitentiary was a tougher environment than the barracks and the place where life sentences were typically served.

President Wilson took four weeks to respond. His response was a surprise, and showed that he studied the issue in depth. He did not agree with Secretary Baker. To the contrary, he agreed with the attorney general that the military did not have jurisdiction to try Witzke. "What action should I take," he asked Baker, "that would not let the guilty man go free—secure his trial in a civil court?"[11]

Not yet twenty-five years old, Lothar Witzke had, it was said, spied for the Germans in the American homeland, caused spectacular acts of sabotage against America including one that damaged the Statue of Liberty, been apprehended at the US/Mexico border with the help of a double agent, and become the sole spy convicted and sentenced to death in the US during World War I. Now he had the attention of President Wilson.

PRISON ESCAPE

It is unclear what, if anything, Witzke knew about the stalled review of his sentence and the debate going on as to whether the military had proper jurisdiction to try him. Probably he knew something, possibly a lot. Did he know that his case had gotten the attention of President Wilson himself? This is unknown. We do know that Witzke was unwilling to sit still and wait out his fate. On the night of August 1-2, 1919, he escaped from Fort Sam Houston. The escape was well-planned and almost worked, despite his isolation within the guardhouse.[12]

The guardhouse at Fort Sam Houston in which Witzke was incarcerated to await hanging was a three-story, yellow brick building flanked on each side by two-story infantry barracks. The first floor of the yellow brick building contained a prison officer's office, guardroom, kitchen, dining room, and a "sally-port" (small entryway). The prisoners' cells were on the second and third floors. Access to the second and third floors was by a single stairway at the bottom of which, on the first floor, was a locked steel wicket. There were three sets of keys, one set each for the sergeant of the guard, the corporal of the guard, and the prison officer. At the second-floor stairway landing there was an anteroom with six cells. On each side of the anteroom was a larger room that contained a large steel cage with additional cells inside the cage. There was also a bathroom, and a toilet separate from the bathroom, on the second floor.

The large cage in the room to the left of the second-floor anteroom was divided into two parts by a steel partition. The left side of the partition was a relatively big, single cell in which several prisoners were housed together. The right side of the partition was subdivided into smaller, single-occupancy cells, each smaller cell separated one from the other by additional steel partitions. Witzke, stripped to his underwear, was housed in one of these smaller cells, the one located at the northeast corner. The goal was to isolate him. No other prisoner was put in the cell next to his. There was a passageway around the entire cage, allowing a sentry to circumnavigate it. However, orders were that the sentry should not walk down the passageway that was parallel to the small cells. There was an insufficient number of guards at the prison, the prison officials did not fully trust them, and in any event the officials did not want the guards wasting time talking to the prisoners, especially to Witzke, who was deemed dangerous. Witzke was nonetheless not totally isolated in his corner cell. The top of the cage was a steel lattice. He would have been able to stand on his cot and talk through the lattice to prisoners in the big cell, on the other side of the partition.

Around midnight on August 1-2, 1919, a prisoner in the cage to the right of the second-floor anteroom told the sentry that he wanted to go to the toilet. According to prison protocol, the sentry was supposed to go to the top of the stairs and call down to the corporal of the guard; the corporal would then unlock the wicket, come up the stairs himself, unlock the prisoner's cell, and accompany the prisoner to the toilet. On this occasion, though, the corporal simply called the sentry, who was reported to be Mexican, to come down the stairs and the corporal handed the sentry the key through the wicket. The sentry then unlocked the prisoner's cell, took him to the toilet, and left him there.

At that moment, another prisoner in the same cage to the right of the anteroom asked to go to the toilet. The sentry, who now had the key, unlocked the second cell, took the second prisoner to the toilet, and left him there with the first prisoner.

Now it was Witzke's turn, in his cell to the left of the anteroom, to ask to go to the toilet. The sentry, using the same key, unlocked Witzke's cell and took him to the toilet as well. The three prisoners seized their opportunity. They jumped the sentry, "wrestled" the rifle away from him, tied him up with towels, gagged him, and ran up the stairs to the third floor where paroled prisoners slept. On the third floor, the bars on one of the windows in the anteroom had been sawed through earlier that day, and the three prisoners eased themselves through the broken bars and out onto the roof of the adjacent barracks. They then ran across the roof, jumped off the end (a two-story jump), and ran away. Meanwhile, the bound sentry managed to free himself and notified the corporal of the guard what happened. About the same time, a sergeant sleeping in the barracks was awakened by the commotion on the roof above him and "raised an alarm."[13]

Someone, presumably the corporal of the guard, telephoned Sergeant Haslam, who was in charge of the prison and was sleeping in his quarters about 200 yards from the prison building. Told of the escape, Haslam telephoned Colonel Gray, the then commanding officer, and requested permission to assemble a search party. Permission was given, and Haslam called out Company G of the Third Infantry, divided them into two patrols of three or four men each, and sent them to search the post and surrounding districts.

An hour later, one of the patrols caught Witzke coming out of a house in a Mexican American village "on the outskirts of the post," dressed in woman's clothing. They grabbed him and brought him back to Haslam. The two other escaped prisoners were never caught. Because of the standing order that he was not allowed to wear clothing in the guard house, Witzke had been wearing only underwear when he escaped. His escape was thwarted because he had to stop to find clothing.

Witzke's brief escape from Fort Sam Houston shows his capacity to conspire with two other prisoners confined in the large cage to the right of the anteroom, notwithstanding his isolation in a small corner cell in the cage left of the anteroom. Most likely the escapees had help from one or more guards, not only to facilitate their communications before the breakout, but also to ensure that the cell key would be handed over to the sentry guarding the second floor who then inexplicably and improperly allowed the three prisoners to go to the toilet at the same time. Also, someone had to procure the proper tools, and then use them without others being aware, to cut the bars on the window through which the prisoners escaped on the third floor. Perhaps the latter was the work of a third-floor parolee, but even then someone such as a guard with access to both the second and third floors would have had to facilitate communications. Sergeant Haslam later insisted in his affidavit that he had patrolled the third floor earlier in the day, and the window bars there were then secure).[14] After some years, Witzke would say that a guard whom he knew as Corporal Harris but whose real name he believed was Willi Dojan assisted him in his escape attempt.[15] Curiously, the escape attempt was never mentioned afterwards as a possible reason to deny clemency for Witzke.

WITZKE TALKS ABOUT BLACK TOM WITH A FORMER NYC POLICE CAPTAIN

Witzke was incarcerated at Fort Sam Houston in Texas from mid-February 1918. Although he was officially considered a dangerous prisoner and there were orders to keep him in isolation, and although he engineered a nearly successful prison break in August 1919, Witzke was even after the prison break not as isolated at Fort Sam Houston as he was supposed to be. He was a good talker, fluent in English, engaging and friendly and easy to like, and guards and officers at Fort Sam Houston talked to him, sometimes seeking information about his alleged sabotage activities before and during the war, and other times just to "shoot the breeze." Three guards (Shores, Haslam, and Voelker) later signed affidavits that were submitted to the Mixed Claims Commission about conversations that they said they had with Witzke or that they overheard in which he allegedly said that he was involved in Black Tom.[16]

Witzke also had notable outside visitors. In mid-September 1919, less than two months after his escape attempt, he was interviewed by Captain Thomas J. Tunney, Special Investigator from MID, in the presence of three officers from Company H, Third Infantry.[17] Tunney had been the highly reputed chief of the New York City Police Department's bomb squad at the time of the Black Tom explosion in late July 1916 and was involved in the initial investigations of that incident. During the war, he took on a second job as a captain and special investigator with the Military Intelligence Division. There, he continued to work on suspected sabotage cases, including Black Tom. He retired from the Police Department in August 1919 but stayed on with MID.

Tunney's jailhouse interview of Witzke lasted several days and touched upon Witzke's personal history, his US activities and acquaintances, his work as a German secret agent, and his final mission when he was captured at the border. Tunney was eager to learn about Witzke's alleged involvement in Black Tom and Kingsland, the two explosions that had captured his attention while he was still with the City's bomb squad. It is unknown whether determining responsibility for those incidents was Tunney's ultimate purpose, or whether Tunney's mandate was to assess Witzke's suitability for a commutation of his sentence.

Witzke presumably had the option to refuse to talk with Tunney in September 1919, but it is understandable that the wily story-teller would have welcomed another opportunity to present himself as an innocent dupe and to further his chance for clemency. The Tunney interview nonetheless presented a challenge for Witzke. The fictional life story he presented at trial had been seriously undermined by the testimony of the prosecution's witnesses and by the documentary evidence presented against him. If he now wanted to come across as believable, but without telling the whole truth, he would have to adjust and rearrange his story once again to accommodate what was now undeniable. What he would tell Tunney, in a series of questions and answers over four days, is puzzling in some ways, as Witzke implicated himself in significant anti-American espionage. Yet, he held firm as to his innocence about the most significant events, Black Tom and Kingsland.[18]

Witzke told the truth about his childhood. He was, he told Tunney, born in Posen, Prussia (now Poznań, Poland), and attended three years of grammar school, nine years of high school, and one year at the Posen Academy. Veracity for the most part ended there. He told Tunney that he left the academy at age seventeen to become a naval cadet, and was promoted to lieutenant in 1915. A naval lieutenant, of course, he never was. Witzke said he spent a year in Valparaiso, Chile, following which he signed on as a seaman to the American steamer *Colusa* bound for the west coast of the United States. He arrived in San Francisco in June or July 1916. This date of arrival was also incorrect and one wonders whether it was an error or a lie; he in truth arrived in San Francisco in late May 1916, giving him enough time to get to know Jahnke and to plan together the Black Tom sabotage, if indeed they did. The German consul employed him as an agent to deliver documents and papers to Chicago and New York, the contents of which he did not know, stating "At that time I was a Naval Officer in the German Navy and I could be trusted with anything."[19] He also carried documents from the New York Consulate back to Chicago and San Francisco, and for the next number of months continued to work in San Francisco for the consul. Innocuous stuff, safely recounted.

In February 1917, as relations between the United States and Germany deteriorated, he left San Francisco and went to Mexico City, intending to make his way back to Germany via Spain. However, the German legation in Mexico City told him that travel to Germany was impossible. The legation offered to find him a job with a German firm in Mexico, but Witzke declined. He went to the Russian consulate and asked for a passport. They issued a passport to him that said he "seemed" to be a Russian citizen, but this was less than he wanted. So he went to Veracruz and persuaded the Russian consulate there to give him a real Russian passport, which they did. This feat impressed the German legation back in Mexico City. They decided that they could make use of someone clever enough to persuade the Russians to give him a passport. They hired Witzke as a secret agent to investigate Allied shipping in Veracruz and Tampico. He also carried documents and papers for them back and forth among these locations. Witzke reported on what goods (especially oil) in what quantities were being shipped out of Mexico. He also investigated a rumor that American and British agents planned to blow up oil properties in Tampico and blame the Germans. All this is basically true.

In May 1917, Witke told Tunney that he was summoned to Monterrey, Mexico. There, he reunited with Kurt Jahnke (after first meeting in the States), who was now chief of the German Secret Service in Mexico. Jahnke sent him to San Francisco to "get in connection with Irishmen, Sinn Féin—and try to liberate the German officials Bopp and von Scheck and others" who were on trial in San Francisco for conspiring to foment revolution against British rule in India "and bring them to Mexico."[20] How Witzke was supposed to accomplish this unlikely mission went unexplained. In any case, back in San Francisco, Witzke said that he delegated the responsibility to two colleagues, named De Lacey and Hornify, and returned to Mexico. His two San Francisco colleagues were arrested shortly afterwards, and Jahnke "begged" Witzke to return to San Francisco to extricate them.

Jahnke also wanted Witzke to meet and deliver documents to a German agent named von Schulenburg who was, Jahnke said, then in charge of German undercover operations on the West Coast.[21] Jahnke also had a new mission for Witzke in San Francisco. Witzke returned to San Francisco carrying letters, invisible ink, a code, and cash, which, after he arrived, he delivered to von Schulenburg at dinner at the Restaurant Hofbrau at Fourth and Market. Following their dinner, von Schulenburg left for Seattle, possibly, according to Witzke, to induce IWW representatives there to make trouble and commit sabotage.[22] He met von Schulenburg one more time, on a train in early November 1917 between Laredo and Mexico City. They talked, but that was all. As presented, Witzke was mostly a courier.

Witzke's other Jahnke-assigned mission in San Francisco was, so he said, to recruit agents from the IWW or other radical organizations to go to Australia and Vladivostok to spread socialist and anarchist ideas and to disrupt the peace. Witzke engaged a "well-known labor agitator" named Jim Larkin to go to Australia for this purpose and two other labor agitators named Leveskovski and McIntyre to go to Vladivostok. He also recruited two women to go to Mexico to be trained as agents and sent to France to join an American "unit" there.[23] Finally, in his dealings with the IWW, Witzke "preached sabotage" and told them he would reward them if he got proof that they did something. "My instructions from my superior was to see if an opportunity offered itself, to blow up places that carried munitions or any other war supplies and to secure agents for this purpose. I received strict orders not to endanger myself in this undertaking as my job was considered far more important,—to start up agitation by inducing agitants for this purpose. We had headquarters in the New Columbia Hotel. . . ."[24] A week or two after offering money, someone tried to take credit and get paid for an oil tanker explosion in San Francisco harbor in September 1917 that Witzke had read about in the newspapers.[25] Witzke was not satisfied with the man's proof and refused to pay him.

Witzke was asked about previous admissions he allegedly made to Altendorf and others regarding his participation in acts of sabotage against the United States, in particular Black Tom and Mare Island. He denied making the admissions and denied any involvement in these events.

Tunney asked Witzke about his relationship with Altendorf. The prisoner seized the chance to deliver what would be his first of several disdainful condemnations of Altendorf over the next several years. Witzke said that he was first introduced to Altendorf by Jahnke at the Hotel Juarez in Mexico City in July 1917. Others in Jahnke's circle told him that Altendorf had worked in England, South America and Cuba "but . . . had never made good." He was never told that Altendorf was a German agent but Jahnke did say that he was "one of our men." Also, the German government sometimes helped out Altendorf with his expenses in exchange for information (Witzke labeled the information "bunk"). "One department tried to shove him to another because he was no good." [26] Altendorf was moved to the Secret Service, to Jahnke, to the captain of a tugboat that towed out the German U-boat *Deutschland*. He ended up as a doctor on a ranch in the north of Mexico that was supposed to be a colony for displaced Germans and Americans of German descent.

As to his relationship with Jahnke, Witzke gave two conflicting accounts of how they met. In his first telling, on the first day of the interview, he said that he was introduced to Jahnke sometime between September and December 1916 at the German consulate in New York City. A clerk at the consulate pointed to Jahnke and told Witzke that he was "an important German." Then the clerk introduced them. They did not, however, become close until Witzke met up with him again in or about May 1917 in Monterrey, Mexico.

On the afternoon of the second day of his interview, Witzke volunteered a "correction" that proved to be a very different account. This time he said that he and Jahnke had first met, briefly, in June or July 1916 in San Francisco, shortly after Witzke landed there. They traveled together across the country to New York City, where they roomed together for about six weeks at One Hundred West Fifty-Sixth Street. He went on to say under further questioning that Jahnke was close to only two men, his assistant Kattenbach and Witzke.

We do not know what prompted Witzke to make his unsolicited correction. Perhaps Tunney knew something that he disclosed to Witzke that compelled Witzke to change his story. In the transcript, it is Tunney who states that Witzke wishes to make a correction. Tunney then dictates the correction, following which Witzke says "that is correct." Clearly the two had talked off the record beforehand.

The "corrected" version of Witzke's relationship with Jahnke is of particular interest in two respects: it fixes the date on which the two met much earlier than the first version does; and it characterizes their relationship as being much closer than initially admitted. This is relevant to assessing the likelihood that the two conspired to blow up Black Tom. If they did not become acquainted until some time in September 1916, then they could not have conspired to commit the Black Tom sabotage at the end of July 1916. However, if they first met as early as June 1916 and were well-enough acquainted to travel cross-country together and room together for six weeks in New York, then it is more credible that they could have been involved in Black Tom.

As we will explain in chapter 6, Witzke and Jahnke in fact first met in San Francisco in late May or early June 1916, and became well-enough acquainted that they started rooming together in San Francisco in early July. They did indeed travel together to New York in September and roomed together there for several weeks. Whether they also travelled to New York in July to reconnoiter Black Tom or commit sabotage there will be analyzed in chapter 12. What matters for purposes of this chapter is Witzke's motive to change the story he was telling Tunney. His first version, if it were true, would eliminate Witzke from suspicion of any connection to Black Tom. His corrected version kept alive the possibility that he was involved. How did that serve Witzke's self-interest? Our guess is that Witzke, still under sentence of death, calculated overnight that his chances of persuading the authorities to keep him alive were better if they believed there might be a link between him, Jahnke, and Black Tom. Also, by September 1920 when the Tunney interview took place, MID, and therefore possibly Tunney, knew about some of Jahnke's activities during the war, including that he was in Mexico in 1917, that he claimed "credit" with Berlin for himself and his people for various acts of sabotage during the war, and that at some point after moving to Mexico he became head of German naval intelligence in North America. Possibly Tunney shared enough of this information with Witzke to make Witzke believe that he (Tunney) knew even more, and therefore Witzke had to tread more carefully than he previously had about his relationship with Jahnke.

WITZKE TALKS ABOUT KINGSLAND
WITH A LAWYER FOR KINGSLAND

During the several months following his failed escape, Witzke had another visitor besides Tunney: Judge Guy Fake, who interviewed Witzke on January 16, 1920. At the time, Fake was both a New Jersey state court judge and an attorney for Agency of Canadian Car & Foundry Company, owner of the Kingsland Ammunition Plant in Kingsland, New Jersey, that was destroyed in an explosion on January 11, 1917. German sabotage was suspected, and the purpose of Fake's interview was to ascertain whether Witzke, who had been implicated by double agent Paul Altendorf in Kingsland as well as in Black Tom, was involved and, if so, to develop evidence that Kingsland could use to defend itself against negligence claims. Fake was unable to obtain a confession from Witzke but said that his "manner and general behavior convinced me that he was guilty of complicity with the Kingsland explosion and that the statements of Doctor Paul B. Altendorf [implicating Witzke] were correct."[27] The interview was not transcribed.[28]

PRESIDENT WILSON CHANGES HIS MIND

The Tunney and Judge Fake interviews took place at the same time that Witzke's military court conviction and death sentence were undergoing further review by the Justice and War Departments, following President Wilson's July 1919 letter to Secretary of War Baker saying that he (Wilson) agreed with Attorney General Gregory's opinion that the military did not have jurisdiction to try Witzke, and asking whether the case should be referred to the civil courts for retrial. At first, a surprised Secretary Baker thought that he could reargue the case to the president. With the help of Acting Judge Advocate General Kreger, he drafted a letter to the President explaining that the Attorney General's opinion had been given without seeing the Review Board's contrary opinion and was based on factual assumptions that were contradicted by the actual evidence produced at trial, such as that Witzke was a German national, not a Russian as the attorney general had assumed, and that he was arrested within a mile of a military encampment whereas the attorney general had wrongly assumed he was not captured in or about a military facility.[29]

Then Baker changed his mind. He decided a better approach would be to ask the attorney general for a new opinion saying that the military had proper jurisdiction after all, based on the changed facts proved at trial. By this time, A. Mitchell Palmer had replaced Gregory as attorney general on March 5, 1919, and it now fell to the new one to render an opinion on the views of his predecessor. Palmer did so on December 24, 1919. The opinion was addressed to the secretary of war. It relied on the new facts proved at trial that Witzke was a German, not a Russian, national, that he had crossed the border at least three times before his arrest and not just once as previously assumed, and that he was arrested only a mile from an encampment "where were stationed officers and men engaged in protecting the border against threatened invasion from the Mexican side." Palmer opined, based on these facts, that the military commission that tried Witzke *did* have jurisdiction to do so. Palmer stressed that he was not overruling his predecessor, "but merely . . . holding that under the entirely different statement of facts" now submitted, "the principles announced in [the Gregory] opinion have no application." Palmer added that the "circumstances attending this submission of my views leads me to request that they be treated as strictly confidential, and not made public." The opinion was not released to the public until 1942 and not officially published until 1949.[30]

The story of Witzke's trial, conviction, and sentence had been a closely guarded secret, unknown to the public. His capture, similarly, was also a closely guarded secret until August 1919 when Altendorf released a long statement, and then published a series of syndicated articles in the *Chicago Tribune* in November 1919, disclosing details of Witzke's Mexican activities and capture at Nogales.[31] On December 27, 1919, three days after the Attorney General issued his opinion, someone leaked the trial story to the *Washington Times*, which reported it on page one of its Saturday evening edition under the banner headline "PRESIDENT STAYS EXECUTION OF GERMAN SPY." The unnamed reporter got the broad outline of the story correct, although not the details and not the spelling of Witzke's name (misspelled "Witke" in the article).

According to the article, "Witke," a German naval officer, was captured entering the United States from Mexico, having been betrayed by a Polish operative of the US military intelligence division. He was court-martialed for plotting against the US and coming to the States "to carry on his work," sentenced to be shot (not hanged), and held "for some months" in a jail at Fort Sam Houston. President Wilson ordered a stay of execution pending resolution of certain questions about whether he should have been tried by civil rather than military authorities. Information at the Justice Department indicated that Witke told the operative who betrayed him (Witzke believed the operative was a German agent) that he was "responsible for the 'Black Tom' explosion."[32] The story was picked up the following day by several national newspapers.[33] The *Atlanta Constitution* obtained a couple of quotations from Secretary Baker elaborating on the point of issue between the War Department and the Department of Justice. No one got wind that that issue had just been resolved.

Although the *Washington Times* story was correct in that Witzke's execution had been stayed pending review, his death sentence had not yet been commuted. That was to come soon enough. On New Year's Day 1920, Secretary Baker, having Attorney General Palmer's new, favorable opinion in hand, sent President Wilson a letter, again recommending that Witzke's sentence be commuted to life in prison.[34] This time, though, Baker was able to tell the President that Attorney General Palmer had issued a new legal opinion that the military court that tried Witzke *did* have proper jurisdiction to do so under Article Eighty-Two of the Articles of War, based on corrected facts not known by Attorney General Gregory when he issued the earlier, contrary opinion.

Baker's strategy worked. Palmer's opinion changed Wilson's mind. It would take five more months, but on May 27, 1920, twelve days after Witzke's twenty-fifth birthday, President Wilson commuted Witzke's sentence. He ordered that "in . . . the case of Lather Witcke, alias Pablo Waberski, the sentence is confirmed and commuted to confinement at hard labor for the term of his natural life." [35] On June 4, 1920, the secretary of war issued General Order Thirty-Two reiterating the charge, finding of guilt, and sentence to be hanged, together with the President's commutation of the sentence to life. The order ended by designating the Leavenworth Penitentary in Kansas as the place of confinement.[36] Witzke's death sentence was now officially revoked, and the prisoner would soon be leaving Texas for Kansas, where he was supposed to spend the rest of his life.

IMPRISONED
AND PARDONED

It would therefore do much to pacify
public opinion in my country and would be
considered a special act of grace by my
Government if the United States of America,
as France did a few months ago, were
now also to set free their last
prisoner of war.
—GERMAN AMBASSADOR TO US ARMY'S
JUDGE ADVOCATE GENERAL, APRIL 1923

On the same day (June 4, 1920) that Order Thirty-Two was issued confirming the commutation of Witzke's death sentence to life at hard labor at
Leavenworth Penitentiary, the army's Adjutant General Guy Henry sent on
behalf of the secretary of war an official copy of the order to the commanding general, Southern Department, Fort Sam Houston, and directed him to
"place Lather Witcke, alias Pablo Waberski, in confinement . . . if not already
confined, and send him, under proper guard, to Leavenworth and deliver him
to the Penitentiary."[1] We know nothing of how Witzke was told about this
change in his fortunes or the details of his transfer. No doubt he was greatly
relieved that his death sentence had been lifted. He arrived at Leavenworth
at the end of the second week of June, spent two or three nights at the disciplinary barracks, and was checked into the penitentiary on June 16, 1920.[2]

LEAVENWORTH PENITENTIARY

Leavenworth Penitentiary in 1920 was an altogether different sort of place
than the guardhouse at Fort Sam Houston. Located in the eastern part of
Kansas, about thirty miles north of Kansas City, at the southwest edge of

Fort Leavenworth, it was the first federal penitentiary of the modern era for civilian convicts.[3]

Congress had authorized the establishment of three such prisons in 1891. Leavenworth was the first of these to be put in operation because there was already a disciplinary barracks there, at Fort Leavenworth, which could be transferred to the Department of Justice instead of building a new facility. The transfer took place in 1895. However, the former disciplinary barracks quickly proved inadequate for the government's needs. In 1896, Congress authorized construction of a new facility to house at least 1,200 prisoners. Construction began the following year using convict labor; it would not be completed until the late 1920s, although civilian convicts held at the former disciplinary barracks were being transferred from 1903 to temporary quarters at the new facility. By 1910 there were 1,000 prisoners housed at the new penitentiary. The cellblocks were completed in 1919. When Witzke arrived in June 1920, there were more than 1,800 inmates housed there, half again as many as were intended by the original design, which had contemplated a separate cell for each inmate.[4]

Leavenworth Penitentiary was a walled city unto itself. The main building was an imposing 336,000 square-foot castle-like structure comprising a central administration building flanked by two large cellblocks that measured 800 feet from end to end, and two smaller cellblocks that angled out from behind the center. The four cellblocks contained 1,200 back-to-back cells facing the outer walls. A grand, domed rotunda that could be seen for miles around topped the administration building.[5] "For staff, it was a glimpse of where they worked; for inmates, it was a dim reminder of their home."[6] The administration building housed offices, kitchen, bakery, cold storage, dining hall, commissary, gymnasium, mailroom, and a chapel. There were other buildings too, including a hospital, power plant, engine room, machine shop, carpenter shop, brick factory, ice plant, furniture factory, and a warehouse. There was also an exercise yard.[7]

Leavenworth was "home" to some of America's most notorious and dangerous criminals, including Robert Panzram, a confessed murderer of twenty-three individuals, and Robert Stroud, the so-called birdman of Alcatraz, all while Witzke was imprisoned there. Stroud, despite the moniker, spent most of his life not at Alcatraz but at Leavenworth, and it was at Leavenworth that he raised and studied birds. He also killed a guard there.[8] Franz von Bopp and Eckhard Schack, the German consul and vice consul, respectively, at San Francisco when Witzke first arrived in America, and by whom Witzke was first employed in the spy business, were also incarcerated at Leavenworth following their convictions in 1918 for violations of US neutrality and for their role in a Hindu-German conspiracy to foment revolution against British rule in India. They were still at Leavenworth when Witzke arrived there.

Witzke's Life at Leavenworth

Witzke was processed into Leavenworth Penitentiary on June 16, 1920, as "Lather Witcke alias Pablo Waberski, Lothar Witzke, German Prisoner of War" and assigned prisoner number 15309.[9] His intake forms record that he was twenty-five years old, 5'7", 155 pounds, had black hair and a fair complexion, smoked but did not use alcohol or drugs, and had once fractured his left patella resulting in "slight crippling." His religion is listed as Lutheran, his education as thirteen years, and his trade, amusingly, as musician, one of 20 self-identified musicians admitted to Leavenworth in 1920. Witzke was the only convicted spy admitted that year.

PERSONAL PROPERTY

Witzke arrived at Leavenworth with the clothes on his back plus a small knife, a notebook, two rings, and a towel.[10] He also had some cash and gold.[11] Prison records show that during his three- to four-year incarceration there he purchased (or on occasion was gifted) numerous additional items. These included substantial quantities of tobacco products (bags of tobacco, cigarette papers, matches, pipe and pipe cleaner, cigars); lots of candy, fruit, and nuts, especially (in the case of fruit) oranges, lemons and dates, and also the occasional cake. Toilet articles included a tooth brush, toothpaste, soap, towels, shaving supplies, toothpicks, talcum and witch hazel. Items of clothing included underwear and socks, pajamas and cloth slippers, garters, shoes, shoe polish, a two-piece suit, sweater, belt, watch and watch chain, and a needle and thread. There was also a variety of more durable goods, including books and magazines (his first book purchase was a concise English dictionary), pen and ink, a mirror, a string instrument plus guitar strings and a violin bow, a set of checkers, a hand ball, and lots of ribbons, silk, poplin, and beads.[12] His very first purchase (during his first week at Leavenworth), even before tobacco and toiletries, was a six-dollar subscription to the *San Francisco Examiner*.[13]

What, if anything, do the items of personal property that Witzke acquired during his time at Leavenworth tell us about the man, apart from the fact that he was a smoker? He seems to have had a sweet tooth (fruit, candy, cake), cared about personal appearance (shoe polish, suit, needle and thread, mirror), and was attentive to his personal hygiene (abundant toiletries). He was a reader (books and magazines), wanted to improve his English language fluency (dictionary), and was interested in world events and West Coast news (newspaper subscription). He wrote letters and perhaps kept a diary (pen and ink). He played games (checkers, handball) and stringed instruments (guitar, maybe a fiddle). Most intriguing are his purchases of ribbons, silk, poplin, and beads, in quantity. Did he do beading and sew or mend clothes for himself, a skill perhaps picked up at sea? Were these meant as presents for women on the outside? We consider below whether even while in prison this ladies' man managed to charm women on the outside for personal gain.

The apparent seamster was also a man of arms. Witzke's personal effects at the time of his capture included a pistol, pistol belt, and cartridges. They were seized by the government as captured munitions of war and never returned.[14]

MONEY

At the time of his arrest on February 1, 1918, Witzke had on his person $693 cash and thirteen Mexican gold coins worth approximately seventy-six dollars.[15] Witzke brought most of this money with him to Leavenworth and turned it over to the Warden for safekeeping. As with other prisoners, the warden allowed him to spend the money. As of mid-March 1921, Witzke had a balance in his account of $395.85.[16]

While in custody, Witzke repeatedly attracted the attention of upper-authorities. We have seen that his conviction was reviewed by President Wilson himself. We will see that his clemency and pardon petitions went up to Presidents Harding and Coolidge. Even the issue of what to do with his small stash of money consumed official attention up to the level of the secretary of war and the Swiss ambassador to the US.

In Washington, the question arose as to whether the money that Witzke was spending was his personal property that he should be allowed to keep or, instead, was German government property, i.e., enemy property that should be confiscated and turned over to the US Treasury. The Acting Judge Advocate General, E. A. Kreger, opined that there was no authority for confiscation if it was Witzke's personal property; it had to be German government property for confiscation to be lawful. According to Kreger, the evidence of ownership disclosed to him was insufficient to decide one way or the other. He noted, however, that the sum at issue was "not so unreasonably large" as to presume it was German property. Therefore, he recommended that the money be left with the warden for the time being, until title could be ascertained "either by proof upon the part of the prisoner . . . or as the result of inquiry and investigation by the proper authorities."[17] The warden agreed to hold the balance until further instructed and Witzke's access to the funds was suspended as of late March 1921.[18]

Other officials then weighed in on the subject of Witzke's money. The army's inspector general opined that the money was enemy property that should be confiscated and turned over to the Treasury. Based on the inspector general's opinion, the secretary of war asked the attorney general to cause the funds to be remitted to the Treasury as a "'Miscellaneous Receipt' (Confiscated Enemy Property)."[19] The managing director of the alien property custodian advised the attorney general that the custodian was no longer demanding the property of enemy aliens "except in very exceptional circumstances" of national interest not presented by the Witzke funds case.[20] The attorney general, without giving reasons, said he did not believe that confiscation was justified. Witzke, for his part, insisted both personally and through representations of the minister of Switzerland, in charge of German interests in the United States, that the funds were his personal property.[21]

Judge Advocate General Kreger was then asked again for a Witzke-related recommendation. There being "no satisfactory proof to the contrary" that the funds were, as Witzke claimed, his personal property, General Kreger recommended that they be "now released for his [Witzke's] use in the same manner as in the case of other prisoners at the Penitentiary."[22] The secretary of war accepted Kreger's recommendation and withdrew his request that the funds be turned over to the Treasury as confiscated enemy property. On September 22, 1921, the Department of Justice notified the warden of this and confirmed that the money could be released for Witzke's use "in the same manner . . . as other prisoners."[23] It had taken six months, but Witzke had his money back.

HEALTH

Witzke was generally healthy during his time at Leavenworth.[24] However, he did see the prison doctor from time to time, and, less often, the prison dentist and prison eye doctor, for various ailments, and he was twice admitted to the prison hospital. He suffered throughout his term from acne and other skin conditions for which he was prescribed a sulphur ointment and other lotions; at one point, he was given permission to shave his head because of scalp disease. He was treated several times for respiratory ailments such as cough and (more seriously) influenza, and in July 1921 for an injured finger. He also suffered regularly from digestive problems. His hospitalizations were for influenza (two nights in March 1922) and, more seriously, twelve nights in May 1923 for what was described in one health record entry (probably mistakenly) as syphilis and in another as erysipelas, a serious skin disorder related to cellulitis.[25] His temperature during this latter illness was as high as 104 degrees for several consecutive days.

CONDITIONS OF CONFINEMENT

Witzke was housed in one of the large dormitory cells of cellblock A. These cells accommodated four to six prisoners and were, according to the warden, "much pleasanter than the smaller, regular, cells" in the prison's other three cellhouses. He was never placed in isolation or confined to any of the prison's punishment cells, a testament to his good behavior throughout his tenure.[26]

WORK; BOILER ROOM ACCIDENT

Witzke was assigned to work in the prison's electric light plant and boiler house, one of the best assignments from a prisoner's standpoint.[27] He was a hard worker and rose to the position of head prisoner's clerk. The prison's daily labor records show that, during most months, he worked weekends as well as weekdays without a day off.[28] Did he work so hard because he was instinctively diligent, because he was bored and it gave him something to do, or because he saw a potential benefit to his standing in the prison or beyond? We cannot know, but his boiler room work would play a role in his ultimate pardon, because of an incident on July 18, 1921.

On Monday, July 18, 1921, just past noon, a blow-off pipe in one of the prison's main boilers exploded, scalding six prisoners who were working in the boiler house at the time, four of them so seriously that they each died from their burns over the next few days.[29] Several prisoners, Witzke among them, were outside at the time of the explosion having lunch; they rushed into the steam-filled boiler house "at serious risk to themselves" to rescue the injured and prevent worse from happening. Worse could have happened. The clouds of steam put the rescuers at risk of being scalded when they entered the boiler room; other boilers (there were six in all) could have exploded.[30] The rescuers were specially commended for their courage by the chief engineer in his report to the warden about the incident.[31] In a subsequent "To Whom It May Concern" memorandum for Witzke's file, the warden wrote that Witzke "exhibited a remarkable degree of courage in immediately entering the boiler room, following the blow-out" and that his efforts and those of his comrades "probably prevented a more disastrous accident."[32] Witzke's bravery would be invoked later by those lobbying on his behalf for a pardon.[33]

Correspondence

Lothar Witzke maintained an extensive and eclectic correspondence during his three years at Leavenworth. Little has survived, but thanks to the prison's correspondence log, we are able to identify many of his correspondents, how much correspondence was carried on with each, and when items were sent and received.[34] Based on this information, we can infer something about the subject matter of these writings.

FAMILY

Witzke wrote many letters to, and received many from, his family in Germany (on average, one or more a week), especially his father, but also his mother and brother Günther. These family letters no doubt reported on his daily life in prison and efforts to obtain his release. It is evident as well from a clemency petition that his mother and father submitted in 1923 on his behalf that he must have shared information about his wartime activities and, in particular, his burning animosity toward the man who betrayed him, the double agent Paul Altendorf.

US MILITARY PERSONNEL

Several of Witzke's correspondents, especially in his first year at Leavenworth, were US Army personnel at Fort Sam Houston, including Corporal Crow, Sergeant Dodd, Captain Rike, and S. C. Kile (who sat in on Witzke's interview at Fort Sam Houston with Judge Fake). One of the first letters he received (in June 1920) was from an S. C. Sobriesik, address Fort Ringgold, Texas. We do not know if this was someone in the army and there is no record in the log of Witzke having written back. The content of his correspondence with army personnel is unknown. The correspondence attests either to his sociability or, more likely, to his enterprising efforts to gather evidence to help his case or his clemency petition.

COMMERCIAL/RETAIL

Witzke regularly corresponded with commercial establishments, many of them for the purpose of making purchases that we know from prison records that he acquired or for other purposes such as banking. These entities included Leet Brothers in Washington, DC, (the printing company recommended to him for obtaining copies of his trial transcript), Montgomery Ward in Kansas City, Pabst Cigarette Company in Pittsburgh, various bead companies in New York including Nelson Bead Co., Imperial Bead Co., and Walco Bead Co., and the First National Bank of Chicago. There were also commercial addressees to whom Witzke wrote and about which nothing is now known, for example Ba“k & Co. of Chicago and G.P. Sharkey of Portland, Oregon.

GOVERNMENTS

Witzke corresponded with various foreign and US government agencies, presumably as part of his campaign for clemency. These included the Swiss Legation, which represented Germany's interests after the war until the re-establishment of diplomatic relations in 1922, the German consulate in St. Louis, and the German embassy in Washington; and, in the case of the US Government, the Department of Justice, the Senate Sub-Committee on Foreign Relations, Senator Borah, President Harding, the army adjutant general, The War Department, and the secretary of war.

FRIENDS

Witzke corresponded with many individuals from across the United States who are identified in the log as "friends." The addresses are wide ranging: Illinois, Michigan, New York, Missouri, Tennessee, Texas, Indiana, Pennsylvania, South Dakota, Louisiana, and Maine; and abroad (apart from Germany), Mexico and Cuba. Most of the addressees have been impossible to trace, for example, James McMurray of Connersville, Indiana, Witzke's first correspondent at Leavenworth, from whom he received mail on June 19, 1920 and to whom he sent a reply on July 16. Of those we have identified, one of the more prominent was William Bayard Hale, a former clergyman and well-known pro-German propagandist who lived on Riverside Drive in New York City. How Witzke came to be acquainted with these individuals is a mystery. Perhaps some of them were part of a network of sympathizers to whom Witzke was somehow introduced and who played a role or were approached by him because they might be able to play a role in his quest for clemency. Among these was Witzke's most frequent correspondent, Mrs. M. E. Johnson, who will be discussed separately below. Mrs. Johnson was not his sole female correspondent. Witzke also wrote from time to time

to women in Germany including, most frequently, a Mrs. S. Rachner, plus a
Miss Solger in Breslau and a Margaret Finger in Hettin (Stettin?). We know
nothing about these women.

A PATH TO A PARDON

Whatever motives, Witzke may have had to pursue the wide-ranging correspondence in which he engaged during his time at Leavenworth—friendship,
love of family, acquisition of poplin, beads, and other items not available at
the prison commissary—there was one overarching objective that informed
his choice of correspondents and the frequency of his writing: obtaining
mitigation of his life sentence, even a pardon. Only a week after arriving at
Leavenworth, he wrote to the War Department saying that he had not been
given a copy of his trial record and asked for one, adding that he was willing to pay for it.[35] The army's adjutant general replied in late July that, according to army records, a copy had already been given to him. However, in
view of Witzke's willingness to pay, he could obtain a photostatic copy from
Leet Brothers in Washington, DC, for twenty-five cents per page (there were
171 pages) who, the Army assured him, did "very satisfactory work" copying records of trial.[36] Witzke contacted Leet Brothers straight away. It must
have taken several tries before he got what he wanted, as the log shows that
Witzke and the Leet Brothers exchanged several letters between August and
December 1920.[37]

Failed Clemency Petitions
(Witzke as His Own Advocate)

Witzke wasted no time in seeking mitigation of his life sentence. He filed
three clemency petitions during his first eighteen months of incarceration at
Leavenworth, the first two with the War Department and the third directly
with President Harding. All were denied.[38]

The prisoner demonstrated some cleverness in advancing the petitions.
For the first petition, he got a letter of commendation from the prison's
warden, saying that his conduct in confinement had been "excellent" since
he arrived.[39] He also enlisted the senior chaplain of the US Army, Major
Cephus C. Bateman, to forward his petition to the War Department. Witzke
probably knew of Bateman from his time on death row at Fort Sam Houston; possibly they had met. Bateman was in San Antonio at the same time,
lecturing there at the school for chaplains. On the morning of September 17,

1918, Bateman prayed at the gallows scaffold at Fort Sam Houston as five of the Black soldiers court-martialed for their role in the prior year's Houston mutiny were hanged.[40] Perhaps in choosing Bateman, Witzke calculated that his application would have a better chance of success than if he wrote the War Department directly.

Somehow, Witzke was also able to attract the attention of other high-level individuals, including a congressman from Chicago's west side, A. J. Sabath. In February 1921, shortly after Witzke's second petition was denied, the warden received a letter from Sabath, on Immigration and Naturalization Committee letterhead, asking whether a petition for pardon or commutation of sentence had been made in the Witzke case. Curiously, the warden replied that he had "no records" of such an application, a strange comment considering the good conduct letter he had written several months before in support of Witzke's first petition.[41] Sabath did not pursue the matter further.

FOURTH PETITION: THE GERMAN GOVERNMENT GETS INVOLVED

Witzke waited a year before filing a fourth clemency petition. This time the recently reopened German embassy got involved. In November 1922, the embassy's Baron von Plessen met twice with the Acting Judge Advocate General, Col. J. A. Hull, to discuss whether executive clemency for Witzke was possible. Hull told von Plessen that it was not yet time to try again. The baron came away with the impression that Hull opposed clemency because Witzke had been accused of sabotage as well as spying. He wrote Witzke about his meetings with Hull and asked Witzke how far the accusations were true, so that he could respond intelligently to the charges.[42]

When Witzke received von Plessen's letter, he decided it was time for a lawyer. The embassy had earlier retained Julius Goebel, a highly regarded professor of legal history at Columbia University, to act as Witzke's counsel. Witzke had not previously contacted Goebel but he did so now, writing to the professor on December 8, 1922.[43] The letter (one of only two letters known still to exist that Witzke wrote while at Leavenworth) was in English, and is strikingly grammatically correct, clear, and well-constructed in argument and rhetoric. Possibly it is a translation of something Witzke wrote in German. Perhaps it was drafted by a third party. Or maybe Witzke's English was just that good. Witzke was adamant in the letter about not being a saboteur:

> My knowledge of these accusations amounts to nothing but the inferences I make, evolved from cross-questioning by Government Agents. In many instances I cannot remember even the names of the towns such sabotage

actions are supposed to have taken place in, nor do I recall the time or conditions. Some of the places mentioned I have never visited, since the duration of my stay in this country, previous to my arrest, amounts only to collectively about seven months.

Witzke then sounds a theme to which he would return in subsequent interviews and affidavits: that the sole source of accusations against him is the "vivid imagination" of Paul Altendorf, someone he says he met accidentally while traveling in Mexico and with whom he was acquainted for a mere fourteen days. Altendorf claimed, Witzke explains, to have elicited from him the information upon which these "chimerical charges" were based, and the War Department accepted such "hearsay evidence," but Witzke insists that he is "not guilty" of the charges. He concludes by listing the acts of sabotage he is said to have committed, including the Black Tom and Mare Island Naval Station explosions, and pointedly notes that he was never prosecuted for sabotage, only spying—the implication being that even the US Government realized that the sabotage allegations against him were a sham.[44]

In early 1923, Germany started a public campaign for Witzke's release, labeling him the last German prisoner of war still incarcerated by the United States. Major US newspapers, including the *New York Times*, picked up the story and began reporting on Witzke's plight. In January 1923, nationalist deputies in the Reichstag took up his cause, announcing that they would interrogate their government about his case. Rumors circulated. Witzke was said to have been held "in solitary confinement in a darkened cell" for half of the last five years. Witzke's father was said to have made numerous, unsuccessful efforts to gain his son's release and return to Germany.[45]

The War Department responded candidly to all of this. Witzke, they confirmed, was the only German prisoner of war still in America. He was also lucky to have escaped the hangman's noose. No, he was not being held in solitary confinement but, yes, he was serving a life sentence, with President Wilson having commuted his death sentence to life in prison at Leavenworth. He would be eligible for parole in 1935. If the German embassy insisted on pursuing release now, they would be told that the department was opposed to any further clemency and that President Harding had already denied the prisoner's own petition for clemency.[46]

One Ohio newspaper, irked that a convicted German spy might be treated more leniently than anti-war American dissidents still incarcerated because of their actions and statements, editorialized sarcastically, "The spy is not considered so dangerous as the political offender who expresses dissenting opinions regarding war, politics or economics. . . . Verily, the alien spy who tries to blow up ships and destroy human lives, is a model human being, according to the imperial view, when compared with the man who ventured to express his dissent from the views of Wilson, Harding and their kind."[47] Witzke is notably described here not just as a spy but as someone responsible for trying to blow up ships.

Meanwhile, out of public sight, Witzke's fourth clemency petition was being reviewed at the War Department. The warden was asked for an update on Witzke's behavior in prison. He responded by forwarding a copy of the prisoner's conduct record, including a copy of the warden's 1922 "To Whom It May Concern" memorandum referencing Witzke's "valuable services" since incarceration as head prisoner's clerk at the prison's power house and describing Witzke's bravery following the July 21, 1921 boiler explosion. The warden added that Witzke's conduct in confinement was "at all times . . . above reproach."[48]

It was not enough. Although Witzke had now served two years and nine months of his sentence and his conduct at Leavenworth to date had been exemplary, clemency was once again denied.[49]

WITZKE'S LETTER TO JUDGE GUY FAKE

In March 1923, shortly before he learned that his latest request for clemency had been denied, Witzke had a visitor at Leavenworth, Guy Fake, the same lawyer representing the owners of the Kingsland Ammunition Plant who had already interviewed him at Fort Sam Houston in early 1920. Like the Fake interview in 1920, no stenographic report was made of the March 1923 interview.[50]

Shortly after the interview, Witzke sent Judge Fake a long letter.[51] By this time, he knew that his latest clemency request had been denied. The letter is unremarkable for its substance in which he denies any role in "Black Tom etc." and accuses Altendorf of fabrications, but is notable for its relative sophistication in argumentation and expression. This was a twenty-eight-year-old German native, by his account a former sailor and secret agent, writing at a level roughly equivalent to that of a native English-speaking journalist. If Witzke in fact penned the letter and did not engage a literate fellow convict to do it for him, the letter shows that Witzke was indeed "exceptionally clever," as Fake asserted, and that his cleverness was manifest even in the medium of written English.

But the letter reveals young Witzke's cockiness as well. He assumed that he could ingratiate himself with Fake by making common cause with the Kingsland lawyer. "After your departure on your last visit" to Leavenworth, he writes:

> I came to the conclusion that you were an entirely different type of man than others who cross-questioned me previously. . . . [Y]ou did not make attempts to trick me, but, conducted your inquiries in a gentlemanly way. At least I am convinced that you were sincerely anxious to clear up this affair of Black Tom etc. . . . without resorting to the framing of evidence. . . . I must admit I liked you, Mr. Fake, and, because of that I felt sorry for you. I seemed to detect a spirit of depression in your manner due perhaps to the valuelessness of my statements, contrary to your expectations.[52]

Witzke then launches an attack on his accuser Altendorf, while maintaining a self-effacing manner. He says that, when first confronted with Altendorf's accusations, he did not think it was possible that such "wild, unconfirmed stories of a monomaniac" could be accepted as evidence. Is it not ridiculous, he asks, to think that a twenty-year-old in 1916, "a stranger in a strange country, hardly able to speak and understand the language properly," which is what he says he was when most of the alleged events took place, could have committed "the most clever exploits imaginable and in quantities unsurpassed by anyone throughout the history of the world"? Witzke's answer to his question is a vigorous "yes."

> I firmly believe, the man [i.e., Altendorf] to be a monomaniac and that he should be confined to an asylum. Read the bunk he passed off on the U.S. military authorities in regard to the spies he caught, the wonderful services he rendered this country during the late war and how cleverly he managed to fool everyone. Conan Doyle is a pauper in imagination compared with Altendorf. . . . No, the whole is nonsense, a fabrication of his too vivid imagination, but due to the war his stories were credited.[53]

Witzke concludes his letter in a self-pitying way, a self-pity that suggests a deeper capacity for duplicity if one believes that Witzke was in truth responsible for what Altendorf accused him of: "As I told you, I realize the futility of convincing anyone. My only hope lays in the chance that some day someone will investigate."

Perhaps he genuinely thought he could win over Fake and was so accustomed to manipulation that he could not see how futile that effort was here. Or perhaps he was merely trying to make the best of a long shot that presented itself, an interview with Kingsland's lawyer. In either case, he seems to have stayed true to the "old Prussian" military discipline that Fake sensed he was wholeheartedly committed to: a duty not to give information against his government. He was willing to lie to get clemency, but not to confess to sabotage or to offer to trade such a confession for his freedom.

Witzke's charm did not work on Guy Fake. But he left Fake impressed all the same. Six years later, in an affidavit provided to the Mixed Claims Commission hearing the United States's sabotage claims against Germany, Fake summarized his two interviews and his impressions of Witzke:

> [The two interviews] satisfied me that Witzke was a man of exceptionally clever intellectual ability and that he is wholeheartedly a disciple of the old Prussian military training. His devotion to what he considered to be his duty which included his duty not to give information against his Government, was little less than a religion with him, and it was impossible to obtain any confession from him respecting his participa tion in the destruction of [Kingsland]. My impression was that about the only crime which he recognized in his code of ethics in connection with his work for his Government, was the "crime" of being "found out."[54]

It was "obvious," Fake concluded, that Witzke was trying to conceal his actual movements; he "admitted . . . that the stories which he had told in his defense at the court martial trial were absolutely false." He seemed to take it as his "duty to make false statements when matters affecting the interests of his country were at stake."[55]

THE GERMAN GOVERNMENT AND WITZKE'S PARENTS ASK FOR CLEMENCY

On April 30, 1923, five weeks after the War Department denied Witzke clemency for a fourth time, the German government formally took on Witzke's cause. Otto Wiefeldt, the German ambassador to the United States, met with Major General Walter Bethel, the army's Judge Advocate General, and asked him to recommend executive clemency in the case. He followed up with a formal request the next day.[56]

The German ambassador made the following points in support of his request. First, although the charges of sabotage were weighing more against clemency than the spying of which he was convicted, there was no evidence that Witzke committed sabotage; indeed, both Witzke and government officials in Berlin confirmed that Witzke "had either never been to the places where the acts of sabotage were committed or . . . was not there at the time of their commission." Second, the accusations against Witzke were based solely on "the wild and erroneous statements" of Paul Altendorf. Third, the government, after extensive investigation, was unable to find evidence that the cipher note signed by the German minister to Mexico emanated from the Imperial government. Moreover, the note could not have been addressed to German consular officials in the United States because diplomatic relations had already been severed. Fourth, the warden at Leavenworth testified both to Witzke's good conduct at Leavenworth and to the remarkable courage he exhibited after the boiler explosion in July 1921, saving lives "at serious risk to himself." Last, other countries, including Germany, had after the war released all prisoners of war, including those convicted of espionage. "It would therefore do much to pacify public opinion in my country and would be considered a special act of grace by my Government if the United States of America, as France did a few months ago, were now also to set free their last prisoner of war." The ambassador assured the judge advocate general that, if Witzke were released, the embassy would "provide for his immediate return to Germany."[57]

A month later, on June 7, 1923, Witzke's parents sent a petition to President Harding requesting a pardon for their son.[58] The petition, organized by the German government to coincide with its own appeal for executive clemency, presented an entirely new narrative of their son's early years as well as disturbing allegations of the attempted murder of Witzke's mother by an alleged surrogate of Paul Altendorf. According to the petition, Witzke left his family home in Germany in June 1913 at age eighteen to join the German mercantile marine. He did so with much enthusiasm, signing onto a sailing ship bound for foreign countries. He wrote "regular and descriptive letters" home about his job and his adventures. He loved his work, difficult though it was, but also looked forward "with great joy" to coming home and reuniting with his parents. The war intervened and prevented his return. The Witzke family fell on hard times. Their last letter from their son was dated January 1918 from Mexico. Then, suddenly, "a ray of light came." A letter arrived from their son from Leavenworth, Kansas. Lothar was alive. Now, by the grace of God, they had "hope to see him again." Little by little, they have since learned of the "hard fate" that overcame him "on account of his having followed the call of duty and placed himself at the service of the honor and liberty of his country." Still, they nurture hope of his being released.

At this point, the petition pivots to the person they see as the real villain of their son's story, not Lothar himself, not the German government, not even the United States: "Mr. President, there is only one person who fears that release of our son and who tries to render void by criminal procedure all steps taken by our Government with a view of obtaining the release of our son. That man is Altendorf . . . a German-Austrian Jew who now calls himself Dr. Bernardo Paul Altendorf, and at present lives in Brooklyn."[59]

For the next five pages, the parents rail against Altendorf, a man who they say was "ill and without funds in a hospital" in Mexico and "sure to die" when their son was introduced to him, took pity, and with friends not only raised the money necessary to save Altendorf's life but also procured for him a position in the Mexican army. "This deed on the part of our son was the misfortune under which he and we with him have to suffer so intensely. For Altendorf, who pretended to be our son's friend, . . . induced him to cross the Mexican border near Nogales. There Altendorf had him arrested by American soldiers. . . . In order to get his high reward and in order to ensure his own safety Altendorf then denounced our son in the most calculated and mendacious way as the originator of all destructions of all military and naval plants in the United States which had occurred during the world war."

The anti-Altendorf diatribe ends with the assertion that a single person could not possibly have done the things that Altendorf said their son had done, especially someone as young as their son with his (then) supposedly limited English language facility. These themes are familiar ones, echoing Witzke's own letter to Judge Fake of April 4 and the Ambassador's letter of May 1, although there are several new details, for example Witzke first meeting Altendorf in a hospital when Altendorf was seriously ill and Altendorf allegedly stealing Witzke's luggage at Nogales. But now comes an entirely new theme, both bizarre and far more nefarious: the alleged murder attempt on Witzke's mother by an Altendorf surrogate.

According to the parents, Altendorf had under his sway a sergeant at Fort Sam Houston named Harriss [sic] whose real name was Willy Dojan, born in Posen, who worked as a sentry at the Fort and who befriended Witzke for the sole purpose of gaining his confidence and prying information from him. He gave Witzke "food and other small luxuries" to make his solitary confinement easier to bear; he pretended to help Witzke with two attempted escapes, supposedly jeopardized his own position at the fort by doing so, and had to flee to Germany where, at Witzke's request, the parents offered Dojan refuge in their home in August 1922. Dojan's purpose (under Altendorf's direction) was to insinuate himself into the confidence of the family and thereby gain access to what were hoped would be documents incriminating Witzke in the acts of sabotage against the United States of which Altendorf had accused him. The parents freely shared Witzke's maritime correspondence with Dojan, which he read eagerly. But he was also desperate to gain access to the family's locked desks. Left alone in the house one day with Mrs. Witzke, he "saw his opportunity and tried to cleave her skull by an exactly calculated and hard blow with the butt-end of a rifle." Due to a chance movement of her head, he missed, tried three more times, then fled when she cried out for help. Mrs. Witzke was gravely wounded. The police investigated but could not find Dojan, presumably because Altendorf had supplied him with identification papers to facilitate his escape. That his motive was to procure incriminating documents, not robbery, was proved by the fact that he did not take with him any of the money, securities, jewels, or silver articles that lay about openly in the house.

The parents were not yet finished. In a final swipe at Altendorf, they introduce into the story, though not by name, the mysterious Mrs. Johnson of Lansing, Michigan, Witzke's most prolific Leavenworth correspondent. Altendorf, they insist, is "still at work and does not abhor from further acts of violence. Thus the house of a woman living in Michigan, with whom our son had corresponded and who takes an interest in his case and has taken steps to procure his release was forcibly entered some time ago and only Lothar's letters were looked through, but nothing else stolen." This, they say, must "undoubtedly" be ascribed to "Altendorf's doings" and to "the doings of the young man who was made a criminal by him [i.e., Dojan]."

The petition ends with a final plea for Witzke's release. "Mr. President, we beg you once more to draw this our deep feeling for our son into benevolent consideration and to fulfill our hearts' most ardent desire." The German ambassador sent copies of the translated petition to the judge advocate general and to the secretary of state, asking the latter to forward a copy to the president.[60]

Mrs. M. E. Johnson

Who was the woman from Michigan with whom Witzke corresponded, who took an interest in his case, and who, according to his parents, had "taken steps to procure his release"? Based on the prison's correspondence log, the individual was Mrs. M.E. Johnson, of Box Seventy-Six, Lansing, Michigan. Witzke first received a letter from her on January 8, 1922. She would become his most frequent correspondent, sometimes signing with the familiar "Eva Estelle." During 1922–1923, they exchanged some 400 communications.

The Lansing City Directory for 1921 lists a "Mrs. Minnie E. Johnson, widow of Bert" (the only M. E. Johnson in the directory, "Mrs." or otherwise) as residing at 1102 N. Larch St., Lansing. The directory says that she was then employed as a credit manager at the Mills Dry Goods Company.[61] She appeared from time to time in the local newspaper. During the war, she was president of the Business Girls' Club, which provided assistance to the wives of American soldiers left destitute when their husbands went to war. Mrs. Johnson was said to have found employment as a sales clerk at the Mills store for one young wife with a two-year old child. When that did not work out because the woman did not like sales, Mrs. Johnson found her another position in a local factory.[62] Mrs. M. E. Johnson was also a member of the local chapter of the American Red Cross, which packed supply boxes for army base hospitals during the war (pajamas, bandages, convalescent robes, shoulder wraps, operating sheets and towels).[63] She was prominent enough locally to be covered in the social pages as well. She attended adult sketch classes at the Lansing Academy of Fine Arts, welcomed her son for a visit from his home in Flint, Michigan, and entertained twelve guests at a Saturday evening Christmas party at her home, the rooms of which were "cheerfully decorated with green and red, and a beautifully decorated Christmas tree centered the room," all in 1922.[64] On a Friday evening in 1923, she entertained "the girls" in the Mills store office with a bohemian dinner at her home.[65]

What impelled Mrs. Johnson to take an interest in the German prisoner Lothar Witzke is a mystery. The bohemian-themed dinner party hints at an interest in things that were central European, though "bohemian" was used at the time to connote a certain kind of spiritedness that need not have had any German association. Perhaps the Business Girls' Club and Red Cross volunteer work during the war manifests a do-good personality that found a suitable object in the plight of America's last German prisoner of war. Whatever the reason, Mrs. Johnson pursued her cause with unrelenting vigor. While none of the letters to or from Witzke has survived, we know the contents of several cables they exchanged, because the prison kept copies. The following are typical. Undated, Lothar to Mrs. Johnson: "Thanks for your kind thoughtfulness. Love, Lothar." March 6, 1922, Mrs. Johnson to Lothar: "Sympathy best wishes speedy recovery . . . Will come if necessary." July 14, 1922: Mrs. Johnson to Lothar: "If illness or trouble wire can I help would come Eva Estelle." July 14, 1922, Lothar to Mrs. Johnson: "Everything OK. My letter left 10th. Thanks inquiring." April 4, 1923, Lothar to Mrs. Johnson: "Many happy returns of the day. Lothar." And so forth. Are these genuine expressions of sympathy, concern, gratitude? Are they speaking to one another in code? Was there a romantic yearning on her part? It is impossible to know.

Final Push for a Pardon

We do not know whether the parents' petition on behalf of their son moved any hearts. We can infer that the German ambassador's intervention moved the decision-makers. In a memorandum to the Secretary of War on June 8, 1923, the judge advocate general advised the Secretary of his earlier meeting with the ambassador, stressing the ambassador's message that Witzke's confinement had attracted the attention of public opinion in Germany and frequent discussion in the Reichstag, and that his release would "do much to pacify public opinion."[66] General Bethel then framed the issue for the Secretary as one of policy. All belligerents employ spying. Death is the usual punishment for spying throughout the world, although spying does not involve the moral turpitude that justifies a death sentence in cases such as murder or rape. As Witzke's death sentence was commuted, death was off the table and the question now before the government was the length of imprisonment. Could the United States now release him without detriment to its interests?

The answer, according to General Bethel, was not straightforward. "It would be a grave mistake for the United States to create the impression throughout the world that it would not in future wars take the severe measures against spies that all nations have heretofore taken." Countries such as France and England had proved during the recent war that they had no qualms about imposing the ultimate penalty. But the United States had not shown such resolve. Witzke's death sentence had been commuted. He had, though, been incarcerated for five years. On balance, therefore, the US had "sufficiently asserted" its policy in respect of spies.

Bethel also raised the subject that had irked the editors of the Ohio newspaper quoted earlier: whether failure to release US citizens still imprisoned for anti-war conduct would be viewed as inconsistent. Bethel thought not. Their actions "savored of treason," whereas Witzke was serving his own country and owed the United States nothing. Finally, regarding the State Department, Bethel advised that they had no objection to Witzke's release. "I recommend," he concluded, "that the unexecuted portion of the confinement in the case of Lothar Witzke be remitted." The American embassies in London, Paris, and Rome all confirmed that Great Britain, France, and Italy had already released the last of their German prisoners of war, including those convicted of felonies.[67]

On August 1, 1923, the day before President Harding's untimely death in San Francisco, General Bethel advised the German ambassador that the matter of Witzke's release was now laid before the secretary of war, and that the secretary had not yet taken any action.[68] The ambassador waited six weeks. There was no further news. On September 11, he delivered a memorandum to the secretary of state, reminding him that two months before he had forwarded a petition for release from Witzke's parents with a request that it be forwarded to the president. He reiterated as well, in summary fashion, the arguments made in his previous communications. The State Department forwarded the Ambassador's memorandum to the secretary of war.[69]

Two weeks later, General Bethel, responding to a request on behalf of the secretary of war for comment and recommendation on the petition of Witzke's parents, again recommended, as he had in his earlier June 8 memorandum to the secretary of war, that the unexpired portion of Witzke's sentence should be remitted.[70] Yet again the matter sat for six weeks. Finally, on November 6, the secretary of war approved the remittance of Witzke's remaining sentence, to take effect November 21, 1923.[71] The following day, November 7, the adjutant general issued, by order of the secretary of war, a formal notice that "so much of [Witzke's] sentence of confinement . . . as shall remain unexecuted on November 21, 1923, is, by direction of the President, remitted."[72]

Getting Ready to Leave Leavenworth

Events now moved quickly as relevant parties (the warden, the prisoner, the German embassy, the US Immigration Service) learned of Witzke's impending release. The German embassy, as promised, took responsibility for arranging transportation to New York and Germany. A Mr. Wilde of Kansas City, representing Germany, was designated to go to Leavenworth on November 21 to take custody of the released prisoner and accompany him to Kansas City. There he would be put on a train to St. Louis and New York, travelling on his own recognizance. The German consul in St. Louis sent the warden a letter of identification for Witzke to carry with him. Mr. Wilde asked for photographs of Witzke and was sent eight copies. The US Immigration Service authorized Witzke to make a "voluntary departure" from the United States under responsibility of the German Government so that deportation proceedings could be avoided. The warden was given immigration forms for Witzke to carry and present to the authorities at his port of departure in order to verify his departure.[73]

We do not know when or how the news of his release was first relayed to the prisoner. Presumably, it came via the Warden, probably on November 12 or 13. Witzke immediately cabled his father in Hannover: "Pardoniert. Reise am einundzwanzigsten November" (Pardoned. Travel on twenty-first November.)[74] He also cabled Mrs. Johnson in Lansing the same day. "Commuted to expire November 21st."[75] She responded quickly, asking if he could arrange to stop in Lansing or Chicago. He replied that deportation was certain, he had no information as to arrangements, but the embassy was in charge and he would no doubt have to leave the day of his release, November 21. He added that his likely route would be St. Louis, New York, Hamburg. Stops at Lansing or Chicago would be impossible because of the added expense and his obligation to follow Embassy instructions. He signed "Lothar."[76]

Someone Forgot to Tell the President

The story of Witzke's sentence commutation broke on November 20, 1923, when the secretary of war announced early in the day that President Coolidge had ordered Witzke released the following day "in as much as all of the other nations associated with the late war had released their prisoners of war" and the German ambassador had guaranteed Witzke would leave the country "at once."[77] Reporters raised the matter later in the day at the White House's semi-weekly press conference. It turned out that no one had told the president what he had supposedly done. The spokesman denied that the president had ever issued such an order, said the president knew nothing of it, and added that the chief would be "little inclined to exercise clemency unless upon extremely good grounds."

As soon as the press conference ended, a miffed White House made inquires about the case at the Justice Department. Justice's records showed that it was a War Department matter. Calls were then placed to the War Department, but it was lunchtime and no one there at the time knew anything about the case. When Secretary of War Weeks returned from lunch and heard what had happened, he went immediately to the White House and met with President Coolidge. The two conferred for some time and the president asked a lot of questions. The secretary walked him through the background of the case, explaining how and why Witzke was being freed. In the end, the President seemed satisfied with the explanation, but he ordered Weeks to "make sure of his ground." When he got back to the War Department, Weeks called in Judge Advocate General Bethel, and the two conferred about the matter once again. It ended with the Secretary announcing that the order for Witzke's release "would stand." The brouhaha was over and Witzke would, indeed, be set free.[78]

Homeward Bound

Five years and four months after being sentenced to death, Witzke was let out of Leavenworth prison, a free man. The warden returned to him his notebook, his knife, and the balance in his personal account of ninety dollars and forty-three cents. He was also given a copy of his official commutation papers plus five dollars that was traditionally given to freed prisoners. The German representative, Mr. Wilde, met him at the prison gate and accompanied him to Kansas City. There, as planned, he was put on a train to New York City. He travelled on his honor, alone.[79]

He left New York on November 29, 1923, shortly after he arrived, on the Hamburg-American line SS *Albert Balin*. Just before the *Balin* sailed, Witzke was upgraded from third to second class, courtesy of the German government.[80] He wore a pair of US Army shoes. It was reported that prison life had left "no traces on the countenance of the former spy, for he was robust and ruddy and looked 23 rather than 30 years old."[81] In fact, he was 28. To reporters at the dock he said, "I'm glad to be going home to my family—or what is left of it. I'll have to find a job first thing. The only trade I have is that of engineer, which I learned at Leavenworth." He made no comment on his wartime activities.[82]

A young and dashing Lothar Witzke, before his capture. The photo was probably taken between 1914 and 1918, when Witzke was in his late teens or early twenties. Bettmann Archive, Getty Images.

Witzke told his American captors that he was Russian, that his family had emigrated to America when he was five years old, and that he was hired out as kitchen help on an English steamer when he was twelve. In fact he was German, spent his school years in Germany, and joined the German merchant marine as a cadet in 1913, after graduation. He sailed on the four-masted, 3166 ton steel barque *J. C. Vinnen* (pictured) from Hamburg to Santa Rosalia (Mexico), Newcastle (Australia), and Valparaiso (Chile). After World War I began, the ship was interned at Valparaiso for the duration of the war. In 1916, Witzke jumped ship and headed for the US. A.D. Edwards Collection. Courtesy of State Library of South Australia.

Witzke's first job after arriving in America in May 1916 was at a soda plant in Keeler, California, deep in the Sierra Nevada Mountains. He quit after two weeks, hiked all day through the high desert to the Olancha rail post (pictured), and caught the night train from there to Los Angeles. Gustafson Collection. Courtesy of California State Railroad Museum Library & Archives.

Master spy Kurt Jahnke (pictured) recruited Witzke to join Germany's intelligence service in the early summer of 1916. Witzke quickly became Jahnke's right-hand man and good friend. It was Jahnke who sent Witzke on his final, fateful trip to Nogales, Arizona, where he was captured.National Archives (College Park), Photographs of American Military Activities, NAID 86711636, Local ID 111-SC-53214.

Jahnke recruited Witzke at the Heidelberg Inn, a popular hangout of the German community in San Francisco. This contemporary postcard ad for the inn says in substance: "I've been deprived of everything long enough. Here I'm a thousand times merrier and happier." Authors' collection.

Morley Avenue, Nogales, Arizona.

Witzke left Mexico City on what turned out to be his final mission to the US on January 16, 1918. He arrived at the border town of Nogales on the evening of January 30, 1918, and checked into the Hotel Central on the Mexican side of the border. He crossed the border on the morning of February 1, 1918, to do some shopping and was arrested seconds later on Morley Avenue, Nogales, Arizona, by two US agents. A stunned Witzke turned deathly pale and stammered "I suppose you think you have caught a German spy." Postcard, 1916, authors' collection.

The Preparedness Day Parade bombing in San Francisco on July 22, 1916, is an act of sabotage some have attributed to Lothar Witzke. Ten people were killed and more than forty seriously injured. This is a photo of the crowd gathered at the corner of Steuart and Market shortly after the bomb exploded there. Bancroft Library, University of California at Berkeley.

Did he do it? The most spectacular act of sabotage of which Witzke was accused was the destruction in July 1916 of the massive Black Tom munitions depot in New York Harbor, the transport station for the bulk of American arms then being shipped to European Allies. Property damage exceeded 500 million in today's dollars. Here, a 1954 Topps bubble gum card depicts the explosion. Authors' collection.

Shrapnel from the Black Tom explosion damaged the torch of the Statue of Liberty, resulting in the permanent closing of an internal staircase that had been used by tourists to climb to the tip of the torch. In this 1912 photo, the Black Tom depot can be seen across the water to the right of the statue. Milstein Division, New York Public Library.

When the US entered World War I against Germany in April 1917, Witzke fled the US for the safe haven of Mexico City, where he continued his espionage activities against the US, including three surreptitious missions back into enemy territory. In this photo, probably taken in late January 1918 during his fateful, final trip from Mexico City to Nogales, Arizona, Witzke (*center*) can be seen on horseback. He learned to ride while he was stranded in Chile. National Archives (St. Louis), Lather Witcke Court Martial File 119966.

Paul Altendorf was the double agent who betrayed Witzke to the Americans and testified against him at his trial. Landau, *The Enemy Within* (New York: G.P. Putnam's Sons, 1937).

While awaiting trial and then execution, Witzke was incarcerated in the guardhouse at Fort Sam Houston, Texas (three-story building, center, flanked on either side by two-story barracks) from mid-February 1918 until June 1920. He escaped briefly in August 1919 by jumping through a broken third-floor window onto the roof of the barracks, running across the roof to the end, then jumping off the roof to the ground below. Courtesy of University of North Texas Libraries, The Portal to Texas History and Austin History Center, Austin Public Library.

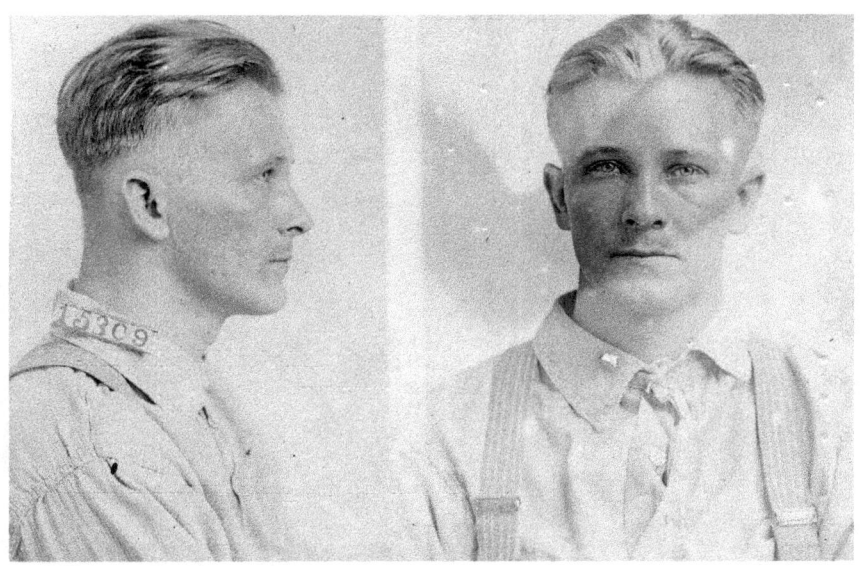

Witzke was convicted of espionage and sentenced to hang in August 1918. In 1920, President Wilson commuted his death sentence to life in prison at Leavenworth Penitentiary, Kansas. The above is his inmate photo from Leavenworth. President Coolidge would pardon and deport him three years later. National Archives (Kansas City), Inmate Case File 15309, NAID 160923963.

Witzke worked in Hankow, China, from 1930 to 1934 as hulk manager for the Hamburg-Amerika shipping line. He was responsible, among other things, for overseeing the coolies who loaded and unloaded the arriving and departing steamers (pictured). Known as a brutal overseer, he sometimes manhandled and injured the coolies working under him. Courtesy of Historical Photographs of China Project and University of Bristol Library, Special Collections.

Witzke met and married Lilli Carstensen while on leave in Germany in 1937. Their firstborn son Dieter and daughter Helga were born in China. This is a photo of Lilli, Dieter, and baby Helga in Hankow circa 1933. Dieter would die of tuberculosis a year later. Courtesy of Christoph and Claudia Moinian.

After he returned to Germany in the mid 1930s, Witzke acquired this comfortable house in Volksdorf, an upscale residential quarter of Hamburg. The home was a "Kapitänshaus," i.e., a house in an area reserved for homeowners who were naval captains or the equivalent. It may have been a gift of the German Government for past services. It remained the Witzke family home until Lilli's death in 1980. Courtesy of Christoph and Claudia Moinian.

After the war Witzke prospered as the CEO of a company that manufactured anti-corrosive and anti-fouling paints for the protection of metal ship bottoms. In 1956, he hosted a lavish wedding for his daughter Helga. Seen in this family wedding photo, left to right, are Lothar Witzke, daughter Helga, son-in-law Hossein Moinian, and Lilli Witzke. Courtesy of Christoph and Claudia Moinian.

Witzke hosting a black tie dinner sometime in the 1950s. Seated at the table are Lothar Witzke (*third from right*), Helga (*second from right*), son-in-law Hossein Moinian (*furthest left*), and Lilli Witzke (*third from left*). The other guests' names are not known. Courtesy of Christoph and Claudia Moinian.

A photo of Witzke in the late 1950s
or early 1960s. He died January 6,
1962. Courtesy of Christoph and
Claudia Moinian.

The Witzke family tombstone,
Friedhof Ohlsdorf Cemetery
in Hamburg, Germany. Three
members of the Witzke family are
buried there: Lothar (May 15, 1895–
January 6, 1962), Lilli (May 3, 1906–
November 17, 1980), and Lothar Jr.
(June 13, 1934–January 16, 1997). The
inscription for Lilli reads: "Our dear
Mother Lilli Witzke in unspeakable
sorrow." There is no inscription
for the father except name and
dates. Courtesy of billiongraves.com.

THE SPY'S
LIFE BEFORE
HIS CAPTURE
AND AFTER
HIS PARDON

6 SAILOR, SPY

What I shall begin I
do not yet know at all.
—LOTHAR WITZKE TO HIS PARENTS,
MAY 21, 1916

The singular life story of Lothar Witzke did not end with his departure from the United States. As told in subsequent chapters, Witzke returned
to Germany, found employment and lived abroad in Mexico, Venezuela and
China. He married and became a father and joined the Nazi Party. In parallel, he served as a key witness for Germany in the long-running sabotage
case brought against Germany by the United States in the 1920s and 1930s.
He served Germany in World War II in Brittany, Athens, and Oslo, and endeavored, during the first part of the war, to infiltrate saboteurs into Great
Britain. He spent his first year after the war as a prisoner (again) in a denazification camp, then became a prosperous chief executive in Hamburg,
even serving a year in the Hamburg state parliament. He died in 1962 in the
arms of a woman who may have been an East German Stasi agent and who
may have murdered him.

Before moving on to the second half of Witzke's life, there are questions
about the first half to try to answer. During his captivity in America, he told
his captors different and contradictory stories about his early life and his time
in America before his capture in 1918. His parents, in their plea for his release
from Leavenworth, introduced the narrative of a young sailor who left home

in June 1913 at age 18 to join the merchant marine and sail the world.[1] He wrote, they said, "regular and descriptive letters about his difficult vocation," a vocation that he loved. His attachment to his parents remained strong, and in July 1914 he wrote to them "with great joy" about the prospective return of his ship to Germany in time for Christmas. Then the outbreak of world war intervened and his communications became fitful. Their last letter from him was dated January 1918, from Mexico. Not until two and a half years later, in a letter sent from Leavenworth penitentiary, did they learn of the fate that befell their son at the hands of Paul Altendorf.

In this chapter, we lay out the story of Witzke's pre-capture life as told in these letters and postcards and seek to resolve the most important discrepancies between the innocent sailor boy narrative of the family correspondence and the other narratives that Witzke, and those with whom he associated, told. The events we describe include Witzke's early twentieth-century schooling in Posen, his life as a merchant marine in 1913-1916, his voyage up the Pacific coast from Chile to San Francisco, his first encounter with the remarkable Kurt Jahnke, and his life as a spy in World War I. These events of Witzke's early life give us glimpses into social conditions in prewar Prussia, the daily lives of German sailors in the World War I era, the British/German naval conflict off the coast of Chile in 1916, and social conditions for German immigrants on the American West Coast in 1916–1917.

SCHOOLING

The earliest writing by Witzke that we have, dated Posen, January 19, 1913, is a curriculum vitae in the style of a letter from his last term at school, perhaps a form letter that he used or planned to use in connection with job applications or as part of an application for the voluntary, one-year military service program for which his education to that point had evidently qualified him.[2] It says that he was born May 15, 1895, in the town of Koschmin, Posen Province, Germany, the eldest of four sons of postal assistant Paul Witzke and his wife Valesca (née Spalding). The family is said to be Prussian of protestant faith. They moved from Koschmin to Posen when the father was appointed telegraph operator (*Telegraphen-Besitzer*) in Posen. There, Witzke attended primary school (at Mittelschule 1) for three years from ages six to nine, then enrolled in the Royal Auguste Viktoria Secondary School (*Königliche Auguste-Viktoria-Gymnasium*), where he remained for several years. At this point in his education, because his career aspiration was to become an officer in the merchant marine, he abandoned the academic track in which he was enrolled and transferred to the local vocational school (the *König-liche Berger-Ober-Realschule*). The transfer put him two years behind where he otherwise would have been had he originally enrolled in the vocational track, but he advanced each year and was due to graduate by Easter 1913. His intent after graduation, he says, was to obtain permission to do voluntary one-year military service.

JOB SEARCH AND THE BIG CITY

Correspondence with his family in June 1913 shows that Witzke sent off for employment brochures with the merchant marine, that he made several short trips in June from his family home in Posen to Bremen, Hamburg, and Berlin, and that, within a few days of learning that the F. A. Vinnen Company was recruiting a small number of applicants for spring and fall voyages, he had procured for himself a position as cadet on one of two Vinnen vessels, the first bound for Santiago, Chile, and the other for Santa Rosalia, Mexico.[3] Young Lothar Witzke was not given to procrastination, and he had the capacity to seize opportunity quickly.

He was a teenager full of wanderlust and a spirit of adventure. This can be gleaned from the ease with which he adapted to unexpected inconvenience and the delight that he took in seeing and doing new things. On his first day in Bremen, he tried to book a room at a cheap hotel near the train station but was told that all hotels in the city were full. He made a good impression on the hotel staff and one of the hotel servants went with him to try to find a room elsewhere, then took him back to his own place and let Witzke sleep on his couch. Witzke got his own room the next night.[4] A few days later, in a letter to his father, he excitedly describes a whirlwind of crowds and restaurants in Berlin (the restaurant dining made possible courtesy of a friend named Ernst Schmolke and a merchant they met named Talbot). He was fascinated by a traffic jam: "Yesterday there was so much traffic at Potsdamer Platz that the carriages and cars as far as you could see stood still and were stuck in stop-and-go traffic. On the sidewalk one had to stop every five minutes." They tried to escape the crowds by having lunch at Aschinger's in Friedrichstrasse, but had to wait half an hour for a table. Later, for dinner, Talbot, whom they had met up with earlier at the English Cafe, took them to the *Landausstellung* where they had roast beef, kohlrabi, and strawberry punch, then to the Café Queen where Witzke drank port and champagne, all paid for by Talbot who, Witzke says, insisted that the young man must "get to know Berlin."[5]

THE J. C. VINNEN

The sailing ship to which Witzke was assigned was the *J. C. Vinnen*, bound for Santa Rosalia, Mexico, on the Baja California peninsula, with a cargo of coal, then Australia, Chile, and back to Germany, a round-trip of an estimated 18 months.[6] The *J. C. Vinnen* was a four-masted, steel-hulled barque measuring 325' x 46' x 25', tonnage 3166 GRT and 2986 NRT. It was launched at Liverpool in 1892 and acquired by the Vinnen Company in 1910.[7] In February 1913, off the coast of Brazil heading back to Germany, the ship's crew recorded seeing the Great Meteor Procession of 1913 from the location 24°29' W, 14°41' S, making it the most southerly known observation of the event.[8]

Witzke had heard about a possible job with the Vinnen line on June 11, 1913.[9] By June 16 he had the job, and by June 21 he was living on board the *J. C. Vinnen*, docked at Hamburg, anticipating departure the following week.[10] He was one of six cadets on board and eager to report his impressions to his family. The first officer was "rather harsh," the second "inexperienced" and "vulgar." He continues to experience new sights and sounds, both on board and on shore leave. He has also already made his first climb to the crow's nest, got dizzy, and climbed down.[11] He saw and listened to his first jukebox while on shore leave in Hamburg. "You insert 10 pfennigs, pick up two receivers, press the number of the song you want to have (from the catalogue) and then you can wonderfully listen to the song."[12]

In another letter to his parents, he describes his work day on the docked ship. Hard work, he says, but work he is already used to: up at half past five, bitter black coffee with hardtack to wake up, then a mix of rolling petroleum barrels onto the ship, carrying salt barrels (each one hundred kg) to storage under deck, and loading coal; then breakfast at eight (lentils with hardtack), work again till noon lunch (salted meat, potatoes, and pea soup), more work till coffee break at four, work again, dinner at six (beans), and in the evening music until lights out at eleven. "There we sit in the bunk and one plays the accordion and we sing. I too can already play something. They always play such melancholic songs . . . 'Little bird fly out into the world / Leave me all alone at home / The only thing I ask of you / Don't forget your mommy.' That is the beginning of a song that I like very much to hear and play."[13]

There was a problem but it had nothing to do with his labors. He was woken up at midnight on his first night, his whole body itching, by something biting his neck. At first, he thought it was his blanket, but he kept getting bitten and could not sleep. Then he was told: bedbugs! The next morning, he went on a bug hunt and caught twenty-four.[14] It would take another week of itching, bites, and bug hunts before he caught and killed the last half dozen of them and was bedbug free.[15] Apart from bedbugs, his principal complaint was bathing. "Washing is very unpleasant here, you go on deck, only keep your pants on and wash with cold water, what a nice thing to do in Cape Horn at 10° below 0."[16] Witzke insists, however, that he loves what he is doing. "The hard work is fun and so are the bugs. You have no idea how much we laugh in one evening when we go on a bug hunt. I haven't had any in three days. . . . The crew's treatment is alright, for we almost only have contact with them during work."[17]

Witzke needed a "few things" for his upcoming voyage and asked his family to send them: six collars, three short-sleeved shirts, three white shirts, a suit hanger, handkerchiefs, a treat (sausages or a cake—"Everyone has something sent to them from home.").[18] Both sausages and a cake arrived a few days later, for which the son was properly grateful.[19]

Sometime during the weekend of June 28–29, 1913, the *J. C. Vinnen* was towed up the Elbe from Hamburg to Cuxhaven, in anticipation of putting out to sea the next day. But the weather was bad, constantly raining and stormy, and their departure from Cuxhaven was delayed. The young Lothar Witzke remained excited. "I'm really enjoying myself," he wrote to his parents, "and look forward to going to sea."[20] On July 2 they were still "lying before Cuxhaven" because of a steady northeast wind. Witzke enjoyed watching the waves, and the ship was large enough not yet to feel them. Then the light up in the foremast blew out. They clambered up the pole and lit the lamps so that they would not be rammed by another ship. "The wind shakes the rope ladder, blows the shirts up and blows out ten matches, only the 11th match will give you fire." Witzke is still enjoying himself. He has begun to keep a diary. There are now eight cadets on board. They are a close-knit group (sing, play cards, sew buttons—"It's really fun"). And then the tug arrives. Two hours later they are in the North Sea. "The waves are mighty. I already fear seasickness," he writes at the end of his last letter home before encountering the open sea. His first voyage had begun.[21]

We will recount in this chapter a few of Witzke's adventures and impressions during his several ensuing voyages sufficient to show how he became a mature adult during this time, and how his life and thinking were shaped by his many months under sail.

The Voyage to Santa Rosalia

Witzke was right to fear seasickness. After one day on the North Sea, he and all of his fellow cadets save one succumbed. "I got it only for a day," he wrote, "but it was all the worse." His cure was to eat "10 potatoes for lunch, without any meat or fat."[22] On July 4, 1913, the *J .C. Vinnen* entered the English Channel, passing the cliffs of Dover and Calais. On July 6, in addition to his daily diary entries, Witzke began the first of four serial letters to his family written during the voyage to Santa Rosalia, to be mailed when his ship made landfall. The letters, penned mostly on Sundays, chronicled the daily life of a cadet at sea, his work and play, his likes and dislikes, his friends and enemies, food, homesickness, the progress of his journey: catching the trade winds, the doldrums, crossing the equator, rounding Cape Horn, storms and calms, the anticipation of landfall after four and a half months of nothing but water.[23]

Witzke's "typical day" at sea evolved as his training and skills developed, but there were roughly two kinds, good weather days and storm days. A sequence of good weather days would begin at 8:00 a.m., then scrubbing or painting or oiling decks until half past noon, rest until half past six, night watch until midnight, sleep until 4:00 the next morning, then a similar cycle but with an earlier start time: up at 4:00 a.m., work until 8:00 a.m., sleep until half past noon, work again until half past six, sleep until midnight, night watch until 4:00 a.m., and so on. Leisure time would involve nothing more than walking back and forth on deck, chatting with friends, smoking, sometimes music, including a makeshift band, a gramophone, singing, even dancing. Witzke, if his letters are to be believed, very much liked his life at sea. "There are not many professions," he wrote, "that allow you to be so lazy."[24]

Storm days were different. During one harrowing storm in August 1913, Witzke suffered a crushed finger and was nearly washed overboard. Coming up on deck as the storm began, he was impressed by the calmness of the crew, each man focused on his task; it helped him quickly to "get used to the unusual." However, as the wind picked up and waves began crashing over the deck, he repeatedly had to hold tight not to be washed away. The force of one wave was so strong that he was pulled loose from his grip and he skidded out of control across the deck from the rail to the mast. The water on deck rose chest high, a heavy gust hit the rigging, the ship listed to one side as if about to tip over. Witzke was sent up to fasten the topsails. It was during this maneuver that the middle finger of his right hand got caught between the mast and an iron ring around the mast to which the sail was attached, crushing his finger. "There was a lot of blood and the whole hand got stiff. I climbed down with one hand and my teeth. After the captain had washed my hand it turned out that no bone was broken, but the finger was pressed flat and had burst." He was sent below to his quarters because he could no longer work or hold on. The living quarters were flooded, water rushing back and forth across the floor, furniture and boxes knocking about. The storm lasted three days, at its height reaching category twelve on the Beaufort scale, a hurricane. Witzke lay in his bunk most of that time, unable to help anymore. After the storm abated, and while the wound healed, he was assigned to the lookout.[25]

Witzke writes that most of the cadets and crew liked him "very much" and "very much" enjoyed working with him. They called him their "comrade from Poland" or, affectionately, "Polak," because he came from Posen. When they wanted something, they always asked him first.[26] There is no reason to doubt Witzke's self-appraisal. He too, for the most part, liked them a lot. The captain was a "fine, quiet man." Witzke's favorite sailor was a seaman from Breslau. He particularly liked working with three Norwegians who shared his watch, first because they taught him English and second because they gave him their fresh bread to eat. Witzke's capacity to learn and master English would play a much greater role in his life than he could imagine. His favorite cadet, with whom he also shared watch, was Otto Laabs, from a town near Stettin. After this voyage, he and Laabs planned to sign on another ship together and to attend helmsman school together at Stettin.[27]

Witzke did, however, dislike two of the helmsman, especially the first. Once during the night watch the second helmsman caught Witzke having tea in his bunk, thought he had been shirking work, and became enraged. He slapped Witzke four times on the face, then made him climb up the topmast for the rest of the night watch. Witzke went to him afterwards, told him he had not been shirking, and that it was wrong to slap him. The second helmsman replied, "Before the voyage is over, you will get your ass kicked a couple more times." This did not sit well with Witzke. He went to his living quarters, pulled out a maritime law book, and discovered that slapping was not permitted for any offense, and that the most punishment that could be administered for a minor offense was some extra work. He decided to complain to the captain. However, before he could do so, the first helmsman, who had disliked him since they first encountered one another in Hamburg before sailing, called on him and asked what had happened between him and the second helmsman. After Witzke told his story, the first helmsman accused him of bossing his comrades around, then slapped him twice in the face. "I suppose you're going to report this to the captain," he sneered. Witzke replied, calmly, that he was indeed going to do so. He then washed, went to the captain, told him what had happened, and asked him whether slapping was permitted. The captain replied no and told Witzke he could insist that the wrongful slappings be noted in the ship's logbook, which would result in each helmsman losing a month's pay. Witzke said that it would not be necessary if the captain told them that slapping was not permitted. The captain did so, gave them a good tongue-lashing as well, and for the rest of the voyage the two helmsmen pretty much left Witzke alone.[28] The young sailor had spunk. It was risky to stand up to the two helmsmen; they were able to make life on board miserable for him. Nevertheless, stand up to them he did, and the result was favorable.

At Santa Rosalia, Mexico

In the late afternoon of Friday, November 21, 1913, the *J. C. Vinnen* arrived at Santa Rosalia roadstead and dropped anchor.[29] The *J. C. Vinnen* had been a long, four and a- half months at sea, around the tip of South America and up the Pacific coast, during which time the crew had seen human beings other than their own shipmates only twice: once when they passed the steamship *Borkum* at the end of July and once in early November when they passed the cruiser *Nürnberg*.[30] The first order of business was mail. The captain brought the mail waiting at Santa Rosalia on board. Witzke's only mail was a postcard dated September 28 and a letter dated October 6. He was crushed not to get more (some of his mail had not gotten through), but glad to get something. As the outgoing mail steamer was leaving the next day (Saturday), he penned a final entry on his open serial letter, then mailed two letters to Germany.[31]

Sunday the 23rd the *Vinnen* was towed to port, and the next day the crew began the laborious task of unloading its cargo of coal, working from 6:30 a.m. to 6:00 p.m six days a week.[32] There were other German ships in the harbor with cadets on board, and the cadets from these other Germans ships (and one or two English ships as well) began socializing with the *J. C. Vinnen* cadets in the evenings, on board the *J. C. Vinnen* because its quarters were judged luxurious relative to theirs.

Witzke's impressions of Santa Rosalia, as recounted in letters to his parents, are sharp-eyed and various. One of his first observations is that many people were walking around wearing cartridge belts; he calls the place "Revolver-town."[33] Everyone, he says, smokes; even little kids smoke cigars. He describes the place, a copper mining town, in some detail and draws a map, noting that all the buildings except the local jail are made of wood. The jail is stone with a corrugated roof. Haircuts are 2.2 marks. Good wine, served in glasses as big as beer mugs, can be had at the two local hotels for thirty pfennigs per drink.[34]

There is a lot in the letters about drunken sailors and violence, not subjects likely to comfort distant parents, but obviously fascinating to Witzke himself. He describes a series of incidents on board the *J. C. Vinnen* in which the ship's craftsmen were so drunk that they began smashing everything in sight, then dragged the first helmsman from his cabin (he had mistreated them during the voyage) and began beating him until they passed out. Later that evening, the drunk sailmaker got into a fight with a sailor. Each repeatedly punched the other until the sailor knocked the sailmaker down and started kicking him in the face. Then he got a knife and was about to stab the other to death when a couple of sober sailors restrained him and took him to his bunk. By the next morning, half the sailors were gone from the ship, one was in jail, and the rest lay drunk in the streets. If that were not enough to distress mom and dad, Witzke goes on to say that these were not isolated incidents limited to a first night's shore leave, but routine occurrences that one simply got used to. Apparently, though, the cadets were not rowdy or injurious to one another. The cadet shore leaves that Witzke describes (Thursday evenings, Saturday evenings, and Sundays) are much tamer affairs: eating jam-filled pancakes and drinking orange lemonade. In a note to one of his brothers, Witzke adds that he has not yet danced "with the ladies," although the cadets often dance among themselves with the accordion playing.[35]

Work unloading the coal progressed quickly, and Witzke was hopeful that their next destination would be San Francisco or Portland. However, it turned out to be, instead, the more distant Newcastle, Australia, a disappointment to cadets who, even if they were no longer homesick, were anxious to return to family and friends.[36]

On Thursday, January 22, 1914, the *J. C. Vinnen* was towed from port to anchorage, and the following day they were at sea, heading for the Pacific Ocean and Australia.[37] They did not carry any cargo, only copper slag as ballast that would eventually be sold to the Australian government.[38] At Newcastle, they would pick up a cargo of coal.

Newcastle, Australia

The *J. C. Vinnen* arrived at Newcastle, Australia, on Sunday, March 22, 1914, after two months at sea.[39] The Pacific voyage was marked, according to Witzke's telling, by severe storms, crossing the international dateline, and homesickness. During one of the storms, Witzke caught a bad cold accompanied by tonsillitis and headaches. He tried the remedy of an old proverb ("head warm, feet cold makes the best doctor poor") by wearing a warm cap and going barefoot for four days, after which he was, he says, "completely recovered." Crossing the dateline was of special interest because, depending on the moment of crossing, the calendar might skip from Saturday to Monday thus jumping over their day off and obliging the cadets and crew to work a straight fortnight. On Friday March 6, close to the dateline, the wind suddenly subsided and they went to sleep thinking they would not cross until sometime Saturday, therefore indeed skipping Sunday. But shortly before midnight a strong thunderstorm suddenly arose, the wind picked up, and they woke at 8:00 a.m. to learn that they had in fact crossed the dateline just in the nick of time, skipping Saturday but not Sunday.[40]

Witzke also described some of the crew's Sunday leisure activities at sea. These included, besides the usual music and dancing, construction of a makeshift gym with a bar and rings for gymnastics and a vaulting buck. He also mentions a curious game in which one player bends over, blind-folded, and the others whack him with bare hands on his butt. One "wins," apparently, by guessing correctly who it is that has whacked you.[41]

Newcastle itself was a welcome whisper of home: "ordinary" houses and shops, an abundance of confectionaries, pubs, and fruit markets, almost no "black or yellow people . . . in contrast to America." There was also a sailors' mission, a kind of clubhouse for seamen with a reading room, billiards room, and large hall where sailors could gather free of charge and play piano, mandolin or guitar, be served tea and cakes on Sunday evenings, and play parlor games on Wednesday evenings with "young ladies from Newcastle society come to play and talk to us."[42] Also, at last, there was a relative abundance of mail from home, to supplement the meager pickings of Santa Rosalia.[43]

Witzke was running short of money. He bought some "necessities" while in Newcastle, including deck shoes, soap, matches, letter paper, an oilcoat, socks, a shirt, and a tropical hat. He also spent freely during his shore leaves. He should nevertheless have had forty-five marks still in safekeeping with the first helmsman with whom he had deposited the money at the beginning of his journey. But it turned out that the first helmsman had been helping himself to Witzke's funds and the funds of other members of the crew that he had been safekeeping, to pay for his own alcohol habit. This the captain had discovered upon reviewing the first helmsman's papers after the first helmsman, drunk, fell into the hold, broke his arm, and was discharged from the ship. One suspects that, even as Witzke was telling his parents that he did not need money, he was hoping that by telling them this story they might choose to send him some at his next port.[44]

Responding to his mother's worry about his future, Witzke insists that he "really likes" his profession. "It's not that bad to be a seaman." The money was good, most of the seamen on sailing vessels were young like he was and wanted to become officers like he did, and he was only a few months shy of qualifying for his able seaman's certificate. His one regret was the long absence from home.[45]

VALPARAISO AND THE OUTBREAK OF WAR

The *J. C. Vinnen* left Australia for Valparaiso, Chile, on May 6, 1914.[46] Witzke had enjoyed himself "marvelously"in Newcastle. As he summarized for his parents in the first segment of the serial letter that he wrote to them on the voyage to Valparaiso, "we were often in the café or at the beach or at the seaman´s mission. But we also did some trips up the river." This harbor life ended when the vessel moved to the coal pier and began loading coal for the return journey east across the Pacific, but the memory of the good times lingered.[47]

In the same letter segment, Witzke revealed to his parents for the first time a darker side of his life at sea, a world not of maritime law books and protective captains but of fist fights and "might makes right" in which Witzke was, fortunately for him, able to hold his own.

> We started with 7 men [i.e., fellow cadets] at the same time, all had the same worries and stuck together tremendously. And the latter is very important, because all sorts of people resort to violence against us, and we have to restrain them. . . . On board fist law prevails and we are fine with that, because you are on good terms with the strongest ones and you just beat the weak ones, when they are rude. . . . At port and also beforehand at sea the petty officer behaved as if he was on top of us. Now that was too idiotic for us, and one time when he attempted to take away our lamp, because we had forgotten to pour petroleum in his, I told him that he cannot have the lamp, and when he got impudent, I just threw him out. But he didn't expect for me to be just there, because he has respect for me, because I am a bit irascible and some aboard have already got a black eye from me. Two days later in the morning he snarled at Fritz, what all that noise so late in the evening was about. Well he chose the right one to speak to, because Fritz just laughed at him and said that was none of his business and whenever he, the master, got drunk with his friends, they made so much more noise. Now it came to a brawl and Fritz beat up the master in such a way that he is letting us be completely at peace.[48]

The voyage to Valparaiso was, because of bad weather, a difficult one. On June 24 Witzke wrote, "Arguably few ships have had such a long and bad journey from Newcastle to Valparaiso as we had. Not only have we had storms very often [they survived four typhoons, Witzke would later learn from the captain], but we are already 50 days at sea today, even though the usual crossing takes only 30-40 days. Constant bad wind, where usually there is only a favorable breeze." They did, though, arrive safely in Valparaiso harbor on June 27, 1914. The ship's work routine there was such that most of the crew got a day of shore leave only every other Sunday. It was Witzke's good fortune, along with a sailor named Christian Grau with whom he would become close, to be chosen as a captain's oarsman.[49] An oarsman was relieved of daily duties on board and, instead, was charged with rowing the captain ashore each day. Once the captain was dropped off at the jetty, the oarsman was free to do as he wished for the rest of the day until it was time to row the captain back to the ship. Normally, this meant the oarsman could nap or shop or grab something onshore to eat. Witzke was eager for the assignment.[50] After two weeks, though, he had still not been ashore because the captain was mostly staying on board. Sundays, the winter storm swells were too high to row across. On other days the captain had so far rarely asked to be rowed ashore due to continuous bad weather; when he did go, it was only to fetch the mail and then return to the ship without spending much time on shore. Therefore, there had not been any opportunity for the oarsmen to spend time ashore.[51]

There was mail. After being delayed by snow in the Andes, it finally arrived and Witzke's haul, including many photographs, was the largest, resulting, he said, in his being "colossally envied." He was sorry to learn that his brother Ottomar (Otti) would have to wear glasses, mentioning, "It must be quite an unpleasant feeling, to constantly have something on your nose." He cautioned a family friend, whom he was told wanted to go to sea, not to sign on with the Vinnen company (there was a lot wrong with Vinnen, he said, including that they did not pay overtime); try the Hamburger Verein Seefahrt instead, he advised, which would look for a good ship out of Hamburg for him.[52]

Witzke's complaints about the Vinnen company escalated as the days passed. Perhaps the bad crossing and the bad weather at Valparaiso had made him cranky. Or maybe he was feeling the pinch of insufficient money. On July 20, 2014, he wrote that there was no way he would stay with Vinnen and that "wild horses couldn't drag me onto such a long journey again." He expressed bitterness about his low pay (five marks per month for a cadet) with no overtime and no bonus for the length of his journey. Once you graduated to the rank of ordinary sailor, Vinnen paid more (twenty marks a month and twenty pfennings per hour for overtime), but their German competition paid much better (thirty to forty-five marks a month plus thirty pfenning per hour for overtime). The British and Norwegians were better still: sixty marks a month and eighty pfennings per hour of overtime, and the food (about which Witzke had not complained before) was "much better" elsewhere.[53]

In the same July 20 letter, Witzke gave his parents a detailed report on his financial condition, which he portrayed as somewhat dire. He retold the story of how the first mate had misappropriated the forty-five marks that Witzke left in his safekeeping and used it to buy alcohol. He shrugged off personal responsibility for any profligate spending of his own ("You will probably wonder about my recklessness regarding expenses sometimes, but that just runs in the blood of a seaman. Money is his weak side.") and asked his father to send him more money. He also mentioned that his new best friend was no longer fellow cadet Otto Laabs, but a sailor (Christian Grau), who was "four heads taller" than Witzke and served as Witzke's fellow oarsman when rowing the captain. The previous Sunday the two had been on shore leave together and they had consumed a large quantity of alcohol and, for the first time in a year, German liverwurst.

Witzke learned about the assassination of Archduke Ferdinand from a local pastor, shortly after arriving in Valparaiso in late June 1914. The event did not raise alarms, at least none that he shared in writing to his parents. He anticipated a layover at Valparaiso of three to four months, then a three- or four-month sail back to Germany, arriving home sometime in January 1915. On August 2, the news came that Germany had declared war on Russia. Witzke assumed that he would be drafted and sent back to Germany straight away.[54] However, by the end of the month it was clear that travel to Europe was out of the question and that he was trapped for the moment in Valparaiso. He worried about the well-being of his family. He thanked his father for twenty-five marks that arrived the previous week. He had, he said, spent seven marks on a new shirt and trousers, and was saving the rest in case he found a way to travel home. It would help subsidize the journey. His hopes for leaving the *Vinnen*, though, were dashed; the German consul was urging German citizens to keep their jobs for now.[55] To make matters worse, the reviled first mate was back on board the *J. C. Vinnen*, having made his way from Newcastle to Valparaiso on another ship, angry as ever and still suffering from the injuries incurred in his fall.[56]

By the end of September 1914, Witzke was in despair. He learned that his father had been called up and his brothers were off to war, and he was fairly desperate to join them. The news in the German press about German victories was countered by contrary stories in the British press and it was hard to know what to believe. About his own circumstances, he wrote that "we are condemned to inactivity and are extremely unhappy. All kinds of efforts are made to get away from here, some go to Buenos Aires over the Andes Mountains, but can't get further from there, the others go up to North America, but those are only the ones that have a lot of money, it is not possible for us boys [i.e., cadets] with our 5 [marks] pay."[57] One piece of goods news, which Witzke reported in a letter to his family at the beginning of November 1914, was that the first mate was leaving the ship for good and the captain would probably be docking his back pay to cover the sums in his safekeeping that he stole (Witzke's forty-five marks included). "You don't need to send me any money," he told his parents, "for I have a place and food for free and then I earn pocket money of 5 Marks a month, I don't need more to live."[58]

THE DRESDEN

On Friday, November 13, 1914, two light cruisers from the German navy, the *Dresden* and the *Leipzig*, put into Valparaiso harbor and dropped anchor.[59] Two weeks earlier, as part of Germany's East Asia Squadron under command of Vice Admiral Maximillian von Spee, the two cruisers along with the *Scharnhorst* (Spee's flagship), the *Gneisenau*, and the *Nürnberg* had defeated Britain's fourth Cruiser Squadron in battle near Coronel off the coast of Chile. Two British ships were sunk, a third was damaged, and 1,654 British officers and sailors were killed. No German ship was sunk or seriously damaged, and not a single German officer or sailor was killed. It was one of the earliest naval battles of World War I and the first defeat of a British naval squadron anywhere in the world in more than one hundred years. The British were stunned.[60]

Two days after the battle, on the morning of November 3, the *Scharnhorst*, the *Geneisenau*, and the *Nürnberg* entered Valparaiso harbor in search of coal, provisions, and intelligence.[61] News of the German victory at Coronel had not yet reached the city. But following visits by the German minister and Consul General to Spee on the *Scharnhorst*, word spread quickly. When the Vice Admiral landed later in the morning, crowds had gathered at the docks, "cameras clicked everywhere," and cheers welcomed him. "The Germans," Spee later wrote, "wanted to celebrate."[62] So, evidently, did the sailors on German merchantmen stranded in Valparaiso harbor by the war, their defenseless ships (like the *J. C. Vinnen*) unable to leave the protection of the neutral harbor for fear of being sunk by the British Navy. Hundreds of German seamen and stokers from these stranded ships offered to join Spee's squadron; 127 were accepted.[63]

Spee was reticent to celebrate. He did agree, however, to attend impromptu festivities at the local German club, where inebriated revelers pressed him to toast his victory with "Damnation to the British Navy!" Instead, he rose to his feet, raised his glass, toasted "the memory of a gallant and honorable foe," then left the club. Walking back to the dock, a woman presented him with a bouquet of arum lilies. "This will do very nicely for my grave," he reportedly said after thanking her for her gift.[64] He knew that the might of the Royal Navy would soon be tracking him to avenge their defeat at Coronel. Indeed, Spee would within two months be killed in battle near the Falkland Islands.

Inexplicably, Witzke does not, in his letters, mention the spectacular German naval triumph at Coronel, the visit of the three German warships to Valparaiso on November 3, or the celebratory welcome they were given by the local German community, although he was surely well-aware of all three. He did briefly mention the subsequent visit of the *Dresden* and the *Leipzig* on November 13: "Last Friday, the two cruisers Leipzig and Dresden were here, from the German ships everyone wanted to join them as a war volunteer, but they didn't take anyone except for some stoker reservists. At night the cruisers left the harbor again and there went the last hope to get home before the end of the war."[65] Why no mention of the German victory at Coronel, Spee's visit to Valparaiso, and the celebration? Perhaps there was a missing letter, though that seems unlikely. Witzke wrote to his family on November 7, 1915, only four days after Spee's visit; there is nothing in that letter about Coronel or Spee in Valparaiso. Other than a missing letter, there is no obvious explanation for these omissions.

On December 8, 1914, Germany's East Asia Squadron, steaming up the east coast of South America for Santa Elena, Argentina, was destroyed in battle at the Falkland Islands. The encounter, though, was not the one Spee had imagined. Faulty intelligence or disinformation, and perhaps hubris, had misled Spee into believing that the Royal Navy ships that were hunting him had not yet reached the Falklands' Stanley Harbour. He therefore thought that he could easily attack and defeat any residual force he might find there, safely re-coal and re-provision, and perhaps kidnap the British governor as a prize. Therefore, instead of steaming past the Falklands to Santa Elena, he detoured into Stanley Harbour. There he was confronted by a British squadron of overwhelming force, under command of Vice Admiral Sturdee, that had been assembled to track and destroy him and that had arrived at the Falklands the day before. The British squadron consisted of two battle cruisers (sufficient unto themselves to defeat the East Asia Squadron), three armored cruisers, and two light cruisers. In the ensuing battle, four of the German squadron's five warships were sunk, and more than 2,000 German seamen were killed. Only the *Dresden* escaped, returning to the west coast of South America to hide in the myriad fiords of Chile for several months before it, too, would be found and destroyed by its British pursuers.[66]

News of the German defeat at the Falklands reached Valparaiso shortly after the battle. Anti-German sentiment had been rising among the local population, exacerbated by a price increase on the German-owned city tram. Rioters smashed windows of German bars and shops and attacked the consulate. Young sailors on shore leave now had to be careful.[67] Witzke was depressed. "Still no option has come up to get away from here," he wrote. "Now that *Scharnhorst*, *Gneisenau*, *Leipzig* and *Nürnberg* are destroyed we can very well give up hope forever. We especially feel the loss of these cruisers as from every ship here some men were so lucky to go with them. From the *J. C. Vinnen*, the carpenter Hermann Hackspill went down with the *Scharnhorst*."[68] Witzke also anticipated a cut in salary by up to half for the entire crew.[69]

Christmas 1914 raised spirits somewhat. Witzke bought himself fruit, sardines, wine, cheese, sausage, cocoa, and sugar. There would also be roast pork.[70] He celebrated twice, once at a party hosted by the local German club for 300 seamen from interned vessels, and the second time on board ship where the roast pork was featured and everyone got drunk.[71] Anticipating the pay cut that would allow him legally to jump ship, Witzke began planning a train trip over the Andes to Buenos Aires. But the captain needed the crew to maintain the ship and so there was no pay cut.[72] In late January 1915, Witzke tried to join the Danish steamer *Transvaal* as a sailor, but its ranks were full.[73] Then, in a letter at the end of January, he told his parents they should not worry about his leaving Valparaiso because there were no more German warships outside Germany to join. "I would have been very happy if I could have joined one of the cruisers [of the East Asia Squadron], but those who have served were given priority."[74]

Meanwhile the *Dresden*, the only cruiser of the East Asia Squadron to have escaped British revenge at the Falklands, was playing cat and mouse along the coast of Chile with a British squadron sent to search for and destroy her. She succeeded in evading detection until March 8, 1915. On that day the

British cruiser *Kent* sighted her not far from Coronel, gave chase, but could not close, and the *Dresden* escaped once more. But not for long. On March 14 the *Glasgow* (seriously damaged at Coronel but now repaired), *Kent*, and *Orama* found her again, anchored in Chilean waters off the coast of the San Fernando Islands (of Robinson Caruso fame). After a five-minute battle, the *Dresden* surrendered. Her crew then scuttled her and rowed ashore. There were nine German dead and fifteen injured. The *Orama* transported the most seriously injured (three officers, twelve seamen) to Valparaiso, where they were taken by ambulance to the German hospital. The rest of the crew was taken on Chilean ships to Valparaiso harbor where they were briefly detained on the *Yorck* before being transferred to Quiriquina Island, where they were interned until the end of the war.[75]

According to Witzke's letters, on Friday morning, February 13 (a month before the sinking of the *Dresden*), Witzke broke his leg in an accident on the *J. C. Vinnen* and was hospitalized for two and a half months; at the hospital, he met and befriended the injured *Dresden* officers and sailors when they were transported there in March. We will address the relevance of this and the other *Dresden* details. But first, we flesh out how Witzke came to be hospitalized with the injured *Dresden* survivors and how he came to know them.

The accident occurred when a punt fell overboard and dangled on a chain by the side of the ship. Witzke wrote to his parents that he was ordered to climb into the punt and keep it from banging into the ship's hull. He did so, but as soon as he got on the chain broke and the punt with Witzke in it dropped into the water. Because the punt had been dangling six meters above the water line, the fall, as Witzke wrote, "was no small thing." He remembered hearing a crack followed by a rapid drop, a hard impact, and the punt filling half up with water. He was moaning and could not breathe. The crew stood at the ship's railing, helpless. He shouted up to them that his knee was broken, that he could not move. During the next half hour, they got him back on deck, laid him on the bridge, and cut the pants off his badly swollen leg. Meanwhile the captain had gotten a doctor to come from a nearby North German Lloyd steamer and called for an ambulance. Witzke was chloroformed and his leg was put in splints and bandaged. Then he was carried ashore on a stretcher, put in the ambulance, and taken to the local German hospital. "I'm telling you," he wrote,

> that was a hell ride, for the roads in Chile are no better than those in Russia. I screamed and cried . . . . After a half hour's ride we arrived at the hospital, I was carefully put to bed, the bandage was taken off and I

felt much better. Then they took two x-rays and it turned out that it was a simple femur fracture right above the joint. Then I lay until Monday without a bandage so the swelling would go down, always got a morphine injection at night and on Monday morning I was chloroformed again, the leg was wrapped and put into an extension bandage. So now I have to lay here until everything is fine again.[76]

Witzke was impressed by the hospital. It was "modern and hygienic," the beds were "sparkling clean," the food was "amazing," and the nurses were "nice and friendly." By the end of his first weekend, he had already had many visits from friends. He predicted his stay would be "a wonderful time, like one big holiday."[77] A few weeks later, he would reaffirm this initial impression. "I think it's wonderful here, nothing but sleeping, reading and eating all day long. The food is impeccable by the way."[78] The worst thing," he said, "is that now there's no chance for me to participate in the war, for in two months the war will be long over."[79] His confidence that the war would be "long over" in two months is at odds with his sense of things in his letters preceding the accident. Perhaps something said in recent mail from the homeland had boosted his confidence.

In mid-March 1915, the injured survivors of the *Dresden* were brought to the German hospital. Witzke refers to them for the first time in a letter home dated April 12. He says that he has had "quite nice chats" with them during the prior four weeks, but on the day he is writing seven of them are being transferred from the hospital to Quirquina Island, south of Vaparaiso not far from Coronel where the interned *Dresden* crew was being held. It will be "very lonely" as a result, Witzke says, because there are only four patients left including him, who are out of bed.

Witzke was released from the German hospital on April 30. He was given a farewell party at which "nurse Hanna" asked to give him her picture. All the nurses promised to knit him a woolen scarf and bring it to him on the *Vinnen,* "Yes! Yes! Mom your boy is always lucky with the girls even if he's not always dressed his best." His leg, though, was still "pretty stiff" and would "never bend completely again." Probably he would not be able to go to sea again unless he developed more flexibility in the leg, and his captain was talking about sending him home by steamer at the end of the war, rather than sail, because it would be too dangerous for him to work on a sailing ship. He would stay in Valparaiso until the war was over, then come home by steamer.[80]

Back on the *Vinnen,* his workload was light because of his leg. But his leg was healing quickly, and he began to worry that if the war did not end soon he would have to stay on the *Vinnen*.[81] In a May 23 letter, he says that he is planning to go back to the hospital to visit the nurses and his "friends from the *Dresden*."[82] Then in early June he writes for a last time about the *Dresden*. The day before his *Dresden* friends were released to Quiriquina, he visited them at the hospital "once more and walked around town with them a bit."[83]

◇　◇　◇

The visit of the *Dresden* to Valparaiso on November 13, 1914, and its sinking in Valparaiso harbor in March of the following year, are key events in the life of Lothar Witzke that must be addressed by any biographer of this German agent, because of Witzke's later claim that he had been an officer on the *Dresden*. It will be recalled that, on the night of the day Witzke was sentenced to be hanged for espionage, the suicide-watch detail guarding him discovered, hidden in his cell, a short note in his handwriting in German, written on cigarette paper, stating, among other things, that he had been a lieutenant on the cruiser *Dresden* that was sunk near Valparaiso, Chile, and that he escaped internment because he lay two months in hospital (implying that he had been among the cruiser's injured when it went down). Two months later, in an interview with Captain Frank Stretton at Fort Sam Houston, Witzke "described in some detail the battle which took place when he was wounded. It appeared a fifteen-inch shell landed on the deck of his boat and exploded. A large fragment of shell struck him just below the knee, knocking him overboard and into the sea which apparently saved him as the boat went down." The interviewer added that, "in speaking of German naval operations, I have noticed that he frequently refers to the Dresden which apparently was the boat on which he was sailing."[84]

If Witzke's claim that he served on the *Dresden* is true, then one of two things must follow. Either Witzke never served on the *J. C. Vinnen*, and the entirety of the family correspondence discussed in this chapter is fabricated, or Witzke joined the *Dresden* during its November 13 visit to Valparaiso, and portions of his correspondence thereafter are fabricated. If the claim is false, then the biographer must explain the purpose of the (false) cigarette paper confession that was hidden in his cell, and that might never have been discovered even if Witzke had been hanged, and in any event the falsity of which could have been ascertained by an examination of contemporaneous records of the cruiser and the *J. C. Vinnen* that existed at the time but have since disappeared.

We address the authenticity of the correspondence elsewhere in this book. If his voluminous correspondence with his family was fraudulent, the scope of the fraud is breathtaking, as it would have involved fabricating numerous items of otherwise innocuous family correspondence. This is entirely implausible.

But it is also difficult to posit a satisfactory explanation for the cigarette paper confession if Witzke had not in truth been on the *Dresden*. Perhaps if he could have been sure that the paper would be discovered before his execution, then a plausible motive might have been the hope that a German naval officer would be better treated in detention while awaiting execution than would someone else. However, the paper was hidden, not placed in a way to ensure discovery, and certainly Witzke would not have known that his cell would be searched on the evening of his sentencing, unless the officers involved in the search were complicit and knew ahead of time that Witzke had "hidden" a paper that they were supposed to "discover." Equally, if its purpose was to secure better treatment by the American guards, it is unclear why Witzke wrote the note in German.

More plausible is that, as a young man about to die for his country in a foreign prison where no one outside the prison even knew of his fate, he wanted to leave some kind of legacy and hoped that after he was gone someone, even a future prisoner in the same cell, would discover his message. But this, too, begs the questions why he hid it and why he wrote in German. Why not be open about the *Dresden* claim? What benefit did secrecy offer, whether the claim was true or not?

The *Dresden*'s logbook survived her sinking, and the British published parts of it in 1915.[85] There is nothing in the published extracts identifying the officers and sailors who served on her, or were taken on board in Valparaiso during her short stop there in November 1914, or were injured when the cruiser was sunk in March 1915.

But there remains a diary of the British surgeon, T. B. Dixon, who served on the *Kent* (the British cruiser that sank the *Dresden*), and who treated the *Dresden* injured, and oversaw their transfer to the German hospital at Valparaiso.[86] Surgeon Dixon's March 14/15 entry describes the sinking of the *Dresden* and his watching a "stream of boats filled with half dressed" survivors making for shore. He was ordered ashore to attend to the wounded and did so. He describes encountering them. There were "about 10 of them lying about . . . all badly wounded." They had received first aid by the time Dixon got there, so he moved onto the verandah of a nearby house, where he met up with two fleet surgeons and three other wounded. The three surgeons "set to work operating on the spot." Orders came to remove the wounded to *HMS Orama*. Apparently, one of the three wounded was taken away and Dixon sat with the other two until the stretchers came. After this, he found two more wounded at other houses and saw to it that they were removed to the *Orama*.

Dixon returned to the *Kent* for lunch, then at 2 pm went across to the *Orama* where he encountered two of *Orama's* surgeons amputating the leg of a German lieutenant above the knee. Dixon was ordered to stay on the *Orama* and accompany the wounded Germans to Valparaiso, which he did. "We worked on, with an interval for dinner, until midnight at compound fractures, etc., and then next morning started again and didn't finish until the late afternoon." He then summarizes, "There were 12 badly wounded Germans and four not so serious. One lieutenant, one midshipman, an engineer and wireless man, and seamen. . . . The lieutenant was assiduous in translating the requests of his men and generally looking after them, although he was in severe pain and must have felt the loss of his right leg and the consequent end of his career in the Navy."

Thus, among the wounded, there was, according to Dixon's diary, only one officer of lieutenant rank, and that officer had had his leg amputated above the knee. This lieutenant could not have been Lothar Witzke because his leg, though injured at the knee, was not amputated. Moreover, we now know the names and ranks of all the *Dresden* wounded who were hospitalized at Valparaiso, thanks to a long-forgotten telegram from the German naval attaché in Washington to the chief of admiralty in Berlin that was published contemporaneously in the *Times* of London.[87] It turns out that the lieutenant with the amputated leg was not the only lieutenant among the wounded; there were two others who were slightly injured. The published telegram establishes that neither of the other two lieutenants, nor any of the other wounded, was named Lothar Witzke.

Witzke, it can now be said with certainty, was not an officer (or non-officer) on the *Dresden* who broke his leg when the cruiser was sunk by the British. Rather, just as described in his letters to his family, he broke his leg in mid-February 1915 in an accident on the *J. C. Vinnen*, and was already in a hospital recovering from his injury when the *Dresden* wounded arrived there the following month. Witzke's cigarette paper confession was a lie.[88]

Witzke may, though, have had an encounter of a different nature with the *Dresden* and Spee's fleet sometime after the Battle of Coronel and before the fleet left Chilean waters for its fateful engagement at the Falklands. In a long interview in 1934 in Hankow, China (where he was then working),

Witzke told the American Vice Consul that, when the war began, all German merchant marine cadets were automatically transferred to the navy and that he saw "active duty" when Spee's fleet arrived off the coast of Chile. "We youngsters were kept busy running ammunition, coal and supplies out from points along the coast to the cruisers, particularly after the German victory at Coronel and before the dash around to the Argentine coast."[89] The statement constitutes an implicit admission by Witzke that he never served as an officer or sailor on the *Dresden*. It also represents an explicit claim that he helped supply Spee's fleet for a time while the *J. C. Vinnen* was interned at Valparaiso.

The claim is plausible in the following sense. The laws of war constrained the number of warships that Spee could send into a neutral port such as Valparaiso at any one time (three), the length of time a single such warship could stay there (not more than twenty-four hours), the amount of coal they could take on (enough only to reach the nearest German port), and the frequency with which they could obtain coal in any port of the same nationality (once only every three months). It was necessary, therefore, for the fleet to be supplied clandestinely offshore. We know that this was done, that various colliers transported stores and coal to the fleet from Valparaiso to Más Afuera 400 miles off the Chilean coast where the fleet was hiding. We also know that hundreds of German seamen and stokers from merchantmen stranded at Valparaiso had offered to join the fleet, and that 127 seamen and stokers had been accepted. At least some of these, maybe most of them, had been accepted to facilitate the transfer of stores and coal from the colliers to the warships.[90]

Witzke made reference to Spee's recruitment at Valparaiso in a letter he wrote shortly after the *Dresden* put into Valparaiso harbor on November 13, 1914.[91] He says nothing in the letter about having volunteered his own services or having participated himself in the clandestine supply effort. His silence does not mean it did not happen. He had reason to fear that his letters might fall into the wrong hands, reason also to protect himself from future reprisals if his participation were discovered. Still, one wonders. His willingness in later years to say he did things that were not true but made him look good (such as that he served as a lieutenant on the *Dresden* and got injured when it was sunk), do not give confidence that he was telling the truth to an American government official in Hankow.

In sum, Lothar Witzke did not serve on the *Dresden* and was not a naval officer. His sole possible connection to the *Dresden* might have involved helping to provide coal to the *Dresden* while it was at Valparaiso. The cigarette paper note of 1918 was therefore a lie to the extent that it spoke of Witzke as a naval officer injured on the *Dresden*. There is no satisfying explanation why Witzke chose to write in German and to conceal in his cell a lie about service on the *Dresden*, especially because the lie could have been readily exposed by documents available at the time. The best explanation is that Witzke was, even at his darkest moment on death row, given to false boasting. It sounded good, even glorious, to present himself as an injured veteran of the ill-fated *Dresden*.

RESTLESSNESS IN VALPARAISO

Once he was out of the hospital, Witzke's letters home became more and more focused on escaping Valparaiso and planning his life after employment on the *J. C. Vinnen* ended. In his May 23, 1915 letter, he wrote that if, as expected, his knee joint remained a bit stiff and weak as a consequence of his accident, he would have to give up his career as a sailor.[92] He pressed his father to write to the trade association to find out whether he could obtain compensation for his pain and suffering.[93] He asked his mother to write to a relative in North America named Arnold that her son was stranded in South America and might travel north to visit him.[94] In July he thought about signing on to the Norwegian sailing ship *Haba* bound for Copenhagen, but decided that his leg was not sufficiently recovered to risk it.[95] His restlessness reached a high pitch in September. "Although we're not doing bad," he wrote, "one hopes from day to day for something fundamental to change and that we be released from our duties or get away in another way. One is in a sort of prison from which, apart from a couple of Sunday walks, one cannot escape, and you can imagine how unbearable this state becomes after a while."[96] Witzke could endure much, but not boredom. And his life to come would to the end be anything but boring.

In October 1915, Witzke complained, as he had before, about Vinnen's failure to promote him. He had graduated from cadet to seaman, but was being denied a promotion to sailor to which he felt entitled by virtue of his months of service; and he asked his father to intervene with Vinnen:

> We unfortunately have not been promoted, we've been ordinary seamen since the 12th month and get 20 Marks a month, but now we've been on board for 27 months already and aren't sailors yet, which we ought to have been since the 24th month, for otherwise every month beyond the 24th is

not calculated in the service period. Couldn't dad contact Vinnen, so our service from the 24th month [onwards] will be calculated as sailors? Even if we don't get sailor's pay, one is glad to get the time on a sailing ship over and done with.[97]

Later in the same month, depressed at not having received any mail for six weeks ("Are you not writing anymore, or is your mail being intercepted?"), and suffering from "deadly boredom," Witzke confessed to his parents that he had toyed with the idea of abandoning ship: "One gets the craziest thoughts. . . . I already seriously considered a couple of times whether one shouldn't run away from board and try one's luck ashore. But there are too many unemployed people running around here, and this always holds one back."[98] As Christmas approached, Witzke's spirits roused a bit, especially when he received a one hundred-mark gift from his parents that he used to buy a long wished-for camera.[99] But he was also, it seems, drinking more heavily, and he was not shy about describing a "big hangover" to his parents.[100] His mother was sufficiently concerned to admonish him: "Please, do not start drinking if you have an opportunity to do it often, because that would be terrible for your future life."[101]

Once the Christmas and New Year holidays passed, boredom and restlessness reasserted themselves. In a letter dated January 20, 1916—his first of the new year— Witzke wrote: "On board everything's as usual, one is pretty vegetating."[102] When his father wrote him that he should not complain about his life, and that compared to the fate of soldiers back home he had no reason to be unhappy, he replied: "But that is just the point, we're doing well and have nothing to do, and that's it! This inactivity becomes unbearable after some time! We're used to all kinds of exertions, and fighting, even if it's just with the elements, is our goal in life, and just when there's something real to fight, we're not in it! Someone else can be content with that!"[103] As much as possible, when not ferrying the captain to shore and back again, he filled his time with photography, following the progress of the postal ships from Holland as reported in the newspapers, and war news.[104] This was January 1916. Young Lothar's path for the rest of 1916 (and thereafter) would more than fulfill his "goal in life" to have "all kinds of exertions."

JUMPING SHIP

On Sunday, April 9, 1916, Witzke jumped ship. The precipitating event, according to a letter he sent his parents announcing the move, was Vinnen's refusal to count his lay days in Valparaiso as credit towards his promotion to sailor.[105] He asked the captain to pay him off and let him go, but the captain refused. So he sold his camera, pulled out the rest of his money, gathered his personal effects, and left. He says that he "found an excellent position," rented a furnished room with an acquaintance, and has since been living "like a lord in France."

> I am earning 8 to 10 P per day on the average, never less than 8, that is 48-60 P per week. Deducting 25 P for room and board leaves me every week still enough spending money. I live with a German family, sleep for the first time in a long time on a mattress, have easy and pleasant work, get excellent and plentiful food,—so, what more does one want? I do not see why I should slave on board ship, day by day from 6-6 o'clock, with poor food and hard work, when the time of voyage is not counted.[106]

Witzke never says what the "excellent position" he found on land was. Did he become involved in some way in intelligence work? Years later, he would say that, when he decided to leave Chile, the German consulate in Valparaiso gave him a secret code with which to identify himself to consular officials in San Francisco. However, there is no evidence to indicate he was doing any intelligence work at the time.

The references to hard work and toiling away on board ship versus the easy and pleasant work he has found on land are curious, given the boredom and light workload that he repeatedly described in his letters of the prior year. Perhaps this was a guilty conscience seeking parental approval for his misbehavior and anticipating their dismay. Paul Witzke was shocked and angry to learn of his son's "dishonorable" conduct. "What you did can only do harm to your future," the father wrote back to his son, "and legally there is no excuse for such a step. . . . Did you consider what it means to commit a breach of contract? What is the use of making money if your honor suffers thereby? Think of the embarrassment in which you place myself and your brothers." He concluded his lengthy reprimand with what amounted to a command: "I expect *with certainty* that you will excuse your step with the captain and resume your post on the ship."[107]

Meanwhile, the son, who would not receive his father's angry reprimand for several months, was encountering unexpected headwinds. Just two weeks after jumping ship and procuring his "excellent" new job on land, there was a labor strike. He could not find other work. The US passenger steamer *Colusa* that plied between Valparaiso and the west coast of the United States was in port, and Witzke made an impulsive decision to head for San Francisco on the *Colusa*.[108]

SAN FRANCISCO

The circumstances of Lothar Witzke's May 1916 voyage to San Francisco, and his life there and elsewhere in North America from the time of his arrival to his arrest in Nogales, Arizona on February 1, 1918 on charges of espionage, would be much disputed in the months and years after his capture. What is not disputed is that he would get his wish for "something fundamental" in his life to change.

According to letters that he wrote to his family and friends, he signed on to the SS *Colusa* as a sailor under the name Hugo Williamson, born in Sweden (the alias was to protect him in case they encountered a British cruiser on the journey).[109] Apparently, though, no one on board believed he was a Swede.[110] The voyage north along the coast of South America included multiple, brief stops up the Pacific coast, then a longer stop at Guayaquil to pick up passengers. Witzke was contemptuous of the captain's recklessness, and described two harrowing incidents in a letter to his friend Christian Grau. At one stop, the captain ran the ship onto a mudbar, two meters from the mast of a sunken schooner sticking out of the water. It took three hours of struggle in the middle of the night to set the ship free. At Guayaquil, the captain drove the ship full steam toward a coast that was close enough for the sailors to see houses distinctly. The ship ran aground and could not get off until high tide lifted it several hours later. There was also an incident closer to San Francisco, when it was discovered that the ship had taken on eight feet of water in its fore section and four feet in its rear. It turned out the ship was leaking seventeen inches per hour and the pumps had to be run constantly for the rest of the voyage.[111]

The *Colusa* arrived at San Francisco on May 21, 1916.[112] The captain offered Witzke fifty-five dollars per month to stay with the ship, which was headed to British Columbia in Canada, but Witzke deemed a visit to Canada too risky for a German national whose homeland was (unlike the United States at the time) at war with Great Britain, and he disembarked in San Francisco. San Francisco, not Canada and not permanent employment at sea, had been his objective from the moment of his decision to join the *Colusa* in Valparaiso. His first letters to his parents and to Christian Grau from San Francisco, both dated May 21, are infused with a new energy and excitement. Barely off the ship, and apparently not yet having even found a place to stay, he was already singing the praises of the city. To his parents: "S.F. is a great city and especially the Panama Exhibition must have been something marvelous. Most of the buildings are still there." To Grau: "What I shall begin I do not yet know at all. . . . My next objective is New York. Whether by land or sea I do not yet know. There is enough work in Frisco because 300 sailors are up in Alaska for the fishing."[113]

Though Witzke's next objective may have been New York (and then Germany), within a few days he was headed, instead, for an obscure mining town 265 miles southeast of San Francisco as the crow flies.

KEELER, CA

Keeler, California, on the eastern shore of Owens Lake deep in the Sierra Nevada Mountains, was in 1916 a twenty-four-hour train ride from San Francisco. It was both the last stop on the Carson and Colorado Railroad and a terminal for steamboats crossing the lake between Keeler and Cartago. Ore from nearby mines and the smelter at Swansea (principally zinc, but also silver, lead and limestone) was transported from Keeler by rail to its final destination in Los Angeles.[114]

There was a soda plant in Keeler, and it was to the soda plant that Witzke made his way at the end of May 1916, only a few days after disembarking in San Francisco. He had been offered a position there as foreman at a salary of two dollars and fifty cents per day plus free board. It is unclear how Witzke came so quickly to be hired for the job. His statement to his parents that work was easy to come by "because 300 sailors are up in Alaska for the fishing" may have explained employment opportunities on ships anchored at San Francisco, but it does not account for employment in remote Keeler.

The individual in charge of the Keeler soda plant at the time that Witzke was hired was a German chemist from Berkeley, California, by the name of Carl Elschner. Witzke would later say, in a 1934 interview, that, as soon as he arrived in San Francisco, he reported to the head of the German Secret Service there (presumably, Consul General von Bopp or Vice Consul von Schack) who directed German espionage throughout that part of the western United States, using a code word given to him in Valparaiso to identify himself. "My youthful appearance, my merchant marine training, and natural talents convinced the 'chief' that I might be of greater service to Germany as a spy than as a naval officer. My service began immediately." If true (aside from the falsity that he had been a naval officer), a recommendation by the German consul general could account for his swift introduction to Elschner and his posting to Keeler. There is some evidence that Elschner himself was a secret German agent who had been directed the previous year by the German general staff in Berlin to set up a spy operation on the West Coast independent of von Bopp. As to why the Germans might have wanted to send a spy to Keeler, a possible answer is that a major new aqueduct for carrying water from the streams that fed Owens Lake to the city of Los Angeles 200 miles to the south had recently been completed. Perhaps Witzke was supposed to reconnoiter the new aqueduct for possible sabotage against it. Whatever the motive, innocent or nefarious, for Witzke's employment, he left for Keeler on May 28, only a week after arriving in San Francisco.[115]

Accommodations at Keeler were primitive, and Witzke, like other plant employees, was housed in a two-man tent. That he did not expect to stay long is evident from the first letter he wrote to his parents from Keeler, a week after arriving there. He had already saved ten dollars, he said, and once he saved a bit more he intended to "look over the United States further." He gave as his mailing address the German Consulate in New York.[116]

For the moment, he seemed content with his work and the isolated location of Keeler. On June 10 he wrote that "it is beautiful and healthful here and the work is easy and interesting." Moreover, the plant "manager, a German chemist," had already promised him a promotion to plant superintendent and a doubling of his salary in a few years, if he stuck around. He said that he could not make up his mind and asked his parents what they thought about it. At the same time, he noted in the very next sentence that Keeler and its surroundings were "dry," meaning it was not permitted to buy or sell alcohol there. Clearly, for all its beauty and healthfulness, Keeler and its soda plant were not, in this young man's mind, Shangri La.[117]

He did not await his parents' answer. A few days later, pressed by the manager to make a two-year commitment and unwilling to do so, Witzke quit his soda plant job and, together with his German tent-mate, set off for Los Angeles. The precipitating event, he said, was a tent fire, started by a stray cigarette butt, which consumed his personal effects and left him with only the work clothes he was wearing.[118] The morning after the fire, the two tent-mates, equipped with a half-liter bottle of water and some biscuits, hiked twenty miles through the high desert to the main rail station to Los Angeles. (Hiring a car to the station would have cost five dollars):

> At 9 we started and walked through the desert, without rest, constantly through sand up to the ankle, until noon. No house, no tree, no water, only rocks, sand and prairie grass. At 12 we were completely parched with thirst and could hardly continue. It is enormously hot in the thin, high air. We

dragged ourselves along for a while, then we found a very small sulphur spring. With our hands we dug a basin and tried to drink the water. It tasted quite awfully like hydrogen sulphide and also smelled like it. At four, when we were already quite desperate, we found a strong sulpher spring. One could not drink the water but we took a bath. We then crept along and found the rails and around 7 we came to a signpost with the inscription "Olancha." The post, in the Wild West, takes the place of houses and men and everything else one is accustomed to connect with a station. We laid ourselves in the sand and waited and half an hour later the train arrived.[119]

THE PLEASURE YACHT FIORGYN

They reached Los Angeles at 10:00 the next morning. An hour later, according to Witzke, he found employment as quartermaster on the American pleasure yacht *Fiorgyn* at a salary of fifty dollars per month. The owner was a local borax millionaire who seldom sailed, and then only on short outings, and therefore the working hours were, in Witzke's words, "great": "four hours work, then 1-1/2 days free." As for the food, "no captain in Germany has anything like it. Eggs with bacon or ham, roast, fruits, cold cuts and other such things." Nevertheless, he did not know how long he would stay, and instructed his parents to continue sending mail c/o the German consulate in New York.[120]

How was Witzke able to secure a cushy job on a luxury pleasure yacht within an hour of arriving in Los Angeles, having trekked twenty miles the previous day through high desert in the summer heat without sufficient hydration and without clothing other than what he was wearing, and then having spent the night in a (presumably) cheap seat on a train to Los Angeles? Could it be that the tent-fire and the twenty mile desert trek were camouflage to entertain friend Grau, that these events never happened, and that Witzke's employment by a Borax millionaire was obtained in the same way as his employment at Keeler: through the connection between Consul General Bopp and the German chemist Elschner, who managed the soda plant and whose mining contacts might easily have included the general manager of the Sterling Borax Company?

As to why Witzke would choose at that moment to take a job on a boat, having decided only a few weeks before to abandon the sailor's life and see America, his 1934 Hankow interview may provide a clue. Witzke says in the interview that, even as he signed on to be a spy, he kept the role of sailor as a cover should he need to explain his presence in West Coast ports (such presence, one can infer, being for the purpose of engaging in acts of espionage there). "A short trip on a coastwise vessel" gave him his first discharge paper, "which endowed me with a definite status as a sailor with experience. It marked the attainment of my first objective," i.e., to explain his presence in any port where he might find himself.[121] This possible explanation of why Witzke chose employment on the *Fiorgyn* is not perfect. Witzke never says in the interview that his "short trip on a coastwise vessel" was his two-week quartermaster job on the *Fiorgyn*. Moreover, in his re-telling of it, the short trip is mixed in with events we know did not occur until a year later (his obtaining certificates of able seaman and lifeboat operator). The explanation is plausible but conjecture only.

Witzke's employment on the *Fiorgyn* was in any event as short-lived as his employment at the Keeler soda plant: a mere two weeks, from June 17 to July 1, according to a chronology of his comings and goings that summer that Witzke himself seems to have prepared in 1916–1917.[122]

WITZKE MEETS KURT JAHNKE

Either just before or just after Keeler and the *Fiorgyn*, Lothar Witzke made the most consequential acquaintance of his young life: the German naval intelligence operative Kurt Jahnke. The two met, or were introduced, at The Heidelberg Inn, a popular hangout of the German and German-American communities in San Francisco.[123] The hapless Gustav Wild, who would fund Witzke's ill-fated chauffeur business the following year and be arrested in 1918 as a suspected accomplice of Witzke in the black powder magazine bombing at Mare Island naval station, was a cashier at the Inn. Located at Thirty-Five Ellis Street, just around the corner from Market Street, the restaurant was easy to miss if you were not looking for it, just a small sign and stairs leading down to a basement door. On the other side of the basement door was what a contemporary restaurant guide called "one of the very few real Bohemian restaurants of San Francisco."[124] In addition to cold beer, hearty food, and decorative details that mimicked the Heidelberg rathskeller, there was camaraderie and nightly music. "It is when the martial strains of 'Die Wacht am Rhein' are heard from the orchestra, which of itself is an institution, that the true camaraderie of the place is appreciated, for then guests, waiters, barkeepers, and even the eagle-eyed, gray-haired manager, join in the swelling chorus, and you can well understand why German soldiers are inspired to march to victory when they hear these stirring chords."[125] It was the perfect venue for recruiting a twenty-one-year-old, homesick sailor to join Germany's naval intelligence service.

Kurt Jahnke, an expatriated German national, was a former US Marine who had been stationed in the Philippines and at Mare Island Naval Station north of San Francisco before his discharge in 1910. After the Marines he became involved in the West Coast's maritime underworld, including the smuggling of illegal Chinese labor into the United States. He was living in San Francisco when World War I began.[126] Unable to return to Germany because the English were stopping neutral flag vessels in the Atlantic to search for German nationals who were subject to military conscription in the home-land, Jahnke offered his services to the German consulate in San Francisco. Vice Consul von Schack hired him to figure out how to get fuel and supplies to Spee's East Asia Squadron then cruising the Pacific, to gather intelligence that would be useful to the Squadron, and to get that information to Spee.[127]

After the East Asia Squadron was destroyed at the Falklands in December 1914, Jahnke was reassigned to more traditional espionage work in the United States and Canada. This meant gathering information about war materials orders placed by the Allies in the US, the nature and volume of arms and munitions production, and the destinations of arms and munitions trans-ports as well as, in Jahnke's words, "shadowing people who were thought to be informers or agents of the Allies." Jahnke also monitored West Coast newspapers for information relevant to the German command, investigated British newspaper propaganda, and established relationships with third-party groups that might be hostile to the Allies and sympathetic to Germany, such as persons in the Indian and Irish independence movements.[128] Additionally, at the time of his first dinner with Witzke, Jahnke was employed as a night watchman by the Morse Detective and Patrol Service.[129]

We do not know the details of Jahnke's first dinner with Witzke. No doubt they downed a stein or two of beer, perhaps shared a plate of the Inn's sauer-braten, and joined the other patrons in singing patriotic German songs that were played by the Inn's orchestra. We do know that the two men got on well, that by the end of the evening Witzke had signed on as Jahnke's sub-agent, and that within a few days or weeks of meeting, they became roommates.[130] Witzke would provide a summary description of his meeting in an affidavit to which he swore a decade later:

> I met in a restaurant which was frequented by Germans and German-
> Americans a Mr. Kurt Jahnke whom I had not previously known. It soon

appeared that like myself he hailed from the Province of Posen and thus we soon became intimate and also discussed my plans for returning home. He explained to me that it was difficult or, rather, impossible to get to Germany and that for this reason he himself had decided to stay in the United States. He also divulged to me that he was holding a position as confidential man of the German Consulate General in San Francisco in the information and intelligence service and that he could use more assistants for his work. I accepted his suggestion to enter this service and after I had been introduced to the other gentlemen employed in the Consulate General, I became for the first time active in the position of an agent for the German Government.[131]

WITZKE THE SPY

Lothar Witzke is mostly remembered for his alleged acts of sabotage—Black Tom, Kingsland, and Mare Island Naval Station. His espionage has received less attention even though it was espionage, not sabotage, that led to his capture, conviction, and sentence to be hanged. He always denied involvement in Black Tom, Kingsland, and Mare Island. He admitted to being a spy. We present and evaluate the evidence that Witzke was a saboteur in Part 3 of this book. Here, we recount what is known about his life as a spy during the year and a half preceding his journey to Nogales and capture there in early 1918. This part of his life had two distinct phases: one, the period before the United States declared war on Germany on April 6, 1917 and two, the period after.

Launching a New Career: Espionage

Witzke's parents were alarmed when they learned that their son had abandoned his quartermaster job on the *Fiorgyn* only days after securing it. "You do not write at all why, and what you intend to do now," Paul Witzke wrote back the day after receiving his son's news. "I cannot give you any advice from here, but if you can do it, use every opportunity to educate yourself further, if possible for the profession you started in."[132] Lothar's response was polite but defiant. "You ask me why I gave up the yacht? America is the strangest country in the world and I should like to come to know it as much as possible. If I wanted to sit still at one place, I could have just as well stayed on the J. C. Vinnen. I do my best to stick to my profession, but it cannot always be done."[133] No mention, of course, of his new trade: spying.

Witzke the spy did not "sit still at one place." His family letters, postcards, and private notebook entries show that, after Keeler and the *Fiorgyn*, he traveled extensively throughout the United States. San Francisco was his base of operations to which he would always return. But the places from which he returned spanned the continent; they included Eureka, Seattle, Salt Lake City, El Paso, Chicago, New York, and the Chesapeake Bay area. By the beginning of 1917, Witzke could tell his parents, "I know now almost all of America. I was in the West, in the Middle and in the East, near the British [i.e., Canadian] and near the Mexican border."[134] His favorite part of the country was the Pacific Northwest, but his longest single trip, made in the company of Kurt Jahnke, was to the east coast. The two colleagues left San Francisco for New York City on October 1 and did not arrive back in San Francisco until December 9, 1916.

Part of Witzke's travel was courier work. He was entrusted to deliver sensitive documents that the German authorities could not risk sending by ordinary mail. "At that time," he told one interviewer, "I was a Naval Officer of the German Navy and I could be trusted with anything."[135] But the bulk of his espionage in 1916 was maritime-related reconnaissance for which his experience as a sailor and his familiarity with port operations and the docks made him especially well-suited. This work was concentrated on San Francisco but required occasional trips to other Pacific coast ports, including Portland, Seattle, and Tacoma in the US and Vancouver and Victoria in Canada. Witzke would observe coastal ship movements and record ships' cargoes and destinations. War materials—lumber and nitrates in particular—were of special interest. He also monitored West Coast ship construction, munitions manufacture, and munitions shipments.[136] In addition to spying, he worked short stints as a painter's helper, a railway motorman, and a lunch cook.[137]

During his early months of service, Witzke moved easily and without incident among the sailors and stevedores with whom he interacted to gather the information he was tasked to obtain. But as the months passed, as war clouds began to blow across the American continent, he grew concerned about his personal safety. He lacked identity papers of a neutral (or Allied) power, an essential cover if the Americans were to turn against Germany. Moreover, his spy portfolio was expanding beyond the comfort zone of the docks. In the first quarter of 1917, Jahnke directed Witzke to try to obtain information that could be used to undermine the credibility of certain witnesses who were expected to testify against Consul General Bopp in a forthcoming trial in which Bopp was accused, among other things, of conspiring to blow up ammunition plants and ships.

Witzke's blond hair and blue eyes made it easy for him to pass as a Dane, a Norwegian, or a Swede. He had signed on to the SS *Colusa* from Valparaiso to San Francisco the previous spring under the name Hugo Williamson, born in Sweden, although his fellow sailors apparently did not believe it. Scandinavian identity papers would, Witzke was sure, provide the perfect cover. As Witzke would later tell it, he found his mark at a dockside bar in San Francisco:

> I came across in a bar a Swedish seaman whose features corresponded closely to mine. He was five feet, seven and one-half inches tall, medium build, blond and with blue eyes. Here was the man I was looking for. The man was drinking a bit and it was easy to strike up an acquaintance with him. I made myself an entertaining bar companion, buying more than my share of drinks and giving him a good time. We became friendly enough to exchange facts of a more personal nature and this led to a show of our identification papers. I almost betrayed my amazement and sheer delight at discovering that his certificate bore no picture. More drinking ensued and we started out on a drunken bust on the Barbary Coast [a local red light district]. While he was dead asleep I ended up this little drama with an automobile ride to a lonely spot on a beach road, where I stole his papers.[138]

Witzke finished off the heist, he says, by overturning the car "to give the authorities something else to worry about." Perhaps Witzke was just propounding a good story for his interviewer (where and how he got a car that was not traceable to him is not explained), but the story is generally believable. His girlfriend, whom he would meet that summer, knew him as Harry Anderson—perhaps the sailor's name whose papers he stole. In any event, Witzke claimed that he got his new papers just in time: the Canadians, he said, picked him up soon afterward in a draft roundup. His new papers saved him.

The Emergence of Pablo Waberski

Despite President Wilson's reelection in November 1916 and his strong personal inclination to keep the United States out of war, events were conspiring otherwise. On January 31, 1917, only days after the sabotage at Kingsland, New Jersey, Germany advised the American government that it would, beginning the following day, engage in unrestricted submarine warfare against all vessels approaching Great Britain. Wilson immediately severed diplomatic relations with Germany and on February 26 asked Congress for authority to arm US merchant ships. On March 1, the Zimmermann telegram went public, further arousing public sentiment against Germany. Sometime during these several weeks, Witzke decided that it was time to get out of town. He may also have been warned by Jahnke that he was "under suspicion." On March 23 he made his move, signing on as a sailor on the coastal steamer *San Pedro*, bound for Mexico.[139] He disembarked at Manzanillo in early April and made his way overland to Mexico City. There he introduced himself to the German Legation, disclosed the intelligence work he had been doing in the US, and offered his services. He was engaged to observe ship movements and the export of oil from Tampico and Veracruz.

Kurt Jahnke, too, escaped to Mexico as war closed in on the US. He and Witzke reconnected there in May 1917. Jahnke was putting together a new team of secret agents to undertake espionage and sabotage against the United States from Mexico. Witzke agreed to join the team. Once again, he would be a subagent of Jahnke. This time, though, his assignments would require him to cross the border into a country at war with Germany, and to move back and forth in and out of enemy territory.

Witzke was not sure that the Swedish identity papers he had stolen a few months before in San Francisco were sufficient cover for such purpose. His Swedish papers were doctored: he had affixed his own photo to someone else's identity. A slip on his part could spell doom. Better, if possible, to obtain properly issued papers—a passport best of all—identifying him as a citizen of an Allied power. He decided he would try to convince the Russians that he was a poor, hungry, out of work Russian mechanic named Paul Waberski who needed a passport to get back to Russia. As he would tell it many years later:

> Garbed in dirty, grease-stained overalls, with my hair unkempt and clotted, a sprouting beard, and a smell that rose to high heaven, I shuffled in the Russian Consulate General in Mexico City, posing as a Russian mechanic. Starting with one of the minor clerks, progressing through the vice consuls and consuls, and then finally up to the consul-general himself. I kept repeating the story I had concocted.
>
> No, I didn't speak Russian, not one word, but it happened that I knew a bit of Polish, as quite a lot of it was spoken around Posen owing to its large Polish element. I explained that I was born in the Russian town of Chenstochowo, and that while a child I had been taken by my parents to the United States, which accounted for my knowledge of English.[140]

Chenstochowo (Częstochowa) was not a random choice. Witzke had vacationed there with relatives several times as a child. He knew the public buildings and the main cathedral with its famous image of the Black

Madonna. He could, therefore, talk knowledgeably about the Russian city where he was allegedly born and had spent his early childhood. Gradually, he wore his interlocutors down. The Russian ambassador, with whom he eventually met, promised to give him identity papers for travel (though not a passport) if he could find a Russian person with a Russian passport who knew him and could vouch for him. According to Witzke, "It chanced that one of the cleverest spies in the pay of Germany in Mexico at that time possessed a genuine Russian passport. This man thereupon accompanied me to the Russian Embassy and promptly convinced the Ambassador that he had known me and my parents for years, and that my story was true in its entirety."[141] The ambassador was persuaded. He gave Witzke a paper, duly stamped, sealed, and with Witzke's photo affixed to it, certifying that Witzke was a Russian citizen. Witzke says he took this document with him to Veracruz, repeated his story to the Russian consul there, and that based on the Embassy's certification of his Russian citizenship, the consul gave him a passport.[142]

It may be that Witzke misremembered or embellished some of the details as to how he acquired his Russian identity. The Russian passport that he was carrying when he was captured at Nogales was issued by the Russian consulate in Mexico City, not Veracruz; it stated that Paul Waberski was a Russian citizen based on a certificate of citizenship issued on May 16, 1917 by the Russian vice consul of Veracruz, not Mexico City, and that he was returning to the United States where he had lived for the past seventeen years, not Russia. Nevertheless, the essential details are believable. Somehow in May 1917 Witzke accomplished the remarkable feat of convincing the Russian authorities in Mexico that, despite his not speaking a word of Russian, he was a Russian national named Paul Waberski and that they should issue him an official passport or paper certifying such.[143] On June 5, 1917, he crossed the border from Mexico to the United States at Laredo, Texas, on what would be the first of three missions for Kurt Jahnke under cover of his new Russian identity. His Alien Head Tax Receipt from the US Immigration authorities at Laredo identified him as a Russian named Pablo Waberski.[144] In the coming months, he would burnish his Russian credentials still further: registering for the draft (June 9) and obtaining able seaman and lifeboat man certificates (June 27), a driver's license (October 17) and a Mexican passport (November 15), all in the name of Paul or Pablo Waberski.[145]

WITZKE'S RETURN TRIPS TO THE US AS PABLO WABERSKI

Witzke made two trips from Mexico to the US during the summer (June 8–July 26) and fall (September 1–November 10) of 1917, using the cover of his new Russian identity.

Personal Life in the United States

We know something of his personal life that summer and fall from investigations done after his capture that are recounted in chapter 2.[146] He met his Berkeley girlfriend Sarah Gillespy at an Irish picnic in Oakland, who knew him as Harry Anderson. They dated throughout the summer and fall, a few dinners at the Heidelberg Inn, probably some dancing. They were intimate at some level and spoke to one another of love. She introduced him to her sister. He wrote to her when he was away. He also two-timed Sarah, picking up women, getting drunk with them, kissing passionately.

Witzke got a driver's license in the fall and bought a Ford car with Gustav Wild, the cashier at the Heidelberg Inn, who had lent him the money for his share. The two had planned to start a jitney business together. But the venture fell through when Witzke could not get a jitney license because he was not a US citizen. He continued to use the car for himself and was never able to repay Wild.

Witzke changed residential addresses a lot and was apparently hard up for cash, once even borrowing from Sarah in order to buy gas. The landlady who rented him a room a few weeks before the end of his fall trip said he was addicted to drink, came in at all hours of the night, slept late, never had visitors, never made phone calls, received lots of calls.

All in all, not an attractive picture of a master spy and saboteur. There was, however, more to Witzke than met the eye.

Professional Life

Kurt Jahnke sent Witzke back to the US to spy, not to play. There is reason to think that his sub-agent delivered. Witzke would later describe his summer and fall missions from Mexico to the US this way:

> On my two trips to the United States it was my task to observe the progress of the trial against the members of the Consulate General who had been arrested and if possible to aid them to flee. I had furthermore been

entrusted with establishing communications with followers of the Irish independence movement (Sinn Fein) and with establishing relations with anarchistic circles, particularly I.W.W. to support these with money if necessary and to send their members into belligerent countries with instructions for the purpose of instigating strikes, riots, mutinies and revolutions. I also was to use these relations with anarchistic organizations to cause their members to commit sabotage against munitions plants and factories on the territory of the United States who were then at war with us. On the first of these trips I was also instructed to call on an agent of the German Government named Shulenberg [Franz Shulenburg, also sometimes spelled Schulenberg or Schulenburg], who worked on the American west coast since the outbreak of the war and to deliver to him papers and invisible inks.[147]

These missions were not inconsequential; Witzke was no mere errand boy. He was being asked to perform intelligence work that required both skill and personal risk. Clearly, Jahnke had a high regard for his subordinate, a regard that he must have acquired during their collaboration the previous year (1916) after Witzke arrived in San Francisco.

(I) INVISIBLE INK FOR SCHULENBURG.

Franz Schulenburg was an early West Coast recruit of the German intelligence service who was mentored by Wilhelm von Brincken, military attaché at the German Consulate in San Francisco.[148] One of Schulenburg's more important assignments, in 1915, was to buy and deliver arms, ammunition, and explosives to Hindu rebels on the West Coast to blow up rail lines in western Canada. The project was conceived by Franz von Papen, the German military attaché at the German Embassy in Washington, DC, and was a joint effort of the embassy and the Consulates in San Francisco and Seattle. Papen paid Schulenburg well for the job but Schulenburg failed to perform. One version of the story has it that he got drunk and never delivered the goods. Another is that the rebels never showed up at the rendezvous site to collect. Whatever the problem, Schulenburg was not content with the payment he had received from von Papen, and proceeded to the San Francisco and Seattle Consulates to collect more. Von Papen was furious when he learned about it and had Schulenburg run out of the US to Mexico. After a short time there, Schulenburg started running guns and ammunition for the Germans in California.[149]

In September 1917, shortly after arriving in San Francisco on his fall trip (not his first, summer trip), Witzke met Schulenburg for dinner at the Hof-

Brau Restaurant on Market Street. He did not know Schulenburg and therefore began by asking him questions about who he was and whom he knew in Mexico. Once satisfied that his dinner guest was indeed Schulenburg, he gave him the invisible ink, letters, code, and cash that he had been entrusted to deliver. After dinner, Schulenburg left for Seattle, possibly, according to Witzke, to induce IWW representatives there to stir up trouble and commit sabotage, although he wasn't sure.[150]

Witzke ran into Schulenburg again, in November, on a train from Laredo to Mexico City. They talked a bit. Schulenburg told Witzke that the US authorities suspected him of causing trouble in Seattle and that he had barely managed to escape from the US. Witzke did not press for details and Schulenburg did not offer them. This was the last time Witzke saw Schulenburg.[151]

Schulenburg would not stay long in Mexico. He returned to California later that month and was arrested in early December in a saloon in San Jose. The police found in his room 150 sticks of dynamite, a coil of fuse, percussion caps, revolver and rifle ammunition, a Maxim silencer, and a "fine Luger type revolver."[152] He was eventually implicated in various plots to blow up government docks and shipping in Seattle, Portland, San Diego, San Francisco, and British Columbia, as well as shipment of dynamite and decoy uniforms to German agents on the Pacific Coast, arranging hiding places for such agents, and shipping wireless supplies to German agents in Mexico.[153]

(II) SINN FEIN; IWW

Witzke's assignment to establish "communications" with followers of the Irish independence movement and "relations" with anarchistic circles was consistent with broader German policy to seek support among anti-British revolutionary, separatist parties (e.g., Sinn Fein, the Hindu Ghadars) and anti-American socialist and labor groups (e.g., IWW). The hope was to provoke loyalists of these causes to engage in disruptive behavior (strikes, riots, rebellion) and sabotage that would interfere with the Allied war effort and divert war resources to combat them.

In his death row interview with Tom Tunney, the former bomb squad chief of the New York City police, Witzke gave specifics of the work he said he did in this regard during his summer and fall trips from Mexico to the US.[154] He recruited, he said, the well-known labor agitator and Irish separatist Jim Larkin to go to Australia "to preach Anarchistic doctrines." With Larkin's help, he also recruited two radicals, Leveskovski and McIntyre, to go to Vladivostok to spread radical propaganda with a view to overturning the government there, creating internal trouble, and "incidentally to blow up munitions stores." Finally, he told Tunney, he recruited two radical women to be trained in Mexico and then sent to France to join an American unit there. Jahnke later told him that one of the women who was of German extraction from Milwaukee, Wisconsin, Alta Miller, worked out and was sent over. The other did not.

Witzke's interactions with Larkin may have been more extensive than Witzke led Tunney to believe, and in any event were corroborated by Larkin himself.[155] Larkin had grown up on the docks of Liverpool and, like Witzke, was at ease in the company of sailors, longshoremen, and the like. He became a union organizer in Liverpool, Belfast and along the Scottish coast, and by the beginning of World War I was the most powerful person in the Irish labor movement. He was also a renowned orator, advocate for Irish independence, and anti-war activist. In October 1914, he went to the US to speak and raise funds for his union; he ended up staying ten years, preaching socialism and communism, organizing underpaid and overworked Irish dockworkers, and campaigning against US entry into the war. After the war he was charged with criminal anarchy, convicted, and incarcerated at Sing Sing for several years until pardoned by Governor Al Smith in 1923 and deported.[156]

Larkin was a special target of German intelligence almost from the moment of his arrival in America. Von Papen, acting through his deputy Wolf von Igel, offered Larkin the position of head of German sabotage operations on the US East Coast. His pitch was if American munitions shipments could be slowed, Germany would break through the Western Front, call for an armistice and recognize a revolutionary government in Ireland. Von Igel also gave him a tour of the service's secret bomb factory in New Jersey. It was around this time that the Germans told Larkin about their "specific plans . . . for destroying the munitions at the Jersey City terminus by means of a loaded barge exploding alongside the pier or jetty." The barge, according to what Larkin was told, "was a Lakawana Railroad barge, it being explained that the detonation from these explosives would result in the explosion of the explosives stored in or about the vicinity."[157]

Larkin declined the offer to run sabotage on the East Coast but stayed in touch with the Germans, and the Germans kept trying. They met again multiple times in New York, Washington, Mexico City, and San Francisco. In San Francisco Consul General Von Bopp asked Larkin to take over West Coast sabotage operations from Vancouver to Guatamala, but again Larkin said no. He was, however, willing to cooperate in other ways, walking a fine line between actions that threatened human life such as sabotage that he would not do, and non-life-threatening actions that were consistent with his broader socialist and anti-capitalist mission or that would otherwise contribute to Irish independence, for example, organizing strikes and stoppages that would slow America's efforts to aid the allies. On one or two occasions, he delivered secret letters for the Germans to their agents in Mexico.[158]

We do not know when Larkin was first introduced to Lothar Witzke. It may have been as early as July 1916 (both men were in San Francisco a short time before the Preparedness Day bombing there) or in early December 1916 when Witzke stopped in Chicago to deliver messages on his way back to San Francisco from New York (Larkin was in Chicago at the same time). We do know that the two met on the West Coast sometime in the summer of 1917 and that Witzke recruited Larkin to go to Australia to proselytize. Larkin reached Australia in late August or early September but was turned away because of his prior record of disturbances and returned to America.[159] The two men met again in Los Angeles in early October. It was probably at this second meeting that Larkin gave Witzke introductions to Leveskovski and McIntyre for the mission to Vladivostok. Witzke later told Tunney that he did not know whether they accomplished anything there because he was captured before they could report back to him.[160] The authors have been unable to discover any further information about Leveskovski and McIntyre or their Vladivostok mission.

After meeting Witzke in Los Angeles, Larkin continued on to Mexico City, crossing the border at Tijuana and delivering letters to German agents in Ensenada. In Mexico City, he met with Minister von Eckhardt. According to Larkin, the Germans showed him detailed maps of oil fields, railway junctions, and ammunition and steel plants in the US, and von Eckhardt tried to recruit him to commit acts of sabotage against these targets. When Larkin refused, relations turned chilly. His wallet and suitcase were stolen from his hotel, he became stranded in Mexico City and he had to wire friends in San Francisco for money to get home. His career as a German agent was done.[161]

(III) FREEING BOPP

The most improbable-sounding of Witzke's missions was his attempt to free members of the German consulate general in San Francisco who were being detained on Angel Island in San Francisco Bay, pending appeal of their convictions for conspiracy to blow up ammunition plants and ships in violation of the Neutrality Act. Consul Franz Bopp and Vice Consul Eckhard von Schack had been free on bail since their convictions and sentencing in early 1917, but after war was declared their bail was revoked and they were detained as dangerous aliens at Fort McDowell on Angel Island.[162]

In his death row interview with Tom Tunney, Witzke told Tunney that, before returning to Mexico at the end of July 1917 from his first trip to the West Coast from Mexico, he delegated responsibility for this assignment to two San Francisco colleagues named De Lacey and Hornify. Lawrence De Lacey was editor of an Irish-American weekly called *The Leader*. Daniel J. Harnedy (the name got slightly mangled in the Tunney interview) was the proprietor of a Mission Street shoe store and a prominent figure in local Irish-American circles who had escaped to America two years earlier after being indicted in England for a political crime.[163]

The plot to extract Bopp and von Schack and spirit them to safety in Mexico actually began in June, shortly after Witzke reached San Francisco from Mexico City, not at the end of his trip. Different extraction methods were considered, including the bribing of guards, getting the guards drunk, effecting a transfer off the Island to a county jail, even landing a boat on the island with armed men to overpower the sentries. Step one was to establish a secure communications link with the two detainees. De Lacey recruited for this purpose an immigration inspector at Angel Island with direct access to Bopp and von Schack named Patrick Farrally. Farrally began carrying written messages between De Lacey and von Schack on June 29. In his initial message, De Lacey reminded the former vice consul that they had met for the first time on February 17 and he assured him that communicating via Farrally was secure, "I can always get a messenger to you, I think . . . Write me fully and this messenger will get the reply to me." He then advised von Schack, in coded language, that although the difficulties of extraction were substantial, Jahnke and Witzke were now on the case, "The little difficulties of removing a friend from his present residence are enormous. J sent a man to me from across the border, and he suggests that you had some financial arrangements contemplated. . . . The whole proposition is simply to get from there; after that a week's wait or so and the border.") The "financial arrangements" were apparently a reference to bribery: who among the guards could be bought? Von Schack was also worried about whether and how a boat could be procured that was fast enough to outrun the patrol boats stationed in the Bay at the entrance of the Golden Gate.[164]

As the summer progressed, the extraction plans proceeded apace. De Lacey's last message indicated that von Schack would be disguised as a clergyman for the escape and that Witzke would be waiting for him at the border, "W is at the border. Will not be back for two or three days. This is German money. Say if you want more. Shall I send you a clergyman's clothes, and make arrangements, or will you? Also where to go and where to stay. Tell no names to soldiers."[165]

This last message from De Lacey may not have been delivered. De Lacey and Harnedy were arrested on August 14, 1917, shortly after the message was written. The messenger Farrally, it turned out, had gone to the authorities when he was recruited in June and disclosed to them what was going on. They persuaded him to play along, to be in effect a double agent, and to gather evidence against the plotters, which he did, sharing with the authorities the contents of every message to and from De Lacey before they were delivered.[166] De Lacey and Harnedy were promptly tried and convicted. De Lacey was sentenced to eighteen months at McNeil Island Penitentiary, Harnedy to one year in the San Francisco County jail.[167] The US attorney admitted when questioned about it that the Government had tried, but failed, to identify "the man from Mexico" referred to in the De Lacey correspondence.[168] Witzke was still undetected.

Witzke told Tunney that, when Jahnke learned about the arrests of De Lacey and Harnedy soon after Witzke's return to Mexico from his summer trip to San Francisco, he "begged" Witzke to go back to San Francisco to extricate them. Witzke, in the guise of Waberski, did go back for a second time at the beginning of September and stayed into November. But if he tried to extract De Lacey and Harnedy during that time, his efforts were unsuccessful even though both plotters were out on bail pending an appeal of their convictions. The following June, the once smooth-shaven De Lacey, then disguised by a heavy growth of beard, was re-arrested trying to flee the country.[169]

In the meantime, Witzke had returned to Mexico City, done reconnaissance work at Manzanillo and Mazatlan harbors to facilitate Germany's expected use of those harbors to shelter German submarines that would be attacking Allied shipping in the Pacific, and begun preparing for his star-crossed journey to Nogales in January where he, like De Lacey, would be betrayed by a double agent and, like De Lacey, would spend the month of June (and many months thereafter) behind bars—including part of that time on death row.

As we have told in Part One the story of Witzke's capture at the border, his ensuing conviction and imprisonment and pardon, we pick up in the following chapters the narrative of Witzke's life story beginning with his return to Germany in 1923.

WEIMAR, ABROAD AGAIN, THIRD REICH

"A past crowded with high
adventure on sea and shore,
intrigue and colorful exploits."
—REGINALD P. MITCHEL, "SPY,"
THE AMERICAN FOREIGN SERVICE JOURNAL
(NOVEMBER 1934)

On November 29, 1923, Lothar Witzke was put on a ship (the SS *Albert Balin*) at New York harbor bound for Germany. He had been released from Leavenworth Penitentiary on November 21, travelled to New York on his own recognizance, and was sequestered at the German Consulate until his date of departure. The *Balin's* passenger list included distinguished individuals, among them the director of the Werner Steel Works at Dusseldorf and the wife of the American Consul at Berlin. Witzke, neatly dressed in a new suit and topcoat, might have boarded the *Balin* unrecognized but for his shoes. The shoes were prison issue, and they attracted the attention of reporters at the dock, who also took note of his aristocratic features, gray eyes, sandy hair, and seemingly excellent health.[1]

Witzke was ill at ease and reluctant to be interviewed. He rolled an unlit cigarette stub between his fingers, tried drawing smoke from it, and smiled only twice, once at being reminded that it was Thanksgiving Day and the other when the interview was over. He spoke fluent English. "As a result of my stay and study at Leavenworth I suppose I have learned to speak English as they do on Main Street," he told the reporters. "We had men from every part of the United States there and now I can tell a Westerner or a Southerner whenever I hear one. The only American's voice I do not care for is the New Englander's." He said he had been well-treated at Leavenworth and had acquired there a "lucrative trade" through his work as chief engineer at the prison's powerhouse. He complained, though, about the prison's lack of study facilities. The only books available were for "the minds of children." Fortunately, he was lent books by prison guards and visitors. He refused to answer any questions about his activities before his arrest, except to say that he had come to America in 1916. As for Thanksgiving, Witzke said: "no man more thankful than I."

> For a long while I waited for death and then for a longer time I feared the ordeal of spending all my years behind prison walls. Now I look out upon life with hope—even torn and troubled Germany after those gray walls will be a paradise for a fellow like me. I am grateful to God for taking care of me and for permitting me again to return to my family and my friends. The war has taken many from me and, no doubt, I shall see strange faces where I had hoped to see those my heart ached for.[2]

Witzke had been eighteen years old when he left Germany to join the merchant marine. He was twenty-eight when he returned. He had already lived an extraordinary life, a life that the Americans came close to cutting short by a hanging that was never done. During the years that followed his return, Witzke would be unemployed in Germany and then employed in the Americas and Asia, he would be married and become a father, he would join the Nazi Party and then the *Abwehr* as World War II approached, and his family would move into a large house in an upscale residential area in Hamburg.

WEIMAR GERMANY

The Germany to which Witzke returned in late November 1923 was convulsed by hyperinflation, political turmoil, and resentment over reparations and the Allied occupation of the Ruhr. On January 11, 1923, the French army had occupied the Ruhr. A dollar in January 1923 cost 17,000 marks; in August, 4,621,000 marks; in September, 98,860,000 marks; in November when Witzke arrived, 2,193,600,000,000 marks.[3]

The German artist George Grosz described shopping in a time of hyperinflation:

> Lingering at the [shop] window was a luxury because shopping had to be done immediately. Even an additional minute meant an increase in price. One had to buy quickly because a rabbit, for example, might cost two

million marks more by the time it took to walk into the store. A few mil-
lion marks meant nothing, really. It was just that it meant more lugging.
The packages of money needed to buy the smallest item had long since
become too heavy for trouser pockets. They weighed many pounds. . . .
People had to start carting their money around in wagons and knapsacks.
I used a knapsack.[4]

In late September 1923, the Weimar government capitulated to the
French occupation of the Ruhr, precipitating a social and political crisis
within Germany. The communists planned an uprising for November 9, 1923.
The far right tried, and failed, to replicate in Munich Mussolini's march on
Rome. Also in November 1923, there was an anti-Jewish pogrom in Berlin's
Scheunenviertel district.[5]

Germany was riven by strife, with opposing nationalists and militarists
on one side, communists on the other, and social democrats occupying a
fragile middle ground. Witzke was vehemently in the nationalist and militarist camp. Five years later, in January 1929, he would summarize his political principles. Referring to what he told American investigators about Black
Tom when they met with him earlier that month in Maracaibo, he wrote, in
English: "I stated that I was a true believer in the black, white and red [i.e.,
the traditional colors of the German Reich] and that it was not my habit to
change my beliefs like a dirty shirt over night and that I was not sympathy
[*sic*] with the present day German Government policy of conciliation." "That
I believed fully in the code of honor of the former German army and navy
officer and if the entire country had been like they, Germany would never
have lost the war."[6] "Every decent German," he added, "must have 'nationalistic tendencies.'"[7] While much of what Witzke said during his testimony
over the years before the Mixed Claims Commission hearing the sabotage
claims between Germany and the United States (recounted in the following
chapter) was curated for the purposes of the German case, this declaration
of belief (contained in a letter, not a witness statement) stands out. As Witzke
was speaking against the then-current Weimar Government, there was no
apparent self-interest in his declaration of principle.

Witzke's 1929 declaration was foreshadowed by a statement that Witzke
had made in February 1918 to Byron Butcher, US special agent involved in
Witzke's arrest. Butcher testified before the military commission that, just
before Witzke was transferred from Nogales to Fort Sam Houston, Butcher
urged him to "tell the authorities" there "his whole story." According to
Butcher, Witzke replied: "No, I can't do that. I am very young to die—22

years old, but I have done my duty. If I told I would be a traitor and that I will never be."[8] This statement was echoed by still another affirmation by Witzke to a British interrogator at his home in 1952 on the subject of Witzke's work in 1939-40 seeking to recruit and infiltrate Flemish agents into the UK. At first Witzke denied to his interrogator ever having recruited agents for such work but he later admitted that he had employed "a group of of 2-3 Welsh nationalists in Antwerp in 1940. . . . When asked for their names and descriptions he said that he had forgotten [their names] but that in any case even if he knew them he would not dream of divulging them. This was because of his code as a former *Abwehr* officer, and because these people were, according to their lights, sincere patriots."[9] Witzke thus had a deep and longstanding ethos of loyalty to his country, to its nationalist ambitions, to its military's code of honor, and to the spycraft that was his work on behalf of his country, including to the agents whom he recruited for such work.

Witzke was eager upon his return to Germany to join with nationalists and others opposed to Weimar and the communists. He had demonstrated during his time in the United States that he was a man of action. Immediately after arriving, he headed for Hanover to see his family, which had moved there from Prussia since the last time that he saw them in 1913. But he quickly made his way to Berlin. There, during 1924, Witzke was in his own words "actively engaged in [anti-Weimar] Nationalistic activities" in Berlin, and had no regular employment.[10] We do not know whether this meant street brawls, protest marches or violence against social democrats, German communists and Jews. All of these occurred in Berlin in 1923–1924.[11] It is easy to imagine that Witzke took part.

We will see in later chapters that the exuberance of Witzke's youth would over time be replaced by self-interested cynicism, an evolution that mirrored that of many in a generation traumatized by Germany's defeat and hyperinflation.[12]

JAHNKE BÜRO AND SEARCH FOR WORK

For six months in 1923–1924 Witzke worked for the Jahnke Büro.[13] The Jahnke Büro was a private investigative agency set up by Kurt Jahnke, with links to nationalists.[14] It was also associated with Admiral Canaris, who had been an intelligence officer on the *Dresden* when it was sunk by the British in 1915 off the coast of Chile. According to Witzke, it was "an extremely high level political intelligence Bureau working mainly through diplomatic channels, with sources in the U.K., Belgium, Holland, France, Russia and the Far East.

. . . Its main consumer was . . . the German Foreign Office."[15] We do not know what Witzke did at the Büro. Presumably he collaborated on projects with his former boss and friend Jahnke and made some pocket money doing so.

In March 1924, Witzke was awarded Iron Crosses, first and second class, for valorous service.[16] The service for which he was decorated must have been his work in the United States and Mexico before his arrest; the awards may also have recognized his steadfastness as a German prisoner of war condemned to death and then life in prison. Whatever the service, Iron Crosses did not pay. Nor did political activity. Witzke needed to move ahead with his life, and conditions in Germany became temporarily calmer after 1924, allowing him to do so.[17] Jahnke, by contrast, would engage in political intelligence work well into the 1930s, reportedly even running informants in London who obtained on an ongoing basis copies of correspondence between Joseph Kennedy, US Ambassador to the Court of St. James, and President Roosevelt.[18]

Witzke began his search for regular work in July 1924 by applying to the German army, marine administration, for leave to take a helmsman examination.[19] Already a seaman, he could earn higher pay as a helmsman. One wonders how Witzke could return to the sea with an injured leg and a limp. Perhaps his leg had healed, or perhaps this was a sign of desperation to find better paying work. Almost a year later, in March 1925, Witzke's residence was near the Hamburg docks;[20] he was evidently hoping that an opportunity would turn up there, but nothing did.

Witzke's helmsman application stated that from 1916 to 1918 he had spent fifteen months at sea. This was false (while it was true that he had spent 15 months at sea, it was not during the years 1916–1918; Witzke was in the United States and Mexico during this time, mostly on land, and a prisoner in the US as of February 1918), and it is curious that Witzke would bend the truth to German authorities to gain employment, as the authorities should have been able to determine without much effort that Witzke was not in the merchant marine (or the German navy) from 1916 to 1918. Perhaps working for Jahnke of naval intelligence counted as naval service. Perhaps Witzke was looking for a naval commission. Even though a letter from the marine administration to the Ministry of Economy lauded Witzke's heroism while he was in the United States, mentioning that he had been sentenced to death for his service to the Fatherland,[21] the helmsmn application led to nothing.

Internal communications among the German representatives acting for Germany in the interstate arbitration against the United States during the 1920s show that they were working with Witzke in March and April 1925 on his first affidavit to be submitted to the Mixed Claims Commission hearing the sabotage claims. In one letter, Witzke complained that he had not been reimbursed his travel expenses from Hamburg to Berlin, attesting to his straightened financial situation.[22]

MEXICO AND VENEZUELA

Though the German economy saw improvement from 1923 to 1925, employment opportunities in Germany were still wanting. Witzke spoke Spanish and had experience of the Americas. He turned his attention to finding work there, and found employment, first in Mexico, and then in Venezuela. The German presence in both countries was longstanding and substantial. The companies that employed him were as of late 1925: the Ford Motor Company in Mexico City; then (until spring 1927) the Veracruz Light & Power Company in Veracruz;[23] and then (through 1929) the Lago Petroleum Company, a US company operating in Maracaibo, Venezuela. How odd that Witzke, an alleged accomplice in an act of sabotage that harmed the Statue of Liberty, and a key witness for Germany in an interstate arbitration against the US, was hired by America's most prominent company, the Ford Motor Company, and then by an American oil company. Witzke evidently was not a notorious figure outside the circle of those interested in the sabotage cases, and in the 1920s one could not instantly access third-party information about an employee.

How Witzke obtained employment in Latin America is unclear. Reinhard Doerries, a leading historian of twentieth-century German intelligence, says that the German Foreign Office devoted considerable attention to Witzke's financial situation due to concern that the former spy would sell his testimony to the Americans.[24] Such concern seems misplaced given what we know of Witzke's patriotism, although economic desperation may temporarily turn the loyalty even of true patriots. In any event, if the Germans were worried about Witzke selling out to the Americans, it is doubtful that they would have placed Witzke with an American employer.

However he got the job, Ford Motor Company, S.A., the Mexican subsidiary of the Detroit-based parent corporation, engaged Witzke in the same year (1925) that this subsidiary became the first automaker to establish production in Mexico. Henry Ford figured that, by putting Mexicans to work, they would have "less time for fighting."[25] Ford remained the only automaker in Mexico until 1938. Ford's first plant was located in a rented warehouse in the La Calandelabria neighborhood on the outskirts of Mexico City. It had 250 employees and in its first year assembled fifty vehicles, using US-made parts. Many of these were Model A, which replaced the Model T in 1928. Ford cars quickly changed the city, leading the government to build Mexico's first two-lane highway, connecting Mexico City to Pachuca.[26]

We do not know what Witzke's work was at Ford in Mexico. He stayed there only about a year before moving on to Veracruz Light & Power Company, an electricity and oil production company in Veracruz, Mexico. The company had obtained in 1907 a one hundred-year concession to provide lighting to the city.[27]

The oil production business in Mexico at the time was thriving. Starting in 1918 and extending into the 1920s, Mexico was second behind only the United States in petroleum output and actually led the world in oil exports. Oil production and exports in and from Mexico peaked in 1921–1925.[28]

Witzke was probably not much interested in the social evolution of Veracruz, much less the ecological impact of oil production on the area. But it would have been hard to miss the effects of the development of oil for a region that had into the early twentieth century been a rain forest where local farmers planted corn and kept cattle. "The oil industry required infrastructure: roads, pipelines, pumping stations, storage tanks, refineries (fourteen total in the region), factories, housing, workshops, telegraph lines and, by the early 1920s, airplane landing strips. Infrastructure alone covered vast areas of the rainforest." "The labor force needed to make these changes possible did not exist in the Huasteca [where Veracruz is located], so the companies had to import it, thus changing the social composition of the region. The oil barons recruited Mexican men by the thousands. At the peak of employment in 1921 there were some 40,000 men on the payroll."[29]

In a system of rigid racial stratification, Witzke would have worked and lived in Veracruz only with expatriates. Oil industry executives and managers were all White Americans and Europeans. So too were the drillers and other skilled workers. Mexicans did the manual labor, and were forbidden from other positions. The segregated world of the oil industry in Mexico was familiar to expatriates from the southern United States: there were Whites-only housing, dining halls, infirmaries, social clubs and swimming pools.[30] It is unlikely that Witzke was bothered. As we will see, during his employment abroad in the 1930s his regard for non-European local workers would be manifestly low; they were bodies to be used.

Witzke could also not have missed the effects of extensive oil spills. Whether he (or anyone in the oil industry) cared is another question. "Between 1904 and 1938, it rained oil in the Huasteca. Forests, mangroves, swamps, marshes, sand dunes and everything in between were blanketed in oil at one point or another. The oil companies didn't lay out pipelines until they could be sure of a return on their investment. Freshly discovered oil spewed out of the land until the pipelines were finished, creating open oil pits, or "dams" from seven to 30 feet deep. By 1918, there were sixty-six oil pools in the Huasteca."[31]

Witzke would also have experienced a natural disaster of a different kind while in Veracruz: on September 28, 1926, a hurricane destroyed most of the city. This would not be the last natural disaster that he would live through while overseas.

Witzke returned to Germany for about six months in 1927 to finalize and sign an affidavit for submission by Germany to the Mixed Claims Commission hearing the sabotage claims. The visit was momentous. He met Lilli Carstensen. Twenty-one years old (eleven years younger than Witzke), she was a beauty, and she was engaged to another man. Witzke could be persuasive with women. Undeterred (and likely stimulated) by the competition, he won her and, within four weeks of meeting, Lothar and Lilli were married. Their marriage would last, and produce three children.

Lilli's childhood had been impoverished and unhappy. Her father died during World War I, and her mother had to take work as a coat check girl at a place of entertainment in Hamburg. An only child, she was often alone. As an adult, she yearned for elegance and status, and her life with her husband would give her the luxury that she needed. Lothar would in later years bring her the current fashion from the catwalks in Paris. Provided with an automobile, Lilli would drive wearing hand-gloves. Lilli was an able pianist and her musical talent would be passed down to later generations; two of her grandchildren became professional musicians.

Lilli likely loved her children, at least the two sons that she would have, if not her daughter, but she was largely incapable of giving or receiving affection, showing none to her daughter and none later in life to her grandkids. Over time, her marriage came to be loveless. And the consequences of a remote mother, we will see, were transmitted to the next generation.[32] Lothar in his way would prove to be a family man, and (unlike Lilli) would be a loving father to his daughter, who resembled him in her intelligence and willfulness. But he was for the most part not a man of sentiment, and he was a womanizer. Often away from home during the decades to come, whether for work or wartime or post-war espionage activities, Lothar may have scarcely been bothered by his wife's closed-up nature, and he likely did not notice it during the head-spinning early days.

Newly married, Witzke found work as of spring 1927 as a laboratory assistant with Lago Petroleum Company in Maracaibo, Venezuela.[33] If the position required laboratory expertise, it is a mystery how Witzke was qualified.

Lothar and Lilli spent almost three years in Maracaibo, another city undergoing social and ecological transformation. As recently as 1920, Venezuela had been the poorest economy in Latin America.[34] Most of the country was rural; the only cities were Caracas, the capital, and Maracaibo, a port city through which passed all exports and imports.[35] In 1922, a massive oil field ("Los Barrosos") was discovered in Maracaibo.[36] The size of the field attracted investment by American oil companies, including Standard Oil Company and Lago Petroleum Corporation (a subsidiary of the American company, Pan American Petroleum and Transport Company).[37]

In 1927, the Lago Company began shipments of crude oil from Lake Maracaibo, which is an inlet of the Caribbean. The ships worked in convoys, timed to the lake's high watermark to ensure the most economical transshipment. The Lago operations in Maracaibo included oil tanks, storage buildings, residential compounds, and an office building.[38] A refinery, one of the world's largest, came on-stream in 1929 in Aruba.[39] Witzke presumably worked in the main managerial offices in an area called "Lago alley" in the outskirts of Maracaibo, near the modern-day avenue 5 *de* Julio.[40]

Life in Venezuela was good for the young couple. They had a house with servants. Lilli even had a pet crocodile. She evidently did not overly cherish the pet. Before the couple moved back to Germany, Lilli had the pet made into a handbag.[41] They likely enjoyed an active social life with the German expatriate community. German businessmen had been established in Maracaibo for a long time before the arrival of the Americans in the 1920s. They had set up country clubs and had inter-married with Venezuelans.[42] Lilli enjoyed life in Venezuela (and soon thereafter in China) because in both places she had a life of status. She tried to act like the movie stars about whom she read incessantly. Evincing glamour, clad in finery, she smoked cigarettes using a cigarette holder.[43]

As they did in Veracruz, the oil companies in Maracaibo operated as states unto themselves, with their own police force. They treated workers however they wished.[44] In 1926, the oil companies began replacing Venezuelan laborers with Chinese workers, who were perceived to be more efficient and docile.[45] The Chinese workers were kept in fenced compounds.[46]

Also as in Veracruz, the ecological devastation in Maracaibo caused by oil production was extreme. Writing in the late 1920s, a US diplomat remarked of Maracaibo:

The waters are covered with oil which is carried up to shore by the waves and blackens all vegetation which it touches. Along the shore are rows of palm trees whose leaves are so covered in oil that they droop to the ground. Oil is spattered everywhere on the vegetation and houses. It is carried into the offices and dwellings on the shoes or the clothes of those who enter.[47]

Some chose to swim in the lake, but only when the breeze was favorable. As reflected in the memoirs of Julia Bornhorst, a German woman living in Maracaibo during the 1920s, a black oil ring would form around the swimmer's neck and feet.[48]

Natural and man-made calamities occured wherever Witzke went during his years working abroad. In Maracaibo, a devastating fire started at the oil production facility on July 21, 1927, and burned down the only shopping center in the city, the "Mercado de Maracaibo."[49]

The lawyers acting for the US before the US/Germany Mixed Claims Commission learned that Witzke was in Maracaibo. They traveled to Venezuela in 1929 to entice, and likely to pressure, Witzke to make admissions about Black Tom. He did not make admissions but, according to the lawyers, he did hint that he knew who was responsible.[50] Witzke alerted the Germans to the visit by the American lawyers. This caused a flurry of activity among the German representatives who were concerned that Witzke, despite having remunerative employment, would betray his country by selling his testimony to the deep-pocketed Americans. One representative who had dealings with Witzke gave a brutal assessment of the man's character: "He is a pretty nasty guy. He bursts of megalomania and pomposity and nothing would upset him more than getting stripped of his nimbus and being exposed as what he is, an ordinary seaman. In his anger, he would probably make up the biggest lies and cause us immeasurable damage."[51]

There was likely in this characterization an element of class-based snobbery toward the man described, inaccurately, as nothing but an "ordinary seaman."[52] We can also be skeptical about the disdain expressed about Witzke's limitations: the wily Witzke may have played the German representative, threatening betrayal and feigning fury, in order to get employment. The concern that Witzke would invent lies to hurt Germany and to help himself seems wrong; the bumblers here were likely the German representatives, not Witzke.

But we would be wrong to dismiss the characterization of Witzke. This is not the only statement to the effect that Witzke was not as smart as he liked to think himself. The other was by a British agent who interviewed him in 1952.[53]

The mix of "megalomania and pomposity" may have been a leitmotiv of critical episodes in Witzke's life. As we will develop in Part III of this book, Witzke enjoyed boasting, even about exploits that he had not done. Later in life, he largely squelched this tendency within his family, saying little to nothing to his children or his son-in-law about his youthful exploits. But there may still have been a very late life outburst, a subject for our epilogue.

It is likely that, because they were worried about Witzke's loyalty, the German authorities promised to find Witzke another, better job. Whether because of such promises or because he was a patriot, Witzke withstood the inducements and pressure from the visiting American lawyers in Maracaibo. He did, however, come under additional pressure from his American boss, William Neunhoffer, the same special agent who played a role in his capture and conviction in 1918.[54] Coincidence or not? Was Witzke's employment by Lago arranged by the *Americans* as a way to exert pressure on Witzke to testify for the Americans? The answer is surely no. It stretches credulity to suppose that Neunhoffer at Lago, ten or eleven years after the events in Texas, told the American lawyers in the arbitration that Witzke was applying for a job, that the American lawyers decided that this would be a way to get access to Germany's star witness, and that the American lawyers then got Lago to give Witzke employment, and all this without the wily Witzke suspecting anything. We know that Witzke suspected nothing from the fact that Witzke got his favorite brother, Kurt, employment at the same time with Lago. Witzke himself also expressed his view that it was a coincidence that his boss was the former secret agent, writing "It is due to the excellent American system of maintaining in the bureaus of all big American firms in foreign countries a former secret service official in a leading position who is still in a certain contact with the Government and to the coincidence that the local head of personnel of the Lago Petr. Co., Mr. Neuenhofer [*sic*], knows me personally from war times, that the Americans ascertained my present address."[55]

In any case, the pressure from his boss caused Witzke to decide that he had to leave his employment at the Lago Company.[56] Witzke created a subterfuge, telling his employers that he was departing Maracaibo for New York in order to testify on behalf of the US.[57] His destination, though, was Germany.

After his brother Lothar's departure, Kurt Witzke found himself in an awkward position. Kurt had been in Maracaibo with his wife and daughter since May 1928, working for Lago as a cashier. His first employment contract was for eighteen months, and his monthly salary was $250. In early 1930 he returned with his family to Maracaibo, and entered another eighteen-month employment, to expire in August 1931, again as a cashier, at a monthly salary of $275. As Kurt told it to the German authorities, Neunhoffer "tried to cause me to make incriminating statements about my brother for the purpose of the sabotage proceedings. However, I always refused to support such schemes. When Mr. Neunhofer [sic] realized that he could not convince me to testify for the Americans, I was suddenly dismissed, and without any compensation for the remaining contract period."[58] Kurt returned to Germany deeply indebted and was incensed about his uncompensated moves back and forth between Germany and Venezuela. He repeatedly solicited the German Foreign Office for financial assistance on the ground that his loyalty to Germany was the cause of his financial straits.[59]

Still another Witzke brother, Ottomar, also made an appearance in Maracaibo in 1930: Ottomar (together with Kurt and their wives) traveled from Germany to Maracaibo in January 1930.[60] Ottomar surely also hoped for employment, but his timing was unlucky, coming three months before Lothar left his employment for good.

Lothar and Lilli returned to Germany in April 1930 aboard the *Frida Horn*, sailing from Maracaibo to Hamburg. Lilli was pregnant with their first child. Life was making Witzke an adult in other ways as well: in 1928 while Witzke was in Venezuela, his father, Paul Witzke died. We have no echo of what his father's death meant for him, but Witzke's earlier choice of Pablo Waberski as his *nom de guerre* may have been a tribute to his father.

Correspondence among the German representatives in the US/Germany arbitration during the spring and summer 1930 shows that the German representatives remained acutely concerned about the risk that, as the Germans phrased it, the Americans would bribe the German witnesses to testify in favor of the Americans. This concern led the German counsel to procure employment for Witzke in Hankow, China, with the Hamburg-America Steamship Line (aka the Norddeutscher Lloyd Steamship Company).[61] The process did not go smoothly: Witzke was dissatisfied with the "small position" first offered to him, and this caused the German representatives a good deal of fuss during spring and summer 1930.[62] Later that year, the Mixed Claims Commission rejected the American sabotage claims. Witzke had been asking about the outcome of the case,[63] and we can assume that Witzke was made aware of the victory to which he contributed.

HANKOW, CHINA

On July 29, 1930, the *Münsterland* departed Genoa, sailing to Shanghai via Port Said.[64] The passenger list includes an entry for Witzke (age thirty-five) and his wife Lilli (age twenty-four). They arrived in Shanghai in late August or early September and left Shanghai for Hankow by river steamer on October 20.[65] The long layover in Shanghai may have been because the medical facilities in Shanghai were superior to those in Hankow, leading the Witzkes to spend a few weeks in Shanghai upon their arrival in China in order for their baby to be born there. In any event they stayed in Shanghai for a few weeks, before going on in mid-October to Hankow with newborn Dieter, a perfect blond-haired, blue-eyed boy, merry and cherished. It is curious that their river steamer's passenger list makes no mention of a Witzke baby traveling with them, whereas it does for other couples.

Hankow, an inland port city at the confluence of the Han and Yangtze rivers, is today part of Wuhan, the capital city of Hubei Province. Hankow was then dominated (commercially) by foreign enclaves.[66] An American travel writer, Harry Franck, described Hankow in the 1920s as "a bustling city wholly Western in its architecture and layout, even though completely surrounded by China, among buildings looming high into the air, with several theaters, even though they offered only American 'movies,' with automobiles dashing their imperious way up and down the river-front Bund."[67]

The concession in Hankow in 1895 was, together with that in Tientsin, Germany's first in China.[68] The postwar period was one of cordiality between China and Germany, whether due to Chinese sentiment that Germans, like the Chinese, were victims of imperialism and unequal treaties or because the Chinese considered that Germany, as a defeated power, posed no threat to China.[69] The German enclave in Hankow developed, together with German colonies in other cities in China, around the local branch of the German-Asiatic Bank and the trade of German firms such as IG Farben and Krupp.[70] Assisted by the Weimar government, the enclave was already in the 1920s sizeable and prospering, featuring government-subsidized German schools, churches, and newspapers.[71] The German community had its own consulate, town hall (*Rathaus*), small shops, men's choir, women's auxiliary, and of course churches.[72]

The German enclave was also fully integrated in the larger expatriate life. Another American traveler (G. H. Thomas) offered this description from November 1936:

> The first-class coaches on the Peking-Hankow Express are the best in all China. They were made with terrific expense by the Pullman Company of Chicago and used to be the regular Shanghai Express. In the Revolution of 1927 they were seized by one of the generals and taken up into Manchuria,

but the Central Government finally got them back and put them on the Peking-Hankow run. . . .

Saturday evening I went out with Hardenbrook (Cornell, 1932) of East-man Kodak and Bob Taylor of the American Consulate and drank some beer. Everyone knows everyone else in Hankow, and after that one evening out in the crowd I know a bunch of them. There is quite a large German group here and at one cafe there were ten or eleven young German fellows singing old German songs. They did an excellent job and were mighty nice chaps. I enjoyed the whole evening, especially hearing the American sail-ors tell stories about the Upper Yangtze and the ships that go there.[73]

Because of its industry and its western influence, Hankow was known as the Chicago of China. But 1930, the year that the Witzkes arrived, was a bad one for Hankow. The war among the armies of the government head-quartered in Beijing, the nationalists whose capital was Nanking, and the communists, disrupted all links between Hankow and the rest of China.[74] The president of the Hankow British Chamber of Commerce described in his annual report for 1930 "broken or dangerous lines of communication, civil warfare, bandits, Communist armies, high taxes and the decline in the price of silver—these are the factors which contributed to making 1930 the worst year that Hankow has known in several decades."[75] The report referred further "to the highly dangerous state of navigation on the Yangtse River, because of bandit and Communist attacks upon shipping."[76]

The warfare between nationalists and communists and the rampant ban-ditry seem barely to have touched the Witzke family. For the Witzkes, it was the good life again, a large villa with servants,[77] and this at a time when Germany was in economic misery following the 1929 crash of the American stock market.

Political developments in Germany did, though, affect Witzke. In 1931 the Nazis established their first party organization in the Far East in Hankow. It was headed by a teacher in the local German school, a Frau von Werder.[78] Af-ter Hitler became Chancellor in January 1933, Nazi-affiliated groups in China "exploded with activity," disseminating political and racial propaganda.[79] To help finance the Nazi campaign in the Reichstag election of March 1933, these groups joined with the China affiliates of the German veteran's move-ment, the *Stahlhelm*, to sponsor a 'Collection for the Struggle Against Com-munism.' They used this slogan to solicit money from Nazi members and other Germans. Germans in China were also encouraged to contribute to the NSDAP's [National Socialist German Workers' Party, i.e., the Nazi party] annual *Winterhilfswerke* [Winter Relief Program], which would direct money to impoverished families in the Reich.[80] Members of the local party groups were ordered to fight communism and to read *Mein Kampf* at least once.[81]

Witzke took some interest in the misery outside the foreign concessions, but it was not sympathetic interest. When he left China in 1934, he took with him an album of photographs, including a series that showed a man (Chinese), handcuffed and rope-tied, being led to an execution place. The last of the photos showed the man's head lying on the ground. Witzke added a caption beneath the photo of the decapitation: "und ab ist die Rübe" ("and off with the turnip [head]").[82] Yes, very Witzke. Sixty years later, Witzke's grandson could still recollect his youthful shock at the photos and at the jocularity of his grandfather's handwritten caption.[83]

Witzke's amusement at the execution may have been in keeping with his conduct while in Hankow. His job was that of "supervisor of river equipment and chief of longshoremen."[84] We know this because he was tracked down in Hankow in December 1933 by the American agent before the US/Germany Mixed Claims Commission and then contacted by the US Consul, who asked Witzke to produce his address book from 1916–1917.[85] The US Naval Attaché reported in October 1935 to the American agent that Witzke "had quite a reputation for brutality in handling the coolies," referencing his "man-handling and injuring coolies."[86] The attaché may have exaggerated, giving the American agent what the attaché imagined that the agent would want to hear about an adverse witness. But there is no reason to question the essential veracity of the report.

The attaché added, "[Witzke] is said to be the same man who was so dangerous and so successful in sabotage in the United States during the World War. . . . It may be taken for granted that [Witzke] has lost a lot of the youthful fire and initiative that made him such a dangerous agent in 1917 and 1918. However, his actions in man-handling and injuring coolies indicate that he still retains his former cruelty and ruthlessness. It will be exceedingly interesting to note where next he appears." [87]

During the first full year that the Witzkes resided in Hankow, the city and its region suffered one of the worst natural disasters in human history. In July/August 1931, catastrophic flooding from engorged rivers inundated Hankow and its region. A Chinese engineer who survived recounted his experience:

> There was no warning, only a sudden great wall of water. Most of Wuhan's buildings in those days were only one story high, and for many people there was no escape—they died by the tens of thousands. . . . I was just coming off duty at the company's main office, a fairly new three-story

building near the center of town. . . . When I heard the terrible noise and saw the wall of water coming, I raced to the top story of the building. . . . I was in one of the tallest and strongest buildings left standing. At that time no one knew whether the water would subside or rise even higher.[88]

It is estimated that 150,000 were drowned in the first inundations, with much worse to come. Famine and disease followed the flooding. Population displacement, stagnant waters and destruction of sanitary systems combined to make a breeding ground for pathogenic microbes that brought dysentery, cholera, typhoid, malaria and schistosomiasis. Measles and smallpox also proliferated because of overcrowding. Two million perished.[89]

The expatriates in Hankow were naturally affected by the flooding but in ways exceedingly mild compared to the desperate Chinese surrounding them. "Their exclusive concessions, located in one of the best-protected areas of the city, were among the last areas to be inundated by the flood. When the waters finally did arrive, foreign residents amused themselves by riding horses through the water or playing tennis on roofs. But before long the novelty wore off. The flood stank, there was no electricity for lights and fans, and the price of vegetables and meat had become extortionate. The solution was to take a ferry to the foreign clubs in the northern part of the city. Unable to indulge in customary amusements—such as horse racing, polo and golf—club patrons stared out onto the flooded grounds, making idle chitchat and drinking."[90]

What Witzke made of this unique calamity we can guess from the lack of any family memory of the event. Witzke and his wife apparently never mentioned their experience of the Hankow flood to their children or grandchildren.[91] Was this because the suffering was not theirs? Perhaps. Silence in this instance would be consistent with Witzke's amusement at the beheading he photographed and lightly dismissed with "and off with the head." But there is another possible explanation. The calamity may have touched too closely upon the family's own pain during their time in China, the death of their son Dieter, discussed below.

After the American Naval Attaché in Hankow found Witzke, and sought without success production of his 1916–1917 address book, there followed a succession of meetings between Witzke and the US Vice Consul there, Reginald P. Mitchel. Witzke spoke openly (if not entirely honestly) with Mitchel about his past, and Mitchel published a revealing article on Witzke in the November 1934 issue of *The American Foreign Service Journal*.[92] Witzke by then was back in Germany.

The article opens with a description of the loading dock at Hankow: "A large German freighter noses its way cautiously against the swirling current of the Yangtze toward her birth at a floating pontoon. Myriad Chinese coolies suddenly transform the scene into a bedlam, grappling with hawsers flung from the ship, making fast the lines, and responding to the megaphone orders marked out by a slightly short, sturdy figure directing mooring operations from the elevated deck of the anchored hulk. The vessel is finally made secure alongside the pontoon, and he lays aside his megaphone."

The magazine reader will have come by this point to appreciate that the subject of the article is the man with the megaphone: "Thus the hulk manager of the Hamburg-Amerika Line at Hankow ends another skirmish with the turbulent river as it courses with flood-season treachery toward the sea, 600 miles away." He is the subject of some sympathy, even pity: "It is an important event in his otherwise drab, monotonous existence, this arrival of a freighter from the Fatherland during the summer high-water period."

The writer evokes the man's childhood and early years, explaining, as though inside the head of the man, that the arrival of the freighter "ever transports him in memory to his childhood days in faraway Posen when he dreamed of sailing the seven seas in command of just such a craft. It has the queer habit too of conjuring up a past crowded with high adventure on sea and shore, intrigue and colorful exploits to remind him that his own life might have flowed into channels other than Central China if Fate had not picked him, as a blonde-haired, blue-eyed youth of 19 to play one of the strangest roles of the World War."

And finally the reveal, "For the stocky, middle-aged hulk manager is Lothar Witzke, the erstwhile Pablo Waberski, reputedly the most notorious spy who operated in the United States during the war and the only secret service agent of the Central Powers to be sentenced to death by the American government." The article is accompanied by a photograph of a handsome Witzke either in his office or at home, looking away from the camera. Witzke is described as middle-aged, though he was then thirty-nine.

The rest of the article offers, purportedly in Witzke's own words, reminiscences of his time as a spy in the United States and Mexico, with a focus on the entertaining story of how Witzke managed to fool the Russian consular agents in Mexico into giving him a Russian passport.[93] Beyond the Russian passport caper, Witzke speaks with precision about German navy ships in the South Pacific and South Atlantic early in the war, and he reveals that he was given a code name already in Valparaiso. He also speaks of espionage activity on the West Coast of the US and Canada.

We have discussed in chapter 6 some of the details offered by Witzke in this interview. Our inquiry here is what the profile in this American magazine tells us about Witzke's state of mind in Hankow in 1934 and more generally what it suggests about the man.

Why would Witzke have spoken to an American consular official on the record about his espionage past? Perhaps he had no clue that his comments would appear in a magazine profile, but this is unlikely; in any case, he told many things to the American consul and apparently obtained no guarantee of confidentiality. Did the German agent authorize the interview? We do not know. The German agent may not have known or cared. Witzke could be trusted not to blab in a way that would harm Germany's interests. The interstate arbitration between Germany and the United States had in any case been won by Germany, though the US was pressing for a rehearing.

Witzke was a pardoned spy; there was no apparent risk to talking about his now harmless subterfuges in obtaining a Russian passport or, even, about other aspects of his past as a spy. The Nazis were in power; Witzke may have felt further empowered by this fact.

Yet, in view of how close-lipped Witzke would later become about his past, apparently never speaking of his American activities even to his family, his volubility on the record with an American consul is striking. Much would happen in Witzke's life and in world affairs between 1934 and the 1950s that could explain why he later came to feel chastened about his time as a spy acting against America.

The article raises the matter of Black Tom. "Witzke's espionage career in the United States is said by one commentator to have constituted 'one of the most extraordinary cases in American history.' The same writer also sketched the ambitious nature of German espionage in the United States and said that 'there were even reports from the British who suspected him of being responsible for the Black Tom explosion in New York Harbor in July, 1916.'" The writer was evidently unaware that, for the American agent before the Mixed Claims Commission, Witzke's responsibility for Black Tom was a certainty, not a rumor developed by the British. When asked about the allegations about his connections to Black Tom, "Witzke today merely shrugs his shoulders and smiles non-committedly."

What are we to make of the fact that Witzke merely shrugged about Black Tom, rather than vehemently denied any role? Perhaps he knew about Germany's triumph up to then in the arbitration, and chose to be coy, no longer feeling the need to deny it. But the interview in its entirety suggests a different explanation: Witzke evidently enjoyed his notoriety as a spy, and may not have wished to disclaim responsibility for spectacular acts of sabotage, whether he did them or not. Witzke's non-denial evasion also echoes what he was reported to have said to American counsel five years earlier in Maracaibo in 1929 when he "'off the record' . . . insisted that he knew nothing of who did the job at Kingsland; but he said Black Tom 'was another matter.'"[94] We return to this in chapter 12, where we assess the evidence of Witzke's role at Black Tom.

Witzke's enduring bitterness about his humiliation at the hands of Paul Altendorf is barely suppressed, though his time with Altendorf was sixteen years past. He calls Altendorf his assistant and interpreter, and attributes his capture to the approbation of Altendorf by the Austrian Embassy, intimating that it was only because Altendorf somehow got the favor of the Austrians that Altendorf came to be trusted by the Germans.

The writer of the article has sympathy for this one-time spy on the world's stage now working a monotonous dead-end job on the docks of Hankow. The writer does not consider that Hankow was a mere stopover for Witzke before he would go on to other adventures.

BIRTHS AND DEATH

In September 1932 Lilli gave birth in China to a daughter that the couple named Helga. Toddler Dieter and baby Helga were cared for by their Chinese nanny ("*ama*").

The family seemed happy, but horror then struck. Both children got tuberculosis.[95] Dieter got it much worse, and Lilli's and Lothar's perfect son died in 1934. Helga would over time become, insofar as she could, the replacement son for her father.

As Helga remained sick with tuberculosis, the family decided to move back to Germany to obtain better medical care for Helga.[96] This meant that they had to leave behind their *ama*, who had been more a mother for Helga than Lilli had been. The separation was scarring for Helga; she would still evoke the pain to her children decades later.[97] As painful as the loss was for Helga, Lilli's inability to connect to Helga (and perhaps to anyone other than her youngest child, still to come) would have caused damage regardless of the lost *ama*. This disability was passed on. Helga as a mother would prove equally incapable of physical affection with her children.[98]

Whether by nature or to distract herself from the loss, Lilli sought refuge in socializing. But it did not work. She may already have had depressive tendencies; if so, they deepened. Lothar, with a wandering eye to begin with, grew distant from his morose wife, and was rarely home. This was already true in China, and it stayed so after their return to Germany.[99]

In 1935, now back in Hamburg, the couple had another son who they named Lothar, after his father. The new son, unlike his father and deceased older brother, was dark-haired and dark-eyed. The father took one look, and pronounced dismissively: "Nein, es ist kein Dieter" ("No, this is not Dieter."). Poor young Lothar—a frightened and sensitive child with an artistic temperament—would struggle to find his way in life. His hopes to be an actor were disdained by his father. Instead, at his father's insistence, he became a bookkeeper at his father's office in the 1950s; but Lothar Jr. was not good with numbers, and the job did not last. He was good with children, and yet he would never have kids. His compass point was always his mother, Lilli. Similar in temperament, they could not let go of one another. He would live with her until the day she died, in 1980.[100]

NAZI PARTY MEMBERSHIP

In May 1932, while in China, within a few months of the formation of the Nazi organization in Hankow, Witzke became a member of the Nazi Party in Hamburg as member number 1168089.[101]

Germany's population in 1932 was sixty-seven million. Nazi Party membership in 1932 was 800,000. That put Witzke in a percentage of 1.2 percent. In a nation whose public sector was dominated by Kaiser-nostalgic conservatives, being a Nazi was not (before 1933) a good career move.[102]

Witzke's membership in the Party did not make him a black sheep in his family; it likely met with approval.

Bundesarchiv files show that, in 1936, his brother Günter (one year younger than Lothar) was an *Oberscharführer*, or staff sergeant, in the SS (*Schutzstaffel*).[103] We do not know how long Günter was a member before 1936, but his rank suggested that he was not a newcomer. Günter left the SS, on good terms, in 1936.

In 1936, Günter's last year in the SS, it had 100,000 members, comprising an elite security organization fanatically loyal to Hitler and to the racial hatred that was his core belief; their responsibility during the war would include running the concentration camps. Whether he had been in the SS for a short time or long time as of 1936, Günter's membership must reflect a certain comfort with the SS's worldview. But his unexplained resignation from the SS at a time that the SS was expanding its power casts doubt on any conclusion that one might make about the implications of Günter's SS membership.

As to brother Ottomar (six years younger than Lothar), Ottomar was an Obersturmführer, or first lieutenant in charge of fifty to one hundred men, in the SA in Hamburg. The SA (*Sturmabteilung*) were the brown-shirted stormtroopers who took the lead in violence against communists and Jews. Family letters from his childhood give no hint that Ottomar would become a thug; as a schoolboy, he took piano lessons. The likelihood that Otto was involved in atrocities depends in part on how long he was in the SA before 1936, and this fact is unknown to us. After the Nazi takeover of the state in 1933–1934, SA violence diminished, as there was less street-fighting to do.[104] But even after 1934, and "precisely because the militants from 1934 onward often lacked the opportunity to engage in the physical violence that during the years of struggle had so successfully served as a means of bonding for SA units, they welcomed opportunities to attack Jews."[105] Moreover, stormtrooper "violence in the years 1933 to 1938 regularly took place in public, in front of the eyes of the local and regional communities. Insulting, spitting at, and beating Jews not only humiliated and terrified the victims of such assaults but also illustrated the new, highly unequal balance of power in German society."[106] We do not know when, if ever, Ottomar left the SA.

As to Kurt, the brother who was closest to Lothar, a declassified CIA document says that Kurt was in the SD (*Sicherheitsdienst*), the intelligence and surveillance agency of the SS, founded by Heinrich Himmler and run by Reinhard Heydrich.[107] Another CIA document, written by a CIA informant in about 1960, reported the following:

> According to the source, [Kurt] Witzke has been in Damascus since 1948. He is considered a very obnoxious person. He came to Damascus together with some other Germans who had been prisoners of war in Italian camps. When Italy agreed to allow these German prisoners to go to Damascus, they made it a condition that Witzke be part of the group. Witzke was not well regarded and was disliked by most of his countrymen. He is a man without scruples. . . .

> What this Witzke, if the name is spelled correctly in the documents, had to do with his past in the Third Reich is unknown to me. But he belonged to the same circle as Brunner and Rademacher, both of whom were wanted for their involvement in the extermination of the Jews.[108]

The evidence therefore is that all three of Lothar's brothers were committed Nazis, and may have been involved in atrocities, though none was pursued as a war criminal.

His brothers' activities are not attributable to Lothar, but his three brothers' memberships in the SS, SA and SD provide familial context to an assessment of the implications of Lothar's membership in the Nazi party. The affectionate family correspondence from the World War I era and Lothar's effort to secure jobs for Kurt and Ottomar at the Lago Company in 1930 show no hint of estrangement.

The sociology and psychology of Nazi party membership are among the most analyzed subjects, and there is material discord among historians. The historiography of Nazi membership has not, though, focused on Germans abroad. For Germans in Germany, those who joined the Party well before 1932 tended to include true believers; pure opportunists flocked to the Party after March 1933 when the Nazis secured power (and the latecomers were derisively labeled "March Violets" by longstanding Nazis). But those who joined the Party in the early 1930s may just not have had the opportunity to join before then or may have lacked exposure to the party through friends and family.[109]

Judging only by the date of his membership, Witzke joined closer to the opportunistic end of the spectrum than to the true believer end. Germany was suffering in 1932 its third disastrous year of economic depression since the 1929 stock market crash; having recovered from hyper-inflation, the Depression that followed so soon was an additional trauma that would push Germany to extremism.[110] Witzke may have hoped, as did millions of Germans, that the Nazi Party would be good for the economy.[111] Or his reasons might have been more self-centered: it is possible that Witzke was advised to join the Party in order to further his opportunities. Or he might have done so for social advancement in the Hankow expatriate community; we have seen that the Nazi group in Hankow was active. Or he might have figured that, as he was already being solicited for contributions to the Party, there was no reason not to formalize the arrangement and secure such advantages as membership might bring. Or there might have been deeper affinity, but if so we cannot know how deep it went.[112] "For most young Germans [of the right ethnicity], National Socialism did not mean dictatorship, censorship, and repression; it meant freedom and adventure. They saw Nazism as a natural extension of the youth movement, as an antiaging regimen for body and mind."[113] Witzke was an adventurer of longstanding, and not given to reflection about the consequences.

Later in the century, the Witzke family, as was the case of numerous German families, wrestled with the fact of his Party membership. Witzke's daughter, Helga, would say: "Ja, aber er war kein Nazi, er war Patriot" ("Yes, but he was not a Nazi, he was a patriot.").[114]

Witzke family life once back in Germany during the 1930s reflected the time. Lilli took child-rearing lessons from Kindererziehung für Nazimütter ("Child-Rearing for Nazi Mothers"). Lothar Jr. and Helga, as every German child at that time, were in the Hitlerjugend (Hitler Youth) and Bund Deutscher Mädel (League of German Girls). But the children refused to attend mandatory activities, and their father did not force them to join. Perhaps he felt the gaze of his anti-Nazi mother-in-law.[115]

The statement of principle that Witzke made in his 1929 letter ("I believed fully in the code of honor of the former German army and navy officer and if the entire country had been like they, Germany would never have lost the war")[116] shows that Witzke was an anti-Weimar militarist and a believer in the *Dolchstoßlegende*, or the Stab-in the-Back-Myth for Germany's loss of World War I, an antisemitic explanation voiced vehemently by the Nazis.[117] His service in the *Abwehr* during World War II was presumably voluntary, as he was beyond the age of military service. The British found it appropriate to intern him for a year in a denazification facility. Near the end of his life he could make a joke about the Nazi genocide of the Jews. His instinctive preference for his blond-haired blue-eyed son over his dark-haired son also likely tells us something.

The family's belief is that neither Witzke nor his daughter Helga, who so closely resembled him, had deep political convictions.[118] But one did not need political conviction to be drawn to the Nazis. In the early 1930s, Nazism "offered a vague but powerful rhetorical vision of a Germany united and strong, . . . a racial community of all Germans working together, a new Reich that would rebuild Germany's economic strength and restore the nation to its rightful place in the world."[119]

While his daughter's defense of her father as a patriot rather than a Nazi sounds overly-protective, we have insufficient ground to say that she was wrong. Nazi ideology was compatible with his convictions such as they were. There is no basis to go further and assign a speculative percentage of true belief versus opportunism to his decision to become a Party member. There is also no basis to believe that Nazi atrocities during World War II would much trouble him, or his brothers.

INTELLIGENCE WORK ANEW

With three kids and a wife to support, we can be sure that upon his return to Germany in 1935 Witzke was focused on securing gainful employment, and

Germany in 1935 offered better prospects for employment than the Germany that he had left in 1929.

By the mid-1930s, "the Third Reich was, on the whole, a success so far as most ordinary Germans were concerned. By this time, unemployment had been all but eliminated, 'order' had been restored, and the country's war industries and armed forces greatly enlarged. Homes, roads (including the famous Autobahn), and all manner of other infrastructure were being built."[120] Germany was, however, far from a prosperous country if the measure is the purchasing power of the average German. In 1939, one of sixty Germans owned a car, compared to one of twenty-five Britons and one of five Americans. And this was despite the substantial state subsidization of the German automobile industry, making the price of an automobile in German artificially low.[121]

We have no information on Witzke's life from 1935 to 1937. These were eventful years in his country. During that time, Hitler bluffed and won when he remilitarized the Rhineland (March 1936), and the Olympics were held in Berlin (August 1936).

As of 1938, a year before the war began, Witzke was a captain at the *Abwehr* Hamburg Intelligence Station, Group II, Sabotage.[122] Witzke's boss at the *Abwehr* Hamburg station, Nikolaus Ritter, began his work with the *Abwehr* on January 1, 1937.[123] Ritter was recruited to join the *Abwehr* because he had lived for a long time in the United States and spoke American English.[124] These commonalities in their life experience could have led the *Abwehr* to seek out Witzke for the same reasons. As Witzke was a captain already by 1938, he may well have been in the *Abwehr* before 1938. His connections through Jahnke to important figures in the German intelligence community likely got him a prized position.[125]

It may be that Witzke joined the *Abwehr* because it provided his best work opportunity, as spycraft and sabotage constituted his recognized expertise in Germany. No doubt he also wanted to serve his country. As an abiding militarist, he may have been an enthusiastic participant in the spread of National Socialism, and he may have considered that he could best help the cause through intelligence work.[126] Whether it helped or hurt Witzke within the *Abwehr* that he was a member of the Nazi party cannot be known. Helmut Groscurth, chief of the *Abwehr*'s Gruppe II (Witzke's department), was among those who plotted in 1938 to overthrow Hitler.[127] The anti-Nazi Groscurth, like the anti-Nazi *Abwehr* chief Wilhelm Canaris, nonetheless continued to serve the Reich.[128] For Nazis and non-party members, Witzke's heroic past would have been a plus, and in January 1939 Witzke found it expedient to have the German Admiralty confirm that he had in 1924 been awarded the Iron Cross, first and second class.[129]

The *Abwehr*'s Group II handled sabotage and uprisings in foreign countries, and included the special operations section known as the Brandenburg Regiment, responsible for "infiltration behind enemy lines (sometimes disguised as the enemy's own troops), . . . seizure of strong points, . . . destruction of enemy bridges and installations, and . . . similar commando missions."[130] Witzke had oversight *inter alia* of British nationals who were ready to engage in sabotage in Great Britain.[131] Witzke's responsibility for infiltrating saboteurs into Britain is evidence that, for the Germans, his US sabotage history was real, not concocted by the United States for the purpose of a damages claim before the US/Germany Mixed Claims Commission.

Already in 1938, Witzke was active in the Netherlands working with *Abwehr* operatives engaged in espionage against Britain. The *Abwehr* used the Netherlands for transmission of messages, and recruited Dutch men and women to spy on the British, for eventual infiltration in Britain, and for false passports. When messages were passed from *Abwehr* operatives in Britain through the Netherlands to Germany, they would end up with Witzke in Hamburg. Ritter and Witzke frequently worked together; Witzke had a knack for impressing his superiors. On one occasion, Witzke joined Ritter in the Hague for a meeting with a beautiful Dutch agent who the Germans had previously recruited.[132] Ritter may have asked Witzke to join this meeting because he knew how well Witzke did with comely women. But this time the chemistry was not there, and the recruit was ill at ease in Witzke's presence. Witzke quickly left the apartment and moved on to other business. The setback, if it even was one, was inconsequential: this was work for which Witzke was well-suited.[133]

KAPITÄNSHAUS (CAPTAIN'S HOUSE)

Witzke's connection to Jahnke may have brought him not just entrée into the *Abwehr* but also a very comfortable house on Farmsener Landstrasse in an upscale residential quarter (Volksdorf) of Hamburg. Witzke may also have benefitted from the support of wealthy Hamburg businessmen with connections to the *Abwehr*. Maintaining such connections was part of the *Abwehr*'s work in Hamburg in the late 1930s.[134] Their home was a "*Kapitänshaus*," in an area reserved for homeowners who were naval captains or the equivalent.[135] Witzke had never been a naval officer, but that evidently did not matter.

Witzke's May 1932 Nazi membership card says that he was then working in China and gives Farmsener Landstrasse in Volksdorf as his address.

It is surprising that Witzke had in 1932 enough money to purchase a rather grand house in Volksdorf, but he may not have purchased it. Witzke family memory, though indistinct on this point, suggests that the house was a reward to Witzke for services rendered.[136] Such services may have been intelligence work done by Witzke during the Weimar and early Nazi eras, or even his loyalty to the fatherland during his time in America.

Whatever the way it came to Witzke, the house, built in the 1920s, was large and comfortable. Its furnishings were expensive, likely purchased in China. Upon entrance, one came into an entry hall. To the left, a dining room, with an exquisite, large round dining table. The tableware was refined, reflecting Lilli's taste. From the dining room, there was access to the somewhat somber living room. The living room was also accessible from the entry hall.

The kitchen had its eating table, and also a door onto the garden in the back.

On the ground floor there was a small guest bathroom where the Pablo Waberski diaries were kept and used. We return in a later chapter to this intriguing family fact.

Toward the back of the house there was a winter garden, with white garden furniture covered by flowered cushions and a view of the outer garden.

The garden was lovely, a lawn with shrubbery, flowers, vegetables, berry bushes and an aged apple tree, all carefully tended by Lilli.

Back inside, a staircase led upstairs where there were three bedrooms and a full bathroom. Lothar Jr's bedroom was small and dark. Helga's room was large and sunlit and had a balcony that overlooked the winter garden. The parents' bedroom looked out at the front of the house; its oak furniture was antique.

The house also had a detached garage and, beneath the garage, a basement that held a small workshop. The family kept the gardening tools there.

The Volksdorf *Kapitänshaus* would survive the war unharmed. Witzke's grandchildren would scamper among its rooms during the 1960s and 1970s, and in 2021 would describe the house in detail and with affection.[137]

STAR WITNESS

"The . . . evidence relating to Witzke and
Jahnke is mainly in the shape of alleged
admissions by Witzke and is intermingled
with his alleged admissions in connection
with the Black Tom Case. This evidence makes
no impression whatever upon us. . . ."
—1930 MCC DECISION, 150

During the sixteen years from 1923 to 1939, as recounted in the preceding chapter, Witzke took part in the street violence of the Weimar era, found employment and lived abroad in Mexico, Venezuela and China, joined the Nazi Party, married and became a father, and became an officer in the *Abwehr* as World War II approached.

This chapter tells a story that proceeded in parallel to those events. It is a story about responsibility for Black Tom, one that unfolded over sixteen years in an interstate arbitration between the United States and Germany. In the arbitration, which began the year that Witzke returned to Germany (1923) and ended as World War II began, the US advanced the position that Witzke and Jahnke were responsible for the sabotage at Black Tom and Kingsland. Germany defended itself, arguing that Witzke and Jahnke were in San Francisco, not the East Coast, at the relevant times. For most of the sixteen-year arbitration, Germany was successful in refuting the American position. It was not until 1939 that the arbitrators, who comprised what was called a Mixed Claims Commission, found in favor of the US position.

The story of this unusual interstate arbitration, a mostly forgotten piece of US/Germany relations in the 1920s and 1930s, is part of the life of Witzke both because he was Germany's star witness and because the evidence assembled for the case is a principal source for Witzke's actions in the Americas in 1916–1917.[1]

THE ORIGINS OF THE MIXED CLAIMS COMMISSION

When the US declared war on Germany in April 1917, President Wilson announced the seizure of private German assets held in the US, to be returned only at the end of the conflict. The seized assets amounted to about $500 million (equivalent in 2020 dollars to about $6.5 billion).[2] The US continued to hold German assets after the war, and the withheld assets contributed to Germany's financial woes after the war.

US private interests, meanwhile, had submitted numerous claims to the US Government for espousal by the Government against Germany for monetary losses suffered by Americans during the war.

Germany needed release of its seized assets. The private US interests clamored for payment of their claims. Reparations payable by Germany to the Allied Powers would not be the solution for US claimants, as reparations did not flow to the US, a non-signatory to the Treaty of Versailles that provided for reparations.

The face-off between US business interests claiming damages from Germany and Germany seeking return of the seized assets of its shippers and others was resolved (or thought to be resolved) in 1921 when the US and Germany concluded a Treaty on the Establishment of Friendly Relations. The Treaty provided that the property of the German government and German nationals that had been seized by the US during the war was to be held by the US until Germany "made suitable provision for the satisfaction . . . of all persons . . . who owe permanent allegiance to the United States of America and who have suffered, through the acts of the Imperial German Government, or its agents, since July 31, 1914, loss, damage, or injury."[3]

The Americans proposed in April 1922 a Mixed Claims Commission to decide the claims, and Germany agreed.[4] The agreement was signed in August 1922.

The proposed Commission was to have three Commissioners, one appointed by each nation and the third to act as Umpire. The US suggested to Germany that, in order to speed ratification by Congress, Germany agree that the Umpire be a respected and neutral American.[5] The prospect of an American Umpire was naturally a concern for Weimar. But Walther Rathenau, who held the dual role of Minister for Foreign Affairs and Minister of Reconstruction, saw the upside if solidarity with the US could lead the Americans to intervene on the reparations issue.[6]

President Harding directed his secretary of state to emphasize in press releases that an American would serve as Umpire.[7] The German Chancellor stressed in a public statement that economic hardship could be reduced by cooperation and good faith.[8]

Germany's bet on the neutrality of the American Umpire was for the most part a winning one. There was a succession of four umpires over the sixteen years that the Mixed Claims Commission functioned. The first and last of these were justices of the US Supreme Court.[9]

THE SABOTAGE CASES

The vast majority of claims submitted to the Commission were quickly resolved. During the 1920s the Commission resolved some 22,000 claims worth $200 million.[10]

The sabotage claims were not even contemplated when the Mixed Claims Commission was established. The original view, as mentioned, was that the explosions at Black Tom and Kingsland were due to worker negligence, not sabotage. It is uncertain what led the companies that owned Black Tom and Kingsland to divert their attention from defending against negligence claims to prosecuting sabotage claims. A possible explanation is that the companies became aware of the series of articles written by Paul Altendorf on his exploits in Mexico with Witzke and others; these articles (published in 1919), as we will see in our last chapter (*Did He Do It? Black Tom*), included multiple allegations of Witzke's boasts about his role at Black Tom.[11] Altendorf's actions thus may have come to influence the life of Witzke even post-imprisonment.

The *Sabotage Cases* were different in nature than most of the claims submitted to the Commission; most claims were minor in scope, absent political implication, and quickly resolved. The sabotage claims, different in all these ways, came to dominate the proceedings. The sabotage allegations were, especially, politically sensitive. It mattered to Weimar Germany that it is not seen as a violator of US neutrality and in that way responsible for the US declaration of war. The imposition of the war guilt clause in the Treaty of Versailles was already more than Germany could accept.[12] Even though it had been the Imperial German government under Kaiser Wilhelm II, not the Weimar Government, that was implicated in the start of the war and that was the alleged violator of US neutrality, there was continuity between the two regimes. Over the course of the Mixed Claims Commission proceedings, several German secret agents who had been operating in the US during the War were engaged by the Weimar Government in prominent positions.[13]

The American Umpires for many years favored Germany's position on the Black Tom and Kingsland *Sabotage Cases*. This would change only in the late 1930s, for reasons described later in this chapter. Until then, it was the American side that rued the choice of an American Umpire, believing that each American umpire "could hardly avoid leaning over backward to avoid any appearance of favoring his own country in any question in which he had to render the final judgment."[14]

◇ ◇ ◇

The Mixed Claims Commission was given the authority to "consider all *written* statements or documents which may be presented to it by or on behalf of the respective Governments."[15] There was no authority to receive *oral* testimony (save for good cause shown), and there was no live testimony or cross-examination before the commissioners.[16] A hearing involving oral testimony and cross-examination was not only a peculiarity of the common law system but also beyond the hope of all involved at the start for rapid settlement. These hopes were dashed in the extreme when the process was taken over by the *Sabotage Cases*. Because there was no oral examination of witnesses, we are able to re-examine the evidence before the Commission with no comparative disadvantage for lack of access to witness testimony in person.

The record in the *Sabotage Cases* was substantial. There were six separate hearings that lasted a total of 60 days; these hearings consisted almost entirely of argument by counsel and presentation by counsel of testimonial and documentary evidence. The parties submitted over 50,000 pages of evidence. The US submitted forty-one briefs; Germany submitted 34.[17]

WITZKE'S TESTIMONY

Witzke made himself available as needed to the German Agent to assist in Germany's defense against the US claims. In March/April 1925, Witzke was in Berlin to meet with the German Agent about his witness statement. In July 1927, Witzke signed his witness statement in Hanover.[18] In January and June 1929, when Witzke was in Maracaibo, Venezuela, working for the Lago Petroleum Corporation, he was interviewed (unsatisfactorily) by the Americans and recounted the American efforts in a follow-up letter to the German Agent.[19] In June 1929, Witzke was back in Berlin to sign another witness statement for Germany.[20] In July 1930, Witzke met with the German agent in Hamburg.[21] In 1933, in Hankow China, as we have also seen, Witzke was tracked down by the US Consul, who asked him to produce his address book from 1916–1917. Witzke declined.[22]

The loyal German did his duty as a witness, allowing the German agent to write up a narrative that suited the German case.

As Witzke told it in his written testimony, he was entirely innocent of any sabotage activities during the period of US neutrality. "I did not have the slightest connection with the destruction of the Black Tom Terminal and the Kingsland Plant."[23] He (or rather the German counsel representing Weimar) was careful to explain that the acts of sabotage that he committed in the US came exclusively after the US entered the war. "I must make a distinction between the time prior to and the period after the American declaration of war. The tasks entrusted to me during these two periods were as different as were the relations between Germany and the US before and after April 6, 1917."[24]

The distinction that Witzke's counsel had him draw between sabotage pre- and post-US neutrality during World War I was essential because under the Treaty of Berlin Germany would be liable to American claimants for damage caused during the period of US neutrality.[25] The sabotage at both Black Tom and Kingsland occurred before the US entered the war. Thus, Germany could avoid liability by submitting evidence that, whatever depredations might have been done by German secret agents to US interests, such actions occurred after April 1917.

The Commission took in all this evidence and ultimately avoided making a decision about Witzke and Black Tom. Instead, after ruling for years in favor of Germany, they found at the end against Germany, but on bases other than the role and credibility of Lothar Witzke.

THE COMMISSION'S 1930 DECISION IN FAVOR OF GERMANY

The Mixed Claims Commission rendered its first major ruling on the merits in October 1930 in Hamburg.[26] The Decision was a victory for Germany.

While questioning the credibility of some of Germany's witnesses, the Commission stated that "we have not the least intention to raise any doubt as to the entire good faith of the present German Government in its management and presentation of these cases, nor of the Agent who has represented Germany as counsel. . . . We believe that the present German Government was entirely prepared to bring out the truth and to take the consequences, whatever they might be."[27] This affirmation would stand for another nine years, until rulings in 1939 by the two American Commissioners that Germany's evidence was fraudulent.

The commission's October 1930 Decision accepted that Germany had authorized sabotage in the US during the period of US neutrality, but as to what German agents had actually done in the US during the period of US neutrality, the Commission made the following statement: "up to the entry of the US into the war there were in the US certain German agents who were, or at least pretended to be, active in sabotage work. But we are also convinced that . . . their pretensions in such reports as they may have made and in their talk with each other were for the most part gross exaggerations of their actual accomplishments."[28] For the commission, therefore, Germany's secret agents in the US were boasters rather than saboteurs.

For Kingsland especially, the Commission found the proof of German responsibility negligible. "In the Kingsland Case, the . . . evidence relating to Witzke and Jahnke is mainly in the shape of alleged admissions by Witzke and is intermingled with his alleged admissions in connection with the Black Tom Case. This evidence makes no impression whatever upon us with respect to the Kingsland Case, but the fact that it does refer to the Kingsland fire as well as to the Black Tom fire tends to weaken the effect of the alleged admissions as to the Black Tom Case. On the evidence we are satisfied that Witzke and Jahnke were not in the east at the time of the Kingsland fire, and eliminate them from further consideration in connection with Kingsland."[29]

Thus, because Witzke's and Jahnke's alleged admissions about Black Tom were intermixed with their alleged admissions about Kingsland, the case for Black Tom was weakened by the weakness of the Kingsland case.

The Commission's disdain for the American case on Kingsland had to do less with their findings as to Witzke and Jahnke than with their findings as to the witnesses Frederick Herrmann and Paul Hilken.[30] These two German operatives originally testified for Germany but then switched and testified for the US. The Commission's assessment of these two witnesses was scathing: "Hilken and Herrmann are both liars, not presumptive but proven. No one could in the light of all their evidence believe anything either says unless something other than his own assertion confirmed his statements."[31] The commission also considered the role and testimony of Friedrich Hinsch, the German captain of a steamer interned at Baltimore and a key witness for Germany, but expressly avoided making a finding as to Hinsch's credibility.[32]

As to Black Tom, the Commission ultimately framed its findings in the negative, as a failure of proof on the American side: "We are not convinced that the [Black Tom] fire was not attributable to Hinsch and Kristoff, although we are convinced that it was not attributable to Witzke or Jahnke. But we are quite a long way from being convinced that the fire was caused by any German agent."[33]

The American case on Black Tom failed in large part because the Commission found Altendorf to be "the chief liar who has appeared in the cases before us, a chief among competitors of no mean qualifications."[34] The Commission also credited Germany's evidence that Witzke was in San Francisco at the time of both Black Tom and Kingsland.[35]

The Commission's findings as to Witzke were never reversed by the Commission's later rulings against Germany. The Commission's choice not to reconsider its findings as to Witzke does not imply that the Commission considered its earlier conclusions final or unassailable; rather, the Commission had no need to reconsider its earlier findings as to Witzke, because it was sufficient for the Commission at the end of the day to make findings based on other parts of the record.

1932, REHEARING DENIED: THE HERRMANN MESSAGE FOUND TOO GOOD TO BE TRUE

After the Commission's denial of the US case on sabotage in 1930, the American agent filed several petitions for rehearing, contending that the Commission had "misapprehended the facts and committed errors of law," and asked to reopen the case for the admission of new evidence.[36]

The new evidence consisted of new testimony from two German-American operatives, Frederick Herrmann (a New Jersey resident) and Paul Hilken (a Baltimore native, whose father was the German consul in Baltimore). Both Herrmann and Hilken had, as noted, originally given testimony on behalf of Germany, denying any role in or knowledge of any sabotage in the US. Herrmann and Hilken then changed their testimony and said that the German agent had suborned their perjury. The Commission continued after 1930 to find both Herrmann and Hilken still to be "liars,"[37] evidently suspecting that they had in some fashion sold their testimony to the Americans.

Besides the still unpersuasive testimony from Herrmann and Hilken, the new evidence proffered by the Americans pertained mostly to a document that came to be known as the Herrmann Message. Frederick Herrmann was among those secret agents who fled to Mexico after the US declaration of war against Germany in April 1917. In Mexico, Herrmann found himself low on funds and could not convince the Resident Minister for the German Empire in Mexico, Heinrich von Eckhardt, to advance him cash.

The Herrmann Message was a plea by Herrmann to his fellow agent Paul Hilken, who had remained in the US, to intervene with von Eckhardt to get the Resident Minister to advance cash to Herrmann. The Message was sent by Herrmann to Hilken from Mexico by courier in January 1917. The coded message was written in lemon juice on the pages of a Blue Book magazine and could be seen only by passing a hot iron over the pages.[38] The vital interest of the Message to the Commission was the reason stated by Herrmann in his Message to justify getting cash, namely, successful acts of sabotage in which Herrmann claimed to have participated.

Decoded, the Message said in part (bracketed text added to identify the coded names): "Have seen 1755 [Eckhardt]. He is suspicious of me. . . . Have told him all reference 2584 [Hinsch] and . . . 7595 [Jersey City Terminal], 3106 [Kingsland]. He doubts me on account of my bum 7346 [German]. Confirm to him through your channels all OK and my mission here. I have no funds. . . ."

At the time of this message, both Black Tom and Kingsland had been destroyed. The Herrmann Message thus showed Herrmann complaining that, despite his having told von Eckhardt in Mexico about the successful exploits, including the destruction of Black Tom ("Jersey City Terminal") and Kingsland, organized by Herrmann and Hinsch and their team in the US, von Eckhardt remained unappreciative and dubious, in part because Herrmann spoke German poorly.

For the American agent, the Herrmann Message was a "smoking gun" with respect to the core issue, Germany's responsibility for the sabotage at Black Tom and Kingsland.

The Commission agreed, in a ruling in 1932 that, if it were authentic, the Message would show that: one, Herrmann and Hilken knew that German agents were responsible for the Black Tom and Kingsland explosions (thus corroborating their revised testimony); and two, Hinsch, Hilken and Herrmann were implicated in the sabotage (thereby discrediting Hinsch's early disavowals of his knowledge or participation in the plots). The American Umpire wrote: "A glance through this translation will indicate that, without reference to any other evidence, [the Hermann Message] is conclusive proof to any reasonable man that (a) Herrmann and Hilken knew the Kingsland fire and the Black Tom explosion were the work of German agents and (b) that Hinsch, Hilken, and Herrmann, undoubted agents, were privy thereto, and (in the light of the record before the Commission) (c) that Kristoff and Wozniak were active participants in these events. As the American Agent has well said, I may utterly disregard all the new evidence produced and still, if I deem this message genuine, hold Germany responsible in both cases."[39]

But the Commission distrusted the witness, Hilken, who found the Message,[40] and, recalling that Herrmann was a liar ("not presumptive but proved"),[41] concluded that the Message was too good to be true for the American side, containing too much to be believed about activities that these agents and operators would have wanted to keep secret.[42]

The Commission dismissed the American petition on December 3, 1932, finding that the new evidence would not be sufficient to reverse the Commission's original opinion.[43]

Those who follow criminal cases reported in the press may assume that witnesses routinely lie in judicial proceedings. Whether true or not in criminal cases, it is rare to find an international arbitral tribunal taking the view in writing that witnesses on both sides perjured themselves. That is, though, what happened here, and the perceived pattern of pervasive perjury hurt the American case for many years, as the US bore the burden of proof. The perjury likely also led the Commission to make as few definitive findings as it could on the basis of the testimonial evidence.

From 1922 through 1932, then, the US case met with nothing but failure. This may have been due in part to superior advocacy on the German side. While the US bore the burden of proof and Germany had the relatively easier task of poking holes in the proof rather than of advancing its own narrative, the skill employed on the German side, their tone, their reasonableness, their acknowledgment of counter-evidence, was, we expect, more effective than the more aggressive tone adopted on the US side, and made the German submissions more convincing. In view of the ultimate findings in the matter, another explanation for the German agent's success would be that the Germans were effective at defrauding the Commission. And another explanation for the aggressiveness of the American side would be legitimate frustration that their rightful claims were being foiled by deception.

THE HERRMANN MESSAGE REVISITED: FRAUD UNCOVERED

In 1933, the American agent filed another petition for rehearing. This petition was granted. The Commission found: "Every tribunal has inherent power to re-open and to revise a decision induced by fraud. . . . If it may correct its own errors and mistakes, *a fortiori* it may, while it still has jurisdiction of a cause, correct an error into which it has been led by fraud and collusion."[44]

More briefing, more evidence, and more hearings followed. By 1939, with widespread American hostility to the Nazi regime, and it being apparent to the German commissioner that the two American commissioners would rule against Germany, the Berlin government ordered the German commissioner to withdraw from the Mixed Claims Commission. On March 1, 1939, the German commissioner did so, charging bias on the part of the umpire, then Supreme Court Justice Owen J. Roberts.[45] Germany may have hoped that the commissioner's withdrawal would incapacitate the Commission,[46] but that is not what happened.[47]

In June 1939, the American commissioner issued an opinion that detailed what he found to be fraud perpetrated by Germany against the Commission in the earlier phase of the proceeding.[48]

With respect to Kingsland, the commissioner found that the series of affidavits submitted by Germany by workers at the Kingsland plant was fraudulent.[49] The commissioner also found that Wozniak's initial testimony had been bought by Germany,[50] and that Hinsch's several written declarations were replete with falsities.[51] In light of this evidence, the American commissioner concluded that German agents engaged in sabotage in neutral countries, including the US, and that, through Wozniak, German agents had played a direct role in the Kingsland fire.[52]

After an exhaustive review of the context, provenance and content of the Herrmann Message, resulting in a finding that the message was authentic,[53] the American commissioner concluded that the German government was liable not only for the destruction at Kingsland but also for that at Black Tom.[54]

Umpire Roberts concurred with the American commissioner's opinion and ordered that the Hamburg Decision of 1930 be set aside. Roberts found that "the Commission was seriously misled" in its initial determinations.[55] As to Germany's responsibility for the sabotage at both Kingsland and Black Tom, the decisive evidence was the Herrmann Message: "As is admitted, the Herrmann message, if genuine, establishes Germany's responsibility in both cases."[56]

On October 30, 1939, the umpire entered an award, with interest, of $31.4 million for the claimants.[57]

Absent at the end of the day was any finding about Lothar Witzke in relation to Black Tom. While the American agent continued to attack the evidence that placed Witzke and Jahnke in San Francisco at the time of the explosion, the Commission took no view.

THE COMMISSION CONCLUDES ITS WORK

Because the German commissioner resigned when it became clear to him that the two American commissioners were going to rule against Germany, the question arises whether the MCC's ultimate findings can be doubted, or dismissed, as biased. Germanophobia was the explanation offered by the German press at the time.[58] But the few German historians who have considered the matter have taken the view that, on balance, Germany's credibility in its submissions before the Mixed Claims Commission was dubious, and that Germany was likely responsible for sabotage in neutral America.[59] As one German historian has written:

> A calm and objective treatment of the politically sensitive sabotage claims in the already tense German-American relations since Hitler had seized power was practically impossible for the Mixed Claims Commission and a disagreement was the logical consequence of this development. One of the reasons for this may also have been the fact that at the same time as negotiations were being held on the activities of German agents in the First World War before the Mixed Claims Commission, German spies were again active in the USA. These subversive activities, which in 1938 led to a series of sensational trials in the USA, cast a very ambivalent light on Germany's credibility with regard to the sabotage claims.[60]

On 10 January 1941, the sabotage claimants received $23.6 million, paid from the funds held in the German Special Deposit Account created in the 1920s for the purpose of the Mixed Claims Commission cases.[61] The Federal Republic of Germany ultimately made payments totaling $97.5 million to cover the MCC awards. These payments were made in annual installments from 1952 to 1978.[62]

Lothar Witzke, the accused saboteur and Germany's star witness, was long gone by the time that the final payments were made.

The build-up to the Second World War was the backstory to the conclusion of the MCC arbitration, and the outcome of the war allowed the final payments due from Germany to the US to be made. The story now to be told is how Witzke served his country in the Second World War in ways far different than the young Witzke had done in America during World War I.

AT WAR AGAIN

"Witzke was Witzke. He did not even need
the proverbial moment of shock before he
instantly got the picture. . . . Witzke
could not help saying with quite a sneer,
'once again, we were damn lucky.'"
-NIKOLAUS RITTER, *COVER NAME:
DR. RANTZAU*, 116-17.

In 1963, a married couple, both doctors, arrived by car at the German/Danish border. They were on a driving trip from Hamburg, The woman tendered her passport. The Danish border police took a look, made an inquiry, and denied her entry. The problem: her maiden name marked her as among the "*unerwünschte Leute*" (unwanted people). The name on the passport: Helga Witzke Moinian. Twenty years after the end of World War II, a German named Witzke would be detained at the Danish border.[1]

US Army files (declassified upon the authors' FOIA request in 2019) contain this description of Witzke from 1944 or 1945: "Short [5'8"], well built, fair hair brushed back, blue-grey eyes, clean shaven, fresh complexion. Walks with a peculiar limp as a result of his wound [elsewhere said to have been suffered on the *Dresden* offshore Chile]. *Is described as a trusted and intrepid officer and is said to have achieved excellent results.*"[2] US Army files also report that Witzke was awarded in March 1942 the War Merit Cross (*Kriegsverdienstkreuz*), a decoration given to military personnel and civilians, and a successor to the Iron Cross awarded during World War I.[3] Witzke was, thus, among those Germans who obtained decorations for valorous service in both world wars.

What had happened in Denmark? What were the "excellent results" achieved by Lothar Witzke during World War II? What did he do to earn a War Merit Cross? We have been able to establish much of what Witzke did during the War. But if there is atrocity in *his* wartime story, it has proved unreachable.

⟡ ◇ ⟡

An *Abwehr* officer as of 1938, stationed in Hamburg, Witzke was associated with the Brandenburg Regiment, a special operations battalion trained for disguise and sabotage, with fluency in a foreign language required.[4] Witzke was identified as a *Sonderführer*, meaning a civilian who had not been trained as a soldier and who was called to military service in a specialist role because of a particular competence. In view of what he would be tasked to do, Witzke's recognized competence was likely undercover work, or more narrowly sabotage. His fluency in English surely also counted.

In 1939–1940 and part of 1941, Witzke worked mostly in occupied Belgium, the Netherlands, and France, with responsibility for infiltration of saboteurs into Great Britain. His operatives were anti-British Welsh and Flemish. In late 1940, Witzke was seen near Brest, organizing fishing vessels to infiltrate agents into the UK. He also found time often to visit his French girlfriend at Douarnenez, a coastal village in Brittany.[5] A British intelligence report from 1941 says: "The most important of the Intelligence Stations on the North Coast of France is Oberleitstelle Brest which is actually engaged in the training, equipment and dispatch of spies and saboteurs to the UK under the direction of Korv. Kap. Schneidewind and his principal assistant Lieut. Lothar Witzke (who was von Papen's Sabotage assistant in the USA during the last war. Sentenced to death by the American court and reprieved by the President.)"[6]

At some time in 1941, Witzke transferred to Greece, where he was sighted by Allied intelligence.[7]

We know from Witzke family correspondence and photographs that he was in Oslo in 1944 and 1945 in civilian clothing.

In 1946, Witzke was imprisoned by the British in Neuengamme denazification camp in the British zone outside Hamburg.

There are, then, five principal phases to Witzke's World War II experience, and we deal with them sequentially in this chapter: (i) 1939-41, mostly in Belgium and Brittany, with the *Abwehr*; (ii) 1941-43, Athens, with the *Abwehr*; (iii) 1944-45, Oslo, likely in a civilian post; (iv) throughout the war, corresponding with and visiting his family in Volksdorf, Hamburg; and (v) 1946, Neuengamme, as a prisoner of the British.

BELGIUM AND BRITTANY, 1939–1941

October 1939. The war has just begun. Germany has conquered Poland, and the Soviet Union has signed a nonaggression pact with Germany. Great Britain and France have declared war on Germany but no hostilities have occurred. Germany hopes that Britain can be pressured to conclude a separate peace with Germany.

A meeting is held in Antwerp, in a block of offices opposite the Canadian Pacific Railway wharf. The objective is sabotage, to be carried out by anti-English Welsh nationalists being trained by the Germans to infiltrate Great Britain in order to sabotage industrial and munitions operations there. At the meeting are (i) Gwilym Williams, a Welsh former constable, polyglot and explosives expert, (ii) a second Welshman named Arthur Owens (alias Snow), (iii) "a powerfully built man who was introduced . . . as the 'Commander'" and who speaks perfect English, (iv) a Major Brasser, *Abwehr* Chief of Air Intelligence, and (v) Major Nikolaus Ritter, the head of *Abwehr* counterespionage with oversight of Britain, including infiltrating agents and, as such, the commander's superior. The meeting takes place over lunch, and lunch is copious, including bottled beer.[8]

The commander takes charge of the conversation. He explains that he wants the Welsh to assist Germany by destroying—in Wales and Bristol, Manchester, Liverpool and Glasgow—dockyards, ships, sheds used for the storage of stores and cotton, electricity generating stations, aerodromes, and munitions factories and dumps. The Germans will supply all necessary material, the only difficulty being the method of supply, whether by submarine or air, and where the drops would be.

In exchange for this help, the Germans will, when terms of peace are made, assure self-governance for Wales.

The commander interrogates the Welshmen at length about the strength and purposes of the Welsh National Movement, and advises that members of the movement find employment in England in order to commit sabotage when the opportunity arises.

The commander says that the German intention is not to deprive England of any territory, but rather to assure self-governance for Wales. The commander gives this explanation of Germany's war aims:

> He further stated that Germany wished to live in peace with England and France, that they did not desire to kill a single Englishman in this senseless war. They had sufficient work in Germany in connection with the National

Socialist movement to keep them occupied for the next hundred years, and for this reason they did not want war. The talk about the Maginot Line being impregnable was all rot as the Germans could walk through it any time they wished, but they did not want to kill their young men or the young men of England and France in doing so. They did not mind forcing matters at all, but were anxious for this silly senseless war to end, as they wanted nothing better than peace with England and France and for this purpose they would appreciate any acts of sabotage committed by the Welsh so as to bring to an end this unnecessary war which serves no useful purpose either to Germany or England and France, and a way to bring this war to a quick conclusion is to cripple England materially so as to make her listen to sense and reason without slaughtering the youth of the various countries concerned in the conflict.[9]

The commander also explains Germany's intentions in Poland: "it was Germany's intention at the proper time to give Russia 200,000 square miles of Polish territory, 80,000 to the Poles; 60,000 to the Jews, and retain 100,000 square miles for herself."

The commander instructs the Welshmen to consider where sabotage materials could safely be stored and where explosives are held and could be stolen, how propaganda could be disseminated among the Welsh, whether Lloyd George (the Welsh former Prime Minister of Great Britain) could be approached with a view to influencing the Welsh to act against England, whether it would be useful for their purpose to give separate and preferential treatment to Welsh troops taken as prisoners, and means of communication, including instruction in wireless transmission. The commander suggests that the Welshman adopt the hobby of stamp-collection as a cover.

The commander gives instruction on incendiarism. This includes demonstration on assembly, with materials at hand.

As they depart, the commander gives Williams fifty pounds, and remarks: "only a fanatic works for nothing. This is for your trouble. If you need more, call upon our friend (Snow). He is authorized to give you what you need."[10]

The next day the Commander has a terrible hangover from the excessive beer drinking.[11]

The Welshmen do not know that the commander is Lothar Witzke.[12]

The Germans do not know that at least one of the two Welshmen (Snow) is a double agent, working for the British while pretending to be working for the Germans.[13]

◇ ◇ ◇

September 1940. Two French fishing boats slip across the English Channel and approach the coast of Kent. Near Dungeness, four men get into row-boats and make their way to shore. It is early morning. The four are *Abwehr* recruits. Their mission is to reconnoiter England's south coast to prepare for the Wehrmacht invasion believed to be just weeks away. The *Abwehr* com-manders, who felt forced to initiate the mission, consider it so hazardous that they name the operation *Himmelfahrt*, or "ascension to heaven."

One of the four, Carl Meier, a twenty-three-year-old Dutch-born Nazi party member, walks a short distance to a coastal village, enters a pub and asks for cider. The landlady, immediately suspicious of both the foreign accent and the fact that the customer did not know that alcohol could not be purchased in a pub at that hour, calls the police. Within hours, the four are arrested.

Interrogated at a MI5 center, all confess and sign lengthy statements. They are charged under England's new Treachery Act. Three, including Meier, are quickly hanged. The fourth argues that he was forced to join the operation; he is imprisoned.[14]

Nothing explicitly links Witzke to this fiasco, but he likely was involved, as he was at the time either chief or second in command of the *Abwehr*'s Brest station. Infiltration of operatives into Great Britain was his job.

Sabotage was a minor story in World War II.[15] But this was not for want of trying, including by Witzke.

Witzke's boss in the *Abwehr*, Nikolaus Ritter, developed in 1939 a con-nection to an American of Boer origin who worked at a factory near Bristol. Because of a bad experience at a British concentration camp during the Boer war, the American was very anti-British, and told Ritter that he was ready to engage in sabotage. Ritter referred the operative to Witzke who knew a middleman who could pass messages to the American. Witzke told Ritter: "Because the factory apparently is making steel structures for aircraft hang-ers, it would be worth the trouble to send those folks a couple of explosive gifts for their engine room." Ritter agreed and said that immediate action was needed by both of them to get the explosives to their operative. "That is what we must do," Witzke said in his quiet manner."[16]

The following weekend, Ritter and Witzke went by train from Hamburg to the Netherlands. In their compartment, they recognized the green of-ficial identity paper of a member of the German foreign office. They gave each other a knowing look and agreed that they would separate from the gentleman in order to avoid being connected on their arrival in Holland to any German officials.

At the German side of the Dutch border, the travelers were obliged to open their suitcases and show their foreign currency. Ritter, traveling under the alias Dr. Bremer, had negligently failed to stash away his foreign currency. When the border official counted the foreign currency, he found that it amounted to more than authorized on Bremer's passport. This would require Ritter to deposit the excess until his return and then to ask an intelligence contact to intervene. These were steps that he wanted to avoid. While trying to figure out what to do, he heard Witzke telling the official quite calmly that he had no currency and needed none. Seizing the opportunity, Ritter got inventive, saying: "I happen to have your currency here with me." As Ritter describes it in his memoirs, "Witzke was Witzke. He did not even need the proverbial moment of shock before he instantly got the picture. Greatly relieved, he said, 'well, then I don't have to try to deceive you, Mr. Inspector. I was afraid Dr. Bremer here forgot to bring it along for me, so just hand it to me, Bremerboy!'" When they got their passports back, "Witzke could not help saying with quite a sneer, 'once again, we were damn lucky.'"[17]

Ritter continues:

> On the Dutch side, everything went without a glitch. In Hengelo, Witzke opened the window and leaned far out to buy a newspaper. There were a few travelers on the platform. Witzke closed the window and, with feigned relaxation, sat in his corner again. . . . Then a little, unassuming man entered our compartment and, with a grouchy greeting, put a brown cardboard suitcase into the baggage net above Witzke's seat. . . . We paid no attention to each other. In Lochem, he disembarked again. He left his suitcase in the net. The only other traveler in our compartment had been sleeping since Oldenzaal and had not heard or seen anything. When we disembarked at Amersfoort, Witzke took the suitcase left by the little man from Hengelo from the overhead net, acting quite naturally, as though it had always belonged to him.[18]

The little man was one of Witzke's agents, "a member of the mysterious group Witzke had developed into a well-functioning border crossing organization."[19] Witzke and Ritter ordered a good Dutch lunch and awaited their train to Rotterdam. Ritter would learn only later what the suitcase contained. He did not need to know. This was Witzke's game and he played it well, identifying operatives in Holland willing and able to participate, for money, in a chain that sent messages and explosives from Germany, through Holland, to

Great Britain. He offered such inducements as were needed, and convinced Dutch customs officials that they had nothing to fear if they worked secretly for him. "He had made astounding deals with these people."[20]

The two arrived in Rotterdam late in the afternoon and checked into a double room at a hotel. In Witzke's suitcase lay two big iron "eggs." These were pineapple-shaped hand grenades. Ritter says that he "did not believe my eyes when I saw Witzke openly put the iron eggs in the closet and push them against the back wall." Upon seeing Ritter's alarm, Witzke calmly responded: "Relax, Doctor Boy. . . . This is an old trick. Come on! Let's go downstairs!"[21]

When Ritter later returned to the hotel room, he startled a house detective searching the room. The house detective excused himself and departed, not having found the grenades. When Ritter later told Witzke about the incident, Witzke "simply smirked. 'Right! I'm familiar with it. If you want to hide something really well, then it's best to leave it exposed and just stick it in some corner. Then nobody will stumble on it.'"[22]

Witzke then met with one of his agents and transferred the grenades into his briefcase. The grenades were on their way to the Boer in Britain. The next evening they were to sail across the channel on a smuggler boat. Industrial explosions followed in Bristol but they were immaterial.[23]

◇ ◇ ◇

Witzke's efforts to infiltrate saboteurs into the UK continued into early 1941.

British intelligence files include correspondence between the Commander and the Welshman Williams in March and April 1940, and report that in late January 1941 the Commander provided the Welshman with a powder tin containing bank notes.[24] Williams by then was working for the British.

The most notable of Witzke's infiltration efforts was an ill-fated voyage by three Cubans into England in late 1940. The Cubans had fought for the Republicans in the Spanish Civil War and later escaped to France. In September 1940 they were contacted by the German Secret Service, who proposed that they carry out work in the UK on behalf of the Germans. The Cubans accepted, claiming (later) that they did so only in order to get out of France, and not because of affinity with the German cause.

The Cubans were transferred by the Germans to Brest, where Witzke instructed them in sabotage. *Abwehr Korvettenkapitaen* Schneidewind was in charge of the operational side, including the purchase of boats, and the briefing of crews and training of agents. The second in command was Lieutenant "Charley" Witzke. The agents and crews reported to him, and he was responsible for providing them with board and lodging; he also assisted in the purchase of boats.

After several abortive attempts to cross the Channel in small boats, manned by crews provided by the German Secret Service, the Cubans finally left France in November 1940 aboard the *Josephine*, captained by Cornelius Everton, a Dutch sailor working for the *Abwehr*. They carried with them explosives camouflaged as canned peas. Their instructions were to obtain employment and carry out sabotage in the Bristol area.

Before their departure, Witzke gave final instructions to the Cubans. They would be landed on the west coast of Britain and were to carry out sabotage in Bristol. Each would be given fifty pounds to maintain himself until he could find work in England. On arrival, they were to report to the Cuban consul, identify themselves as refugees from Germany, and ask for employment, preferably in a factory. Witzke promised them a large monetary reward and future employment with the victorious Germans.

During their voyage across the channel, the Cubans threw most of their sabotage material overboard.

On arrival at Fishguard, England, the *Josephine* was intercepted by a British naval patrol, and all of those on board were sent to London for routine interrogation. The Cubans, together with Evertsen, confessed and were imprisoned in the UK for the duration of the war, and then deported, the Cubans to America and Evertsen to Holland.[25] Another fiasco for the *Abwehr*.

◇ ◇ ◇

It is likely that, during his time running the Brest office, Witzke was involved in operations in at least two Breton seacoast villages, Douarnenez and Le Touquet.

Witzke's French mistress lived in Douarnenez, a seacoast village where the *Abwehr* operated boats for patrol and infiltration.[26] We know of one German action that occurred in that seacoast town while Witzke was in Brittany running *Abwehr* Section II. As reported by a German seaman: "In October 1940 I was ordered by *Abwehr* Section II to land two agents unobserved in Sligo Bay in north-west Ireland. For this enterprise I commandeered one of the famous French tunny-trawlers, the *Anni Braz Bihen* out of Douarnenez; I camouflaged the vessel suitably and made her ready for sea, and on the day fixed for sailing I was sent a crew of four Frenchmen with a Dane as engineer."[27] Witzke likely organized this effort.

The *Abwehr* also operated in Le Touquet, another Breton seacoast town.

Le Touquet was a point of departure for *Abwehr*-instigated missions to the UK, with boats typically sent first from Brest to Le Touquet before departure to the UK.[28] The *Abwehr* office in Le Touquet reported to Brest, and Witzke was sighted by British intelligence in Le Touquet in 1940-1941. We do not know what he was doing there, but we do know what German troops did there. They pillaged the town and, in 1943, demolished the famed Atlantic Hotel and shipped its parts to Germany by train. On each car was written: "Dons des français à leurs amis allemands" ["Gifts from the French to their German friends]."[29] There is no evidence that Witzke was among the pillagers, and no basis to speculate that he was. But he would have known all about what happened there while he was still in Brittany.

As demobilized French soldiers returned home, some of those who had retained their fighting spirit tried to join the Free French forces under de Gaulle in Britain. The way to do that was via fishing boats departing from Breton ports. In the opposite direction came de Gaullist intelligence operatives. The consequence was that, once the Germans abandoned the hope of invading England (Operation SeaLion), coastal patrol was added to Witzke's responsibilities in Brittany. This meant trying to keep Free French volunteers from fleeing to Britain and the English and French resistance from infiltrating France. It was a daunting task for the *Abwehr* to control the innumerable coves and small fishing villages that dotted the rocky coast of Brittany.[30] This was neither spycraft nor sabotage, and it is likely that Witzke delegated coastal patrol to others.

In view of Germany's effort to prevent American armaments from reaching the Allied Powers while the United States was a neutral during World War I, the question arises whether Germany, through the *Abwehr* and its famed saboteur of US armaments, made similar efforts while the US was a neutral during World War II before Pearl Harbor in December, 1941. The answer is no, at least not through the *Abwehr*. The *Abwehr* had learned that sabotage of US industry was ineffectual, no matter how destructive and spectacular isolated acts of sabotage might be, and could hasten US entry.[31] The *Abwehr*'s only preparations for acts of sabotage in the event of war with the US were in Mexico, where agents were supposed to link up with anti-American Irish elements in the US and by that means plan sabotage against shipping and armament factories.[32] Nothing came of it.

Witzke spoke Spanish and had spent substantial time in Mexico during

World War I, including conspiring to sabotage the oil fields at Tampico that served the British. He would have been ideally suited for the role of liaison with any Mexican operations that the Germans were considering during World War II. But we have found nothing that links him to any of it.

While the *Abwehr* forswore sabotage in the United States, other elements of the German command, pushed by Hitler to bring the war to American soil, obliged their leader and infiltrated saboteurs (all Germans who had lived in the US) into the US by U-boat in June 1942 (six months after Pearl Harbor and thus after the US was at war against Germany). The saboteurs' mission was to blow up American war plants, bridges, and transportation facilities, and also to set explosive devices in department stores and railroad stations to terrorize the public.[33] Divided in two units, they landed at Amagansett, Long Island, and near Jacksonville, Florida. They were quickly caught because two of them were anti-Nazi and went to the FBI. There was extensive publicity in the US about the captures but none of course in Germany and Witzke may not even have heard about it.

Germany's sabotage efforts in the United States during World War II were, ultimately, even less effectual than those during World War I.

US Army files report, as mentioned, that Witzke was awarded the War Merit Cross (Kriegsverdienstkreuz), a decoration awarded to military personnel and civilians.[34] We know from the date of the award—March 1942—that the decoration was for his service with the *Abwehr* from 1939 to 1941. Ritter's memoirs attest to Witzke's excellence in spycraft and in running operatives. The first-hand accounts of Witzke's dealings with agents and double agents demonstrate his mastery, his verbal facility, his calm, his sense of humor and even his enjoyment of his role. While the results of his actions seem minimal in context, the quality of his efforts was clear enough to his superiors that he was decorated.

ATHENS, 1941–1943

Witzke was sighted by British intelligence sources in Thessaloniki in May 1941, at a time that he was still primarily engaged in *Abwehr* activities in France and Belgium. He was reported to be in Athens in November 1941, February and May 1942, and May 1943. An *Abwehr* officer interrogated in July 1945 by British intelligence reported that Witzke was in Athens from late summer 1941 to April 1942; we return below to this interrogation.

Greece fell to the *Wehrmacht* in April 1941. Germany allowed Italy to occupy most of Greece (until the Italians abandoned the war in September 1943), but reserved to itself the sectors that mattered most, including Athens, the Piraeus and Thessaloniki.

The invasion of Greece in 1941 and the ensuing occupation disrupted the Greek agrarian economy. Within months after the occupation of Greece began in April 1941, Athens suffered starvation on a scale that was worse than anywhere in occupied Europe outside the concentration camps.[35] The famine peaked in the winter of 1941–1942, and was worst in Athens. Some 250,000 people died directly or indirectly as a result of starvation.[36]

This was the Greece that greeted Witzke in 1941, "in a shack in the refugee quarter of Dourgouti [in Athens], forty-year-old Androniki P. lay slumped by the door, covered in an old blanket, having sold the rest of her possessions to buy food. Her husband, who had died several days earlier, lay inside. Her three children sat crying, but she was too weak to help them. In another hut in Ayios Georgios, an unemployed worker lay unable to move, while his children clustered around his bed, asking for bread."[37]

Witzke likely was no more bothered by this than was Hermann Göring, who commented: "We can't be overly concerned with starving Greeks. That's a misfortune that will befall many other peoples."[38] The immiseration and enfamishment of the conquered countries, especially to the east, was part of the bargain that Nazi leadership made with the German people (of the requisite race). These countries were systematically plundered of food and goods.[39]

German occupation of Greece fit the pattern. For most of the Germans occupying the country, even for many of the philhellenes among them, Greece was there to be exploited.[40] The exploitation was accomplished through one-sided business deals, or more directly through looting, or sexually. There is evidence, as we will see, that Witzke took part in all of this, except the looting.

A British intelligence report says that Witzke was in Greece as an assistant to an individual identified as Schifebauer.[41] It is likely that this was a misspelling of Schiffbauer, an *Abwehr* officer in Greece in 1941–1942. An interview in July 1945 by British intelligence of an *Abwehr* agent named Hans Jurgen Kirchner offers a comment on Schiffbauer:

> Hptm (Captain) Schiffbauer. DOB 1895. Was in the film industry before the war. Served as an artillery officer during the last war. At the end of 1941 and in 1942 was head of AST (Gruppe II) Athens. In summer 1942 took over the same position in Salonica where he remained until Oberstlt Strojil replaced him early in 1943. Was then transferred to the Personnel Dept. of the O.K.W., believed as a Major. Was not highly thought of; Eisenberg and Iwan Kirchner thought he was an idiot.[42]

Witzke would not have let an "idiot" deter his activities, whether such activities were for personal profit, sexual adventure, or managing agents.

The same July 1945 interview of an *Abwehr* agent (Kirchner) that described Witzke's superior in Greece, Schiffbauer, presents us with the following description of Witzke in Greece: "Used to be a sailor, but also worked on dry land in the Norddeutsche Lloyd [aka the Hamburg America line]. From late summer 1941 to April 1942 was employed in Gr. II of AST Athens as controller of agents. When KIRCHNER was there he saw him very little and learnt very little about him; he had the impression that WITZKE was more interested in his own private business affairs and in young girls. Later is believed to have left the Abwehr."[43] A physical description was also provided, including the characterization of Witzke as "stout."[44]

Kirchner seems to have known nothing of Witzke's successes running agents in Belgium and Brittainy, let alone of Witzke's exploits in the Americas during the First World War. Or perhaps he did not care. The interrogation of this *Abwehr* agent in July 1945 is nonetheless revealing about Witzke's relationships, as a forty-seven-year-old participant in Germany's occupation of Greece, to three important subjects: money, food, and females.

We noted in an earlier chapter that Witzke purchased during the late 1930s a comfortable house in a posh residential quarter in Hamburg. Witzke evidently had become something of the entrepreneur, and the German occupation of Greece was an appealing place for an *Abwehr* officer or German businessman "interested in his own private business affairs." "James Schaeffer, an American oil executive working in Greece, summed it up: 'the Germans are looting for all they are worth, both openly and by forcing the Greeks to sell for worthless paper marks, issued locally.'"[45] One Sonderführer "had been seeking access to Balkan chrome supplies on behalf of Krupps before hostilities broke out. Now in Wehrmacht uniform, he marched into the offices of Greek mining concerns and secured several long leases at favorable rates."[46] "Shell was forced to sell its Greek plant to the Germans after being warned that unless it agreed to the sale it would be charged with sabotage and its property confiscated. Tobacco stocks lying in the warehouses of northern Greece, leathers, cotton cloth and silk cocoons were all confiscated or bought up at prewar prices and sent north to the Reich."[47]

Witzke's ability (discussed below) to provide for his family on the home front even when conditions back in Germany became most dire suggests that Witzke derived benefits from his service in occupied Europe. The comment by Kirchner, the interrogated *Abwehr* agent, that Witzke was more interested in his private business than in his *Abwehr* duties may have been a gripe by an individual who disliked Witzke. But it likely also reflected a gradual disillusionment on the part of Witzke in the greater cause, leading him to a narrowed view of his interests. It was during the course of Witzke's service in Greece that Germany invaded the USSR and became caught in a lethal drain of manpower and resources. Witzke would have been among those in a position to understand the change in Germany's prospects. Those at home subjected to constant bombing raids needed no further evidence.[48] As a young man and prisoner of the Americans, Witzke repeatedly manifested his allegiance to the fatherland by his refusal to confess anything to his US interrogators, even at the risk of his life. That attachment to country and cause faded by the middle of the second world war.

As to food, the photographs of Witzke during his time in Mexico and the United States as a young man in his twenties show a handsome and slender adventurer. The photograph in the magazine article about him in China shows that he retained his good looks at age 39. A family photograph of Witzke in Oslo in 1944 or 1945 shows a no longer young-looking or so slender man in his late forties. At a time when Greeks were dying by the thousands of famine, "stout" Witzke had ample to eat.[49]

As to women, Witzke's womanizing was well-established before his time in Greece. The new detail is his interest in *young* women. Perhaps his taste in women had not changed; perhaps, as he aged, the age of the women who interested him remained unchanged. We will find this penchant manifested at the most important Witzke family event of the 1950s, the wedding of his daughter, Helga.

◈   ◇   ◈

The last reported sighting of Witzke in Greece was in May 1943. If Witzke's time in Greece came to an end around then, he would have not been there when the Italian occupation gave way, in September 1943, to German occupation. And he would have been gone before the brutal partisan and anti-partisan combat that consumed much of Greece as of late 1943.[50]

During the time that we know that Witzke was in Greece, there was one spectacular act of sabotage by the Greek resistance, working with the British, that would have caught his attention either because it disrupted his business activities or as an echo of his past in the United States. In late November 1942, Greek partisans destroyed the Gorgopotamos viaduct that carried the railway line connecting Athens with the north. The railway to Athens was inoperative for several weeks.[51]

As was the case wherever Witzke served during the war, the Nazis' treatment of the Jews would have been known, and likely visible, to Witzke during his time in Greece, though the deportations from Greece to the death camps came mostly once Witzke was in Oslo.[52]

OSLO, 1944–1945

Witzke was based in Oslo throughout 1944 and through April 1945. Germany had invaded Norway in order to secure the shipping routes used to transport iron ore from Sweden to Germany. Norway's ports were also used as bases for the battle with the British for control of the North Sea. During the war, ships, including tankers, were outfitted at the Oslo shipyards for use in the polar theater.[53] Control of shipping to and from Norway was, thus, strategically vital to Germany, and Witzke's job in Oslo was to monitor the shipyards.

Photographs sent home and kept by his family show Witzke in civilian dress seated at a desk in an office.

Witzke's letters home in 1944 reported that he worked long hours and that his work involved ships and visits to the shipyard. If his activities were less benign than monitoring the shipyard, he was not telling. On March 3, 1944, Witzke wrote: "I have to work during the day today and in the evenings one is tired and goes to sleep. On Sundays I usually visit my ships and watch what people are doing and if the ships are in good condition. It's a pity I can't ski because everyone goes skiing here on Sundays."

A letter to Helga in October 1944 gives us a sense of Witzke's morning routine in Oslo:

Dear Helgamäusel! Pappi made a proper fool of himself early this morning. First I had slept in, looked for the clock and it was 7 hours 10 minutes. So, I went out of the bed, into the bathroom in a hurry, quick shave, made tea and had breakfast. It was already 10 minutes to eight and I should be at the office at 8 o'clock. During breakfast I turn on the radio and while I chew my bread I hear the radio announcer say, "It is 6:42." I look at my clock and it was 7:42 and then I look out of the window and it was quite bright already, so I thought the announcer must have gone mad. Then he announces again, 6:45. That's enough; I phone my office but no one takes the call. I call the directory assistance and I'm astonished to hear that the clock was put forward by an hour. Well, I still had a lot of time then, and so I thought I'd write my Helgamausel a quick letter.

◇ ◇ ◇

Norway was the idyllic posting for a German soldier during World War II. It was presumably the same for a German civilian operative. Even for Norwegians, other than Jews, the occupation was relatively benign. The Germans treated Norwegians relatively well, and, though there was a small resistance movement, Norwegians were generally civil toward the occupying force.[54] Peace in Norway was maintained by the substantial German occupying force, including 6,000 SS troops. Unlike Denmark, the quality of the army units stationed in Norway was high, because Hitler was concerned throughout the war about a British invasion of Norway that never materialized. The high-quality German troops in Norway saw virtually no combat during the occupation of Norway. In 1945, while the homeland was being destroyed, German units in Norway took Sundays for rest and relaxation.[55]

Through the very end:

> German discipline remained high. German combat units, ordered to disarm, complied promptly. . . . Even when no British or Norwegian forces were at hand, German commanders proceeded to disarm their own troops—the first time in history that a superior military force disarmed itself without having suffered a military defeat. Discipline was maintained on the trip home. Units stuck together, officers and men continued to observe the chain of command, and the German forces returned to Germany with a feeling that while their country had been defeated, they and their units were still unbowed. Not until they returned to Germany would the utter devastation and total ruin that had befallen their mother country sink home.[56]

Witzke, by contrast, had traveled back and forth to Germany several times and already knew the situation at home. It is unimaginable that he told himself in 1945 what he told himself in 1918, namely, that Germany had been defeated due only to a stab in the back or insufficient military ardor.

Witzke had time in Oslo for recreation. In July 1944, he tells his family, "I have been swimming a few times as well, in fact out by the shipyard; we have rowboats there, one rows out to the fjord with them and jumps into the water." His letters home paint a picture of Norwegians going about their ordinary business. But there are hints of scarcity. A letter to Helga on February 27, 1944 reports that "the Norwegians are now out and about with their skis. Little mouse [his nickname for Helga], I can't get a sleigh for you. I would have liked so much to gift you one but they don't sell them anywhere." A concern about obtaining a sleigh as a gift for his daughter was a concern unimaginable for most families in Europe in 1944.

Witzke also had time for entertainment, including of the kind that he could report back to his family. A letter to Helga in October 1944 reports: "one could go to the theatre but this year it is closed. Now and then one goes to the cinema and recently I saw "*Circus Renz.*" Are you also going to the cinema now and then or is it too dangerous with all the alarms?"

In a letter to Helga in September 1944, Witzke commiserates about the hardship caused by Allied air raids and reports about his acquisition of a bicycle for recreation:

> It's really bad now with the alarms, I see. You can't get any rest any more. Here we only had alarms twice when the English laid down mines into the fjord so that our ships couldn't go in or out. . . . I have so much to do here, as I have to do Mr Kölln's work now as well. But that doesn't hurt, as that way I'm always occupied. Otherwise it is too boring, sitting here all alone without you in Norway. I'd rather be at home now and be able to work in the garden. . . . Mammi wrote me she got a nice pearl necklace for you. The joy was great, I guess. I bought a bicycle recently and ride it around in the evenings and on Sundays. It is a very pretty new bike with a front brake and an electric lamp that gets its power from a little dynamo that's attached to the front wheel.

The wartime gift of a pearl necklace for Helga attests to the family's access to cash.

Even in the darkening days for the Reich of February 1945, Witzke could write, "Dear Helgamäusel! I also have gone skiing every Saturday and Sunday, even today where there was a lot of mud already and it was no fun."

Aker Brygge is today a wharf in Oslo lined with restaurants and shops, featuring summertime *al fresco* dining. It was for a century one of Oslo's most important shipyards, and Witzke's responsibilities surely included oversight of the Aker shipyard. At the time of his letter to Helga about the change to daylight savings time, shipyard employees, organized by a Norwegian resistance group, the Pelle-gruppen, were smuggling dynamite into their workplace. The dynamite was stored until explosives, hidden in the pockets and lunch boxes and toolboxes of the shipyard workers, could be brought onto the ships docked there. The explosions occurred, on November 23, 1944, a few weeks after Witzke's letter to Helga, and they destroyed six ships, including one warship. The Pelle group was later betrayed to the Germans and most of the group was tortured and executed by the Gestapo in February and March 1945.[57]

Witzke's work took him back to Germany from time to time, including to Hamburg in August 1944, and to Berlin in April 1945, a fraught month in German history. He traveled sometimes by plane and sometimes by boat. In a letter home in September 1944, he describes a boat trip and his resolute efforts to procure sweets for his family and sustenance for himself:

> I have arrived here [Oslo] safely and the journey was quite nice. We had strong winds on the Baltic Sea but in return no air raids. I drank lots of milk in Copenhagen and ate a good pork roast. In Sweden there was no confectionery, sadly, but instead I got some chocolate bars and sweets for you; they're going to Hamburg tomorrow by coastal steamer. You will have to pick them up at the office then. Other than that there's a lot of work here again. The pig at the shipyard is big and fat and is going to be slaughtered next week. The other two are still too small to be slaughtered, but Christmas will be the time. Now we're looking for a goat, and geese and chickens so we can raise them.

The reference to a stopover in Sweden leads one to wonder whether he was meeting there with undercover agents in that neutral nation. The reference to his Hamburg office is also of interest; if this was a commercial enterprise, that would be consistent with a US Army file that says that Witzke after 1941 left the *Abwehr* for the *Hermann Göring Reichswerke*.[58]

To the extent that Witzke's work in Norway involved counterintelligence, he would have recognized what he was up against: in the winter and spring 1944, a group of saboteurs began operations in and around Oslo to disrupt the production of armaments for Germany. They became known as the Oslo Gang and they were never caught.[59] If Witzke had responsibilities in Denmark, he would have observed a similar story there as of the summer of 1944, when the Danes, encouraged by German defeats in the east and west, launched a series of successful sabotage actions against factories supplying the German war effort.[60] The response in September 1944 was mass arrests and deportations directed at the no-longer-reliable (from the German standpoint) Danish police force.[61]

Witzke's last surviving wartime letter home on April 16, 1945, was in the final days of the Reich. He writes: "Dearest Helgamäusel! Pappi has to write you quickly, as one doesn't know how long the postal service will still be working. So, as you see, I have landed well in Oslo. I flew on a Lufthansa aeroplane from Berlin to Copenhagen and then I took the train from there.

Now have been here for 4 days already and I have to work every day."[62] It would be of great interest to know what Witzke needed to do in Berlin at that dire time in German history, when the Soviets were already devastating the city. Whatever it was, someone in a position of power authorized resources to allow Witzke to travel back and forth between Berlin and Oslo. Equally intriguing is what, at that time, was still keeping Witzke so busy in Oslo.

We do not know how Witzke made it home from Oslo in May 1945, but he managed.[63]

✧　✧　✧

Witzke's longtime friend and mentor, Kurt Jahnke, resurfaced during Witzke's time in Oslo. The evidence for this is that Witzke later told British intelligence during an interview at his home in Hamburg in 1952 that he had seen Jahnke the last time in 1944.[64] Even if the two saw one another after that, we can trust the remembered meeting, which likely took place on a trip by Witzke back to Germany, because Witzke would have been motivated in 1952 to understate his contacts with Jahnke.

Jahnke's survival to 1944 attests to the man's singular skills. Walter Schellenberg, the chief of the SD wrote in his memoirs that he met Jahnke in 1937 as a conduit to Reinhard Heydrich and described Jahnke as "a key figure in the German Secret Service . . . and a remarkable man."[65]

In the wake of Pearl Harbor, after a brief period of increased influence, Jahnke's star waned. Because he had been close to Rudolf Hess, Hitler suspected him of complicity in his deputy's flight to Scotland on the eve of the invasion of the Soviet Union. He was denounced to Heydrich in a Gestapo report that asserted that Jahnke was a British agent. The story of the denunciation gives us a measure of the man.

In March 1942, while [Jahnke] was in Switzerland reviewing with his Chinese friends the possibilities of a separate peace with Japan, Gestapo chief Heinrich Mueller gave Heydrich a 30-page report detailing Jahnke's association with the British Secret Service. The report stated categorically that Jahnke was in Switzerland at that very moment, not to work on a Sino-Japanese peace, but to receive new instructions from his British contact. On his return from Switzerland, Jahnke was confronted with the accusation by Heydrich and Schellenberg, but they drew from him only an enigmatic rejoinder. "Your whole life," he said, "has inclined you toward systematic suspicion, but I think you are big enough to overcome that. What is important is a man's real character—and there you can trust your instinct."[66]

Considered too useful to be done away with, Jahnke survived that crisis, as he did the incessant infighting within the Nazi intelligence apparatus.[67] During the war, Jahnke "led a very secluded life, mostly on his estate in Pomerania, particularly after his Berlin villa had been completely destroyed in an air raid. He had a very wide circle of acquaintances, . . . all of which he had, however, collected for his own purpose."[68]

FAMILY LIFE AT VOLKSDORF DURING THE WAR

Witzke's daughter Helga preserved a trove of correspondence exchanged with her father while he was in Oslo. Her children, in turn, preserved these letters, together with photographs of their grandfather (both in Oslo and during the 1950s back in Germany), and they have generously made all this available to the authors. From this correspondence and these photographs, we have learned about the family situation during the war, and about Lothar as a father and family man.

The subject matter covered in the correspondence is unsurprisingly mostly mundane. We see Witzke's affection for Helga and the frequency with which he writes to her compared to his fewer letters to (and from) his son, Lothar Jr. His correspondence also contains a few stern lectures to his children about proper behavior and diligence in household chores to help their mother.

Much of the correspondence reads like a father on a business trip writing to his twelve-year old daughter. On January 24, 1944, Witzke wrote to Helga from Oslo:

> My dear, little Helga-maus! Your letter gave me great joy. You can already write wonderfully with the new pen. I should now come home to you quickly, otherwise the rabbits [in Volksdorf] will bite each other so much. But as much as I would like to, I can't come now, as Mr Kölln [Witzke's colleague in Oslo] has gone to Germany. And one of us has to be here at all times. But please, try to get wire already whenever you can, and I will make you a nice stable when I come. I have got you a set of stamps of Norway which I include in this letter. If you want some from Sweden and Denmark as well, just write me.

The Witzkes almost to the end of the war had enough to eat thanks to Lilli's gardening, and packages sent by papa Lothar, including a radio and a fifty-liter barrel of French red wine. Helga had a particular memory that, upon a visit home during the war, Witzke and Lilli enjoyed an evening drinking some of the wine that he had brought with him. Such plunder of the occupied territories kept innumerable German families more or less well fed through 1944.[69] "German soldiers literally emptied the shelves of Europe. They sent millions of packages back home from the front. . . . When one asks the now elderly witnesses about this period in history, their eyes still gleam at the memory of . . . the velvet, silk, liqueurs, and coffee from France, the tobacco from Greece, . . . and the tons of herring from Norway. . . ."[70] France, Greece, Norway, all countries where Witzke spent the war. Norway especially was a prized source for herring. "Considering that normal weekly meat and fish rations in Germany at this point [1944] were 350 grams (less than a pound), the herring imports [from Norway] represented a nutritional increase of around 50% for German housewives. Moreover, that figure includes only officially permitted imports—it doesn't take into account vacationers' prohibited but tolerated practice of bringing fish back with them on passenger trains."[71] This was true of families of ordinary *Wehrmacht* soldiers; one must assume that Witzke had amply more opportunity for self-enrichment than did soldiers.

A letter from Witzke to Helga on March 3, 1944, is mostly about food, "Is it still that cold at yours that you can go ice skating? The 30 eggs were quite nice, were they? You could all properly feast once again. And so there was canned milk as well, that sounds like a great thing. I want to depart from here soon now and visit you all in Hamburg. I want to see that I can stay over Easter. I still have to dig over the garden after all. I have a lot to do there, too." A month later, food and danger are the subjects of a letter from Witzke to Helga:

> We [in Oslo] got 2 little pigs that we want to fatten now. Their food is the waste from our ships. Mammi writes that the planes are already flying low above our houses. You have to be very careful there, and already go into the house at pre-alarm, because they're shooting at people with their weapons on board. Our garden [at Volksdorf] is also very nice and everything bloomed neatly. It looks like we're going to have a lot of apples and pears this year, what do you think, my Mausel? I see Mammi's carrots sprouted after all, and now she has 7 rows. So you will have lots of carrots. . . . Did the chairs and table for the veranda arrive?

Furniture for the veranda in 1944! A fortunate family.

Inevitably, the war intrudes in the family correspondence and references to the deterioration in Germany's situation become frequent. In a letter from Oslo dated February 12, 1944, Witzke tells Helga, "I hope the children from Hamburg won't have to be evacuated, because then I would be all alone with

Mammi when I come back to Hamburg." Air raids have interrupted Helga's schooling, and he laments on February 20, 1944, "I suppose you aren't learning too much anymore with all the alarms." Witzke urges his daughter to stay away from the front door because of air raid strafing fears, and he is mystified that her mother allows her to be in danger's way. By April 1944, mail delivery between Norway and Germany has become imperilled: "Today the mail arrived that was in the aeroplane which was shot down. It was all wet and I could hardly read Mammi's letter. I was lucky that we weren't shot down."

In November 1944, Witzke discusses with Helga the Russian landing in the north of Norway and whether that poses a threat to his safety. "It is not so bad yet with the Russians in Norway. They are all the way north, about 2000 km away from us and there are tall mountains covered in thick ice and snow. The Russians won't have it easy to reach Oslo. So we don't need to worry yet." As the Allies advance, deprivation appears in the correspondence: no Christmas presents in 1944; Witzke has run out of money ("I'd like to give you and Butzi [Lothar Jr.] some skis but I'm out of money."); travel is no longer possible between Oslo and Hamburg and between Norway and Sweden ("I will probably not be able to go to Sweden, the Swedes don't want to grant me an entry permit."). During the winter of 1944–1945, Helga's school is closed because of coal shortages.

The Witzke family survived, notwithstanding devastation all around them.[72] During the last week of July 1943, the Allied air forces, especially the RAF, intensively bombed Hamburg in an operation named Gomorrah. The bombing created a firestorm that suffocated those in bomb shelters and swept up people on the street. The city center, industrial zones and port area were destroyed. But Volksdorf, distant enough from the center, was unharmed and never bombed.

The family remained in their own house. It was a big and beautiful home, and it survived intact. They never had to take in refugees.[73] This set of circumstances by itself put the Witzke family in a tiny category of Germans on the home front.

But the deprivation touched the Witzke family. There were days late in the war that Helga ate nothing but turnips. After the war, when food became available, on at least two occasions Helga ate so much that she became seriously ill. Later, when she had kids and cooked for them, her meals were almost always too much, and everything had to be eaten. Helga would be part of prosperous West Germany's *Fresswelle*, the eating wave.

One detail about life at Volksdorf during the War attests to a measure of hardship, and even bears slightly upon the ultimate question that this book addresses (whether or in what way Witzke was responsible for Black Tom). Witzke wrote before the War a diary of the exploits of Pablo Waberski in Mexico. Helga read during the War her father's accounts of Waberski's exploits, and extolled the diary to her children as a veritable literary work, a combination of stirring fantasy and reality, adding to her well-stocked store of admiration of her heroic father. The Pablo Waberski diary has not, however, survived because, while the patriarch was off at war (or imprisoned by the British), Lilli kept the diary in the bathroom in the Volksdorf house and the family used the pages of the diary as toilet paper until it was no more. In a world where toilet paper was scarce, this was pragmatism on the part of Lilli. To what extent the demise of the diary reflected Lilli's resentment of her husband's other life, we cannot speculate. Helga came terribly to regret that she did not preserve the diary.

Until the end, Witzke regularly managed to make visits home. From Oslo on May 13, 1944, he writes: "I think I will come for the summer holidays after all. Your holidays last until 20 August and I want to come in early August already. Let's go swim properly then. I hope the weather will be good then and warm. Or don't they open the bath at Volksdorf any more during summer?"

His visits home were not those of a soldier traumatized and shattered by the war. Witzke was calm, making his way, serving his country.

Witzke's ability to supply his family with goods during the direst days of the war suggests that he was sufficiently high up to pull this off. Perhaps, alternatively, he was a smuggler. As his Oslo work involved shipping and ports, smuggling and pilfering food and supplies are easily imaginable.

Years later, Helga would tell her children that their grandfather was not involved in "the dirty business."

NEUENGAMME, 1946

Hamburg and its region fell within the British zone of occupied Germany. As of September 1945, the British set up the former Nazi concentration camp at Neuengamme as Civilian Internment Camp Number Six for displaced persons, surrendered German army personnel and forced laborers. "The initial concern was not that individual activities might have been criminal, but whether they were a danger to the security of the British forces."[74]

A British officer described the work done at Neuengamme:

> Most individuals arrested in the Hamburg area fell into arrestable categories: members of SS, senior officials of the Nazi apparatus and government,

Justices, court officials, senior Army and naval officers (U-boat command-
ers) and members of the Hamburg *Abwehr* (Nazi intelligence). They were
brought to Neuengamme where they completed an initial questionnaire
and it was our task to interrogate and assess them. We had to write-up a
report on each of them. It was extremely hard work because we were always too few to cope with the number of people brought to the camp.[75]

As a former *Abwehr* agent from Hamburg, Witzke was in at least one
arrestable category, and he was interned in the British Zone at the Neuengamme Civil Internment for more than a year, from November 30, 1945, to
December 23, 1946.[76]

The British imprisoned close to 100,000.[77] Those suspected of war crimes
were prosecuted before criminal tribunals. Denazification was for those believed to have committed lesser wrongs.[78] The absence of records saying that
Witzke was ever tried as a war criminal shows that he was not seen as one.
It sufficed that he had been in the *Abwehr*. There was, inevitably, no moral
precision as to who was interned and who not.[79]

We have been unable to recover any records of Witzke's internment at
Neuengamme, though there must once have been records documenting why
he was arrested, what transpired during his interrogations while a prisoner,
and why he was released. The absence of surviving records as to Witzke
may be due to the fact that few records have survived.[80] We have but a single
stray reference to Witzke at Neuengamme from the British Intelligence files,
reporting that he admitted in 1952 to British interrogators that, while at
Neuengamme, he encountered a German major who had previously been a
secretary to Jahnke.[81] The *Bundesarchiv* contains a reference to Witzke having
been registered at a British discharge center on April 6, 1946, together with
the Admiral of the Aegean task force.[82] That admiral was Werner Lange, who
was a prisoner of war from May 8, 1945 to November 30, 1946, overlapping
Witzke's time at Neuengamme.[83] We have been unable to contextualize the
report beyond observing that Witzke was in Greece during some of the time
that Lange was fleet commander there.

Treatment of prisoners at the denazification facilities was harsh though
incomparable to the treatment of prisoners under the Nazi regime. "A submission by internees from November 1946 claimed that 478 internees at Neuengamme had been physically mistreated and that 1,979 had been robbed."[84] If
Witzke was mistreated, his family did not hear about it.

Witzke's superior at the *Abwehr*, Nikolaus Ritter, was also imprisoned,
together with others from the Hamburg Intelligence Station, as of May 1945

at Neuengamme. This was six months before Witzke would be imprisoned at Neuengamme, and Ritter does not mention Witzke. One wonders why it took the British six months to find and intern Witzke. By the time that Witzke was there, Ritter and the others had been transferred to another facility.[85] The conditions that Ritter describes likely applied to Witzke's prison time as well. "Furniture and sanitary facilities had been removed, and ten of us were squeezed into a room for four. The food rations were barely enough to keep us alive. There was no diversion of any kind except for the endless roll calls every morning and every evening. In between, we were allowed to go out into the courtyard and into a pasture surrounded by barbed wire."[86]

Upon his release from Neuengamme just before Christmas 1946, Witzke had spent more than six years of his life as a prisoner, five in federal prisons in Texas and Kansas, and one at a denazification facility outside Hamburg. There is no evidence that he was scarred by the experience. He may have counted himself lucky.

Lilli managed reasonably well while Lothar was at Neuengamme. An English officer took a liking to her, and supplied her with coffee that otherwise could hardly be procured by Germans. Using the illicitly obtained coffee, Lilli went on the black market and sold the coffee for critical household provisions.

The reader will wonder what Lilli gave in return for the steady supply of a commodity as valuable as coffee. It is unimaginable that there was no *quid pro quo*. At the very least, there had to have been an intimate friendship.[87]

When Witzke was released by the British, the Hamburg that he found was shattered and desperate:

The winter of 1946–1947 was the worst in living memory. The river Elbe froze and ships carrying essential supplies could only reach the port through a channel cut by icebreakers. Unable to dock at the wharves, they had to unload into lighters in mid-stream. In January and February, 85 people froze to death, and a further 200 died each month from inflammation of the lungs. Due to a shortage of coal, the supply of electricity was reduced to maintain essential services. The suburban railways ceased to run, trams stopped at 8.00 p.m. and theatres and cinemas remained closed. Building was at a standstill. Because no coal was available for domestic heating, there was massive thieving of coal from freight trains arriving in the marshalling yards, with crowds of up to 30,000 taking part.[88] The deprivation was such that factory production in the British sector and elsewhere in Germany plummeted. The reason was that German workers did not have enough food to sustain productive work for a factory day.[89]

This desperation did not much touch the Witzke family. Just as Lothar sailed through the war uninjured and untraumatized, and just as Lilli, with Lothar's help, avoided extreme deprivation on the home front, the Witzke family would prosper during the post-War period. This is the subject of our next chapter.

What, after all, did Witzke do in Denmark, or elsewhere, that would cause his name twenty years after the war still to be *non grata*? This remains an unanswered question about the life of Lothar Witzke. It is inexplicable that an *Abwehr* agent not known to have been a war criminal and who was never stationed in Denmark would have been, still in the 1960s, on a Danish list of unwanted persons. Even in the immediate post-war era, Danish authorities were concerned much more with Danes who had collaborated than with Germans who had done their duty as German soldiers or operatives.[90] Was Witzke listed not because of World War II activities but because of espionage activities during the Cold War? Possible, but equally implausible because recently declassified CIA files show little interest in the man. Was Helga simply mistaken, and was she held at the border for reasons unrelated to the Witzke name? Possible but doubtful, as she was a smart woman and she told her children with certainty that the issue was the name. One would have thought that, confronted at the Danish border by this eruption of the past, Helga would have asked Lilli for answers. But this was not the way of the Witzke family.

The sole family memory of Witzke's wartime activity.aside from such of his activities in Oslo that he chose to recount in his family correspondence, was that he worked clandestinely "behind the lines" in anti-partisan activities.[91] It is impossible to square this family memory, as reported later by his daughter Helga to Witzke's grandchildren, with anything that we know of Witzke's wartime story. Witzke was in two countries at times and places where there was anti-German partisan activity (Greece and Norway), but he was not behind the lines in either. The most that can be said is that Witzke worked in Brittany and Belgium with operatives who themselves were behind the lines in Britain, but Britain of course was not an occupied country and there was no partisan or anti-partisan activity there. The family memory may be an instance of a story transformed as it was retold from generation to generation, or it may be that Witzke himself transposed some of the facts to make himself more heroic. He told little else about his wartime activities. Any tendency that he had toward braggadocio was silenced by his service during this war.

The first-hand descriptions that we have of Witzke at war present a man of confidence, a master of spycraft, a commander of men, with verbal facility and ready humor. He made many contacts. His past had paved the way for a position of responsibility during the war. He was decorated for what he accomplished. He did not lack for women, money or food. All in, he had a good war. His wartime experience likely set him up for his next act.

PROSPERITY

"Ein Mann beugt sein Knie für niemandem."
(transl: "A man kneels for no one.")
WITZKE TO HELGA, HAMBURG, CA 1954

Witzke family photographs from the 1950s show celebrations.[1] White linen tablecloths. Wine glasses drained and refilled. The men in tuxedos, their wives in dresses or gowns. Several of the celebrations are at Hamburg's Anglo-German Club, an expensive setting "deliberately modelled on a traditional English gentlemen's club and . . . intended to cater for the city's elite."[2] Life in West Germany was good in the 1950s for many former Nazis.

WORK, AND ESPIONAGE?

After the war Witzke took employment at the Hamburg-based Rahtjen company (sometimes misspelled Rathjen) and he became CEO in June 1950.[3] At his death Witzke was credited with having led the company's successful rebuilding after the war.

The Rahtjen company was founded in 1856 by Johann Rahtjen, who had developed anti-corrosive and anti-fouling paints, primarily for the protection of metal ships' bottoms from rust and vegetable or animal growth, either in salt or fresh water. The paint was distinguished both by its color composition and by its shorter dry time compared to the competition. The paint was widely used on warships and commercial steamships, including steamships of the German lines *Norddeutscher Lloyd* and *Hamburg-America*.[4] During the nineteenth century and until the end of World War I, the company operated in partnership with an English firm, Suter, Hartmann & Ratjen's Composition Co., Ltd.[5] After World War I, Rahtjen severed its ties to Suter Hartmann and reconstituted in Germany as Joh. Rahtjen GmbH. The company seems to have prospered during the inter-war period, but fell on hard times during World War II. At some time, probably not before 1960 and possibly not until after Witzke's 1962 retirement, Rahtjen was acquired by the English textile giant Courtaulds.[6] In 1970, years after Witzke's death, Rahtjen merged with another German company, and the name disappeared.

Witzke was unqualified in several ways to run the Rahtjen company. He had no experience of paint or paint manufacturing. He had no business executive expertise. He had no experience running an enterprise. But he had experience of ships, ship construction and ship maintenance. He surely had long known of Rahtjen paint. His naval education and background, plus his accomplishments in the two wars, would have made him a plausible candidate for a position at a company ravaged by the war, even assuming that the position was secured for him by powerful friends.

His family suspected at the time, and suspects to this day, that his employment at Rahtjen was a front for espionage activities. But if his work was a cover for espionage, he was a resourceful multi-tasker, because Rahtjen was not a fictive or shell company. The company's majority shareholder was a British company, Pinchin, Johnson & Associates. The position of chief executive officer had to be a demanding one. Witzke was fetched early every morning by his chauffeur. The business trips that caused him to be repeatedly absent from home for extended times were a prime reason for the family's suspicions. But Witzke sometimes invited Lilli to join him on his trips and, as Lilli had no interest and lacked the temperament, Helga instead would accompany her father. She spoke decent English, and English was needed. It is unlikely, though not out of the question, that he brought along his daughter on business trips that were a cover for espionage.

Could his family not have known for sure that Witzke remained a spy even while serving as Rahtjen's CEO? Yes. A big talker and, in his youth, almost a fatal boaster, he never spoke to his daughter or son-in-law about his espionage and sabotage activities, past or ongoing (if ongoing). Witzke as a prisoner had been tight-lipped with his interrogators, telling them nothing of use to the Americans about the sabotage allegations. That self-constraint in the service of his country was likely a departure from his natural inclination. Neither Witzke nor his daughter was modest. They liked and needed to talk, and Helga would even exaggerate their accomplishments. Perhaps Witzke learned a life-long lesson.

All that his children (and grandchildren) were told about Witzke's past was that he had been imprisoned for two years in a dark cell because of sabotage of an oil refinery in Central America. This never happened, but the admission of sabotage is of interest, notwithstanding that it is transposed to a place that rendered Witzke guiltless of the sabotage at Black Tom or elsewhere in the United States. Aside from the fictional oil refinery sabotage, and aside from his quasi-fictional diary recounting the adventures of Pablo Waberski, no stories about the family patriarch's past have survived in family memory. Nor, apparently, did his family press him for stories. It may have been a cultural norm for German families in the 1950s not to interrogate their fathers too closely about the past.

Ritter's memoirs include an epilogue on the post-war fate of his Hamburg group. He discusses several from his Hamburg team, but not Witzke, a curious omission.[7] One explanation could be that Ritter, who lived in Hamburg after the war, knew that Witzke continued to act as a spy, and Ritter may have judged it prudent to make no mention of Witzke, even though the book was written after Witzke's death.

If Witzke remained after the war a spy, for whom?

Hamburg was in the British occupation zone. Witzke was imprisoned by the British for a year at Neuengamme. The British were majority shareholders in the Rahtjen company. Witzke frequented the Anglo-German Club in Hamburg. The British were plausible new spymasters for this erstwhile *Abwehr* operative. Was Witzke recruited while at Neuengamme?

In April 1952, the British intelligence service twice interviewed Witzke as part of their investigation of Kurt Jahnke's past (and potentially ongoing) espionage activities. The report said: "While his manner is thawing out he still only gives snippets of information and then solely on 3rd parties who may be able to supply direct information." With respect to the main object of the interrogation, the British agent reported: "The general trend of Witzke's conversation confirmed case officer's previously held opinion, namely that Witzke was from 1923 onwards much more in Jahnke's confidence than he has so far admitted."[8] Witzke broadly indicated a willingness to work with British intelligence to gather information about Jahnke, but it appears that he in fact provided nothing.

Notes of the first of these interviews, at Witzke's home in Hamburg on April 8, 1952, tell the following:

His manner while not unfriendly, was cool (he offered the case officer neither a drink nor a cigarette). Case Officer's general impressions may be summarized as follows:

a) No success was achieved by direct specific questioning of Witzke. He invariably either replied that he had not been sufficiently in Jahnke's confidence to know the answer, gave general replies, or refused to answer.

b) He is by no means quite the astute Machiavellian figure which might be supposed. He twice contradicted himself rather grossly in the course of the interview.[9]

It is evident that the interrogator did not think (or know) that Witzke was an agent working for the British. It is possible that the interrogator was uninformed. But it is more plausible that he would have known, or at least been told to stay away from Witzke.

Another possibility is that Witzke was a double agent, working ultimately for the *Stasi*, notwithstanding his vehement anti-communism. If so, he would not have been alone among unreconstructed Nazis working (against their convictions such as they were) for the East Germans by spying on West Germans, especially the Hamburg business elite. The *Stasi's* penetration of Hamburg business circles in the 1950s was deep, and they made use of executives of real companies, not only shells.[10] Many Germans of Witzke's generation had dark pasts that they wanted to keep buried. It is unlikely that the *Stasi* could have made use of Witzke's sabotage history during World War I, as this had been notorious, among the Americans at least, for decades. Perhaps there were acts during World War II lost to us, but known to the *Stasi,* that were used to blackmail Witzke. Searches in *Stasi* files for a mention of Witzke have led nowhere. It is not realistically possible that the *Stasi* had no file on Witzke. There are therefore two alternative explanations for our not finding a Witzke file: either our searches were inadequate or the Witzke file has been destroyed.

General Reinhard Gehlen, the *Wehrmacht's* intelligence chief for the Eastern Front during World War II, established at the end of the war ties with the United States, and maintained his intelligence network by employing numerous former Nazis and known war criminals to spy for the west against the east.[11] The Gehlen Organization was quickly penetrated by spies working for the Soviets and the *Stasi*, due in part to the organization's use of former Nazis who were susceptible to blackmail.[12] We have no evidence that Witzke was connected to the Gehlen Organization, but he would have sympathized with their anti-communist aims, and if, as his family suspected, he engaged in espionage even after World War II, it is plausible that he did so as part of this organization. If that were the case, that would not answer whether he was one of those who the *Stasi* reached.

The family's suspicion that their patriarch remained a spy even during the 1950s, using his legitimate business as a cover, is plausible but ultimately not proved. However, the circumstances of Lothar Witzke's death, which we recount in the Epilogue, add to their suspicions.[13]

THE DEUTSCHE PARTEI

Witzke's post-war politics reflected his undiminished belief in strength and discipline. He was a member of the *Deutsche Partei*, described generously as a gathering place for conservatives and nationalists and less generously as the party for unreconstructed Nazis.[14] The *Partei*, founded in 1947, thrived nationally in the late 1940s, and obtained two ministerial posts in Konrad Adenauer's cabinet after the 1949 elections.[15] The 1949 elections marked the *Deutsche Partei*'s high point. After 1952, the *Partei* formed a coalition with the centrist Christian Democratic Union and Free Democratic Party. By 1957, the coalition splintered; the *Partei* was considered too right-wing and was excluded. In 1957, the *Partei* failed to gain five percent of the vote and lost its position in the Hamburg Parliament.

The Hamburg branch of the *Deutsche Partei*, dominated by former National Socialists, was considered extremist even within a party considered radically right-wing by many Germans. In 1952, the year that Witzke served in the Hamburg Parliament as a party representative, the local branch was entirely under the control of extremists and former National Socialists.[16] One may wonder how this could have been allowed by the occupying British. The answer is that denazification, pursued robustly in the immediate aftermath of the war, had given way to the complexities of distinguishing degrees of culpability, reviving the country, and above all the exigencies of the cold war.[17]

Witzke was evidently a favored member of the Hamburg branch of the *Deutsche Partei*. He was put forward to serve in the second *Hamburgische Bürgerschaft* (Hamburg Parliament) from 1949 to 1952. According to the election laws of the *parliament*, each qualifying party established a list of its members to be designated for parliamentary service based upon how many votes the party received. In the 1949 election, the *Deutsche Partei* got 13.1 percent of the votes, good enough for nine parliamentary seats. Witzke was number ten on the list. In September 1952, he was designated to replace fellow party member Gerhard Nagel, who died in July 1952.[18] His service lasted only through 1953.

Witzke seems not to have spoken up as a member of parliament. His name is not mentioned on the list of speakers in 1952 or 1953, and he advanced no motions or proposed legislation. The issues of the time in Hamburg were barely ideological. Politicians in the city of all parties were concerned with reparation of the devastated city, reconstruction of the harbor, and housing.

If Witzke were a spy, would he have served in the local Hamburg Parliament? Yes. The East Germans evidently considered that such service provided both superior cover and extra opportunities for espionage. The *Stasi's* penetration of the Hamburg parliament during the 1950s was not less than its penetration of German business circles.[19]

FAMILY LIFE

Family life for the Wtzkes during the 1950s was constrained, notwithstanding material comfort. Lothar and Lilli rarely entertained. They rarely attended church. Any friendships that Witzke maintained were not shared with his family. Having been a sailor as a young man, Witzke never sailed with his family. Having been a world traveler, Witzke no longer enjoyed travel abroad. When he and his family would return to Germany from a vacation in Austria, he would say: "Finally back to civilization." Vacations within Germany were preferred; Lilli's favorite destination was Grömitz, a little seaside resort on the Baltic Sea.

We should not, though, imagine that theirs was a life of confinement. In March 1953,[20] during his time as a member of parliament, Witzke joined the Anglo-German Club and the club became the go-to place for drinking, dining and socializing by him and his wife. Founded in 1948 by Sir John Dunlop, the High Commissioner of the British military government, and modeled on upper class men's clubs in London, the Club's purpose was to promote business and cultural exchange between Germany and Great Britain.[21] Lilli, with an afinity for status and refinement, enjoyed her husband's membership in such an exclusive club. We do not know what her husband liked about the Club, but he also presumably enjoyed the status that membership conveyed, and likely used it to maintain or gain business contacts, or for espionage.

Beyond the Anglo-German Club, the family photographs attest to a social life and dining out at fine restaurants. As does some of the family correspondence. In January 1958, Lilli wrote to her son-in-law on his twenty-eighth birthday:

> You turned 28 now, didn't you? You were born in 1930? So was my first-born, my little Dieter. It is funny that I've gotten another son having the same age, isn't it? . . . On Thursday Pappi invited me and Butzi [Lothar Jr.] to eat at Ching's and on Tuesday to the Anglo-German Club, we dined

finely there once again. It was a good opportunity as Pappi has foreigners here. A new, very elegant Chinese restaurant opened here, we want to go there next time. It's a shame we didn't get round to eating at Ching's at Christmas, as the two of you also like to eat there. But the time was too short. Yesterday Pappi and I went to the 'festival of seafaring' in *Planten un Blomen* but it wasn't very exciting, very mixed audience.[22]

Witzke was an autocrat at home and he would not have been an outlier among German men in his imposition of his wishes at home. "Germany in the 1950s, like America and Britain and other Western countries during this decade, experienced a conservative interlude, where relations between the sexes appeared to retreat to something like their pre-war shape. Women . . . returned to home and children."[23] His wife Lilli wanted to have cousins and aunts over for Sunday coffee, a tradition, but Witzke forbade that, for reasons unknown. He also forbade her to play the piano because, he said, it got on his nerves. Why he lost his taste for music is unknown: as a young man at sea, he took delight in music and song, taught himself to play musical instruments and upon his entry to Leavenworth even stated his trade, facetiously or not, as musician.

Witzke also had lost over the years his interest in reading. Though he had been an avid reader in prison in the United States, he now rarely read books. Witzke would have followed, though, the news in print, and Hamburg in the post-war era was a breeding ground for journalism in West Germany. In Hamburg in 1947 *Der Spiegel* was founded by a leftist journalist, Rudolf Augstein. In succeeding years, the conservative press baron Axel Springer founded in Hamburg the woman's magazine *Constanze*, the *Hamburger Abendblatt, Die Welt,* and, most successfully, the *Bild-Zeitung*.[24]

Witzke had never had a taste for high culture. This did not change in the 1950s. While Lilli would have loved to attend classical concerts, he insisted upon musicals, featuring women with long legs. Their marriage was not, though, a clash between her high and his low culture. Lilli also loved *kitsch*. Her grandchildren recall that, during the 1960s, she watched for hours every year the televised doings of the Carnival in Cologne and Mainz. It was their first experience of TV. Lilli would have been an ideal viewer of the 1950 German film, *Schwarzwaldmädel*, the most popular film of the post-war era in Germany. It told the story of a German city-dweller who journeys to the countryside to find his soul and, inevitably, a pure German country girl.[25] This was the true German spirit that (many Germans chose to believe) the Nazi era had somehow slightly distorted.

BROTHERS

Lothar (born in 1895) was the oldest of four brothers. The others were: Günter, born a year after Lothar; Kurt, born a year after Günter; and Ottomar, born in 1901.

Lothar's correspondence with his family while he was a sailor during the World War I years is filled with references to and questions about his brothers; there was also correspondence directly among the brothers that has not survived. Günter was on the western front during the war. Kurt was also at war, at a front undisclosed. Ottomar was still at school. Judging only from the correspondence of the time, the family was close-knit and caring. Lothar was still looking out for his brothers as of 1930, when he found jobs for Kurt and Ottomar with the Lago company; there was a brief period when all three were together in Maracaibo. The closeness among the brothers did not survive the decades.

Though Lothar was closest to Kurt, the two did not remain in contact after the war. Kurt was reportedly imprisoned in Italy in 1945 and then sent to Syria where he consorted with Nazi war criminals, Alois Brunner and Franz Rademacher, who had been involved directly with the genocide of the Jews.[26] The Syrians found it expedient to employ former Nazis to assist in both their war against Israel in 1948 and repression of their own population. Kurt, who had been in the SD, made a living by working for the Syrian intelligence agency, and organizing weapons deliveries among Arab countries.[27] When Kurt attended his brother Lothar's funeral, in January 1962, his appearance was a shock; the family had not known that Kurt was still alive. After Lothar's death, Kurt stayed in intermittent contact with Helga. By then, Kurt had left his wife and home. Kurt had a daughter, Ada; Helga and Ada socialized on a few occasions during the 1970s.

There was no reported post-war contact between Lothar (or his family) and his brothers Günter and Ottomar. The latest information that we have about Günter and Ottomar is their membership in the mid-1930s in the SS and SA, respectively, and this comes from archival research.

LOTHAR JR.

Lilli wanted Lothar Jr. (the family called him "Butzi") to be an actor. Lothar Sr. insisted that his son be an accountant, working for Witzke's company. Lothar Jr. was unsuited in every way to work for his father as an accountant. A sensitive artistic type, he had no head for numbers and crumpled under his father's gaze. Lothar Jr.'s time working for his father led to a severe emotional/psychological breakdown on the part of Jr., followed by one year in a sanitarium. After coming home from the sanitarium in 1956, Lothar Jr.'s parents could not deal with him. They sent him to Munich, where Helga was studying, saying in effect: you deal with him. In Munich, Lothar Jr. became psychotic. He came to believe that he was the reincarnation of Hitler and a great conductor and that he would start a new revolution. The psychosis passed.

Lothar Jr. lived most of the rest of his life in a room in Volksdorf next to Lilli. He was involved in a series of lawsuits and petty criminal matters. He eschewed ambition. When he was asked what he did for a living, he would answer: "my sister is a doctor." Her achievement was the best that he could do.

A letter to his brother-in-law (Hossein Moinian) in January 1958 gives us an instance of Lothar Jr speaking for himself:

> I just said to Mommy that I've developed a remarkable ability to waste my time. But it is really quite an accomplishment how I am passing the time—now that I don't write any more. But somehow the evening always comes—I don't even know how—and then you'll find me cheerfully sitting in front of the television set. Mommy and I sometimes spook around the house at 2 a.m. and can't get ourselves to go to bed. And then I get up only at 1 p.m. Mommy usually cooks my lunch in the evening and she often says that she wouldn't be surprised if I don't get up until the evening.

Lilli suffered a stroke in 1975. Lothar Jr took care of her for her five remaining years. After she died in 1980, Lothar Jr. sold the captain's house that his father had bought in the late 1930s. The purchase price was about 600,000 DM. Helga and Lothar Jr. agreed that he would get three-fourths and she one-fourth of the purchase price.

After Lilli's death, Lothar Jr. got married and bought an apartment near the old house. He started a real estate business, buying apartments and renting them out. His last project was to buy properties in Spain; it did not work out. Lothar Jr. died of complications of diabetes at age sixty-two, in 1997.

We have from his niece and nephew (Helga's daughter and son) two retrospectives on their uncle; they differ but are reconcilable. For the niece (Claudia Moinian), Lothar Jr. "in his last years at last lived his own life with a woman who we didn't like very much, but he didn't care, and he was finally free from a family where he was not accepted." For his nephew (Christoph Moinian), Lothar Jr. was "broken by his own sensitivity, on the one hand, and by the harshness of his father and of life itself, on the other. He never managed to stand on his own two feet, despite his manifest talent."

HELGA

We know from the prison guards at Fort Sam Houston that Witzke, then a twenty-three-year-old prisoner, was a good talker, fluent in English, engaging and friendly, easy to like. We find in Helga echoes of Witzke as a youth. Intelligence. Volubility. Ease in learning languages. Arrogance. Stubbornness. Conservative politics combined with a disinclination to abide authority figures. She always voted the CDU (Christian Democratic Union), West Germany's center-right party, and hated the left-leaning SPD (Social Democratic Party), Willy Brandt in particular.[28] But she was not interested in politics, and lacked ideology.

Helga's character as described by her children brings to mind some of the impressions derived by Judge Fake from his two meetings with young Witzke in 1920 and 1923: "[The two interviews] satisfied me that Witzke was a man of exceptionally clever intellectual ability and that he is wholeheartedly a disciple of the old Prussian military training. . . . My impression was that about the only crime which he recognized in his code of ethics in connection with his work for his Government, was the 'crime' of being 'found out.'"[29]

Helga tried her best to emulate her father. She adored and admired him for being a self-made man, for his competence, for becoming a CEO, for being a member of the Hamburg Parliament. For his manliness, in short. But she revered him from a distance. He was away from home a lot. This was true in China, it was true during World War II, and it was true during the 1950s.

Beyond the sadness of Lothar Jr., the family was in many ways not a close family. After high school, Helga went with two friends to Italy for three months. Her parents did not know where she was or for how long and seemed not to care until Helga was supposed to start work as a secretary for her father. Then her father went to the consulate in Hamburg to ask them to investigate where she was. To the extent Helga felt neglected, though, blame was never directed at her father. For Helga, the problem was that there was no heart-to-heart connection between her and her mother. This went two ways. When Lilli in the 1970s suffered a debilitating stroke, Helga reported the news emotionlessly to her kids.

Helga had her first boyfriend when she was eighteen or nineteen. He was an artist. Her father forbade the relationship. Helga obeyed him, and ended the relationship.

Father and daughter had a bigger tension when Witzke refused to pay for her medical studies because he wanted her to be a proper woman, at home, a wife and mother. She did part-time jobs to pay for her own studies.

She wanted to show her father that she could study and succeed without him. Strong, like her father, she was the type never to give up. Because she had little money at the time, she had spartan meals. This was how she met her husband. He was a medical student with money, and she saw him at the butcher shop ordering meat that she could not afford.

There is a sternness and rigidity displayed by the later Witzke that is far from the flexible, easy-going adventurer of his early letters. One might have expected the sailor who jumped ship at Valparaiso and headed for North America (and was severely reprimanded for it by his father) to be more tolerant later in life of his daughter's medical ambitions. The calcification that sometimes comes with age may be the explanation.

HELGA'S WEDDING

In the mid-1950s, Helga presented to her family a new boyfriend, Hossein Moinian, a fellow medical student from a wealthy and westernized Iranian family. We might predict that Witzke would have a hostile reaction to the prospect of a brown-skinned foreigner of Iranian descent marrying his daughter. We would be wrong. The two men had an immediate affinity. Witzke recognized in Moinian another man's man, an adventurer in his own way, who had left Iran for Germany without speaking a word of German, and was making his career as a professional (a physician). Witzke's willingness to accept Helga's non-Christian and light-brown skinned husband into the family suggests that he was not fixated on racial purity. Witzke was surely aware, though, that Persians would have been categorized by the Nazis as Aryans.

For Moinian, Witzke would be the doting father that he never had back home in Iran. Between the two, there was love and respect. The two shared something else as well. Helga, having grown up revering her womanizing father, married another womanizer. Like her mother before her, Helga suppressed her knowledge of this marital reality.

The wedding of Helga in 1956 to Hossein Moinian was a major event for the Witzke family. The wedding took place at a church in Hamburg and the reception was at the swanky Hotel Atlantic in Hamburg. The father of the bride was proud to pay for such an affair.

Once the guests were assembled, Witzke stood up to give the welcome toast. Twice he started and twice he had to stop because he was crying. He then gave up. Helga later recounted the story as a nice one, but without deep emotion on her part or, in her memory, from her father. Just a nice story. Was he already drunk? Probably not. Was he nervous about public speaking? Probably not. How then do we explain this eruption of sentiment? Witzke's grandson offers this: "Maybe there was a heart, which wanted to express itself."

Among the guests was a very attractive daughter of friends of the parents of the bride. As Helga would later describe it to her children, this woman caused the groom's brother (also a womanizer) to fall for her. The father of the bride took notice of her as well.

Lothar Witzke was enjoying his daughter's wedding. The heady occasion and the wine loosened his social guard such as it was. He liked women, and for a lifetime they had liked him back. Why should it not be the same for this lovely young thing? He approached her. He flirted with her, and this did not go unnoticed by his wife and daughter. But he went further this time than they could imagine. Amid his daughter's wedding celebration, visible to all, Lothar Witzke got down on his knees before the comely guest and declared his love. He was not teasing; he was trying to get her.[30]

Helga was angry and embarrassed, but she found ways to excuse his conduct. As Helga later told the story, the responsibility was in significant part that of the woman. The groom's reaction? He found it funny. He too liked the young woman.

A surviving photograph (reproduced at page 124) of a formal reception echoes this family melodrama. The photograph is of the Witzke family, together with a few guests. The celebrants have moved their chairs into a semi-circle around the table in order to face the camera. Perhaps other photographs, not surviving, show those at the table posed and smiling toward the viewer. The surviving photograph catches the family and their guests unguarded and unposed, interacting, and with no one facing the camera. To the extreme left sits Helga's husband, speaking with a satisfied smile to the very attractive young woman to his left. To her left sits Lilli, looking unhappily at the woman who is occupying the attention of her son-in-law at this reception. Across the table sits an aged but sprightly Witzke, grinning. To his left, Helga is turned completely toward her father, speaking animatedly. Witzke is not looking at his daughter. He is looking in the direction of the young woman across the table. His countenance suggests that he is pleased. He may be inebriated.[31]

The moment captured by the camera seems to be a precursor to Witzke's imminent and public declaration of passion. And the distressed look on Lilli's face suggests that she is aware of the lure that this young woman had for the men in the Witzke family. She would not have been totally surprised.

She knew her husband well enough. Their marriage by the 1950s was distant and unhappy. In later years, Lilli was persistently ill, talked often about her medications, and never about her husband.

NO APOLOGIES

Witzke was among those who thought that he and Germany had nothing to apologize for. His guiltlessness for the events of the Nazi era would not have distinguished him from millions of Germans who considered that they were the ones who suffered most.[32] As one historian has expressed the point:

> In surveys carried out on behalf of the American military government in the postwar years, when asked the question whether National Socialism was "a bad idea, or a good idea badly carried out," the population of the American Zone consistently showed a plurality for the view that it had been "a good idea," and showed an actual majority for that and "no opinion" combined. The view that Nazism had been simply and unequivocally a 'bad idea' was never held by more than forty percent of respondents, and by the end of the third post-war winter that number had declined to around thirty percent with double that number—sixty percent—now insisting that Nazism had been a "good idea" gone wrong.[33]

The genocide of European Jewry was not a matter that bore contemplation.[34]

German intellectuals in the years after the war and especially in the 1960s and 1970s would examine Germany's quest to remake its identity in the debris of Nazism.[35] Among these was the German filmmaker, Rainer Werner Fassbinder, whose 1978 film "The Marriage of Maria Braun" is a critique of what he saw as Germany's failed effort to remake its spirit. The film's heroine, Maria Braun, makes her way in the post-war world, befriending (and more) the American occupying force. The film's first image is a photograph of Hitler on the wall of the registry office where Maria and her fiancé are during the war years about to exchange their marriage vows. Allied bombs destroy the office before their vows are exchanged. The film ends with Maria's posh post-war house exploding while a German radio announcer recounts with almost hysterical fervor the final minutes of West Germany's victory in the 1954 World Cup. For Germans, their *Weltmeisterschaft* (FIFA world championship title) signaled that "Wir sind wieder wer" ("We are somebody again"). The film offers no comfort as to who or what Germans had again become.[36]

Witzke would have scoffed at this critique. Not given to introspection, the struggle to realize an identity, whether on the personal or national level, was of no moment to him. Disinterested in looking inwards, he was equally disinterested in looking back. He was a man of action.

In around 1960, when Witzke was a bit deaf, he and Helga were at a café in Hamburg. Pointing to a man sitting nearby whose attire showed him to be an observant Jew, Witzke said, "Da sitzt noch einer, den sie vergessen haben zu vergasen." In English, "There's another one sitting there who they forgot to gas." Helga became angry, not least because, being hard of hearing, her father had spoken loudly. The casually expressed anti-Semitism forces us to wonder whether Witzke was more of a true Nazi than his family's memory allowed.

After his death, Helga's family often talked with disgust about the Nazis, with no mention of their father/grandfather.

On a rare visit to church in the 1950s, Witzke observed a believer kneeling at prayer. His reaction was disgust, "Ein Mann beugt sein Knie für niemanden." "A man kneels to no one." His life experience taught him that self-reliance alone mattered.

THE SPY
AS SABOTEUR

DID HE DO IT?
WEST COAST SABOTAGE

I have many lives on my conscience
and I have killed many people
and will now kill more.
—LOTHAR WITZKE TO PAUL ALTENDORF,
QUOTED IN LIPSCOMB SPECIAL
BORDER REPORT, FEBRUARY 2, 1918

The evidence is clear and convincing that Lothar Witzke was a German spy in the US and Mexico during World War I.[1]

Was Witzke also a saboteur in the Americas during World War I? Paul Altendorf, the double agent responsible for Witzke's capture in January 1918, told Special Agent Byron Butcher at Nogales just after Witzke was captured that Witzke had boasted to him about having committed several acts of sabotage during 1916–1917, including the black powder magazine explosion at Mare Island Naval Station near San Francisco, the disabling of the boilers on the *Minnesota*, the crippling of a ship in the Gulf of Mexico, and, most spectacularly, the explosion of the Black Tom munitions depot in New York harbor.[2] At Witzke's trial, Altendorf testified under oath about the boasts about Mare Island, the *Minnesota*, and Black Tom, and added a new one, a boast by Witzke about burning down a lumber mill in Oregon.[3] A year later, in a series of articles in the *Chicago Tribune*, Altendorf gave more detail about these boasts, saying that Witzke had bragged about ruining the *Minnesota's* boilers, starting a devastating forest fire in Oregon, causing a munitions ship explosion, and causing the Black Tom explosion.[4] Another source, the former military attaché at the German Consulate in San Francisco, Wilhelm von Brincken, suggested in 1920 that Kurt Jahnke and Lothar Witzke may have been responsible for the horrific Preparedness Day Parade bombing in July 1916.

In contrast to his admissions under oath about espionage, Witzke never made any such admission of sabotage. In the case of Black Tom, Witzke issued vigorous denials, though off the record he was on two occasions coy about whether he had any role at Black Tom.

The closest that Witzke came to a public admission regarding sabotage was a carefully curated statement in his 1927 affidavit submitted to the Mixed Claims Commission that, after the US entered the war in 1917, he was:

> entrusted with establishing communications with followers of the Irish independence movement (Sinn Fein) and with establishing relations with anarchistic circles, particularly I.W.W. to support these with money if necessary and to send their members into belligerent countries with instructions for the purpose of instigating strikes, riots, mutinies and revolutions. I also was to use these relations to cause their members to commit sabotage against munitions plants and factories on the territory of the United States who were then at war with us.[5]

This statement, made after his pardon and his return to Germany, constitutes an admission that Witzke did, or intended to do, only those things that Altendorf and William Gleaves had testified at trial that he was tasked by Jahnke to do on the mission to Nogales when he was captured. None of this implicated Witzke in Black Tom, or Kingsland, or the devastating acts of West Coast sabotage that he supposedly bragged about to Altendorf. In other words, he was admitting what the German agent had determined could safely be admitted (because each act came after the US and Germany were belligerants) and in any case was undeniable.

On one other occasion, in 1929 in an interview in Venezuela, Witzke reportedly told Amos Peaslee, chief counsel for the American claimants before the Mixed Claims Commission, and Leonard Peto, vice president of one of the claimants, that he had done sabotage work during the war, "but he repeated over and over again that no one would ever find out what it was."[6]

In this chapter, we examine the evidence as to Witzke's responsibility for the acts of sabotage on the West Cost about which Witzke allegedly boasted to Altendorf or of which he was suspected by the German attaché Von Brincken. Black Tom will be separately discussed in the following chapter. For each alleged act of West Coast sabotage, to the extent that we find it unlikely that Witzke had a role, we consider whether the circumstances suggest that

Altendorf fabricated the boast or whether Witzke did indeed make the boast, albeit falsely. This set of circumstances will, in turn, figure in our ultimate assessment of whether Witzke was responsible for the Black Tom sabotage, because that assessment turns in part on a view as to both Altendorf's credibility and Witzke's boastfulness.

SHIP EXPLOSIONS

In his February 1918 statement to Butcher, in his military trial testimony, and in his *Chicago Tribune* series, Altendorf said that Witzke boasted to him about disabling the *Minnesota's* boilers, causing a munitions ship to explode, and crippling a ship in the Gulf of Mexico. Other than the *Minnesota*, Witzke did not identify the names of the ships. Because Jahnke claimed credit with Berlin for several fires or explosions on ships that were identified, and because Witzke was Jahnke's chief assistant from July 1916 to February 1918, it may be that Witzke helped with, and was referring in his boasts to, one or more of the ship fires and explosions mentioned by Jahnke. We discuss below the *Minnesota* and several other ship explosions that occurred while Witzke was on the West Coast.

The *Minnesota*

Altendorf made his first, and most detailed, statement about Witzke's *Minnesota* boast in his Butcher debriefing of January 31, 1918. The boast, according to Altendorf, occurred on the January 1918 trip from Mexico City to Nogales, during an overnight stop in Guadalajara while the two were out drinking together: "Waberski . . . claimed that while working as a mechanic of the 'U.S. *Minnesota*' he had ruined or disabled the boat's boilers." Altendorf repeated the boast in his trial testimony in similar terms, except that he omitted the detail about Witzke working as a mechanic on the ship, and this time he gave as the setting of the boast a dinner at Jahnke's house in Mexico City on the night before the two men left for Nogales at which Jahnke and another German agent were also present: "[Waberski] told me that he was the cause of the boilers in the Minnesota blowing up, that he ruined the boilers in the Minnesota." Altendorf recounted the boast a third time, more briefly, in one of his *Chicago Tribune* articles: "[At a supper in Mexico City] Waberski boasted . . . that he had ruined the boilers of the transport Minnesota."[7]

As discussed in chapter 2, the Military Intelligence Division investigated the *Minnesota* boast before Witzke's August 1918 military trial at Fort Sam

Houston. The investigators reached no firm conclusion, and the investigation was terminated when Witzke was convicted.

The SS *Minnesota*, a civilian steamer, was in 1915-1917 the largest US flag merchant ship in the world.[8] Owned by the Great Northern Steamship Company until January 1917, it sailed between Seattle and Shanghai, carrying grain to the Far East and Chinese silks back to America.[9] In the fall of 1915 it was chartered to British interests and left Seattle for England on November 14, 1915, carrying 16,000 tons of cargo (wheat, canned salmon, lumber, hops, and frozen halibut).[10] In early December 1915, the Port Captain of San Francisco began receiving distress signals from somewhere off the coast of lower California. It was the *Minnesota*, powerless and drifting at sea, all six of its boilers having collapsed. Sabotage was suspected. Tugs were dispatched, the *Minnesota* was towed to San Francisco, and an investigation was commenced.[11]

Because of the time and place of the *Minnesota's* boiler failure, Witzke could not have been responsible. At all relevant times (November-December 1915) Witzke was in Valparaiso, Chile. He would not make his first visit to the United States until May of the following year, six months after the event. Moreover, the investigation of the incident concluded beyond doubt that the boiler collapse was caused not by sabotage or foul play, but by the mechanical failure of aging boilers, all of which needed to be replaced before the voyage could resume.[12] New boilers (of American manufacture) were procured while the ship idled at San Francisco, and on February 14, 1917, the *Minnesota* resumed its long-delayed journey.[13] Witzke therefore did not ruin or disable the SS *Minnesota's* boilers.

Did Altendorf make up the story or did Witzke falsely boast?

Altendorf is not likely to have known on his own the story about the *Minnesota's* boilers. He had been in Mexico the whole time. He was not a seaman and, from what we know of his life in Mexico, he did not frequent ports or hang out with seamen, other than Witzke. As far as we know, he did not read American newspapers. To be sure, he was capable of inventing a story that made Witzke responsible for the *Minnesota's* ruined boilers, but only if he knew about the boiler story to begin with.

By contrast, it is plausible, even likely, that Witzke knew of the *Minnesota* boiler incident. He had spent a good deal of time in San Francisco from May 1916 to the end of 1917. The *Minnesota* story was covered in the local newspapers and updated from time to time as the ship remained idle in San Francisco, awaiting new boilers. Witzke frequented bars and restaurants near the docks where the incident may even have been discussed among the seafaring crowd. He was most likely in San Francisco in mid-February 1917 when the ship, with much fanfare, finally left San Francisco for England. Witzke would also have known that the incident occurred six months before his arrival in the US and that the investigation ruled out foul play. However, except for Jahnke (with whom Witzke had apparently shared his true biography), the story that Witzke was telling about himself was that he had been in America, and on the West Coast, for much longer. Therefore, there was little risk that those to whom he was boasting, whether just Altendorf (the only audience in Altendorf's original telling) or Altendorf plus two or three others (according to Altendorf's later versions), would have known enough to contradict him. Jahnke would have known but had no incentive to undercut Witzke. Certainly Witzke, if he was falsely boasting, could not have guessed that Altendorf would be repeating the boast several weeks later to a US investigator who might know or be able easily to determine that the *Minnesota's* boilers had not been the target of sabotage.[14]

In summary, the *Minnesota* was not sabotaged and, even if it had been, Witkze could not have been responsible. The alleged boast by Witzke that he had sabotaged the *Minnesota* was therefore a lie either by Altendorf or by Witzke. Because of the unlikelihood that Altendorf would have known on his own about the *Minnesota*, it is more likely that Witzke boasted falsely about the *Minnesota* than that Altendorf made up the story.

Munitions Ship Explosion

Altendorf wrote in one of his 1919 *Chicago Tribune* articles that, at a dinner in Mexico City in January 1918 the night before he and Witzke left for Nogales, Witzke boasted to a group of dinner guests that included, besides Altendorf himself, Kurt Jahnke and two other German agents, that he had found employment as a sailor and had caused a munitions ship explosion. Altendorf did not provide more detail. Altendorf had not mentioned a munitions ship explosion before his *Chicago Tribune* articles, either in his February 1918 statement to Byron Butcher or in his August 1918 trial testimony. What likely happened in the interim was that Altendorf learned that, in early 1917, three officials of the German Consulate in San Francisco (consul Franz von Bopp, vice consul E. M. von Schack, and military attaché Wilhelm von Brincken) were convicted in a San Francisco court of directing German agents to destroy munitions vessels sailing from Pacific coast ports to US allies during the period of neutrality. If so, that event either refreshed Altendorf's memory that destruction of a munitions ship had been an additional boast by Witzke over dinner in Mexico or caused Altendorf falsely to "remember" a purported boast about a munitions ship explosion.

That German agents on the west and east coasts of the United States engaged in acts of sabotage during the period of neutrality against cargo ships bound for Allied nations is undisputed.[15] Numerous examples of bombs and other incendiaries being planted in munitions ships were presented at the trial of Bopp, Schack, and Brincken. Although not identified at the time of trial, Kurt Jahnke was later named by attaché Brincken as one of the agents employed for this purpose.[16] Witzke, as Jahnke's number two man, would have been a natural suspect as well, but for the fact that he had not yet arrived in America and had not yet started working for Jahnke at the time that the three consular officials were arrested. Altendorf did not, of course, know this; as far as he knew, Witzke had been a resident of the West Coast when the attacks occurred. Also, it is more than likely that similar attacks, directed by others, continued thereafter, including after the US declared war on Germany. Indeed, as will be discussed later in this chapter in connection with the Preparedness Day Parade bombing, von Brinken would say in 1920 that Jahnke had approached him after his (von Brincken's) arrest and release on bail for incendiary devices to plant in a munitions ship in the summer of 1916, when Jahnke and Witzke were already acquainted and working together. It is entirely plausible, therefore, that Witzke engaged in sabotage against one or more munitions ships. However, we have not been able to identify any particular attack on a munitions ship to which Witzke can be linked.

In summary, Altendorf's assertion for the first time in one of his 1919 *Chicago Tribune* articles that Witzke had boasted to him about blowing up a munitions ship on which he served as a sailor is suspect because he had not previously reported such a boast either in his original debriefing at the time of Witzke's capture or at Witzke's trial. The allegation about the boast was made only after Altendorf had settled in the United States and after it was reported in the American press that such bombings had been commissioned by officials at the German consulate in San Francisco. Also, nothing ties Witzke to any particular ship bombing, much less to a bombing on a ship on which Witzke was employed as a sailor (part of the boast Altendorf reported). We are inclined, therefore, to believe that Altendorf fabricated this boast.

That said, it is likely that Witzke engaged in munitions ship sabotage even if he did not boast to Atlendorf about it. He admitted in his 1927 affidavit for the Mixed Claims Commission that, before the US entered the war, part of his job as a spy was to reconnoiter munitions ships on the West Coast that were bound for the Allies, and part of his mission after the US entered the war was to induce others to engage in sabotage against munitions plants. Additionally, German attaché von Brincken reported that Jahnke had come to him at the Consulate asking for bombs to plant on munitions ships, this at a time when Witzke was himself in San Francisco and serving as Jahnke's number two. These admissions, together with von Brincken's report, point to Witzke's likely involvement in one or more munitions ship bombings.

Cargo Vessels

Besides munitions ships, cargo vessels were targets of German sabotage, as the Germans were eager to interrupt the supply of all war materials, not just munitions, destined for Allied countries. Jahnke claimed credit with Berlin for several such attacks, including against the steamer *Margaret*, the tanker *J. A. Moffett*, and the steamer *O. M. Clark*. We consider now whether Witzke may have been an accomplice in these attacks. As Altendorf did not say that Witzke mentioned any of these to Altendorf, this portion of our inquiry does not implicate either Altendorf's credibility or Witzke's boastfulness. The issue, rather, is more simply: is there evidence that links Witzke to any of these accidents or acts of maritime sabotage?

On June 24, 1917, four days after leaving the Columbia River (in Oregon) for China with a cargo of lumber, a fire was discovered in the hold of the steamer *Margaret*. It was towed back to Astoria (at the mouth of the Columbia River).[17] British intelligence reported to the Americans that Jahnke claimed credit for the fire.[18] We have not been able to find additional information on the fire, which suggests that it was not consequential.

Witzke was at the time on the US West Coast. He registered with the Selective Service in San Francisco on June 5, and he obtained Able Seaman and Lifeboat Efficiency certificates in San Francisco on June 27. Whether he was in the Portland/Astoria area in Oregon in between those dates is not known, although his Alien Head-Tax receipt issued at Laredo on June 5 when he crossed the border from Mexico into the United States lists his destination as Portland, Oregon, suggesting that he may have been there during the summer of 1917 before returning to Mexico. The sole facts connecting Witzke to the *Margaret* are, thus, that he was on the West Coast at the time under the direction of Jahnke (who was then in Mexico) and that British intelligence reported that Jahnke was taking credit with Berlin for the explosion. Witzke never boasted to Altendorf about the *Margaret* fire.

Another ship explosion for which Jahnke claimed credit (in his intercepted communications with Berlin) occurred on September 26, 1917, on the Standard Oil tanker *J. A. Moffett*. The tanker was docked at the time in San Francisco bay at Point Richmond wharf, taking on 61,000 gallons of fuel oil. The explosion tore off the top of the forward deep tank (which was empty), blew up the deck plates, killed two men, and threatened the lives of eighteen others who were working on the ship. Damage was estimated at $10,000 (more than $200,000 in 2020 dollars). Initially, the explosion was thought to be an accident, the result of collected gas ignited by a spark that was in turn caused by hobnailed shoes worn by the two men working at the steel side of the tank who were hosing it down preparatory to its being filled with gasoline (or perhaps by a hammer, or the lighting of a match, as one of the dead men was said to be an "inveterate smoker").[19]

There were three investigations of the explosion. The conclusion was "causes unknown." The damage, apart from the loss of life, was less serious than first reported because, although the forward tank was destroyed, the blast was upward and the ship's hull was therefore largely unaffected. The fuel oil was saved.[20]

It is tempting to tie Witzke to this explosion. He was in San Francisco at the time. (The day after the explosion, he wrote a postcard to his aunt Bertha, postmarked San Francisco September 28, saying that he had recently returned to San Francisco.)[21] He was dating a girl from Berkeley, the suburban San Francisco town adjacent to Richmond, and therefore he likely knew his way around the area. The explosion was on the waterfront, where Witzke had specially prepared himself to operate without attracting suspicion; and, as he said in his 1934 Hankow interview, from the time he landed in the United States in May 1916 he had been building up his cover as an experienced sailor, in order to be able to work on American coastal vessels and to explain his presence in any port where he might find himself doing espionage work.[22] In Mexico earlier that spring, he had been tasked with reconnoitering oil shipments from Tampico and Veracruz, from which it can be presumed he acquired knowledge of tankers, how they loaded oil cargoes, and the like. Plausible, but just speculation. There is no hard evidence that Witzke was involved in the attack on the *J. A. Moffett*. Nor did he boast to Altendorf about any such involvement.

According to an April 3, 1918, intercepted cable to his superior in Antwerp, Jahnke credited "my people" with destroying the SS *Clark* in 1917.[23] The *Clark* was the steamer *O. M. Clark* that was severely damaged in a fire that started shortly after midnight on December 7, 1917, while taking on oil in Los Angeles. The ship had left Portland on November 30 bound for Callao, Peru, carrying a cargo of one million feet of lumber. The ship was completely gutted by the fire and had to be beached. The loss including cargo was estimated at $230,000 (more than $4.6 million in 2020 dollars).[24] The steamer was eventually repaired and returned to service at the end of February 1918. The reconstruction cost, though substantial ($30,000 plus charter loss of $50,000), was less than the originally estimated damage.[25] The cause of the fire was never determined.

Witzke was one of Jahnke's "people," therefore a potential suspect. However, as he was in Mexico from mid-November (when he crossed the border at Laredo) until his capture at Nogales on February 1, 1918, he could not have planted a time-bomb on the ship at Portland in late November and could not have set the fire in San Pedro on December 7. Witzke was not the culprit and was not involved, unless, somehow, he engaged the one who was.

Gulf of Mexico Ship Explosion

Witzke's most detailed ship explosion boast, according to Altendorf, concerned a ship in the Gulf of Mexico. Altendorf described the conversation with Witzke in his end-of-January 1918 statement to Butcher:

> In speaking of his exploits Waberski said that at one time he had crippled a boat in the Gulf of Mexico by taking a red hot coal in a glove he had soaked in water for 24 hours and dropping the coal into a hole he had prepared leading to the dynamite magazine. He safely reached the far end of the boat before the explosion took place.[26]

The detail about the coal in the glove gives the story facial credibility but on examination is dubious. The term "dynamite magazine" would typically refer to a small building on land in which dynamite was stored, *e.g.*, in a mining camp or logging camp, whereas a ship's magazine where ammunition is stored would be called a "powder magazine" or simply a "magazine." Witzke, having been a cadet and then a sailor on the *J. C. Vinnen*, as well as having worked (briefly) in a mining area (Keeler) and perhaps a logging camp in the American northwest, would have known the difference and would not have used the term dynamite magazine to refer to a ship's magazine. Of course, assuming the boast was truthful, it is possible that Altendorf (not familiar with maritime or mining vocabulary) misheard or misremembered, or that Butcher or Lipscomb was familiar with the term dynamite magazine but not powder magazine, and used the former term in the report of Altendorf's debriefing.

Altendorf did not reference this boast in his testimony at Witzke's trial, or in his subsequent *Chicago Tribune* articles, unless his mention in the latter that Witzke told him "he had found employment as a sailor and had blown up a ship carrying munitions" was a reference to the Gulf of Mexico dynamite magazine boast. The latter is unlikely. Altendorf was a colorful storyteller. If he meant the dynamite magazine boast, he would have retold that story in all its detail, if anything embellishing it with still more detail, not less. Was he in effect, therefore, "walking back" the boast by not retelling it? Perhaps, although it was not in Altendorf's nature to walk anything back.

In any event, if the dynamite magazine boast was truthful, the event would likely have occurred at a Gulf port while the target ship was docked there, not at sea. (Presumably Witzke would not have blown up a ship at sea on which he was sailing, for fear of sinking his own ship and drowning.) The only Gulf ports that Witzke is known to have visited were Tampico and Veracruz. We have not been able to identify any ship explosion or fire linked to those two cities during the times that Witzke may have been there. German agents were thought to be responsible for a fire on the American oil steamer *Santurce*, which burned and sank in the Gulf in late June 1917 during a voyage from Tampico to the United States, carrying a cargo of oil and gasoline. All of the crew were rescued. The cause of the fire was not known.[27] Witzke left Mexico in early June 1917 and was on the US West Coast from June 8 to the end of July. The most he could have done, therefore, was engage someone else to set the fire, not set it himself. Moreover, the facts of the *Santurce* fire do not otherwise conform to the hot coal story.

Was the Gulf dynamite magazine story a false boast by Witzke or did Altendorf fabricate it? The fact that Altendorf told the story to Butcher in his first debriefing, coupled with the relative detail of the story, suggests that Altendorf was telling the truth about what he heard; he had more to gain at that time by being truthful. However, the fact that he did not repeat the story (an entertaining one) raises doubts. Had he really heard Witzke make such a colorful boast, one would expect him to retell it (if anything, with additional embellishments), not suppress it. Therefore, this is a much closer call than the *Minnesota* boast. By a hair's breadth, we conclude that this was a false boast by Witzke, not a fabrication by Altendorf.

LOGGING CAMP FIRES

Altendorf told Byron Butcher that Witzke had boasted to him about setting forest fires in the Pacific Northwest. He repeated the allegation in his trial testimony and in his *Chicago Tribune* articles. In particular, Altendorf told Butcher at the end of January 1918 that, while out drinking in Guadalajara, Witzke boasted that he "caused the fires in the Oregon logging camps last fall."[28] Similarly, but giving it a different setting, Altendorf testified at Witzke's trial in August 1918 that Witzke told him and several guests at a dinner in Mexico City on the night before they left for Nogales that he had worked at a mill in Oregon and "fixed the wood to burn down this mill." Altendorf then repeated a version of this story in his 1919 *Chicago Tribune* articles, with Witzke boasting to guests at the dinner that "as a lumberjack in Oregon he had started a disastrous forest fire."[29]

There were bad forest fires in Oregon (and other Pacific Northwest locations including Idaho and Washington state) during the summer 1917, some of which began under suspicious circumstances, although most had burned out by early fall due to heavy rains. The documents place Witzke in San Francisco during the summer 1917: on June 9 (Selective Service Registration), June 26–27 (Lifeboat Man and Able-Seaman certificates), and July 15 (postcard to Aunt Bertha). Otherwise his whereabouts on any particular day are unaccounted for. When he crossed the border at Laredo on June 5, he listed Portland (not San Francisco) as his destination. He had been in Oregon and Washington before, during the previous August, and knew something of the region.

There were two major sets of fires in June and early July 1917: the first began during June 13–16; the second began in the second week of July.[30] Others would follow as the summer wore on. Arson was suspected in a fire that began on the night of July 14 at the Lester Lumber company works, in the Monsanto area of western Washington state (roughly midway between Portland and Seattle); it spread quickly to a nearby camp. Suspicion of arson was aroused because the telephone wires had been cut. Also, there was an IWW camp with twenty-five residents less than a mile from the Lester camp, thus focusing suspicion on the IWW, although IWW involvement was never proved.[31] If Witzke himself started the Lester camp fire, then he could not have been in San Francisco the next day where his postcard to his Aunt Bertha was postmarked on the fifteenth. But he need not have set the fire himself. One of Witzke's mandates that summer from Jahnke was to incite IWW members and encourage sabotage against American war efforts.

Arson and the IWW were suspected in other fires as well, including one at the Wheeler lumber company camp in Tilamook County near Portland and the Sheridan lumber camp on Mill Creek in Polk County, south of Portland near Salem.[32] Fires continued to erupt and spread, especially to the south of Portland, causing significant damage.[33] Arson or carelessness was suspected in several of them. In late August, a weary and frustrated forester noted the importance of lumber to the war effort and pleaded with his fellow countrymen to help find the arsonists, "It is puzzling to understand why the men who are setting these fires, if they are American citizens, cannot realize that they are interfering with the war program of the government. . . . At this time when the lumbering industry is so vital to the welfare of the nation the lumber concerns are under a serious handicap when they have to remove men from the logging camps and put them to fire fighting. It is the patriotic duty of all persons in the fire zone to do all they can to bring these incendiarists to light."[34]

Did Altendorf fabricate the logging camp fires boast? We think not. He reported the boast to Butcher at his first opportunity, when he had the most to gain from being, or being seen as, truthful. His subsequent retellings added a bit of detail that may have been embellishment but was not inconsistent. Additionally, there is no reason to think that Altendorf, having spent the prior fall in Mexico working with General Calles, would have known about forest fires that fall in Oregon (indeed, he may not even have known that Oregon was a state of the United States). He may have seen, from rifling through Witzke's papers in Guadalajara while Witzke was in a drunken sleep, that Witzke's Alien Head-Tax receipt, issued at Laredo on June 5 when Witzke crossed the border into the US for his summer visit, listed Portland as his destination. But it does not follow that Altendorf would have known about or therefore linked Witzke to Oregon forest fires in the fall.

We thus conclude that Witzke boasted to Altendorf about causing logging camp fires in Oregon. Was Witzke's boast truthful or false? Whether Witzke was himself an arsonist, or instigated others to commit arson, or misappropriated the arson of others in order to portray himself as a successful saboteur, we cannot know. The most that can be said based on the evidence available to us is that Witzke had been in Oregon and Washington, he could have been there at the time of the fires, and setting such fires or instigating others (such as IWW workers) to do so was consistent with his mission to the West Coast.

DUPONT TACOMA WORKS EXPLOSION

Jahnke took credit with his superiors for an explosion at the DuPont powder works near Camp Lewis in Tacoma, Washington, during 1917.[35] There were two explosions there that year. Jahnke himself was in Mexico, not the United States, at the time of both explosions, and his role therefore could have been no more than that of a planner. The first explosion occurred during the early

morning of June 10 when half a ton of black powder exploded, killing a work-
man and blowing a graining mill to smithereens. The shock was heard for
miles. The estimated property loss was $5,000 (approximately $100,000 in
2020 dollars).[36] The second explosion occurred in the black powder corning
mill on the evening of October 21. No one was in the mill at the time and no
one was killed or injured, but the building in which the dynamite blew up
was destroyed. The estimated property loss was $4,000 (about $80,000 in
2020 dollars).[37] Both explosions were initially thought to be accidents, but
the official causes were never determined.

Witzke was on the US West Coast both times, the first during his summer
trip from Mexico to the States and the second during his fall trip.

On his summer trip, he had crossed the border at Laredo, listing Portland
as his destination. However, he appears to have been in San Francisco, not
the Pacific Northwest, on June 9 because he registered with the US selective
service there on that day. If so, his being in the Tacoma area early the next
morning to commit sabotage is improbable.

As for October 21, he wrote a postcard to his Aunt Bertha dated that
day and postmarked San Francisco the following day. It is improbable that
he was in the Tacoma area on the evening of the twenty-first committing
sabotage, unless the postcard was written earlier than the twenty-first and
was then posted on the twenty-second by someone else for the purpose of
establishing an alibi. The postcard is curious in several respects. Though
written to his Aunt Bertha in Zurich (it ends by saying "cordial greetings to
mother, father, brother, grandmother, Paul and Elly and yourself"), it is addressed to "Mr. Witzke" in Posen, Germany, not to Aunt Bertha in Zurich,
Switzerland. Moreover, Witzke would always include a first name, or at least
a first initial, in his address; this time there was no first name or first initial.
Finally, as Witzke had three brothers, Kurt, Otto, and Gunther, the closing
reference to "brother" in the singular is odd. The October 21 postcard alibi is
therefore suspect. However, beyond the fact that Witzke was close to Jahnke,
that Jahnke took credit for these explosions, and that Witzke but not Jahnke
was on the West Coast at the time, there is no evidence linking Witzke to
these explosions.

MARE ISLAND

The deadliest sabotage of which Witzke reportedly boasted was the black
powder magazine explosion at the Mare Island Navy Yard near San Francisco on July 9, 1917. The blast destroyed 128,000 pounds of powder, killed six

(including a mother, father, and their two young daughters who lived near the powder magazine), and injured thirty-eight. It also destroyed a specially built structure known as building no. 40 in which the powder was stored.[38]

According to Altendorf (as recounted to Special Agent Byron Butcher), Witzke told Altendorf over a bottle of wine at Guadalajara "that he had blown up a black powder magazine of 250,000 pounds near San Francisco (Mare Island), one morning about five o'clock. Waberski reportedly bragged that sixteen lives had been lost, including at least six children. He reportedly asserted that he was working for the American government as a mechanic on the island at the time of the explosion and laid wires to accomplish the sabotage."[39] Altendorf repeated the substance of the alleged boast in his trial testimony in August 1918, this time saying that the boast had been made to guests at a dinner in Mexico City the night before he and Witzke left for Nogales. Then, in his *Chicago Tribune* articles, he said that a priest-friend of Witzke had told him about Witzke's Mare Island exploit. He did not repeat that Witzke himself had made the boast.[40]

Some details of the Mare Island explosion as recounted by Altendorf are wrong. First, the blast occurred at 7:55 a.m., not 5:00 a.m. when Witzke reportedly said that he "heard it" while lying in bed. Second, in Altendorf's first telling of the boast to Byron Butcher, Witzke supposedly "bragged that sixteen lives had been lost including six children," whereas the correct number of fatalities was six including two children. Third, the amount of powder blown up was 128,000 pounds, not the 250,000 pounds that Altendorf said Witzke boasted of having destroyed.

The official board of inquiry convened to investigate the explosion concluded unanimously that "the explosion was not an accident, but was due to the deliberate act of some person or persons unknown." However, it was unable to produce a suspect or any evidence of how the explosion occurred.[41]

Neither Lothar Witzke nor Kurt Jahnke was a suspect during the official inquiry. The name Lothar Witzke was not even known to investigators at the time. Kurt Jahnke was known, both to the Secret Service and the Bureau of Investigation, and should have been a suspect, or at least a person of interest, for three reasons.

First, Jahnke had been on a Secret Service watch list for several years because of his suspected prior criminal activities.[42]

Second, Jahnke was stationed at Mare Island Navy Yard after he enlisted in the US Marines in 1909.[43]

Third, and most important, in early 1916 Jahnke dropped by the San Francisco office of the Bureau of Investigation with a remarkable story to tell about threats to the Mare Island Navy Yard. He said that in December 1915 he had been approached on Kearney Street by a man named Lang, who once was connected to Mare Island. Lang told Jahnke that "there were things he could do at Mare Island that would be of advantage to the Fatherland." Lang also said he had a source named Lynch who was close to the mayor of Vallejo (the town where the Mare Island Navy Yard was located). Then in January 1916, Jahnke said, a second man whose name he did not know also approached him on the street and said there was "work he could do" at Mare Island. Jahnke gave as his reason for telling this to the bureau that he thought it might be related to a recent theft of a naval code of a warship docked at the Naval Yard. The theft of the code was not public knowledge, which should have aroused the Bureau's interest in Jahnke in particular, but the bureau did not follow up.[44]

Why did Jahnke, a German agent himself, tell this story to the Bureau of Investigation? Maybe he was already forming the intent to attack the powder magazine at Mare Island should the US join the war against Germany and imagined that his disclosure to the bureau would divert suspicion. Maybe his reasoning was still more obscure. Either way, his story should have been of interest to the board of inquiry, especially given Jahnke's shady past and prior marine service at Mare Island.[45]

In January 1918, a person with intimate knowledge of Germany's sabotage activities on the West Coast told the Secret Service that he suspected Kurt Jahnke had been involved in perpetrating the Mare Island explosion.[46] That person was Lieutenant Wilhelm von Brincken, former military attaché at the German consulate in San Francisco, recently released from prison after serving 18 months for his role in blowing up ships leaving West Coast ports with war supplies bound for American allies and for his part in a German-Hindu plot to foment revolution against British rule in India. Von Brincken was also the consulate's designated handler for bomb-makers. He was quick to tell the service that he had nothing tangible linking Jahnke to the explosion, but his suspicion was grounded in personal experience. On an earlier occasion, von Brincken had been asked to procure dynamite for Jahnke to blow up a ship in the harbor that was loading war supplies for the allies. Von Brincken surely had a motive for turning state's evidence, as it earned him a reduced sentence relative to his co-conspirators and enabled him to remain in the US after the war.

Von Brincken's "suspicion" launched a multi-month search for Jahnke that took Secret Service agents to waterfront hangouts, saloons, cheap hotels and boarding houses all over San Francisco as well as south to Los Angeles,

Watts, Long Beach, San Diego, and Ensenada (Mexico) and north to various destinations in Oregon, including Portland, Coos Bay, Roseburg, Marshfield, Bunker Hill, Bandon, Northbend shipyards, Coquille, Cushman, and Florence. In March 1918, the Service got a naval intelligence report that Jahnke had been in Monterey in November 1917 working on sabotage plans with an Irish lodge to burn woodyards, shipyards, and an aviation station, and to "dispose" of government witnesses at the Hindu plot trials. It is not clear whether the report meant Monterey, California, or Monterrey, Mexico. The Secret Service made a thorough search of Monterey, California, and failed to find Jahnke.[47]

The closest anyone came to finding and catching Jahnke was during the winter or early spring 1919. An American agent in Guatemala learned from what were thought to be reliable sources that Jahnke was employed as an attaché at the German legation in Mexico City. A plan was put in motion (apparently with the blessing of Guatemala's president) to lure Jahnke to Guatemala for propaganda purposes, where he would be seized upon his arrival and turned over to the American authorities. But the US State Department nixed the plan.[48]

The problem with fingering Jahnke for the Mare Island explosion is that he was already in Mexico when it occurred, having fled the United States in May 1917 after the US declared war on Germany. At most, therefore, he could have been involved in the planning only from a distance. By contrast, Lothar Witzke, Jahnke's principal assistant at the time, was in the US on July 9, 1917, most likely in San Francisco. (On June 27 he had obtained a lifeboat man and able seaman certificates in San Francisco; on July 15 he sent to his Aunt Bertha in Zurich a picture postcard postmarked San Francisco.) Jahnke had sent him from his safe haven in Mexico to the American West Coast for the summer. His mission was (among other things), according to Witzke himself, to establish relations with the Irish independence movement and anarchistic circles on the West Coast such as the IWW, to support them with money as necessary, and "to use these relations with anarchistic organizations to cause their members to commit sabotage against munition plants and factories on the territory of the United States who were then at war with us."[49] It is no stretch to interpret that mission to include an attack on the powder magazine of a major American naval station.

However, apart from Witzke's alleged boast to Altendorf that he did it, there is nothing to link Witzke to the crime. Further, while the boast as recounted by Altendorf was relatively detailed, the details did not perfectly fit what we know of the crime. Von Brincken's speculation is intriguing. He was as likely as anyone to know about what Germans were doing on the West Coast and who was doing it in the first days after the United States entered the war. But von Brincken could give only speculation about, not knowledge of, who did it. His 1920 articles in the *San Francisco Bulletin* suggesting that the Preparedness Day explosion in 1916 was a botched German/Jahnke attempt to blow up a ship at the docks loading war supplies for Europe, not an attack on the parade (see "The Preparedness Day Parade Bombing" subsection below), do not weigh one way or the other with regard to the Mare Island explosion. Further, as recounted in chapter 2, following Witzke's capture in February 1918, the US Intelligence Service made its own concerted, and unsuccessful, effort to link Witzke to the crime. They interviewed Witzke's acquaintances, and they showed his photo to various persons at the naval station connected to the ammunition depot. They looked at the photos of every person employed at the depot around the time of the explosion. They investigated contractors. They could not find a link between Witzke and the explosion. In sum, Witzke's connection to the Mare Island explosion is plausible but far from established.

We think it likely that Altendorf was telling the truth when he said that Witzke boasted about causing the Mare Island explosion. Our reasons are similar to those stated with regard to the other boasts. Alttendorf included the boast in his first debriefing by Butcher, at a time when he had incentive to prove his credibility and to tell the truth. He repeated the substance of the boast at Witzke's trial, under oath, although he weeded out one element of the story that was factually false (the number killed) and left out other arguably contestable details (that Witzke was employed there as a mechanic at the time by the US government, that Witzke "laid a wire" that caused the explosion). It is not clear why he would tell less of the story at trial, but less does not mean that the allegation of the boast is suspect.

Regarding whether the boast was truthful, the evidence is insufficient to reach a conclusion or even to assess probabilities. The most that can be said is that Witzke was at the time Jahnke's right-hand man and was in San Francisco on a Jahnke-directed mission when the explosion happened, that blowing up a black powder magazine at a US navy yard was consistent with that mission, that Jahnke had prior connections to Mare Island, and that the local German official in San Francisco with long-standing connections to Germany's local saboteurs suspected that Jahnke was involved. However, the concerted effort that was made after Witzke was captured and before his trial to link Witzke to the explosion was not successful. We are left with the possibility that Witzke was involved, but no reliable evidence apart from the boast itself.[50]

THE PREPAREDNESS DAY PARADE BOMBING

Despite the US policy of "strict neutrality" in the first years of World War I, there were those, especially Republicans, who urged "preparedness," i.e., strengthening the US military, making it ready, in case the United States, too, became embroiled in the war. The preparedness movement gained momentum as the war progressed. Even President Wilson, staunch advocate of neutrality, said that he favored preparedness, and went so far as to lead one of the preparedness parades that movement advocates held in various cities to rally support. San Francisco was a city with both fervent preparedness advocates and fervent opponents—the latter fearing, among other things, that the very act of urging preparedness increased the chances of going to war.

In 1916, the preparedness movement in San Francisco scheduled a huge preparedness parade for July 22, 1916. Trouble was feared. Presumed radical activists, worried that the United States was edging closer to entering the war, had sent anonymous letters to civic and commercial leaders, threatening violence. The police were out in force to prevent it. In addition, union/management tensions in the city were high; two weeks before, the parade's Grand Marshall, railroad magnate Thornwell Mullally, had crushed a strike by the city's streetcar workers.

At 2:06 in the afternoon of July 22, about half an hour after the parade commenced, a suitcase bomb exploded at the southwest corner of Market and Steuart Streets, immediately in front of the Ferry Exchange Saloon. At the time, more than 50,000 marchers (including fifty-two bands) were marching up Market Street, watched and cheered by 100,000 spectators lining both sides of the street. Ten people were killed and more than forty were seriously injured by the blast.

Within days of the bombing, five individuals were indicted and charged with murder: the radical labor agitator Thomas J. Mooney, his wife Rena Mooney, his assistant Warren Billings, and two other union activists, Israel Weinberg and Edward Nolan. In separate trials, Thomas Mooney and Warren Billings were convicted; Mooney was sentenced to hang, Billings was sentenced to life in prison. Rena Mooney and Israel Weinberg were acquitted. Edward Nolan was never tried. In November 1918 the governor of California commuted Mooney's death sentence to life in prison.

Even before the verdicts against Thomas Mooney and Warren Billings were handed down, serious doubts were raised about their guilt and the fairness of their trials. It was later established that both were framed by a prosecutor who knowingly relied on perjured testimony and fabricated evidence. There was not much forensic evidence because the police botched the first hours of the investigation, by for example hosing down the area around the blast before any evidence there could be gathered. Twenty-one years after his wrongful conviction, Mooney was pardoned and released from San Quentin on January 7, 1939. Billings, though never pardoned, was given a full commutation of sentence nine months after Mooney's pardon and was released from Folsom Prison on October 17, 1939. The identity of the real bomber(s) is still unknown.

Many theories have been advanced over the years as to who the bomber was, Lothar Witzke being one of the suspects.[51] The Witzke theory (or the "German Theory" as it is more generally known and as it is referred to below) is the one relevant to this book. However, in order to evaluate the German Theory, it is necessary to present what is uncontested about the evidence and then to summarize the more plausible theories of cause that compete with it.

Several points are uncontested. First, the bombing was not an accident; most of those killed were struck by shrapnel from the bomb.

Second, some physical evidence survived the hosing of the bomb area, including pieces of torn fabric, two locks, small pieces of twisted metal, unexploded cartridges and exploded bullets of various calibers, several pieces of four-inch wrought steel pipe, and several pieces of a malleable iron cap. The two locks were thought to be for a suitcase and a bag. None of the metal pieces was from a metal suitcase frame. The iron cap likely screwed over one end of the pipe. Explosive experts who examined the pipe fragments at the time were unanimously of the view that they came from a single length of pipe and that the explosion occurred inside the pipe, causing it to burst outward. The pipe probably contained either dynamite or nitroglycerine and was likely hidden in a suitcase packed with cartridges and metal scraps. Shoes were found that had been blown off the feet of the victims, suggesting that the explosion occurred at sidewalk level.

Whether the bomb was dropped or placed on the sidewalk was disputed. The physical evidence was insufficient to say with certainty what the explosive was, how it was triggered, or whether the bomb was placed or dropped. If it was a suitcase bomb, then most likely it was detonated by the acid-fuse method. If the bomb was made to be thrown or dropped, most likely nitroglycerine was used.[52]

Third, there were eyewitnesses. One group of seven witnesses testified to seeing a man or men place a suitcase in front of the Ferry Exchange Saloon. Another group of four witnesses testified to seeing a falling object. Those who saw someone set down a suitcase differed as to the size and color of the suitcase, whether the man who left it was or was not clean-shaven, what he wore, and how tall and heavy he was. However, six of the seven agreed that he was dark complexioned or looked Mexican, Portuguese or Spanish. Those who saw something fall also had differing recollections. The most precise of the four described a black object, twelve to fourteen inches long, three and a half or four inches in diameter that "disappeared behind the people standing on the sidewalk" just before the explosion. Yet another witness testified to seeing a man on the roof. Years later there surfaced a long-distance photo taken one minute before the explosion, showing such a man.

As to theories of who the bomber was, there are plausible alternatives to the German Theory. All of them fit what an early commentator called the "passionate hater" profile, i.e., an individual or group of individuals, each having his or their own reason to target the parade or its bystanders, and each theory having some evidence to back it up: a fanatical labor radical or opponent of the "open shop"; a fanatical pacifist; a fanatical pro-Mexican; a fanatical pro-German. Also possible would be that someone did it as a frame-up to discredit one of these groups, *i.e.*, someone sympathetic to the open shop or to militarism and war with Germany or Mexico, seeking to discredit activists on the other side who would be blamed for the deed.[53]

LABOR AGITATORS

A popular theory at the time was that labor did it, even if Mooney himself did not. Certainly, labor was among the groups opposed to war preparedness and therefore opposed to the Preparedness Day Parade, not to mention labor's special antipathy to the parade's strike-breaking grand marshal. Many of the anonymous threat letters sounded labor, IWW, and anti-militarist themes. For example, one anonymous letter to the hawkish editor of a local paper read in part: "Your extreme activity in promoting and glorifying militarism marks you as the most vicious and dangerous 'jingo' of all your brutal, greedy, thieving and war-making class. . . . The immediate 'extermination' of you and your evil class, is going to be the sole and patriotic duty of the EMPLOYEES LIBERTY LEAGUE."[54]

How labor would have benefited from the bombing is less clear. Absent the swift arrest of Mooney and Billings (though they were labor agitators, they were not popular with the mainstream labor movement), a bombing would surely have resulted in increased scrutiny and distrust of union labor (already under siege). Similarly, although anti-war activists opposed preparedness, it is unclear how killing and maiming parade spectators would have furthered their cause. In any event, no credible suspect ever emerged from this group. Later commentators have mostly discounted the theory.

ANTIWAR ANARCHISTS

The historians Paul and Karen Avrich state categorically in their 2012 book about Alexander Berkman and Emma Goldman that the bombing was an anti-militarist protest by the San Francisco branch of Gruppo Anarchico Volonta, disciples of the Italian anarchist Luigi Galleani. The authors cite "interviews and undisclosed sources" of Paul Avrich, as well as testimony by Galleani at his 1918 deportation hearing in Boston.[55] While there were likely sound reasons to hide the identities of Paul Avrich's interviewees and undisclosed sources, anonymous sources cannot be evaluated when assigning guilt. As for Galleani's testimony, it adds little to the anarchist theory. Galleani said at his November 1918 hearing, in response to questions from the deportation investigator, that he knew with "mathematical certitude" that Mooney was innocent, and that he was "positively sure that it was not Mooney who threw the bomb." By November 1918 lots of people were sure that Mooney had been framed and therefore did not commit the crime. To say so publicly did not constitute an admission, or even an implication, of one's own guilt.

MEXICANS

Four eyewitnesses said that they saw a man who looked Mexican place a suitcase at the corner of Steuart and Market. There were reasons why a Mexican fanatic or revolutionary might have targeted the July parade. American troops, led by General Pershing, had invaded Mexico in March 1918 in pursuit of Pancho Villa. In late June, a substantial battle had been fought on Mexican territory, with loss of life on both sides. Anti-American sentiment among Mexicans was high. Two Mexicans had recently been apprehended trying to blow up a US supply warehouse at Nogales. Three weeks before the parade bombing, a bomb in a restroom on a train had exploded as the train was pulling into Oakland. Mexicans were suspected, although never apprehended. Three itinerant Mexican farm workers, one with a suitcase, had been on the train. Two got off at Richmond (a San Francisco suburb) and the third was discovered by a suspicious conductor in the toilet of the smoking car, apparently trying to avoid paying extra fare; he then jumped off the train as it was slowing, two minutes before the explosion. Perhaps most damning, the Mexican theory seemed to explain why the corner of Steuart and Market was targeted: local newspapers had been reporting for several days that the bullet-torn battle flag of the First California Volunteers, who had fought in the Spanish-American War, would be taken out of the State Museum and carried in the parade by Spanish American War veterans. The veterans, according to the papers, would be lining up on Steuart Street.[56]

One journalist and two lawyers who studied the Preparedness Day bombing concluded that the Mexican theory was the most likely explanation.[57] A not insignificant flaw, though, is that newspapers reported that the veterans were scheduled to march out onto Market Street at 1:15, not 2:06 p.m. (the time the bomb went off). Even if the bomber anticipated a late start to the parade (which happened), it is unlikely that he would have guessed that the veterans would pass the corner of Steuart and Market, as they did, at precisely 2:06 p.m.[58] Moreover, apart from these four eyewitnesses (there were others who saw it differently), there was nothing concrete pointing to a Mexican perpetrator.

ANONYMOUS LETTER WRITERS

Several diligent (they have also been called obsessed) investigators at the time believed that the writer or writers of threat letters sent anonymously to civic and commercial leaders (some 200 letters in all) perpetrated the crime. It was eventually determined, with the help of chirography experts, that these letters were written by two individuals, probably a man and a woman. In 1918, someone calling himself "John Doe for now" even sent an anonymous confession, with numerous similarities in printing and style to some of the earlier threat letters. Eventually, suspicion focused on Frederick and Leone Esmond, two Canadians who had previously lived in the United States and England. Their residence in 1916 was unknown, but in 1917 Frederick was employed by the IWW on the West Coast, had allegedly made seditious remarks to informants, and worried about being drafted into the Army. Leone was supposedly a radical socialist and had reportedly visited Japan in late 1917 for the purpose of recruiting Japanese converts to the IWW. In 1918 Frederick was jailed for alleged complicity in a bombing of the California governor's mansion, then later tried, convicted, and jailed at Leavenworth for immigration act violations.

In 1920, while Frederick was at Leavenworth, the investigators of the anonymous letters obtained samples of his handwriting. They found a hand-writing expert willing to testify that his handwriting matched parts of the anonymous letters, including the confession. Other handwriting experts disagreed. Another difficulty was that, at the time the confession was mailed, Frederick was already at Leavenworth. He could have smuggled out the let-ter, but this was just more complication to the theory. As for Leone, she was actually indicted by a grand jury in 1921 for complicity in the Prepared-ness Day bombing, but the charges were dropped shortly thereafter. After Frederick served his sentence at Leavenworth for immigration violations, he was released. The couple disappeared and, with their disappearance, any lingering interest in their possible involvement in the Preparedness Day bombing waned.

CONFESSIONS

Over the years, several unrelated individuals (in addition to "John Doe for now") confessed to the crime.[59] The most compelling confession was that of Louis J. Smith, an American of German descent. In 1915, working with C. C. Crowley (Consul Bopp's chief agent at the time), Smith was involved in the Tacoma bombing of an ammunition barge whose cargo was ultimately destined for Vladivostok. One person was killed. Smith was then ordered by Bopp to Detroit, from which venue he was supposed to destroy trains and bridges in Canada as well as powder works at Gary, Indiana, and Ishpem-ing, Michigan. He escaped indictment and prison by betraying Crowley and turning state's evidence. Smith died in Cleveland in 1922. In 1929, it came to light that he had made a deathbed confession regarding the Preparedness Day bombing to his sister, Dora Monroe. The confession was first disclosed by an elderly veteran, Frank Stephens, a friend of Mrs. Monroe, in a letter to Senator Thomas Schall of Minnesota, who had recently published an article arguing that Mooney and Billings were innocent. Schall released the let-ter to the press, the press descended on Stephens, and the story gets rather muddled from there.

As best can be sorted out, the elderly veteran Stephens first met Smith in 1915 at the home of Smith's sister, at which time Smith supposedly told him that he was a German agent. The two met again in 1919, got into conversa-tion about (among other things) the Mooney trial, and Smith told Stephens that he knew for a fact that Mooney was innocent. In 1922, shortly after Smith died, Stephens visited Dora Monroe, who told him that her brother had confessed to her before he died that he had done the Preparedness Day bombing. At first, when confronted with the story by reporters in 1929, Dora Monroe denied it. However, when pressed, she admitted that it was true, and gave a detailed account of the confession, the gist of which was that Louis Smith was overcome by grief and guilt that he had caused an innocent man to languish in prison, he wanted to relieve his conscience before he died by telling someone, and therefore did so. He had, he told her, been promised $10,000 to blow up an automobile in the parade, $2,000 up front and $8,000 when the job was done. He and two accomplices brought the bomb in a suitcase from Seattle to San Francisco, went to the spot in the parade where they had been told their target would be, but could not see it. So, they climbed to the roof of a building, got to the roof six minutes before the bomb was set to explode, looked around but still could not see a car. Not wanting to blow himself up and his companions, he threw the bomb down onto the street, fled the building, and headed out of town. (He was never paid the $8,000 balance because he did not bomb the car.)

Ott Monroe, Dora's son, had overheard part of his uncle's confession to his mother, and corroborated the details. Moreover, it turned out that in November 1916, only a few months after the bombing, Louis Smith had similarly confessed to his brother Alonzo, who lived in Wheeling, West Virginia. According to Alonzo, his brother Louis told him that he had thrown a dynamite bomb from the roof of a building into the parade and that he had two accomplices, one of them named Joe. Alonzo could not remember the other name.

Then Dora Monroe changed her story. She asserted, among other things, that Thomas Mooney was standing next to Louis Smith on the roof of the saloon when Smith threw the bomb. Her changed story was a sensational reversal of the original story that Stephens said he was told both by Smith and by Dora. It also undercut Smith's alleged motive for repenting: his guilty conscience that Mooney, an innocent man, was in prison for a crime he did not do. Eventually, Dora Monroe repudiated her changed story, but by then her credibility was in tatters.

Notwithstanding the reversals, elements of Smith's purported confession made sense, in particular that he had been hired to target an automobile in the parade. There was only one such automobile, that of Andrew Gallagher, the San Francisco city supervisor. Gallagher, a prominent labor leader, was the only labor leader to support preparedness and the parade. It was plausible that whoever hired Smith to do the deed (the Law-and-Order Committee of the San Francisco Chamber of Commerce was one suspect) was trying to create a split in the labor movement by murdering Gallagher.

But there are problems with the substance of Smith's confession. Smith said he had thrown the bomb forty feet, an exaggeration at best. One eyewitness saw one person on the roof, not three. There is also the curious fact that the confession tracked the prosecution's discredited theory that the bomb was a time bomb that was thrown. Why use a time bomb, if your target was an automobile in a parade that was randomly driving up and down the parade line, and whose location therefore at any given moment could not be known in advance?

GERMAN SABOTAGE

The most compelling theory of who was responsible for the bombing is that it was the work of a German agent. The twist is that, according to the final version of this theory, the target was not the parade itself but a ship docked near the ferry terminal loaded with explosive material bound for the Allied Powers. According to the theory, the agent was carrying a suitcase bomb down Pine or California Street, trying to cross the street to the Ferry building to access the docks and the target ship, but could not get across because of all the barricades and people in the way. The staging area for the parade was the Embarcadero area at the bottom of Market, immediately in front of the Ferry Terminal and the docks, as well as Steuart Street. The agent, unable to get past the barriers and the crowds, and time running out (so the theory goes), left the suitcase in front of the ferry exchange saloon and retreated.[60]

That a German saboteur may have been responsible for the bombing first surfaced in the spring of 1918, but without the he-was-not-targeting-the-parade twist. A story published in the *San Francisco Daily News* on April 25 reported that the United States had obtained a "circumstantial confession" from an unnamed confessor saying that German government agents were responsible for the explosion, that its purpose was to "terrorize Americans," and that an individual now hiding in South America was the person who threw the bomb. The next day the *News* identified the alleged perpetrator—a man named Jahnke—and reported that an international search for him was underway. The *News* also reported that the source of its story was a nurse who had cared for a sick member of the Baron von Brincken family (von Brincken had been military attaché at the German consulate in San Francisco during the period of neutrality), that she overheard alarming information suggesting German terrorism was connected to the Preparedness Day and Mare Island explosions, that she communicated this information to the San Francisco police, and that they took her to the Secret Service for further debriefing.[61] The chief of the Secret Service bureau in San Francisco denied knowledge of a confession but admitted that the Secret Service and the Justice Department were aware of the allegation about German sabotage and were investigating.[62]

The *News* story died down relatively quickly. However, it included a photo of Kurt Jahnke. On April 27, an individual named Pedersen called at the Secret Service office and announced that he had seen someone resembling Jahnke on Preparedness Day at Natoma Street, by the rear entrance of a firehouse being built on a lot facing the Street between Third and Fourth Streets. Pedersen was employed at the time as a mortar-mixer for the construction. He said that the man who looked like Jahnke appeared around noon and was carrying a dress suitcase that was brown but not new. The man talked to the foreman. There were small pieces of iron stored in a rear shed that were cut from reinforcements used in the concrete work. Pedersen thought that the iron might have been used in the bomb, and that the man resembling Jahnke might have stored the pieces there. Pedersen added that there was a second, short man with Jahnke. Both men, he said, stayed about five minutes. He described Jahnke as being about twenty-eight years old, 5'10" or 11", with a dark swarthy complexion, Austrian-looking, bony, 170 or 180 pounds, wearing a soft hat.[63]

Pedersen came back two days later. He repeated his story but amended the location of the firehouse. This time he said that the firehouse was on Howard just below Third and ran back to Hunt Street. He also gave the address of the foreman he had mentioned.[64] The Secret Service found the story suspicious. They thought Pederson was probably a set up, possibly by Mooney supporters who would later accuse the service of ignoring an important lead if they did not follow up. They forwarded the information to the police department for further investigation. A week later, San Francisco's chief of police reported back that, following investigation, his department concluded there was "nothing tangible whatever to connect the incident with the explosion at Stuart [sic] and Market Sts. during the Preparedness Day Parade."[65] That ended any further investigation of whether German sabotage was linked to the parade, although the hunt for Jahnke continued.

Two details of Pedersen's story that seem not to have interested the Secret Service were: Pedersen's description of the man at the construction site, including his estimate of the individual's height as 5'10" or 5'11", and that there was a second, shorter, man present. The height description of the taller man matched the height description of Jahnke that von Brincken gave the Service during his January interview.[66] We know from Witzke's prison record that he was 5'7", i.e., three or four inches shorter than Jahnke, and therefore he could have been the shorter man.

At the time that Pedersen came forward with his story, the Secret Service did not know that Lothar Witzke existed, much less that he had been interrogated by a military intelligence officer at Fort Sam Houston just two months before.[67] Had they known, they might have been interested in a detail of that interrogation that intersected with Pedersen's story in an intriguing way. Witzke had told his interrogator that, after arriving in San Francisco from Mexico in early July 1917, he obtained employment as a painter from the Nullay-Ready Employment Agency "on Howard Street, between Third and Fourth." They sent him to paint a wood shack on Bay Street.[68] There was no Nullay-Ready agency in San Francisco, and Bay Street was in another part of the city, but there was a Murray-Ready Employment Agency on Howard Street between Third and Fourth, a mere stone's throw from the firehouse and shed that featured in Pedersen's story. Given Witzke's habit of presenting to his interrogators narratives that were false but were based on real places and events in his life and the lives of his acquaintances so that he could keep his false stories straight, it is likely that he was familiar with the precise neighborhood of Pedersen's story, perhaps even the very construction site and shed of which Pedersen spoke. This might be dismissed as a coincidence, but there were other coincidences as well involving Witzke and Preparedness Day that we will discuss below and that cumulatively are not easy to dismiss.

In early fall 1920, the German Theory resurfaced, this time advanced by Baron Wilhelm von Brincken himself, the alleged 1918 "circumstantial confessor" and former military attaché at the German consulate, and this time including the twist that the target was a munitions ship, not the parade. Von Brincken had recently been released from McNeil Island prison in the Puget Sound after serving eighteen months of two concurrent, two-year sentences for (i) conspiring to violate US neutrality by directing agents to bomb tunnels and bridges in Canada and destroy munitions vessels sailing from Pacific coast ports to US allies and (ii) his role during 1915–17 in the Hindu-German conspiracy to foment revolution against British rule in India. Consul Bopp and Vice Consul von Schack, among others, had been convicted of the same crimes and were still in prison.[69]

Von Brincken's version of the German Theory was published by the *San Francisco Bulletin* on October 26, 1920, as part of the last serial of von Brincken's memoirs that the *Bulletin* began publishing in August.[70] Von Brincken gave it as his belief that the Preparedness Day bomb was intended for a ship loading war material at the harbor front a block from the parade's starting point. He named Kurt Jahnke as the likely perpetrator, and said that not long before the incident he had been asked, and refused, to provide Jahnke with dynamite to blow up an English ship then at the wharf. "If such a person, von Brincken concluded, 'were to have gone down Pine or California street that day,' he would have encountered an obstacle—the crowd." Von Brincken posited that the bomber then cut across Market, started down Steuart, "saw this was crowded too, and abandoned the lethal suitcase next to the saloon wall."[71]

The German Theory is a compelling explanation of the bombing for several reasons. First, the German Consulate in San Francisco was the operations center for German espionage and sabotage on the West Coast during the period of neutrality. The head of operations was the Consul General, Franz Bopp, assisted by vice consul Baron E. H. von Schack and attaché Lieutenant Wilhelm von Brincken.[72] Although all three were indicted in late 1915 for the first of the two conspiracies for which they ultimately went to prison, they remained free even after their January 1917 convictions, pending appeal. It was not until April 1917, after the United States entered the war, that they were re-arrested and interned on Angel Island as enemy aliens. Their indictments for the German-Hindu conspiracy occurred three months later. Thus, the Consulate was open for espionage and sabotage business, with Bopp *et al.* fully engaged, until the final hours of neutrality in April 1917. The Preparedness Day parade was during that period.

Second, the consulate accumulated, in von Brincken's words, "a regular museum of bombs" and other deadly instruments. One of von Brincken's duties was to receive the inventors of bombs. They came, he said, by the hundreds and offered up many devices, some quite ingenious. Consul Bopp himself was particularly intrigued by a thermos bottle bomb that he would take apart and put back together over and over.[73] Thus, the Consulate was privy to the latest sabotage bomb technology.

Third, blowing up ships sailing from West Coast ports with cargoes of munitions and other war supplies destined for Allied countries was a particular objective of the German Government. Bopp, von Schack, and von Brincken would eventually be convicted for such activities.

Fourth, according to Gentry, the author of *Frame-Up*, there *was* a ship in the harbor on July 22 with a cargo of war materials bound for the allies who opposed Germany, "in fact several, one of them berthed only a block from Steuart and Market."[74] Further, von Brincken says in one of the *Bulletin* articles that, after telling Jahnke that he did not have any dynamite to give him, he asked Jahnke what he wanted the dynamite for and Jahnke replied: "Oh, there is some damned English ship loading acid for the manufacture of explosives in the bay and I want to blow the ship up. I had some 40% dynamite, but it is not strong enough. I want some 60% stuff."[75] Explosive experts at the time concluded that the explosive used in the Preparedness Day bomb was either dynamite or nitroglycerine (the two most common types of bomb explosives in use at the time), that the explosion itself was not a powerful one, and that, if dynamite was used, it was probably a single stick of no more than 40 percent strength.[76]

Fifth, there is von Brincken's speculation that the bomber started out walking down Pine or California, both of which run parallel to one another and diagonally to Market Street, each intersecting and ending at Market, two and one blocks respectively above Steuart. Why Pine or California? As it happens, the German consulate was located at the corner of Sansome and Pine.[77] If one were at the German consulate and wanted to take the shortest route to the ferry terminal and wharf area while avoiding the crowds of spectators lining Market, then Pine or California would have been the route. Von Brincken's thought was, apparently, that the bomber started out at the German consulate. Did von Brincken know more than he was telling? After all, he was by his own admission the consulate's designated handler for bomb makers. Nevertheless, he insisted that his version of the German Theory was speculation only.

Sixth, von Brincken's narrative was apparently corroborated by former vice consul von Schack, who was still in prison when von Brincken's *Bulletin* story was published. Von Schack, worried about becoming the target of German assassins when he got out of prison and returned to Germany, sent to his lawyer a letter, to be turned over to the United State in the event of his assassination, giving a "full account of attempts made to destroy cargoes at San Francisco and other Pacific coast ports."[78]

Seventh, the German Theory could explain the many unexploded cartridges and exploded bullets of various calibers at the scene. If the goal was not to harm parade participants and spectators but rather to destroy powder or other explosive materials loaded on a nearby ship, then the purpose of the cartridges and bullets may have been to trigger further explosions once the initial explosion happened.

Eighth, several years later an odd and possibly important detail was added to the German Theory in the form of an affidavit made in 1926 by the then seventy-three-year-old founder of *The Sporting News*, Alfred H. Spink. The affidavit was made public in 1928, shortly after Spink's death. According to the affidavit, during 1914–1916 Spink and his wife Bertha lived in Oakland, California, next door to the former German consul to the Marshall Islands, Powell Mertz, and his wife, a German Countess. Mertz was also, apparently, an undersecretary at the German Consulate in San Francisco.[79] Bertha Spink spoke German. The two women became best friends. The Mertzs did not have a telephone. When a telephone was needed, they would use the Spinks' phone. Alfred Spink and Powell Mertz often discussed explosions that occurred on the West Coast. Also, "whenever an explosion took place, Mr. Mertz . . . would call up San Francisco and conduct long conversations." After the Victoria Bridge explosion in Canada, Mrs. Mertz invited Mrs. Spink to a celebration at the Germania Cafe in San Francisco. (Bertha declined.)

In the days leading up to the Preparedness Day Parade, Mertz told Spink that he was anxious to get away from Oakland because "there have been some terrible carryings on over here, I do not approve of them . . . and I am exceedingly anxious not to be implicated." Several days before the parade, Bertha told Alfred that something awful was going to happen in San Francisco, that the Mertzs had warned her not to go to the Preparedness Day Parade, and that they should stay out of San Francisco that day altogether. Although Alfred Spink went to work every day in San Francisco, he stayed home on the twenty-second, heeding his wife's warning from the Mertzs. It turned out that the Spinks' phone was being tapped because of Mertz's calls, a fact Spink learned when, shortly after the parade explosion, a representative of the district attorney's office in San Francisco called at the Spinks' home and told Spink that they had overheard Mertz on a number of calls.[80]

Ninth, there is the curious blank in Dr. Heinrich Alpert's diary for 1916. In 1915 Alpert was Germany's commercial attaché in Washington, DC, responsible for trying to impede American industrial output. On July 24, 1915, during a visit to New York City, he accidently left his briefcase on the Sixth Avenue elevated train. The Secret Service, which had been tailing him, got the briefcase and discovered in it most of Alpert's future plans and prospects. (The blunder earned Alpert the nickname "Minister Without Portfolio.") Alpert kept a detailed diary, and American intelligence later got hold of it as well. Apparently, Alpert was "meticulous" in making daily entries. However, in 1916, two sets of pages were blank: July 22–25 (the Preparedness Day explosion was on July 22) and July 28–August 4 (the Black Tom explosion in New York was July 30). Coincidence, perhaps, but eye-catching that the dates of two of the most consequential explosions in 1916 should go unremarked in the diary of the German diplomat responsible for trying to slow US industrial output.[81]

Finally, as to the possible involvement of Jahnke and/or Witzke, there is reason to suspect it. By the summer 1916, Jahnke had probably replaced C. C. Crowley as Bopp's chief operative and was, in any event, one of Bopp's top two agents.[82] Although Witzke had been in the States for only two months, he and Jahnke had started working together some weeks before and were already roommates.[83] Von Brincken's *Bulletin* memoirs put Jahnke in San Francisco at the time of the parade bombing. Witzke's whereabouts on July 22 are less certain, although San Francisco is a strong possibility. His declaration of intention to become a US citizen is dated July 25 San Francisco, suggesting he was in San Francisco three days after the parade. However, his single address book entry for the dates July 14-23 reads "San Francisco-Eureka." Does that mean he was in San Francisco on the first date and Eureka on the last one, or something else? Not clear.[84]

As discussed at the beginning of this chapter, in sworn affidavits submitted to the Mixed Claims Commission in the Sabotage Cases, both Jahnke and Witzke admitted that, throughout the period of neutrality (which ended April 1917), they were engaged in the surveillance of war material shipments to Germany's opponents in the war. Jahnke stated: "I engaged in making observations as to the war material orders which had been placed in the United States by the Allies; in ascertaining the nature and volume of arms and munitions production; in finding out the destination of arms and munitions transports. . . ."[85] Witzke stated: "As a sub-agent of Jahnke the task was assigned to me to make observations in San Francisco and in other places in the west of the United States as to the movements of ships of the allies, the cargo and destination of such ships, ship construction, manufacture and shipments of munitions. . . ."[86] Although both men denied committing acts of sabotage on US territory during neutrality (to have admitted to such acts would have exposed Germany to liability before the Mixed Claims Commission for Black Tom and Kingsland, as both occurred during the period of neutrality), there is von Brincken's statement that Jahnke told him shortly before Preparedness Day that he was looking for dynamite to blow up a ship in the harbor; and, according to Paul Altendorf, Witzke boasted to him and others about having committed similar acts of sabotage after the US declared war.[87]

There is also Witzke's boast, reported by Altendorf: "I have many lives on my conscience and I have killed many people." Of the numerous acts of sabotage of which Witzke has been accused, the Preparedness Day bombing was much the most lethal, both in terms of lives lost and serious personal injury inflicted.

Lastly, there is the curious coincidence of Jahnke's listed residential address that seems to have escaped the notice of other commentators. At the time that Witzke met Jahnke, Jahnke was employed as a detective by the Morse Detective and Patrol Service.[88] The San Francisco Directory for 1916 contains two entries for Jahnke. The first says that "Curt" Jahnke, a laborer, resides at 669 Clay St. The second says that "Jahnke-Borden C.A." is a patrolman with the Morse Patrol who resides at 669 Clay Street.[89] (C. A. Borden was a Jahnke alias, based on his mother's maiden name.) But the 1916 edition was for the year ending June 1916. Jahnke's entry in the 1917 Directory for the year July 1916 to June 1917 says Jahnke-Borden C. A. is a patrolman with Morse Patrol who resides at 115 Market Street.[90] 115 Market is less than a block from the Ferry Exchange Saloon at Steuart and Market. Is that where Witzke and Jahnke resided when they started living together? Were they living only a block from where the bomb was dropped or planted on Preparedness Day? Quite a coincidence, especially if they had nothing to do with it. How convenient, if they did: Jahnke and/or Witzke would have gotten to the corner of Steuart and Market, seen that they could not make it to the wharf in time because of the parade participants still lined up on Steuart, and decided to abandon the suitcase bomb in front of the saloon and then disappear into the crowd and return to their apartment a few doors further up the street. That Witzke lived in the immediate neighborhood of the explosion is further corroborated by information in Witzke's Declaration of Intention to become a US citizen dated July 25, 1916, three days after the Preparedness Day bombing.[91] There, Witzke says that he resides at 134 Folsom St. ("Clipper House"), which was between Spear and Main (the two cross streets immediately above Steuart). Thus, whether Witzke's correct address at the time was 115 Market or 134 Folsom Street, he was residing only steps away from the location of the bombing.

Means, motive, and opportunity: all were present here. The circumstantial evidence linking Jahnke and Witzke to the Preparedness Day bombing is substantial.

Nevertheless, there are reasons to be cautious about reaching a conclusion of guilt, apart from the lack of direct evidence. Several aspects of the circumstantial evidence cast doubt on a conclusion about Witzke's role.

- Only von Brincken's version of the Germany Theory (that the target was a war supply ship in the harbor, not the parade) makes sense. The Germans were suspected of many acts of sabotage during the period of neutrality, but not of terrorism. The incidents to which they were linked all had as their purpose interruption of the flow of American-made war supplies to their enemy, not terrorizing the American public. The Preparedness Day bombing, if the parade was the target, was an act of terror. For this reason, the affidavit of Albert Spink is particularly hard to credit insofar as it implies foreknowledge that something awful would occur at the parade. That would mean that the Germans deliberately committed an act of terror against San Francisco parade participants and spectators. Perhaps the warning to Spink, if there was one, about something awful happening, was a reference to an anticipated ship bombing at the wharf rather than a bombing at the parade.

- Von Brincken's version of the theory is undermined to the extent that the bomb in the suitcase was wrapped in metal scraps, not just bullets. The uncontested physical evidence included small pieces of metal that did not come from a metal suitcase. The bullets were presumably intended to ignite additional explosions in the ship's cargo once the initial explosion occurred. But the small pieces of metal are harder to explain if the purpose of the bomb was a ship's cargo, not terror. Shrapnel has no purpose other than to inflict injury upon human flesh; many of the most severe parade wounds were in fact caused by the shrapnel and bullets. Maybe the small metal pieces can be explained by the need to pack the pipe bomb securely and the immediate availability of cheap scraps that were expected to scatter harmlessly in the ship's cargo bay, not rip human flesh. But the shrapnel is concerning.

- Von Brincken may have had reasons other than the truth to speculate as he did. When he got out of prison in January 1920, his marriage was over. His wife had divorced him, changed her name, and was seeking custody of their children. He was in danger of being deported back to Germany, where his having turned state's evidence against his fellow diplomats in the German-Hindu conspiracy trial would not be well regarded. He was therefore desperate to stay in the United States, to be near his children, to have a future. By the time the *Bulletin* published his version of the German Theory, he had changed his name to Roger Beckwith, remarried a beautiful Los Angeles divorceé, and inherited an enormous fortune from an uncle in Denmark. Perhaps he thought his story would enhance his chances to be allowed to stay in America, where he would always be available to be interviewed by the US Government and others about his story. His story portrayed himself as a lover of the United States, despite his service at the Consulate. In the end he was allowed to stay. He became a Hollywood actor and appeared over a long career in more than seventy movies, including the 1937 film "The Prisoner of Zenda" with Ronald Coleman, Douglas Fairbanks, Jr., Raymond Massey, and David Niven.

To conclude: several of the theories discussed above, besides the German one laying blame on Jahnke and Witzke, are plausible explanations of the Preparedness Day bombing, sufficiently so that settling without reservation on any one theory would be reckless, absent dramatic new information not likely to emerge.

CONCLUSION

Was Witzke a saboteur on the West Coast as well as a spy? We believe Altendorf when he says that Witzke boasted to him about having committed acts of sabotage against the United States, particularly those boasts that Altendorf reported to Butcher in his first full in-person debriefing at about the time Witzke was captured. Were Witzke's boasts truthful or false? Here it gets more complicated. It is certain that some of Witzke's boasts were false, *e.g.*, the *Minnesota* boiler boast. That does not mean that all his boasts were false, but one demonstrated instance of a false boast raises some doubt as to the veracity of his other reported statements.

Circumstantial evidence supports the possibility that some of the boasts were true (the northwest logging campfires, the Mare Island bombing), but there is no hard evidence. Similarly, there were other acts of sabotage about which Witzke did not boast that can be plausibly connected to him (one or more munitions ship bombings and cargo ship bombings), including several to which Jahnke made claim for himself and his people (the steamer *Margaret* fire, the *J. A. Moffett* tanker explosion); and at least one (the Preparedness Day Parade bombing) about which suspicion of his involvement emerged over time. Again, however, there is no hard evidence, only inference.

Even though Witzke cannot be definitively linked to any particular act of West Coast sabotage, it stands to reason that he engaged in, or was involved in the planning of, some such acts. The esteem in which he was held by Kurt Jahnke, the important mission to Nogales to which he was assigned by Jahnke, the cipher message entrusted to his care, his carefully curated 1927 affidavit to the Mixed Claims Commission admitting involvement at some level in acts of sabotage similar to those that were part of his Nogales mission (just not the ones of which he was accused in the sabotage cases), all point to Witzke having been a saboteur. But at least with regard to West Coast sabotage, we cannot conclude that a preponderance of the evidence connects Witzke to any particular incident.

DID HE DO IT?
BLACK TOM

"I realize the futility of convincing
anyone. My only hope lays in the chance
that some day someone will investigate."
—LETTER, WITZKE TO JUDGE FAKE,
APRIL 1, 1923

INTRODUCTION

Witzke's life story is worth telling even if during his time in the United States he was a secret agent with no involvement in the sabotage at Black Tom. But unlike any of his other adventures, the sabotage at Black Tom tailed Witzke's life. The US pursued a claim against Germany for sixteen years before the Mixed Claims Commission for the sabotage at Black Tom, relying on the testimony of multiple witnesses who swore that Witzke told them that he was responsible for Black Tom. Germany scoffed that Witzke would have confided such a deed to any of the US witnesses and presented Witzke as its star witness for the defense. While a prisoner in the US after his conviction for espionage, Witzke was interrogated about his role at Black Tom. The consensus of historians is that Witzke was responsible for Black Tom, and his biographer's motivation to connect him to Black Tom is strong.

A leading German historian on twentieth-century German intelligence operations, Reinhard Doerries, has concluded, "Whether Kurt Jahnke and his right-hand man Lothar Witzke had some part in or themselves orchestrated these two most spectacular sabotage cases [Black Tom and Kingsland] in the

United States during World War I, cannot be determined with absolute certainty even today."[1] We do not need absolute certainty. Is there a probability?

We evaluate in this chapter the evidence for and against Witzke's responsibility for the sabotage at Black Tom, setting out first the case that he did it and then the case that he did not. This analysis has not been done before. Most historians have assumed that Witzke was involved in Black Tom and presented dramatic descriptions of Witzke and Jahnke on a rowboat on the Hudson River on July 29–30, 1916.[2] None, though, has analyzed the evidence about Witzke. A secondary source cited by many is Henry Landau, *The Enemy Within: The Inside Story of German Sabotage in America* (1937).[3] Landau worked with US counsel before the Mixed Claims Commission, and he writes a compelling story, but his book is a wholesale adoption of the American position before the Mixed Claims Commission, and its utility is undermined by an absence of footnotes.[4]

The following passage from Jamie Bisher, *The Intelligence War in Latin America, 1914–1922* (2016), is representative of the historical studies that assert that Witzke was involved in Black Tom:

> Lieutenant Lothar Witzke received an extraordinary apprenticeship in the black arts of espionage and sabotage. He escaped Chilean internment early in the war, but instead of returning to Germany like his SMS Dresden shipmate Wilhelm Canaris, he remained in Latin America. He learned Spanish and tradecraft while working as a courier between German consulates. In May 1916 he was sent to San Francisco disguised as a seaman on a US ship, SS Calusa, and began working for Consul General Franz von Bopp, initially as courier, then graduating to saboteur. Mentored by Kurt Jahnke, he took a job as a mechanic at the Mare Island Naval Shipyard in Vallejo, California and planted the notorious bomb that blew up a huge black powder magazine killing ten adults and six children in spring 1916. Witzke's superior performance earned him a permanent transfer to Jahnke's sabotage team and a trip to New York City. He participated in the Black Tom operation that rattled Manhattan on July 30, 1916, and in the incendiary attack on the Kingsland munitions factory on January 11, 1917.[5]

We have established that, contrary to what is said in this passage, Witzke did not serve on the *Dresden*.[6] Nor did Witzke escape from internment; he jumped a merchant marine ship, stayed for a while in Valparaiso, and then made his way to California. We have also seen that the evidence for Witzke's role in the Mare Island sabotage is contestable (and this sabotage occurred in any case in summer 1917, not in spring 1916). Whether it is probable that

Witzke participated, as asserted, in the Black Tom operation (or Kingsland) remains to be determined.

The Case That He Did It
WITZKE'S ADMISSIONS

The core of the American case about Black Tom before the Mixed Claims Commission was the sworn written testimony by multiple witnesses that Witzke said separately to each of them that he was responsible for the sabotage at Black Tom. Such testimony remains the core of the case for Witzke's involvement in Black Tom.[7]

Of the many witnesses against Witzke, one matters far more than the others: Paul Altendorf, the double agent who convinced the Germans in Mexico, including Jahnke and Witzke, that he was working with them while he was in truth working for the Americans.

Altendorf

Immediately after Witzke's apprehension at Nogales, Arizona, on February 1, 1918, Altendorf was twice debriefed by the Americans about his dealings with Witzke. The reports of the interviews written up by the Americans are two of the earliest recorded reports of what Altendorf said that Witzke said to him, and reflect Altendorf's freshest recollection. Both debriefings were done by Byron Butcher, Special Secret Service Agent at Nogales, who then reported his interviews to Captain Joel Lipscomb, who included the contents of the debriefings in reports to the War Department.[8]

The first report, dated February 2, 1918, contains the following narrative about a discussion between Witzke and Altendorf during their trip north from Mexico City to the US/Mexico border on or about January 16, 1918:

> Waberski [Witzke] also informed A-1 [Altendorf] over a bottle of wine that he had blown up a black powder magazine of 250,000 pounds near San Francisco (Mare Island), one morning about 5 o'clock. Waberski bragged that sixteen lives had been lost, including six children. . . .
>
> Waberski also claimed that while working as a mechanic of the U.S. '*Minnesota*' he had ruined or disabled the boat's boilers. . . . In speaking of his exploits Waberski said that at one time he had crippled a boat in the Gulf of Mexico by taking a red-hot coal in a glove he had soaked in water for 24 hours and dropping the coal into a hole he had prepared leading to the dynamite magazine. . . .

"I also did the work in New Jersey, with Yenky [Jahnke], when the munition barges were blown up and piers wrecked," asserted Waberski to A-1. "We were out in a small boat and the waves nearly swamped us and we came near drowning. The hardships of this piece of work were many, but it was all for 'The Fatherland.' The German ambassador and Yenky think very highly of me for my work, and I am very proud to have done it. I am a man they know can depend upon," said Waberski. "I have many lives on my conscience and I have killed many people and will now kill more," added the German to A-1. . . . He stated to A-1 that he had operated in the United States with von Bernstorff and Yenky."[9]

Such conversation took place, according to Altendorf, in January 1918, six months after Witzke, Jahnke and Altendorf had first met in the summer in Mexico City. Jahnke was not present. Witzke was drinking wine. The second report, dated February 7, 1918, contains the following statement:

> Both Yenky and Waberski explained to the Agent A-1, at various times, that they were responsible for the large munition explosion in New Jersey, Yenky explained that following the explosion they were adrift in a small boat and nearly perished. He is still suffering severely from stomach trouble as the direct result of his exposure following the explosion.[10]

In this second telling, there were multiple undated conversations and the speakers were indiscriminately both Jahnke and Witzke.

Both reports present two notable (alleged) details. One is that Witzke (and Jahnke) said that he and Jahnke were together on a small boat on the Hudson River when the explosion occurred. The other is that their boat nearly swamped. In the first telling to Butcher, the implication is that the explosion caused waves that nearly swamped their boat, but this is not explicit. In the second report, there is no mention of a wave, and one could conclude that the explosion itself somehow caused injury to Jahnke. Altendorf addressed the subject of inconsistencies in his statements in an affidavit submitted to the MCC in 1929: "In so far as minor differences may appear in reports they are either errors in quoting me or they are the result of honest differences in recollection on minor points which I doubtless had in various interviews, and also resulted in part from the fact that I discussed at different interviews different aspects of the matters."[11]

Germany's witnesses testified before the Mixed Claims Commission that this was all invented by Altendorf, and that no mention whatsoever of Black Tom was made by Witzke or Jahnke. But were that so, Altendorf would not have known by February 1918 (or earlier, in January, 1918) that Black Tom was even an act of sabotage, let alone that it had a possible connection with German operatives. The Black Tom explosion was reported in the international press, but the primary coverage was in the US press; Altendorf arrived in Mexico in 1917 and would not by 1917 have read any US press about Black Tom. Even if he somehow had read an account, the initial conclusion by investigators had been that negligence was the cause of the explosion at Black Tom.[12] There is therefore no way that Altendorf could have guessed on his own that the explosion at Black Tom was an act of sabotage that could be attributed to Lothar Witzke. Rather, Altendorf must have heard about Black Tom from a German operative in Mexico, and the most likely such source would have been Witzke himself, just as Altendorf said.

There is also no other way to explain that Altendorf's February 1918 debriefings both mention New Jersey as the site of the sabotage. Altendorf, a Polish native who had spent no time in the United States as of February 1918, would not have known that Black Tom was in New Jersey. He had to have been told about Black Tom by someone in Mexico in late 1917 or early 1918. The most likely source was, again, Witzke himself, just as Altendorf said.

Further, if Altendorf were fabricating, it is hard to explain why he would have said that Witzke and Jahnke were on a rowboat that almost swamped and why he would have included Jahnke as a participant. It is true that innocuous details can make a fabrication more credible, and this is what Witzke (and later the German agent) argued that Altendorf was doing, by shamelessly transposing a slightly similar story that he had heard from Jahnke about an incident in the harbor of Veracruz in which Jahnke was with Witzke and almost drowned.[13] This explanation requires that one find Altendorf to be a calculated liar of an egregious nature. Altendorf's record of service for the Americans makes it difficult to believe that he was mendacious to that degree.

At the time that he was debriefed in February 1918, Altendorf was employed by US intelligence (and would remain so until April 1, 1919), he had successfully informed US intelligence about multiple German operatives in Mexico, and he had triumphantly delivered to American authorities a spy bearing a coded note. That spy (Witzke) was to be tried for espionage. The authorities investigating Witzke were all West Coast-based, and hence had a keen interest in Altendorf's reports of Witzke's statements about acts of sabotage on the West Coast, several of which (Mare Island and the *Minnesota*) the authorities would duly investigate. While Altendorf might have been the object of even higher esteem if the prisoner that he delivered turned out also to be responsible for Black Tom on the East Coast, the marginal benefit to Altendorf of fabricating a confession about Black Tom was hardly worth the risk to his status. Altendorf was on solid ground with the Americans. Just how solid was documented by the Americans themselves.

Two months after Witzke's arrest, a memorandum from another US double agent in Mexico, William Neunhoffer, to the Bureau of Investigation in Washington endorsed the accuracy of Altendorf's earlier intelligence reports from Mexico and described him as an "absolutely reliable" informant, because everything that Altendorf said about which Neunhoffer had personal knowledge was true.[14] A year after Witzke's arrest, Altendorf told a lawyer, Guy Fake, representing the owner of Kingsland (Fake was also Witzke's correspondent while Witzke was at Leavenworth) that in Mexico City Altendorf had heard Witzke saying that he was responsible for the explosion at Kingsland.[15] This caused Fake to investigate Altendorf's credibility and he obtained from Altendorf a series of letters from US government and military personnel attesting to Altendorf's merit and credibility. One such letter, from H. S. Dickey, Captain, US Army, Department of Intelligence, said: "Dr. Altendorf has shown the greatest evidence of dedication to his work, loyalty to the American government, and wonderful resourcefulness in working up his cases."[16] Another, from Brigadier General J. A. Ryan, said: "Dr. Altendorf is a fine linguist and a man of exceptional talent for secret service work. . . . He is devoted to the American Forces and I deem him competent to perform the duties of a Captain of the Intelligence Department, to which Department he would be a valuable acquisition."[17]

The division superintendent of the Bureau of Investigation in San Antonio, Charles E. Breniman, also endorsed Altendorf: "He is a man who possesses exceptional ability as an investigator, speaks a number of foreign languages, is pain-staking and careful in his work, and his reports are always received with the most implicit confidence. His wide experience, splendid education and natural qualifications would make him a most valuable man to any investigating branch of the government.[18]

The sole negative statement by American authorities about Altendorf's truthfulness turned out to be unjustified. The US Consul at Nogales in November 1918 wrote about Altendorf: "I regard him as a man of very little principle and believe that in order to strengthen his cases on which he was employed, that he exaggerated and did not always tell the exact truth."[19] The falsification that particularly troubled the consul was Altendorf's charge that a certain Maria Wilkinson was the mistress of Captain Joel Lipscomb. There was a follow-up to this critique of Altendorf, from the War Department's Major

Barnes: "It might be said, however, in justice to Altendorf that much of his criticism of Captain Lipscomb has since proven to have had substantial foundation."[20]

The ire of the US intelligence community during the early 1920s after the appearance in the press of Altendorf's descriptions of his exploits in Mexico attests in a different way to the veracity of Altendorf's accounts. While the intelligence community was displeased to have their operations made public, there was no suggestion that Altendorf's dramatic accounts were false or exaggerated.[21]

Altendorf's reliability is additionally corroborated by a conversation between Witzke and Special Agent Byron Butcher, as reflected in a contemporaneous report by Butcher about a conversation that he had with Witzke on February 14, 1918.[22]

The Witzke/Butcher conversation took place two weeks after Witzke's arrest. It occurred at a train station in Arizona where the two were en route to San Antonio. The conversation took place in the open, without other witnesses, and was described by Butcher as a "chat," suggesting that it was spontaneous and informal. Butcher transcribed the conversation from memory within three or four hours of speaking with Witzke.[23] The dialogue reported by Butcher has the ring of authenticity and, while Butcher may have been motivated to assure the conviction of a foreign agent charged with espionage, the details of the reported dialogue were not needed for a conviction. There is, in short, no reason to doubt that Butcher's report accurately reflects what Witzke said.

Their conversation began by Witzke asking Butcher what he thought the US authorities would do with him. "Pablo," Butcher replied, "I tried to tell you the other day that the best thing for you would be to tell the whole thing. . . . *As you have already guessed, we know nearly all about you.* We are in war now, and also as you know spies are hung. . . . The only possible chance you have is [to] tell them all you know." Witzke replied, "No, I can't do that. I am very young to die, 22 years. But I have done my duty. If I told you I would be a traitor and that I will never be."[24]

Butcher pressed for a confession, and Witzke remained steadfast.

B. Pablo, that is the chance we all take who do this work. It is legitimate as long as you do not get caught, but when you are caught you have to pay the penalty.

W. Yes, I know it. I will probably be the first man to die in the United States for my country, won't I?

B. Yes, probably the first, though I hear that one or two more have been caught since you were here. You think it over, for the wa[y] I see it, your only chance now is to tell all.

W. No, I think I will go through with it. I had planned to live in Mexico after the war, but now I can never do that.

B. Is there any word or message I can give Lupe, if she should come to the border? [Lupe Garcia, from Mazatlan, was supposedly the fiancée of Waberski.]

W. You can tell her that I will never come back.

B. It is great work, Pablo, and I have tried to treat you as I would expect you to treat me under the same circumstances.

W. If you are ever my prisoner, I will take good care of you. No, to tell would make me a traitor, I can't do it.

———

W. [. . .] The most I can say is I wish you luck. You are doing your work and I have been doing mine. What kind of a trial will I get?

B. I do not know, as yet, how they will try you.

W. Will it be published in the papers?

B. I don't know, probably not.[25]

The "chat" ended with the following exchange:

W. *You know all the details all right and I think that it was that Doctor Altendorf who told you, as I told him a lot of things in conversation.*

B. I think the Doctor and Siegel will talk when we get them and tell all they know.

W. How much did you pay the Doctor to do this on me.

B. If we get him, he will probably get the same pay as you.[26]

Witzke's statement—"You know all the details all right, and I think it was that Dr. Altendorf who told you, as I told him a lot of things in conversation"—was the closest Witzke would come in his multiple interrogations to an admission. But what was he admitting? The answer depends upon what Butcher had said to Witzke that the Americans knew about Witzke. Witzke had been interrogated by Butcher and others for two weeks before their railroad platform chat. The interrogations surely focused on the purpose of Witzke's mission to Nogales, and on other West Coast matters. Any interrogation about Black Tom or Kingsland would have been perfunctory. Butcher likely said that the Americans knew that Witzke was a German spy, and probably went no further. Witzke's statement that the Americans got "all the details" from Altendorf most likely referenced the Nogales espionage mission and cannot be taken as an implicit admission about Black Tom.

Witzke's statement to Butcher is nonetheless consequential because Witzke was saying that (i) he had in fact made statements to Altendorf about his espionage activities, (ii) such statements were not false boasts, and (iii) he presumed that Altendorf's reports were accurate. His comment to Butcher contains no intimation that Altendorf's reports had to have been invented because Witzke had never said anything incriminating to Altendorf, though this would have been the moment to suggest that Altendorf was fabricating for pay.

The German agent before the Mixed Claims Commission repeatedly assailed Altendorf's character, and the attacks, which had an ethnic component, drew blood. The Germans repeatedly referred in their submissions to Altendorf as an Austrian Jew. Altendorf's response, in his 1929 affidavit, was: "I have no particular prejudices against either Austrians or Jews, but it happens that I am neither an Austrian nor a Jew. I was born in Krakow and am now an American citizen. I am a Protestant and am not and never had been a member of the Jewish faith. My ancestry is chiefly Lutheran and Roman Catholic."[27] One can imagine the reaction of the German representatives to this testimony. They produced Altendorf's birth certificate, showing that his birth was registered at the Hebrew Registry in Krakow.[28] One cannot, though, jump from Altendorf's defensiveness (or willingness to lie) about his own story to conclude that he lied outright about what he was told by Witzke about Black Tom. There are too many indicators of Altendorf's credibility regarding Witzke's statements about Black Tom.

Though the MCC was disdainful of Altendorf, it nonetheless found that German agents had made admissions about Black Tom more or less as Altendorf testified that they had.

Altendorf's statements that Witzke told him that he was responsible for Black Tom are credible. On this basis alone, there is a fair case that Witzke was responsible for the sabotage at Black Tom.

Corporal John Shores was one of the guards at Fort Sam Houston where Witzke was confined after his arrest in February 1918.

Shores signed an affidavit in September 1919, saying that he had heard (or overheard) Witzke say, about two months previously, that he and another un-named fellow "blew up" Black Tom.[29] The date of the affidavit was the last day of the interviews of Witzke by Thomas J. Tunney, the former chief of the New York City Police Department's bomb squad and newly Special Investigator for the US Military Intelligence Division. Either Tunney asked around at the prison whether anyone had heard Witzke say anything about Black Tom or Shores heard about the interviews and came forward.

There was nothing in it for Shores to invent a confession by Witzke. To find a motivation for Shores to lie, one would need to posit enmity between Shores and Witzke. But there is no evidence of that.[30]

But why would Witzke have made such a statement, especially in or about July 1919 as alleged? Witzke would in September 1919 spend four days with Tunney assiduously denying any role at Black Tom and insisting that he never said to Altendorf anything about Black Tom. Yet, according to Shores, Witzke had freely mentioned two months previously that he had blown up Black Tom. It is likely that Witzke was at the time hoping to secure a pardon, an effort that would occupy Witzke for three years. It would have been entirely against his interest to have made such a self-incriminating statement. One explanation for the reported statement by Witzke to Shores is that, for one moment anyway, Witzke wanted to boast, whether truthfully or falsely.[31]

During the MCC proceedings, Shores gave testimony in 1926 that was much more detailed than his September 1919 affidavit:

> Witzke told me that he had blown up Black Tom. I asked him who was with him when he did this, and he said that his partner Jahnke was with him. He said that he and Jahnke got a boat and went over and set off the explosion, and then got into the boat again to make their getaway. He said that the boat was overturned by the explosion; that Jahnke went under the boat and he lost track of him, because it was in the night; and that he himself swam ashore, but was nearly drowned.[32]

While Witzke's accomplice was unidentified by Shores in his report two months after the alleged conversation occurred, seven years later Shores purported to remember that it was Jahnke. Shores also could supply seven years later the new details that their boat was swamped by the explosion and that Witzke swam ashore separately from Jahnke.

Witzke's reply (in a witness statement in 1927) was:

> Shores was one of the guards at the prison of the Fort Sam Houston. He was not one of the few people who, during my time in prison, met me in a somewhat friendlier manner and I altogether maintained a reserved and incommunicative attitude towards him. The allegation that I told him I had exploded the Black Tom is sheer invention. I am of the decided opinion that even the American authorities at the time did not credit the brief testimony which he gave. . . .
>
> In the affidavit submitted now. . . . Shores attempts to lend a greater semblance of credibility to his former testimony by adding a number of details. That this new statement is fabricated is evident from the following . . . [33]

The detailed testimony that Shores submitted in 1926, written by the American agent for the Mixed Claims Commission, is not credible. None of the rowboat details had been mentioned in 1919. And while some of the new details (*e.g.*, that Witzke swam ashore separately from Jahnke) differ from the rowboat narrative that the American agent had been advancing, the focus on the swamped rowboat tracks too conveniently the core narrative that the American agent wanted the Commission to accept, based upon Altendorf's statements. Shores' 1919 affidavit, by contrast, does not have these infirmities, and there was no identifiable motivation for Shores to invent the conversation. While it remains difficult to understand why Witzke would have said off-handedly to Shores what he steadfastly denied to Tunney, the Shores 1919 affidavit must weigh in the balance in favor of the view that Witzke said what Shore said that he did. Witzke may have been swept up by a momentary urge to boast. Shores' testimony that Witzke said that he blew up Black Tom with another agent thus corroborates Altendorf's testimony that Witzke said that he did it with Jahnke.

Haslam

Second Lieutenant George Haslam was another officer at Fort Sam Houston charged with guarding Witzke from December 1918 to December 1919. He was the officer in charge of the prison on the night of Witzke's attempted escape that was foiled only because Witzke lacked clothing. Having made no report at the time of any conversations with Witzke, Haslam testified seven years later (in an affidavit in April 1926), without giving details of time or place or context, that "Witzke told me that he, with another man, had blown up Black Tom," and that "a rowboat, in which he was, was overturned by the explosion of a drifting ammunition barge."[34]

The Americans argued to the Mixed Claims Commission with respect to Haslam's testimony:

> Were Sergeant Haslam to be examined by the Commission, it would perceive the type of soldier that he is, rugged but of exact statement, a man whose word is not to be doubted. His unprompted statement that Witzke told him that his row-boat had been overturned by the explosion of "a drifting ammunition barge" is a striking piece of evidence, for this must have referred to the explosion of the *Johnson 17*, an incident of which Witzke would hardly have known had he not been on the scene.[35]

The praise for Haslam's honesty is impressive, and the German agent accepted that Haslam was a truthful individual.[36] But one must wonder, as noted with respect to Shores' report, why Witzke would at this critical juncture (post-conviction and pre-pardon) have made any self-incriminating comments.

And yet, Haslam had no motivation to invent the detail about the barge, and the American agent likewise had no need to adduce testimony that the rowboat was overturned by the explosion of a drifting barge, as other testimony already attributed the overturning to waves and Altendorf's original version was that the boat was nearly swamped. But if Haslam was not inventing, why would Witzke have said or invented such a detail? One is left, again, to posit boasting, though this would have been counter to Witzke's efforts to obtain a pardon.

The Haslam testimony, on balance, weighs in favor of the view that Witzke said to him, as he had said to Altendorf, that he was responsible for Black Tom.

KRISTOFF'S STATEMENTS

Michael Kristoff, a native Slovakian and (hence) Austrian national by birth, was the alleged third man in the sabotage of Black Tom.

Kristoff was employed in July 1916 at a factory adjacent to Black Tom. He disappeared from his job after the Black Tom explosion and never claimed his wages. Immediately after the explosion, his aunt (with whom he was living in Jersey City) went to the local police and told them that Kristoff had returned home early in the morning on July 30, 1916, crying "What I do? What I do?"[37] Kristoff was interrogated by the Jersey City police in September 1916 and released for lack of evidence of a connection to the disaster.[38]

Starting in October/November 1916 and lasting to April 1917, Kristoff was befriended by an investigator (Alexander Kassman) who pretended to be an anarchist while in truth he worked for the owner of the Black Tom terminal (Lehigh Valley Railroad Company). The gist of the multiple reports by Kassman was that Kristoff repeatedly told Kassman, both separately and in the presence of Kristoff's friend David Grossman, that he blew up Black Tom together with two Germans.[39]

As Kassman wrote:

> I asked him, "Say, Michael, how were you working for the explosion in Black Tom? This must be a hard job." *He then told me that in the middle of the night with two men he came over to Black Tom.* One man told Michael Kristoff to watch the place all around and he, Michel Kristoff, with another man went to a big steamboat with ammunition aboard. "On the ship where I was there were small cases of powder. I put between the cases two pieces of dynamite, and lit it. The explosion should be about half an hour later."
>
> "Around the ship where I put the dynamite were steamboats and on the boats were cars of ammunition. My friend also put on one boat between the cars and half an hour later there was an explosion [*sic*].
>
> "The powder that was on the ship in the cars after the explosion blew up all the ammunition that was around in Black Tom."
>
> I then said to Michael Kristoff, "The two men who were with you are anarchists." *Michael Kristoff told me that the two men belonged to a German group.* I then asked him, "Where is the place of the German Group?" He told me that he knows only two of the men. I then asked him, "How do you know this man and where did you meet this man the first time?" Michael Kristoff said, "I will tell you some other time."[40]

Kristoff's statement preceded the Altendorf February 1918 debriefings by many months, and Altendorf would not have known of Kristoff's statement. Kristoff's statement that there were two Germans working with him therefore independently corroborates the content of the Altendorf debriefings on the core point that there were two Germans—identified by Altendorf as Jahnke and Witzke—responsible for the Black Tom sabotage. Kristoff never identified his two accomplices, though Kassman pressed him for names.[41]

Most of those who investigated Kristoff were skeptical about his supposed role at Black Tom. There were multiple reasons for this.

One is that Kristoff came across as mentally deficient. A psychiatrist who examined Kristoff in August 1916 found him to be "a person of such low order of mentality and so lacking in mental capacity as to be unable to carry through any project of the kind."[42] This may have been nativist bias against an immigrant with poor English. The man was able to hold a job. He was able to identify whether there were two Germans acting with him on July 30. Nativist bias or not, Kristoff was far from an ideal source of information. He enlisted in the US Army in 1917, was incarcerated in 1921 for petty larceny, and was then re-arrested in July 1921 on the charge of having made a false statement at the time of his enlistment in the US Army in 1917. The prosecutor argued that he enlisted to try to avoid suspicion for his involvement in Black Tom.[43]

Another reason for skepticism about Kristoff was (and is) that his reported statements about Black Tom were confusing in their detail (there were, for example, no steamboats with cars at Black Tom), but the explanation may be that Kristoff's English was poor. "Cars" might have been "cases" of ammunition.

A third reason for skepticism was that there were doubts about the honesty of the investigator (Kassman) who wrote up the reports of Kristoff's statements (and whose testimony ten years later before the Mixed Claims Commission introduced material changes in his reports that conformed them to the US case, *e.g.*, he changed "steamboats" to "barges").[44] Kassman purported to have received corroboration about Kristoff's role from a friend of Kristoff, David Grossman, who reportedly said that he also had heard Kristoff say in his presence that he, Kristoff, was responsible with two others for Black Tom. But Grossman denied all of this in a deposition.[45] For the Commission, Kassman's testimony was canned testimony. "Nor do we like the fact that the language of the admissions is always substantially exactly the same and is very brief, whether it is quoted from Kristoff or (in one instance) from Grossman, who is alleged, after having emphatically told Kristoff in Kassman's presence that he must never under any circumstances say anything about Black Tom, to have told Kassman at a later interview alone just what Kristoff told Kassman and in the same brief, crisp language."[46] The Commission's dismissal of the Kristoff statements does not, though, account for the remarkable coincidence that both Kristoff and Altendorf, neither knowing of the other, said that there were two Germans involved in the sabotage.

Whatever doubts there were about Kassman, it is difficult to dismiss as an invention the report that there were two Germans involved in the sabotage. Neither Kristoff nor Kassman had any reason to invent that specific number of German operatives. Many months later, Altendorf, not knowing of Kristoff's statements or of Kassman reports, would report that he was told the same about Black Tom.

Kristoff's reported testimony that he was accompanied by two Germans doing the sabotage at Black Tom is on balance credible evidence and, even though Kristoff never identified who the two Germans were, no pair of Germans other than Jahnke and Witzke has ever been suggested or alleged by any source. The Kristoff evidence thus weighs in favor of the view that Witzke was involved in the Black Tom sabotage.

THE TWO-WEEK GAP IN WITZKE'S HANDWRITTEN CHRONOLOGY OF HIS SUMMER 1916

In a 1927 affidavit submitted to the Mixed Claims Commission, Witzke referenced what he called a "notebook" that, he said, supported his testimony that he was in San Francisco in late July 1916.[47] The "notebook," actually an address book, became an important and much contested document in the MCC case because crammed into two pages in the midst of the address book there is what purports to be a chronology of Witzke's activities during 1916 and 1917.[48]

The reader will instantly wonder: what does the chronology say about where Witzke was and what Witzke was doing on July 29–30, 1916? The answer is: nothing, because there is a two-week gap in the chronology from July 24 to August 7, 1916. The two-week gap appears to reflect an effort to conceal where Witzke was during the time. While there are other gaps in the chronology, these other gaps indicate either that Witzke was in transit from place A to place B on the dates given and was resident in place B until the next travel entry, or that Witzke had jobs suggested by proximate entries in the chronology. The transit explanation does not work for this two-week gap because the entry immediately before July 24 reads "San Francisco-Eureka 14 July-23 July" and the entry immediately after reads "Eureka-Seattle 8 August-13 August." This implies that Witzke was in Eureka during the two-week gap, but Witzke has never so suggested and nothing so indicates; further, as discussed below, three items of correspondence place Witzke in San Francisco during this two-week period, contradicting a prolonged Eureka residence.

When one considers the two-week gap in the Witzke chronology along side the analogous gap in the diary of the New York-based German operative, Doctor Heinrich Albert,[49] the suspicion that Witzke was concealing something grows only stronger.

In addition to the omission of any entry for the critical period in late July and early August 1916, the chronology in Witzke's address book is suspect in multiple other ways.

First, the chronology stands out from the rest of the address book both for being a chronology rather than a notation of names and addresses and for being crammed into two pages. It also stands out for being written mostly in pen, whereas the rest of the address book was written in pencil. There is, in short, nothing natural about the chronology.[50]

Second, there are pages ripped out of the address book just after the chronology.

Third, while we cannot be certain, the handwriting of part of the chronology (the top right of two pages) appears to have been done by a different person than the rest.[51]

Fourth, Germany strenuously resisted production of the address book during the MCC arbitration.[52] Germany's explanation was that Witzke refused to allow production because he was concerned that the American representatives would harass individuals identified in his address book. Witzke had reason to fear harassment given what happened to his family in 1922 during a visit to his home by a former guard at Fort Sam Houston, Willy Dojan, who attacked Witzke's mother in an apparent effort to obtain Witzke's papers.[53] But our review of the entirety of the address book suggests that there were few, if any, names in the address book that could have been a legitimate source of concern for Witzke. (A contemporary perspective would question why the address book could not have been produced with redactions, but the address book consists almost entirely of names and addresses and therefore redaction might reasonably not have occurred to Witzke or the German agent.) Germany's resistance to production therefore suggests that Germany considered that there was something to hide.

In summary, the Witzke handwritten chronology raises substantial suspicion that it was hiding something about where Witzke was and what he was doing in late July 1916.

SUDDENLY CIRCUMSPECT CORRESPONDENCE WITH HIS FAMILY IN SUMMER 1916

Witzke's correspondence to his family seems suspiciously curated from the time of his arrival in San Francisco. He told his parents about his jobs and his wages, and nothing else. One may dismiss this as the reserve of a young man telling the minimum to his parents. But the letters that he sent while a sailor had much more detail.

The content of Witzke's correspondence during the summer 1916 is still more odd. In June, Witzke still wrote frequently to his family, even if his correspondence had become opaque. Then in July, silence, except a postcard dated July 26 and postmarked San Francisco July 28, in which he said very little except that he had met a nice man (Jahnke, but not naming him) and that his mailing address is still New York. Then, on August 2, a short letter to his parents postmarked San Francisco, mentioning Jahnke by name, profession (detective) and little else. The conclusion is fair that he was leaving out much more than he was telling.

THE JAHNKE EVIDENCE

Kurt Jahnke was both Witzke's superior and Witzke's most important companion during his years in the Americas.[54] They formed, in Henry Landau's prose, "one of the most deadly teams of saboteurs in history."[55]

Their relationship was more than one of expedience.[56] The two spent substantial time together in San Francisco in summer 1916, traveled together across the United States and then spent three months together on West Fifty-Sixth Street in Manhattan in late 1916. They shared an interest in women, as Jahnke was also reported to be "very fond of women."[57] After Witzke's arrest in February 1918, Jahnke retrieved Witzke's personal effects in Mexico City, including his private notebooks, and delivered them to Witzke's parents in Hanover.[58] Upon his return to Germany after being pardoned by President Coolidge, Witzke for a time was employed by the Jahnke Büro.

The older, more accomplished and impressively talented Jahnke undoubtedly influenced Witzke. The interview of Witzke by a British intelligence agent in 1952 revealed Witzke's enduring connection to and admiration for his mentor. "The general trend of Witzke's conversation confirmed case officer's previously held opinion, namely that Witzke from 1923 onwards was far more in Jahnke's confidence then he has so far admitted."[59] "While not willing to be cross-questioned he is quite willing to talk generally about Jahnke who would appear to fascinate him."[60] Witzke held the view that it was thanks to Jahnke that Canaris was made head of the *Abwehr*.[61]

Jahnke surely saw in Witzke an appealing, intrepid and loyal young man. And likely something else, more specific: a young man who, despite his youth, had extensive experience of ships and ports. The tasks assigned by Jahnke to Witzke show that Jahnke recognized that Witzke's expertise was in maritime matters, including observation of ports and ship movements. Jahnke presumably also knew that Witzke could handle himself on a boat. If Jahnke was involved in reconnoitering or detonating Black Tom from the riverside, Witzke would have been the perfect accomplice.[62]

To the extent that there is evidence that Jahnke participated in the sabotage at Black Tom, the case for Witzke's participation is strengthened. Conversely, to the extent that the evidence points away from Jahnke, the case for Witzke's participation diminishes. Part of the evidence for Jahnke's role at Black Tom is the testimony, assessed above, of Altendorf and others that

Witzke told them that he and Jahnke were responsible for Black Tom. There is additional evidence, considered here, that pertains to Jahnke independent of the alleged admissions by Witzke.

An affidavit submitted to the Mixed Claims Commission in 1931 by a British agent (Casimir Palmer) purported to recount in some detail the agent's encounter with Jahnke fourteen years previously, in February 1917:

> Shortly after the Bernstorff Party returned to Berlin in February, 1917, Kurt Jahnke was brought to me at the Parisian Rotisserie, on Eighth Avenue, near 42nd Street, New York. . . . Jahnke professed to be in want of funds at the time and claimed to have been rather badly treated by the Intelligence Office in New York. He offered to make a statement, in consideration of payment of a sum—$1000—and a guaranty of immunity, telling the details of the Black Tom destruction, and naming the men who actually participated in causing the disaster. Jahnke himself claimed credit for arranging the whole affair, and as I remember it named four men who actually took part. The only name which is distinctly remembered is "witzke," which was recalled to my mind by the Altendorf articles in the papers in 1920 or 1921. I distinctly remember that Jahnke stated that fires were started at two or more separate and distinct points around the property. . . .[63]

The problem with this affidavit is that the same agent (Palmer) wrote up a *contemporaneous* report of his conversation with Jahnke in 1917. The report says that in February 1917 Jahnke told him that he was "short of funds and has intimated that for a sufficient sum of money and guaranty of immunity for himself he will tell all about the Black Tom explosion of July 1916, and the principals involved."[64] The 1917 report does not say that Jahnke said or implied that he himself was involved at Black Tom. Nor, of course, does the report mention Witzke, and Palmer acknowledged in his 1931 affidavit that he had already as of then read or been told about the Altendorf articles that featured Witzke. Taken together, Palmer's affidavit and report constitute meager evidence that Jahnke (or Witzke) was responsible for Black Tom. They suggest, rather, only that Jahnke knew who was responsible for Black Tom.

Other evidence on Jahnke comes from a document in British Intelligence files that says, "In 1917 he was carrying out sabotage at Monterey, and at about that time was responsible for the blowing up of a large ammunition dump in New Jersey. This exploit, which apparently entailed a great deal of personal danger for Jahnke, earned him considerable renown among his associates and has been regarded as one of the outstanding successes of his career."[65]

How much can be made of this British intelligence report of what the British believed that the Germans believed? Not much.

The "associates" who reportedly held Jahnke in renown for blowing up Black Tom are unidentified, but one can derive from the report that they were German colleagues in Mexico. That Jahnke was held in renown by them does not amount to much evidence that Jahnke was responsible for Black Tom, because Jahnke may have wanted it to be thought that Black Tom was his doing, even though it was not, and there is evidence, discussed later, that, while Jahnke at one point asserted to his colleagues in Mexico that he had done Black Tom, he thereafter tacitly retreated from such assertion.

Had it been the German command that believed Jahnke responsible for Black Tom, this would amount to something because a falsity in this circumstance would have carried risk for Jahnke. One would also hesitate to assume that the German command were dupes to believe it.[66] But as it is more likely that the "associates" were Jahnke's colleagues in Mexico, this document weighs negligibly in favor of Jahnke's role at Black Tom.

That Jahnke *claimed* responsibility and that this claim was, to his benefit, accepted at least for a time by some of his German colleagues is relevant to our inquiry even if the claim was false, because, if it was to Jahnke's benefit to assert responsibility for Black Tom, then it may have been in Witzke's interest to do the same, even if untrue.

PENNEWITZ STATEMENT

Robert Pennewitz was a Dutchman (or perhaps German) who submitted to the Mixed Claims Commission in 1935 a statement in which he claimed to have worked as an operative for the German admirality from 1915–18 and to have knowledge of Witzke's role at Black Tom.[67] The MCC Commissioners ignored the statement.

According to Pennewitz, the Admiralty dispatched two secret agents—an American named Henry Alt and an Alsatian named Victor Blank (or Blanc)— into Mexico in spring 1916. From Mexico, they crossed the US border using a weakpoint previously discovered by Witzke. The two then traveled to New York where Witzke met up with them and introduced them to a man named Christof. Christof was knowledgeable of Black Tom. As Pennewtiz recounted:

> Henry Alt, Victor Blanc and Christof went together to Black Tom from the waterside at night, they did not carry explosives in their boat, the purpose was to get knowledge of the location and how the plant was guarded.

On a night late in July 1916 they decided to do their work. Again they reached Black Tom by water in a boat.

They looked the situation over carefully from the water, then they went ashore and placed brandpatronen and time-bombs in several freight cars loaded with ammunition. Then they returned to the boat and seeing a freighter anchored, they placed a timebomb on the freighter also.

They especially placed two timebombs in each car, to be sure of the explositon.

After finishing this job, they rowed to the New Jersey shore, then Henry Alt and Victor Blanc left Chistof alone, went to New York, where they were met by Lothar Witzke and all three went back to Mexiko.[68]

Pennewitz further said that in November 1916 Witzke guided Alt and Blanc back over the Mexican border into the USA, spent time with them in New York, and Alt and Blanc then carried out the Kingsland sabotage. Witzke thereafter helped the two to get back again to Mexico.

The Pennewitz statement offers corroboration of Kristoff's alleged assertions that he was directly involved in the Black Tom sabotage and had worked with two other operatives and, broadly, of Altendorf's testimony that it was reported to him that the Black Tom detonations were set by men in a rowboat. Jahnke is notably absent in Pennewitz's version, and this absence is plausible. It is difficult to understand why Jahnke would have traveled across the continent to participate in a Hinsch-led operation, and even more difficult to accept that Jahnke himself would have been in a rowboat planting bombs. Witzke's role in the Pennewitz version also makes sense: it is unclear that he would have had the time to reconnoiter the site and it is plausible that he would have been in a supervisory role.

Against reliance on the Pennewitz statement are the following considerations: (i) there is no mention anywhere else known to us of Alt or Blanc; (ii) Pennewitz's account is inconsistent in multiple ways with the Witzke/Jahnke roles supposedly confessed by Witzke; (iii) Pennewitz says that Alt and Blanc used in spring 1916 a weakpoint in the US/Mexico border to cross from Mexico into the US, but the evidence is incontrovertible that Witzke had not been at or near the border as of spring 1916; (iv) while Pennewtz has Witzke masterminding the Kingsland sabortage, the evidence otherwise connecting Witzke to Kingsland is very thin; and (v) Pennewitz's statement was put forward nineteen years after the events described.

In summary, though the Pennewitz statement offers in important ways the most plausible version of the sabotage at Black Tom, its introduction of two operatives nowhere else mentioned raises major doubt. So too does the very belated submission of his statement. On balance, the Pennewitz statement weighs in favor, but not materially, of a Witzke role at Black Tom.[69]

WITZKE'S DEDICATION TO GERMANY'S OPERATIONS IN THE AMERICAS

The case that Witzke was responsible for Black Tom is supported indirectly by the evidence that German agents were responsible for Black Tom and by Witzke's dedication to furthering Germany's interests in the Americas during World War I.

Germany's sabotage campaign in the Americas was documented by a January 1915 telegram from the German Foreign Office that authorized sabotage in the United States against suppliers of munitions to the Allied Powers, "In United States sabotage can reach to all kinds of factories for war deliveries; railroads, dams, bridges must not be touched there. Under no circumstances compromise Embassy, and equally Irish-German propaganda."[70]

Before von Rintelen left the scene in 1915, he was already organizing the placement of incendiary devices, in particular exploding cigar-sized lead tubes, in munitions-laden ships bound for Europe.[71] German agents also conducted biological attacks and tried to organize labor strife at docks where munitions were to be loaded and shipped.[72]

It was established before the Mixed Claims Commission that two German operatives in the United States were, at a meeting with the German General Staff in February 1916 in Berlin, directed to pursue sabotage in the US.[73]

While denying responsibility for Black Tom and Kingsland, Germany admitted in its submissions to the Mixed Claims Commission that it committed sabotage during the period of US neutrality, "We do not contest that a number of things were done in the United States during the period of neutrality which were illegal or illegitimate: and I do not deny that a number of agents were sent to the United States for the purpose of doing damage to supplies destined for the Allied Powers. They were authorized and instructed to commit acts which were not in accordance with neutrality, but the number was very, very small. To speak of a systematic campaign of sabotage in the United States . . . is absolutely unjustified."[74]

Germany further admitted that German secret agents pursued sabotage as of 1915 in Mexico[75] and in Canada,[76] and as of April 1917 in the United States.[77] A leading German historian has concluded that "the surviving documents leave no doubt that from the beginning of the war until February

1917 projects were constantly being carried out that egregiously violated American neutrality. . . ."[78]

The Herrmann Message is, in any case, proof that German agents in the United States were responsible for Black Tom.[79] The coded message, sent by Frederick Herrmann in January 1917 from Mexico by courier to Paul Hilken, was written in lemon juice on the pages of a Blue Book magazine. Decoded, the message said in part (bracketed text added to identify the coded names): "Have seen 1755 [Eckhardt]. He is suspicious of me. . . . Have told him all reference 2584 [Hinsch] and . . . 7595 [Jersey City Terminal], 3106 [Kingsland]. He doubts me on account of my bum 7346 [German]. Confirm to him through your channels all OK and my mission here. I have no funds. . . ."[80] As both Black Tom and Kingsland had been destroyed at the time of this message, the Herrmann Message shows Herrmann complaining that, despite his having told Minister von Eckhardt in Mexico about the successful exploits organized by Hinsch and his team in the US, including the destruction of Black Tom ("Jersey City Terminal") and Kingsland, von Eckhardt remained unappreciative and dubious, in part because Herrmann spoke German poorly.

The Mixed Claims Commission agreed that, if it were authentic, the Hermann Message would show that Hinsch, Hilken and Herrmann were German agents who were implicated in the sabotage (thereby discrediting Hinsch's early disavowals of his knowledge or participation in the plots).[81] In June 1939, after an exhaustive review of the context, provenance and content of the Herrmann Message, the American Commissioner concluded that the message was authentic.[82] The Umpire concurred with the American Commissioner's Opinion.[83] The Commission's findings are thorough and convincing as to the Germans' culpability for Black Tom.

When Witzke was captured at the border in February 1918, he was carrying a coded document identifying the bearer as a secret agent of the Reich entitled to protection, assistance and funding by German consular officers in Mexico. Witzke later admitted that he had been serving as a German spy on the West Coast since May 1916[84] and that his purpose at the time of his capture was to foment insurrection and sabotage in the US.[85] Witzke was, thus, an admitted secret agent as of April 1917 at the latest, working for a nation that had since August 1914 pursued espionage and sabotage in the US, including at Black Tom.

Witzke was awarded the Iron Cross for his service to Germany in the

Americas. While the award was conferred in 1924 after Witzke's return to Germany, Altendorf wrote in 1919 that Witzke had boasted in 1918 about the award.[86] It is unimaginable that Altendorf fabricated this conversation, as it was a true story. As Witzke was already aware in 1918 that he would be honored, the award had to be for what he had already accomplished in the Americas in service to Germany. This does not show that Witzke had a role at Black Tom, but Black Tom was the most sensational success achieved by the Germans in the Americas.

Witzke's character and principles suited him for a role as a daring saboteur. He was ready to die for his country. After Witzke's arrest in February 1918, Byron Butcher, US special agent involved in the arrest and initial interrogation, reported that, during a chat on the railroad platform, when he (Butcher) urged Witzke to tell the US authorities his true story, Witzke replied: "No, I can't do that, I am very young to die, twenty-two years old, but I have to do my duty, and I will never be a traitor."[87] His adherence to a code of honor as he saw it was more than a moment's vainglory. In January 1929, Witzke gave a statement of his political principles in a letter to the German agent (referring to what he had said to American investigators when they met with him earlier that month in Maracaibo). While Witzke wrote his letter in German, the passage that follows is Witzke quoting himself in English, "I stated that I was a true believer in the black, white and red [*i.e.*, traditional colors of the German Empire] and that it was not my habit to change my beliefs like a dirty shirt overnight and that I was not in sympathy with the present day German government policy of conciliation. That I believed fully in the code of honor of the former German army and navy officer and if the entire country had been like they, Germany would never have lost the war."[88] For Witzke, then, Germany lost the war not in the field but because of insufficient loyalty or bravery by the populace as a whole. "Every decent German," he said, "must have 'nationalistic tendencies.'"[89]

Witzke's heroism during the boiler explosion at Leavenworth prison in July 1921 shows that he was physically intrepid.

Witzke's political convictions by themselves show nothing about whether he was in a rowboat on the Hudson River in July 1916, but where, as in his case, militarism is combined with youthful risk-taking and physical bravery, one has the portrait of an individual who would not hesitate, if so requested (let alone ordered) by his superiors, to blow up a munitions depot whose munitions were destined to arm Germany's enemies.

The openness of American society likely contributed to the willingness of Witzke (and other German operatives) to commit acts of sabotage that violated US neutrality. On September 6, 1916, five weeks after Black Tom, Witzke wrote to his mother, "I could not write during the last days because I took a 10 days' trip to the country from which I returned only yesterday. I had a wonderful time in the country, eating, drinking, sleeping—that was the best recreation. How well it agreed with me you can judge from the fact that I gained seven pounds in ten days."[90] On January 5, 1917, Witzke wrote to his parents, "I know now almost all of America. I was in the West, in the middle and in the East, near the British and near the Mexican border. . . . I like the USA very well, one earns so much that one can live and have a little pleasure besides."[91] The freedom to roam the country that Witzke manifestly felt reveals an ease with life in the US, not just of money and food but also of security from the authorities.

Witzke was enthusiastically dedicated to advancing Germany's sabotage efforts in North America, and he was given the Iron Cross for his efforts. The most spectacular of Germany's operations in the Americas was the sabotage at Black Tom. Witzke would have leapt at the opportunity to serve the fatherland in this way.

SUMMARY

The case for Witzke's responsibility for the sabotage at Black Tom rests on the following: (i) Altendorf's February 1918 reports that Witzke told him that he had blown up Black Tom; (ii) the corroborating testimony of the prison guards, Shores and Haslam, that Witzke told them that he had blown up Black Tom; (iii) Kristoff's reported statements that two Germans did the sabotage with him; (iv) the inexplicable two-week gap in Witzke's handwritten chronology of his doings in the summer of 1916, paired with the same gap in Ahrendt's diary; (v) the Pennewitz statement that Witzke worked with Kristoff and two others to do the job; and (vi) the evidence of Germany's responsibility for Black Tom and of Witzke's dedication to Germany's pursuit of sabotage in the Americas during World War I.

The Case That He Didn't Do It

The case against Witzke's connection to Black Tom starts with the evidence that Witzke was nowhere near New York anytime during July 1916.

THE EVIDENCE OF WITZKE'S WHEREABOUTS IN JULY 1916

There is substantial documentary evidence that places Witzke (and Jahnke) in San Francisco in late July 1916. There is no evidence, other than Altendorf's statements (and Witzke's other reported boasts) that Witzke said he was at Black Tom, that places Witzke in New York in late July 1916. This mix of evidence and lack of evidence weighs materially against the conclusion that Witzke was responsible for Black Tom.

Witzke's Testimony

Witzke gave sworn testimony before the Mixed Claims Commission that he was in San Francisco, not New York, on July 29-30, 1916:

> From the evidence submitted to me I see that the Black Tom explosion took place during the night from the 29th to 30th July 1916. I can state for an absolute certainty that at that time I was not in New York at all but was in the west of the United States. With the exception of the time after my release from prison in 1924 I have been east in the United States and in New York, only on one single trip in my life. On this first and only trip to the east I started out together with Jahnke on September 25, 1916, arriving in New York on October 1, 1916. I base this statement on my notebook and it is also in full accordance with my recollection. Naturally I cannot now anymore give from memory reliable data as to where I stayed in each and every week and each and every month of the years 1916 to 1918. Yet I remember quite positively that it was only after a stay in the west of the United States of at least three months that I undertook this first and only trip to New York, a clear recollection of which I also retain on account of the manifold new impressions which I received on that occasion.
>
> Furthermore I can state from memory that it was in San Francisco that I learned of the Black Tom explosion which as an extraordinary event had caused a sensation all through the United States and was discussed on the front page of the newspapers. I was present when it was talked about by the people in the restaurant, one of whom was Jahnke.[92]

Witzke's Handwritten Chronology

We have discussed above the suspicions raised by the 1916-17 chronology in Witzke's address book, and we will return again to this subject below. Whatever suspicions are justifiably raised, however, all of the entries for Witzke in the summer 1916 are in the Pacific Northwest, not the East Coast. While the two-week gap in the chronology for the period covering Black Tom makes the chronology obviously inconclusive regarding Witzke's whereabouts at the critical time, the chronology by itself offers support only for a West Coast presence.

The geographic case against Witzke's involvement in Black Tom does not in any case rest on the chronology because three other documents, if genuine, placed Witzke in San Francisco on July 25, July 28, and August 2, 1916. These documents are discussed in the next sections.

July 25 Declaration

One document placing Witzke in San Francisco in late July 1916 is a July 25 declaration by Witzke of intention to become a US citizen.[93] The July 25 US citizenship declaration is significant to the extent that it shows that Witzke himself was in San Francisco to submit it. The authors tried unsuccessfully to determine whether personal presence was required at the time and place. Even assuming that appearance by the declarant was required, the declaration was not accompanied by a photograph. Therefore, it would have sufficed that an individual roughly matching the description in the declaration appear as a stand-in. The declaration describes Witzke as White, fair complexion, 5'6", 180 pounds, blonde hair, blue eyes. Others could have served as a stand-in.[94]

The American agent argued that the declaration was concocted as an alibi for Black Tom, noting that there is no basis to believe that Witzke wanted to become a US citizen and there is no evidence that Witzke followed up on the declaration. But US citizenship could have served Witzke as a cover for his espionage activities generally, without regard to Black Tom. The German agent argued before the Mixed Claims Commission that the declaration's authenticity was borne out by the circumstance that Witzke did not invoke it when allegations about Black Tom were made during his trial or during the subsequent years when he was interviewed in prison by, among others, Detective Tunney and Judge Fake. Nor did he mention this alibi when he prepared his 1927 declaration before the Mixed Claims Commission. Presumably, a carefully constructed alibi would have been the first resort of Witzke and of the German agent to prove his innocence. Yet, capture, imprisonment and a death sentence might cause anyone to overlook facts of his prior life, and the German agent's explanation for not raising the citizenship declaration until late in the game was in fact that Witzke remembered it only later, after he inspected his papers.[95] The late invocation of the declaration therefore does not add to the inquiry.

Even if Witzke himself filed the July 25 declaration on that date, it would still have been possible for him to be in New York on July 29, but the timing would have been such that he would have arrived in New York only as of 9:40 a.m. on July 29, just fifteen hours in advance of the explosion.[96] The American agent's argument was that "the preparations were of course made in advance, probably after months of planning and investigating in New York."[97] This is likely true, as there is substantial evidence that Hinsch was in New

York during the days preceding the sabotage.[98] But, unless one posits that the July 29-30 dates were not fixed and that the Germans were flexible enough to carry out the sabotage at such time as all participants were assembled, it is implausible that the German operatives would have cut it so close, arranging for an alibi that brought Witzke to New York just hours before the sabotage that he was supposed to do himself. A plan of that nature would have meant that the Germans were counting on there being no train delays and no need for Witzke to survey the site or the river. The effort to explain away the July 25 citizenship declaration by imagining a last minute trans-continental train ride is therefore unconvincing. More convincing is the objection that, as the declaration lacked a photograph, it would have been easy for someone other than Witzke to submit it.[99]

In any case, Witzke's July 25 citizenship declaration, while inconclusive standing alone, weighs in favor of a finding that he was in San Francisco in late July 1916.[100]

Correspondence

Two more documents placing Witzke in San Francisco are a postcard from Witzke to his parents postmarked July 28, and signed "Lothar," and a letter from Witzke to his parents dated August 2, also signed "Lothar," together with an envelope stamped "San Francisco, August 2, 1916."[101] The question to consider is whether these two items of correspondence were mailed by Witzke on the given dates or created just to serve an alibi, whether mailed by someone else or fabricated.

We have reviewed all of the extensive correspondence between Witzke and his family from 1913 onwards, and we are convinced by the content that the correspondence is, overall, genuine. To conclude otherwise would be to posit a breathtaking fabrication by Germany, reconstructing intimate family correspondence, together with backdated envelopes and postcards, spanning years. It does not, however, necessarily follow that the few critical items of correspondence from the last week of July 1916 are authentic; these may have been fabricated even absent a vast conspiracy to create fraudulent evidence. Moreover, even if genuine, someone other than Witzke could have mailed them on July 25 and August 2 from San Francisco.[102] German secret agents in the United States were smart enough to employ a classic alibi technique of this kind. And it would have cost them little effort. Finally, even though this alibi was not a sure thing (for the reasons set out in the next paragraph), some alibi was better than none and it is unclear what better alibi was available to Witzke.

There is all the same substantial reason to doubt that the letter and post-card from San Francisco in late July 1916 were mailed by someone else or fabricated to serve an alibi. If Jahnke and Witzke in July 1916 wanted to create an alibi by placing themselves in San Francisco rather than in New York, it is implausible that they would do so by means of a postcard and a letter not just dated and stamped that week but also *actually mailed to Germany*. If they were worried about being caught, their concern could only have been that they might be found by the Americans and prosecuted then and there. If so, they would have needed then and there the evidence to support an alibi. They would not likely have sent their evidence to Germany during the war, notwithstanding that the wartime correspondence between Witzke and his family did get through with some regularity. Hence there is no good argument that the correspondence of late July that placed Witzke in San Francisco was mailed by someone else or fabricated to establish an alibi.

JAHNKE'S WHEREABOUTS

A parallel debate was had before the Mixed Claims Commission about Jahnke's whereabouts the week of Black Tom. Most of the testimony, as we have seen, places Witzke with Jahnke. Were the evidence to show that Jahnke was, as he claimed, in San Francisco that week, any conclusion as to Witzke's role would be cast in doubt.

Germany argued before the MCC that the evidence proved that Jahnke was in the Bay Area throughout the summer of 1916. Jahnke so testified,[103] and the German agent submitted records from the Morse Detective and Patrol Service that showed, or purported to show, that Jahnke was at work in the Bay Area throughout the summer of 1916 and, in particular, was guarding the Anglo-London-Paris National Bank in San Francisco on July 29–30, 1916.[104] The American agent contested this evidence, arguing that the time records may have been falsified to serve as an alibi.[105] There followed a battle of affidavits as to whether anyone in 1929 could recall having seen Jahnke in that Bank on those days in 1916.[106] It is no surprise that evidence as to Jahnke is wanting. He was a master secret agent.

One historian is certain that Jahnke was in New York, not in San Francisco, at the time of Black Tom:

> The day after the explosion, Jahnke and Witzke rushed back to San Francisco. Jahnke went to some effort to conceal his brief absence from San Francisco; evidence later submitted to the German-American Mixed Claims Commission (MCC) included a time sheet for the Morse Agency

showing Jahnke had worked on the night of 28 July, thus making it impossible for him to have been in New Jersey at the time of the explosion. However, other testimony revealed that someone else had worked for Jahnke on the night in question. In addition, more than 20 witnesses clearly identified Jahnke in the New York area on the night of 29 July.[107]

The reader's attention may have been caught by the assertion in the last sentence in the quoted passage that more than twenty witnesses testified reliably that they saw Jahnke in theNew York area on the night of July 29, 1916. Were that so, that would be decisive, demonstrating that Jahnke lied about his whereabouts at the time of the Black Tom sabotage and that Witzke also lied that he saw Jahnke in San Francisco at the time. But the sources cited by this historian for his assertion include no eyewitness testimony. The evidence as to Jahnke's whereabouts offers no support for Jahnke's presence in the New York area in late July 1916. Nor does it prove the contrary.

In summary, though there are questions about the reliability of the documents placing Witzke in San Francisco or elsewhere in the Pacific Northwest in late July 1916, the documents overall stand up to scrutiny. In any case, the imperfect nature of the West Coast evidence is not evidence of an East Coast presence. No document from the summer of 2016 places Witzke on the East Coast.

Even if, therefore, one accepts that it is probable that Witzke said what Altendorf and the others swore that he said about his responsibility for Black Tom, one must seek to reconcile those statements with the evidence placing Witzke on the West Coast in late July 1916, nowhere near Black Tom. That reconciliation will come later in this chapter.

THE JAHNKE CABLE

The Jahnke-related evidence as to Black Tom goes beyond the issue of his whereabouts in July 1916. While the geographic evidence would be dispositive were one to find it conclusive as to Jahnke's presence in San Francisco in July 1916, we find it inconclusive. However, there is additional evidence that weighs against Jahnke's role at Black Tom.

A document preserved at the British National Archives at Kew Gardens appears to be a 1918 summary, prepared by the British Intelligence Department, Naval Staff, of an intercepted cable from Jahnke to Berlin in 1917, arguing why he (Jahnke) was more suitable than Frederick Hinsch to run Germany's Mexico operations. In the cable, as summarized, Jahnke claims that he had "destroyed the Japanese SS *Shin-no Karu*, the American vessels *J. A. Moffett*, and *O. M. Clark*, and the British SS *Margaret*; also, the Dupont works at Tacoma. Jahnke further states that he reports movements of American troops, that he is causing strikes and mutinies; also, that an American attack on Tampico is impending and Mexico has offered Clipperton Island to Japan, and finally recommends submarine attacks on American coast from Mexican base."[108]

What is *un*mentioned in this list of exploits is what matters. In a context in which Jahnke had every motivation to cite Black Tom, had he been responsible in any way for that sabotage, Black Tom went unmentioned. Unlike the rest of the Jahnke-related evidence that we have, the cable comes from Jahnke himself (summarized by the British anyway). This document, even though it is a report rather than the original, weighs materially against the conclusion that Jahnke was involved.

The October 1917 cable takes on still more significance in light of a document that recounts an explosive exchange between Jahnke and Hinsch that took place in Mexico City in 1917, likely some time before the cable was sent, regarding credit for Black Tom.

The document, preserved in the Bundesarchiv in Berlin among other MCC papers and internal correspondence exchanged among the German representatives, seems to be a verbatim summary (in German) of portions of an English-language affidavit signed in 1938 by a former German operative in Mexico, Frederick Hadler, who was then cooperating with the Americans and who may have been a double agent in 1917.[109] The document tells of a meeting among German operatives in Mexico City in 1917. The relevant portion is (emphasis added):

> Dilger was an energetic man and had wide authority to raise money to finance the work that he was doing. . . . Captain Hinsch was in the Dilger group of agents. . . . Another man that came from the United States (San Francisco) was Kurt Jahnke. Jahnke apparently carried on some activities of his own, but he had very little connection with Hinsch and the group with which I was working, although he was financed by von Eckhardt. Some time after his arrival *it was reported by Anton Dilger to Hinsch that Jahnke had told Minister von Eckhardt that he, Jahnke, had caused the Black Tom and other fires and explosions in the United States. Hinsch then became very indignant and shouted that he himself had brought about the*

Black Tom explosion. Prior to this Hinsch had been very close-mouthed about his activities in the United States but after this incident Hinsch no longer hesitated to speak openly about the house about those things. On one occasion Jahnke came to the house on Calle Chihuahua and *Hinsch accused him of making false claims, and there was a terrific dispute.* I left the room in the course of the dispute as it became so heated I did not think it discreet for me to remain. Hermann and Anton Dilger, however, remained in the room. Finally, Hinsch, Herrmann and Dilger determined to make a report to the General Staff.[110]

The date of the meeting is not said, but it appears from the narrative of events given in the affidavit to have been in the summer of 1917 or shortly thereafter.

As seen here, there is ample evidence that Hinsch was directly responsible for overseeing the Black Tom sabotage. The account of the summer confrontation in combination with the October 1917 cable tells us that, while Jahnke asserted responsibility for Black Tom, once he was confronted by Hinsch on the subject, Jahnke stopped taking credit.

THE TWO-WEEK GAP IN WITZKE'S HANDWRITTEN CHRONOLOGY OF HIS SUMMER 1916—REVISITED

Had Witzke been trying to create an alibi for Black Tom, the chronology in his address book was his opportunity to do so, and he did not try to do so. It would have been so easy to write that he was in San Francisco (or anywhere other than near New York) during late July and early August 1916, but instead his chronology leaves those two weeks unaccounted for.

It is difficult to posit an explanation for the omission of those two weeks if one assumes that Witzke was responsible for Black Tom and wanted to conceal this. An omission of the two weeks from the chronology hardly would have sufficed in this hypothesis.

This conclusion is strengthened if one assumes, as the evidence suggests, that the chronology was created separately from the rest of the address book, and *a fortiori* if it was created later than the rest. Under this hypothesis, Witzke had time to reflect on the purpose of the chronology, and yet inexplicably chose to say nothing about late July 1916.

There are several unanswered questions relating to the chronology (who wrote it and why and when, and why there was a two-week gap in mid-summer 1916), but none of these uncertainties amounts to evidence of a Witzke role at Black Tom. Germany's resistance to production of the address book, even if unjustifiable, may have had nothing to do with Black Tom. Germany and Witzke may have been concerned that the address book would lead the Americans to other acts that violated US neutrality.

EVIDENCE THAT THE GERMAN MCC REPRESENTATIVES BELIEVED WITZKE DIDN'T DO IT

The correspondence exchanged internally among German representatives before the Mixed Claims Commission suggests on balance an expectation that truthful evidence from Witzke would help Germany.

An example of such correspondence (quoted above in *Weimar, Abroad Again, Third Reich*) is an April 1929 complaint by a German representative about Witzke's exaggerated self-importance, the writer concluding that Witzke must be placated because, "in his anger, he would probably make up the biggest lies and cause us immeasurable damage."[111] Such comment, made in a letter to another German representative, indicates a belief that truth from Witzke would serve Germany's defense.

Another example is a letter to Witzke in April 1925 in which the German agent made suggestions for the wording of Witzke's affidavit and then added: "Your statements, if you want to make them, of course must be absolutely true, so you can swear to them at any time."[112]

Another example is a July 14, 1930 telegram about a search by Witzke for documents held by him or his family. The German representative reports that Witzke told him that he and Jahnke bought train tickets for a trip on September 26, 1916, from San Francisco to New York and that they may have used their real names and this might be found in the train company's records. This led the German representative to ask the German consulate to look for train records for July 1916 in order to demonstrate that there was no record of Witzke or Jahnke traveling to New York in July. The German representative evidently believed that Witzke and Jahnke were not in New York in July 1916.[113]

There is also correspondence dated July 14, 1930, in which a German representative reports that Witzke commented that it took 4.5 days to get by train from San Francisco to New York, and that hence the American argument that Witzke could have departed San Francisco on July 25 and arrived in New York on July 30 could be correct. There is no defensiveness in this; Witzke's reported comment about the time needed to go by train from San Francisco to New York in no way intimates that this was in fact what he did in late July 1916. That same month (July 1930), Witzke wrote to the German agent that he had turned over all the correspondence found in his family house, and added: "I am thus squeezed out like a lemon. Now nothing is left."[114]

Against the above, there is a letter from German representative de Haas on August 4, 1930, circulating an affidavit by Witzke regarding correspondence with his family, and adding the comment: "the American side must not be given time to verify the authenticity of the claims made and the documents provided in the affidavit."

It is possible that Germany's representatives did not know the truth, or did not want to know the truth. But the tone and content of most of this correspondence indicate a sincere belief by the German representatives, and by Witzke himself, that Witzke was not responsible for Black Tom or Kingsland.

NO MENTION OF BLACK TOM IN THE PARDON RECORD

The German agent argued to the Mixed Claims Commission that there was important circumstantial evidence that the American authorities themselves did not credit the testimony of those who said that they had heard Witzke admit to Black Tom. Had the Americans credited such reports, the German agent argued, the United States would have acted to prosecute Witzke, and to pursue Germany, as of 1918 for the sabotage of Black Tom. Instead, the US did nothing with the information that it had as of 1918: it did not add sabotage to the espionage charges against Witzke before the military tribunal; and the US then proceeded to pardon Witzke without any discussion of Witzke's supposed responsibility for one of the greatest acts of sabotage in US history.

That there was no prosecution of Witzke in the US for Black Tom is of little consequence. The prosecutor before the Military Tribunal had physical evidence (the coded cipher) to corroborate the testimony about espionage, and none regarding sabotage; this made it much easier to prosecute Witzke only for espionage. Additionally, the prosecution was West Coast-based; sabotage on the East Coast was outside their jurisdiction.

But the pardon story cannot readily be explained away. It is curious at the least that no written comment was made to presidents Wilson or Coolidge that the man whose sentence was reduced and who was then pardoned was believed to be responsible for an act of sabotage that killed several, destroyed millions of dollars in munitions, blew out the windows of downtown Manhattan and damaged the Statue of Liberty. There is, though, a possible explanation: the evidence is that the Americans did not focus on Black Tom until later, when the Mixed Claims Commission proceedings were under way, and it was only then that the view became widespread among Americans that Witzke was responsible for Black Tom. The silence about Black Tom in the pardon history therefore weighs only immaterially against Witzke's responsibility for Black Tom.

A HISTORY OF BOASTING

Witzke was on occasion a false boaster. It is therefore possible that he told Altendorf what Altendorf reported, but that what he told Altendorf was untrue.

The prime example of a false boast by Witzke concerned the *USS Minnesota*. Altendorf said that Witzke told him that he was responsible for the supposed sabotage of the *USS Minnesota*. Altendorf could not have invented this detail because he could not have known about the *Minnesota*. He could have heard about it only in Mexico from a German operative, and there is no reason to doubt that, just as Altendorf swore, he heard about it from Witzke.

As explained in chapter 11, there was no known explosion on the *USS Minnesota* and Witzke could not have been responsible for the explosion on the *SS Minnesota*. Witzke thus was a man who on at least one occasion took credit for an alleged act of sabotage that he did not do (and that, as discussed in chapter 11 was not even an act of sabotage).

The *Dresden* story is an instance in which Witzke used his knowledge of a real incident to invent a false claim that he was there. Witzke evidently took what he learned about the *Dresden* while at the German hospital in Valparaiso to shape his later claim that he himself had been injured while serving on the *Dresden*. We have established that this was untrue.

It seems not to have occurred to Altendorf that Witzke's boasts about his exploits might have been false. This is curious because Altendorf repeatedly stressed that the man had a penchant for boasting. In an article in the *Chicago Tribune*, Altendorf described how easily Witzke could be cajoled into boasting:

> [On or about Jan. 14, 1918, I] returned to Jahnke's house in good time for supper. At the table were Jahnke, Waberski, Kettenbach, Gaebel and myself. When an opening presented itself, I started fishing for information, baiting the hook with fulsome flattery for Waberski. Thus encouraged, he launched into a boastful account of his achievements as a German secret agent in the United States for all of which he had been rewarded by his grateful Kaiser with the Order of the Black Eagle with two bars. He taunted Jahnke with the fact that he had received no decorations.
>
> *Waberski boasted* that with Jahnke he had caused the Black Tom explosion in New York harbor in July 1916, which caused a loss of many millions of dollars and several lives; that he had found employment as a sailor and had blown up a ship carrying munitions; that he had ruined the boilers of the transport Minnesota; that as a lumberjack in Oregon he had started a disastrous forest fire, and other crimes.[115]

Once launched, Witzke reportedly could not stop himself, even if this meant that he painted himself as a psychopathic murderer:

> He wound up by turning to me and saying: "I have laid many people in the cemetery. If you are not straightforward with me, I will put you there."
>
> At the time I thought this an idle boast. Later he told me privately and in all seriousness that he had murdered a number of persons with his own hand. One of these was a woman with whom he lived a short time in New York City while operating in that vicinity; another was a woman in Mexico City.[116]

In another newspaper article in 1919, Altendorf had Witzke boasting again:

> *Wabirski boasted* to me that he had blown up several munitions plants and stores of explosives, including the Black Tom explosion in New York, resulting in the death of a number of persons, including women and children; blew up some ships and caused disastrous fires in the forests of the Pacific northwest. He also boasted of a number of individual murders, for all of which services he had been decorated by Germany with the Black Eagle of the second grade with two bars. [117]

When boasting is false, the falsity may be mere embellishment or exaggeration, or it may be entirely made-up. Witzke's statement that he committed sabotage on the *Minnesota* fits cleanly within the category of entirely false boasting. Witzke was not in or near the US when the *Minnesota* was damaged. His false boast about the *Minnesota* would be an especially close cousin to a false boast about Black Tom, if the latter was false.

The context may explain boasting even by an agent otherwise cautious. The setting was gatherings of German agents in Mexico, where they felt safe and free to brag about exploits from their time in the US. Witzke in Mexico in 1917 was just twenty-two years old. He was far from home and there was a war far away that he wanted to be part of, and this may have allowed him to be loose-lipped or inventive in a way that he would not have been elsewhere.

Why would Witzke have falsely boasted about Black Tom if he was not even there? Because it made him appear more heroic. He also may have thought that word of an exploit of this scale would secure Altendorf's allegiance on their trip north to the US border.

Witzke may not have been the only German operative in the Americas prone to false boasting. The Mixed Claims Commission in its 1930 decision declined to rely on the evidence of alleged admissions by the German under-cover agents *inter alia* because it considered that the German operatives repeat-edly exaggerated their accomplishments: "up to the entry of the US into the war there were in the US certain German agents who were, or at least pretended to be, active in sabotage work. But we are also convinced that . . . their preten-sions in such reports as they may have made and in their talk with each other were for the most part gross exaggerations of their actual accomplishments.[118]

UNRELIABLE TESTIMONY

In light of Witzke's history of boasting, it is not decisive whether Altendorf and others were being truthful when they said that Witzke told them that he did it. Even if he did say so, he may have been falsely boasting.

We have concluded, as explained earlier in this chapter, that the Altendorf debriefings of February 1918 are credible evidence that Witzke told Altendorf that he was responsible for Black Tom. The statements of Shores and Haslam also weigh slightly in favor of the conclusion that Witzke told them that he did it. But Altendorf's testimony is anything but airtight. There is much more to say about his credibility, and none of it is favorable, as will be set out here. As to the several other witnesses (other than Shores and Haslam) who swore that Witzke told them he was responsible for Black Tom, their testimony amounts to nothing, as will also be explained.

Altendorf Revisited

Written Narrative of Mexico Trip

Altendorf prepared in late January and February 1918 an eleven-page nar-rative of his January 1918 trip to Mexico.[119] The narrative is detailed and persuasive. The narrative was done in January and/or February 1918, and it reads as a fresh recollection, rather than as an invented story.

Altendorf's Mexico trip narrative covers the same time period and same events as Altendorf's February 1918 briefings to Butcher in which Altendorf recounted the admissions supposedly made by Witzke and Jahnke about their responsibility for Black Tom (and Kingsland). The trip narrative reports sev-eral statements by Witzke, including that he had killed many and would not hesitate to kill Altendorf if Witzke came to suspect Altendorf of treachery.

But the narrative includes nothing about Black Tom (or Kingsland).

The focus of the Mexico trip narrative is Altendorf's own doings, not statements by Witzke. It may be that Witzke's boasts or admissions about Black Tom came to Altendorf's mind only in the context of the Butcher briefings that concerned Witzke. But the omission in Altendorf's Mexico trip narrative of a mention of Witzke's statements about Black Tom casts doubt on the credibility of Altendorf's assertions to Butcher that Witzke made statements to Altendorf about Black Tom.

Butcher Debriefings

In his Butcher debriefings in February 1918, Altendorf implicated an innocent man, Gustav Wild, as an accomplice of Witzke in the July 9, 1917 bombing of the Mare Island Naval Station near San Francisco.[120] It is implausible that Witzke would have disclosed to Altendorf the name of an accomplice otherwise unknown to Altendorf. Much more likely is that Altendorf, who had searched through Witzke's belongings with Butcher after Butcher brought them back across the border from the Mexican side of Nogales, saw the Wild entry in Witzke's notebook or heard Butcher and Lipscomb discuss it, and then decided to claim that Witzke had told him that Wild was his accomplice in the Mare Island plot.

Altendorf was ready from the start to invent admissions if he considered that the inventions would add to Altendorf's stature as a source.

August 1918 Trial Testimony

Six months after the statements made in February 1918 immediately following Witzke's capture, Witzke's espionage trial was held, and Altendorf was a key Government witness.

Altendorf had said in February 1918, as explained above, that the conversation during which Witzke took responsibility for Black Tom and other acts of sabotage occurred in *January 1918* during their trip north from Mexico City to the US border. At the military trial, Altendorf testified that the incriminating conversation occurred in *August 1917* in Mexico City at a dinner with Jahnke and Witzke (both of whom he had met for the first time only a few hours before):

Q. From the conversation with Waberski at this dinner, did you learn who he was?

A. Yes, sir, in talking there he talked about where *they were laying mines off an island in New Jersey, and how a wave came up and almost washed away Yahnke, and that Waberski helped to save Yahnke.*

Q. What were they doing, if you know, in New Jersey?

A. They were also *preparing for the big explosion that happened* in New Jersey.

Q. In whose interest was this explosion caused?

A. This was in the interest of Yanke and Waberski, by direct orders from the German Ambassador, Von Bernstorff.[121]

To accept that this conversation occurred as recounted, within hours of Altendorf and Witzke meeting one another for the first time, one must accept that Witzke was a reckless fool, and acted that way with Jahnke present. The timing is simply implausible. Jahnke made this point during his written testimony before the MCC in 1927:

> No such conversation took place in my presence, on the day when we met, nor at any other time. That in Mexico, where we actually felt ourselves continually watched and spied upon by the agents of the countries at war with us, a man, who theretofore had been an entire stranger to us, should have been given by us, on the very first day our meeting him, information on strictly confidential matters, such as the activities of the Secret Service, is, in itself, I think so highly improbable that I need add no further explanations to my denial.[122]

Altendorf also included in his trial testimony quoted above the assertion that he was told that Black Tom was done "by direct orders from the German Ambassador, Von Bernstorff." Even if we accept that Witzke made at some time in some place some reference about Black Tom to Altendorf, it is implausible that he would have added that it was done by direct order from the German Ambassador because, first, it is doubtful that the German ambassador, von Bernstorff, would have been aware in advance of Black Tom as a target, let alone would have given the go-ahead,[123] and this means that Witzke was likely inventing this, if he said it, and second, because Witzke would have had no cause to specify the authorization; he was working with Jahnke and that amply sufficed as authorization. The add-on reference by Altendorf to von Bernstorff appears to have been an invention designed to give the Americans what Altendorf thought they needed for a conviction: testimonial evidence that Witzke was acting on behalf of Germany.

Also damning to the credibility of Altendorf's trial testimony is what he said about the denominations of the bills that he supposedly saw Jahnke hand to Witzke:

Q. Did he [Jahnke] give him [Witzke] anything else?

A. Yes, sir, $1000 American paper, Gold money, and 800 pesos was in Mexican Gold money.

Q. This money, this $1000 was in Gold certificates?

A. Yes, sir; there were $500 in twenties, and the rest was in tens. . . .

Q. Did he tell Waberski where to get more money?

A. Yes, sir, he had on his card to every German consul on the border that he could go to them and get money, on his identification card; it was a recommendation to all German consuls, from German Ambassador Herr Von Echhardt.[124]

This testimony is not believable because Altendorf could not have known just from observation how much money Jahnke gave to Witzke, much less the precise denominations of the paper currency and the amounts of each. Altendorf did not mention the currency or denominations in any of his Butcher debriefings. It is likely that Altendorf learned from Butcher or Lipscomb the sums that Witzke was carrying when he was captured (approximately $1,000), and then fabricated a story about seeing the amounts and denominations that Witzke was given in Mexico City based on what Altendorf was told that Witzke had on his person in Nogales.[125]

Fake Interview (1920)

The Kingsland lawyer, Guy Fake, first interviewed Witzke at Fort Sam Houston in January 1920, and got nothing.[126] Fake then met with Altendorf on May 27, 1920, at Fake's offices in New Jersey.[127] Fake's contemporaneous report of that conversation says that, with respect to Black Tom, Altendorf said, "*Kurowski [elsewhere identified as Fiodor Wozniak, the prime suspect at Kingsland]*[128] *told me [Altendorf] that he was out in a boat with Kurt Jahnke in Jersey on some river laying wires to destroy munitions.*"[129] Fake also reported that Altendorf, conveniently, told him that Wozniak [aka Kurowski] told Altendorf that "Yancke [Jahnke] and Waberski [Witzke] had two men employed inside the [Kingsland] plant and when the explosion happened Yancke and Waberski ran away and went to San Francisco."[130]

There is nothing to corroborate Witzke's supposed responsibility for organizing the Kingsland explosion. There is also nothing to corroborate Wozniak's supposed role at Black Tom. Wozniak was the Kingsland guy, not the Black Tom guy. Altendorf either had gotten confused by the questions (a generous interpretation) or was giving the lawyer for Kingsland what the lawyer hoped to hear, even if that meant fabrication.

Kingsland aside, Altendorf's statement to Fake about what he heard about Black Tom is that Jahnke's accomplice on the boat was not Witzke but Kurowski (Wozniak). All other reports have Witzke on the boat with Jahnke.

Within a week of Fake's report of his May 24, 1920 conversation with Altendorf, Altendorf signed an affidavit on June 4, 1920.[131] This affidavit repeated his statements to Fake about Witzke's boasts about his responsibility for organizing the Kingsland sabotage. As to Black Tom, the affidavit spoke generally of Witzke's boasts of responsibility, with no mention of any boat; the affidavit also referenced the statement by Kurowski (Wozniak) that he and Jahnke did "some destruction work for the German Government near New York," but without any detail of a boat ride.

The conclusion must be that by 1920 Altendorf was desperately trying to sell his services, and he was ready to do so without regard to truth-telling. Altendorf's mendacity as of 1920 undermines his trustworthiness in 1918.

Congressional Testimony (1920)

On January 22, 1920, Altendorf testified under oath before the US Senate Committee on Foreign Relations. Under oath, Altendorf twice swore that he was a US citizen. Yet, he was not; he became a citizen in 1924.[132]

The US Commissioner who presided over the Mixed Claims Commission weighed these lies against the above-mentioned commendations of Altendorf submitted by the American agent. A report prepared by Kibby Munson for the Commissioner in 1930 observed, "any effect this character evidence might have is seriously impaired by the untrue statements made under oath by Altendorf regarding his race, education and citizenship without apparent reason in the record for making these untrue statements."[133] The Commission declined to rely on Altendorf in any way, and this refusal was a central reason why the United States lost before the Mixed Claims Commission for some fifteen years before proof of the Herrmann Message's authenticity finally turned the case against Germany in 1939. For the Commission, Altendorf was "the chief liar" among a long list of lying witnesses.[134]

The more statements that Altendorf made, the more inconsistencies there were. As well summarized by the German agent in a brief to the Mixed Claims Commission:

> The incident of the boat was told in four different ways. According to the first version, both Witzke and Jahnke were nearly swamped and almost drowned by the waves *after blowing up barges and wrecking piers*; according

to the second version, *Jahnke* was almost washed away by a wave when *he and* Witzke were laying mines off an island in New Jersey, and Witzke saved him; according to the third version, given in *Altendorf's* newspaper articles, Jahnke fell out of the boat *while reconnoitering Black Tom Island* in New York Harbor in preparation for the great explosion there on July 29, 1916; and, according to the fourth version, in the preliminary statement given to Mr. Fake, Altendorf placed an altogether different individual, *Karowski*, the man who, he alleged, caused the fire at the Kingsland plant, in the boat "laying wire on some river near New Jersey to destroy munitions."[135]

The fabrications that bothered the Commission (e.g., about his own biography) together with others that we have identified (e.g., about Gustav Wild and about the currency denominations) and the inconsistencies in his statements could suffice for the reader to conclude that Altendorf had no credibility.

While, as explained, we depart from the view taken by the Mixed Claims Commission and we accept that, just as Altendorf said, Witzke likely told Altendorf that he and Jahnke together took action regarding Black Tom, the facts set out in this section show why the call is a close one. In any case, our conclusion about Altendorf goes only as far as accepting that Witzke told him in essence what Altendorf reported. Whether this is what likely happened in New York Harbor on July 29–30, 1916, is another matter.

Other Witnesses for the US

The US presented written testimony by several other witnesses about Witzke's responsibility for Black Tom. These witnesses fall into three groups: (i) another double agent, Gleaves; (ii) another prison guard responsible for watching over Witzke, Ingram; and (iii) residents of Nogales, Mexico, at the time of Witzke's January 1918 arrival there, Sholars and Colton.

Gleaves

William Gleaves was a British intelligence agent involved in the events that led to Witzke's arrest in Nogales, Arizona, in February 2018. While pretending to Witzke to be serving the German cause, Gleaves was working for the British and collaborating with US intelligence. Gleaves was an ideal double agent in that he was Black, and the Germans believed that a Black person could easily be convinced to act against the United States.

Gleaves testified live before the military tribunal in August 1918 that was trying Witzke for espionage. His testimony made no mention of statements supposedly made by Witzke in Mexico City as to his previous activities in the United States under the direction of the German authorities. Yet, as a witness for the prosecution, such admissions would have had bearing on the case. According to Gleaves' later testimony before the Mixed Claims Commission, Witzke allegedly said that he had blown up ammunition plants in the US at the direction of German authorities, admissions that would have identified Witzke as a German agent, the very purpose of the prosecution. Instead, Gleaves' testimony about Witzke's activities mentioned nothing other than planning for insurrection among Black US soldiers.[136]

By contrast, Gleaves testified as follows in an affidavit submitted in 1927 by the American agent to the Mixed Claims Commission:

> I was first introduced to Lothar Witzke by the German Consul in Mexico. . . . Witzke . . . told me that he, for a long time had been doing business for the Germans in the United States in blowing up properties that were furnishing supplies to the Allies and he frequently discussed this with me *in numerous conferences that we had after that time in Mexico City*. I met with him and some of the other German operators *from time to time in different hotels in Mexico City*. . . . *He talked with me and with other people in my presence a great many times* about munition properties that he had blown up in New Jersey. . . . The subject of his sabotage work in the United States was a topic of common conversation among us, and I understood from what he said and what the other German officials and operators told me that he had been employed by the Germans for such work for a long time in the United States and that he had taken part in several destructions.[137]

Gleaves' testimony before the MCC is not credible.

First, as presented by Gleaves' testimony, Witzke was an exceedingly foolish and reckless boaster, exposing himself and his co-saboteurs to risk for the sake of his vanity. As Gleaves was not German, any explanation that Witzke may have been loose-lipped among fellow Germans or German speakers (such as Altendorf) would not apply. According to Gleaves, Witzke boasted openly about his sabotage exploits in the United States to a wide circle that included a newcomer. Such testimony makes Witzke out to be a fool, and makes it inexplicable that Jahnke would ever have trusted him.

Second, it is scarcely credible that Gleaves would not have mentioned Witzke's alleged boasts when Gleaves testified before the military tribunal. Rather, it is much more likely that Gleaves gave the American agent what the agent wanted several years later, a story that neatly fit the American agent's theory of the sabotage case. Forced, as we are, to judge which version might be true and which false, we readily select the version that Gleaves presented in person and under oath, unmediated by a lawyer drafting words for him.

In addition, Gleaves' trial testimony was roughly contemporaneous with the events discussed, and his affidavit was done nine years later.

Third, Gleaves' live testimony before the military tribunal shows that the story that he gave nine years later to the Mixed Claims Commission could not have happened. That story, to recall, was that Witzke boasted about Black Tom in Gleaves' presence *numerous times in Mexico City*. Yet Gleaves testified before the military tribunal that he met Witzke for the first time at 10:00 p.m. on January 15, 1918, that the meeting held that night was the only one between Witzke and Gleaves in Mexico City, and that Gleaves departed for Nogales the next morning.[138] As the affidavit came nine years after his trial testimony, and as the affidavit was written by the American agent, we have no hesitation, faced with this contradiction, to prefer Gleaves' trial testimony.

Gleaves was, thus, ready in 1927 to give the American agent what it wanted, even if that meant departing from the truth. The American agent was careless not to check the 1927 affidavit against Gleaves' August 1918 testimony. It does not follow that nothing that Gleaves said should be trusted. But this is of no consequence to our inquiry because Gleaves said nothing in August 1918 relevant to Black Tom. Accordingly, Gleaves' testimony, both oral and written, adds nothing credible to the evidence about Witzke and Black Tom.

Ingram

John Ingram was a prison guard at Fort Leavenworth. He signed in 1929 an affidavit submitted by the American agent to the Mixed Claims Commission, saying that Witzke told him he had "pulled a job in New Jersey" that "had to do with destruction of some property," and had handled "plenty of 'soup,'" which meant "high-explosives."[139] As with the other testimony, one must question why Witzke would have said this to a prison guard, other than to boast against his self-interest at a time when he hoped for a pardon. One must also consider the context of after-the-fact canned testimony by other American witnesses. Similar considerations apply to an assessment of Ingram's testimony, though his recollection of the slang supposedly used by Witzke ("pulled a job" and "soup" for explosives) has the ring of authenticity.

Ingram's testimony on balance is of negligible weight in an assessment of Witzke's involvement in Black Tom.

Sholars

Oscar Sholars was the proprietor of the Root Beer Garden in Nogales, Mexico.[140] He saw Witzke shortly before his arrest. Sholars testified: "When Waberski [Witzke] came into my store he was recognized by several customers who told me that he was a well-known German agent who had been very successful in the United States in causing the destruction of some of the biggest ammunition plants there."[141]

Witzke's testimony was that no one other than Altendorf and Gleaves knew that he was a German agent, and that Sholars' testimony is not credible.[142]

Sholars' testimony suggests that Witzke had widely advertised not just his secret agent status but also his sabotage exploits, and had developed a notoriety akin to that of a local celebrity. Even if it had become known in Nogales that there was a ring of German secret agents circulating in town, and even if such knowledge was deemed safe, this is not the same as proclaiming responsibility for sabotage. It is difficult to reconcile this reckless extravagance with what we otherwise know of Witzke, including the trust that Jahnke placed in Witzke. An explanation may be that there was a broad ring of German operatives in Nogales, and Witzke may have believed that he was speaking only among friends, but this is bending over backwards in favor of crediting this testimony.

On balance, Sholars' testimony is not credible.

Colton

William Colton was a US resident of Nogales, Sonora, and was an acquaintance of Gleaves. Colton would later become the proprietor of Sholars' Root Beer Garden in Nogales.

A written declaration was submitted for Colton before the Mixed Claims Commission in 1927. His testimony was that he met Witzke a single time, in Nogales, and at that meeting "Witzke . . . explained to me that . . . he was . . . going to proceed into the United States to continue his work of blowing up properties. . . . When I asked him if he had much experience in that line he told me that he had blown up some of the biggest ammunition plants in the United States."[143]

Witzke's testimony was that he did not recollect Colton, and he denied having said anything to Colton about sabotage activities.

To credit Colton's testimony, we need to accept that Witzke met Colton, a Black US citizen, for the first time at the border and, although he intended to slip over the frontier the next day disguised as a Russian, he told Colton about his plan "to proceed into the United States to continue his work of blowing up properties there," and then added that he had already "blown up some of the biggest ammunition plants in the United States." This is doubtful, though a motivation could be imagined: Witzke perhaps felt the need to assure the confidence of his confederates by telling or boasting about his experience doing espionage and sabotage work.

Colton's 1927 testimony is not consistent with the testimony given by Gleaves before the Military Tribunal in August 1918. At the trial, Gleaves described his meetings with Witzke in Nogales, and they do not include a meeting with Colton and Witzke.

Colton's witness declaration has zero weight.

In summary, the testimony of the US witnesses before the Mixed Claims Commission appears largely contrived to help the US position and is not credible. The accumulation of canned testimony creates a momentum of disbelief, reducing the credibility even of those who might have told the truth.

THE MCC'S FINDINGS

The Mixed Claims Commission in its final decision of 1939 against Germany did not mention Witzke. The MCC had no need to identify which German operatives were responsible for the sabotage at Black Tom and Kingsland, as it was enough for the American case to show, as they did through the Hermann Message, that German agents were responsible. While the MCC set aside its rulings that Germany's responsibility was unproven, and condemned Germany for fraudulent testimony, the MCC did not expressly revisit, or hence overturn, its 1930 findings as to Witzke's role. Those findings were that Witzke and Jahnke were on the West Coast at the time of Black Tom and Kingsland. One cannot know whether the MCC would have set aside its findings as to Witzke, had it been necessary to do so.

The MCC also chose not to revisit its scathing rejection of Altendorf's crediibilty ("the chief liar who has appeared in the cases before us, a chief among competitors of no mean qualifications"). One must wonder whether the MCC had, at the end of the day, any regret about such disdain given the ultimate finding that Germany was the side that presented perjured testimony and fraudulent submissions. Even judging by the rulings made in 1930, the disdain for Altendorf is at tension with the MCC's finding that the admissions made were more or less as Altendorf had testified but were not dispositive because they were more likely false boasts.

Looking at the combination of what the MCC found about the Altendorf/Witzke evidence in 1930 and did not later revise, it is fair to infer that, for the

MCC, (i) Witzke made admissions about Black Tom, (ii) Witzke was likely on the West Coast at the time of Black Tom, and (iii) Witzke's admissions were, thus, likely false boasts.

SUMMARY

The case that Witzke did not do it rests on the following:

- The evidence places Witzke and Jahnke on the West Coast in July 1916. No reliable evidence places either of them anywhere near New York in July 1916.
- In a cable touting his exploits in the Americas, Jahnke in 1917 did not mention Black Tom. If Jahnke was uninvolved, the case that Witzke was involved diminishes materially.
- Witzke's chronology for 1916–1917 was an easy opportunity for Witzke to create an alibi as to his whereabouts in late July and early August 1916, but he instead left those weeks unaccounted for, suggesting that he considered that there was no need to create a record that put him on the West Coast at the time of Black Tom.
- Internal correspondence suggests that the German representatives before the Mixed Claims Commission wanted the truth to come out with respect to Witzke and Black Tom, because they believed that Witzke was not responsible for Black Tom.
- If the Americans believed that Witzke was responsible for Black Tom, they likely would have referenced this in the extensive correspondence regarding Witzke's pardon. But Witzke's connection to Black Tom went unmentioned.
- Witzke was a boaster and there is one significant instance of false boasting about a supposed act of sabotage that he could not have done and that was not even an act of sabotage (the damage to the SS *Minnesota*).
- Altendorf may have given credible debriefings in February 1918 about what Witzke told him, but Altendorf thereafter gave multiple conflicting accounts of the substance of Witzke's boasts about Black Tom, thereby undermining his credibility with regard to any one account. The supposedly corroborating testimony by other witnesses has close to zero weight.
- The MCC found and never revised its findings that Witzke was on the West Coast at the time of Black Tom and that any admissions that he made about Black Tom were false boasts.

Other Considerations
WITZKE FAMILY MEMORY

This book was conceived and written long after the death of Lothar Witzke, long after the deaths of his wife Lilli and son Lothar Jr., and also after the deaths of his daughter Helga and his son-in-law Hossein Moinian. Insofar as we have information from the Witzke family, our sources are the grandchildren, Helga's children. They never met their grandfather. Their information about their grandfather is derived from conversations with their parents, from time spent with Witzke's wife Lilli (their grandmother), from preserved family correspondence and photographs, and from time spent in the house in Volksdorf.

Until contacted by the authors, Witzke's grandchildren had never heard of Black Tom.

What are we to make of the absence of any family recollection, at least insofar as reported to the authors, of Witzke's responsibility for Black Tom (or Kingsland) or any other acts of sabotage in the United States?

One possible explanation is that the grandchildren are protective of their family legacy, and have concealed from the authors anything that might implicate their grandfather in crimes in America almost one hundred years ago. We believe that the grandchildren hid nothing from us. They in fact have come to suspect that Witzke *was* responsible for brazen acts of sabotage during World War I, and have the conviction that he was a spy to the time of his death. Moreover, as our chapters on Witzke's life after America attest, the grandchildren have been eager and forthcoming contributors to this biography.

Another possibility is that Helga and her husband (and her brother) were protective of the family legacy, and hid from their children the bad things that they knew about their grandfather. We cannot dismiss this possibility, but we find it unlikely based on what we know of the extensive conversations between Helga and her kids about her childhood and her parents, recollected conversations that have supplied some of the material for the chapters on Witzke's life in the 1930s, 1940s and 1950s. Helga shared much of an intimate nature with her daughter, Claudia, including about conflicts with her father; it is implausible that Helga withheld bad facts about her father's past in America.

Family secrecy set aside, then, what are we to make of there being no family memory of Witzke's involvement or non-involvement in sabotage in the United States in 1916–1917?

The most cautious conclusion would be that nothing is to be made of it. On this view, Witzke for whatever reason simply did not speak, at least to his daughter and son-in-law, of what he had done in America, and there is no implication to be derived one way or the other from such reticence.

And yet, if he did not do it, how tempting it must have been for Witzke, living in American-dominated West Germany in the 1950s, to say to his family, in substance: "the Yanks tried for 16 years to prove that I was responsible for Black Tom, but I wasn't."

Conversely, if Witzke *was* responsible for one or more acts of sabotage in America, would it not have been tempting for him, one evening over a drink or three with, for example, his son-in-law, to say: "Ah, if you knew of the things that I did in the Americas and how much I got away with. Sure, they got me for espionage for a few years, but there was so much more. Sixteen years in arbitration and they could never prove what I did on the Hudson River."

The most likely explanation for Witzke's silence about his past is that he, like his daughter, was someone who did not look back.[144] What mattered to each of them was action in the moment. On this view, the absence of Witzke family memory on the subject of Witzke's involvement in Black Tom or other acts of sabotage does not tip the balance either way about whether he did it.

WHAT ABOUT KINGSLAND?

Altendorf said that Witzke was responsible for both Black Tom and Kingsland. Witzke and Jahnke concededly spent several months in New York in late 1916 and therefore were in a position at least to organize the Kingsland sabotage. We set out in this section the evidence for Witzke's involvement in Kingsland, and assess its implications for Witzke in relation to Black Tom.

According to Altendorf, Witzke made multiple admissions as to Black Tom, but only two purportedly tied Witzke not just to Black Tom but also to Kingsland. The American agent did not even consistently claim before the MCC that Witzke was involved in Kingsland.[145] But for Gleaves, the other witnesses that the US agent submitted to corroborate Altendorf's testimony testified to what Witzke supposedly said only about Black Tom, not about Kingsland. Moreover, while Altendorf provided colorful detail about Witzke's reported admissions about Black Tom (two men in a rowboat on the Hudson River, swamped by a wave), there was a paucity of detail about Kingsland.[146]

A week after the Kingsland sabotage, the German agent Paul Hilken received a January 19, 1917, letter from a German agent named Carl Ahrendt. The postscript to the letter reads, "Yours of the 18th just received and I am delighted to learn that the von Hindenburg of Roland Park won another victory. I had a note from March who is still at McAlpin. Asked me to advise his brother that he is in urgent need of another set of glasses. He would like to see his brother as soon as possible on this account."[147]

The evidence before the Mixed Claims Commission established that "Hindenburg of Roland Park" was a reference to Hilken, who lived in the Roland Park subdivision of Baltimore. The "victory" was a reference to the Kingsland operation. Herrmann's code name was "March," and the "glasses" he was requesting were the incendiary cigars.[148] The point, for our purposes, is: nothing about Witzke (or Jahnke).

As we have seen in an earlier chapter, the Mixed Claims Commission in its 1930 Decision was vehement and dismissive about the American evidence about Witzke and Jahnke in relation to Kingsland. The Commission found the US case on their link to Kingsland so weak that this weakness, in the Commission's view, undermined the US case as to Black Tom as well. "In the Kingsland Case, the . . . evidence relating to Witzke and Jahnke is mainly in the shape of alleged admissions by Witzke and is intermingled with his alleged admissions in connection with the Black Tom case. This evidence makes no impression whatever upon us with respect to the Kingsland case, but the fact that it does refer to the Kingsland fire as well as to the Black Tom fire tends to weaken the effect of the alleged admissions as to the Black Tom case. On the evidence we are satisfied that Witzke and Jahnke were not in the east at the time of the Kingsland fire, and eliminate them from further consideration in connection with Kingsland."[149]

Though the evidence is negligible that Witzke and Jahnke were at Kingsland in January 1917, it remains possible that they were involved in organizing the sabotage there. Witzke spent time in New Jersey during his autumn 1916 trip to New York City with Jahnke. On October 12 he sent to his mother a picture postcard, dated October 10, with a photo on it of the Buena Vista Hotel and Restaurant on the Hudson River in Edgewater, New Jersey, opposite 153rd Street. (The short text of the card is innocuous, wishing his mother a happy birthday.)[150] He also spent time during the same trip in the Chesapeake Bay area, as he reported in a letter to his parents dated January 5, 1917. Paul Hilken, the paymaster for the Kingsland sabotage, lived in the nearby Baltimore suburbs. Witzke may have visited Hilken during his trip to the Chesapeake Bay. But these tidbits of travel detail are just that. They do not begin to link Witzke to the Kingsland fire.

In summary, it is unlikely that Witzke was involved directly in the Kingsland sabotage. At most, he and Jahnke were involved in the planning in the months before January 1917. But the evidence for this is negligible and does not amount to a likelihood.

What does this imply about the evidence for Black Tom? If, as we find, Witzke was unlikely involved at Kingsland, this means either that Altendorf was inventing his stories or that Witzke was inventing for his own self-glory a connection to Kingsland. The MCC commissioners soundly judged that the unreliability of the evidence linking Witzke to Kingsland undermined the reliability of the evidence linking Witzke to Black Tom. Though we find that conclusion sound, we do not, as we need not, rest our assessment of the evidence respecting Black Tom on the evidence pertaining to Kingsland. A full exposition of the Kingsland story would be a distraction from Black Tom.

Conclusion

There is substantial evidence that he did it.

Altendorf's accounts in February 1918 are credible reports that Witzke told Altendorf that he was responsible for Black Tom. Altendorf would not have known about Black Tom, or that Black Tom was in New Jersey, without having been told by a German agent in Mexico in 1917 or early 1918. The details in Witzke's boasts about Black Tom—the pairing with Jahnke and the swamped rowboat—were unlikely to have been invented by Altendorf and likely had to come from Witzke. Witzke's statement to Butcher that the Americans know from Altendorf what Witzke said or did is a material validation of Altendorf's veracity. Altendorf had scant motivation to invent wholesale in February 1918 when he was a respected double agent working for the Americans. To dismiss his reports in their entirety, one would need to assign small value to *inter alia* Witzke's statement to Butcher that he expected that the Americans had gotten the truth from Altendorf, and to the commendations by US intelligence about the confirmed accuracy of Altendorf's reports overall. We do not believe that Altendorf fabricated the entirety.

The contents of Altendorf's February 1918 debriefings were partially corroborated by an independent source, Michael Kristoff, who told investigators in 1916–1917 that he was working with two unidentified Germans. No pairing of German agents other than Jahnke and Witzke has ever been identified.

The Altendorf and Kristoff reports find contextual validation from the German sabotage campaign in the Americas in 1916 and Witzke's role therein. In May 1916, Witzke, injured in the merchant marine, had made his way from Chile to California and reported to the German consulate there, volunteering for such service as the consulate might direct. He was in his mid-twenties, can-do and adventure-seeking. It was wartime, and Witzke wanted to serve his country. The setting was propitious for him to play a role in whatever activities, including sabotage, were being organized by his compatriots.

Witzke admitted to pursuing sabotage after the United States entered the War, and he also admitted to sabotage in Mexico. The man was not a small-time secret agent. When he was captured at the border, he was carrying in code a document that identified him as a secret agent employed by the Reich and entitled to assistance and protection and funding at any German consulate in Mexico. Witzke was a clever and effective operative, a militarist and loyal German, an individual who gained the trust of his superiors both as a young man in San Francisco in 1916, again in the *Abwehr* during World War II, and later when he became the chief executive of a paint company in Hamburg in the 1950s. Kurt Jahnke was an operative at a higher level. The two teamed up. As the Herrmann message shows, German secret agents in the US destroyed Black Tom.

The 1935 report of the agent Robert Pennewitz offers a narrative that plausibly ties together several strands of evidence, while avoiding key counters to some of that evidence. According to Pennewitz, Witzke was not at Black Tom itself, but was in New York supervising the three agents, including Kristoff, who detonated Black Tom. Pennewitz's version is consistent with Witzke arriving in New York just hours before Black Tom, as he would have needed himself to reconnoiter the site. His version also plausibly leaves Jahnke out of the picture, neutralizing the objection that Jahnke would not likely have crossed the continent to take part in a Hinsch-led operation and would not likely have been in a rowboat on the Hudson detonating a munitions dump.

Yet, there is still more evidence that Witzke did not do it.

The documentary evidence places both Witzke and Jahnke on the West Coast during July 1916. Three documents show that Witzke was probably in San Francisco in late July 1916: a July 25 declaration by Witzke of intention to become a US citizen submitted in San Francisco; a postcard from Witzke to his parents postmarked July 28, and signed "Lothar"; and a letter from Witzke to his parents dated August 2, also signed "Lothar," together with an envelope stamped "San Francisco, August 2, 1916." There was also his handwritten chronology that covers the summer of 1916; while it has a two-week gap in late July and early August, all its entries otherwise are made in the Pacific Northwest or in California. None of these documents presents an airtight case for Witzke's whereabouts, but they cumulatively place him on the West Coast in July 1916.

If Witzke did it, he would have done it with Jahnke, whether or not Jahnke himself was in New York for the event, and the evidence as to Jahnke suggests that Jahnke was not responsible, directly or indirectly, for Black Tom: the cable that Jahnke wrote from Mexico in 1917 lists his exploits against the Americans, and Black Tom is not one of them.

Witzke could have included in his handwritten chronology an entry for late July and early August 1916 placing him on the West Coast, but he eschewed that easiest of alibis, suggesting that he considered that there was no need for an alibi.

The private correspondence among the German representatives shows that Witzke said that he was not in New York in July 1916 and they believed him.

While we have endorsed Altendorf's essential credibility as to the Black Tom allegations, Altendorf had a history of prevarication, and it appears that the Americans themselves did not much believe in the Black Tom allegations: if they had, one would expect some mention of it in the extensive internal correspondence discussing Witzke's pardon.

As to the Pennewitz version, while the notion that Witzke, without Jahnke, oversaw the sabotage at Black Tom, but did not himself detonate the munitions is a tempting version, there is no other source that mentions the agents Blanc and Alt who were supposedly responsible with Kristoff for the detonation, and Pennewitz's silence until 1935 raises doubt about his reliability. His statement also contains details that are contradicted by known facts. As an isolated and uncorroborated version of the event, it cannot bear the weight of persuasion.

We are left with a conflict between Altendorf's 1918 reports that we find essentially accurate and the evidence that placed Witzke (and Jahnke) on the West Coast in July 1916. There is one way to reconcile this conflict. Witzke falsely boasted. This is not, though, just an expedient way to resolve the conflict. Witzke had a history of boasting, including a key instance in which he boasted of an act of sabotage that he could not have done, the boiler explosions on the SS *Minnesota*.

It remains possible that the evidence placing Witzke on the West Coast in July 1916 was concocted and that Witzke and Jahnke traveled across the continent to do the deed on July 30, 1916. The temptation for the biographer of Witzke is strong to conclude that they did. But the evidence on balance weighs the other way. Based on what we know, the probability is that, though Black Tom tailed Witzke his entire life, he did not do it.

EPILOGUE: DEATH OF A SPY

Lothar Witzke died suddenly on January 6, 1962, five months short of his sixty-seventh birthday.[1] The day of his death was his first day of retirement. As he walked out the door that day, he called to his wife and daughter, who stood at the top of the staircase: "*Und heute starte ich den ganz großen Coup.*" In English: "Today I'm getting started on the biggest feat yet."[2]

Witzke was buried in Hamburg. His tombstone shows that his wife Lilli died in 1980 and was buried with her husband. Their son, Lothar Jr., was buried there in 1997.[3] Their daughter, Helga, died in 2014 and was buried with her husband, Hossein Moinian. Helga and her husband are survived by three children and two grandchildren.

Two notices of Witzke's death appeared in a local evening newspaper, the *Hamburger Abendblatt*.[4] One, from his family, mourned the death of their beloved husband, father, brother, son in law and brother-in-law. The other, written by his employer, Johann Rahtjen GmbH, paint factory, mourns the passing of their CEO, who thanks to his strong character helped to reconstruct and expand the company since 1950.

Neither of the death notices suggests any fame or infamy. Neither mentions any uncertainty about the circumstances of his death. The notices are indistinguishable from millions of other such notices of lives lived without drama. A happy family man. A successful company man. They suggest that Witzke was, in the end, just an ordinary (if superior) man ending an ordinarily accomplished life. No news article or magazine obituary commemorated this singular figure. Can we reconcile these quotidian notices with the life of the most sinister German saboteur of World War I, a man who was convicted of espionage and sentenced to be hanged and who received a US presidential pardon? We must accept that a biography unimaginable to most of us would hardly have been irregular for a German who died in 1962. But still, the contrast between Witzke's death notices and what we know of his life is surprising.

The Hamburg police investigated Witzke's death. They told his wife that he died of a sudden heart attack. But they told his daughter something else.

They told Helga that Witzke died in bed with a woman.[5] Efforts to find any surviving police report have been unavailing.

◇ ◇ ◇

Forty years after the death of her father, Helga Witzke Moinian received a visitor, surnamed Saidowsky. He said that he was an amateur historian, researching the life of Lothar Witzke. He was formerly from East Germany. He told Helga that Witzke had been responsible in his youth for thousands of deaths, blowing up ships and an oil refinery in Latin America.[6] He said that Witzke had remained a spy throughout the 1950s, working for the British, and that his paint company was a front owned by the British. He offered this as well: Witzke was killed by the woman whom he bedded on the day of his death, and she was a Stasi agent.[7]

For the family, it was evident that the "amateur historian" was himself a former Stasi agent. His stories of Witzke's responsibility for maritime deaths and a refinery explosion are not borne out by the evidence. The authors have sought Stasi files on Witzke, but have found none, and it is unknown whether any ever existed.

The aftermath of the visit by the "amateur historian" was a painful one for Witzke's daughter. Until then, she kept a photograph of her revered father by her bed. After that, she put the photograph away. It was not the supposed revelations of his deep past that bothered Helga. It was the continued lies; it was the secret life that her father led during the 1950s and that he had concealed from her. She came to think that he was unknown to her, and that their closeness was a mirage. Witzke's lies caught up with him, sabotaging after his death his relationship with the person with whom he was closest, his daughter.

There was something grandiose in Witzke's last pronouncement to his family, as he exited the Volksdorf home on the day of his death. The greatest feat yet, by an individual who was said to be responsible for the most spectacular act of sabotage in US history? The greatest feat yet, by a man who escaped a Texas prison only to be captured in the clothing of a Mexican peasant woman? The greatest feat yet, by a man who as a prisoner at Leavenworth rescued the victims of a boiler explosion at the risk of his own life? The greatest feat yet, by the only German agent during World War I in the United States who was captured, convicted, sentenced to death, and then obtained a presidential pardon? The greatest feat yet, by the man who was decorated in two world wars?

Witzke was unforeseeably spared the noose in 1918 and given a second chance at life. But if we accept Altendorf's stories as true, a measure of megalomania cursed Lothar Witzke from early on to his last day. If the story of the Stasi agent is true, Witzke on the last day of his life could not see that the woman in bed with him was using him, not wanting him. Franz von Papen said that it was "the German warrior's supreme disgrace—to die in bed."[8] A thought of a similar nature may have crossed Witzke's mind on his last day.

What was the feat that Witzke planned the day of his death? Did that feat relate to his death? The mysteries that shadowed the life of the once notorious spy and saboteur continued to the day of his death.

NOTES

INTRODUCTION

1. "Frequently Asked Questions About the Statue of Liberty," National Park Service, accessed 5 September 2019, https://www.nps.gov/stli/planyourvisit/get-the-facts.htm.
2. Quoted in Jules Witcover, *Sabotage at Black Tom: Imperial Germany's Secret War in America, 1914–1917* (Chapel Hill, NC: Algonquin Books, 1989), 311.
3. Sidney Sutherland, "German Spies in America, Part Five—War on Two Coasts," *Liberty*, March 21, 1931, 50.
4. For example, Jules Witcover, *Sabotage at Black Tom*; Chad Milman; *The Detonators* (New York: Little, Brown & Co., 2006); Herbert Landau, *The Enemy Within* (New York: G. P. Putnam Sons, 1937.
5. Bill Mills, *Agent of the Iron Cross: The Race to Capture German Saboteur-Assassin Lothar Witzke During World War I* (Lanham, MD: Rowman & Littlefield, 2023).

PROLOGUE. SABOTAGE ON THE HUDSON

1. Mena Reiss, Affidavit, February 14, 1925, US letter exh. J, MCC, RG 76, EN PI 143/13, Ser. US Exhibits Filed Under the Letters A through S, 1923?–1939?, Box 1 (NACP), 19. Mena Edwards became Mena Edwards Reiss when she married in October 1917. Ibid. "Eastman Girls" refers to attractive young women in early ads of the Eastman Kodak Company who were depicted using an Eastman Kodak camera, the point being to suggest both that attractive young women used these cameras and that an Eastman Kodak camera was so easy to use that even a woman could manage it. See "Magazine Ads," http://kodakgirl.com/kgmagazineads.htm.
2. The several German operatives mentioned in this chapter are listed alphabetically and identified summarily in table 1.
3. Henry Landau, *The Enemy Within* (New York: G.P. Putnam's Sons, 1937), 43.
4. Franz von Papen, *Memoirs of Franz von Papen* (London: André Deutsch, 1952), 56. See also A. A. Hoehling, *Women Who Spied* (New York: Dodd, Mead & Co., 1967), 79.
5. Von Papen's Memoirs and Mena Edwards' testimony cannot be reconciled. One or the other lied, not just with respect to details but as to the essence. Von Papen's memoirs and other writings have been criticized as unreliable and self-serving. "Papen's account of his activities in America is perhaps the most self-serving and erroneous section of his Memoirs, regarded as notoriously unreliable." Richard W. Rolfs, *The Sorcerer's Apprentice: The Life of Franz von Papen* (Lanham, MD: University Press of America, 1996), 21n19. See also George O. Kent, "Problems and Pitfalls of a Papen Biography," *Central European History* 20, no. 2 (June 1987): 191–97, https://doi.org/10.1017/S0008938900012590. To accept von Papen's word means that Edwards fabricated the entirety of her testimony. We do not believe that she did, although parts of her testimony are questionable. See note 7 below.

6. All quoted statements by Mena Edwards are taken from Reiss, Affidavit, February 14, 1925, MCC, US letter exh. J.

7. It is evident that Mena Edwards later gave the American representatives before the Mixed Claims Commission what they wanted to hear and, as such, her testimony needs to be considered skeptically. This was acknowledged even by those who worked on the American side. See Landau, *The Enemy Within*, 148 ("It seems likely that she drew somewhat on her imagination"). We refer in this prologue to what we consider to be her less contestable assertions.

8. Michael Warner, "The Kaiser Sows Destruction: Protecting the Homeland the First Time Around," *CSI Publication* (2007), https://www.cia.gov/library/center-for-the -study-of-intelligence/csi-publications/csi-studies/studies/vol46no1/article02.html.

9. Acting General Staff to Military Attaché, German Embassy (Washington DC), Telegram, January 24, 1915, GER exh. XXXIV-A and B, MCC, RG 76, P 51, Ser. German Exhibits and Translations re Sabotage Cases, ca. 1922–1939, box 1019 (NACP). An English translation of the telegram is quoted at MCC, "Certificate of Disagreement and Opinion of the American Commissioner," June 15, 1939, *Rep. of Int'l Arb. Awards*, vol. 8 (New York: United Nations, 2006), 254, https://legal.un.org/riaa /cases/vol_VIII/1-468.pdf. German MCC Exh. XXXIV.

10. The telegram, intercepted by British intelligence and turned over to the Americans, became a central part of the US case against Germany before the MCC for damages arising from the sabotage campaign by Germany in the US. *1939 Certificate of Disagreement*, 253 et seq.

11. "The record in this case proves conclusively that Rintelen's activities in this country were connected with inoculating horses and cattle, the destruction of piers and elevators and munitions factories; that he was furnished with incendiary devices by a German chemist. Dr. Scheele, who manufactured bombs and other incendiary material, not only for Rintelen, but for other saboteurs." *1939 Certificate of Disagreement*, 257. See also Comment by German Agent, Transcript of Oral Arguments, US vs. Germany, September 18–30, 1930 (The Hague, Netherlands), MCC, RG 76 (NACP), 213: "Rintelen . . . tried to organize sabotage against Allied ships carrying munitions from the United States, a fact that has been known in the United States for a long time, because his activities were discovered shortly after they had started"; and Franz von Rintelen, *The Dark Invader: Wartime Reminiscences of a German Naval Intelligence Officer* (London: Lovat Dickson Ltd., 1938), 92 et seq.

12. Michael Warner, "The Kaiser Sows Destruction: Protecting the Homeland the First Time Around,"*CSI Publication* (2007), https://www.cia.gov/library/center-for-the -study-of-intelligence/csi-publications/csi-studies/studies/vol46no1/article02.html.

13. Von Rintelen, *The Dark Invader*, 189 et seq.

14. Ibid.

15. 1939 Certificate of Disagreement, 292–94. Also present were German Army Major Hans Marguerre, serving on the Political Section of the intelligence department of the German General Staff, and Rudolph Nadolny, Liaison Officer between the Foreign Office and the General Staff. *1939 Certificate of Disagreement*, 256.

16. Landau, *The Enemy Within*, 46.

17. *1939 Certificate of Disagreement*, 295–301.

18. Landau, *The Enemy Within*, 46–47.

19. Ibid., 78.

20. Ibid., 78.

21. Von Rintelen, *The Dark Invader*, 115

22. Sidney Sutherland, "German Spies in America, Part Seven—The Black Tom Tragedy," *Liberty*, April 4, 1931, 54.

23. Sutherland, ibid., 55; Landau, *The Enemy Within*, 80.

24. "First Explosion Terrific," *New York Times*, July 31, 1916; "The Dark Invader and the Black Tom Explosion," Weird N.J., accessed Nov. 14, 2020, https://weirdnj.com /weird-news/the-dark-invader-and-the-black-tom-explosion/.

25. There was also a party at the Hotel Astor in New York on August 4. "On Friday, August 4th, Hinsch attended a party on the roof of the Hotel Astor given by Hilken in celebration of the Black Tom explosion. (Hilken's diary for 1916, Ex. 911, Ann. A; Ex. 976, Ann. E, p. 58; Ex. 986, Ann. A, p. 76)." *1939 Certificate of Disagreement*, 314.

26. "First Explosion Terrific," *New York Times*, July 31, 1916. Consistent with this view, *The New International Year Book: A Compendium of the World's Progress for the Year 1916* (New York: Dodd, Mead & Co. Inc. 1917), 222–23, discussed the Black Tom explosion within the category of "Fire Protection," and noted that "there were numerous losses in fires in plants devoted to the manufacture of war munitions or where such supplies were collected for shipment." *New International Year Book*, 223.

27. The evidence as to Hinsch and Kristoff was summarized, but not at the time accepted, by the Mixed Claims Commission in its Decision of October 1930. Judicial Decisions, 25 *Am J. Int'l L.* 147, 159–68 (1931).

28. *1930 MCC Decision*, 159–68.

29. Chad Millman, *The Detonators* (New York: Little Brown & Co., 2006), 24. See also "Many Explosions Since War Began," *New York Times*, July 31, 1916.

30. The sabotage campaign was not decisive of the US declaration of war in April 1917. Other factors predominated (the U-boat attacks on US shipping, cultural affinities, the Zimmermann Telegram fiasco, and the interests of US banks to intervene to preserve their markets and debtors in England and France). Of these, unrestricted U-boat attacks were most decisive. Adam Tooze, *The Deluge: The Great War and the Remaking of the Global Order, 1916–1931* (New York: Penguin Group, 2014), 57–58. As to banking and commercial relations, "American loans established not simply Britain's subordination to Wall Street, but a condition of mutual dependence. The more that Britain borrowed in America and the more it purchased, the harder it would be for Wilson to detach his country from the fate of the Entente." Ibid., 49. The timeline in March 1917 reveals what immediately precipitated the US declaration of war that followed in April 1917: March 1, Zimmermann Telegram made public; March 18, three American merchant ships sunk with heavy loss of life; March 19, the Russian czar is overthrown and the Kerensky government established, making the Allied Powers a suitably pro-democracy team for the idealistic US president (this would change as of November 1917 when the Bolsheviks seized power); March 20, Wilson's cabinet unanimously declares for war; March 21, Wilson convenes a session of Congress for April 2 in order to seek a declaration of war.

31. Address of the President of the United States Delivered at a Joint Session of the Two Houses of Congress, April 2, 1917, 65th Congress, 1st Session, Senate, Document No. 5 (Washington: Government Printing Office, 1917), reproduced at https://www.loc .gov/law/help/digitized-books/world-war-i-declarations/ww1-gazettes/US-address -of-president-to-congress-April-1917-1-OCR-SPLIT.pdf.

32. Address of President Wilson delivered at Washington, D.C., Flag Day, June 14, 1917 (Washington: Government Printing Office, 1917), reproduced at https://archive .org/details/addressofpresideo2wilsonw/page/n1/mode/2up.

33. David M. Kennedy, *Over Here: The First World War and American Society* (New York: Oxford University Press, 1980), 75–88.

34. Ibid., 66–67.

35. Ibid.

36. "How serious these events were taken in the United States can be seen from a report by Max Warburg . . . about his talks with Americans in the Hague in March 1918: 'The mood in America was so bitter towards Germany [the Americans told him] because so many deceitful things, some of which became known only little by little, had happened. First, there had been the various explosions in the factories, which, as evidence had shown, were brought about in America on German orders, at a time when America was not yet at war with us. . . .'" Reinhard R. Doerries, *Imperial Challenge, Ambassador Count Bernstorff and German-American Relations, 1908–1917*, trans. Christa Shannon (Chapel Hill: University of North Carolina Press, 1989), 143–44.

37. One historian believes that "the reason that the secret agents fled the US for Mexico after war was declared was not their safety but, rather, the need to be in contact with headquarters in Germany, which with the departure of the German ministry in the US now had to be done through von Eckhardt, the German minister to Mexico, and also because von Eckhardt had funds to finance espionage and sabotage." Landau, *The Enemy Within*, 112. Their flight was likely also motivated by anti-German hysteria in the US following the declaration of war. See Kennedy, *Over Here*, 66–69.

38. Kurt Jahnke, Affidavit, November 24, 1927, GER exh. P, MCC, RG 76, EN P 51, Ser. German Exhibits and Translations re Sabotage Cases, ca. 1922–1939, vol. 2 (NACP), 3. See also Friedrich Katz, *The Secret War in Mexico* (Chicago: University of Chicago Press, 1981), 414. Jahnke was "probably the most intelligent of all the German agents" in America and the only one of them "who was to play a prominent role in Germany after World War I." Ibid.

39. Lothar Witzke, Affidavit, July 19, 1927, GER exh. Q, MCC, RG 76, EN P 51, Ser. German Exhibits and Translations re Sabotage Cases, ca. 1922–1939, vol. 2 (NACP), 4–5.

40. Lothar Witzke to Guy L. Fake, April 1, 1923, US order exh. 352-A, MCC, RG 76, EN PI 143/14, Ser. Printed US Exhibits, 1929?–1939?, vol. 6 (NACP).

1. CAPTURED AT THE BORDER

1. Jay Bellamy, "The Zimmermann Telegram And Other Events Leading To America's Entry into World War I," *Prologue Magazine* 48, no. 4 (2016), https://www.archives .gov/publications/prologue/2016/winter/zimmermann-telegram.

2. "German leaders and the German government under the Emperor Wilhelm II . . . exhibited an astonishing degree of confidence in their nation's military and economic power as well as cultural superiority, coupled with a devastating ignorance or underestimation of American military and economic strength." Reinhard R. Doerries, *Imperial Challenge, Ambassador Count Bernstorff and German-American Relations, 1908–1917*, trans. Christa Shannon (Chapel Hill: University of North Carolina Press, 1989), 2; Reinhard Doerries, "The Politics of Irresponsibility: Imperial

Germany's Defiance of United States Neutrality during World War I," in Hans Tre-
fousse (ed.), *Germany and America: Essays on Problems of International Relations
and Immigration* (New York: Brooklyn College Press, 1980), 3–20. Walther Nicolai,
director of the intelligence division of the German General Staff, considered even
US *economic* capabilities to be unimportant. Russel Duane Van Wyk, *German-
American Relations in the Aftermath of the Great War: Diplomacy, Law, and the
Mixed Claims Commission, 1922–1939* (PhD diss., University of North Carolina at
Chapel Hill, 1989), 20.

3. Sidney Sutherland, "German Spies in America, Part Three—Von Papen at the
   Helm," *Liberty*, March 7, 1931, 36.
4. For additional background on the Mexican Revolution and civil war, Mexico's
   relations with Germany, and the German Secret Service operation in Mexico during World War I, see Friedrich Katz, *The Secret War in Mexico: Europe, the United
   States, and the Mexican Revolution* (Chicago: Univ. of Chicago Press, 1981); John D.
   Eisenhower, *Intervention! The United States and the Mexican Revolution, 1913–1917*
   (New York: Norton, 1993); Mark Wasserman, *The Mexican Revolution: A Brief History with Documents* (Boston: Bedford/St. Martin's, 2012); Barbara Tuchman, *The
   Zimmermann Telegram* (New York: Random House, 1958).
5. Except as otherwise noted, this account of Witzke's meetings with Jahnke and his
   journey from Mexico City to the border is based on four articles written by Paul
   Altendorf and published in the *Chicago Tribune* from November 20 to 23, 1919,
   entitled "On Secret Service in Mexico." The four articles were part of a longer series
   of syndicated articles by Altendorf published between November 3 and December
   2, 1919, in the *Tribune* and other newspapers.
6. According to British intelligence reports at the time (the British were monitoring
   Jahnke), the Spanish steamer that Jahnke met at Veracruz was the SS *Alfonse XIII*.
   M.I.1.a, "Extracts from report on the Mexican situation," August 23, 1918, Jahnke
   Kurt, KV 2/755, 122, 124 (TNA-UK).
7. The Industrial Workers of the World, known by its initials as the IWW, was an anti-
   war, anti-capitalist organization of mostly unskilled, low-wage workers.
8. Guns were expensive and hard to come by in Mexico City at the time; Altendorf
   knew Calles well because he had been a physician for Calles's regiment the previous
   fall and served on Calles's staff.
9. Paul Altendorf, "On Secret Servkice—in Mexico, Article 20," Chicago Tribune, November 22, 1919.
10. Jamie Bisher, *The Intelligence War in Latin America, 1914–1922* (Jefferson, N.C.: Mc-
    Farland & Co., Inc., 2016), 186.
11. Testimony of US Consul E.M. Lawton, Trial Hearing Record, 100–4, August 16–17,
    1918, US v. Witcke alias Waberski, RG 153, Ser. Court Martial Case Files, 1917–1938,
    File Lather Witcke, alias Pablo Waberski, 119966 (NASL); Statement of Doctor Con-
    rad von Schoech to Byron Butcher, February 4, 1918, in Lipscomb, Special Border
    Report re Foreigners: German Activity, February 8, 1918, US order exh. 315, MCC,
    RG 76, EN PI 143/14, Ser. Printed US Exhibits, 1929?–1939?, vol. 6 (NACP).
12. There is no Russian city named Winski. It is unclear whether Witzke deliberately
    misstated his birthplace or if the immigration inspector misheard him. Perhaps he
    said Minsk.

13. Testimony of Charles Beatty, Witzke Trial Record, 65–72; Memorandum, Utley to Department Intelligence Officer, Southern Department [R.L. Barnes], August 7, 1918, RG 165, Ser. MID Correspondence, 1919–1941, File 10541-268/Item 169 (NACP).

14. Testimony of William Gleaves, Witzke Trial Record, 52–54; Von Schoech, Statement to Butcher, February 4, 1918, in Lipscomb, Special Border Report, February 8, 1918, MCC, US order exh. 315.

15. Testimony of Byron Butcher, Witzke Trial Record, 72–100.

16. This account of Altendorf's biography is based on Altendorf's syndicated articles in the *Chicago Tribune* (n. 5 *supra*), especially Articles 2 and 3 (November 4 and 5, 1919), and on his testimony at Witzke's trial, Witzke Trial Record, 6–43. See also Bill Mills, *Treacherous Passage: Germany's Secret Plot Against the United States in Mexico During World War I* (Lincoln: Univ. of Nebraska, 2017), 38–40. According to Mills, Altendorf also spoke Yiddish. Ibid., 38. An account, albeit uncritical, of Altendorf's life during the several years after Witzke's capture can be found at ibid., 129–45, 178–92. Over the years, Altendorf offered conflicting versions of his biography that put into question his credibility. For example, in 1929 he stated in an affidavit filed with the Mixed Claims Commission that he left Krakow at age fourteen and never returned, thereby contradicting his testimony at Witzke's trial (on which we have relied here) that he was trained in medicine at Jagiellonian University in Krakow. See G. Kirby Munson, "Witzke and Jahnke," MS, rev. July 25, 1930, MCC, RG 76, EN PI 143/83, Ser. Notes of the Law Clerk Concerning Evidence in the Sabotage Cases, 1930–1930 (NACP), 3–4. This and other discrepancies affecting Altendorf's credibility are discussed in detail in Ch. 12, *Did He Do It? Black Tom.*

17. William Gleaves, Affidavit, January 31, 1927, US exh. 339, MCC, RG: 76, EN: PI 143/14, Printed US Exhibits (1929?–1929?), vol. 2 (NACP), paras 2–3.

18. Karl Baedeker. *The United States, with Excursions to Mexico, Cuba, Puerto Rico and Alaska,* 4th ed. (Leipzig: Karl Baedeker, 1910), 640.

19. Military Attaché R. M. Campbell (American Embassy, Mexico) to Chief, Military Intelligence (Washington), Memorandum re Revolutionary Group, March 18, 1918, US order exh. 342, MCC, RG 76, EN PI 143/14, Ser. Printed US Exhibits, 1929?–1939?, vol. 6 (NACP).

20. Altendorf, "On Secret Service in Mexico, Article 3," *Chicago Tribune,* November 5, 1919.

21. Testimony of R.M. Campbell, Witzke Trial Record, 60–64.

22. Ibid.

23. Altendorf, "On Secret Service in Mexico, Article 20," *Chicago Tribune,* November 22, 1919.

24. Ibid.; Testimony of Paul Altendorf, Witzke Trial Record, 24–25; Butcher Testimony, Witzke Trial Record, 75.

25. Altendorf, "On Secret Service in Mexico, Article 20," *Chicago Tribune,* November 22, 1919; Altendorf Testimony, Witzke Trial Record, 28–29.

26. Altendorf, "On Secret Service in Mexico, Article 22, *Chicago Tribune,* November 24, 1919" and Articles 27–28, November 28, 1919.

27. Altendorf, "On Secret Service—in Mexico, Article 1," *Chicago Tribune,* November 3, 1919.

28. Date of resignation: Altendorf, "On Secret Service in Mexico, Final Article," *Chi-*

cago Tribune, December 2, 1919. Text of commendation: Dickey (Army Dept. Intelligence Officer) to To Whom It May Concern, March 24, 1919, quoted in Altendorf, "On Secret Service in Mexico, Article 1," *Chicago Tribune*, November 3, 1919. The Dickey memorandum is cited, but not quoted, by Mills, *Treacherous Passage*, Notes for p. 179, as "Memorandum from Captain H.S. Dickey to Director of Military Intelligence Division, 'Subject: Paul Bernardo Altendorf—Informant A-1,' November 6, 1918, NARA, RG 165, Records of the War Department and Special Staffs, Military Intelligence Division, File 51-45." Altendorf received strong commendations from other officials as well. *For example*, on April 9, 1919, Major R. L. Barnes writes to Colonel Garrison that Altendorf is "one of the most successful men whom I have ever seen in undercover work and possesses an uncanny qualification for working into the confidence of others," RG 165, Ser. MID Correspondence, 1919–1941, File 10541-268/108 (NACP), 23–24. Similarly, Captain Henry Pratt to Colonel Martin, April 10, 1919, cites references from several other individuals "who have a knowledge of Dr. Altendorf's services rendered during the present war," including Gen. J. A. Ryan and Special Agent Byron Butcher, and several Department of Justice officials. RG 165, Ser. MID Correspondence, 1919–1941, File 10541-268/108 (NACP), 25.

29. Butcher Testimony, Witzke Trial Record, 75–76. The search took place in Lipscomb's office.

30. Butcher Testimony, Witzke Trial Record, 77, 83, 88; Joel A. Lipscomb, Special Border Report re German Activity, Foreigners: Latar Witcke alias Pablo (Paul) and Harry Waberski, February 2, 1918, US exh. 228, MCC, RG 76, EN PI 143/14, Ser. Printed US Exhibits, 1929?–1939?, vol. 1 (NACP).

31. Butcher Testimony, Witzke Trial Record, 99; Lipscomb, Special Border Report, February 7, 1918, MCC, US exh. 228; Lipscomb to Department Intelligence Officer, Fort Sam Houston, Memorandum, "Subject: Waberski," June 29, 1918, RG 165, Ser. MID Correspondence, 1919–1941, File 10541–268/125 (NACP).

32. Butcher Testimony, Witzke Trial Record, 77, 90; Lipscomb Testimony, Witzke Trial Record, 106–7; Lipscomb, Special Border Report, February 7, 1918, MCC, US exh. 228. Witzke also had on him a small notebook containing notes, a list of his travel expenses from his journey to Nogales, and the names and addresses of several women. Henry Landau, *The Enemy Within* (New York: G. P. Putnam's Sons, 1937), 121. The small notebook has been preserved as part of Witzke's court martial case file: RG 153, Ser. Court Martial Case Files, 1917–1938, File Lather Witcke, alias Pablo Waberski, 119966 (NASL).

33. Lipscomb Testimony, Witzke Trial Record, 110–11; Assistant Intelligence Officer [Lipscomb] to Department Intelligence Officer [Barnes], Memorandum, "Subject: Paul Witzki, alias Pablo Waberski," February 6, 1918, RG 165, Ser. MID Correspondence, 1919–1941, File 10541-268/20.

34. Both the "list of expenses" and the "items to be purchased" are pages in the small notebook that Witzke had on him when he was captured. See note 31 sup.

35. Lipscomb Testimony, Witzke Trial Record, 111–12.

36. Butcher Testimony, Witzke Trial Record, 96–98; Memorandum of Statement made by Pablo Waberski [alias of Witzke] to Byron Butcher at Calabasas Station, Arizona, February 14, 1918, in Photostatic Copy of Report of Wm. Neunhoffer re Pablo Waberski, February 25, 1918, US order exh. 288, MCC, RG 76, EN PI 143/14,

Ser. Printed US Exhibits, 1929?–1939, vol. 6 (NACP). The interrogation (in fact, a conversation), took place while Butcher and Witzke were waiting for the train to take them from Nogales to San Antonio. Joel Lipscomb to Department Intelligence Officer, Fort Sam Houston [Barnes], Memorandum re "Pablo Waberski," February 16, 1918, RG 165, Ser. MID Correspondence, 1919–1941, File 10541-268/16 (NACP) .

37. Waberski [alias of Witzke], Statement to Butcher at Calabasi Station, February 14, 1918, MCC, US order exh. 288.

2. WHAT WAS HIS CRIME?

1. Joel Lipscomb to Department Intelligence Officer, Fort Sam Houston [Barnes], Memorandum re "Pablo Waberski," February 16, 1918, RG 165, Ser. MID Correspondence, 1919–1941, File 10541-268/16 (NACP); Altendorf, "On Secret Service in Mexico, Article 21," *Chicago Tribune*, November 23, 1919.

2. Lothar Witzke, Affidavit, July 19, 1927, GER exh. Q, MCC, RG 76, EN P 51, Ser. German Exhibits and Translations re Sabotage Cases, ca. 1922–1939, vol. 2 (NACP), 14–15. Witzke's assertion that he was "bound hand and foot for two weeks" at Nogales is contradicted by a statement he is said to have made to his captor Byron Butcher at the end of his two weeks in custody at Nogales, while the two were waiting at the Calabasas station for a train that would transport Witzke to Fort Sam Houston to await trial. Butcher told Witzke, "I have tried to treat you as I would expect you to treat me under the same circumstances," to which Witzke responded, "If you are ever my prisoner, I will also take good care of you." Butcher Testimony, Witzke Trial Record, 97.

3. Ibid., 15.

4. Letter reproduced in E. V. Spence to Dept. Intelligence Officer, Southern Dept., Fort Sam Houston, Memorandum re Pablo Waberski, German Agent, June 25, 1918," RG 165, Ser. MID Correspondence, 1919–1941, File 10541-268/186 (NACP).

5. Witzke would provide other (often contradictory) narratives over the next decade. We address these other narratives elsewhere in this book as appropriate.

6. Statement of Pablo Waberski When Questioned by Major R. L. Barnes, February 18, 1918, MID, File 10541-268/29.

7. There is no Russian city named Winske. It is unclear whether Witzke deliberately misstated his birthplace or if the immigration inspector misheard him. Perhaps he said Minsk.

8. E. V. Spence to Department Intelligence Officer, Memorandum re Pablo Waberski alias Lathar Witcke, April 10, 1918, MID, File 10541-268/90.

9. The interview was summarized by Joel Lipscomb, the US Intelligence Officer at Nogales, in Joel A. Lipscomb, Special Border Report re German Activity: Foreigners, Latar Witcke alias Pablo (Paul) and Harry Waberski, February 2, 1918, US exh. 228, MCC, RG 76, EN PI 143/14, Ser. Printed US Exhibits, 1929?–1939?, vol. 1 (NACP). This appears to be the earliest of Altendorf's several accounts of that trip. In a series of newspaper articles that Altendorf published in 1919, Altendorf says that, after Witzke's arrest, Butcher asked Altendorf to "have a rest" and "make out a full report on my operations in Mexico to date. I 'rested' fifteen days, for my report filled one hundred typewritten pages and was in English, a language with which up to that

time I had little more than a bowing acquaintance." Altendorf, "On Secret Service in Mexico, Article 21," *Chicago Tribune*, November 23, 1919. The authors have been unable to find any one hundred--page memo by Altendorf. There does exist an undated eleven-page typed, single-spaced memo titled "My Trip to Mexico" signed "A-1" (Altendorf's code name): RG 165, Ser. MID Correspondence, 1919–1941, File 10541-268/205 (NACP). The undated copy of the memo we have was in the possession of Major Barnes and was forwarded to an unidentified recipient on August 10, 2018. Perhaps this was the memo to which Altendorf refers in his 1919 article, although it is much shorter.

10. Joel A. Lipscomb, Special Border Report re German Activity, Foreigners: William Gleaves, February 4, 1918, US exh. 226, MCC, RG 76, EN PI 143/14, Ser. Printed US Exhibits, 1929?–1939?, vol.1 (NACP).

11. As explained in chapter 1, the IWW (also known as the Wobblies) was an anti-war, anti-capitalist organization of mostly unskilled, low-wage workers. It was founded in Chicago in 1905. In 1917 (the year the United States entered the war) it claimed 300,000 card carrying members, although the number of actual dues paying members was closer to 60,000. Vincent St. John, "The I.W.W.—Its History, Structure and Methods" (Chicago: Industrial Workers of the World, 1919), http://www.library .arizona.edu/exhibits/bisbee/docs/019.html.

12. The cable is quoted in Lipscomb, Special Border Report, February 2, 1918, MCC, US exh. 228. See also Special Agent to C.E. Breniman, February 5, 1918, RG 165, Ser. MID Correspondence, 1919–1941, File 10541-268/13 (NACP). In later accounts, including six months later at Witzke's trial, Altendorf would identify the target as Byron Butcher. How he came to know that Butcher was the target is a mystery since Witzke never confessed.

13. The substance of the Altendorf and Gleaves debriefings was reported to Alexander Bielaski, Chief of the Bureau of Investigation in Washington, in a memorandum dated March 7, 1918. The memorandum summarized Witzke's (Waberski's) mission as follows: "The proof seems conclusive that Waberski and others entered into a conspiracy in Mexico to cause to be committed depredations in the United States and it is reasonably well-established that Waberski and his group planned to incite an insurrection in this country. It also seems quite conclusive that the I.W.W. Organization was to be the medium through which the culprits would act. Waberski was arrested immediately after crossing the line and therefore no overt acts were committed on this side; and so far as the proof shows, no part of the conspiracy was formed in the United States." Chief, Bureau of Investigation, Department of Justice to Mr. Bielaski, Memorandum re Pablo Waberski alias Lathar Witcke, March 7, 1918, US order exh. 341, MCC, RG 76, EN PI 143/14, Ser. Printed US Exhibits, 1929?–1939?, vol. 6 (NACP). For the twenty-first century reader, the notion of German spies conspiring in Mexico to subvert the US may seem farcical. How could Germany matter to Mexico or Mexico to Germany? But this would be a failure of historical perspective. Wilhemine Germany was expansionist, and the Kaiser had an enduring fantasy of an alliance of Mexico and Japan against the US. Barbara Tuchman, *The Zimmermann Telegram* (New York: Random House, 1958), 28–51.

14. In Lipscomb, Special Border Report, February 4, 1918, MCC, US exh. 226, Lipscomb reports that Witzke said five men, not six.

15. Dietz was one of the group of six (or five) that had left Mexico City together for Nogales, but Gleaves had not seen him for several days. He turned up in Nogales on the evening of February 1, arriving by automobile with another member of the party known as "Schmidt" and a third man whom Gleaves did not know. Dietz told Gleaves that the threesome would return to Hermosillo the next morning, although Gleaves later came to believe that they were headed to Naco to cross into the United States. Gleaves regarded Dietz as more dangerous than Witzke because, he explained to Butcher, "Dietz and Schmidt had caused the Tampico fires last October." Dietz's mission, as far as Gleaves understood it, was to go to the New Mexico coal fields "where the Germans had a large following among the IWW and miners from New Mexico," and then proceed to Piedro Negras for the meetings there.

16. For comments on German underestimation of US economic and military might, see Reinhard R. Doerries, *Imperial Challenge: Ambassador Count Bernstorff and German-American Relations, 1908–1917*, trans. Christa Shannon (Chapel Hill: University of North Carolina Press, 1989), 2.

17. "By the fall of 1915 a full-scale assault on 'hyphenism' was underway. The term was by no means new to public debate but in the context of a world war that threatened to engulf the United States it acquired a new currency, especially in the rhetoric of Theodore Roosevelt." Frederick C. Luebke, *Bonds of Loyalty: German-Americans and World War I* (DeKalb, Illinois: Northern Illinois University Press, 1974), 140.

18. "It would appear more than likely that the former Pinkerton man and German agent, Kurt Jahnke, who had established important connections with Irish-American groups, played his part in the manipulation of Irish revolutionaries for German aims. . . ." Doerries, *Imperial Challenge*, 155–56. The German campaign to win over the Irish in America ultimately failed. Ibid., 76.

19. Operative C-308, Report re Sarah Gillespy and Jerelli," February 6, 1918, RG 165, Ser. MID Correspondence, 1919–1941, File 10541-268/18 (NACP).

20. Willard Utley to R.L. Barnes, Memorandum re Pablo Waberski, August 18, 1918, RG 165, Ser. MID Correspondence, 1919–1941, File 10541-268/197 (NACP), para. 21.

21. This is the only instance of which we are aware that Witzke used the alias "Harry Anderson." In June 1917, his lifeboat man and able-seaman certificates were issued in the name of Pablo Waberski. The San Francisco Crowley-Langley Directory for the year ending June 1917 lists "Harry Anderson, seaman" as residing at 273 4th Street, which was located between Howard and Folsom. We do not know if this was the same Anderson.

22. Operative C-308, Report, February 6, 1918, MID, File 10541-268/18.

23. Utley to Barnes, Memorandum, August 18, 1918, MID, File 10541-268/197, para. 21.

24. See cable from Special Agent Breniman (Fort Sam Houston) to Western Department (San Francisco), February 3, 1918 ("Military authorities Nogales holding German spy name LATHAR WITCKE traveling with Russian passport under name PABLO WABERSKI has confessed participation several explosions in United States including Mare Island and implicated German named WILD now working as checker in large German restaurant San Francisco"), quoted in Don E. Rathbun, Report re Pablo Waberski, March 7, 1918, RG 165, Ser. MID Correspondence, 1919–1941, File 10541-268/52 (NACP); Major R.L. Barnes to Dept. Intelligence Officer, Western Department, Memorandum re Pablo Waberski, July 11, 1918, RG

165, Ser. MID Correspondence, 1919–1941, File 10541-268/130 (NACP) (stating that informant A-1, i.e., Altendorf, had implicated Wild in the Mare Island bombing). See also Joel Lipscomb, "Special Border Report Regarding a Man Named Wild," February 2, 1918, US exh. 228-A, MCC, RG 76, EN PI 143/14, Ser. Printed US Exhibits, 1929?–1939?, vol. 1 (NACP).

25. We assess Altendorf's credibility in detail in chapter 12. Re the search of Witzke's baggage, see Capt. Joel A. Lipscomb to Department Intelligence Officer, Fort Sam Houston, Memorandum re Waberski, June 29, 1918, RG 165, Ser. MID Correspondence, 1919–1941, File 10541-268/125 (NACP).

26. Rathbun, Report, March 7, 1918, MID, File 10541-268/52.

27. Curiously, and apparently coincidentally, Witzke had also worked in Keeler for the same company the year before, a fact not known by the authorities at the time Wild was being investigated but discovered a decade later during the sabotage cases arbitration.

28. Utley to Barnes, Memorandum, August 18, 1918, MID, File 10541-268/197, para. 16.

29. Rathbun, Report, March 7, 1918, MID, File 10541-268/52.

30. Motor Vehicle Department, Operator's License for Pablo Waberski, October 17, 1917, Trial Record, Exh. 11, August 16–17, 1918, US v. Witcke alias Waberski, RG 153, Ser. Court Martial Case Files, 1917–1938, File Lather Witcke, alias Pablo Waberski, 119966 (NASL).

31. Utley to Barnes, Memorandum, August 18, 1918, MID, File 10541-268/197, para. 7.

32. Ibid., 14–15, para. 23.

33. Ibid., 15, para. 29.

34. Ibid., 15, para 29.

35. Watkins to Military Staff (Washington), Telegram, September 30, 1918, RG 165, Ser. MID Correspondence, 1919–1941, File 10541-268/206 (NACP).

36. Lipscomb, Special Border Report, February 2, 1918, MCC, US exh. 228.

37. Background regarding the Cipher Bureau is based on the following: Memorandum, R. H. Van Deman, "Subject: A brief resume of a certain period in the military intelligence service of the United States Army," April 8, 1949, Box 106, Memoirs of Major General R. H. Van Deman, US Army Intelligence Center Library (Fort Huachuca, AZ); Marc B. Powe, "A Sketch of a Man and His Times," in *The Final Memoranda*, ed. Ralph E. Weber (Wilmington: Scholarly Resources Inc., 1988), ix–xxiii.

38. An office of naval intelligence had been set up in the Navy three years before.

39. Military attaches and operatives were still sending unsolicited information including about the war to Washington from abroad, however, the information was not being systematically filed and it was not being distributed to the armed services and government agencies most in need of it.

40. Van Deman Memorandum, April 8, 1949, 33–34.

41. Ibid.

42. Ibid., 35. The novelist, according to the historian Joan Jensen, was Gertrude Atherton. Joan Jensen, *The Price of Vigilance* (Chicago: Rand McNally & Co., 1968), 117–18.

43. Powe, "A Sketch," xviii.

44. David Kahn, The *Reader of Gentlemen's Mail: Herbert O. Yardley and the Birth of American Codebreaking* (New Haven: Yale, 2006), 20–21.

45. See Herbert Yardley, *The American Black Chamber* (Indianapolis: Bobbs-Merrill

Company, 1931), 140. Yardley says that MI-8 had the cryptogram in hand by "early in February, 1918." According to a copy of *Black Chamber* annotated by William F. Friedman, the precise date was February 7, 1918. Friedman was a highly regarded cryprographic officer in World War I. A prolific author and teacher, he would eventually become chief cryptoanalyst for what came to be known as the US Signals Intelligence Service. National Security Agency/ Central Security Service, "William F. Friedman 1999 Hall of Honor Inductee," https://www.nsa.gov/History/Cryptologic -History/Historical-Figures/Historical-Figures-View/Article/1623026/william-f -friedman/; Britannica, "William F. Friedman and Elizebeth S. Friedman," https:// www.britannica.com/biography/William-F-Friedman-and-Elizebeth-S-Friedman. We cite his annotations several times below.

46. Yardley, *Black Chamber*, 142.
47. Ibid., 169–70.
48. Van Deman, writing several decades after the event and apparently relying on Yardley's account, says simply that "the coded message found on [Witzke's] person [was] sent to the Military Intelligence Branch where it was submitted to the Code and Cipher Section and decoded during a single night." Van Deman Memorandum, April 8, 1949, 37, 63.
49. Yardley to Van Deman, March 3, 1918, quoted in Friedman annotation at Yardley, *Black Chamber*, 168.
50. Van Deman to Yardley, February 28, 1918, informing Yardley that Churchill had sent the cryptogram to Manly that day. Quoted in Friedman annotation at Yardley, *Black Chamber*, 168.
51. Testimony of John Manly, Witzke Trial Record, 126.
52. Friedman annotation, at Yardley, *Black Chamber*, 140, 170. See also the War Depart-ment's loose sheet of paper on which is typed the cipher together with a German decipherment with English translation, stamped "Solved May 18, 1918," RG 165, Ser. MID Correspondence, 1919–1941, File 10541-268/106 (NACP). Friedman in an an-notation at Yardley, 170, quotes the Official Record as saying, "Miss Edith Rickert assisted Capt. Manly in the decipherment of the Waberski message more than any-one else. Others that helped some are Victor Weisskopf, Capt. Powell, and myself. signed Yardley."
53. Testimony of John Manly, Witzke Trial Record, 125–28.
54. Ibid., 131.
55. Quoted in Kahn, *Gentleman's Mail*, 44.
56. Testimony of Manly, Witzke Trial Record,129. See, by way of comparison, the original translation in MCC, File 19541-268/106, which is slightly different. The translation was cleaned up for the trial. Also, the punctuation in the translation is all spelled out in the actual message.
57. Van Deman to Barnes, Telegram, May 17, 1918, RG 165, Ser. MID Correspondence, 1919–1941, File 10541-268/105 (NACP).
58. Barnes to Military Staff (Washington), Telegram, May 20, 1918, RG 165, Ser. MID Correspondence, 1919–1941, File 10541-268/108 (NACP).
59. Van Deman to Barnes, Telegram, May 21, 1918, RG 165, Ser. MID Correspondence, 1919–1941, File 10541-268/112 (NACP).

3. TRIED AND CONVICTED FOR SPYING

1. As Major Barnes, the intelligence officer for the Southern Department at Fort Sam Houston, put it in a cable to Van Deman in May 1918, "It is not believed that we should turn [Waberski] over to circuit court as public trial would require exposure [of] two valuable undercover informants. Penalty he would receive probably would be few years imprisonment which would not justify their exposure. Unless there is possibility of his being executed think no trial advisable." Barnes to Military Staff, Telegram, May 20, 1918, RG 165, Ser. MID Correspondence, 1919–1941, File 10541-268/108 (NACP).

2. The order, a copy of which the authors have not been able to find, is referenced in G. S. Hornblower to Capt. D. Keppel, Memorandum re Pablo Waberski (Question of military jurisdiction), May 22, 1918, RG 165, Ser. MID Correspondence, 1919–1941, File 10541-268/120 (NACP), para. 6.

3. Charles Harris III and Louis Sadler, "The Witzke Affair: German Intrigue on the Mexican Border, 1917–18," *Military Review* 59, no. 2 (February 1979): 36, 46. For a more detailed summary of the rivalry between Gregory and Van Deman, see Joan Jensen, *The Price of Vigilance* (Chicago: Rand McNally & Co., 1968), 117–25. See also William Corson, *The Armies of Ignorance: The Rise of the American Intelligence Empire* (New York: Dial Press, 1977), 41–75. On the origins and jurisdiction of the Bureau of Investigation, see "A Brief History, the Nation Calls, 1908–1923," Federal Bureau of Investigation (website), https://www.fbi.gov/history/brief-history; "Federal Bureau of Investigation, History," Federation of American Scientists (website), https://fas.org/irp/agency/doj/fbi/fbi_hist.htm. Prior to 1908, the Treasury Department had some federal investigative responsibilities as well, including the Secret Service and counterfeiting, both of which responsibilities it retained after the bureau was constituted.

4. Acting Judge Advocate General James J. Mayes to Chief of Military Intelligence Branch, 1st Ind., May 31, 1918, RG 165, Ser. MID Correspondence, 1919–1941, File 10541-268/? (NACP). We do not know to which MID file 10541-268 document this 1st Ind. was affixed. Our copy was located between file 10541-268/193 and file 10541-268/197. Possibly it was an indorsement to Hornblower's May 22, 1918, memorandum to D. Keppel, MID, File 10541-268/120 (supra, note 2). See also Memorandum for Gen. Crowder, "Subject: Court-martial jurisdiction over spies," attached to Opinion of Judge Advocate General, "Discipline: Spies Triable by General Court-Martial," April 6, 1918, *Opinions of the Judge Advocate General of the Army 1918*, 2 vols. (Washington: Government Printing Office, 1919), 2:252–53; Hornblower to Keppel, Memorandum, May 22, 1918, MID, File 10541-268/120.

5. *Ex Parte Quirin*, 317 US 1 (1942).

6. See Matthew Shapanka, "The Crime of Terrorism: Military and Civilian Approaches to Prosecuting Terrorists," *The Federal Lawyer* 56 (Sept. 2009), 32–39, 35: "The application of [President George W.] Bush's order [establishing a military commission in 2002 for those accused of terrorism] to those captured outside the United States fundamentally differentiates his plans for military commissions from other similar plans. In both the case of Waberski and the case of the Nazi saboteurs [captured on Long Island during World War II], those prosecuted were captured

inside the United States; both were accused of violating the laws of war in so doing; and neither was captured in the course of a military operation. Those detained at Guantanamo and deemed eligible for prosecution by military commission have all been captured abroad in the course of military operations in Afghanistan and Iraq."

7. *See Hamdan v. Rumsfeld*, 548 US 557 (2006).

8. US v. Witcke alias Waberski, RG 153, Ser. Court Martial Case Files, 1917–1938, File Lather Witcke, alias Pablo Waberski, 119966 (NASL). The case file includes, besides the trial transcript itself, correspondence, cables, and memoranda about the case written subsequent to the trial, much of it concerning appeals and applications for leniency or pardon.

9. Brig. Gen. James A. Ryan, Brig. Gen. James J. Hornbrook, Col. Augustus C. Macomb, Col. Irvin L. Phillips, and Lt. Col. Charles H. Errington.

10. Witzke Trial Record, 4.

11. The prosecution presented nine witnesses and fourteen documentary exhibits. The four main witnesses were: Altendorf and Gleaves, who testified about meeting Witzke in Mexico City, his mission to the US, and their trip with him to Nogales; special agent Butcher, who testified about his employment of Altendorf as a US secret agent, his instructing Altendorf to join the German Secret Service in Mexico as a double agent, and a conversation he had with Witzke, after he was captured, about spying; and the cryptographer John Manly, who explained how the cipher message was deciphered. The other witnesses were the US military attaché in Mexico City in charge of US counterespionage there, Maj. R. M. Campbell, who testified about the German Secret Service in Mexico and his January meeting with Altendorf in which Altendorf disclosed that he was a US secret agent and gave Campbell a "mass of papers" containing important intelligence information to be forwarded to the authorities in the US; the immigration inspector at Nogales at the time Witzke crossed the border, Charles Beatty; US Consul at Nogales, E. M. Lawton; and Agent Lipscomb. Each of the four testified as to what he knew about Witzke's admission to the US, his capture, and the search of his personal effects. Agent Lipscomb also testified about US military establishments in or near Nogales. In addition, Special Agent William Neuenhoffer, who had been stationed in Mexico City to investigate German activities there, testified about seeing Witzke and Altendorf together in Mexico City. The fourteen documentary exhibits were photographs, the code, the cipher message, and other documents recovered from the search of Witzke and his personal effects after he was captured.

12. Altendorf Trial Testimony, Witzke Trial Record, 15, 17, 28–29.

13. Gleaves Trial Testimony, Witzke Trial Record, 46–47, 49.

14. Butcher Trial Testimony, Witzke Trial Record, 93, 96–98.

15. Witzke Trial Record, 98.

16. Ibid., 17, 19, 30, 47, 55.

17. Ibid., 163–65.

18. Ibid., 165.

19. Ibid., 165–66.

20. Ibid., 7–9, 37–40.

21. Ibid., 39–40.

22. Ibid., 40–41.

23. Ibid., 160–61.

24. Ibid., 161.

25. Ibid., 161–63.

26. Witzke Testimony, Witzke Trial Record, 136–60. Barnes's February 18 interrogation is discussed in chapter 2, supra.

27. Ibid., 137.

28. Witzke Testimony, Witzke Trial Record, 142.

29. Closing arguments: The defense's closing argument is at Witzke Trial Record, 160–61 163–65, 168–69. The prosecution's closing argument is at Witzke Trial Record, 161–63, 165–67. Verdict and sentence: Witzke Trial Record, 169–70.

30. As we will see in the following chapter, American authorities, troubled by the assertion of military jurisdiction over Witzke, debated for many months after the trial the meaning and purpose of the broad language "or elsewhere" of Article 82 of the Articles of War. Even if that language were strictly applied, there was still no evidence that Witzke "lurked" anywhere.

31. Affidavits of Pvt. Henry Brackett, Col. Roy Stephens, and First Lt. Charles Miller, each dated August 20, 1928, annexed to Commanding General Ryan to army adjutant general, Memorandum re Lathar Witzke, alias Pablo Waberski, August 20, 1918, RG 153, Ser. Court Martial Case Files, 1917–1938, File Lathar Witcke, alias Pablo Waberski, 119966 (NASL).

32. Ibid (annexes include copy of cigarette paper and translation). According to Brackett, the reason Stephens searched for the razor where he did was that, when Witzke was brought back to his cell after the first search, he "glanced up to a certain corner" of the cell. Brackett says that he reported this to Miller when he told him about the razor. Apparently, shortly after the cigarette paper was discovered, MID asked Altendorf to interview another prisoner at the guard house (Czelaski), with whom Witzke was thought to be friendly, about the cigarette paper note. According to Altendorf's report of the interview, MID suspected that the note was intended for delivery to Czelaski (or someone else in the guard house) for further forwarding to another individual. (Altendorf told Czeslasi that he, Altendorf, was probably the intended ultimate recipient of the note.) Czeslaski said he had talked three times with Witzke, including once in the bath house where Witzke asked him if there were other German prisoners at Fort Sam Houston. Czeslaski responded by cautioning Witzke not to speak German with him and to "be careful." Czeslaski never responded directly to Altendorf's explicit question about the note. Excerpt, Altendorf to Intelligence Officer Southern Department, August 27, 1918, RG 165, Ser. MID Correspondence, 1919–1941, File 10541-268/185 (NACP).

4. ON DEATH ROW

1. J. M. Ryan to General Samuel T. Ansell, October 4, 1918, RG 153, Ser. Court Martial Case Files, 1917–1938, File Lather Witcke, alias Pablo Waberski, 119966 (NASL). The case file includes correspondence, cables, and memoranda relating to the case as well as the trial record.

2. Reginald Hall to Edward Bell, September 25, 1918 (copy in authors' file). Bell was the first secretary of the US embassy in London to whom Hall first showed the

            intercepted Zimmermann cable in 1917 that was a contributing factor to the US's entry into the war.

3. Ansell to Commanding General Southern Department, October 22, 1918, Witzke Case File 119966.

4. The Review Board was comprised of three members: the Chief of the First Division [R. M.] Millar and two Judge Advocates, [C. C.] Tucker and E.R. Keedy.

5. Attorney General's letter: Letter, Attorney General Gregory to President Wilson, November 25, 1918, Witzke Case File 119966. See also Bettman to Review Board member Keedy, Memorandum re the question of jurisdiction of military tribunals over case of Pablo Waberski and similar ones, November 5, 1918, ibid., on which the Attorney General's letter was based. The Attorney General's letter was later published as an opinion of the Attorney General: Thomas Gregory, "Trial of Spies by Military Tribunals," 31 *Op. Att'y Gen.* 356 (1920). Supreme Court case: *Ex Parte Milligan*, 71 US (4 Wall) 2 (1866).

6. "Review by the Board of Review (First Division)," May 20, 1919, Witzke Case File 119966. The Review was based on an original report by Judge Advocate (Lt. Col.) Mark Guerin. At the Request of then Acting Judge Advocate General E. A. Kreger, Guerin also prepared a separate memorandum addressing in detail the question of whether Nogales, Arizona was, at the time, in the "zone of operation" of the United States, answering the question in the affirmative. Mark E. Guerin to General Kreger, Memorandum re Trial by Military Commission of Lather Witcke, alias Pablo Waberski," May 7, 1919, Witzke Case File 119966.

7. "Review by the Board of Review (First Division)," May 20, 1919, Witzke Case File 119966.

8. Ansell to Kreger, Memorandum, [n.d.], Witzke Case File 119966. Then Acting Judge Advocate General Kreger had circulated the Review Board's opinion to several colleagues, including former Acting Judge Advocate General Ansell, soliciting their views. Kreger to Ansell, Memorandum re U.S. vs. Witcke, alias Waberski (CM. 119966), May 25, 1919, Witzke Case File 119966.

9. RGH to General Kreger, Memorandum, [n.d.], Witzke Case File 119966. Edith Cavell was an English nurse working in Brussels when the Germans invaded in 1914. She hid Allied soldiers who had been abandoned when the Allies withdrew from the city. The hidden soldiers eventually made it to neutral Holland but Cavell was arrested, convicted of treason, and executed by a German firing squad.

10. Secretary of War Newton D. Baker to President Wilson, June 26, 1919, Witzke Case File 119966.

11. President Wilson to Secretary of War Baker, July 19, 1919, Witzke Case File 119966.

12. This account of the escape is based on the following affidavits of the guards who were on duty at the time. George D. Haslam, Another Affidavit, April 14, 1926, US exh. 335, MCC, RG 76, EN PI 143/14, Ser. Printed US Exhibits, 1929?–1939?, vol. 2 (NACP).; A. H. J. Voelker, Affidavit, December 16, 1926, US exh. 336, MCC, RG 76, EN PI 143/14, Ser. Printed US Exhibits, 1929?–1939?, vol. 2 (NACP). The affidavits were given some seven years after the event, in connection with the Sabotage Cases arbitration. Although the details of the escape of a notorious German spy would no doubt be etched in the memories of those who were then guarding him, the passage of time between the event and the date of the affidavits is substantial.

13. Haslam Affidavit, MCC Ex. 335.

14. Ibid.

15. See Public Prosecutor's file re criminal proceedings against Dojan for attempted murder of Lothar Witzke's mother, [n.d.], GER exh. LXVI-A, RG 76, EN 51, Ser. German Exhibits and Translations re Sabotage Cases, ca. 1922–1939, vol. 8, (NACP) and German Agent, Memorandum concerning Public Prosecutor's file no. 4F990/22 re investigations against Dojan in connection with attempted murder, [n.d.], GER exh. LXVI-B, MCC, RG 76, EN P 51, Ser. German Exhibits and Translations re Sabotage Cases, ca. 1922–1939, vol. 8 (NACP), 47 (concerning examination of Lothar Witzke before the Public Prosecutor, March 4, 1924). See also John Harris to Lothar Witzke, July 14, 1921, copy attached to Petition, Paul and Vally Witzke to President Harding, June 7, 1923, Witzke Case File 119966. In the letter, Harris writes, "When you see Lieut. Stratton Provost Marshall of San Antonio give him my best regards and tell him I'm enjoying my freedom very much. But how in the hell did he get that plan of that key?" "Stratton" may be a reference to Capt. F. P. Stretton, who was stationed at Fort Sam Houston at the time of the escape attempt.

16. John Shores, Affidavit, March 21, 1926, US exh. 333, MCC, RG 76, EN PI 143/14, Ser. Printed US Exhibits, 1929?–1939?, vol. 2 (NACP); George D. Haslam, Affidavit, April 14, 1926, US exh. 334, MCC, RG 76, EN PI 143/14, Ser. Printed US Exhibits, 1929?–1939?, vol. 2 (NACP); George D. Haslam, Affidavit, April 23, 1929, US order exh. 198, MCC, RG 76, EN PI 143/14, Ser. Printed US Exhibits, 1929?–1939?, vol. 6 (NACP); Voelker, Affidavit, December 16, 1926, MCC, US exh. 336 (quoting what Corporal John Shores told him he heard Witzke say).

17. Lothar Witzke, Examination by Thomas J. Tunney, September 16–17, 1919, US exh. 24, MCC, RG 76, EN PI 143/14, Ser. Printed US Exhibits, 1929?–1939?, vol. 1 (NACP). The three officers were Major R. B. Woodruff, Capt. F. P. Stretton, and Cpl. Henry A. O'Brien.

18. For the differing, earlier accounts that Witzke gave, see chapter 1, supra (the Butcher/Lipscomb interrogations), chapter 2, supra (the Barnes/Spence interrogations), and chapter 3, supra (Witzke's trial testimony).

19. Witzke, Examination by Tunney, September 16–17, 1919, MCC, US exh. 24, 66.

20. Bopp was convicted in May, 1918 for his part in the Hindu-German plot. "San Francisco Consuls Sentenced to Prison," *New York Times*, May 1, 1918. He had been convicted the previous year of conspiracy to violate the Sherman Act in plotting to blow up munitions ships carrying munitions bound for the allies. "Bopp and His Associates Are Convicted," *San Francisco Chronicle*, January 11, 1917.

21. Not to be confused with the decorated German military officer in World War I, diplomat, and ambassador to Russia in World War II, also named von Shulenburg, who was executed in 1944 for his part in the 26 July plot against Adolf Hitler.

22. Landau says Shulenberg (Landau's spelling of the agent's name) visited Seattle on May 11, 1916, in connection with an unsuccessful scheme to employ Hindu coolies in the Canadian northwest to dynamite railroad bridges and tunnels. Henry Landau, *The Enemy Within: The Inside Story of German Sabotage in America* (New York: G.P. Putnam's Sons, 1937), 31–32. Shulenberg, penniless and in poor health, was arrested in San Jose in December 1917 and confessed. Ibid.

23. One of these women, Witzke said, did not work out; the other did. The latter was named Alta Miller from Wisconsin.

24. Witzke, Examination by Tunney, September 16–17, 1919, MCC, US exh. 24, 77.

25. Perhaps the explosion on the oil tanker *J. A. Moffett* on the morning of September 25, 1917, while the vessel was docked at nearby Richmond. Two men were killed. "Richmond Walls Crumble from Ship Explosion," *San Francisco Chronicle*, September 26, 1917.

26. Witzke, Examination by Tunney, September 16-17, 1919, MCC, US exh 24, 61.

27. Guy L. Fake, Affidavit, August 18, 1924, US exh. 10, MCC, RG 76, EN PI 143/14, Ser. Printed US Exhibits, 1929?-1939?, vol. 1 (NACP), para. 24. In December 1919, Altendorf told Fake that Witzke had admitted to him that he was involved in the Kingsland explosion. Ibid., para. 21.

28. Captain Sherman Kile of MID, who was stationed at Fort Sam Houston at the time, participated in the interview with Judge Fake. Kyle would later submit an affidavit to the Mixed Claims Commission, stating among other things that he and Judge Fake questioned Witzke in particular about "some foreigner whom Judge Fake suspected had been working with Witzke in connection with the destruction of the Kingsland Plant. Witzke admitted, as I recall it, some foreigner had travelled with him from New York back to Mexico after his stay in New York at 100 West Fifty Sixth Street, and he admitted this this man was also connected with work for the Germans, but he did not give any definite information as to the nature of the man's work nor any satisfactory information as to their relations between themselves." Sherman Kyle, Affidavit, March 1, 1927, US exh. 628, MCC, RG 76, EN PI 143/14, Ser. Printed US Exhibits, 1929?-1939?, vol. IV (NACP); Sherman Kyle, Affidavit, September 27, 1928, US exh. 560, MCC, RG 76, EN PI 143/14, Ser. Printed US Exhibits, 1929?-1939?, vol. 3 (NACP).

29. Kreger to Baker, Memorandum re Case of Luther Witcke alias Pablo Waberski, August 12, 1919 (with enclosures), Witzke Case File 119966. Secretary Baker with Kreger's help also drafted a letter to be sent to new Attorney General A. Mitchell Palmer to the same effect. Ibid.

30. Letter, Attorney General Palmer to Secretary of War Baker, "Trial of Spy by Court Martial," December 24, 1919, 40 Op. Att'y Gen. 561 (1949) (For an explanation of why Palmer repudiated Gregory in secret, see Cox to Biddle, July 2, 1942 and Biddle to Holtzoff, July 2, 1942, Papers of Alexander Cox, Box 61, FDR Library, cited at Louis Fisher, *Military Tribunals and Presidential Power: The American Revolution to the War on Terrorism.* (Lawrence: Univ. of Kansas, 2005), 89n78.

31. "Airs German Plot in Latin America," *New York Times*, August 24, 1919; Paul Altendorf, "On Secret Service in Mexico, *Chicago Tribune*, November 3, 1919, to December 2, 1919.

32. "President Stays Execution of German Spy," W*ashington Times*, December 27, 1919.

33. "German Spy Causes Clash at Washington," *Atlanta Constitution*, December 28, 1919; "President's Reprieve Saves German Spy," *New York Times*, December 28, 1919.

34. Baker to President Wilson, January 1, 1920, Witzke Case File 119966. The letter summarized the recent history of the case: Witzke's trial by military commission in August, his conviction for violating the 82nd Article of War, and his sentence to be hanged. It noted that the reviewing authority had approved the sentence, the Acting Judge Advocate General had recommended that the sentence be commuted to twenty years, had then transmitted the record to the President with his own recommendation that twenty years was too light and should be changed to a life

sentence of hard labor at Leavenworth Penitentiary. It also contrasted the factual assumptions upon which Gregory's prior legal opinion was based with the real facts established at trial and confirmed by the Review Board: that Witzke was a German national not a Russian; that he crossed several times into the United States during the twenty-four hours preceding his arrest and was not arrested immediately the first time he set foot in the United States; and that when arrested he was in the vicinity of military encampments where US Army officers and men were stationed who were patrolling the Mexican border where an invasion was threatened from the Mexican side.

35. Order of President Wilson, May 27, 1920, Witzke Case File 119966.
36. Gen. Orders, No. 32, War Department, *General Orders and Bulletins: War Department 1920* (Washington: Government Printing Office, 1921).

5. IMPRISONED AND PARDONED

1. Adjutant General Guy V. Henry to Commanding General, Southern Department re Lather Witcke, alias Pablo Waberski, June 4, 1920, RG 153, Ser. Court Martial Case Files, 1917–1938, File Lather Witcke, alias Pablo Waberski, 119966 (NASL). In their haste to notify Fort Sam Houston of the commutation and to hustle Witzke off to Leavenworth, the official copy sent to Fort Sam Houston misidentified the Order as No. 118 rather than No. 32. A corrected copy was sent the next day. Henry to Commanding General, June 5, 1920, Witzke Case File 119966.
2. Lothar Witzke, Memorandum of interview by Leonard A. Peto and Amos J. Peaslee at Maracaibo, Venezuela, January 9, 1929, US exh. 552, MCC, RG 76, EN PI 143/14, Ser. Printed US Exhibits, 1929?–1939?, vol. 3 (NACP); Intake Card for Lather Witcke, Leavenworth Penitentiary, File 15309/images 3–4, RG 129, Ser. Inmate Case Files, 7/3/1895-11/5/1957, File U. Inmate File of Lothar Witzke (aka Luther Witzke, aka Lather Witcke) (NAKC), https://catalog.archives.gov/id/117690150.
3. Strictly speaking, the very first federal penitentiary was the US Penitentiary in Washington, DC, operated by the federal government from 1831 to 1862. There were also several federal territorial prisons. Todd Kerstetter, "Leavenworth Penitentiary," in *Encyclopedia of the Great Plains*, ed. David J. Wishart (Lincoln: University of Nebraska-Lincoln, 2011), http://plainshumanities.unl.edu/encyclopedia/doc/egp. law.025.xml.
4. Paul W. Keve, *Prisons and the American Conscience: A History of U.S. Federal Corrections* (Carbondale: South Illinois Univ. Press, 1991), 36, 38, 40–41, 53; Kenneth LeMaster, *U.S. Penitentiary Leavenworth* (Charleston, Chicago, Portsmouth and San Francisco: Arcadia Publishing, 2008), 7–8; United States Penitentiary in Leavenworth, Kansas, *Annual Report 1919-1920* (Leavenworth: U.S. Penitentiary Press, 1921), 22 [reproduction: Microfilm, 1897–1925 (New York: New York Public Library, 1992)].
5. Keve, *Prisons*, 41; LeMaster, *Penitentiary Leavenworth*, 14.
6. LeMaster, *Penitentiary Leavenworth*, 18.
7. Leavenworth Penitentiary, *Annual Report 1919-20*, 74–83; "General Arrangement, United States Penitentiary, Leavenworth, Kans.," (map, 1916) in *Manufacturing in Penitentiaries, Report of the Commission on Equipping United States Penitentiaries for Manufacturing Articles Used by the United States Government*, 7240 H.doc. 1752,

December 2, 1916, https://congressional-proquest-com.ezproxy4.library.arizona
.edu/congressional/docview/t45.d46.7240_h.doc.1752_map_1?accountid=8360.

8. Keve, *Prisons*, 58–59.

9. Witzke Intake Card, Leavenworth, File 15309/images 3–4. Witzke is identified on an-
cillary intake forms by yet other names besides those on his Intake Card, e.g., Luther
Witzke. See "Health Record of Luther Witzke," Leavenworth, File 15309/image 186.

10. Deputy Warden's Office receipts dated June 16, 1920, Leavenworth, File 15309/im-
ages 122, 129, 136.

11. Ibid., image 129.

12. "Record of Articles Received by Prisoners, L. Witcke," Leavenworth, File 15309/im-
ages 32–37.

13. Letter, Chief Clerk to *San Francisco Examiner*, June 22, 1920, Leavenworth, File
15309/image 84. The one year subscription cost Witzke $6.

14. Second Ind., H. A. White to Adjutant General, December 1, 1920, Witzke Case File
119966.

15. Fort Sam Houston to Warden Leavenworth Penitentiary, Telegram, December 14,
1920, Leavenworth, File 15309/216; Third Ind., Adjutant Saxon to Army Adjutant
General, February 7, 1921, Witzke Case File 119966. The cash was comprised of 18
twenty-dollar bills, 33 ten-dollar bills, and three dollars in American silver coins.
The gold coins were comprised of five twenty peso gold pieces, seven ten peso gold
pieces, and one five peso gold piece.

16. Army Adjutant General to Warden Leavenworth Penitentiary, March 19, 1921, Leavenworth, File 15309/image 85.

17. Fifth Ind., Kreger to Adjutant General, March 15, 1921, Witzke Case File 119966.

18. First Ind., Warden to Army Adjutant General, March 22, 1921, Leavenworth, File
15309/image 85.

19. Secretary of War to Attorney General, April 15, 1921, summarized in Secretary of
War to Attorney General, June 1921, Witzke Case File 119966.

20. See Second Ind., Adjutant General to Judge Advocate General, May 22, 1921 and 3rd
Ind., Judge Advocate General to Adjutant General, June 10, 1921, with enclosure,
Witzke Case File 119966.

21. See Second Ind., Judge Advocate General to Army Adjutant General, July 21, 1921,
Witzke Case File 119966.

22. Ibid.

23. Letter, Attorney General to Warden, September 22, 1921, Leavenworth, File 15309/
image 55.

24. "Health Record of Luther Witzke," Leavenworth, File 15309/images 186–87. See also
miscellaneous requests from Witzke to see a doctor, ibid., images 184–85.

25. Skin conditions: "Hospital Sick Report," ibid., image 186; shaved head: Physician to
Deputy Warden, July 12, 1923, ibid., image 183; grippe: Hospital record (admitted
March 2, 1922, discharged March 4, 1922), ibid., image 176; syphilis / erysipelas: Hos-
pital records (admitted May 2, 1923, discharged May 14, 1923), ibid., images 174, 186.

26. Warden to Superintendent of Prisons Heber H. Votow, February 23, 1923, Leavenworth, File 15309/image 151.

27. Ibid.

28. "Individual Daily Labor Report" for periods ending June 30, 1921, 1922, and 1923,
ibid., images 58–59, 137–40.

29. "Six Prisoners Scalded," *Leavenworth Post*, July 20, 1921; "Boiler Explosion Claims Another," *Leavenworth Post*, July 29, 1921; "Report of Physician," Leavenworth Penitentiary, *Annual Report 1921–22*.
30. J. A. Kirwin, "Black and White Heroes in Gray," *Leavenworth Post*, July 24, 1921.
31. Chief Engineer to Warden W.I. Biddle, July 21, 1921, Leavenworth, File 15309/images 69–70. See also Letter, Chief Engineer Carl Jensep to Warden, July 21, 1921 (revised version of p. 2 of earlier letter of same date, adding one name to the list of those commended for their courage), ibid., image 169.
32. Warden, "To Whom It May Concern," January 31, 1922, ibid., image 102.
33. Less widely remarked, but pointedly noted in an opinion piece published in the *Leavenworth Post* by the editor of the inmate newspaper "New Era" several days after the accident, was that there were both White and Black prisoners who were victims and rescuers, and the rescue itself was color-blind. "When we are in danger of death," the author wrote, "we don't stop to choose the color of the skin which is to help us save our lives. We don't yell 'Nigger'—we cry 'Help.' In this case the white boys did their utmost to save the colored boys and the colored lads did their best to rescue the white men." Of particular note was a "colored runner" for the Boiler House named Mitchell—probably James H. Mitchell (prisoner #13228), who "covered his head with a blanket and descended into that fiery pit when it was trying to snuff out the lives of his fellows. He brought up three men, two white and one colored." Overcome by the effort, Mitchell was himself then "carried to the hospital." "Why," the author ended his piece by asking, "can't this spirit of good fellowship—this commendable show of brotherhood—manifest itself all the time?" Kirwin, "Back and White."
34. "Letters" registries for Witzke, June 1920-November 1923, Leavenworth, File 15309/images 38–47.
35. See Second Ind., Judge Advocate Martin to Army Adjutant General, July 23, 1920, Witzke Case File 119966. The 2nd Ind. Says that the Judge Advocate General's office received a communication to this effect from Witzke dated June 23. The prison's correspondence log for Witzke indicates that on June 23 and 24 he sent communications to the War Department c/o a Chaplain Bateman; presumably, one or both of these was the communication referred to in the 2nd Ind.
36. Adjutant General Redington to Warden, July 27, 1920, Leavenworth, File 15309/image 60.
37. "Letters" registry, July-December, 1920, ibid., image 46.
38. First petition: 4th Ind., Acting Judge Advocate General E.A. Kreger to Army Adjutant General, January 17, 1921, Witzke Case File 119966; Memorandum, Army Adjutant General to Judge Advocate General, January 29, 1921, ibid.; Army Adjutant General Redington to Warden, January 29, 1921, Leavenworth, File 15309/image 82. Second petition (for reconsideration): Army Adjutant General to Warden, "Subject: Case of General Prisoner Lather Witcke alias Pablo Waberski," February 12, 1921, Leavenworth, File 15309/image 81. Third petition (to President Harding): "Letters" registry for Witzke, July-December 1921, Leavenworth, File 15309/image 42; Second Ind., Acting Judge Advocate General Hull. To Army Adjutant General, November 7, 1921, Witzke Case File 119966; Letter, Army Adjutant General to Warden, November 22, 1921, Leavenworth, File 15309/image 51.
39. Second Ind., Warden to Adjutant General, December 23, 1920, Leavenworth, File 15309/image 63.

40. "Embryo 'Holy Joes' Taught by Senior Army Chaplain," *Trench and Camp* (Deming, New Mexico), June 2, 1918; "Five Pay Penalty of Houston Mutiny," *The Houston Post*, September 18, 1918. We can reasonably infer that Bateman was Witzke's intermediary with the War Department because Witzke's prison correspondence log for June-December 1918 shows that all of his correspondence addressed to the War Department was care of Bateman.

41. A. J. Sabath to Warden, February 18, 1921, Leavenworth, File 15309/image 71; Warden to A. J. Sabath, February 23, 1921, ibid., image 72.

42. See Assistant Attorney General Ottinger to Acting Judge Advocate General Hull, November 9, 1922, Witzke Case File 119966; Hull to Ottinger, November 11, 1922, ibid. We know of von Plessen's letter to Witzke only because it is referenced in Witzke's letter to Julius Goebel, discussed in the following paragraph of the text.

43. Witzke to Professor Goebel, December 8, 1922, Witzke Case File 119966. Curiously, neither Von Plessen's letter to Witzke, nor Witzke's to Goebel, is recorded in the prison's correspondence log. The log does show that Witzke mailed something to the German Embassy in Washington on December 1. Perhaps he sent a post-dated copy of the Goebel letter to the embassy so that von Plessen would know its contents, and the embassy then forwarded it to the professor. Or perhaps he sent the embassy a German language draft, which the Embassy then translated and sent on to Goebel.

44. Witzke's list of sabotage allegations against him included several items that, as far as the authors have been able to determine, were never alleged by Altendorf or anyone else, including ammunition factories in Chicago and Connecticut and the mysterious disappearance of the naval collier Cyclops with its crew of 306 in March 1918, a time when Witzke was already in custody at Fort Sam Houston! Was Witzke embellishing to try and make Altendorf look as ridiculous as possible?

45. "Plea for German Prisoner," *New York Times*, January 6, 1923.

46. "U.S. Will Refuse to Free War Spy," *Baltimore Sun*, January 7, 1923; "Parole Is Now Expected for Witzke, German Spy," *New York Times*, January 7, 1923; "Release of Witzke, Spy, Denied German Embassy," *Baltimore Sun*, January 10, 1923.

47. "Two Views of Federal Prisoners," *The Coshocton Times*, January 11, 1923.

48. Second Ind., Warden to Army Adjutant General, February 27, 1923, Leavenworth, File 15309/image 87. A copy of the warden's "To Whom It May Concern" memorandum is at ibid., image 86. The original date of the memo was January 31, 1922 but the date "Nov 13" is handwritten above January 31, indicating that Witzke's good conduct continued through 1922.

49. Third Ind., Army Adjutant General to Judge Advocate General, March 7, 1923, Witzke Case File 119966; Fourth Ind., Judge Advocate General Bethel to Army Adjutant General, March 9, 1923, ibid.; Army Adjutant General to Warden, March 24, 1923, Leavenworth, File 15309/image 88.

50. Guy L. Fake, Affidavit, November 29, 1929, US order exh. 352, MCC, RG 76, EN PI 143/14, Ser. Printed US Exhibits, 1929?–1939?, vol. 6 (NACP), 2.

51. Witzke to Fake, April 1, 1923, MCC, US order exh. 352-A.

52. Ibid.

53. Ibid.

54. Guy Fake, Affidavit, March 6, 1929, US exh. 627, MCC, RG 76, EN PI 143/14, Ser. Printed US Exhibits, 1929?–1939?, vol. 4 (NACP).

55. Ibid.
56. German Ambassador to Judge Advocate General Walter Bethel, May 1, 1923, Witzke Case File 119966.
57. Ibid.
58. Petition, Paul and Vally Witzke to President Harding, June 7, 1923, Witzke Case File 119966. The original was in German. The Case File copy is a translation.
59. Ibid.
60. German Ambassador to Judge Advocate General Bethel, July 14, 1923, Witzke Case File 119966.
61. Lansing, Michigan, *City Directory* (1921), 502, reproduced at https://www.ancestry .com/interactive/2469/7258614?pid=434851580&treeid=&personid=&rc=&usePUB =true&_phsrc=MCN198&_phstart=successSource.
62. "Work Found for Soldier Wives by Business Girls," *Lansing State Journal*, June 27, 1916.
63. "Red Cross Packs Boxes of Supplies," *Lansing State Journal*, March 27, 1917.
64. "Lansing Becoming Artists' Colony as Academy Here Interests Many," *Lansing State Journal*, June 7, 1922; "Personals," *Lansing State Journal*, November 6, 1922; "Christmas Party," *Lansing State Journal*, December 26, 1922.
65. "Bohemian Dinner," *Lansing State Journal*, February 12, 1923.
66. Judge Advocate General Bethel to Secretary of War, Memorandum, June 8, 1923, Witzke Case File 119966.
67. Great Britain: Note, First Secretary, American Embassy, London to Assistant Military Attache, American Embassy, London, Note, August 13, 1923, and Assistant Military Attache, American Embassy, London to War Department, Memorandum re Release of German Prisoners, August 15, 1923, ibid.; France: Military Attache, American Embassy, Paris to War Department Washington, D.C., Memorandum re Release of German Prisoners, May 18, 1923, and 1st Ind. thereon, War Department to Judge Advocate General, June 6, 1923, ibid.; Italy: Chief, M.I. 5 to Military Attache, American embassy, Rome, Memorandum re-Release of German Prisoners, May 1, 1923, and First Ind. thereon, Military Attache, American Embassy, Rome to Army Chief of Staff, July 23, 1923, ibid.
68. Judge Advocate General Bethel to German ambassador, Washington, D.C., August 1, 1923, Witzke Case File 119966.
69. Acting Secretary of State Phillips to Secretary of War, September 13, 1923, with attached Memorandum, German Ambassador to State Department, September 11, 1923, Leavenworth, File 15309/images 98–102.
70. Fourth Ind., Judge Advocate General Bethel to Army Adjutant General, Sept. 26, 1923, Witzke Case File 119966.
71. Army Adjutant General's Office to Judge Advocate General, November 7, 1923, ibid.
72. Army Adjutant General, "A.G. 383.6 Witcke, Lather (9.13.23) Prisoner," November 7, 1923, Leavenworth, File 15309/image 206. The same day the Secretary of War notified the Secretary of State of Witzke's sentence remission and asked him to advise the German embassy. He explained that the November 21 release date was chosen in order to give the German Ambassador sufficient time to arrange for Witzke's return to Germany, as the Ambassador had promised to do. He also asked that the German ambassador communicate and coordinate with the warden. Secretary of

War Weeks to Secretary of State, November 7, 1923, ibid., image 115. Technically, the remission of Witzke's sentence was a commutation, not a pardon. A commutation reduces the length of a convicted person's sentence but does not expunge his conviction or the legal consequences thereof. A pardon goes further and extinguishes the consequences of the conviction. The term "pardon" is often used colloquially to refer to both. Witzke himself used both terms when explaining what happened, and some contemporary newspapers called his release a pardon. Although we are careful in this section not to use the term pardon, elsewhere in the book we adopt the colloquial convention and use the term pardon both to refer to Witzke's bid for clemency and to the remission of his sentence.

73. German Government correspondence: German Consul (St. Louis) to Warden, November 15, 1923, Leavenworth, File 15309/images 113–14; German Agent Wilde to Warden, November 17, 1923, ibid., image 112; Warden to German Agent Wilde, November 19, 1923, ibid., image 111. Immigration Service correspondence: Warden to Inspector in Charge, Immigration Service, November 12, 1923, ibid., image 105; Inspector in Charge to Immigration Bureau, Washington, Telegram, November 16, 1923, ibid., image 107; Inspector in Charge to Commissioner-General of Immigration, November 16, 1923, ibid., image 106; Warden to Inspector in Charge Reynolds, Immigration Service, November 16, 1923, ibid., image 195; Inspector in Charge Reynolds to Warden Biddle, November 19, 1923, ibid., image 109; Inspector in Charge to Commissioner of Immigration, November 19, 1923, ibid., image 110.

74. Lothar Witzke to Paul Witzke, Cablegram, November 13, 1923, Leavenworth, File 15309/image 103.

75. Witzke to Mrs. M.E. Johnson, Telegram, November 13, 1923, Leavenworth, File 15309/image 95.

76. M.E. Johnson to Witzke, Telegram, November 14, 1923, Leavenworth, File 15309/image 214.; Witzke to Mrs. M.E. Johnson, November 14, 1923, ibid., image 94.

77. "Lone German Spy Convicted In U.S. Will Go Free Today," *Washington Post*, November 21, 1923.

78. Ibid. See also "Spy Is Released Without Orders From President," *Atlanta Constitution*, November 21, 1923.

79. Witzke, Interview by Peto and Peaslee, January 9, 1929, MCC, US exh. 552

80. "German Spy, Witzke, And Host of Aliens Bid Adieu to U.S.," *Atlanta Constitution*, November 30, 1923.

81. Ibid. His age was 28, not 30.

82. Ibid.; "Pardoned Spy Sails for His Homeland, *New York Times*, November 30, 1923.

6. SAILOR, SPY

1. Petition, Paul and Vally Witzke to President Harding, June 7, 1923, RG 153, Ser. Court Martial Case Files, 1917–1938, File Lather Witcke, alias Pablo Waberski, 119966 (NASL).

2. Lothar Witzke, "My CV," January 19, 1913, Lothar Witzke, Correspondence (originals) comprising 84 letters and cards, 1913–1916, GER exh. XCCII-A/ 5, MCC, RG 76, EN P 51, Ser. German Exhibits and Translations re Sabotage Cases, ca. 1922–1939, vol. 16 (NACP). Witzke gave two subsequent, slightly different accounts

of his education. In 1919 he told an interviewer that, after three years of grammar school and nine years of high school, he attended Posen Academy for a year. Lothar Witzke, Examination by Thomas J. Tunney, September 16–17, 1919, US exh. 24, MCC, RG 76, EN PI 143/14, Ser. Printed US Exhibits, 1929?–1939?, vol. 1 (NACP). In or about 1953, after finishing a one-year term as a member of the Hamburg Parliament, he submitted a short personal biography stating that he had graduated at grade 13 from the gymnasium (i.e., the academic track) before entering the merchant marine. Hamburg State Archive. The authors believe that the 1913 "My CV" is the most accurate one.

3. Mother to L. Witzke, June 10, 1913, MCC, GER exh. XCII-A/6; L. Witzke to Mother, June 11, 1913, MCC, GER exh. XCII-A/8; and L. Witzke to Father, June 16, 1919, MCC, GER exh. XCII-A/9.

4. L. Witzke to Mother, June 11, 1913, MCC, GER exh. XCII-A/8.

5. L. Witzke to Father, June 16, 1919, MCC, GER exh. XCII-A/9.

6. L. Witzke to Parents, June 21, 1913, MCC, GER exh. XCII-A/10.

7. Lars Bruzelius, "A Catalogue of Four-Masted Barques and Ships, 1892 Osborne," http://www.bruzelius.info/Nautica/Ships/Fourmast_ships/Osborne(1892).html.

8. "Astronomy Sleuths Chase 100-Year Meteor Mystery," https://www.space.com/19410-100-year-meteor-mystery-photos.html. The Great Meteor Procession occurred on February 9, 1913. The report in the *Vinnen's* log book is dated February 10. Several other observers besides the *Vinnen* crew reported seeing the procession on February 10. Possibly there was a second procession of meteors a few hours after the first.

9. Mother to L. Witzke, June 10, 1913, MCC, GER exh. XCII-A/6 and L. Witzke to Mother, June 11, 1913, MCC, GER. Exh. XCII-,A/8.

10. L. Witzke to Mother, June 11, 1913, MCC, GER exh. XCII-A/8 and L. Witzke to Father, June 16, 1913, MCC, exh. 9.

11. L. Witzke to Parents, June 21, 1913, MCC, GER exh. XCII-A/10.

12. L. Witzke to Parents, June 24, 1913, MCC, GER exh. XCII-A/11.

13. L. Witzke to Parents, June 29, 1913, MCC, GER exh. XCII-A/1.

14. L. Witzke to Parents, June 21, 1913, MCC, GER exh. XCII-A/10.

15. L. Witzke to Parents, June 26, 1913, MCC, GER exh. XCII-A/12.

16. L. Witzke to Parents, June 29, 1913, MCC, GER exh. XCII-A/1.

17. L. Witzke to Parents, June 24, 1913, MCC, GER exh. XCII-A/11.

18. L. Witzke to Parents, June 21, 1913, MCC, GER exh. XCII-A/10.

19. L. Witzke to Parents, June 24, 1913, MCC, GER exh. XCII-A/11.

20. L. Witzke to Parents, June 30, 1913, MCC, GER exh. XCII-A/3.

21. L. Witzke to Parents, July 2, 1913, MCC, GER exh. XCII-A/13.

22. L. Witzke to Parents, July 6-August 3, 1913, MCC, GER exh. XCII-A/14.

23. The four serial letters (GER exh. XCII-A/14–17), were written between July 6 and November 21, 1913.

24. L. Witzke to Parents, October 12-November 21, 1913, MCC, GER exh. XCII-A/17.

25. L. Witzke to Parents, August 31-October 8, 1913, MCC, GER exh. XCII-A/16.

26. L. Witzke to Parents, July 6-August 3, 1913, MCC, GER exh. XCII-A/14.

27. Ibid.

28. L. Witzke to Parents, August 10–17, MCC, GER exh. XCII-A/15.

29. L. Witzke to Parents, October 12-November 21, 1913 and November 30, 1913, MCC, GER exh. XCII-A/17 and 18.

30. Excerpt, L. Witzke to Parents, date uncertain, MCC, GER exh. XCII-A/sub-exh. 100. See also L. Witzke to Parents, July 6–August 3, 1913, MCC, GER exh. XCII-A/sub-exh. 14 ("On Thursday [July 24] the Lloyd cargo steamer *Borkum* passed by so closely that we could recognize people") and L. Witzke to Parents, October 12–November 21, 1913, MCC, GER exh. XCII-A/sub-exh. 17. "Last Monday we were all very happy, for we met the small cruiser *Nürnberg*. . . . It was about 2pm when the man in the lookout reported a steamer which turned out to be a battleship as it approached. It did not seem to intend to come near us, but when we raised the German flag, it turned around, also raised the German flag and came towards us. You can imagine how we cheered. Our captain, however, was not too pleased with this, for the steamer signaled (probably a misunderstanding) as an order "Go to Mazatlan!" The old man now feared that either war had broken out or that something was wrong. In the meantime the cruiser had come alongside and slowed down. Our whole crew had assembled on the foredeck, some also hung in the topmasts and the officers stood on the bridge. Both sides shouted out three hurrays, then one officer from the other ship took the megaphone and asked: "Where are you heading?" Our old man replied: "To Santa Rosalia!" The others went on asking: "How was the weather?" "Thank you, good, except for Cape Horn!" From the other side again: "Do you have any mail to Mazatlan?" "No thank you!" "Is everything alright on board?" Then our captain spoke: "Would you like to give a report about us?" "Yes, will do." "Today we've been 131 days at sea!" "How many?" "131 days!" "Safe journey!" "Thank you, the same to you." One of our sailors who knew how to signal had a lively conversation with the cruiser's signaler."

31. L. Witzke to Parents, October 12-November 21, 1913, MCC, GER exh. XCII-A/17 and L. Witzke to Parents, November 30-December 7, 1913, MCC, GER exh. XCII-A/18.

32. L. Witzke to Parents, November 30-December 7, 1913, MCC, GER exh. XCII-A/18.

33. L. Witzke to Parents, October 12-November 21, 1913, MCC, GER exh. XCII-A/17.

34. L. Witzke to Parents, November 30-December 7, 1913, MCC, GER exh. XCII-A/18.

35. Ibid.

36. Ibid.; L. Witzke to Parents, December 28, 1913, MCC, GER exh. XCII-A/20.

37. L. Witzke to Parents, January 25, 1914-March 8, 1914, MCC, GER exh. XCII-A/25 and 26.

38. L. Witzke to Parents, May 10, 1914-July 6, 1914, MCC, GER exh. XCII-A/33.

39. L. Witzke to Parents, March 29, 1914, MCC, GER exh. XCII-A/27.

40. L. Witzke to Parents, January 25, 1914-March 8, 1914, MCC, GER exh. XCII-A/25 and 26.

41. Ibid.

42. L. Witzke to Parents, March 29, 1914, MCC, GER exh. XCII-A/27.

43. Ibid.; L. Witzke to Parents, April 12, 1914 and April 26, 1914, MCC, GER exh. XCII-A/28 and 30.

44. L. Witzke to Parents, April 19, 1914 and May 5, 1914, MCC, GER exh. XCII-A/29 and 31.

45. L. Witzke to Parents, April 26, 1914, MCC, GER exh. XCII-A/30.

46. L. Witzke to Parents, May 5, 1914 and May 6, 1914, MCC, GER exh. XCII-A/31 and 32.

47. L. Witzke to Parents, May 10, 1914-July 6, 1914, MCC, GER exh. XCII-A/ 33.
48. Ibid.
49. At school Witzke had belonged to a rowing club, and therefore could claim special skill at rowing.
50. L. Witzke to Parents, May 10, 1914-July 6, 1914, MCC, GER exh. XCII-A/. 33.
51. L. Witzke to Parents, July 12, 1914, MCC, GER exh. XCII-A/34.
52. L. Witzke to Parents, May 10, 1914-July 6, 1914, MCC, GER exh. XCII-A/33.
53. L. Witzke to Parents, July 20, 1914, MCC, GER exh. XCII-A/35.
54. L. Witzke to Parents, August 2, 1914, MCC, GER exh. XCII-A/36.
55. L. Witzke to Parents, August 30, 1914, MCC, GER exh. XCII-A/37.
56. L. Witzke to Parents, September 6, 1914, MCC, GER exh. XCII-A/38.
57. L. Witzke to Parents, September 21, 1914, MCC, GER exh. XCII-A/39.
58. L. Witzke to Parents, November 1, 1914, MCC, GER exh. XCII-A/40.
59. L. Witzke to Parents, November 16, 1914, MCC, GER exh. XCII-A/41; "Extracts from the Log of the Dresden, With Comments on Her Career," *The Naval Review*, vol. 3, Iss. 3 (1915), 412–38, https://books.googleusercontent.com/books/content?req =AKW5QaeCARZuKUGMIosuO1KV605CBzFC6ZvcSkd3y-cO6vKmX6079byd LPO2msSIdYoSGyTYx9MHO349z2R1HH-sZrYZKFqSijcakjOByl8bsSXcLDs KbsvzhJLRE-sGS82ofERy7CdZI1spRcDcYmje79MsrCnHqa_AEC2ZsQrMgvsVa TFIQNDi8oRFZnxPuNDuQ9vtnlhx5rUW8aegkgXMaG2zd5GONyMIO27BP3 mc8kQ8ohu_tuhCdu2_ZmOEo7GPZAeiky_D.
60. "Battle of Coronel," https://www.britishbattles.com/first-world-war/battle-of-coronel/.
61. Barrie Pitt, *Coronel and Falkland* (London: Cassell, 1960, reprint Sharp Books, 1918), 79. For the time being, the *Dresden* and the *Leipzig* stayed behind at Más Afuera where the East Asia Squadron had taken refuge after the battle. Under the laws of war, Spee could not send more than three warships into Valparaiso, a neutral port, at the same time and the warships could not stay in a neutral port longer than twenty-four hours. There were also restrictions on coaling. The warships could take on enough coal only to reach the nearest German harbor, and they were prohibited from coaling again for three months at another port of the same country. Accordingly, it was necessary to find German or other sympathetic merchantmen to refuel his squadron clandestinely outside the main ports. A. Neville Hilditch, *Coronel and the Falkland Islands* (London and Toronto: Oxford Univ. Press, 1915) 9–10; Robert Massie, *Castles of Steel: Britain, Germany, and the Winning of the Great War at Sea* (New York: Ballantine Books, 2003), 236.
62. Massie, *Castles of Steel*, 237.
63. Pitt, *Coronel and Falkland*, 83.
64. Ibid., 79–82.
65. L. Witzke to Parents and Brothers, November 16, 1914, MCC, GER exh. XCII-A/41.
66. Pitt, *Coronel and Falkland*, 103–85. The British suffered ten fatalities and fifteen wounded at the Falklands battle.
67. L. Witzke to Parents, December 5, 1914, MCC, GER exh. XCII-A/42.
68. L. Witzke to Parents, December 13, 1914, MCC, GER exh. XCII-A/ 43.
69. L. Witzke to Parents and Siblings, December 20, 1914, MCC, GER exh. XCII-A/44.
70. Ibid.
71. L. Witzke to Parents and Siblings, December 26, 1914, MCC, GER exh. XCII-A/45.

72. L. Witzke to Parents and Siblings, January 3, 1915, MCC, GER exh. XCII-A/46.

73. L. Witzke to Parents, January 26, 1915, MCC, GER exh. XCII-A/47.

74. L. Witzke to Parents, January 30, 1915, MCC, GER exh. XCII-A/48/64.

75. Pitt, *Coronel and Falkland*, 193–94; Massie, *Castles of Steel*, 283–86; "The Sinking of the Dresden," *Naval Review*, vol. 3, Iss. 3 (1915), pp. 439–40; Log of the *Orama* for March 16, 1915, http://oldweather.s3.amazonaws.com/ADM53-69709/ADM53-69709-100_1.jpg; Ginger Historian, "The hunt for the SMS Dresden," February 28, 2015, http://boredhistorian.blogspot.com/2015/02/the-hunt-for-sms-dresden.html; "Dresden Crew on Island, Three Hundred of the Men at Quiriquina, Off Chilean Coast," *New York Times*, March 19, 1915. The captain of the *Dresden* and the Chilean government took the position that the *Dresden*, because she had been in neutral Chilean waters for more than twenty-four hours, should have been entitled to protection under international law, not attacked. Among *Dresden's* uninjured survivors was Wilhelm Canaris, who would later become head of the *Abwehr* (Germany's military intelligence service) from 1935 to 1944.

76. L. Witzke to Parents, February 16, 1915, MCC, GER exh. XCII-A/50.

77. Ibid.

78. L. Witzke to Parents, March 8–13, 1915, MCC, GER exh. XCII-A/52.

79. L. Witzke to Parents, February 16, 1915, MCC, GER exh. XCII-A/50.

80. L. Witzke to Parents, May 1, 1915, MCC, GER exh. XCII-A/sub-exh. 55. Witzke concluded his thought by writing, "They are going to draft us anyway once we come over, so I'll see whether I can stay with the military." It is unclear what Witzke meant by this sentence. Once the war was over and he could go home, why would he be drafted upon arriving in Germany? In any event, the idea of a future career in the military seems to have been on his mind.

81. L. Witzke to Parents, May 8, 1915, MCC, GER exh. XCII-A/56.

82. L. Witzke to Parents, May 23, 1915, MCC, GER exh. XCII-A/59.

83. L. Witzke to Parents, June 9, 1915, MCC, GER exh. XCII-A/61.

84. Capt. Frank P. Stretton to Dept. Intelligence Officer, Memorandum re Lothar Witzke, alias Pablo Waberski," October 2, 1919, RG 165, Ser. MID Correspondence, 1919–1941, File 10541-268/234 (NACP).

85. "Extracts from the Log of the Dresden, With Comments on Her Career," *The Naval Review*, vol. 3, Iss. 3 (1915), 412–38; "The Sinking of the Dresden," ibid., 439–40.

86. T.B. Dixon, *The Enemy Fought Splendidly: Being the 1914–1915 diary of the Battle of the Falklands and Its Aftermath* (Dorset: Blandford Press, 1983).

87. "German Wireless News," *Times of London*, March 20, 1915, citing a telegram signed Boy-Ed to the Admiralty in Berlin. The seriously wounded were Captain-Lieutenant Wiebitz, chief helmsman Max Zents, chief-engineer Gaffrey, sailors Karle and Cramens, boatsman's mate Brass, torpedo engineer Kunge, and radio engineer Molgedy. The slightly injured were Lieutenants Richards and Max Schmidt, sailors Scrugeis Reizer, Karl Schmidt, and Mondovitz, chief boatsman's mate Warnemünde, and chief sailor Kühl. The article also reports that Captain-Lieutenant Wiebitz died of his injury. In fact, he survived and remained a prisoner until the end of the war. There was an unsuccessful effort made during the war to repatriate him on compassionate grounds. British Foreign Office: Prisoners of War and Aliens Department: General Correspondence from 1906, Reference FO 383/59 (1915) (British National Archives), http://discovery.nationalarchives.gov.uk/browse/r/r/C2617301.

88. All historians (to our knowledge) who have written about Witzke and referenced the *Dresden* have accepted his *Dresden* story as true. *For example,* Bill Mills, *Agent of the Iron Cross: The Race to Capture German Saboteur-Assassin Lothar Witzke During World War I* (New York: Rowman & Littlefield, 2023), 11–12. "One of the youngest members of the *Dresden* crew to escape from Chile was naval cadet Lothar Witzke. . . . Witzke survived the Falklands Islands battle and was a party to the elusive cat-and-mouse struggle with the British navy in the waters of Tierra del Fuego. During the *Dresden's* final engagement at Isla Más a Tierra, the young midshipman received a shrapnel wond that tore into his left leg and fractured his patella (kneecap). For the rest of his life, Witzke would walk with a delayed stride. . . . Captured after the battle, he was taken aboard the *Orama* with the other seriously wounded sailors and transported to a hospital in Valparaiso." See also Henry Landau, *The Enemy Within: The Inside Story of German Sabotage in America* (New York: G.P. Putnam's Sons, 1937, facsimile reprint, London: Forgotten Books, 2018), 34; Sidney Sutherland, "German Spies in America: Part Eleven—Witzke," *Liberty,* May 2, 1931; Charles Harris III and Lewis Sadler, "The Witzke Affair: German Intrigue on the Mexican Border, 1917–18," LIX/2 *Military Review* (February 1979), 37; Richard B. Spence, "K.A. Jahnke and the German Sabotage Campaign in the United Sates and Mexico, 1914–1918," *The Historian* 59, no. 1 (Fall 1996), 99–100; Chad Millman, *The Detonators* (New York: Little, Brown & Co., 2006), 80.

89. Reginald P. Mitchell, "Spy," *The American Foreign Service Journal* 11, no. 11 (November 1934), 581–82.

90. Laws of war: Hilditch, *Coronel and the Falkland Isla*nds, 9–10; clandestine supply and recruitment: ibid. and Pitt, *Coronel and Falkland*, 83–84.

91. L. Witzke to Parents, November 16, 1914, MCC, GER exh. XCII-A/41.

92. L. Witzke to Parents, May 23, 1915, MCC, GER exh. XCII-A/59.

93. Ibid.; L. Witzke to Parents, June 9, 1915, MCC, GER exh. XCII-A/61. This was not Witzke's first such request to his father. Responding to a similar request from his son in January 1915, Paul Witzke had written to Vinnen about the issue and got a reply dated November 23, 1915, saying that performance, conduct and age were relevant factors for promotion as well as length of service, that the company had not heard from the captain in some time, and that they would write him about the issue. Vinnen & Co. to Paul Witzke, November 23, 1915, MCC, GER exh. XCII-A/78.

94. L. Witzke to Parents, May 23, 1915, MCC, GER exh. XCII-A/59.

95. L. Witzke to Parents, July 17, 1915, MCC, GER exh. XCII-A/67.

96. L. Witzke to Father, September 15, 1915, MCC, GER exh. XCII-A/72.

97. L. Witzke to Parents, October 3, 1915, MCC, GER exh. XCII-A/73.

98. L. Witzke to Parents, October 21, 1915, MCC, GER exh. XCII-A/74.

99. L. Witzke to Parents, December 26, 1915, MCC, GER exh. XCII-A 80.

100. L. Witzke to Parents, December 6, 1915, MCC, GER exh. XCII-A/79. See also, e.g., L. Witzke to Parents, November 21, December 14, and December 26, 1915, MCC, GER exh. XCII-A/77, 66, and 80.

101. Mother to L. Witzke, February 13, 1916, Lothar Witzke, Correspondence (originals and translations) comprising 24 letters and cards, 1916–17, GER exh. LXXXVI/11, MCC, RG 76, EN P 51, Ser. German Exhibits and Translations re Sabotage Cases, ca. 1922–1939, vol. XI (NACP).

102. L. Witzke to Parents, January 20, 1916, MCC, GER exh. XCII-A/sub-exh. 82.

103. L. Witzke to Parents, December 31, 1915, MCC, GER exh. XCII-A/81.
104. L. Witzke to Parents, December 26, 1915 and February 27, 1916, MCC, GER exh. XCII-A/80 and 84.
105. L. Witzke to Parents, April 10, 1916, MCC, GER exh. LXXXVI/1. In 1924, the Vinnen company issued a certificate with somewhat different dates and information about Witzke's service on the *J. C. Vinnen*. It stated that Witzke was employed on the ship as a cadet from June 18, 1913 to June 17, 1914, as an ordinary seaman from June 17, 1914 to June 17, 1915, and as an able-bodied seaman from June 17, 1915 to April 1, 1916, and that according to reports made at the time by the ship's captain, Witzke's "conduct and service have always been satisfactory." The certificate, under cover of a letter from the Vinnen company to the German Foreign Office dated March 2, 1929, was part of the evidence submitted by Germany to the Mixed Claims Commission during the Sabotage Cases arbitration. F. A. Vinnen & Co. to Foreign Office, March 2, 1929 with attached certificate, Vinnen & Co. to German Foreign Office, March 2, 1929, GER exh. LXV, MCC, RG 76, EN P 51, Ser. German Exhibits and Translations re Sabotage Cases, ca. 1922–1939, vol. 8 (NACP).
106. Ibid.
107. Father to L. Witzke, June 1, 1916 MCC, GER exh. LXXXVI/13.
108. L. Witzke to Parents, May 21, 1916, MCC, GER exh. LXXXVI/2. The *Colusa* had arrived at Valparaiso from San Francisco on or about April 23. "Steamship Movements," *Indianapolis Star*, Apr. 23, 1916. In his 1934 interview at Hankow, Witzke hinted that his decision to go to San Francisco may have been more calculated than his letters imply, that it was the German Consulate in Valparaiso that suggested he go, and that they gave him a code word for purposes of identifying himself to the German authorities in San Francisco after he got there. Mitchell, "Spy," 582. If true, this would help explain the ease with which Witzke made contact with the German Consul General in San Francisco and the speed with which he was apparently integrated into Germany's West Coast espionage activities, discussed below. Still, his letters are compelling evidence that he was bored with his life at Valparaiso, angry with his employer Vinnen, and restless to move on. Whatever role the Consul General may have had in his decision to leave, impulse was surely the driving force.
109. Ibid. See also Alien Crew List for SS *Colusa* Arriving at Port of San Francisco May 21, 1916, in California, Passengers and Crew Lists, 1882–1959, M1416—San Francisco, 1905–1954, at 1052, accessed via Ancestry.com. Christian Grau, Witzke's shipmate and friend on the *J. C. Vinnen*, told a German interviewer in 1929 that it was his recollection that Witzke joined the *Colusa* at Valparaiso as a stowaway, with the help of an officer on that ship. Richard Paulig, Affidavit *inter alia* testifying to his interviews on May 2 and 3, 1929 with Christian Grau, September 2, 1929, GER exh. XCII-G, MCC, RG 76, EN P 51, Ser. German Exhibits and Translations re Sabotage Cases, ca. 1922–1939, vol. 16 (NACP). Grau's recollection is consistent with what Witzke himself told an interviewer in 1934 in Hankow, China. He said then that he began his journey to San Francisco as a stowaway, was discovered, and then was employed on the ship at Arica as a sailor. Mitchell, "Spy," 582. Curiously, Witzke also told his Hankow interviewer that he posed on the *Colusa* as a Dane. The ship's crew list cited above, though, lists his supposed nationality as Swedish.
110. L. Witzke to Christian Grau, May 21, 1916, MCC, GER exh. XCII-E.

111. Ibid.
112. "Colusa in from South," *San Francisco Examiner*, May 22, 1916.
113. L. Witzke to Parents, May 21, 1916, MCC, GER exh. LXXXVI/2; L. Witzke to Christian Grau, May 21, 1916, MCC, GER exh. XCII-E. We do not know when these letters were mailed. Perhaps Witzke started them on the 21st but didn't finish them until a few days later.
114. "California Ghost Town," http://www.ghosttowns.com/states/ca/keeler.html; "Weird California, Keeler," http://www.weirdca.com/location.php?location=370. In 1913, water from nearby streams that fed Owens Lake began to be diverted by aqueduct to Los Angeles to serve the needs of that growing city. Owens Lake gradually dried up and Keeler slowly died. Dept. Of Public Service, *Complete Report on the Construction of the Los Angeles Aqueduct* (Los Angeles: Dept. of Public Service, 1916); "Strange Geographies: the Little Town that Los Angeles Killed," http://mentalfloss.com/article/22793/strange-geographies-little-town-los-angeles-killed.
115. Elschner and second spy operation: Tracie Provost, "The Great Game: Imperial German Sabotage and Espionage Against the United States, 1914–1917" (PhD diss., University of Toledo, UMI Microform, 2003), 126 n. 210, citing MCC Affidavit of Carl von Moltke, August 31, 1931; aqueduct: "Owen's Valley's Los Angeles Aqueduct," http://www.owensvalleyhistory.com/ov_aqueduct/page19.html and Dept. of Public Service, *Complete Report on the Construction of the Los Angeles Aqueduct* (Los Angeles: Dept. of Public Service, 1916); San Francisco departure date: Lothar Witzke, Notebook (original), 1916–17, GER Ann. 130, MCC, RG 76, EN P 61, Ser. German Annexes to Expert Opinion Deposition of Albert S. Osborn Relating to Sabotage Cases, ca. 1922—ca. 1938, box 1036 (NACP). Elschner, who was also a member of the US Geological Survey, was arrested February 16, 1918, in San Francisco as a "dangerous enemy alien." He was accused of involvement in a plot to blow up a British government cable station in the Hawaiian Islands, where he had been doing a survey assignment the week before an explosion damaged the station. "Federal Employee Is An Alleged Plotter," *Los Angeles Times*, February 17, 1918. Nothing seems to have come of the charge.
116. L. Witzke to Parents, June 4, 1916, MCC, GER exh. LXXXVI/3.
117. L. Witzke to Parents, June 10, 1916, MCC, GER exh. LXXXVI/sub-exh. 4.
118. Witzke told a similar story to a German interviewer in 1929 about the tent fire, adding that the primitive living conditions deterred him from wanting to stay in Keeler. Affidavit of Richard Paulig, September 2, 1929, MCC, GER exh. XCII-g. On or about June 21, he sent his brother Otto a picture postcard from San Pedro called Camping in the Desert, showing a large tent. He wrote, "I lived for three weeks in this type of tent and in the same part of the country. Found it very agreeable." L. Witzke to Otto Witzke, June 21, 1916, Lothar Witzke, Correspondence (originals and translations) comprising 27 picture postcards, 1914–17, GER exh. CXXVII-A, MCC, RG 76 (NACP). According to Witzke's address book, he was at Keeler from May 28 to June 16. Witzke, Notebook (original), 1916–17, MCC, GER Ann. 130.
119. Excerpt, L. Witzke to Christian Grau, [n.d.] (probably written in late June 1916), MCC, GER exh. XCII-F.
120. L. Witzke to Parents, June 25, 1916, MCC, GER exh. LXXXVI/5. The name of the yacht is misspelled in the body of the letter as "Figorin." The "borax-millionaire"

who owned the *Fiorgyn* was Thomas Thorkildsen, general manager of the Sterling Borax Company of Los Angeles. The yacht was a palatial schooner-rigged vessel, 117 feet long, equipped with gas engines. The previous summer it had sailed from Chicago to San Francisco via the Panama Canal, a record for the longest voyage of any yacht of her class. "Private Yacht," *Los Angeles Times*, March 3, 1916. For a short, well-told history of the Sterling Borax Company, see Ruth Cornwall Woodman, "Lang—the Sterling Borax Company" (unpublished), http://www.elsmerecanyon .com/tickcanyon/borax/ruthwoodman/ruthwoodman.htm.

121. Mitchell, "Spy," 582.

122. Witzke, Notebook (original), 1916–17, MCC, GER Ann. 130. We return to the subject of this notebook, or address book, in chapter 12. In an affidavit dated January 27, 1930, submitted to the Mixed Claims Commission, Thorkildsen said, after being shown Witzke's photograph, that he did not think Witzke was ever quartermaster on his yacht. Thomas Thorkildsen, Affidavit, January 27, 1930, US exh. 756, MCC, RG 76, EN PI 143/14, Ser. Printed US Exhibits, 1929?–1939?, vol. 7 (NACP). It is not surprising that, twelve years after Witzke's brief service, Thorkildsen would not recognize the photograph of someone who had worked for him only two weeks and whom he would have seen, and briefly, only a handful of times.

123. Lothar Witzke, Affidavit, July 19, 1927, GER exh. Q, MCC, RG 76, EN P 51, Ser. German Exhibits and Translations re Sabotage Cases, ca. 1922–1939, vol. 2 (NACP); Kurt Jahnke, Affidavit, November 24, 1927, GER exh. P, MCC, RG 76, EN P 51, Ser. German Exhibits and Translations re Sabotage Cases, ca. 1922–1939, vol. 2 (NACP).

124. Clarence Edwords, *Bohemian San Francisco: Its Restaurants and Their Most Famous Recipes; The Elegant Art of Dining* (San Francisco: Paul Elder and Company, 1914), 46.

125. Ibid.

126. Marine Corps. Service: "Kurt A. Jahnke" in *U.S. Marine Corps Muster Rolls, 1798–1958*, Microfilm Publication T977, ARC ID 922159, R.G. 187 (National Archives, Washington, D.C.), accessed via Ancestry.com database; Richard B. Spence, "K.A. Jahnke and the German Sabotage Campaign in the United Sates and Mexico, 1914–1918," *The Historian* 59, no. 1 (Fall 1996): 91, citing "Kurt A. Jahnke," Service Record, U.S. Marine Corps, File #33906, National Personnel Records Office (Military Personnel Records), Navy Reference Branch, in Federal Bureau of Investigation (FBI), File #62-5394, "Kurt A. Jahnke," FOIPA #240,106. Smuggling: Secret Service Daily Reports (San Francisco), March 8, 1918, RG 87, Ser. Daily Reports of Agents, 1875–1938, File San Francisco: volumes 14–16, April 1, 1917–July 31, 1918 (2 of 2)/images 308, 313–14 (NACP), https://catalog.archives.gov/id/152411462; San Francisco residence: Jahnke, Affidavit, November 24, 1927, MCC, GER exh. P.

127. Jahnke, Affidavit, November 24, 1927, MCC, GER exh. P.

128. Ibid.

129. See entry for "Jahnke" in *Crocker-Langley San Francisco Directory for the Year Ending June 1916* (San Francisco: H.S. Crocker Co., 1916), 994; Landau, *The Enemy Within*, 34.

130. L. Witzke to Parents, August 2, 1916, MCC, GER exh. LXXXVI/6. "Have been on land for three weeks and am living with an acquaintance of mine from Posen. He is a very nice man, his name is Kurt Jahnke."

131. Witzke, Affidavit, July 19, 1927, GER exh. Q.

132. Paul Witzke to Lothar Witzke, October 8, 1916, MCC, GER exh. LXXXVI/17.

133. Lothar Witzke to Paul Witzke, November 29, 1916, MCC, GER exh. LXXXVI/ 15.

134. Lothar Witzke to Parents, January 5, 1917, MCC, GER exh. LXXXVI/8.

135. Courier work: Witzke, Affidavit, July 19, 1927, GER exh. Q, 3. "I could be trusted": Witzke, Examination by Tunney, September 16–17, 1919, MCC, US exh. 24, 66.

136. Witzke, Affidavit, July 19, 1927, GER exh. Q, 3; Mitchell, "Spy," 582.

137. Witzke, Notebook (original), 1916–17, MCC, GER Ann. 130.

138. Mitchell, "Spy," 582.

139. Buildup to war: see, e.g., Michael Howard, *The First World War: A Very Short Introduction* (New York: Oxford University Press, 2002), 81–95; and Jay Bellamy, "The Zimmermann Telegram And Other Events Leading To America's Entry into World War I," *Prologue Magazine* 48, no. 4 (2016), https://www.archives.gov/publications /prologue/2016/winter/zimmermann-telegram. Jahnke warning: Mitchell, "Spy," 582. Sailor on San Pedro: Witzke Affidavit, Ex. Q, 4.

140. Mitchell, "Spy," 583.

141. Ibid.

142. Ibid., 582–83.

143. Trial Hearing Record, exh. 5 (introduced at 70), August 16–17, 1918, US v. Witcke alias Waberski, RG 153, Ser. Court Martial Case Files, 1917–1938, File Lather Witcke, alias Pablo Waberski, 119966 (NASL).

144. Trial Hearing Record, exh. 12 (introduced at 89).

145. Ibid., exhs. 4 (introduced at 68), 7 (introduced at 79), 8 (introduced at 80), 11 (introduced at 88) and 9 (introduced at 82).

146. Except for a few picture postcards to his family, there is no surviving correspondence from this period.

147. Witzke, Affidavit, July 19, 1927, GER exh. Q.

148. Not to be confused with the decorated German military officer in World War I, diplomat, and ambassador to Russia in World War II, also named von Schulenburg, who was executed in 1944 for his part in the 20 July plot against Adolf Hitler.

149. Provost, "The Great Game," 49, 126–27.

150. Witzke, Examination by Tunney, September 16–17, 1919, MCC, US exh. 24, 71–72.

151. Ibid.

152. "Prison At Presidio," *Santa Cruz Evening News*, December 6, 1917.

153. "Notorious German Dynamiter Held Here," *San Francisco Examiner*, December 25, 1917.

154. Witzke, Examination by Tunney, September 16–17, 1919, MCC, US exh. 24.

155. James Larkin, Affidavit, January 2, 1934, US exh. 990-A, MCC, RG 76, EN PI 143/11, Ser. US Exhibits, ca. 1923–1939, Box 15 (NACP).

156. There are several well-researched biographies of Larkin. For example, Emmet J. Larkin [no relation], *James Larkin: Irish Labor Leader, 1876–1947* (Cambridge: MIT Press, 1965); Donal Nevin, *James Larkin: Lion of the Fold; The Life and Works of the Irish Labour Leader* (Dublin: Gill & McMillan, 2006).

157. Meeting with von Igel: Larkin, *James Larkin*, 207–8, citing Larkin, Affidavit, January 2, 1934, MCC, US exh. 990-A; Jules Witcover, *Sabotage at Black Tom: Imperial Germany's Secret War in America, 1914–1917* (Chapel Hill, NC: Algonquin Books, 1989), 298–99, citing Larkin, Affidavit, January 2, 1934, MCC, US exh. 990-A. Jersey

City terminus plans: Witcover, *Sabotage at Black Tom*, 298–99, quoting from Larkin, Affidavit, January 2, 1934, MCC, US exh. 990-A.

158. Offer re West Coast sabotage: Larkin, *James Larkin*, 215–16, citing Larkin, Affidavit, January 2, 1934, MCC, US exh. 990-A. Delivering letters to Mexico: Larkin, *James Larkin*, 217, citing Larkin, Affidavit, January 2, 1934, MCC, US exh. 990-A.

159. "Jim Larkin Not To Be Allowed," *Dundee Evening Telegraph*, August 30, 1917 ("To Land in Australia. Melbourne, Wednesday. In connection with the report that James Larkin the Irish agitator, is on his way to Australia Mr. Hughes replying to a question in the House of Representatives today said instructions had been given to prevent Larkin from landing in Australia— Reuter"); Nevin, *James Larkin*, 510 ("On 25 July 1917 a cable from London was published that James Larkin was on his way to Australia via USA. His entry into Australia was prevented as it was thought that from his previous record for disturbances, the visit was for the purpose of creating strife in this country to secure his brother's release").

160. Witzke, Examination by Tunney, September 16–17, 1919, MCC, US exh. 24.

161. Larkin, *James Larkin*, 217–18, citing Larkin, Affidavit, January 2, 1934, MCC, US exh. 990-A.

162. "Consul of Germany and His Aid Indicted," *New York Times*, February 9, 1916; "German Consul Guilty in Munitions Case," *New York Times*, January 11, 1917; "Consul Bopp Is Sentenced," *New York Times*, January 23, 1917; "Bopp Group in Danger of Confinement," *San Francisco Examiner*, March 28, 1917; "Plan for Interning Germans Dropped," *San Francisco Examiner*, April 5, 1917; "Ram Chandra jailed with Other Hindus," San Francisco Examiner, April 8, 1917. By the time of their detention at Angel Island in connection with the Neutrality Act violations, Bopp and Schack, among others, were also on trial for conspiring to foment revolution against British rule in India—the so-called Hindu-German plot. "San Francisco Consuls Sentenced to Prison," *New York Times*, May 1, 1917.

163. Tunney interview: Witzke, Examination by Tunney, September 16–17, 1919, MCC, US exh. 24; De Lacey and Harnedy background: "2 Jailed As Heads of Plot to Free Bopp," *San Francisco Examiner*, August 15, 1917; "Arrest Two for Plot to Release German Consul," *The Rockford Morning Star*, August 15, 1917; "De Lacey, 2 Others Guilty of Bopp Plot," *San Francisco Examiner*, September 9, 1917.

164. "De Lacey Writes of Spies to Schack," *San Francisco Examiner*, September 5, 1917; "Letters from De Lacey Sent to Von Schack," *San Francisco Examiner*, September 5, 1917.

165. "Escape As Clergyman Was Planned," *San Francisco Examiner*, September 6, 1917.

166. "Arrest Two for Plot to Release German Consul," *The Rockford Morning Star*, August 15, 1917; "2 Jailed As Heads of Plot to Free Bopp," *San Francisco Examiner*, August 15, 1917.

167. "De Lacey Writes of Spies to Schack," *San Francisco Examiner*, September 5, 1917; "De Lacey, 2 Others Guilty of Bopp Plot," *San Francisco Examiner*, September 9, 1917; "Condensed Telgrams," *Bay City Times*, September 17, 1917.

168. "Money Given By De Lacey, Says Witness," *San Francisco Examiner*, September 6, 1917.

169. "Editor Who Plotted to Free Interned Germans Is Taken Into Custody on Bench Warrant," *Riverside Enterprise*, June 2, 1918.

7. WEIMAR, ABROAD AGAIN, THIRD REICH

1. "Pardoned Spy Sails for His Fatherland," *New York Times*, November 30, 1923.
2. Ibid.
3. Richard J. Evans, *The Coming of the Third Reich* (New York: Penguin Group, 2003), 105; Adam Tooze, *The Deluge: The Great War and the Remaking of the Global Order, 1916–1931* (New York: Penguin Group, 2014), 443.
4. George Grosz, "A Little Yes and a Big No," trans. L.S. Dorin (Dial, 1946), 124, quoted in "The Weimar Republic: The Fragility of Democracy," https://www.facinghistory.org/weimar-republic-fragility-democracy/economics/personal-accounts-inflation-years-economics-1919–1924-inflation. "A woman sitting down in a café might order a cup of coffee for 5,000 marks and be asked to give the waiter 8,000 for it when she got up to pay an hour later." Evans, *Third Reich*, 106.
5. Molly Loberg, *The Struggle for the Streets of Berlin: Politics, Consumption and Urban Space, 1914–1945* (Cambridge: Cambridge University Press, 2018), 99–100.
6. Lothar Witzke to Privy Councillor Hossenfelder, January 12, 1929, GER exh. LVI-C, MCC, RG 76, EN P 51, Ser. German Exhibits and Translations re Sabotage Cases, ca. 1922–1939, vol. 7 (NACP), 3.
7. Witzke to Hossenfelder, January 12, 1929, MCC, GER exh. LVI-C, 5. He continued: "On question, I said: 'that I hope the future may bring a change some day and that until such time I would hold myself in reserve subject to call.' When further asked, I said, 'that my belief was the present republican Government sincerely wants to clear up the old matters between themselves and their old enemies, thinking that this policy is to the best of Germany's interest. I said that political conditions in Germany are all up turned and the different parties, even Government offices pulling in different directions, more or less following their personal political beliefs." Ibid., 3–4.
8. Testimony of Byron Butcher, Trial Hearing Record at 111, August 16–17, 1918, US v. Witcke alias Waberski, RG 153, Ser. Court Martial Case Files, 1917–1938, File Lather Witcke, alias Pablo Waberski, 119966 (NASL).
9. Three-page enclosure entitled "Lothar Witzke/Kurt Jahnke" [n.d.] accompanying letter from D.J.J. to Ronnie, May 12, 1952, Witzke Lothar, KV 2/2296, 13–14 (TNA-UK).
10. Lothar Witzke, Memorandum of interview by Leonard A. Peto and Amos J. Peaslee at Maracaibo, Venezuela, January 9, 1929, US exh. 552, MCC, RG 76, EN PI 143/14, Ser. Printed US Exhibits, 1929?–1939?, vol. 3 (NACP), 1977.
11. "As inflation reached its climax in October and November 1923, crowds demonstrated, broke display windows, robbed bakeries, and raided public markets. Antisemitic riots broke out in Berlin's Scheunenvertiel, where crowds assaulted people and ravaged property." Loberg, *The Struggle for the Streets of Berlin*, 155–56. "Banned from government zones, demonstrators instead flocked to shopping districts as sites that promised crowds and attention. By the end of the Weimar Republic, they deliberately targeted commercial sites for the publicity potential as well as for their ideological value. Members of diverse parties distributed fliers outside department stores and at Potsdamer Platz. National Socialists in particular focused on these areas as locations of 'Jewish' commerce. At Christmas, Communists marched through the streets of West Berlin to show class divides." Ibid., 149–50.

12. "Hyperinflation became a trauma whose influence affected the behaviour of Germans of all classes long afterwards. It added to the feeling in the more conservative sections of the population of a world turned upside down, first by defeat, then by revolution, and now by economics. It destroyed faith in the neutrality of the law as a social regulator, between debtors and creditors, rich and poor, and undermined notions of the fairness and equity that the law was supposed to maintain. It debased the language of politics, already driven to hyperbolic over-emphasis by the events of 1918–19. It lent new power to stock fantasy-images of evil, not just the criminal and gambler, but also the speculator and, fatefully, the financially manipulative Jew." Evans, *Third Reich*, 111.

13. Enclosure re Lothar Witzke/Kurt Jahnke, KV 2/2296, 13–14. This was not the only sign of a connection between Jahnke and Witzke that exceeded immediate expedience in the Americas. After 1918, while Witzke was imprisoned in the United States, Jahnke visited Witzke's family in order to turn over to his parents Witzke's correspondence and address book retrieved by Jahnke in Mexico in early 1918. Lothar Witzke, Affidavit re authenticity of his letters and cards [Group 2], June 20, 1929, GER exh. LXXXVI-A, MCC, RG 76, EN P 51, Ser. German Exhibits and Translations re Sabotage Cases, ca. 1922–1939, vol. 11 (NACP), 5.

14. "The office headquarters from which [Jahnke] pulled the threads of what are reported to be rather diverse operations involving contacts in various parts of the world, were probably on his estate in Pomerania. Who employed his services and what type of activity he directed from there, is still a matter of speculation." Reinhard Doerries, "Tracing Kurt Jahnke: Aspects of the Study of German Intelligence," in George O. Kent (ed.), *Historians and Archivists: Essays in Modern German History and Archival Policy* (George Mason University Press 1991), 38. See also Bryan Clough, *State Secrets: The Kent-Wolkoff Affair* (Brighton: Hideaway Publications, Ltd., 2005), 228.

15. Enclosure re Lothar Witzke/Kurt Jahnke, KV 2/2296, 13–14.

16. He received the Iron Cross, First Class, on March 15, 1924. Bundesarchiv to coauthor, email, February 3, 2020.

17. In November 1923, the month of his return, the German central bank stopped monetizing government debt, a step that would eventually end hyperinflation in Germany. In February 1924, the Allies agreed to end their occupation of the Ruhr and to grant the German government a more realistic reparations payment schedule. This was known as the Dawes Plan. The Dawes Plan stretched payments until the 1980s (Tooze, *Deluge*, 454). Payments were financed in large part by an international loan headed by Wall Street (Tooze, 457). The Young Plan in January 1930 further reduced Germany's reparations obligations. "Britain and France increasingly functioned as conduits for a cycle of payments that ran from the United States to Germany and back again. After the Young Plan, France retained only 40 percent of its reparations payments, Britain barely 22 percent. The rest was passed on to the United States for war debts" (Tooze, 489).

18. [Illegible] to Dowgill, February 16, 1940, Jahnke Kurt, KV 2/755, 101–2 (TNA-UK).

19. Application by Witzke for admission to helmsman examination, July 1, 1924, Hamburg State Archive 111–1, Senat. Nr. 11500

20. Paul Witzke to German Foreign Ministry, March 28, 1925 (handwritten note on let-

ter from Foreign Ministry to Paul Witzke, March 25, 1925), German Foreign Ministry Archive, R95271/K193123.

21. Head of Marine Administration to Ministry of Economy, July 2, 1924. Hamburg State Archive, 111-1, Senat. Nr. 11500.

22. L. Witzke to G. Heuser, Apr. 17, 1925, German Foreign Ministry Archive, R95271/K193205.

23. Witzke, Interview by Peto and Peaslee, January 9, 1929, MCC, US exh. 552.

24. Reinhard Doerries, "Tracing Kurt Jahnke: Aspects of the Study of German Intelligence," in George O. Kent (ed.), *Historians and Archivists: Essays in Modern German History and Archival Policy* (Fairfax, VA: George Mason University Press, 1991), 42–43n29. Doerries reaches that conclusion from the "German records relating to the Claims Commission," but he neither references specific correspondence nor provides dates. Ibid.

25. Paul H. Hearn, "Henry Ford and Mexico," *The Chesterfield Advertiser*, 1922.

26. "Ford cumple 95 años en nuestro país," *Carplanet*, June 24, 2020, 3.

27. *The Mexican Year Book: A Statistical, Financial, and Economic Annual, Compiled From Official and Other Returns, 1911* (London: Forgotten Books, 2017).

28. "In 1921 Mexico accounted for 25 percent of the world's output of petroleum, making it the second most important producer after the United States. Over the next nine years Mexican output declined continuously and precipitously. By 1930, output was only 20 percent of what it had been in 1921, and Mexico accounted for only 3 percent of world production. Mexico would not again reach its 1921 levels of output until 1974. It never regained its 1921 market share." Stephen Haber, Noel Maurer, and Armando Razo, "When Institutions Don't Matter: The Rise and Decline of the Mexican Oil Industry," Hoover Institute Publication, https://web.stanford.edu/class/polisci313/papers/Haber-RazoFeb25.pdf.

29. Myrna Santiago, "ENERGY: Black Rain: Veracruz 1900–1938," *Berkeley Review of Latin American Studies* (Spring 2007), https://clas.berkeley.edu/research/energy-black-rain-veracruz-1900%E2%80%931938.

30. Ibid.

31. Ibid.

32. Christoph Moinian and Claudia Moinian (Witzke's grandchildren), interview by coauthor, November 2019. "Numerous wells also caught fire. The worst conflagration took place at Well #3 in San Diego de la Mar, which spurted a black column of oil and burst into flames on the Fourth of July, 1908. The explosion was so large that the earth sank and left gaping holes like two mouths. . . . Dos Bocas remains the largest oil spill and fire in history: about 420 million gallons of oil buried 30 square miles of forest, swamps, mangroves and marshes in oil." Ibid. "By comparison, the 1989 Exxon Valdez spill was 10.8 million gallons and the 1991 Gulf War spills and fires lost 240 million gallons. When the fire burned itself out, a toxic lake remained. Poisonous gases rose in clouds from its waters. One hundred years later, the lake is still there." Ibid.

33. Witzke, Interview by Peto and Peaslee, January 9, 1929, MCC, US exh. 552. We know from a letter from Witzke's brother, Kurt, that Witzke was a laboratory assistant. K. Witzke to Limmer, March 21, 1931, PA AA RZ207/95287.

34. Macpecri Media, *El Desafío de la Historia: Petróleo, Mucho Más que Oro Negro,* vol. 30, https://www.amazon.com/Petróleo-mucho-más-que-oro-negro-ebook/dp /B01AF7WK0A.

35. See Ebelio Espínola Benitez, *Los Comerciantes Alemanes en Maracaibo,* http:// ve.scielo.org/scielo.php?script=sci_arttext&pid=S1011–22512006000100012.

36. See Argenis Malavé, *Maracaibo: ciudad de 3 fundaciones* (2015), 259, http:// biblioteca.clacso.edu.ar/Venezuela/ceshc-unermb/20160829053753/MC3F.pdf, referring to the phenomenon known as "el reventón," whereby nearly 100.000 barrels of petroleum were produced daily. See also Macpecri, *El Desafío de la Historia.*

37. Lago Petroleum was apparently acquired by a subsidiary of Indiana Standard Oil in 1925. Parker Thomas Moon, *Imperialism and World Politics* (New York: MacMillan, 1929), 451. Indiana Standard then bought control of Pan American. See Max Winkler, *Investments of United States Capital in Latin America* (Boston: World Peace Foundation Pamphlets, 1929), 165–66.

38. Manuel Taborda, "Petróleo y clase obrera, or'igenes de la clase obrera venezolana," *CLACSO,* 2016, 60.

39. Ibid., 75.

40. Juan José Martín Frechilla y Yolanda Texera (comp), *Petróleo nuestro y ajeno: la ilusión de la modernidad,* Colección ciencias Sociales, 2005, 18.

41. Moinian and Moinian, interview, May 2019.

42. Espínola Benitez, "Los Comerciantes Alemanes en Maracaibo 1900–1930," *Paradigma* 27, no. 1 (December 2006), 349–63.

43. Moinian and Moinian, interview, May and November 2019.

44. Tomas Straka, *La nación petrolera* (2016), 270, https://www.unimet.edu.ve/unimet site/wp-content/uploads/2013/02/La-Nacion-Petrolera-Venezuela-1914–2014.pdf.

45. Straka, 270.

46. Malavé, *Maracaibo,* 251.

47. Nikolas Kozloff, "The Oily History of Offshore Operations: From Venezuela to the Gulf," Huffpost, last modified May 25, 2011, https://www.huffpost.com/entry /the-oily-history-of-offsh_b_559781.

48. Loren Puerta Bautista, Los paisajes petroleros del Zulia en la mirada alemana (1920–1940)," (PhD diss., Universidad Central de Venezuela, 2008), 86.

49. Malavé, *Maracaibo,* 117.

50. Henry Landau, *The Enemy Within* (New York: G. P. Putnam's Sons, 1937), 185.

51. de Haas to von Prittwitz, April 19, 1929, transl., PA AA RZ207/95287.

52. The reference to Witzke as an "ordinary seaman" also suggests that the German representatives understood that Witzke had never been a naval officer. We have confirmed this to be so, as discussed in chapter 6.

53. See infra chapter 10.

54. K. Witzke to Limmer, March 21, 1931, PA AA RZ207/95287.

55. Witzke to Hossenfelder, January 12, 1929, MCC, GER exh. LVI-C, 2. Landau says that the Neunhoffer employed by Lago was not William Neunhoffer but rather William Neunhoffer's brother. Landau, *The Enemy Within,* 183. Landau's view is corroborated by Witzke's brother Kurt who, in a letter written in March 1931 to the German Foreign Office, describes Lago's Head of Human Resources as "a certain Mr. Neunhofer [*sic*], an American, who was the brother of a well-known American

secret agent during the war. This former secret agent had testified in the sabotage processes for the American government." K. Witzke to Limmer, March 21, 1931, PA AA RZ207/95287. It is immaterial whether Neunhoffer was the agent or his brother. We go with Witzke's account: he had to have known if his Lago boss was the same Neunhoffer whom he had known in Mexico.

56. K. Witzke to Limmer, March 21, 1931, PA AA RZ207/95287. The letter from Witzke's brother, Kurt, complains about pressure applied by Neunhoffer to get confessions from Lothar and Kurt about Lothar's supposed sabotage activities.

57. Paulig to de Haas, October 6, 1930, PA AA RZ207/95287.

58. K. Witzke to Limmer, March 21, 1931, PA AA RZ207/95287.

59. Paulig to de Haas, October 6, 1930, PA AA RZ207/95287. See also Report, [illegible] to von Bülow, Dieckhoff, and Limmer, March 4, 1931, PA AA RZ207/95287; Report, [illegible] to Dieckhoff (?), March 9, 1931, PA AA RZ207/95287.

60. K. Witzke to Limmer, March 21, 1931, PA AA RZ207/95287.

61. Dr. Tannenberg (German Agent) to Dr. Schütte (Hamburg-Amerika-Linie), July 15, 1930, PA AA RZ207/95283; Glässel (Norddeutsche Lloyd) to de Haas (German representative in the MCC case), April 17, 1930, PA AA RZ207/95281; Böger (Hamburg Amerika Linie) to de Haas, April 23, 1930, PA AA RZ207/95281; de Haas to Dr. Schüttel, May 10, 1930, PA AA RZ207/95281.

62. For example, de Hass to Schütte, May 10, 1930, PA AA RZ207/95281; Reginald P. de Haas to German Agent, Telegram, June 11, 1930, PA AA RZ207/95281, together with de Haas note thereon, [n.d.], re meeting with Witzke. The back-and-forth led Witzke not to depart on the *Münsterland* from Hamburg on July 18, and instead to stay in Hamburg after July 18 and travel by road to and lodge in Genoa, at the government's expense, and board the *Münsterland* there, for departure on July 29. Tannenberg (German Agent) to Schütte, July 15, 1930, PA AA RZ207/95283.

63. Paulig to Witzke, May 2, 1930 ("Regarding the sabotage case, unfortunately there has been no decision yet."), PA AA RZ207/95281.

64. There are two Passenger Lists giving two different departure dates (July 18 and July 29). It is the July 29 List that includes a reference to Port Said. Hamburg State Archive, Hamburger Passagierlisten, Departure Date: July 18, 1930, Volume: 373–7 I, VIII A 1 Band 381, p. 2272, microfilm K1983; Hamburg State Archive, Hamburger Passagierlisten, Departure Date: July 29, 1930, Volume 373–7I, VIII A 1 Band 381, p. 2413, microfilm K1983.

65. "Passenger List," *North China Herald*, Oct. 21, 1930.

66. The foreign concessions were those of the British, French, Germans, Russians and Japanese. The German concession was formally ended in 1917 and administered thereafter by the Chinese, but the change had little effect on the lives of the German residents.

67. Harry A. Frank, *Roving Through Southern China* (New York: The Century Company, 1925), 75.

68. Kurt Bloch, *German Interests and Policies in the Far East* (New York: Institute of Pacific Relations, 1940), 2.

69. Bloch, *German Interests*, 11.

70. Donald M. McKale, "The Nazi Party in the Fast East, 1931–45," *Journal of Contemporary History* 12, no. 2 (1977): 293, www.jstor.org/stable/260218 (accessed June 28, 2020).

71. McKale, "The Nazi Party," 292.

72. McKale, "The Nazi Party," 293.

73. Gould H. Thomas, *An American in China 1936-1939: A Memoir* (New York: Greatrix Press, 2004), 167.

74. "A slashing offensive got underway today when northern alliance forces began advancing along a wide front in Hunan and Shantung provinces in an effort to push through to the Yangtze river and Nanking. . . . A counter attack was reported launched by Gen. Chiang Kai-Shek, head of the Nanking government forces. . . . Marshal Feng Yu-Hsiang, the so-called 'Christian general,' was commanding the northern alliance troops in the Honan sector, west of Shantung. This offensive has as its objectives Hankow. . . ." "New Offensive Started in China War," *Richmond Record-Herald*, August 7, 1930.

75. "1930 Troubles Gave Hankow a Bad Year," *New York Times*, May 17, 1931.

76. Ibid.

77. Moinian and Moinian, interview, May 2019.

78. McKale, "The Nazi Party," 292.

79. Ibid., 293.

80. Ibid., 294.

81. Ibid.

82. Christoph Moinian, email exchange with coauthor, August 2019.

83. Moinian and Moinian, interview, May 2019.

84. Report No. 390 by US Naval Attaché, Peiping, China, October 11, 1935, RG 165, Ser. MID Correspondence, 1919–1941, File 10541-268, Box 3453 (NACP).

85. Landau, *The Enemy Within*, 273–75. After what seems to have been consultations with the German Agent, Witzke declined to produce the address book. Ibid. The document or documents that Witzke was asked to produce were throughout the MCC case referred to as "notebooks." Having found the original document ultimately produced by the German Agent on behalf of Witzke, we have ascertained that "notebook" was a misnomer. The document in question was in fact an address book, and that is how we reference it.

86. Report by US Naval Attaché, Peiping, China, October 11, 1935. File 10541-268, Box 3453. A twenty-first century sensibility reacts to the Attaché's reference to "coolies." The term was widely used at the time for effectively indentured Asian workers, and its wide use is some context for Witzke's treatment of Chinese workers. President Roosevelt in 1938 used the term in one of his "Fireside Chats" (Number 13, 24 July 1938), telling a story about "two Chinese coolies" arguing in a crowd. The 1879 Constitution of the State of California declared that "Asiatic coolieism is a form of human slavery, and is forever prohibited in this State, and all contracts for coolie labour shall be void." Carroll D. Wright, *Labor Laws of the United States* (Washington: Government Printing Office, 1904), 129.

87. Report by US Naval Attaché, Peiping, China, October 11, 1935. File 10541-268, Box 3453.

88. This is recounted by Jin Shilong, Senior Engineer at the Hubei Flood Prevention Agency. "1931 China Floods," Wikipedia, accessed August 1, 2019, https://en.wikipedia.org/wiki/1931_China_floods.

89. Chris Courtney, "Central China flood, 1931," DisasterHistory.Org, accessed August 1, 2019, https://disasterhistory.org/central-china-flood-1931.

90. Chris Courtney, "Picturing disaster: The 1931 Wuhan flood," Chinadialogue, September 11, 2018, https://chinadialogue.net/en/cities/10811-picturing-disaster-the -1931-wuhan-flood/.

91. We surmise this based on the fact that Witzke's daughter, Helga, confided much to her children, especially her daughter, Claudia, and never mentioned the Hankow flood. Nor did Lilli ever mention the flood to her grandchildren.

92. Reginald P. Mitchel, "Spy," *The American Foreign Service Journal* (November 1934), 581–83, 627.

93. While the author purports to be quoting Witzke, and the substance of the remarks attributed to Witzke is surely accurate, it is unlikely that the words quoted are Witzke's. It is unlikely, for example, that Witzke would have used a phrase such as "the war clouds already had begun to blow faintly over the States."

94. Landau, *The Enemy Within*, 185.

95. We do not know whether tuberculosis was a byproduct of the flooding. The accounts that we have read do not mention tuberculosis as one of the diseases that spread.

96. Witzke's grandchildren believe that the return was in 1935, Moinian and Moinian, email exchange, February 2021, but an item in The China Press shows that "Mrs. L. Witzke and child" were on the M.S. Sauerland that departed Shanghai on March 14, 1934, for Hamburg. "M. S. Sauerland Off For European Ports," *The China Press,* Mar 14, 1934, ProQuest Historical Newspapers: Chinese Newspapers Collection, A1. A passenger list for a riverboat arrival at Shanghai a week earlier shows "Mr. and Mrs. Witzke." "Passenger List," *The North China Herald*, March 14, 1934, ProQuest Historical Newspapers: Chinese Newspapers Collection, 436. It may be that Witzke took his family by boat to Shanghai, then returned to Hankow and traveled solo thereafter to Germany.

97. Moinian and Moinian, interview, May 2019.

98. Moinian and Moinian, interview, November 2019.

99. Moinian and Moinian, interview, May 2019.

100. Ibid. We return to Lothar Jr's story in Chapter 10.

101. BArch R 9361-IX KARTEI/49291267. The membership card shows Witzke's residence as Hamburg. We have investigated without success whether it would have been possible for Witzke to join the party while in China, giving Hamburg as his German address.

102. See, by way of comparison, William Brustein, *The Logic of Evil: The Social Origins of the Nazi Party, 1925–1933* (New Haven: Yale University Press, 1998), arguing that people joined the Nazi Party not because of Hitler's irrational appeal or charisma or anti-Semitism, but because the party was perceived to offer more benefits to more people than did the other political parties in Weimar Germany, showing Nazi supporters to have been no different from citizens anywhere who select a political party or candidate who they believe will promote their economic interests. See also Gary King, Ori Rosen, Martin Tanner, and Alexander F. Wagner, "Ordinary Economic Voting Behavior in the Extraordinary Election of Adolf Hitler," *The Journal of Economic History*, December 1, 2008, https://www.cambridge.org/core/journals /journal-of-economic-history/article/abs/ordinary-economic-voting-behavior-in -the-extraordinary-election-of-adolf-hitler/8C79A0AB9DA174B7D81A6EB313B1E DFC (distinguishing the reactions of the unemployed from the poor but employed

to the Depression that started in 1929 and worsened through 1932, the former flocking to the German Communist Party and the later disproportionately joining the Nazi party).

103. BArch R 9361-III 228317(Günter Witzke); BArch R 9361-III 569905 (Ottomar Witzke).
104. Daniel Siemens, *Stormtroopers: A New History of Hitler's Brownshirts* (New Haven: Yale University Press, 2017), 155, 178, 186.
105. Ibid., 192.
106. Ibid.
107. This document is referenced in an article written by a Swedish historian of Nazi war crimes, Niclas Sennerteg. "Vem var den mystiske mr Witzke i Damaskus?," https://sennerteg.wordpress.com/2015/05/25/vem-var-nazisten-kurt-witzke-i-syrien/.
108. Ibid.
109. See Brian Ault, "Joining the Nazi Party before 1930: Material Interests or Identity Politics?" *Social Science History* 26, no. 2 (2002): 273–310, doi:10.2307/40267779.
110. "The [Weimar] Republic seemed [as of 1929] to have weathered the storms of the early 1920s. . . . It would need a catastrophe of major dimensions if an extremist party like the Nazis was to gain mass support. In 1929, with the sudden collapse of the economy in the wake of the Stock Exchange crash in New York, it came." Evans, *Third Reich*, 230.
111. "As Germany plunged deeper into the Depression, growing numbers of middle-class citizens began to see in the youthful dynamism of the Nazi Party a possible way out of the situation." Ibid., 246.
112. "'We cannot know.' If used sparingly, this is one of the strongest phrases in the biographer's language. It reminds us that the suave study-of-a-life we are reading, for all of its detail, length and footnotes, for all its factual certainties and confident hypotheses, can only be a public version of a public life, and a partial version of a private life. Biography is a collection of holes tied together with string. . . ." Julian Barnes, *The Man in the Red Coat* (New York: Alfred A. Knopf, 2020), 114.
113. Götz Aly, *Hitler's Beneficiaries*, trans. Jefferson Chase (New York: Holt Paperbacks, 2008), 14.
114. Moinian and Moinian, interview, May 2019. To substantiate that he was a nationalist, his grandchildren point to Witzke's routine comment when returning to Germany from Austria after a vacation. "Ah, at last a civilized country [*ordentliches Land*] again."
115. Ibid.
116. Witzke to Hossenfelder, January 12, 1929, MCC, GER exh. LVI-C, 3.
117. Evans, *Third Reich*, 150. "The widespread belief on the right that the German army had been 'stabbed in the back' by revolutionaries in 1918 translated easily into antisemitic demagogy. It was, men like Ludendorff evidently believed, 'the Jews' who had done the stabbing, who led subversive institutions like the Communist Party, who agreed to the Treaty of Versaillees, who set up the Weimar Republic." The stab in the back explanation also required particular myopia to conditions in Germany in November 1918. By 1918, Allied industry was mass producing tanks and gas, and German industry was far behind, the convoy system had become effective in protecting Allied shipping against German U-boats, and there were not enough U-boats on the German side, Germans were malnourished, both at home and on the front, and US entry in the war guaranteed that the Allies would stay far ahead in the

supply of food, steel, munitions and equipment. With the arrival of the Americans, the Central Powers were also outnumbered on the Western front by two to one. The disparity in numbers plus the prospect of a vast army of enemy tanks pushed Ludendorff to launch the spring offensive in 1918 in an effort to win the war at once. When that effort failed, Germany had no chance to win. In August 1918, during a surprise Allied attack at Amiens, German troops surrendered en masse. Ludendorff was worried that this was a precedent that would repeat itself. Richard J. Evans, *The Third Reich in History and Memory* (Oxford: Oxford Univ. Press, 2015), 27–32.

118. Moinian and Moinian, interview, November 2019.

119. Evans, *Third Reich*, 257.

120. Frederick Taylor, *1939, A People's History of the Coming of World War II* (New York: W. W. Norton & Company, 2019), 107.

121. Ibid., 195–201.

122. Nikolaus Ritter, *Cover Name: Dr. Rantzau*, trans. Katharine Wallace (Lexington Ky: University Press of Kentucky, 2019) (German original, 1972), 84–85.

123. Ibid., 5.

124. Ibid., xi.

125. British intelligence files report that "at the outbreak of [World War II], Jahnke, at Canaris' request, set about the proper organization of Abt. II of the Abwehr." Memorandum re "Kurt Jahnke," July 30, 1941, Jahnke Kurt, KV 2/755 (TNA-UK). "Abt. II" was where Witzke worked. Jahnke may have placed Witzke there. We have discussed in chapter 6 the persistent legend, to which Witzke contributed, that he had served as a naval officer on the *Dresden*. Had this been true, Canaris would have been one of his shipmates. But it is untrue.

126. By 1938, the character of National Socialism was manifest. In 1938, Austria became part of the Reich (March), the Munich Agreement was signed (September), and there was a nationwide anti-Jewish pogrom, *Kristallnacht* (November). In the immediate wake of *Kristallnacht*, the Nazi regime promulgated the Regulation for Elimination of Jews from the Economic Life of Germany, forcing Jews to transfer all businesses into Aryan hands and requiring Jews to make restitution of one billion Reichsmarks for the damage done on *Kristallnacht*. Jews were forbidden to attend concerts and museums and all Jewish pupils were expelled from German schools.

127. Taylor, *1939*, 50.

128. Ibid. Service with the *Abwehr* should not be confused with service in other Nazi organizations designed to control peoples within the occupied territories, such as the Gestapo or SD (*Sicherheitsdienst*), the Nazi Party intelligence service led by Reinhard Heydrich. The *Abwehr* was generally not comprised of hardened Nazis and its operatives "were not the most motivated individuals in Germany's war effort. Some were avoiding the trenches; some opposed Hitler and sought refuge in an organization reputedly tolerant toward dissidents; some exploited the opportunities of clandestine operations to dodge work and to obtain the advantages of unvouchered funds to enrich or enjoy themselves. Despite the presence of many serious hardworking, patriotic members, the Abwehr had the reputation of being a bloated inefficient, corrupt agency." David Kahn, "Covert Warfare: The Final Solution of the Abwehr," in John Mendelsohn, *Covert Warfare: Intelligence, Counterintelligence, and Military Deception During the World War II Era* (New York: Garland Publishing, Inc., 1989).

129. BArch B 563/Marine V/HPK-W-7/341).
130. "The members of the Abwehr were not themselves spies. Rather they supported the agents. They recruited, trained, equipped, assigned, disguised, inserted, communicated with, paid, and sometimes withdrew agents." Kahn, "Covert Warfare."
131. Ritter, *Cover Name*, 85.
132. Ibid., 92.
133. Ibid., 84–85, 91–92.
134. Ibid., 21.
135. Moinian and Moinian, interview, May 2019.
136. Moinian and Moinian, email exchange with authors, November 2022.
137. Moinian and Moinian, email exchange with coauthor, March 2021.

8. STAR WITNESS

1. Witzke was called "Germany's star witness" by the principal lawyer for the sabotage claimants, Amos Peaslee. See Reginald Hall & Amos Peaslee, *Three Wars With Germany* (New York: G. P. Putnam's Sons, 1944), 110 (quoting a letter from Peaslee to Hall dated January 21, 1929).
2. See Daniel A. Gross, "The U.S. Confiscated Half a Billion Dollars in Private Property During WWI," *Smithsonian Magazine*, July 28, 2014, https://www.smithsonian mag.com/history/us-confiscated-half-billion-dollars-private-property-during-wwi -180952144/; Russel Duane Van Wyk, "German-American relations in the aftermath of the Great War: Diplomacy, law, and the Mixed Claims Commission 1922–1939" (PhD diss., University of North Carolina at Chapel Hill, 1989), 36.
3. Charles I. Bevans, Treaties and other International Agreements of the US of America, 1776–1949, vol. 8 (Department of State Publication, 1971), 146. See also Stephen M. Schwebel, *International Arbitration: Three Salient Problems* (Cambridge: Grotius Publications Ltd., 1987), 216; W. Michael Reisman and Christina Skinner, *Fraudulent Evidence Before Public International Tribunals: The Dirty Stories of International Law* (Cambridge: Cambridge University Press, 2014), 23–24. The Treaty, known as the Treaty of Berlin, did more than provide for the Commission. As its title declares, the Treaty ended the war between the US and Germany, a necessary act as the US had in 1919 rejected the Treaty of Versailles.
4. Manfred Jonas, "Mutualism in the Relations between the US and the Early Weimar Republic," in Hans Trefousse, ed., *Germany and America: Essays on Problems of Internationals Relations and Immigration* (New York: Brooklyn College Press, 1980), 45–46; Van Wyk, "German-American relations," 49.
5. Peter Buckingham, *International Normalcy: The Open Door Peace with the Former Central Powers, 1921–1929* (Wilmington DE: Scholarly Resources, Inc., 1983), 113.
6. Jonas, "Mutualism," 45–46; Van Wyk, "German-American relations," 61.
7. Jonas, "Mutualism," 46.
8. Van Wyk, "German-American relations," 63.
9. The first Umpire was Justice William R. Day of the US Supreme Court. After Justice Day withdrew for health reasons in 1923, he was replaced by then American Commissioner, Judge Edwin Parker; Parker served until his death in 1929. Roland Boyden, the US Agent, then became Umpire in 1930; he died in 1931. Supreme Court Justice Owen Roberts then served for the duration of the Commission. H. H.

Martin, *Final Report of H. H. Martin Acting Agent of the US Before the Mixed Claims Commission US and Germany* (Washington, DC: Gov. Printing office, 1941), ii–iii.

10. H. H. Martin, *Final Report*, 92–97; Van Wyk, "German-American relations," 13.

11. Van Wyk, "German-American relations," 125, note 5, offers this view but without citation to sources showing how and when the companies decided to pursue sabotage claims.

12. Van Wyk, 128 ("accepting financial liability for the sabotage cases would seem proof in Germany, as well as the rest of the world, that the US had reason to enter the war against the Central Powers in April 1917. Such a verdict would deliver a devastating blow at a time when Weimar's assault on 'the War Guilt Clause' found adherents even among Germany's former enemies.").

13. Karl Boy-Ed and Rudolf Nadolny each served as German ambassador to Turkey during the 1920s; Nadolny also served as ambassador to Russia and as the head delegate to the disarmament conference in Geneva in the 1920s. Kurt Jahnke became a member of the Reichstag during the 1920s. Franz von Papen became German Chancellor on June 1, 1932.

14. Henry Landau, *The Enemy Within* (New York: G. P. Putnam's Sons, 1937), 132. Landau worked with the American counsel. The date of his book, 1937, was shortly before the tide finally turned in favor of the Americans.

15. Agreement between the US and Germany Providing for the Determination of the Amount of the Claims Against Germany, signed at Berlin, August 10, 1922, Art. VI, https://history.state.gov/historicaldocuments/frus1922v02/d216 (emphasis added).

16. Certificate of Disagreement and Opinion of June 1939, in "Mixed Claims Commission (United States v. Germany) constituted under the Agreement of August 10, 1922, extended by Agreement of December 31, 1928," *Rep. of Int'l Arb. Awards* 8 (Washington D.C.: UN Publication, 2006), 103, https://legal.un.org/riaa/cases/vol _VIII/1–468.pdf. "The Agreement of August 10, 1922, between Germany and the United States, which established this Commission and is the foundation of its jurisdiction, does not authorize it to issue subpoenas for witnesses or to administer oaths and take the oral testimony of witnesses."

17. Reisman and Skinner, *Fraudulent Evidence*, 28, citing L.H. Woolsey, "The Arbitration of the Sabotage Claims Against Germany," *Am. J. Int'l L.*, 33 (1939), 737, 737.

18. Lothar Witzke, Affidavit, July 19, 1927, GER exh. Q, MCC, RG 76, EN P 51, Ser. German Exhibits and Translations re Sabotage Cases, ca. 1922–1939, vol. 2 (NACP), 1, 21.

19. Lothar Witzke to Privy Councillor Hossenfelder, January 12, 1929, GER Exh. LVI-C, MCC, RG 76, EN P 51, Ser. German Exhibits and Translations re Sabotage Cases, ca. 1922–1939, vol. VII (NACP); see also Lothar Witzke, Affidavit, March 20, 1929, GER exh. LXXI, MCC, RG 76, EN P 51, Ser. German Exhibits and Translations re Sabotage Cases, ca. 1922–1939, vol. VIII (NACP), 1.

20. Witzke, Affidavit, July 19, 1927, GER exh. Q.

21. Tannenbaum (German Agent) to L. Witzke, July 15, 1930, R95283/196868–69.

22. Landau, "*The Enemy Within*," 273–75.

23. Witzke, Affidavit, July 19, 1927, GER exh. Q, 1.

24. Ibid.

25. As the Commission stated in its Decision of October 1930, "Germany and the US, now friendly nations, have entered into an agreement under which Germany accepts liability for such damage during neutrality to citizens of the US, if the damage

resulted from acts of her authorized agents." Judicial Decisions, 25 *Am J. Int'l L.* 147, 148 (1931).

26. Ibid., 149.

27. Ibid., 149.

28. Ibid., 150.

29. Ibid., 150.

30. These individuals are introduced in the prologue, table 1.

31. 1930 MCC Decision, 151. The Commission commented further as to Herrmann: "Whether he now means to tell the truth or means to lie, he is testifying solely because of the fact that he has lost his position in Chile, that the German Government has not taken care of him, and that by testifying he has secured the chance to get back to the US with a guaranty of immunity. We do not imply or think that anything improper was done to induce him to testify, merely that it is sufficiently obvious that Herrmann would not have turned his coat if the German government or the German legation in Chile had offered him appropriate inducements, and that having turned his coat because of advantage to himself he is pretty sure to be in a mental attitude in which hostility to Germany and desire to make good with the claimants play a substantial part. And there is nothing about Herrmann of which we feel so sure as that he *will lie if he thinks lying worthwhile from his own point of view.*" Ibid., 151–52 (emphasis in original).

32. "Hinsch, the man whom Herrmann connects with himself in the [Kingsland] story, has denied it. His denial contains plausible details, but we could not rely on it if we felt that Herrmann was now telling the truth, for though we have no evidence that Hinsch is a liar, there is a strong presumption that he might be under circumstances which pointed to his guilt." Ibid., 151.

33. 1930 MCC Decision, 150. The Commission elaborated: "We cannot be sure that Kristoff did not set fire to Black Tom or take some part in so doing. We cannot be sure that Graentsor or Grantnor, or Graentnor was not Hinsch, and that Hinsch did not employ Kristoff and others who are unknown. But it will be sufficiently clear from the foregoing that, as we have said, the evidence falls far short of enabling us to reach the point, not merely of holding Germany responsible for the fire, but of thinking that her agents must have been the cause, even though the proof is lacking." Ibid., 168.

34. Ibid., 158.

35. Ibid., 158.

36. Ibid., 182.

37. Ibid., 86.

38. This was standard spycraft at the time. "Like the classics, lemon juice and urine, application of a hot iron brought up the message." Alan Furst, *Dark Star* (New York: Random House, 1991), 288–89.

39. 1939 Certificate of Disagreement, 115.

40. "As respects the production of the message, I find that it comes from a source which the Commission has held unworthy of belief." Ibid., 116.

41. Ibid., 117.

42. "But enough has been said to show in how extraordinary a manner this document dovetails with all the important and disputed points of claimants' case and how pat all these references are, not to the request for funds but to the claimants' points of

proof, — this aside from the absurdity of sending this unnecessary information into an enemy country to a suspected spy then under surveillance." Ibid., 119.

43. Ibid., 122.
44. Ibid., 9.
45. Letter of German Commissioner, Victor Huecking, dated March 1, 1939, referenced in 1939 Certificate of Disagreement, 241.
46. 1939 Certificate of Disagreement, 252; Van Wyk, "German-American relations," 390–92.
47. "If it be possible for one National Commissioner, whether under the express order or with the tacit consent of his Government, thus to bring to naught and render worthless the work resulting from the expenditure of thousands of dollars and years of careful research, and thus to defeat the very purpose for which the Commission was constituted under the Treaty of Berlin, such a result would make a mockery of international arbitration." 1939 Certificate of Disagreement, 245.
48. Ibid., 226–468.
49. Ibid., 284–91.
50. Ibid., 265–84.
51. These falsities are detailed in the 1939 Certificate of Disagreement, 313–25.
52. Ibid., 347–49.
53. The commissioner's analysis of the Herrmann Message occupied over 100 single-spaced pages of his Opinion. Ibid., 349–454.
54. Ibid., 458.
55. Decision of Commission by Umpire dated October 30, 1939, referenced in 1939 Certificate of Disagreement, 459 para. 5.
56. Ibid., 459 para. 6.
57. Reginald Hall & Amos Peaslee, *Three Wars With Germany* (New York: G. P. Putnam's Sons, 1944), 188 (the amount with interest was $55 million).
58. Völkische Beobachter, June 18, 1939, trans. "The arbitrariness of this anti-German action is . . . without any doubt," quoted in Burkhardt Jähnicke, *Washington und Berlin zwischen den Kriegen: die Mixed Claims Commission in den transatlantischen Beziehungen* (Baden Baden: Nomos, 2003), 291.
59. See Jähnicke, *Washington und Berlin*, 290–93; Reinhard R. Doerries, "Die Tätigkeit deutscher Agenten in den USA während des Ersten Weltkrieges und ihr Einfluß auf die diplomatischen Beziehungen zwischen Washington und Berlin," in Reinhard R. Doerries, ed., *Diplomaten und Agenten: Nachrichtendienste in der Geschichte der deutsch-amerikanischen Beziehungen* (Heidelberg: Universitätsverlag C. Winter Heidelberg GmbH, 2001), 31.
60. Jähnicke, *Washington und Berlin*, trans., 293.
61. Van Wyk, "German-American relations," 393.
62. Ibid., 394–95.

9. AT WAR AGAIN

1. After a few hours, the family was allowed to enter the country. Further details are lost. Christoph Moinian and Claudia Moinian (Witzke's grandchildren), interview by coauthor, November 2019.
2. US Army Declassified Case File NW# 63388, Doc ID 33709561, 4 (emphasis added).
3. Ibid., 6.

4. Ibid.
5. Entry, Nov. 1940, Chronology, n.d., Witzke Lothar, KV 2/2296 (TNA-UK), 7.
6. Ibid., Entry, Jan. 1941, 8.
7. Ibid., Entry, Nov. 1941, 8.
8. Gwilym Williams, Report, October 7, 1939, Selected Historical Papers from the GW Case, KV 2/468 (TNA-UK). The meeting is also described in Ladislas Farago, *The Game of the Foxes* (New York: David McKay Co., 1971), 225–26; John Humphries, *Spying for Hitler: The Welsh Double-Cross* (Cardiff: University of Wales Press, 2012), 37–43; and James Hayward, *Hitler's Spy: The True Story of Arthur Owens, Double Agent Snow* (New York: Simon & Schuster, 2012), 69–70. Ritter, without reference to this particular meeting, corroborates generally Farago's facts, and explains that, the facts having been exposed by Farago, Ritter was satisfied that he could safely tell his story without concern about exposure of his operatives or fellow agents. Nikolaus Ritter, *Cover Name: Dr. Rantzau*, trans. Katharine Wallace (Lexington KY: University Press of Kentucky, 2019) (German original, 1972), xvi–vii, 2–3.
9. Ibid. We would be wrong to consider Witzke's comments about German war aims as nothing but guile, albeit they were self-serving and reflected Nazi propaganda. Though the war had begun, few at that time imagined the total war that would ensue. Frederick Taylor, *1939: A People's History of the Coming of World War II* (New York: W. W. Norton & Company, 2019), 284. ("Somehow, the Führer's constant assurances that he was a man of peace had sunk into the national consciousness. By 1939, ordinary Germans for the most part believed him.")
10. Memorandum, October 28, 1939, KV 2/468 (TNA-UK).
11. James Hayward, *Hitler's Spy: The True Story of Arthur Owens, Double Agent Snow* (New York: Simon & Schuster, 2012), 69–70, 182.
12. That the Commander was Witzke can be derived from the totality of the information and sources, including US Army Declassified Case File NW # 63388, Doc ID 33709561, 5. Witzke "was responsible for the dispatch of a number of saboteurs to the U.K. (summer of 1940)" and "concerned with sending sabotage parties to UK (Jan 41)." Farago, who interviewed several of the agents involved, identifies the Commander as Witzke. Farago, *Game of the Foxes*, 225–26. James Hayward does as well. Hayward, *Hitler's Spy*, 69–70.
13. The British considered both Williams and Snow to be their agents, acting as double agents pretending to be working for the Abwehr. Ritter insists in his memoirs that Snow was loyal to Germany and that the British were the ones tricked. Ritter, *Dr. Rantzau*, 212–13.
14. "Secrecy and firing squads: Britain's ruthless war on Nazi spies," *The Guardian*, Aug 28, 2016, https://www.google.com/url?sa=t&rct=j&q=&esrc=s&source=web&cd=&cad=rja&uact=8&ved=2ahUKEwjHxdOKwdPuAhUhmeAKHQAaCHoQFjADeg QIBxAC&url=https%3A%2F%2Fwww.theguardian.com%2Fworld%2F2016%2Faug %2F28%2Fbritain-nazi-spies-mi5-second-world-war-german-executed&usg=AOv Vaw3DyLvyoOZVmo1WyGYBUcBL
15. "Let it be said at once that the sabotage efforts both of the German Abwehr and of Germany's enemies achieved but very modest results. Only the sabotage attack by British and Norwegian Commandos on the Norsk-Hydro heavy-water installations in Ryukan in 1942, can claim to have been truly effective. . . ." Paul Leverkuehn,

Germany Military Intelligence, trans. R. H. Stevens and Constantine FitzGibbon (Auckland, NZ: Pickle Partner Publishing, 1954), loc. 802 of 3106, Kindle. Leverkuehn was Chief of the Abwehr's Istanbul Station. Ibid., loc. 74 of 3106.

16. Ritter, *Dr. Rantzau*, 115–16.

17. Ibid., 116–17.

18. Ibid., 117.

19. Ibid., 117.

20. Ibid., 117.

21. Ibid., 117–18

22. Ibid., 118.

23. Ibid., 118–19.

24. Gwilym Williams, Chronology written in Swansea, Wales, February 1, 1941, Selected Papers from GW Case, KV 2/468 (TNA-UK).

25. [n.a.], Report on the Case of Cornelius Evertsen and the "Josephine" Expedition, November 1940, Cornelius Evertsen, KV 2/546 (TNA-UK). The *Josephine* fiasco is also described in John Humphries, *Spying for Hitler*, 83–92.

26. Entry, Nov. 1940, Chronology, n.d., Witzke Lothar, KV 2/2296 (TNA-UK), 7.

27. Leverkuehn, *Germany Military Intelligence*, loc. 1843 of 3106.

28. Report on the Case of Cornelius Evertsen and the "Josephine" Expedition, November 1940 (TNA-UK), 3.

29. "Chronologie du Touquet-Paris-Plage," Wikiwand, https://www.wikiwand.com/fr/Chronologie_du_Touquet-Paris-Plage, trans. ("De 1940 à 1944, plus de 40 000 soldats allemands occupent la ville (Le Touquet), hôtels et villas sont pillés. En 1943, ils démolissent le prestigieux hôtel Atlantic au profit de l'organisation Todt afin d'en récupérer les matériaux qui sont envoyés en Allemagne par train. Sur chaque wagon, était inscrit "dons des français à leurs amis allemands").

30. Leverkuehn, *Germany Military Intelligence*, loc. 1602 of 3106.

31. Ibid., loc. 895 of 3106.

32. Ibid.

33. David J. Danelski, "The Saboteurs' Case," *Journal of Supreme Court History* (1996): 61.

34. US Army Declassified Case File NW# 63388, Doc ID 33709561, 6.

35. Mark Mazower, *Inside Hitler's Greece: The Experience of Occupation, 1941–44* (New Haven: Yale University Press, 1993), 22.

36. Ibid., 41.

37. Ibid., 37.

38. Quoted in Götz Aly, *Hitler's Beneficiaries*, trans. Jefferson Chase (New York: Holt Paperbacks, 2008), 248.

39. "The Nazi leadership did not transform the majority of Germans into ideological fanatics who were convinced that they were part of the master race. Instead it succeeded in making them well-fed parasites." Ibid., 324.

40. "By the time the Wehrmacht entered Greece, the string of victories across Europe had given the troops a sense of almost superhuman invincibility. Their behavior fascinated one young American in Athens. He wrote that morale and discipline had been replaced by 'a corporate realisation of power which runs through the German army from generals to privates. They all appear to have a massive sense of undeviating strength (with almost sadistic overtones) which creates a psychology difficult for outsiders to understand.'" Mazower, 23.

41. The misspelling was picked up and copied by the Americans. US Army Declassified Case File NW# 63388, Doc ID 33709561, 5. Witzke "was rumoured . . . to be posted to Athens as SCHIEBAUER's assistant (May 1942)." The spelling of "rumoured" confirms that the Americans were adopting the British intelligence reports on Witzke.

42. File No. SIME/00.101,903, SIME Report No. 4, 13, www.cia.gov/library/reading room/docs/Waldheim. The file was declassified in 2000 in accordance with the Nazi War Crimes Disclosure Act.

43. File No. SIME/00.101,903, SIME Report No. 4, 22, www.cia.gov/library/reading room/docs/Waldheim.

44. Ibid.

45. Mazower, *Hitler's Greece,* 24.

46. Ibid., 24.

47. Ibid., 25.

48. Richard J. Evans, *The Third Reich in History and Memory* (Oxford: Oxford Univ. Press, 2015), 141. "During the war, and especially from 1943 onwards, as Allied bombing raids became more frequent and more destructive, [the German] people began to look to their own future rather than rally around the national community so insistently propagated by the Nazi Party."

49. A grainy photograph in US Army files from the war likewise shows a no longer youthful looking Witzke, and the accompanying description says that he is "stocky." US Army Declassified Case File NW# 63388, Doc ID 33709561, 3.

50. "With the Italians disarmed, the Third Reich was now in sole charge in Greece, and the Wehrmacht's campaign against the *andartes* [Greek partisans] became the central issue of Axis occupation policy." Mazower, *Hitler's Greece*, 155. Some of the declassified intelligence reports place Witzke as of late 1941 in the state-owned conglomerate, *Hermann Goering Reichswerke.* This bloated conglomerate, which became the largest company in the world in 1942, focused on coal and steel but its operations extended to oil, armaments and shipping. Its activities and geographic scope were so vast, and our information about Witzke's connection (if any) to the conglomerate is so scant, that we have no basis to speculate as to what Witzke's role might have been.

51. Mazower, *Hitler's Greece* , 138.

52. Ibid., 235.

53. For a photograph of a tanker being outfitted in Akers shipyard during the war, see https://www.history.navy.mil/our-collections/photography/numerical-list-of-images /nhhc-series/nh-series/NH-71000/NH-71366.html.

54. "Fearful of German retaliation, the Norwegian Home Front, with the support of the exiled Norweigian Government and SOE, 'decided early on in the war to keep a low level of armed resistance, mainly restricted to sabotage actions to disrupt German efforts to mobilise Norwegian personnel and resources for war purposes.'" Claire M. Hubbard-Hall, "The Nazi Intelligence Matrix: The Gestapo outside Germany, 1939-1945," *Global War Studies* 12/1 (2015): 29 (quoting Tom Kristiansen, "Closing a Long Chapter: German-Norwegian Relations 1939–45: Norway and the Third Reich," in John Gilmour and Jill Stephenson, eds., *Hitler's Scandinvian Legacy* [London: Bloomsbury Academic, 2013], 93).

55. Richard Petrow, *The Bitter Years: The Invasion and Occupation of Denmark and Norway, April 1940–May 1945* (New York: Morrow Quill Paperbacks, 1974), 328–29.

There was, to be sure, scarcity relative to peacetime. Hein Klemann and Sergei Kudryashov, *Occupied Economies: An Economic History of Nazi-Occupied Europe, 1939-1945* (London: Berg, 2011), 404.

56. Petrow, *The Bitter Years*, 342.

57. https://en.wikipedia.org/wiki/Pelle_group.

58. US Army Declassified Case File NW# 63388, Doc ID 33709561, 3, 7.

59. Petrow, *The Bitter Years*, 239.

60. Ibid., 275.

61. Ibid., 288–89.

62. Witzke's reference to taking a train from Copenhagen to Oslo is curious or maybe just imprecise. One needed at the time to take a ferry from Copenhagen to Malmo in order to cross from Denmark to Sweden, and from there to take a train to Oslo.

63. According to information supplied by Witzke when he later became a member of the Hamburg parliament in 1952, Witzke during World War II worked for the *Abwehr* in Hamburg with Colonel Nikolaus Ritter and saw active service in the final years of the War. This latter detail is untrue unless service in civilian clothing was considered active service. Family photographs show Witzke in civilian dress in Oslo in 1944, looking comfortable and early middle-aged; family correspondence includes letters from Witzke in April 1945 from Oslo. See, by way of comparison, Reinhard Doerries, "Tracing Kurt Jahnke: Aspects of the Study of German Intelligence," in George O. Kent (ed.), *Historians and Archivists: Essays in Modern German History and Archival Policy* (George Mason University Press, 1991), 41n20, accepting the statement that Witzke "saw active service in the final years" of World War II.

64. Interview of Lothar Witzke, April 8, 1952, referenced in three-page enclosure entitled "Lothar Witzke/Kurt Jahnke," [n.d.], accompanying letter from D.J.J. to Ronnie, May 12, 1952, Witzke Lothar, KV 2/2296 (TNA-UK).

65. Walter Schellenberg, *The Labyrinth: Memoirs of Waler Schellenberg, Hitler's Chief of Counterintelligence*, trans. Louis Hagen (Cambridge, MA: Da Capo Press, 1956), 23.

66. Farago, *Game of the Foxes*, 565–66.

67. Schellenberg, Labyrinth, 238–39, 259–60; Doerries, "Tracing Kurt Jahnke," 38.

68. Interview (trans.) of Walter Schellenberg, August 23, 1945, Jahnke Kurt, KV 2/755 (TNA-UK), 12.

69. "The women of the Third Reich [became] accustomed to . . . [t]he packages their husbands . . . constantly sent back from the German-occupied countries between 1941 and 1944 [that] contained staple and gourmet items that supplied well beyond the minimum calories necessary for human survival." Götz Aly, *Hitler's Beneficiaries*, 2. But see Richard J. Evans, *The Third Reich in History and Memory* (Oxford: Oxford Univ. Press, 2015), 177. "Aly is certainly wrong in his claim that, even during the war, the German people had 'never had it so good.'"

70. Aly, *Hitler's Beneficiaries*, 97.

71. Ibid., 103.

72. "Nobody could live on what they were officially allowed to buy; a huge black market, run by escaped foreign workers, emerged, wild gangs engaged in regular shootouts with the Gestapo. Diseases like tuberculosis, boosted by malnutrition and debilitation, rose sharply in incidence in 1944." Richard J. Evans, *The Third Reich in History and Memory* (Oxford: Oxford Univ. Press, 2015), 322.

73. The sole addition to their home during the war was Lilli's mother, who lived in an apartment in Hamburg and somehow survived the firestorm and thereafter came to live with the family in Volksdorf.

74. Helen Fry, *Denazification: Britain's Enemy Aliens, Nazi War Criminals and the Reconstruction of Post-war Europe* (Stroud UK: The History Press, 2010), https://www.thehistorypress.co.uk/publication/denazification/9780750951135/.

75. Statement by Dennis Goodman (Hermann Gutmann), in the uniform of the Eighth King's Royal Irish Hussars, quoted in Helen Fry, *Denazification.*

76. Two-page report of interrogation accompanying letter from D.J.J. to Ronnie, May 15, 1952, Witzke Lothar, KV 2/2296 (TNA-UK), 10.

77. "While older studies suggested the British interned 68,500 people, the real figure exceeded 90,000 and probably approximated 100,000." Andrew H. Beattie, "'Lobby for the Nazi Elite'? The Protestant Churches and Civilian Internment in the British Zone of Occupied Germany, 1945–1948," in *German History* 35, no. 1 (March 1, 2017): 43–70, https://doi.org/10.1093/gerhis/ghw140. "After Germany's capitulation, roughly 320,000 Germans were interned in the four occupation zones according to subsequent Allied decisions— with about 93,000 of these in the British zone." Marco Kühnert, "Module T: Internment, Re-Education and Punishment: The British Internment Camp at Neuengamme, 1945–1948," NS— Geschichte, Institutionen, Menschenrechte, https://www.ns-geschichte-institutionen-menschenrechte.de/module_T.html.

78. David Cohen, *Transitional Justice in Divided Germany After 1945* (U.C. Berkeley War Crimes Studies Center), 12–13, https://www.ocf.berkeley.edu/~wcsc/wp-content/uploads/Papers/cohen-trans-justice-germany.pdf.

79. Henry E. Collins, *Mining Memories and Musings: Autobiography of a Mining Engineer* (Ashire Publishing Ltd, 1985), 39 et seq. "In November 1945, I was consulted on a list of persons to be arrested as important Nazis. I was horrified to see a number of names of key men in the coal industry. . . . I was able to have the names erased from the list because the persons concerned were vital to the recovery of coal production" (quoted in Christopher Knowles, *Winning the Peace: The British in Occupied Germany, 1945–1948* [New York: Bloomsbury Publishing Plc, 2017], 216–17n97).

80. See Alyn Bessmann, a historian of Neuengamme, Email to coauthor, May 7, 2020. "We have searched long and hard but without any results for [records of prisoners at Neuengamme CIC No. 6]. The only files we could trace offering individual-related data from the Neuengamme internees are the Detention Reports and Detainees Personal Record Sheets from several British internment camps in The British National Archives, reference WO 309/1707 to 1785 (see "Wisch-Zwillinger," The National Archives, accessed January 26, 2021, https://discovery.nationalarchives.gov.uk/details/r/C173498). But these files are rather incomplete and Lothar Witzke is not mentioned.").

81. Three-page enclosure entitled "Lothar Witzke/Kurt Jahnke" [n.d.] accompanying letter from D.J.J. to Ronnie, May 12, 1952, Witzke Lothar, KV 2/2296 (TNA-UK), 14.

82. Bundesarchiv Berlin to co-author, July 27, 2020. Discharge centers were set up by the occupying forces to register and process Germans, whether soldiers or *Abwehr* or other, seeking reentry into civilian life.

83. "Werner Lange," Bordgemeinschaft der Emdenfahrer, accessed January 26, 2021, http://www.bgef.de/dieschiffe/emdeniii/chefetage/lange-werner.html.

84. Andrew H. Beattie, *Allied Internment Camps in Occupied Germany: Extrajudicial Detention in the Name of Denazification, 1945–1950* (Cambridge: Cambridge University Press, 2020), 182.

85. Ritter, *Dr. Rantzau*, 200.

86. Ibid.

87. The probable quid pro quo would have placed Lilli in a very large category of German women "fraternizing" with occupying soldiers in exchange for food. Petra Goedda, "From Villains to Victims: Fraternization and the Feminization of Germany, 1945–1947," *Diplomatic History* 23, no. 1 (Winter 1999): 1–20.

88. Knowles, *Winning the Peace*, 112 (footnotes omitted). A first-person account of the deprivation in Hamburg in 1946–1947 is given by an occupying British soldier who fell in love with and married a German woman. Harry Leslie Smith, *Love Among the Ruins: A Memoir of Life and Love in Hamburg* (London: Icon Books, Ltd., 2012).

89. Frederick Taylor, *Exorcising Hitler: The Occupation and Denazification of Germany* (New York: Bloomsbury Press, 2011), loc. 3968 of 7921, Kindle.

90. Henrik Lundbak (Museumsinspector/Curator, Collections and archives of The Museum of Danish Resistance) to the authors, Email, March 31, 2020.

91. Moinian and Moinian, interview by coauthor, May 2019.

10. PROSPERITY

1. The family stories recounted in this chapter were described to the coauthor during interviews with Witzke's grandchildren, Christoph Moinian and Claudia Moinian, in May and November 2019, in February 2021, and in correspondence from 2019 to 2023.

2. Christopher Knowles, *Winning the Peace: The British in Occupied Germany, 1945–1948* (London: Bloomsbury Publishing Plc., 2017), 120.

3. The Rahtjen's company's few surviving archives of the period include the 6 June 1950 contract that designated Witzke as CEO, and a 28 June 1950 contract that reconstitutes the company's shareholding.

4. The formal name of the Hamburg America Line was Hamburg-Amerikanische Packetfahrt-Actien-Gesellschaft (HAPAG).

5. The founding and 19th century history of the company is described in *Holzapfel's Co. v. Rahtjen's Co.*, 183 US 1, 1–3 (1901), and in "The Suter Hartmann Rahtjen's Composition Company of London," *New Zealand Press*, vol. 63, issue 12736, 23 February 1907, p. 11, https://paperspast.natlib.govt.nz/newspapers/CHP19070223.2.76.

6. *Opera Mundi Europe, A Weekly Report on the Economy of the Common Market*, No. 425 (September 7, 1967), p. L [pdf. p. 23], http://aei.pitt.edu/81932/1/OM0118.pdf; Funding Universe, "Courtauld's plc History," http://www.fundinguniverse.com/company-histories/courtaulds-plc-history/.

7. From 1954 on, Ritter was the managing director of the German Aid Society in Hamburg. Nikolaus Ritter, *Cover Name: Dr. Rantzau*, trans. Katharine Wallace (Lexington: University Press of Kentucky, 2019) (German original, 1972), 2.

8. Two-page report of interrogation accompanying letter from D.J.J. to Ronnie, May 15, 1952, Witzke Lothar, KV 2/2296 (TNA-UK), 10.

9. Report of Interrogation, KV 2/2296, 13.

10. Helmut Stubbe da Luz, *Heldenhafte "Tschekisten"? "Kundschafter des Friedens"? Begleitband zur Ausstellung Hamburger Politiker als DDR-Spione im Kalten Krieg* (Hamburg: Bibliothek der Helmut-Schmidt-Universität, 2015).

11. Tamara Feinstein, ed., "The CIA and Nazi War Criminals, National Security Archive Posts Secret CIA History, Released Under Nazi War Crimes Disclosure Act," *National Security Archive Electronic Briefing Book No. 146*, February 4, 2005, https://nsarchive2.gwu.edu/NSAEBB/NSAEBB146/index.htm.

12. Richard Breitman, Norman Goda, Timothy Naftali, and Robert Wolfe, *U.S. Intelligence and the Nazis* (Washington, DC: National Archive Trust Fund Board, 2004), 8–9, https://doi.org/10.1093/hgs/dcio28.

13. Might the reason for his trips have been women? Doubtful. There is little reason to think that he needed these trips to find women or to be with women. He was able to find women where he was, and he was not the type to take a long trip to accommodate a woman. And the invitations to his wife and daughter contradict an adulterous purpose.

14. "It was a strange combination of a regional ultra-conservative pressure group and a collection point for Nazi remnants (it had originally been re-founded in 1946 as a direct successor to the so-called 'German-Hanoverian Party', which between 1866 and 1933 had campaigned for the restoration of the Hanoverian monarchy that had been dispossessed by Bismarck)." Frederick Taylor, *Exorcising Hitler*, 6291 of 7921 (Kindle edition).

15. Helmut Stubbe-da Luz, "*Die Deutsche Partei in Hamburg: Wurzeln, Anfänge, Umfeld, Erfolge und Niedergang*," in *Zeitschrift des Vereins für Hamburgische Geschichte, Bd. 79* (Hamburg: Bibliothek der Helmut-Schmidt-Universität Hamburg 1993), 249

16. Ibid., 257.

17. Perry Biddiscombe, *The Denazification of Germany: A History 1945–1950* (Tempus Publishing Ltd. 2007).

18. Stubbe da Luz, "Die Deutsche Partei in Hamburg," 255; information supplied to the authors on June 20, 2018, by Bürgerschaft der Freien und Hansestadt Hamburg Bürgerschaftskanzlei Parlamentarische Informationsdienste.

19. Stubbe da Luz, *Heldenhafte "Tschekisten."*

20. Britta Doering, administrator of the Anglo-German Club of Hamburg, email exchange with coauthor, April 2021.

21. "Elite Hamburg British club angers expats with men-only policy," *The Local: Germany's News in English*, Sept. 13, 2017 (quoting the Club's president on the Club's origins), https://www.thelocal.de/20170913/hamburgs-anglo-german-club-angers-expat-brits-with-men-only-policy/.

22. *Planten un Blomen* is an urban park in central Hamburg.

23. Taylor, *Exorcising Hitler*, loc. 6568 of 7921, Kindle.

24. Ibid., loc. 6461–72 of 7921.

25. Ken Moulden, "Fassbinder and the Search for Identity in *The Marriage of Maria Braun*," *Literature & Aesthetics* 16(2) December 2006, 242.

26. Niclas Sennerteg, "Vem var den mystiske mr Witzke i Damaskus?," https://sennerteg.wordpress.com/2015/05/25/vem-var-nazisten-kurt-witzke-i-syrien/.There was a relatively substantial community of Nazis in Syria in the immediate postwar era, many fleeing prosecution. Philippe Sands, *The Ratline: Love, Lies and Justice on the Trail of a Nazi Fugitive.* (New York: Alfred A. Knopf, 2021), 178, 183, 228–29, 250.

27. https://archive.org/details/BEISSNERFRIEDRICHWILHELM-0059/
    BEISSNER%2C%20FRIEDRICH%20WILHELM_0059?q=%22Kurt+Witzke%22.
28. Brandt, a democratic socialist, was leader of the SPD from 1964 to 1987 and served as
    Chancellor of the Federal Republic of Germany (West Germany) from 1969 to 1974.
29. Guy Fake, Affidavit, March 6, 1929, US exh. 627, MCC, RG 76, EN PI 143/14, Ser.
    Printed US Exhibits, 1929?–1939?, vol. IV (NACP).
30. Incongruent with his womanizing, photographs of Witzke during the 1950s show a
    man prematurely aged. He looked 80, not 60.
31. Witzke liked to drink, but considered that his drinking was not excessive. His son-
    in-law (a physician) would admonish him for his drinking. Witzke would reply:
    "It's not too much! I'm drinking only sip by sip."
32. "Superlatives that placed the suffering of the Germans high above the suffering of
    other nations sluiced through the [postwar] German press, through brochures and
    tracts." Harald Jähner, trans. Shaun Whiteside, *Aftermath, Life in the Fallout of the
    Third Reich, 1945–1955* (London: Penguin Random House, 2019), 301. "When they
    were asked to give Jews back what they were owed, many 'Aryanizers' [asserted]
    their own misfortunes and their difficulties in keeping themselves afloat. This state
    of mind was enabled by the fact that it was shared by the vast majority of Germans,
    and therefore rarely encountered any critique. The lack of guilty feelings, the inten-
    tional, supportive blindness allowed people to reject, en masse, all responsibility for
    Nazi crimes. Instead of showing empathy for the victims of Nazism, they endlessly
    pitied their own fates." Geraldine Schwarz, *Those Who Forget: My Family's Story in
    Nazi Europe*, trans. Laura Marris (New York: Scribner 2017), 71.
33. Frederick Taylor, *Exorcising Hitler*, loc. 4082–83 of 7921, Kindle.
34. "For decades there was no widespread engagement with the murder of millions;
    that only began with the Auschwitz trials that lasted from 1963 until 1968." Harald
    Jähner, *Aftermath*, 324. That was convenient for Witzke, who died in 1962.
35. "The political and cultural revolution of the 1960s, driven mostly by young people
    who had been barely old enough for kindergarten at the end of the war, affected
    West Germany more intensely than any other Western country, up to and including
    America. Suddenly, after 20 years of restoration and reconstruction but relatively
    little re-evaluation, there were ageing war criminals on trial before West German
    courts, there was talk of the Holocaust (largely ignored in the 1950s), there was a
    national debate about the country's past and where it should be heading. In effect,
    the debate that might have been had in the years immediately following the Ger-
    man defeat . . . finally began to take place more than twenty years later." Taylor,
    Exorcising Hitler, loc. 337 of 7921, Kindle.
36. Another take on this film is offered in Jähner, *Aftermath*, 157: "It was not until 1979
    that Rainer Werner Fassbinder made a film to commemorate the 'disloyal' post-
    war German woman. While materialism is a central theme in *Die Ehe der Maria
    Braun* (*The Marriage of Maria Braun*), the dignity emanated by Hanna Schygulla
    in the title role testifies to an appropriate regard for the importance of the liberated
    woman as a force for social change. One recurring motif in the film, incidentally,
    is the American cigarette, mythically charged as both black market currency and
    as bait. At the start of the film Maria is given a cigarette by her African-American
    boyfriend, and at the end, in the middle of the economic miracle, she blows her
    house up with one after forgetting she's turned the gas tap on."

11. DID HE DO IT? WEST COAST SABOTAGE

1. In 1927, in an affidavit submitted to the Mixed Claims Commission in the sabotage cases, Witzke admitted under oath that he became a German agent in 1916 shortly after arriving in San Francisco from Valparaiso and that his assigned tasks included reporting on Allied ship movements on the US West Coast, ship cargo and destination information, ship construction, munitions orders, and manufacture and shipment of munitions. These activities, according to an interview that he gave in China several years later, focused on ships carrying nitrate and lumber, especially nitrate, "as we were watching very closely the movements of all materials of war along the Pacific Coast." Lothar Witzke, Affidavit, July 19, 1927, GER exh. Q, MCC, RG 76, EN P 51, Ser. German Exhibits and Translations re Sabotage Cases, ca. 1922–1939, vol. 2 (NACP), 3. Kurt Jahnke, Witzke's immediate superior, also submitted a sworn affidavit to the Mixed Claims Commission in which he corroborated Witzke's admission. Kurt Jahnke, Affidavit, November 24, 1927, GER exh. P, MCC, RG 76, EN P 51, Ser. German Exhibits and Translations re Sabotage Cases, ca. 1922–1939, vol. 2 (NACP), 9, 3: "Lothar Witzke was one of my sub-agents whom I met in the spring of 1916. . . . I engaged him for the service which I described previously in this statement . . . [i.e., collecting] observations and information of all kinds which might be of value to the leading military and political bureaus in Germany [including] making observations as to the war material orders that had been placed in the United Sates by the Allies; in ascertaining the nature and volume of arms and munitions production; in finding out the destination of arms and munitions shipments. . . ." In 1918, traveling as a Russian national named Pablo Waberski, Witzke was captured at the US-Mexican border with a code book and a cipher message from the German ambassador that identified him as a secret agent and instructed German consuls in Mexico to forward his coded messages to the embassy as consular dispatches. Based in part on the code book and cipher message, a military tribunal in August 1918 convicted Witzke of being a spy under Article Eighty-Two of the Articles of War.

2. Joel A. Lipscomb, Special Border Report re German Activity, Foreigners: Latar Witcke alias Pablo (Paul) and Harry Waberski, February 2, 1918, US exh. 228, MCC, RG 76, EN PI 143/14, Ser. Printed US Exhibits, 1929?–1939?, vol. 1 (NACP), 631–33.

3. Testimony of Paul Altendorf, Trial Hearing Record at 9, 18–19, August 16–17, 1918, US v. Witcke alias Waberski, RG 153, Ser. Court Martial Case Files, 1917–1938, File Lather Witcke, alias Pablo Waberski, 119966 (NASL).

4. Paul Altendorf, "On Secret Service In Mexico, Article 18," *Chicago Tribune*, November 20, 1919.

5. Witzke, Affidavit, July 19, 1927, GER exh. Q, 5–6.

6. Reginald Hall & Amos Peaslee, *Three Wars with Germany* (New York: G.P. Putnam's Sons, 1944), 109.

7. Lipscomb, Special Border Report, February 7, 1918, MCC, US exh. 228., 632; Altendorf Testimony, Trial Record, 18; and Altendorf, "On Secret Service in Mexico, Article 18," *Chicago Tribune*, November 20, 1919.

8. There was in 1916–1917 another ship named *Minnesota,* the other one being a navy ship. The navy ship—the USS *Minnesota*—was a Connecticut class battleship commissioned in 1907. It circumnavigated the globe in 1908–1909 as part of President

Roosevelt's Great White Fleet, then operated along the Atlantic coast and in the Caribbean, including along the east coast of Mexico in 1913–1914 during the Mexican Revolution. It was placed in reserve in November 1916, then returned to service in April 1917 after the US entered the war (based at Tangier Sound, Chesapeake Bay) and was used as a training ship for gunners and engineers. We have found no evidence of a boiler explosion on the ship. There is in any case nothing in Witzke's history to suggest that he was ever in the vicinity of the ship. Naval intelligence told MID that no one with Witzke's name or any of his aliases had ever served on the *Minnesota*. Churchill to McCauley, July 17, 1918, RG 165, Ser. MID Correspondence, 1919–1941, File 10541-268/147 (NACP); Wells to Churchill, August 9, 1918, ibid., 166. The USS *Minnesota* can thus be excluded from consideration.

9. Photolibrarian, "SS Minnesota, Merchant Ship," https://www.flickr.com/photos/photolibrarian/30234473733.

10. "Minnesota Is On Way to Atlantic," *Spokane Daily Chronicle*, November 15, 1915.

11. "Hill Liner Is in Trouble Limping to San Francisco," *San Francisco Chronicle*, December 2, 1915; "Minnesota's Boilers All Put Out of Commission," *San Francisco Chronicle*, December 7, 1915; "Minnesota Is Being Slowly Towed to City," *San Francisco Chronicle*, December 9, 1915; "Disabled Hill Steamer Is Near Port, Minnesota Believed Victim of A Plot," *San Francisco Chronicle*, December 11, 1915; "Minnesota To Get In Tomorrow, Thorough Probe To Follow," *San Francisco Chronicle*, December 12, 1915.

12. "No Evidence Of A Plot On Minnesota," *San Francisco Chronicle*, December 17, 1915; "New Boilers Must Be Put In Minnesota," *San Francisco Chronicle*, December 22, 1915 (quoting the US Supervising Inspector: "The Government's investigation of the Minnesota is complete. I am satisfied that the ship left Seattle in seaworthy condition and that the boiler troubles which caused her to put back to this port were purely of a mechanical nature").

13. "American "Boilers," *San Francisco Chronicle*, December 23, 1915; "Giant Liner Minnesota, the great freighter sails today for New York, via the Panama Canal," *San Francisco Chronicle*, February 14, 1917. By then the ship had been sold to new owners.

14. Another possibility is that Altendorf may have heard Witzke boast about ruining a ship's boilers, and got the name of the ship wrong. Such a possibility cannot be ruled out, but we find it the least likely of the possibilities. In his telling and retellings, Altendorf never waivered about the ship's name. He repeated it each time without a hint that he might be misremembering it. There is one slight discrepancy in the way Altendorf identifies the *Minnesota* in his statement to Butcher and in his *Chicago Tribune* articles. In the former he says "U.S. *Minnesota*," in the latter "the transport Minnesota." The prefix "U.S." is meaningless as a ship prefix; it should be either USS (designating a military ship—United States Ship) or SS (meaning a civilian steam-powered ship, also called a steamer). Perhaps this was an error of Altendorf's memory or Butcher's transcription; Witzke would have known the difference. The term "transport" can refer to a civilian cargo ship, but is more often used to designate a military ship that transports personnel or military supplies. The USS *Minnesota* was a battleship, not a military transport, although beginning in March 1919 (several months before Altendorf publishing his *Chicago Tribune* series) it served for a time as a transport for returning veterans from France.

15. Henry Landau, *The Enemy Within* (New York: G. P. Putnam's Sons, 1937), 23–27.

16. Curt Gentry, *Frame-up, The Incredible Case of Tom Mooney and Warren Billings* (New York: W. W. Norton & Co., Inc., 1967), 465–66.

17. "With Fire in Hold," *Oakland Tribune*, June 25, 1917.

18. D.I.D. to Bell, [n.d.], Summary, Jahnke Kurt, KV 2/755 (TNA-UK), 134.

19. "Oil Tanker Explosion Kills Two," *San Francisco Examiner*, September 26, 1916; "Blast Cause On Ship Unknown," *San Francisco Examiner*, September 28, 917.

20. Ibid.; "Dock & Deck," *Oakland Tribune*, September 28, 1917.

21. Lothar Witzke to Aunt Bertha, September 27, 1917, Lothar Witzke, Correspondence (originals and translations) comprising 27 picture postcards, 1914–1917, GER exh. CXXVII-A/25, MCC, RG 76 (NACP).

22. Reginald P. Mitchel, "Spy," The American Foreign Service Journal (November 1934), 582.

23. Landau, *The Enemy Within*, 173. See also Summary D.I.D. to Bell [n.d.], KV 2/755, 134.

24. "Steam Schooner O. M. Clark Burns While Taking Oil," *Oregon Daily Journal*, December 7, 1917; "$230,000 Ship Fire, San Pedro," *Stockton Daily Evening Record*, December 7, 1917.

25. "Steamer O. M. Clark Towed to Long Beach," *San Pedro News-Pilot*, February 20, 1918.

26. Lipscomb, Special Border Report, February 7, 1918, MCC, US exh. 228, 632.

27. "US Tank Steamer Victim of Raiders," *Tulsa Democrat*, June 30, 1917; "American Oil Steamer Burns at Sea; Is Work of German Agents," *El Paso Morning Times*, July 1, 1917.

28. Lipscomb, Special Border Report, February 7, 1918, MCC, US exh. 228, 637.

29. Altendorf Testimony, Witzke Trial Record, 13; Altendorf, "On Secret Service in Mexico, Article 18," *Chicago Tribune*, Nov. 20, 1919.

30. "Forest Fires Are Menacing Big Industry," *Salem Statesman Journal*, July 22, 1917.

31. "Logging Firms Blame Firebugs," *Statesman Journal* (Salem), July 15, 1917.

32. "Forester Suspects Timber Fires Have Been Set By I.W.W.," *Oregon Daily Journal* (Portland), July 18, 1917.

33. *See, e.g.,* "Forest Fires Seem To Be Spreading in Timber To The South," *Oregon Daily Journal* (Portland), July 22, 1917.

34. "Forest Fire Situation Is Much Worse," *Statesman Journal* (Salem), August 24, 1917.

35. D.I.D. to Bell, Summary, May 2, 1918, Jahnke Kurt, KV 2/755 (TNA-UK), 134.

36. "Powder Mill Blows Up," *Tacoma Times*," June 11, 1917; "Powder Plant Destroyed," *Great Falls Tribune (Montana)*, June 11, 1917.

37. "Dupont Explosion Rocks Countryside," *Tacoma Times*, October 23, 1917.

38. "Secret Probe in Blast Is Rushed by US Sleuths," *San Francisco Examiner*, July 10, 1917; "Mare Island Explosion Not An Accident, Says Report," *Official US Bulletin*, August 27, 1917, 8; T. Roosevelt (Acting Secretary of the Navy) to Hon. Julius Kahn (Member of Congress), House Committee Hearing on Naval Affairs, *Hearings on Sundry Legislation Affecting the Naval Establishment, 1923–1924*, 68th Cong., 1st Sess. (Washington: Government Printing Office, 1924), 1026–28.

39. Lipscomb, Special Border Report, February 7, 1918, MCC, US exh. 228, 631–32.

40. Altendorf Testimony, Witzke Trial Record, 18 ("He [Waberski] said, 'I have done wonderful things in San Francisco; I blowed up 250,000 pounds of black powder, I was lying at 5:00 o'clock in the morning when I heard it, and I laughed, I knew there were women and children in it, but I laughed and knew that I had done it for the Fatherland'"); Paul Altendorf, "On Secret Service in Mexico: Article 17," *Chicago Tribune*, November 19, 1919 ("He [the priest-friend of Witzke] had a very good time

with [Witzke], he said, on a certain trip on which that gentleman blew up 250,000 pounds of black powder, killing a number of people and doing a lot of damage").

41. "Not An Accident, Says Report," *Official US Bulletin*, 8. It was thought that there were two explosions: The first was a high explosive of some sort that had been placed in the corner of the building and was detonated with a spark; the second explosion was the black powder in the magazine being detonated, apparently by the first explosion. The cause of the initial spark was unknown.

42. Secret Service Daily Reports (San Francisco) for March 24 and April 12, 1915, RG 87, Ser. Daily Reports of Agents, 1875–1938, File San Francisco, volumes 8–10, November 1, 1913–July 31, 1915 (2 of 2)/images 526–27, 624–25 (NACP), https://catalog .archives.gov/id/152404913; Secret Service Daily Reports (San Francisco) for February 11, 1916, RG 87, Ser. Daily Reports of Agents, 1875–1938, File San Francisco, volumes 11–13, August 1, 1915–March 31, 1917 (1 of 2)/image 991 (NACP), https:// catalog.archives.gov/id/152406087.

43. Jahnke served part of the year as well in the Philippines. "Kurt A. Jahnke" in *U.S. Marine Corps Muster Rolls, 1798–1958*, Microfilm Publication T977, ARC ID 922159, R.G. 187 (National Archives, Washington, D.C.), accessed via Ancestry.com database; Richard B. Spence, "K.A. Jahnke and the German Sabotage Campaign in the United Sates and Mexico, 1914–1918," *The Historian* 59, no. 1 (Fall 1996): 91, citing "Kurt A. Jahnke," Service Record, U.S. Marine Corps, File #33906, National Personnel Records Office (Military Personnel Records), Navy Reference Branch, in Federal Bureau of Investigation (FBI), File #62-5394, "Kurt A. Jahnke," FOIPA #240,106.

44. The Justice Department report of Jahnke's visit to the Bureau of Investigation is summarized at Secret Service Daily Reports (San Francisco), February 6, 1918, images 1954–55, 1957. See also Spence, "Kurt Jahnke," 99, citing MID, File #10541-367/34, "Jahnke, C. A. alias Yenky, A.," Dept. of State, Office of the Counselor, 19 March 1918; #10541-367/79, Lt. Utley to Dept. Intelligence Officer, So. Dept., 8 August 1918; #10541-367/81, "A. Jahnke, German Spy," 10 August 1918; USDS, File #862.20212/1101, Lansing to American Embassy, London, 11 April 1918.

45. An unsourced version of this story has Jahnke foreshadowing the 1917 explosion more explicitly. Landau writes: "In order further to divert suspicion from himself and to display his patriotism as a naturalized American citizen, [Jahnke] boldly walked into the office of the Secret Service in San Francisco on February 10, 1916, and reported to the agent in charge that he had discovered a plot to blow up the navy yard at Mare Island. However, as the source of his information was an overheard conversation between alleged German agents whose whereabouts were unknown to him, the authorities paid little attention to his warning." Landau, *The Enemy Within*, 34. The authors have reviewed the San Francisco Secret Service Daily Reports for February 10, 1916 as well as for the rest of February, and were not able to corroborate Landau's version.

46. Secret Service Daily Reports (San Francisco) for January 25, 1918, RG 87, Ser. Daily Reports of Agents, 1875–1938, File San Francisco: volumes 14–16, April 1, 1917-July 31, 1918 (1 of 2)/images 1874–75, 1878 (NACP), https://catalog.archives.gov/id/152409462.

47. *See, e.g.*, Secret Service Daily Reports (San Francisco) for March 21, 1918, RG 87, Ser. Daily Reports of Agents, 1897–1938, File San Francisco, vols. 14–16, April 1, 1917-July 31, 1918 (2 of 2)/images 394–95, https://catalog.archives.gov/id/152411462.

48. Secret Service Daily Reports (San Francisco) for March 4, 1919, RG 87, Ser. Daily

Reports of Agents, 1875–1938, File San Francisco, vols. 17–19, August 1, 1918–August 31, 1919 (1 of 2)/image 1759 (NACP), https://catalog.archives.gov/id/152412747.

49. Witzke, Affidavit, July 19, 1927, GER exh. Q, 5–6.

50. Recently, a theory that was emphatically rejected at the time has been revived: that the culprit was Ordinance Man Neil Damstedt, who was the only person in the building next to the explosion when it occurred. Damstedt certainly had means and opportunity, but seemed to lack motive. Now Stephen Ruder, an intelligence analyst with NCIS, has suggested a motive: that Damstedt was in fact angry and depressed. His wife was ill, his son was unemployed, his two daughters were still living at home, and Damstedt himself had been demoted and his pay cut in half a week earlier. See Stephen Ruder, "Who Really Blew Up Mare Island?" *Naval History Magazine* 36, no. 3 (June 2022).

51. One of the best summaries of these theories including the evidence for each is the appendix titled "Whose Bomb?" in Curt Gentry, *Frame-Up: The Incredible Case of Tom Mooney and Warren Billings* (New York: W. W. Norton & Co., 1967), 441–47. See also Ernest J. Hopkins, *What Happened in the Mooney Case* (New York: Brewer, Warren & Putnam, 1932), 46–74; Richard Frost, *The Mooney Case* (Stanford, CA: Stanford University Press, 1968), 489; Paul and Karen Avrich, *Sasha and Emma: The Anarchist Odyssey of Alexander Berkman and Emma Goldman* (Cambridge, MA: Harvard University Press, 2012), 265–66; Jeffrey A. Johnson, *The 1916 Preparedness Day Bombing: Anarchy and Terrorism in Progressive Era America* (New York: Routledge, 2018), 151–52. Our account of the theories leans heavily on Gentry. Gentry names Witzke as the possible perpetrator.

52. In the acid-fuse method, dynamite can be exploded by an acid such as nitrate in an open vial with a cotton wick. The acid climbs the wick, sets the powder on fire, and the dynamite explodes when the heat reaches a certain temperature. Apparently, expert bomb-makers can time the explosion to the minute. If the bomb uses nitroglycerine, the bomb's explosion can be triggered by any sudden jarring motion, such as dropping or throwing it. Gentry, *Frame-Up*, 443.

53. Hopkins, *What Happened*, 49–50.

54. Quoted in Gentry, *Frame-Up*, at 14.

55. Avrich and Avrich, *Sasha and Emma*, 265–66. Paul Avrich died in 2006. His daughter took his notes and unfinished manuscript, added research of her own, and completed the book half a dozen years later.

56. Hopkins, *What Happened*, 59–74; Gentry, *Frame-Up*, 453–57.

57. The three, according to Gentry, were Ernest Jerome Hopkins, an editor at the *San Francisco Bulletin* at the time of the bombing and author of the book *What Happened in the Mooney Case*, cited earlier; and two of the lawyers who represented Mooney at different times during the case's twenty-year saga, Bourke Cockran and George Davis. Gentry, *FrameUp*, 456. Davis had been a newsboy selling papers to Preparedness Day parade spectators at Market and Montgomery, in front of the Palace Hotel, when the bomb when off.

58. Gentry, *Frame-Up*, 456–57.

59. The confessions are summarized at Gentry, *Frame-Up*, 447–50, 469–74. Our account of Louis Smith's confession is based on Gentry's summary of it.

60. Both Frost and Gentry favor this theory. See Frost, *The Mooney Case*, 489, and Gentry, *Frame-Up*, 477.

61. The *Daily News* stories were reprinted in "Says Blow-up of S.F. Parade Was German Plot," *Modesto Evening News*, April 25, 1918, and "Mooney Plot Is Thickening," *Riverside Daily Press*, April 26, 1918. The *News* story claimed as well that Jahnke had been hired to carry out the Mare Island bombing.

62. Ibid. Secret Service reports indicate that, in the fall of 1917, a lawyer representing von Brincken gave the Secret Service information potentially implicating Consul Bopp and Vice Consul Schack in the Mare Island bombing. Then in January the service interviewed both the nurse who would later be mentioned in the *News* story as well as von Brincken himself. Both provided leads about possible German sabotage including at Mare Island, but not regarding the Preparedness Day bombing. Von Brincken mentioned Kurt Jahnke numerous times and suggested he might know something about Mare Island. Efforts were begun to locate Jahnke. In March, when rumors started reaching the service about Jahnke or other German agents possibly being involved in the Preparedness Day bombing (this, before the story broke in the *Daily News*), von Brincken was approached again and, through his lawyer, denied any knowledge of it. The service continued to try to track down Jahnke, but told the head office in Washington that it was not working on the theory that the Mare Island and Preparedness Day bombings were linked. Secret Service Daily Reports (San Francisco) for October 10 and 12, 1917 and January 5, 18, 19 and 25, 1918, RG 87, Ser. Daily Reports of Agents, 1875–1938, File San Francisco: volumes 14–16, April 1, 1917–July 31, 1918 (1 of 2)/images 1054, 1057, 1063–65, 1740–41, 1828, 1835–36, 1874–75 (NACP), https://catalog.archives.gov/id/152409462; Secret Service Daily Reports (San Francisco), March 6, 7, and 29, 1918, volumes 14–16 (2 of 2)/images 295–96, 298, 305, 457, https://catalog.archives.gov/id/152411462.

63. Secret Service Daily Reports (San Francisco), April 27, 1918, volumes 14–16 (2 of 2)/images 660–63.

64. Secret Service Daily Reports (San Francisco), April 29, 1918, volumes 14–16 (2 of 2)/images 670–72.

65. Secret Service Daily Reports (San Francisco), May 6, 1918, volumes 14–16 (2 of 2)/images 718–19.

66. "33–35 yrs; 5 ft 10 or 11 in; 160 lbs; swarthy, pimply face; blond hair; light eyes, small and ratty; rough dresser." Secret Service Daily Reports (San Francisco), January 25, 1918, volumes 14–16 (1 of 2)/images 1874–75.

67. "Statement of Pablo Waberski When Questioned by Major R. L. Barnes," February 18, 1918, MID Correspondence, 1917–1941, RG 165, Ser. MID Correspondence, 1919–1941, File 10541-268/29 (NACP).

68. Ibid., 13.

69. Von Brincken, who pleaded guilt to the Hindu-German plot charges and turned states' evidence against his fellow conspirators, was treated more leniently at sentencing. The Hindu-German conspiracy trial is famous in the annals of American litigation because of the pageantry of the Hindu defendants' dress and, on the last day of the trial, the courtroom assassination of the chief defendant, Ram Chandra, by one of his fellow defendants, Ram Singh. Singh was then shot dead by a US marshal. "All But 1 Guilty in Hindu Plot," *San Francisco Examiner*, April 24, 1918; "Names of Guilty in Hindu Plot and Disposition of Others Involved," ibid; "Baron Brincken Is Given His Release," *Charlotte News*, January 9, 1920.

70. See A. P. Chew, "Evidence Given by German Agent Tends to Clear Mooney, Billings,"

Minneapolis Star, November 3, 1920 and Gentry, *Frame-Up*, 464–66. Brincken previewed some of the details in earlier articles in the series.

71. Gentry, *Frame-Up*, 466.

72. Landau, *The Enemy Within*, 23.

73. Chew, "Evidence Given By German Agent"; Gentry, *Frame-Up*, 457.

74. Gentry, *Frame-Up*, 466. The assertion is unsourced. We have not been able to verify or refute the statement.

75. Ibid., 465. It is not clear whether Brincken is saying that this particular English ship was the Preparedness Day target.

76. Ibid., 442. Forty percent dynamite strength means that it contains 40 percent nitroglycerine, 10 percent wood pulp, and 50 percent nitrate of soda.

77. See ibid., 466.

78. Chew, "Evidence Given By German Agent."

79. The Oakland Directory listed their respective addresses as 474 and 472 44th Street. Polk-Husted Directory Co., *Oakland, Berkeley and Alameda Directory, 1915*. https://archive.org/details/polkhusteddirect1915polk/page/n561/mode/2up.

80. The Spink-Mertz narrative, and the quotations from Spink's affidavit, are from Hopkins, *The Mooney Case*, 55–58. See also Gentry, *Frame-Up*, 467–68. Spink made his affidavit, and disclosed it to the Mooney defense team, in 1926 after his wife died. He had promised her not to go public with the story while she was alive, to protect them and the Mertzs. The Mooney defense team discovered that Mrs. Mertz was still alive and tried to contact her in Germany. The German Government refused to let her be interviewed. Gentry, *Frame-Up*, 468.

81. Gentry, *Frame-Up*, 457, 469.

82. Landau, *Enemy Within*, 33–34.

83. *See, e.g.*, Jahnke, Affidavit, November 24, 1927, MCC, GER exh. P, 9; L. Witzke to Parents, August 2, 1916, Lothar Witzke, Correspondence (originals and translations) comprising 24 letters and cards, 1916–1917 ["Group 2" correspondence], GER exh. LXXXVI/6, MCC, RG 76, EN P 51, Ser. German Exhibits and Translations re Sabotage Cases, ca. 1922–1939, vol. 11 (NACP).

84. The address book is discussed in more detail in chapter 12, infra.

85. Jahnke, Affidavit, November 24, 1927, MCC, GER exh. P, 3.

86. Witzke, Affidavit, July 19, 1927, GER exh. Q, 3.

87. There are other hints of sabotage committed during neutrality. See, e.g., Jahnke Affidavit, November 24, 1927, MCC, GER exh. P, 6: "He [Wunneberg] further informed me tht he had been given instructions, and furnished material, for placing incendiary and explosive bombs on departing vessels of the Allies, when opportunity offered."

88. See L. Witzke to Parents, August 2, 1916, MCC, GER exh. LXXXVI/6: "I am . . . living with an acquaintance of mine from Posen. He is a very nice man, his name is Kurt Jahnke and he is a private detective."

89. Crocker-Langley, San Francisco Directory for 1916, 994, https://archive.org/details/crockerlangleysa1916sanfrich/page/994/mode/2up . C.A. Borden was one of Jahnke's aliases, according to Secret Service reports about him.

90. Crocker-Langley, *San Francisco Directory for 1917*, 1059, https://archive.org/details/crockerlangleysa1917sanf/page/1058/mode/2up.

91. Lothar Witzke, Declaration of Intention to become US citizen, July 25, 1916, GER exh. N, MCC, RG 76, EN P 51, Ser. German Exhibits and Translations re Sabotage Cases, ca. 1922–1939, vol. 2 (NACP).

12. DID HE DO IT? BLACK TOM

1. Reinhard Doerries, "Tracing Kurt Jahnke: Aspects of the Study of German Intelligence," in George O. Kent (ed.), *Historians and Archivists: Essays in Modern German History and Archival Policy* (Fairfax, Virginia: George Mason University Press, 1991), 33. Doerries also writes: "There are a number of circumstantial indicators that would tend to suggest that both operations would have appealed to the sense of action of such men as Jahnke and Witzke" (34).

2. *For example,* Richard B. Spence, "K.A. Jahnke and the German Sabotage Campaign in the United States and Mexico, 1914–1918," *The Historian* 59, No. 1 (Taylor & Francis Online, Fall 1996): 89–112, has written: "According to Witzke's later confession, confirmed by other evidence, he and Jahnke planted bombs among some 13,000 tons of explosives with the help of Hinsch and his men. The day after the explosion, Jahnke and Witzke rushed back to San Francisco." Spence, 102. Tracie L. Provost, *The Great Game: Imperial German Sabotage and Espionage against the United States, 1914–1917* (PhD diss., University of Toledo, UMI Microform, 2003), has written: "On the night of Saturday July 29, 1916, three German saboteurs infiltrated the New Jersey Terminal. Lothar Witzke and Kurt Jahnke arrived by boat shortly before midnight. They brought with them time fuses, incendiary devices, and explosives provided by Hermann and Hinsch. A third accomplice, Michael Kristoff, arrived by land. Together they set several small fires and timed explosive devices in boxcars containing TNT." Provost, 131 (un-footnoted). Chad Millman, *The Detonators: The Secret Plot to Destroy America and an Epic Hunt for Justice* (New York: Little Brown & Co., 2006) has written: "As Jahnke and Witzke rowed toward the Statue of Liberty, and Black Tom Island beyond, they knew that Kristoff was walking toward the target. Jahnke and Witzke had been given explosives, detonators, a target, a patsy, a getaway route, and a safe house". Millman, 90. Bill Mills, *Agent of the Iron Cross: The Race to Capture German Saboteur-Assassin Lothar Witzke During World War I* (New York: Rowman & Littlefield, 2023), has written: "a rowboat bearing Kurt Jahnke and Lothar Witzke drew ever closer to the lonely depot. Witzke was a skilled oarsman from years of rowing boats on the Baltic as a naval cadet, and his powerful frame effortlessly propelled the craft across the dark water" Mills, 33. We have found a single scholar (in a published dissertation) who takes a contrarian view of Germany's responsibility for the sabotage at Black Tom, opining that the evidence does not show Germany's responsibility, but his view does not turn on the evidence as to Witzke. Russel Duane Van Wyk, "German-American relations in the aftermath of the Great War: Diplomacy, law, and the Mixed Claims Commission 1922–1939" (PhD diss., University of North Carolina at Chapel Hill, 1989).

3. Henry Landau, *The Enemy Within* (New York: G.P. Putnam's Sons, 1937).

4. Landau acknowledges that he worked with counsel for the American claimants in the Sabotage Cases.Landau, *The Enemy Within*, ix.

5. Jamie Bisher, *The Intelligence War in Latin America, 1914–1922* (Jefferson, NC: McFarland & Co., Inc., 2016), 183 (footnotes omitted). More recently, the work of Jules

Witcover, *Sabotage at Black Tom* (Chapel Hill, NC: Algonquin, 1989), is frequently cited as authority for Witzke's involvement and culpability. Like Landau's, Witcover's book lacks footnotes.

6. There is a consensus among historians of the *Sabotage Cases* and Black Tom that Witzke served on the Dresden. For example, Landau writes: "By the beginning of the war [Witzke] was a well-built, athletic young fellow, good looking with keen blue eyes, fair hair, and ruddy complexion, serving aboard the cruiser Dresden in South American waters. He also had the usual sailor's fondness for wine, women, and song. After many months of excitement, during which the Dresden was alternately playing havoc with Allied shipping and hiding from British warships, she was eventually caught and sunk. Witzke's leg was broken in the action, and together with other survivors of the crew he was interned in Valparaiso. . . . Early in 1916 he escaped; and as a seaman, under an assumed name, he succeeded in reaching San Francisco in May 1916 on board the S.S. Calusa." Landau, *The Enemy Within*, 35. Spence writes: "In March 1916 the German Admiralty named Jahnke chief for *N. und S. Angelegenheiten* for the western United States. To assist him, Berlin dispatched Lothar Witzke, a young naval officer, who reached San Francisco in May. Witzke was a former crewmember of the cruiser *SMS Dresden*, sunk by British guns off the coast of Chile in 1915. One of Witzke's comrades on that vessel was Wilhelm Canaris, future chief of the *Abwehr* and later collaborator with Jahnke in anti-Nazi intrigue." Spence, "K.A. Jahnke and the German Sabotage Campaign," 99–100 (footnote omitted). Mills echoes these writers: "One of the youngest members of the *Dresden* crew to escape from Chile was naval cadet Lothar Witzke." *Agent of the Iron Cross*, 11. But the consensus is wrong, as we have established above in our *Sailor* chapter.

7. There was no oral testimony before the Mixed Claims Commission. As we have the written record, plus other information unavailable to the Commission, we are in a position to make an independent evaluation of the Black Tom testimony.

8. There is no basis to question the accuracy of Butcher's reports of what Altendorf reported: Butcher had no motivation to exaggerate what Altendorf told him about Black Tom; Black Tom was not part of the US charges of espionage; Black Tom was also an East Coast matter and Butcher's superiors were responsible for the West Coast; the sabotage cases before the Mixed Claims Commission were years in the future, and were contemplated by no one at the time.

9. Joel A. Lipscomb, Special Border Report re German Activity, Foreigners: Latar Witcke alias Pablo (Paul) and Harry Waberski, February 2, 1918, US exh. 228, MCC, RG 76, EN PI 143/14, Ser. Printed US Exhibits, 1929?–1939?, vol. 1 (NACP), 631 (emphasis added).

10. Joel A. Lipscomb, Special Border Report re German Activity, Foreigners: Yenky [Jahnke], February 7, 1918, US exh. 227, MCC, RG 76, EN PI 143/14, Ser. Printed US Exhibits, 1929?–1939?, vol. I (NACP), 619–20 (emphasis added).

11. Paul Altendorf, Affidavit, January 16, 1929, US exh. 561, MCC, RG 76, EN PI 143/14, Ser. Printed US Exhibits, 1929?–1939?, vol. 3 (NACP).

12. This changed by 1919, as shown by Tunney's interview of Witzke in September 1919. During that year as well, Altendorf had his several articles on his exploits published.

13. Witzke introduced this explanation in 1919 in his jailhouse interview by Captain Tunney. Lothar Witzke, Examination by Thomas J. Tunney, September 16–17, 1919,

US exh. 24, MCC, RG 76, EN PI 143/14, Ser. Printed US Exhibits, 1929?–1939?, vol. 1 (NACP), 87–88.

14. William Neunhoffer to A. Bruce Bielaski, March 20, 1918, US order exh. 289, MCC, RG 76, EN PI 143/14, Ser. Printed US Exhibits, 1929?–1939?, vol. 6 (NACP).

15. Guy L. Fake, Affidavit, August 18, 1924, US exh. 10, MCC, RG 76, EN PI 143/14, Ser. Printed US Exhibits, 1929?–1939?, vol. 1 (NACP), para. 21.

16. Quoted by Altendorf in Altendorf, "On Secret Service—in Mexico, Article 3" *Chicago Tribune*, Nov. 3, 1919. We see no reason to doubt the authenticity of the letter or quotation. It would have been easily disprovable had Altendorf invented it.

17. Brig. Gen. J. A. Ryan to "To Whom It May Concern," October 23, 1918, NARA RG165, Records of the War Department and Special Staffs, Military Intelligence Division, File 51-45/18 (NACP).

18. C. E. Breniman to "To Whom It May Concern," October 26, 1918, RG 165, Ser. MID Correspondence, 1919–1941, File 51-45/17 (NACP).

19. Capt. Ray Powell, Memorandum of Conversation with Mr. E. N. Lawton, United States Consul at Nogales, Sonora, November 8, 1918, MID, File 51-45/[illegible] (NACP). Powell is reporting his conversation with Lawton.

20. Major E.L. Barnes, Memorandum for Colonel Garrison re Dr. P. B. Altendorf, April 9, 1919, MID, File. 51-45/31 (NACP).

21. See Bill Mills, *Treacherous Passage: Germany's Secret Plot against the United States in Mexico during World War I* (Lincoln NE: Potomac Books, 2017), 192ff.

22. Memorandum of Statement made by Pablo Waberski [alias of Witzke] to Byron Butcher at Calabasas Station, Arizona, February 14, 1918, in Photostatic Copy of Report of Wm. Neunhoffer re Pablo Waberski, February 25, 1918, US order exh. 288, MCC, RG 76, EN PI 143/14, Ser. Printed US Exhibits, 1929?–1939, vol. 6 (NACP).

23. Ibid.;Testimony of Byron Butcher, Trial Hearing Record at 96, August 16–17, 1918, US v. Witcke alias Waberski, RG 153, Ser. Court Martial Case Files, 1917–1938, File Lather Witcke, alias Pablo Waberski, 119966 (NASL).

24. Waberski [alias of Witzke], Statement to Butcher at Calabasi Station, February 14, 1918, MCC, US order exh. 288 (emphasis added).

25. Ibid. (emphasis added).

26. Ibid.

27. Altendorf, Affidavit, January 16, 1929, MCC, US exh. 561.

28. Birth Certificate of Bernard Altendorf, GER exh. XL-A, MCC, RG 76, EN P 51, Ser. German Exhibits and Translations re Sabotage Cases, ca. 1922–1939, box 1020 (NACP). The American representative, Kibby Munson, joined in the disdain of Altendorf's effort to deny his origin. As Munson noted, "The German brief spoke of Altendorf as an Austrian Jew. Altendorf did not like this designation. . . ." G. Kirby Munson, "Witzke and Jahnke," MS, rev. July 25, 1930, MCC, RG 76, EN PI 143/83, Ser. Notes of the Law Clerk Concerning Evidence in the Sabotage Cases, 1930–1930 (NACP), 4. Altendorf's denial of his ethnic origin was not his only prevarication about his life. Altendorf was born in 1875 and he stated in a 1929 affidavit submitted to the Mixed Claims Commission that he had not been in Krakow since 1889. Altendorf, Affidavit, January 16, 1929, MCC, US exh. 561, 4. But he also swore (before the military tribunal that heard the espionage case against Witzke in August 1918) that he had been educated at Krakow University, Altendorf Testimony, Witzke Trial

Record, 6, an impossibility because it would mean that he was attending Krakow University at age 14.

29. John Shores, Affidavit, September 20, 1919, US exh. 24-A, MCC, RG 76, EN PI 143/14, Ser. Printed US Exhibits, 1929?–1939?, vol. 1 (NACP).

30. Shores' report is given some corroboration by an affidavit done seven years later for the American agent. The affidavit was by Captain Voelker, the Post Adjutant at Fort Sam Houston: "In September, 1919, I think, . . . one Corporal John Shores, on duty as Corporal of the Guard, heard Witzke say that he [Witzke] with another man, whose name I do not know, had blown up Black Tom. On hearing the story I reported it to Col. Gray, the Commanding officer of the Post. Col. Gray remarked that Witzke had already been tried and convicted as a spy, and that in his opinion this matter was un-important as to Witzke." A.H.J. Voelker, Affidavit, December 16, 1926, US exh. 336, MCC, RG 76, EN PI 143/14, Ser. Printed US Exhibits, 1929?–1939?, vol. 2 (NACP). The Captain's comment that he was told that the admission was of no consequence because Witzke had already been convicted, and as a spy, not a saboteur, likely re-flects the American Agent's effort to explain why the US, if they believed that Witzke was a saboteur, had taken no action against Witzke for his alleged sabotage.

31. Another explanation is that Witzke might have hoped that his "admission" would be reported up the chain of command and that his execution would be delayed while his claim was investigated. Whether his admission had anything or not to do with New York Police Captain Tunney showing up two months later, we do not know. But Tunney did question Witzke about Black Tom and Kingsland.

32. John Shores, Affidavit, March 21, 1926, US exh. 333, MCC, RG 76, EN PI 143/14, Ser. Printed US Exhibits, 1929?–1939?, vol. 2 (NACP).

33. Witzke then discussed the roles and ranks of sentries to show that the individuals who purportedly heard confessions could not have been present. Lothar Witzke, Affidavit, July 19, 1927, GER exh. Q, MCC, RG 76, EN P 51, Ser. German Exhibits and Translations re Sabotage Cases, ca. 1922–1939, vol. 2 (NACP), 17–18.

34. George D. Haslam, Affidavit, April 14, 1926, US exh. 334, MCC, RG 76, EN PI 143/14, Ser. Printed US Exhibits, 1929?–1939?, vol. 2 (NACP).

35. Brief for the Underwriters in support of the Memorials filed by the Underwriters and by the Lehigh Valley Railroad, filed July 25, 1928, MCC, RG 76 (NACP), 190–91.

36. Transcript of Oral Arguments, US vs. Germany, September 18–30, 1930 (The Hague, Holland), MCC, RG 76 (NACP), 288.

37. John Rigney, Affidavit, January 21, 1927, GER exh. LV, RG 76, EN P 51, Ser. German Exhibits and Translations re Sabotage Cases, ca. 1922–1939, box 1021 (NACP), para 6.

38. As stated by the MCC in their October 1930 Decision: "the fact that Kristoff was discharged makes it certain that at the least the Jersey City police had not sufficient evidence to make the charge against him, and it is significant also that they did not keep Kristoff under surveillance or do anything else towards pushing the matter fur-ther. Their judgment is important, for they certainly had a good deal of the evidence now so strongly relied upon." Judicial Decisions, 25 Am J. Int'l L. 147, 161 (1931).

39. Alexander Kassman, Affidavit, January 24, 1927, US exh. 329, MCC, RG 76, EN PI 143/14, Ser. Printed US Exhibits, 1929?–1939?, vol. 2 (NACP).

40. Comment by US Agent, 1930 MCC Oral Argument, 232–33, quoting Alexander Kassman, Annex to Affidavit, January 24, 1927, US exh. 329, MCC, RG 76, EN PI 143/14, Ser. Printed US Exhibits, 1929?–1939?, vol. 2 (NACP) (emphasis added).

41. MCC October 1930 Decision, 165.

42. George King, Affidavit, February 28, 1929, GER exh. LII, MCC, RG 76, EN P 51, Ser. German Exhibits and Translations re Sabotage Cases, ca. 1922–1939, box 1020 (NACP).

43. "Seized as Suspect in Black Tom Case," *New York Times*, July 6, 1921.

44. MCC October 1930 Decision, 163: "Where Kristoff in the alleged admissions speaks of 'steamboats' at Black Tom upon which he and his companions set fires, Kassman in his affidavit speaks of 'barges.' There were no 'steamboats' at Black Tom, but there were 'barges.'"

45. David Grossman, Deposition, [n.d.], GER exh. XLI, MCC, RG 76, EN P 51, Ser. German Exhibits and Translations re Sabotage Cases, ca. 1922–1939, box 1020 (NACP).

46. MCC October 1930 Decision, 164. One historian of World War I has written this: "Kristoff reportedly told Kassman that rich friends had provided the funding for the Black Tom operation. One of the alleged backers, David Grossman, lived in Bayonne. Kassman arranged to meet Grossman and gleaned more details of the plot from him. Grossman denied knowing the money had been for sabotage. But, Grossman told Kassman, he later learned Kristoff had served as a lookout while another man placed dynamite on a small boat beneath the piers and a third put explosive charges between railroad cars loaded with ammunition. In spring 1917 Kristoff vanished. Grossman refused to testify, but his interrogation helped police identify two other men—Lothar Witzke, a naval officer with an intelligence background, and Kurt Jahnke, a naturalized American citizen with connections to the German consulate in San Francisco." Michael S. Neiberg, "World War I Intrigue: German Spies in New York!," https://www.historynet.com/world-war-i-intrigue-german-spies-in-new-york.htm. The last sentence is the one of interest. Were it true that Grossman's report of his conversations with Kristoff led the police to identify Witzke and Jahnke as the two other actors at Black Tom, this would be a source for Witzke's (and Jahnke's) participation at Black Tom independent of the testimony of Altendorf and the other witnesses presented by the US Agent to the Mixed Claims Commission. But there is no source cited for this historian's statement, and we are aware of none that could have been cited. There is no police report known to the authors that identifies Witzke and Jahnke. The US agent before the Mixed Claims Commission did not assert that New Jersey police had determined or even suspected that Witzke and Jahnke were involved in the Black Tom sabotage.

47. Witzke, Affidavit, July 19, 1927, GER exh. Q.

48. Lothar Witzke, Notebook (original), 1916–1917, GER Ann. 130, MCC, RG 76, EN P 61, Ser. German Annexes to Expert Opinion Deposition of Albert S. Osborn Relating to Sabotage Cases, ca. 1922—ca. 1938, box 1036 (NACP). The address book was produced by Germany to the American representatives in 1937. By then, the focus of the arbitration was elsewhere, and little attention was paid to the address book. It appears to the authors that no one has examined the address book in the intervening 85 years, and it took a sustained effort by the authors to find the original in the National Archives at College Park, Maryland. The analysis that follows is based on our examination of the original.

49. Albert was Germany's commercial attaché in the United States and its chief paymaster for propaganda and sabotage activities. He infamously fell asleep on a New York subway, woke suddenly at his stop, and in his hurry to exit accidentally left his briefcase on the train. His briefcase was retrieved by a Secret Service agent who had

been tailing him and turned out to contain numerous papers documenting some of Germany's nefarious activities in the US during the period of neutrality. Albert, like Witzke, also kept a diary and the diary separately fell into the hands of US authorities. Like Witzke's diary, Albert's diary turned out to be blank for the last week of July and the first week of August, 1916, *i.e.*, the two week period surrounding Black Tom, even though Albert rarely missed a day, much less a two week period. Landau, *The Enemy Within*, 99–100, 309.

50. There is a possible explanation why the chronology was crammed into the two particular pages that were chosen. The two pages were "S" pages in the address book, and many of the entries in the chronology concern and begin with "San Francisco."

51. The authors consulted an experienced handwriting expert, Jeffrey Luber, a forensic document examiner employed by the Suffolk County (NY) Crime Laboratory. Luber's view is reflected in the sentence to which this note applies.

52. Witzke first mentioned his address book to the German Agent in the summer of 1927. He then found the book among his papers in Hanover but declined to give it to the German Agent because it contained names and addresses of individuals and, he said, he was concerned about harassment by the American Agent. Paulig, Affidavit, March 25, 1929, filed as Annex 12 to Report of German Agent, August 1, 1929, MCC, RG 76, EN PI 143/17 (NACP). In April 1929, Witzke consented that the address book be submitted only to the commissioners. He also consented at that time that two pages of the book containing the chronology be filed before the Commission. But he continued to refuse in 1929 to allow the American agent to receive the address book. Lothar Witzke, Affidavit, July 29, 1930, GER exh. CXXVI, MCC, RG 76, (NACP). The address book was ultimately produced in its entirety in 1937.

53. Dojan, a native German who was a guard at Fort Sam Houston (where he was known as Corporal Harris) and later served as a witness to supposed admissions by Witzke about Black Tom, was, according to Witzke, sent by US interests to Germany in 1922 to befriend Witzke's family and to obtain whatever papers were kept at the house. While hosted by Witzke's unknowing and welcoming parents at their home in Hanover, Dojan was, on September 13, 1922, discovered by Witzke's mother going through private family papers, presumably searching for evidence of use to the Americans. A physical altercation ensued and Dojan was said to have caused grievous harm to Witzke's mother. Witzke's father, Paul Witzke, immediately reported the attack to the Hanover police. The story is substantiated both by the contemporaneous report by Paul Witzke to the Hanover police on September 13, 1922, and by a June 1923 letter from Witzke's parents to President Harding, seeking a pardon of their son. Witzke's parents would not have gone to the police with an invented story of an assault on Witzke's mother, and it would have been reckless on their part to add a fabricated story to their letter to the US President seeking clemency for their son. Public Prosecutor's file re criminal proceedings against Dojan for attempted murder of Lothar Witzke's mother, [n.d.], GER exh. LXVI-A, RG 76, EN 51, Ser. German Exhibits and Translations re Sabotage Cases, ca. 1922–1939, vol. 8, (NACP); German Agent, Memorandum concerning Public Prosecutor's file no. 4F990/22 re investigations against Dojan in connection with attempted murder, [n.d.], GER exh. LXVI-B, MCC, RG 76, EN P 51, Ser. German Exhibits and Translations re Sabotage Cases, ca. 1922–1939, vol. VIII (NACP); Petition, Paul and

Vally Witzke to President Harding, June 7, 1923, Witzke Case File 119966 (National Archives at St. Louis).

54. According to the German agent before the MCC, Witzke and Jahnke even came from the same hometown. MCC 1930 Oral Argument, 282. This was reported as well by British Intelligence based on their post-war interrogation of Witzke. British National Archives Reference KV-2-2296.

55. Landau, *The Enemy Within*, 34.

56. A letter written by Witzke to the German Agent in 1929 from Maracaibo has a curious sentence. Describing the efforts of American interrogators to obtain from Witzke admissions about Black Tom, Witzke wrote: "Jahnke (member of Diet, Kurt), I declined to discuss upon the ground that Jahnke has different political tendencies and I did not wish to have anything to do with him personally." Lothar Witzke to Privy Councillor Hossenfelder, January 12, 1929, GER Exh. LVI-C, trans., MCC, RG 76, EN P 51, Ser. German Exhibits and Translations re Sabotage cases, ca. 1922–1939, vol. VII (NACP). We dismiss as not credible Witzke's statement about wanting to keep his distance from Jahnke; that was a self-serving way to avoid giving the Americans any information about Jahnke. But Witzke had no reason to fabricate his statement that he and Jahnke had different political tendencies. The difference would have been that Witzke was to the right of Jahnke. Perhaps Witzke suspected that Jahnke sympathized with the communists, a suspicion that Witzke would voice in 1952 to British interrogators.

57. R. Townsend to Intelligence Inspector Vesey, September 17, 1941. Jahnke Kurt, KV 2/755 (TNA-UK) (reporting interview with Augusta Kell-Pfeffer, who was in prison in Great Britain as a suspected spy for Germany and who knew Jahnke during the 1930s).

58. Lothar Witzke, Affidavit re authenticity of his letters and cards [Group 2], June 20, 1929, GER exh. LXXXVI-A, MCC, RG 76, EN P 51, Ser. German Exhibits and Translations re Sabotage Cases, ca. 1922–1939, vol. XI (NACP), 5.

59. Two-page report on interrogation of Witzke on April 21, 1952, accompanying letter from D.J.J. to Ronnie, May 15, 1952, Witzke Lothar, KV 2/2296, 9-10 (TNA-UK).

60. Three-page enclosure entitled "Lothar Witzke/Kurt Jahnke" [n.d.], reporting on interrogation of Witzke on April 8, 1952, accompanying letter from D.J.J. to Ronnie, May 15, 1952, Witzke Lothar, KV 2/2296, 13 (TNA-UK).

61. Ibid., 15.

62. At school, Witzke was a member of the school's rowing club. His strength and prowess as a rower were recognized by the *Vinnen*'s captain. When the *J. C. Vinnen* docked at Valparaiso, Witzke was chosen by the captain to be one of the captain's two oarsmen while the ship was anchored there. The oarsmen were on call every day to row the captain to shore and back. The job superseded what would otherwise have been the oarsmen's daily duties on board ship and was coveted. During the time the captain was onshore, the oarsmen were free to do whatever they wanted. L. Witzke to Parents, May 10, 1914-July 6, 1914, MCC, Ger. exh. XCII-A/33.

63. Casimir Pilenas Palmer, Affidavit, May 2, 1931, US exh. 896-A, MCC, RG 76, EN PI 143/11, Ser. US Exhibits, ca. 1923–1939, Box 10 (NACP).

64. Casimir Pilenas [Palmer], Report by British Operative No. 45 re Jahnke, February 2, 1917, US exh. 896-B, MCC, RG 76, EN PI 143/11, Ser. US Exhibits, ca. 1923–1939, Box 10 (NACP).

65. Memorandum, July 5, 1941, enclosing Note, "Kurt Jahnke," Jahnke Kurt, KV 2/755 (TNA-UK).

66. Attesting to Jahnke's reputation for sabotage in the Americas without reference to Black Tom, a German agent turned by the British told British Intelligence that "in 1939 Canaris asked Jahnke, who of course had sabotage background, to help him build up Abteilung II. Jahnke did, in fact, assist in the formulation of the Lehrregiment 600 Z.b.v., a sabotage organization in Belgium Holland and France, and in the study of USA politics and sabotage possibilities in the States." Interview of code name "Dictionary" [Carl Marcus], April 5, 1945. Jahnke Kurt, KV 2/755 (TNA-UK). Similarly, a German woman imprisoned by the British as a suspected spy told British intelligence in 1940 that she was told by a German agent that "Jahnke had done very useful sabotage work during the last war in the U.S.A." R. Townsend to Intelligence Inspector Vesey, September 17, 1941, Jahnke Kurt, KV 2/755 (TNA-UK) (reporting interview with Augusta Kell-Pfeffer, who was in prison in Great Britain as a suspected spy for Germany and who knew Jahnke during the 1930s).

67. Robert Pennewitz to MCC, May 1935 and enclosure, "My Evidence Concerning the Black Tom and Kingsland Sabotage" [n.d.], RG 165, Ser. MID Correspondence, 1919–1941, File 10541-268/285 (NACP).

68. Ibid., 4.

69. It remains to be mentioned that one historian, Jules Witcover, has written that a *watchman* who worked for the one of the barge companies at Black Tom reported that, shortly after midnight on July 30, he saw a small rowboat bearing two men moving slowly from the farthest Black Tom pier toward Bedloe's Island, which sits due east of Black Tom. Soon afterwards, he testified, he saw a small fire in one of the boxcars, and then went off duty, having been unable to find a watchman employed by the owner of the site to deal with the fire. Jules Witcover, *Sabotage at Black Tom: Imperial Germany's Secret War in America, 1914–1917* (Chapel Hill, NC: Algonquin Books, 1989), 161. The authors have seen several reports by watchmen at Black Tom but have not found the one mentioned by Witcover. Witcover's book is unfootnoted.

70. Acting General Staff to Military Attaché, German Embassy (Washington DC), Telegram, January 24, 1915, GER exh. XXXIV-A and B, MCC, RG 76, P 51, Ser. German Exhibits and Translations re Sabotage Cases, ca. 1922–1939, box 1019 (NACP). An English translation of the telegram is quoted at MCC, "Certificate of Disagreement and Opinion of the American Commissioner," June 15, 1939, *Rep. of Int'l Arb. Awards*, vol. 8 (New York?: United Nations, 2006), 254, https://legal.un.org/riaa/cases/vol_VIII/1-468.pdf.

71. "The record in this case proves conclusively that Rintelen's activities in this country were connected with inoculating horses and cattle, the destruction of piers and elevators and munitions factories; that he was furnished with incendiary devices by a German chemist. Dr. Scheele, who manufactured bombs and other incendiary material, not only for Rintelen, but for other saboteurs." *1939 Certificate of Disagreement*, 257. See also Comment by German Agent, 1930 Argument, 213: "Rintelen . . . tried to organize sabotage against Allied ships carrying munitions from the United States, a fact that has been known in the United States for a long time, because his activities were discovered shortly after they had started." Landau lists "the names of forty-seven ships on which bombs of other incendiary devices were found while en

route to Allied countries from American ports," and notes that this practice ceased abruptly when the US declared war on Germany in April 1917 and German operatives fled to Mexico. Landau, *The Enemy Within*, 36.

72. Hinsch testified as follows:

> I attempted at first to instigate strikes among the stevedores in ports, and furnished for that purpose negroes hired by me at the time with circulars which I caused to be distributed in Norfolk, Newport News and Baltimore. After that, we attempted to infect horses and mules transports with anthrax germs. I used the negroes also for that purpose. Finally, we manufactured so-called dumplings in order to cause fires on munitions ships and ships with contraband. I used Ed Felton and his negroes also for this purpose.
>
> Q. When did you start these activities?
> A. In May, 1916, after I had talked with Rintelen personally.

Friedrich Hinsch, Examination by Tannenberg, September 3, 1930, GER exh. CXXVIII, MCC, RG 76 (NACP), 109. The Baltimore sabotage cell is well-described in Dwight R. Messimer, *The Baltimore Sabotage Cell: German Agents, American Traitors, and the U-Boat Deutschland During World War I* (Annapolis MD: Naval Institute Press, 2015).

73. "It is now thoroughly agreed, both by the witnesses for Germany and the witnesses for the United States, that authority for sabotage was directly given to Hilken and Herrmann in a meeting with "Sektion Politik" of the German General Staff by Captains Nadolny and Marguerre in Berlin in February, 1916." *1939 Certificate of Disagreement*, 265.

74. Comment by German Agent, 1930 Oral Argument, 210; see also ibid., 276.

75. Describing efforts to set fire to the Tampico oil fields in Mexico, comment by American Agent, 1930 Oral Argument, 23; see also *1939 Certificate of Disagreement*, 257.

76. "The General Staff is anxious that vigorous measures should be taken to destroy the Canadian Pacific in several places for the purpose of causing a lengthy interruption of traffic." Comment by German Agent, 1930 Oral Argument, 203; German Foreign Office to German Ambassador in the US, Telegram, December 3, 1915, quoted in W. Reginald Hall, Affidavit, December 28, 1926, US exh. 320, MCC, RG 76, EN PI 143/14, Ser. Printed US Exhibits, 1929?–1939?, vol. 1 (NACP); *1939 Certificate of Disagreement*, 259. See also Reinhard R. Doerries, *Imperial Challenge—Ambassador Count Bernstorff and German-American Relations, 1908–1917*, trans. Christa Shannon (Chapel Hill NC: Univ. N. Carolina Press, 1989), 178–80.

77. Witzke himself admitted to this. "I must make a distinction between the time prior to and the period after the American declaration of war. The tasks entrusted to me during these two periods were as different as were the relations between German and the United States before and after April 6, 1917." Witzke, Affidavit, July 19, 1927, GER exh. Q, 1.

78. Doerries, *Imperial Challenge*, 187. See also Arthur S. Link, Forward to Doerries, *Imperial Challenge*, xiv: "The German government . . . mounted a massive campaign on American soil of intrigue, espionage, and sabotage unprecedented in modern times by one allegedly friendly power against another. It revealed better than anything else the true attitude of the German leaders toward the United States. It was an attitude of hostility and contempt."

79. The Hermann Message is discussed in detail in *chapter 7, Star Witness*.
80. Ibid.
81. 1939 Certificate of Disagreement, 156 (referencing 1932 Decision).
82. The Commissioner's analysis of the Herrmann Message occupied over 100 single-spaced pages of his Opinion. *1939 Certificate of Disagreement*, 349–454.
83. Decision of Commission by Umpire, October 30, 1939, para 6 at p. 312. MCC, RG 76 (NACP).
84. "As a sub-agent of Jahnke the task was assigned to me to make observations in San Francisco and in other places in the west of the United States as to movements of ships of the allies, the cargo and destination of such ships, as to ship construction, manufacture and shipments of munitions, orders given to munition factories and as to the development of the war and munition industries, and also to collection information of all kind which might be of value to German official agencies." Witzke, Affidavit, July 19, 1927, GER exh. Q, 3.
85. Witzke, Affidavit, July 19, 1927, GER exh. Q.
86. Altendorf, "On Secret Service—in Mexico, Article 18," Chicago Daily Tribune, November 20, 1919, 19.
87. Waberski [alias of Witzke], Statement to Butcher at Calabasi Station, February 14, 1918, MCC, US order exh. 288.
88. Witzke to Hossenfelder, January 12, 1929, MCC, GER exh. LVI-C, 3.
89. Ibid., 5. He continued: "On question, I said: 'that I hope the future may bring a change some day and that until such time I would hold myself in reserve subject to call.' When further asked, I said, 'that my belief was the present republican Government sincerely wants to clear up the old matters between themselves and their old enemies, thinking that this policy is to the best of Germany's interest. I said that political conditions in Germany are all upturned and the different parties, even Government offices pulling in different directions, more or less following their personal political beliefs.'" Ibid., 3–4.
90. Lothar Witzke, Correspondence (originals and translations) comprising 24 letters and cards, 1916–17 ["Group 2" correspondence], GER exh. LXXXVI/7, MCC, RG 76, EN P 51, Ser. German Exhibits and Translations re Sabotage Cases, ca. 1922–1939, vol. XI (NACP).
91. Witzke, Correspondence, 1916–17, MCC, GER exh. LXXXVI/8.
92. Witzke, Affidavit, July 19, 1927, GER exh. Q, 6–7.
93. Lothar Witzke, Declaration of Intention to become US citizen, July 25, 1916, GER exh. N, MCC, RG 76, EN P 51, Ser. German Exhibits and Translations re Sabotage Cases, ca. 1922–1939, vol. 2 (NACP).
94. It is curious that Witzke's weight was given as 180 lbs. That is overweight for a young man who was 5'6". The photographs of Witzke on his trip from Mexico to Nogales in January 1918 show him to be trim, not overweight. According to Witzke's intake form at Leavenworth, the day he arrived there (June 16, 1920) he was 5'7" and weighed 155 lbs. Two alternative explanations arise: (i) the simple one is that Witzke could have lost weight between June 1916 and June 1920; (ii) the conspiratorial one is that Witzke's stand-in weighed 180 lbs. An additional curiosity is that Witzke also filed in May 1916 a Declaration of Intention and Petition for Naturalization. Perhaps it was a two-step process. At the least, the July 1916 Declaration

shows that, within a very few days of Witzke's arrival for the first time in the US, he was creating a cover for espionage activities.

95. *1930 Oral Argument*, 293.

96. July 25, 1916, the date that Witzke applied for US citizenship in San Francisco, was a Tuesday. In 1916, the Overland Limited had a scheduled departure from San Francisco at 6:00 p.m. Tuesday and a scheduled arrival in New York on July 29, at 9:40 a.m. Saturday morning. Brief for Claimant [Lehigh Valley Railroad Company], filed March 22, 1928, MCC, RG 76 (NACP), 14, note. See also de Haas to ?, Telegram, July 14, 1930, German Foreign Ministry Archive, R95283/K196857–58 (internal German Foreign Office correspondence confirming that Witzke could have departed San Francisco on July 25 and arrived in NYC the morning of July 30).

97. Reply Brief for the Underwriters, March 15, 1929, MCC, RG 76, EN P 45, Ser. German Memorandums, Briefs et al relating to the Sabotage Cases, ca. 1928–1939, Box 1153 (NACP), 28.

98. *1939* Certificate of Disagreement, 314.

99. If Jahnke had preceded Witzke to NYC by some number of days, that would make the close timing less of an issue. Another, or related, possibility is that July 29–30 might not have been a date written in stone; the plan might have been to execute once all perpetrators were in place, with Wtizke being the last to arrive.

100. Inexplicably, the lawyer to whom an investigation of the Witzke part of the case was delegated by the US Commissioner (Kibby Munson) said in his findings that it was uncontested by the American Agent that Witzke was in San Francisco on July 25 for his citizenship application. G. Kirby Munson, "Witzke and Jahnke," MS, rev. July 25, 1930, MCC, RG 76, EN PI 143/83, Ser. Notes of the Law Clerk Concerning Evidence in the Sabotage Cases, 1930–1930 (NACP), 66. To the contrary, the American Agent did contest the July 25 application's genuineness.

101. L. Witzke to Parents, July 26, 1916, MCC, GER exh. CXXVII/4; L. Witzke to Parents, August 2, 1916, MCC, GER exh. LXXXVI/6. The August 2 letter says that I "have been on land for three weeks." Germany argued that this proved that he had been in San Francisco for three weeks as of August 2, 1916, and, thus, far from Black Tom. Brief of the German Agent under Order of the Commission of October 5, 1929, filed March 22, 1930, MCC, RG 76, EN P 45, Ser. German Memorandums, Briefs et al relating to the Sabotage Cases, ca. 1928–1939, Box 1153 (NACP), 17–18.

102. The American Agent disputed that the postmark was August 2, suggesting that it might have been August 12. We have examined the original envelope that contained Witzke's August 2 letter to his parents. The postmark is clearly marked August 2, 1916. Witzke vouched for the authenticity of the 1916–17 correspondence in a 1929 affidavit. Witzke, Affidavit re 1916–17 correspondence, June 20, 1929, MCC, GER exh. LXXXVI-A.

103. Jahnke, Affidavit, November 24, 1927, MCC, GER exh. P, 1.

104. Morse Detective Agency, Records, 1916 in William Ruwe, Affidavit, December 21, 1929, US Exh. 738, MCC, RG 76, EN PI 143/14, Ser. "Printed US Exhibits, 1929?–1939?, vol. VII (NACP); 1930 Brief on Behalf of Germany, 20–30.

105. *1930 Brief on Behalf of Germany*, 28–30. Landau describes it this way: "Following out the usual practice of secret service agents everywhere, he established a cover for himself by joining the Morse Patrol, a night watchman agency, in San Francisco. Whether he actually did the work himself or obtained a substitute is not

known, but he achieved his object of having his name on the daily work sheets—a convenient alibi if suspected of sabotage in other parts of the country." Landau, *The Enemy Within*, 34.

106. 1930 Brief on Behalf of Germany, 30–34.

107. Spence, "K.A. Jahnke and the German Sabotage," 102 (footnote omitted).

108. "Summary of letter from D.I.D. to Mr Bell (U.S.A.), in continuation of previous Memoranda communicated by D.I.D. to U.S. Govt.," [n.d.], Jahnke Kurt, KV 2/755 (TNA-UK).

109. Frederick W. Hadler, Affidavit, Extract of Exh. 1005, Annex A, April 1, 1938, German Foreign Ministry Archive, RZ 211-95377/K485922–25.

110. Ibid.

111. De Haas to von Prittwitz, trans., April 19, 1929, German Foreign Ministry Archive, R95281/171–76.

112. [Gustav Heuser (German Foreign Ministry)] to Lothar Witzke, trans., April 6, 1925, German Foreign Ministry Archive, R95271/K193192–95.

113. De Haas to ?, telegram, July 14, 1930, German Foreign Ministry Archive, R95283/ K196857–58.

114. Lothar Witzke to Dr. Tannenberg, trans., July 12, 1930, German Foreign Ministry Archives, R95283/K496865.

115. Altendorf, "On Secret Service—in Mexico, Article 18," *Chicago Daily Tribune*, Nov. 20, 1919 (emphasis added).

116. Ibid.

117. "Airs German Plot in Latin America," *New York Times*, August 24, 1919.

118. 1930 MCC Decision, 150.

119. A-1 [P.B. Altendorf], "My Trip to Mexico," [Jan/Feb, 1918], MID, File 10541-268/205 (NACP).

120. Major R.L. Barnes to Dept. Intelligence Officer, Western Department, Memorandum re Pablo Waberski, July 11, 1918, RG 165, Ser. MID Correspondence, 1919–1941, File 10541-268/130 (NACP) (stating that informant A-1, i.e., Altendorf, had implicated Wild in the Mare Island bombing).

121. Altendorf Testimony, Witzke Trial Record, 7–9.

122. Jahnke, Affidavit, November 24, 1927, MCC, GER exh. P, 12–13.

123. Doerries, *Imperial Challenge*, 189–90.

124. Altendorf Testimony, Witzke Trial Record, 20.

125. Lipscomb's February 2 report says Witzke had on his person when captured "approximately $1000 in American currency and Mexican gold. The gold was in a money belt and the currency bound around the calves of his legs with handkerchiefs." Lipscomb, Special Border Report, February 2, 1918, MCC, US exh. 228.

126. Fake, Affidavit, August 18, 1924, MCC, US exh. 10, para. 24.

127. Ibid., para. 27.

128. Ibid. Landau also identifies Kurowski (sometimes spelled as Karowski) as Wozniak. Landau, *The Enemy Within*, 203–4, 258–61.

129. Fake, Affidavit, August 18, 1924, MCC, US exh. 10, para. 27 (emphasis added).

130. Ibid.

131. Paul Altendorf, Affidavit, June 4, 1920, US exh. 87, MCC, RG 76, EN PI 143/14, Ser. Printed US Exhibits, 1929?–1939?, vol. 1 (NACP).

132. See Munson, "Witzke and Jahnke," MS, rev. July 25, 1930, MCC, 5.
133. Ibid., 7. Munson wrote his report six years after the US had (in the Immigration Act of 1924 [the Johnson-Reed Act]) closed its borders to most immigration, and US citizenship had become a prize sparingly granted.
134. 1930 MCC Decision, 158.
135. 1930 Brief on Behalf of Germany, 196.
136. Gleaves Testimony, Witzke Trial Record, 46–47.
137. William Gleaves, Affidavit, January 31, 1927, US exh. 339, MCC, RG: 76, EN: PI 143/14, Printed US Exhibits (1929?–1939?), vol. 2 (NACP), para. 6.
138. Gleaves Testimony, Witzke Trial Record, 44–49.
139. John Ingram, Affidavit, August 17, 1929, US exh. 732, MCC, RG 76, EN PI 143/14, Ser. Printed US Exhibits, 1929?–1939?, vol. 7 (NACP).
140. Witzke, Affidavit, July 19, 1927, GER exh. Q, 14.
141. Oscar Sholars, Affidavit, February 6, 1927, US exh. 349, MCC, RG: 76, EN: PI 143/14, Printed US Exhibits (1929?–1939?), vol. 2 (NACP), 1311.
142. Witzke, Affidavit, July 19, 1927, GER exh. Q, 14.
143. William Colton, Affidavit, February 11, 1927, US exh. 350, MCC, RG 76, EN PI 143/14, Ser. Printed US Exhibits, 1929?–1939?, vol. 2 (NACP).
144. Witzke in this was representative of the postwar German mindset. As a German historian has commented, "According to the spirit of the age it was not important where someone came from, but only where they wanted to go." Harald Jähner, trans. Shaun Whiteside, *Aftermath: Life in the Fallout of the Third Reich, 1945–1955* (London: Penguin Random House, 2019). 321.
145. See, for example, 1930 Oral Argument, 14, where the agent argues that Jahnke, Witzke and Kristoff were responsible for setting fire to Black Tom, and that Hinsch, Wozniak, Herrmann and others were responsible for Kingsland.
146. There is detail about Kingsland provided by Altendorf in his June 4, 1920 Affidavit. MCC, US exh 87, but this Affidavit was not contemporaneous with Altendorf's conversations with Witzke and the detail provided in the Affidavit is absent in Altendorf's contemporaneous reports. Moreover, Altendorf in 1920 was zealously providing the Kingsland representatives what he though they wanted or needed. We therefore dismiss this detail as not credible.
147. 1939 Certificate of Disagreement, 85.
148. Ibid.
149. *1930 MCC Decision*, 150.
150. L. Witzke to mother, October 10, 1916, MCC, GER. exh. CXXVII/9. The picture postcard is postmarked October 12, 1916.

EPILOGUE. DEATH OF A SPY

1. Berlin Document Center; Freiund Hansetadt Hamburg, Senat, Staatsarchiv, Handschriftensammlung, Burgerschaftsmitglieder 1859–1959, No. 601.
2. Christoph Moinian and Claudia Moinian (Witzke's grandchildren), interview by coauthor, May and November 2019. The grandchildren's memories of what their mother, Helga, told them about Witzke's final words at home are conflicted. Another version has Witzke saying "mache" instead of "starte," which would be

translated as "today I'm doing the biggest feat yet," and make the intended act more imminent.

3. "Gravestones: Friedhof Hamburg-Ohlsdorf 0030," grabsteine.genealogy.net, accessed February 1, 2021. https://grabsteine.genealogy.net/tomb.php?cem=2006&tomb=503 &b=&lang=en.

4. Death Notices, *Hamburger Abendblatt* (Ian 1962).

5. Moinian and Moinian, interview, May and November 2019.

6. This detail notably echoes what Helga told her children was written in the Pablo Waberski notebooks. This raises the question whether Helga mixed up these memories in recounting these stories to her children (or, possibly, her children mixed these memories in their retelling to the coauthor).

7. Moinian and Moinian, interview, May and November 2019.

8. McKenzie Porter, "The Men Who Tried to Capture Canada," Maclean's, July 15, 1950, https://archive.macleans.ca/article/1950/7/15/the-men-who-tried-to-capture-canada.

BIBLIOGRAPHY

Altendorf, Paul Bernardo. "On Secret Service in Mexico." *Chicago Tribune*, November 3, 1919–December 2, 1919.

Aly, Götz. *Hitler's Beneficiaries*. Translated by Jefferson Chase. New York: Holt Paperbacks, 2008.

Anonymous. "Extracts from the Log of the Dresden, With Comments on Her Career." *The Naval Review* 3, no. 3 (1915): 412–38.

Anonymous. "The Sinking of the Dresden." *The Naval Review* 3, no. 3 (1915), 439–40.

Ault, Brian. "Joining the Nazi Party Before 1930: Material Interests or Identity Politics?" *Social Science History* 26, no. 2 (2002): 273–310.

Avrich, Paul, and Karen Avrich. *Sasha and Emma: The Anarchist Odyssey of Alexander Berkman and Emma Goldman*. Cambridge, MA: Harvard University Press, 2012.

Baedeker, Karl. *The United States, with Excursions to Mexico, Cuba, Porto Rico, and Alaska: Handbook for Travellers*. 4th ed. Leipzig: Karl Baedeker, 1909.

Beattie, Andrew H. *Allied Internment Camps in Occupied Germany: Extrajudicial Detention in the Name of Denazification, 1945-1950*. Cambridge: Cambridge University Press, 2020.

———. "Lobby for the Nazi Elite? The Protestant Churches and Civilian Interment in the British Zone of Occupied Germany, 1945-1948." *German History* 35, no. 1 (March 1, 2017): 43–70.

Biddiscombe, Perry. *The Denazification of Germany: A History, 1945-1950*. Tempus Publishing Ltd. 2007.

Bisant, David. "William Gleaves and the Capture of Lothar Witzke." *National Security Agency Newsletter* 47, no. 7 (July 1999): 4–6. https://archive.org/details/nsa_newsletter_1999_07/page/n3?q=%22Lothar+Witzke%22.

Bisher, Jamie, *The Intelligence War in Latin America, 1914-1922*. Jefferson, NC: McFarland & Co., 2016.

Bloch, Kurt. *German Interests and Policies in the Far East*. New York: Institute of Pacific Relations, 1940.

Breitman, Richard, Norman J. W. Goda, Timothy Naftali, and Robert Wolfe, *U.S. Intelligence and the Nazis*. Washington, DC: National Archive Trust Fund Board, 2004, https://doi.org/10.1093/hcgs/dci028.

Brustein, William. *The Logic of Evil: The Social Origins of the Nazi Party, 1925-1933*. New Haven: Yale University Press, 1998.

Bruzelius, Lars. "A Catalogue of Four-Masted Barques and Ships, 1892." *Osborne*. http://www.bruzelius.info/Nautica/Ships/Fourmast_ships/Osborne(1892).html.

Buckingham, Peter. *International Normalcy: The Open Door Peace with the Former Central Powers, 1921-1929*. Wilmington DE: Scholarly Resources, Inc., 1983.

Clough, Bryan. *State Secrets: The Kent-Wolkoff Affair*. Brighton: Hideaway Publications, Ltd., 2005.

Cohen, David. *Transitional Justice in Divided Germany After 1945*. U.C. Berkeley War Crimes Studies Center.

Colby, Frank Moore. *The New International Year Book: A Compendium of the World's Progress for the Year 1916*. New York: Dodd, Mead & Co., 1917.

Collins, Henry E. *Mining Memories and Musings: Autobiography of a Mining Engineer*. Ashire Publishing Ltd, 1985.

Corson, William. *The Armies of Ignorance: The Rise of the American Intelligence Empire*. New York: Dial Press, 1977.

Danelski, David J. "The Saboteurs' Case." *Journal of Supreme Court History*. 1996, 61–82.

Dixon, T. B. *The Enemy Fought Splendidly: Being the 1914–1915 Diary of the Battle of the Falklands and Its Aftermath*. Dorset: Blandford Press, 1983.

Doerries, Reinhard R. *Imperial Challenge: Ambassador Count Bernstorff and German-American Relations, 1908–1917*. Translated by Christa Shannon. Chapel Hill: University of North Carolina Press, 1989.

———. "Die Tätigken deutscher Agenten in den USA wahrend des Ersten Weltkrieges und ihr EinfluB auf die diplomatischen Beziehungen zwischen Washington und Berlin." In *Diplomaten und Agenten—Nachrichtendienste in der Geshichte der deutsch-amerikanischen Beziehungen*, edited by Reinhard Doerries, 11–52. Heidelberg: Universitatsverlag C. Winter Heidelberg GmbH, 2001.

———. "The Politics of Irresponsibility: Imperial Germany's Defiance of United States Neutrality during World War I." In *Germany and America: Essays on Problems of International Relations and Immigration,* edited by Hans Trefousse, 3–20. New York: Brooklyn College Press, 1980.

———. "Tracing Kurt Jahnke: Aspects of the Study of German Intelligence." In *Historians and Archivists: Essays in Modern German History and Archival Policy*, edited by George O. Kent, 27–44. George Mason University Press, 1991.

Dooley John F. "John Manly and the Waberski Cipher Solution." In *Codes, Ciphers and Spies, Tales of Military Intelligence in World War I*, 193–206. New York: Copernicus Books, 2016.

Edwords, Clarence E. *Bohemian San Francisco: Its Restaurants and Their Most Famous Recipes; The Elegant Art of Dining*. San Francisco: Paul Elder and Company, 1914.

Eisenhower, John D. *Intervention! The United States and the Mexican Revolution, 1913–1917*. New York: Norton, 1993.

Evans, Richard J. *The Coming of the Third Reich*. New York: Penguin Group, 2003.

———. *The Third Reich in History and Memory*. Oxford: Oxford Univ. Press, 2015.

Farago, Ladislas. *The Game of the Foxes: The Untold Story of German Espionage in the United States and Great Britain in World War II*. New York: David McKay Co., 1971.

Federal Bureau of Investigation. "A Brief History: The Nation Calls." https://www.fbi.gov /history/brief-history.

Federal Bureau of Investigation. "Federal Bureau of Investigation: History." https://fas.org /irp/agency/doj/fi/tbi/hist.html.

Feinstein, Tamara, ed. *The CIA and Nazi War Criminals: National Security Archive Posts Secret CIA History Released Under Nazi War Crimes Disclosure Act*. [Washington, DC]: National Security Archive, 2005. PDF. https://nsarchive2.gwu.edu/NSAEBB /NSAEBB146/index.htm.

Fisher, Louis. *Military Tribunals and Presidential Power: The American Revolution to the War on Terrorism.* Lawrence: Univ. of Kansas, 2005.

Frank, Harry A. *Roving Through Southern China.* New York: The Century Company, 1925.

Frost, Richard. *The Mooney Case.* Stanford, CA: Stanford University Press, 1968.

Fry, Helen. *Denazification: Britain's Enemy Aliens, Nazi War Criminals, and the Reconstruction of Post-War Europe.* Stroud UK: The History Press, 2010. https://www .thehistorypress.co.uk/publication/denazification/9780750951135/.

Gentry, Curt. *Frame-Up: The Incredible Case of Tom Mooney and Warren Billings.* New York: W. W. Norton & Co., 1967.

Goedda, Petra. "From Villains to Victims: Fraternization and the Feminization of Germany, 1945–1947." *Diplomatic History* 23, no. 1 (Winter, 1990): 1–20.

Gregory, Thomas. "Trial of Spies by Military Tribunals." *Op Att'y Gen.* 31 (1920): 356.

Gross, Daniel A. "The U.S. Confiscated Half a Billion Dollars in Private Property During WWI." *Smithsonian Magazine,* July 28, 2014. https://www.smithsonianmag.com /history/us-confiscated-half-billion-dollars-private-property-during-wwi-180952144/.

Grosz, George. "A Little Yes and a Big No." Translated by L. S. Dorian Dial, 1946, 124. Quoted in "The Weimar Republic: The Fragility of Democracy." http://www.facinghistory .org/weimar-republic-fragility-democracy/economics/personal-accounts-inflation -years-economics-1919–1924-inflation.

Hall, Reginald, and Amos Peaslee. *Three Wars with Germany.* New York: G. P. Putnam's Sons, 1944.

Harris, Charles, III, and Louis Sadler. "The Witzke Affair: German Intrigue on the Mexican Border, 1917–1918." *Military Review* 59, no. 2 (February 1979): 36–50.

Hayward, James. *Hitler's Spy: The True Story of Arthur Owens, Double Agent Snow.* New York: Simon & Schuster, 2012.

Hilditch, A. Neville. *Coronel and the Falkland Islands.* London and Toronto: Oxford Univ. Press, 1915.

Hoehling, A. A. *Women Who Spied.* Madison Books, 1967.

Hopkins, Ernest J. *What Happened in the Mooney Case.* New York: Brewer, Warren & Putnam, 1932.

Howard, Michael. *The First World War: A Very Short Introduction.* New York: Oxford University Press, 2002.

Hubbard-Hall, Claire M. "The Nazi Intelligence Matrix: The Gestapo outside Germany, 1939–1945." *Global War Studies* 12, no. 1 (2015): 12–37.

Humphries, John. *Spying for Hitler: The Welsh Double-Cross.* Cardiff: University of Wales Press, 2012.

Jähner, Harald. *Aftermath: Life in the Fallout of the Third Reich, 1945–1955.* Translated by Shaun Whiteside. London: Penguin Random House, 2019.

Jähnicke, Burkhardt. *Washington und Berlin zwischen den Kriegen: die Mixed Claims Commission in den transatlantischen Beziehungen.* Baden Baden: Nomos, 2003.

Jensen, Joan M. *The Price of Vigilance.* Chicago: Rand McNally & Co., 1968.

Johnson, Jeffrey A. *The 1916 Preparedness Day Bombing: Anarchy and Terrorism in Progressive Era America.* New York: Routledge, 2018.

Jonas, Manfred. "Mutualism in the Relations between the United States and the Early Weimar Republic." In *Germany and America: Essays on Problems of International*

Relations and Immigration, edited by Hans Trefousse, 45–46. New York: Brooklyn College Press, 1980.

Kahn, David. "Covert Warfare: The Final Solution of the Abwehr." In Mendelsohn, John. *Covert Warfare: Intelligence, Counterintelligence, and Military Deception During the World War II Era*. New York: Garland Publishing, Inc., 1989.

———. *The Reader of Gentlemen's Mail: Herbert O. Yardley and the Birth of American Codebreaking*. New Haven: Yale, 2006.

Katz, Friedrich. *The Secret War in Mexico: Europe, the United States, and the Mexican Revolution*. Chicago: Univ. of Chicago Press, 1981.

Kennedy, David M. *Over Here: The First World War and American Society*. New York: Oxford University Press, 1980.

Kent, George O. "Problems and Pitfalls of a Papen Biography." *Central European History* 20, no. 2 (June 1987): 191–97. https://doi.org/10.1017/S0008938900012590.

Kerstetter, Todd. "Leavenworth Penitentiary." In Encyclopedia of the Great Plains, edited by David J. Wishart. Lincoln: University of Nebraska-Lincoln. http://plainshumanities. unl.edu/encyclopedia/doc/egp.law.025.xml.

Keve, Paul W. *Prisons and the American Conscience: A History of U.S. Federal Corrections*. Carbondale: South Illinois Univ. Press, 1991.

Kiesselbach, Wilhelm. *Problems of the German-American Commission*. Translated by Edwin H. Zeydel. Washington, DC: Carnegie Endowment for International Peace, 1930.

King, Gary, Ori Rosen, Martin Tanner, and Alexander F. Wagner. "Ordinary Economic Voting Behavior in the Extraordinary Election of Adolf Hitler." *The Journal of Economic History*, December 1, 2008. https://www.cambridge.org/core/journals /journal-of-economic-history/article/abs/ordinary-economic-voting-behavior-in-the -extraordinary-election-of-adolf-hitler/8C79A0AB9DA174B7D81AEB3131EDFC.

Klemann, Hein A. M., and Sergei Kudryashov. *Occupied Economies: An Economic History of Nazi-Occupied Europe, 1939–1945*. London: Berg, 2011.

Koenig, Robert. *The Fourth Horseman: One Man's Secret Mission to Wage the Great War in America*. New York: Public Affairs, 2006.

Kozloff, Nikolas. "The Oily History of Offshore Operations: From Venezuela to the Gulf." Huffpost.com. https:www.huffpost.com/entry/the-oily-history-of-offsh_b_559781.

Kristiansen, Tom. "Closing A Long Chapter: German-Norwegian Relations 1939–45: Norway and the Third Reich." In *Hitler's Scandinavian Legacy*, edited by John Gilmour and Jill Stephenson, 73–100. London, Bloomsbury Academic, 2013.

Kühnert, Marco. *Module T: Internment, Re-Education and Punishment: The British Intern- ment Camp at Neuengamme, 1945–1948*. NS— Geschichte, Institutionen, Menschen- rechte. https://www.ns-geschichte-institutionen-menschenerechte.demodule_T.html.

Landau, Henry. *The Enemy Within*. New York: G. P. Putnam's Sons, 1937.

Larkin, Emmet J. *James Larkin: Irish Labor Leader, 1876–1947*. Cambridge: MIT Press, 1965.

LeMaster, Kenneth. *U.S. Penitentiary Leavenworth*. Charleston, SC: Arcadia Publishing, 2008.

Leverkuehn, Paul. *Germany Military Intelligence*. Translated by R. H. Stevens and Constantine FitzGibbon. Auckland, NZ: Pickle Partner Publishing, 1954.

Loberg, Molly. *The Struggle for the Streets of Berlin: Politics, Consumption, and Urban Space, 1914–1945*. Cambridge: Cambridge University Press, 2018.

Luebke, Frederick C. *Bonds of Loyalty: German-Americans and World War I*. DeKalb, Illinois: Northern Illinois University Press, 1974.

Macpecri Media. "Petroleo, Mucho Mas que Oro Negro." *El Desafío de la Historia* 30. https://amazon.com/Petroleo-mucho-mas-que -oro-negro-ebook/dp/B01AF7WK0A.

Malavé, Argenis. "Maracaibo: Ciudad de 3 Fundaciones." 2015, 259. http:biblioteca.clacso .edu.ar/Veneuzuela.ceshc-unermb/20160829053753/MC3F.pdf.

Manchester, Harland. "The Black Tom Case." *Harper's Magazine*, December 1, 1939, 60–69.

Martin, H. H. *Final Report of H. H. Martin, Acting Agent of the United States Before the Mixed Claims Commission, United States and Germany*. Washington, DC: Gov. Printing Office, 1941.

Massie, Robert K. *Castles of Steel: Britain, Germany, and the Winning of the Great War at Sea*. New York: Ballantine Books, 2003.

Mazower, Mark. *Inside Hitler's Greece: The Experience of Occupation, 1941–44*. New Haven: Yale University Press, 1993.

McKale, Donald M. "The Nazi Party in the Fast East 1931–1945." *Journal of Contemporary History* 12, no. 2 (1977): 293. www.jstor.org/stable/260218.

Messimer, Dwight R. *The Baltimore Sabotage Cell: German Agents, American Traitors, and the U-Boat* Deutschland *During World War I*. Annapolis MD: Naval Institute Press, 2015.

Millman, Chad, *The Detonators*. New York: Little Brown & Co., 2006, 24.

Mills, Bill. *Agent of the Iron Cross: The Race to Capture German Saboteur-Assassin Lothar Witzke During World War I*. New York: Rowman & Littlefield, 2023.

———. *Treacherous Passage: Germany's Secret Plot Against the United States in Mexico During World War I*. Lincoln, Nebraska: Potomac Books, 2017.

Mitchell, Reginald P. "Spy." *The American Foreign Service Journal* 11, no. 11 (Nov. 1934): 581–83, 627.

Moon, Parker Thomas. *Imperialism and World Politics*. New York: MacMillan, 1929.

Morgan, Edward M. "Court-Martial Jurisdiction over Non-Military Persons Under the Articles of War." *Minnesota Law Review* 4, no. 2 (January 1920): 79.

Moulden, Ken. "Fassbinder and the Search for Identity in *The Marriage of Maria Braun*." *Literature & Aesthetics* 16, no. 2 (December 2006): 240–51

Neiberg. Michael S. "World War I Intrigue: German Spies in New York!" https://www .historynet.com/world-war-i-intrigue-german-spies-in-new-york.html.

Nevin, Donal. *James Larkin: Lion of the Fold; The Life and Works of the Irish Labour Leader*. Dublin: Gill & McMillan, 2006.

Petrow, Richard. *The Bitter Years: The Invasion and Occupation of Denmark and Norway, April 1940–May 1945*. New York: Morrow Quill Paperbacks, 1974.

Pitt, Barrie. *Coronel and Falkland*. Sharp Books, 1918. Reprint, London: Cassell, 1960.

Porter, McKenzie. "The Men Who Tried to Capture Canada." *Maclean's*, July 15, 1950. https://archive.macleans.ca/article/1950/7/15/the-men-who-tried-to-capture-canada.

Powe, Marc B. "A Sketch of a Man and His Times." In *The Final Memoranda*, edited by Ralph E. Weber, ix–xxv. Wilmington: Scholarly Resources, 1988.

Provost, Tracie. *The Great Game: Imperial German Sabotage and Espionage Against the United States, 1914–1917*. PhD diss., University of Toledo, UMI Microform, 2003.

Puerta Bautista, Loren. "Los paisajes petroleros del Zulia en la mirada Alemana (1920–1940)." PhD diss., Universidad Central de Venezuela, 2008.

Reisman, W. Michael, and Christina Skinner. *Fraudulent Evidence Before Public*

International Tribunals: The Dirty Stories of International Law. Cambridge: Cambridge University Press, 2014.

Ritter, Nikolaus. *Cover Name: Dr. Rantzau*. Translated by Katharine R. Wallace. Lexington, KY: University Press of Kentucky, 2019.

Rolfs, Richard W. *The Sorcerer's Apprentice: The Life of Franz von Papen*. Lanham MD: University Press of America, 1996.

Ruder, Stephen. "Who Really Blew Up Mare Island?" *Naval History Magazine* 36, no. 3 (June 2022). https://www.usni.org/magazines/naval-history-magazine/2022/june/who-really-blew-mare-island.

Sands, Philippe. *The Ratline: Love, Lies and Justice on the Trail of a Nazi Fugitive*. New York: Alfred A. Knopf, 2021.

Schelenber, Walter. *The Labyrinth: Memoirs of Walter Schellenberg, Hitler's Chief of Counterintelligence*. Translated by Louis Hagen. Cambridge, MA: Da Capo Press, 1956.

Schwarz, Géraldine. *Those Who Forget: My Family's Story in Nazi Europe*. Translated by Laura Marris. New York: Scribner 2017.

Schwebel, Stephen M. *International Arbitration: Three Salient Problems*. Cambridge: Grotius Publications Ltd., 1987.

Sennerteg, Niclas. "Vem var den mystike mr Witzke i Damaskus?" *Niclas Sennerteg* (blog), May 25, 2017. https://sennerteg.wordpress.com/2015/05/25/vem-var-nazisten-kurt-witzke-i-syrien/.

Siemens, Daniel. *Stormtroopers: A New History of Hitler's Brownshirts*. New Haven: Yale University Press, 2017.

Smith, Harry Leslie. *Love Among the Ruins: A Memoir of Live and Love in Hamburg, 1945*. London: Icon Books, Ltd., 2015.

Spence, Richard B. "K. A. Jahnke and the German Sabotage Campaign in the United Sates and Mexico, 1914–1918." *The Historian* 59, no. 1 (Fall 1996): 89–112.

St. John, Vincent. *The I.W.W.: Its History, Structure and Methods*. Chicago: IWW Publishing Bureau, [1917]. https://archive.org/details/iwwitshistorystroostjo/page/n3/mode/2up.

Straka, Tomas. "La Nación Petrolera: Venezuela, 1914–2014." 2016. https://www.unimet.edu.ve/unimestite/wp-content/uploads/2013/02/La-Nación-Petrolera-Venezolana-1914–2014.pdf.

Stubbe-da Luz, Helmut. "Die Deutsche Parte in Hamburg: Wurzeln, Anfange, Umfeld, Erfolge und Niedergang." In *Zeitschrift des Vereins für Hamburgische Geschichte*, Bd. 70. Hamburg: Bibliothek de Helmut-Schmidt-Universität Hamburg, 1993.

———. "Heldenhafte *Tschekisten Kundschafter des Friedens?*" *Beglaliband zur Ausstellung Humburger Politiker als DDR-Spione*. Kalten Krieg. Hamburg: Bibliotek der Helmut-Schmidt-Universitat, 2015.

Sutherland, Sidney. "German Spies in America." *Liberty Magazine*, February 21, 1931–May 16, 1931.

Tagg, Lori. "Moments in MI History: World War I Counterintelligence Agents Get Their Man February 1918." *Military Intelligence Professional Bulletin* 43, no. 3 (July/Sept. 2017): 74–75.

Taylor, Frederick. *Exorcising Hitler: The Occupation and Denazification of Germany*. New York: Bloomsbury Press, 2011.

———. *1939: A People's History of the Coming of World War II*. New York: W. W. Norton & Company, 2019.

Tooze, Adam, *The Deluge, The Great War, and the Remaking of the Global Order, 1916–1931.* New York: Penguin Group, 2014.

Tuchman, Barbara. *The Zimmermann Telegram.* New York: Random House, 1958.

Tunney, Thomas J. *Throttled! The Detection of the German and Anarchist Bomb Plotters.* Boston: Small, Maynard & Company, 1919.

Van Deman, Ralph H. "Memoirs of Major General R. H. Van Deman," unpublished manuscript [n.d.]. US Army Intelligence Center Library. Fort Huachuca, AZ.

Van Wyk, Russel Duane. *German-American relations in the Aftermath of the Great War: Diplomacy, Law, and the Mixed Claims Commission, 1922–1939.* PhD diss., The University of North Carolina at Chapel Hill, 1989.

Von Rintelen, Franz. *The Dark Invader: Wartime Reminiscences of a German Naval Intelligence Officer.* London: Lovat Dickson Ltd., 1938.

Warner, Michael. *The Kaiser Sows Destruction: Protecting the Homeland the First Time Around.* Center for the Study of Intelligence, 2002.

Wasserman, Mark. *The Mexican Revolution: A Brief History with Documents.* Boston: Bedford/St. Martin's, 2012.

Weber, Ralph E., ed. *The Final Memoranda: Major Ralph H. Van Deman, USA Ret., 1865–1962; Father of Military Intelligence.* Wilmington: Scholarly Resources Books, 1988.

Winkler, Max. *Investments of United States Capital in Latin America.* Boston: World Peace Foundation Pamphlets, 1929.

Witcover, Jules. *Sabotage at Black Tom: Imperial Germany's Secret War in America, 1914–1917.* Chapel Hill, NC: Algonquin Books, 1989.

Yardley, Herbert. *The American Black Chamber.* Indianapolis: Bobbs-Merrill Company, 1931. https://archive.org/details/american-black-chamber-ii-watermark/mode/2up?q=Yardley%2C+the+american+black+chamber (annotated copy of William Friedman).

INDEX

Page numbers in **bold** type indicate illustrations.

ingramcontent.com/pod-product-compliance
ng Source LLC
rsburg PA
1349191025
300028B/408